D1760922

Counterflows to Colonialism

INDIAN TRAVELLERS AND SETTLERS IN BRITAIN 1600–1857

Michael H. Fisher

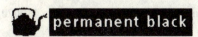

permanent black

Published by
PERMANENT BLACK
D-28 Oxford Apartments, 11 IP Extension,
Delhi 110092

and

'Himalayana', Mall Road,
Ranikhet 263645

Distributed by
ORIENT LONGMAN PRIVATE LIMITED
Bangalore Bhopal Bhubaneshwar Calcutta Chandigarh Chennai
Ernakulam Guwahati Hyderabad Jaipur Kolkata
Lucknow Mumbai New Delhi Patna

First published 2004 in hardback
First paperback printing 2006

ISBN 81-7824-154-4

Printed by Pauls Press, New Delhi 110020
Binding by Saku Binders

Contents

Contents

List of Charts, Images, Maps, and Tables

*(Italicized items denote colour images,
between pp. 176 and 177)*

List of Abbreviations

BL	British Library
Court Minutes	Minutes of the Court of Directors, Oriental and India Office Collections, B/ series
CPC	Imperial Record Office, *Calendar of Persian Correspondence*
Diary	Dyce Sombre Diary, L/L Boxes 63-5, BL
FPC	Foreign Political Consultations, NAI
FSC	Foreign Secret Consultations, NAI
GLRO	Greater London Record Office
HMS	Home Miscellaneous Series, BL
IGI	International Genealogical Index
Lascar Papers	Marine Department, Papers Relating to the Care of Lascars, 1793-1818, L/MAR/C/902, vols 1-2, BL
MSA	Maharashtra State Archives
NAI	National Archives of India
OBP	Old Bailey Proceedings, Guildhall Library
PDHC	Political Department, Home Correspondence, L/PS/ series, BL
PP	United Kingdom. Parliament. *Sessionals*
PRO	Great Britain, Public Record Office, Kew
WAC	Westminster Archive Centre
WBSA	West Bengal State Archives

Acknowledgements

Completing this vast project—a study of the tens of thousands of people from India who travelled or settled in Britain between 1600 and 1857—has only been possible through the generous assistance of many people and institutions. No work has hitherto considered the full range of people who ventured from India to Britain over this period, interacted with society there, generated representations of both Britain and India, and usually returned to India bearing and disseminating knowledge often discordant with that projected by British colonialism. Nonetheless, several scholars have written about important aspects of these issues. The most extensive study of Asians who immigrated to Britain is the pioneering work of Rozina Visram, with whom I have frequently and productively exchanged references and ideas over the past decade. I have also gained considerable insights from conversations with scholars considering different aspects of the Indian presence in Britain, including G. Balachandran, Jill Barber, Antoinette Burton, William Dalrymple, Simon Digby, Rebecca Gang, Gulfishan Khan, Shompa Lahiri, Philippa Levine, Rosie Llewllyn-Jones, John McLeod, Prafulla Mohanti, Satadru Sen, Kate Teltscher, Kusum Vadgama, Gauri Viswanathan, and Lynn Zastoupil. In the appropriate chapters I have recognized their written work and that of others who have preceded me.

The evidence essential for this book could only be found through research into manuscripts and publications in Persian, Urdu, and English, located in archives and libraries on three continents. In Britain, I spent much particularly productive time in the British Library, Family Records Centre, Greater London Record Office, Guildhall Library, Hertford Local Library and Archives, Public Record Office, Stafford County Record Office, Westminster Archives Centre, and William Salt Library. In India, especially valuable archives and libraries include the Aligarh Muslim University Library, Maharashtra

State Archives, National Archives of India, and West Bengal State Archives. In the United States, the Huntington Library holds unique manuscript letters while the libraries of the universities of Chicago, Michigan, and Wisconsin and Oberlin College were especially valuable for rare secondary sources. I sincerely thank all the archivists and librarians at these institutions who assisted me.

Generous financial support for this research came from the American Council of Learned Societies, the American Institute for Indian Studies, Oberlin College, and the University of Michigan. None of these organizations, however, is responsible for the contents of this book.

Many people, far too numerous to mention, have heard presentations based on this project and provided me with excellent suggestions for improvement. Among my most valued audiences were scholars at Aligarh Muslim University; Allahabad University; Delhi University; Barnard College; Centre for the Study of Social Sciences, Kolkata; Columbia University; Dartmouth College; George Washington University; Huntington Library; Indian National Labour Institute; Jamia Milia Islamia; Jawaharlal Nehru University; John Carroll University; Mumbai Study Group; Nehru Centre (London); North Carolina Center for South Asia Studies; Pennsylvania State University; Sahitya Akademi; University of California at Berkeley; University of Michigan; Victoria Memorial Library; and Yale University.

I would like to especially thank Paula Richman for closely reading drafts of the chapters. I would like to dedicate this book to her and Roswita, my earliest and greatest supports.

Note on Transliteration

Relying so heavily as this book does on original documents from several languages, it faces problems of transliteration: balancing technical consistency against respect for spellings used by the people it studies. Over this long period, people varied widely in the spellings of their names. For example, one Indian scholar-teacher wrote his name 'Abdool Alee' but his friend and colleague wrote his 'Hassan Ali', neither of which reflects current transliteration protocols. Further, many of the original names have been so Anglicized as to be unrecognizable in any original Indian form. By retaining these original spellings of names and terms wherever possible, rather than forcing a uniform schema on them, I thus retain their chosen English forms. For technical terms that I transliterate directly from Persian or Urdu, however, I use the standard forms found in most recent scholarship, but without diacritical marks, as these are usually unnecessary for scholars and distracting for others.

Introduction

Counterflows

People from India have been travelling to or settling in Britain since the early 1600s, about as long as Britons have been sailing to India. Most histories of Britain, India, and colonialism, however, tend to neglect these Indians. The mainstream of colonialism undoubtedly consisted of the movement of Britons outwards as they traded, conquered, and ruled India. Yet, a mounting 'counterflow' of Indians entered Britain, living there and producing knowledge in ways that compelled British responses. By the mid nineteenth century, tens of thousands of Indian seamen, servants, scholars, soldiers, students, envoys, royalty, officials, merchants, tourists, and settlers had all journeyed to Britain. Once there, Indian men and women participated variously in British society according to their class, gender, regional origin, religion, caste, and individual circumstances, through friendships, negotiations, and conflicts with Britons and each other. In multifarious contested ways, their self-representations and deeds influenced British attitudes and policies towards them as individuals and towards India generally. Some settled, but most returned after months or years of living in Britain, bringing back to India direct information about Britain. Colonialism, as it developed over time, shaped these interactions and representations of self and 'other'. Colonialism powerfully altered what being 'Indian' meant, culturally and legally, in Britain—meanings which often developed quite differently in India. This book surveys and analyses the range of Indians who ventured to Britain during the 250-year transition to colonialism, the many reasons why they undertook this voyage, their diverse lived experiences and actions there, and contrasting representations of self and other by Indians as well as Britons.

To learn about these Indians in Britain, we must consider the full range of surviving manuscript and published source materials. This evidence, located in India and Britain, reflects their perspectives as well as those of Britons. Some twenty Indians variously wrote books in Arabic, English, Nepali, Persian, and Urdu about their experiences there, assessing and often critiquing as well as praising aspects of Britain. Some published their books in Britain, others simply circulated them as manuscripts among their peers in India. Dozens printed self-advertisements or pamphlets in the British press. Many more wrote autobiographical letters or petitions, or testified before Parliament, London law courts, and at meetings of East India Company stockholders or directors. Conversely, dozens of Britons recorded their impressions of the conversations, comportment, and appearance of Indians in Britain. British official census, parochial, tax, judicial, and other documents recorded thousands of Indians, intermixed with Britons. British artists depicted Indians of several social classes in Britain, illustrating how they were perceived there. However, the burgeoning British colonial archive preserved the largest amount of information about Indian travellers and settlers, as the East India Company sought to identify, control, maintain, and return them to India. Only indirect evidence remains about much of the personal social intercourse between Indians and Britons, including their conversations and intimate relationships. When assembled, these diverse materials enable a study of colonial relations as measured and recounted primarily by Indians, instead of Britons.

This book uses these multiple, often contrasting, sources about this vast range of people over two-and-a-half centuries to develop not a single historical narrative but rather many intertwined ones. It stresses changes and disjunctures, as well as continuing themes. Competing British authorities and individuals in India and Britain followed contradictory policies and practices, while various Indians tried divergent strategies in dealing with them. Contending Indians found allies among British factions and individuals, and vice versa. Each chapter of this book presents brief biographies of Indians who were both characteristic of their class, gender, and background at that time, but who were also distinctive—for instance because they more extensively recorded their own accounts or made themselves particularly noted by Britons.

The book begins in the early 1600s, with the pre-colonial period, when Indians were relative rarities in Britain. The transition to colonialism enabled increasing numbers of Indians to make the passage to Britain and also complicated their roles and receptions there. The very meaning of being 'Indian' in Britain went through substantial change over the centuries. By the early nineteenth century many Indians had developed communities and social circles in Britain, yet British attitudes were hardening against them as colonialism penetrated virtually all aspects of society in Britain and India. The book concludes in 1857, on the eve of 'high colonialism', after which many aspects of life for Indians in Britain altered significantly.

By highlighting the words and acts of Indians in Britain, this book complements the much larger body of writing by and about the Britons around them. Many histories of colonial India concentrate on Britons as they conquered and ruled the subcontinent. Similarly (with a few notable exceptions), most histories of Britain pay little heed to people from India there.[1] Yet, representations by Indians directly in the British public sphere often contrasted with British 'Orientalist' constructions of Indians, which have been far more extensively studied.[2] Some scholars have begun to consider Indians who travelled to Britain, especially concentrating on the post-1857 period, when their reception and roles differed considerably from the earlier period.[3] This book, however, focuses on the first 250 years of passages by Indians into Britain, because interactions between Indians and Britons then were more contingent and diverse than in the post-1857 period.

[1] Even most histories of imperial Britain do not discuss Indians in Britain. See Louis, ed., *Oxford History*.

[2] For recent expositions of the ways English culture 'constructed' India, see Ballantyne, *Orientalism*; Cannadine, *Ornamentalism*; Daunton and Halpern, *Empire*; Dirks, *Castes*; Inden, *Imagining India*; Mackenzie, 'Empire and Metropolitan'; Washbrook, 'Orients'.

[3] See Fryer, *Staying Power*; Gerzina, *Black London*; Myers, *Reconstructing*; Innes, *History*; Visram, *Asians* and *Ayahs*. For the later period, see Burton, *At the Heart*; Gundara and Duffield, *Essays*; Guptara, *Black British*; Lahiri, *Indians*; Lindborg, ' "Asiatic" '; Panayi, *Immigration*; Ramdin, *Making*, and *Reimagining*; Reeves, *British Racial*; Rich, *Race*; Scobie, *Black Britannia*; Shyllon, *Black People*; Tabili, 'Construction' and *'We Ask'*; Vadgama, *India*; Viswanathan, *Outside*.

Identities: 'Indians', 'Britons', and 'the Company', 1600 to 1857

The changing and contested meanings of being 'Indian' in Britain form a central theme of this book. Around 1600, the terms 'Indian' and 'Briton' both had a range of denotations and connotations, none identical to their usage in English today. No one could realistically have imagined how colonialism by the East India Company would develop over the coming centuries. The Indian subcontinent had never been entirely united under a single ruler, although over the seventeenth century an increasing portion had come under the Mughal empire. Most people held strong class, gender, and ethnic affiliations.[4] Further, many of the earliest people who went to Britain were outside mainstream Indian society and often already living transculturally: international seamen, or members of 'trade diaspora' communities— Armenians, Parsis, or people of mixed European-Indian ancestry. Far more Muslims than Hindus went to Britain, often supported by traditions of travel through the wider Islamic world that already linked Europe and Asia. Although, from the mid eighteenth century, British authorities occasionally termed as 'Indians' people of solely European ancestry who had settled in India, I do not do so. Rather, this book heuristically reserves the term Indian for people from territories today called India, Pakistan, Bangladesh, and Nepal who were not of exclusively European ancestry.

In 1600, virtually no Indians had clear knowledge of Britain or its peoples. The earliest Indians thus voyaged to an almost unknown place. As soon as Indians began to return, they brought back with them first-hand knowledge of that distant island, knowledge which supplemented and often contradicted British self-representations that were increasingly prevalent in India. Yet, due to the relatively late development of publishing in India, until the early nineteenth century these Indian accounts about Britain circulated only in limited ways, orally or through manuscripts. This absence of a cumulative and coherent body of comprehensive knowledge about Britain meant that many subsequent Indian travellers discovered Britain anew. Thus, even a well-educated visitor in the late eighteenth century had, in Partha

---

[4] Here ethnic means regional, 'caste' (*jati*), and/or religious identities.

Chatterjee's words, no 'prior mental map imprinted on his mind telling him how England ought to be seen'.[5] This allowed fresh insights but also often disadvantaged Indians relative to Britons, both in Britain and in India, especially as British knowledge of India increased.

In 1600, England was a struggling kingdom on the southern part of a relatively marginal European island. Eventually, the regions within this island united, and concepts of the British nation-state and empire haltingly emerged through heated debate as well as civil and foreign wars. Rapid economic change within Britain brought class-consciousness and conflict. For centuries, however, controversies remained about 'Britishness', including debates about the inclusion within that term of Catholics, Protestant Dissenters, and Jews, as well as people from India. Thus, especially in the earlier chapters, 'British' and 'Britain' are useful—although anachronistic—shorthand categories.

In Britain, cultural identifications of 'the East', 'the East Indies', and 'India', as well as the peoples who lived there, all shifted inconsistently over the centuries. Given their initial vague knowledge of these areas and peoples, Britons often conflated everyone eastward from the South African Cape to the Philippines as 'Indians', 'Orientalists', or 'Asiatics' (among other terms). Through the seventeenth century, Britons largely regarded the Orient as holding vast wealth and power, access to which was worth the risk of a long and dangerous voyage. Once in India, Britons often stood as petitioners, seeking to appease or employ Indian intermediaries who could intercede on their behalf with established political authorities and commercial networks. Yet, as British travellers, merchants, and soldiers brought back firsthand accounts, Anglocentric depictions of the Orient accumulated and circulated through the burgeoning English print media. Less noticed by historians, Indian travellers and settlers in Britain also contributed incrementally to this body of knowledge about themselves and their homelands. This book shows how changing representations by Indians and of Indians resonated with growing British economic, military, cultural, and political assertions there, primarily exerted through the East India Company.

[5] Partha Chatterjee, 'Five Hundred Years'.

From its foundation in 1600, the East India Company provided the main means for movement between India and England—for Indians as well as Britons. Indeed, this book takes as its chronological limits the period from the Company's initial chartering in 1600 to its replacement by the British Crown as ruler over India in 1858. Yet, while 'the Company' thus forms a major unit of analysis, it was not homogeneous over this period.[6] During the seventeenth century, rival English bodies of merchants vied for access to trade in Asia until they merged as the United East India Company in 1709. Until the mid eighteenth century, the Company largely confined itself to commerce, and to defending its trading posts against more powerful local rulers and rival European companies. Thereafter, Parliament increasingly took over parts of the Company's administration. Throughout the Company's history, contending factions and interests among its shareholders and directors struggled against each other. Nevertheless, the Company's virtual monopoly over shipping between India and Britain until the early nineteenth century proved profound in ensuring the dependence upon it of most Indians who made this journey, whether as seamen in British employ or paying passengers.

Further, British authorities and public opinion generally regarded the Company—and specifically its Court of Directors in London—as accountable for 'Indians', variously defined, both in distant India and, more immediately, in Britain. Parliament, indeed, determined that the Company ultimately bore legal as well as moral responsibility for indigent Indians in Britain.[7] The Company's directors generally recognized these obligations, usually motivated by their desire to remove Indians from British public discourse and back to India. Further, in the service of colonial control, the Company's growing colonial archive amassed vast statistical and descriptive evidence about India and Indians. These extensive acquisition policies preserved the words of Indians in Britain through their many original letters, petitions, narratives, bonds, and other self-representations. In Bernard

---

[6] See Chaudhuri, *English East India Company*, and Sutherland, *East India Company*.

[7] Although the Company's legal liability diminished between 1834 and 1854, the moral obligation continued. See Part III of this book.

Cohn's words, 'many [of British colonialism's] major effects were un-intended, as those [Indians] who were to be the objects produced by the formation [of colonial knowledge] often turned it to their own ends.'[8] Therefore, the Company's multiple, complex, and often con-tradictory roles appear as continuing themes.

By 1858, following the 'mutiny', Indian and British identities and relations had changed dramatically as many on both sides had come to identify themselves and each other as opposing peoples. Within India, haltingly from the mid eighteenth century, the Company's British and Indian employees seized political, military, and economic power away from a range of regional and Mughal successor states and European rivals. Between 1757 and 1857, the Company annexed two-thirds of Indian territory while the remaining third came under its indirect rule through subordinated Indian 'princes'.[9] For the first time in history, one government had power over virtually all of India.

Differences certainly remained among Indians, based on class, gen-der, and ethnic identities. Yet, broader and more incorporative Indian self-definitions were developing across the subcontinent, fostered by British transregional administrative structures as well as new modes of communication and transportation, and widespread shared resent-ment against colonialism. In particular, many Indians in Britain gain-ed the perspective to see the full extent of British colonialism and to consider all of India, and all other Indians in Britain, as sharing much. Thus, we can feel more comfortable writing about 'India' and 'Indi-ans' as consensual categories from the mid nineteenth century.

By this time, British self-definitions were also more firmly estab-lished. Widespread conceptions of the British nation had emerged out of long wars, particularly against the Catholic French in continental Europe, Asia, Africa, and the Americas.[10] While debates remained over what the British empire actually meant or should mean, a number of interrelated factors led many Britons to regard Indians collectively as essentially different from Britons.[11] These factors included the furious

---

[8] Cohn, *Colonialism*, p. 22.

[9] See Fisher, *Politics*.

[10] See Colley, *Britons*.

[11] See Harrison, *Climates*; and Metcalf, *Ideologies*.

fighting of 1857 in India; the spread in Britain of constructions of 'races' as biological, immutable, and hierarchically ranked; the penetration of colonialism into virtually all aspects of British society and economy; and Orientalist cultural appropriations of 'the East'. Yet, shifting British cultural identifications of 'India' comprised only one factor in the actual lived experiences of individual Indians in Britain.[12]

It is naturally impossible to identify all the tens of thousands of Indians who went to Britain over this period. Evidence about many has not survived, or has survived only in fragments. Nor, from this remove, can anyone prove who was the first Asian or Indian to reach Britain—although many writers have advanced their own candidates.[13] Additionally, Indians, by any definition, were not the only people from Asia who came to Britain.[14] Nevertheless, the increasingly extensive links between India and Britain, particularly through British colonialism, argue for the logic of this book's definition of its subject: Indians in Britain.

Complexities of Context, Gender, Class, and Ethnicity

The lived experiences and accomplishments of Indians who ventured to Britain varied in their historical context as well as their gender, class, ethnicity, and individual circumstances. To reflect this, each of the book's three parts concentrates on a different time period, within which each chapter considers particular categories of Indians. Since each Indian in Britain had unique roles and relationships, each chapter also highlights selected individuals, relating them to the book's overarching themes.

Part One focuses on the pre- and early-colonial periods. Chapter One shows the ways that the earliest Indians—including merchants,

[12] Matar demonstrates for earlier centuries the difference between the personal reception of Muslim visitors to Britain and the negative images of Muslims in British literature, especially drama. Matar, *Islam in Britain*, and *Turks, Moors, and Englishmen*.

[13] See Das, 'Early Indian Visitors'; Digby, 'Eighteenth Century Narrative'; Qadir, 'Early Muslim Visitors'; Seth, *History of Armenians*; Taifoor, 'Sheikh I'tesamuddin'; Williams, *Black Hills*.

[14] See Ng, *Chinese*; Parker, 'Chinese People'; Peacock, *Lee Boo*.

seamen, male and female servants, and the wives of Britons—functioned in England during the seventeenth and early eighteenth centuries. Chapter Two considers how, during the late eighteenth century, expanding colonial rule shaped the experiences in Britain of increasing numbers of Indians from each of these categories, plus Indian diplomats and political agents.

Part Two examines the transitional phase, from the late eighteenth century to the 1830s, as colonial patterns intensified in Britain and India. There were now so many Indian settlers and travellers that each chapter can address a separate type. Chapter Three studies Indian scholar-officials who educated Britons about Indian culture, individually and at colleges in Britain. Chapter Four discusses Indian seamen, who made British imports from India possible but who had to contend with British efforts to control them. Chapter Five traces the highly controversial, changing, and inconsistent British legal definitions of and cultural attitudes to Indian women and men of all classes in Britain. Chapter Six analyses Indian servants and slaves who established temporary or permanent places for themselves in British society.

Part Three explores the decades leading up to 'high colonialism', each chapter concentrating on a particular type. Chapter Seven demonstrates how various Indian agents, diplomats, and royalty developed sophisticated strategies for manoeuvring within the British public sphere. Chapters Eight and Nine detail how some Indians—including Anglicized officials, pensioned princes, soldiers, businessmen, and students—regarded Britain in different ways, as a site for enjoyment, improvement, and justice. Finally, Chapter Ten reconstructs how various classes of Indians in Britain developed their own social circles and communities during the decades to 1857.

Certain themes link these three parts and ten chapters. Throughout, gender and class, as constructed by Indians as well as Britons, remained key interrelated factors in both colonialism and its counterflows, cross-cutting ethnic identities and correlating with power. Scholars have demonstrated how many Britons characterized their presence in India as masculine and increasingly disparaged most Indian men as effeminate and/or childlike.[15] In India, many British men of all classes

[15] See Sinha, *Colonial Masculinity*.

had sexual relationships with subordinated Indian women.[16] Their children formed an 'Anglo-Indian' or 'Eurasian' community, larger in number than 'pure' Europeans, but increasingly marginalized by British society.[17] In contrast, relatively few European women present in India were available to Indian men as wives, mistresses, or sex-workers.[18] Further, there was sometimes a defensiveness in élite Indian male attitudes towards their own community's gender practices, and a tendency to try to 'reform' Indian women as a way to recover religious 'purity', self-esteem, and political power. Thus, colonial practices were highly gendered and class-based.

For the counterflow of Indians going to Britain as well, gender and class remained complex factors. Each of the book's three parts discusses the Indian wives and children of Britons. Their status in British society depended on their husband's or father's social class and his treatment of them. An élite Indian wife was subordinated by gender to British men of her husband's class but simultaneously empowered by his class over British male and female servants. Men of mixed ancestry might enter the highest circles of British society and politics, including Parliament, depending on their wealth and degree of Anglicization. Indian wives and children of Britons, however, were never numerous in Britain and their relationship with British society became increasingly problematic due to colonialism.

Many Indian women went to Britain as servants or slaves. Some stayed on, marrying and merging into British society. Like many lower-class British women, some were subject to sexual exploitation, with little redress available to them: some entered the workhouse, others went home pregnant or with small children born in Britain. More prominent were Indian noblewomen, whose 'exotic' attractiveness captured many British imaginations, although their direct personal interactions with British society were usually highly limited by purdah—their practice of seclusion. The experience in Britain of Indian women generally differed from that of Indian men of the same class there, reflecting both Indian and British patriarchal values and laws.

Overall, many more Indian men than women entered Britain. Dozens of Indian men of all classes had marriages or liaisons with

---

[16] See Ghosh, 'Colonial Companions' (Ph.D., 2000).
[17] See Hawes, *Poor Relations*.
[18] See Arnold, 'European Orphans'.

British women (in addition to the thousands who employed British sex-workers). Indeed, marriage with a British woman often provided the main means of entry into British society for an Indian male settler. In order to marry legally, these men had to be Christians, or convert— at least nominally—to Christianity. British laws however gave Indian men more control over property than they did to married British women—including to the British women that Indian men married. Thus, cultural constructions of gender often aligned Indian and British men of the same class against British women.

The relationships between conceptions of gender and biological 'race' shifted over time. Through the eighteenth century, sexual relations between Indian men and British women were relatively unremarked upon in Britain. By the early nineteenth century, British (male) authorities began paying far more attention to them, often believing Indian men needed protection from predatory British women. These attitudes contrast powerfully with widespread British hostility from the later nineteenth century onwards to 'miscegenation', particularly between British women and non-White men.[19]

Gender also provided a central criterion for Indian assessments of British society. Many Indian male authors, writing for either British or Indian audiences, criticized British society for the immodest dress and deportment of British women, including élite British women. These men found such women titillating or shocking or both since, in India, respectable Indian women remained secluded from men external to their household, and most British women lived aloof from Indian men. Thus, many Indian commentators on Britain, like European ones on the rest of the world, measured local society on the basis of their valuation of its treatment and behaviour of its women. Gender was not the only distinguishing factor among Indians in Britain.

Another continuing theme throughout the book is the ethnic diversity among Indian settlers and travellers. Not all Indian regions, 'castes', or religious communities responded similarly to opportunities to travel to Britain or had the same experiences there. The people most willing to undertake the journey usually had the most extensive prior links with Europe. The frontier of British–Indian interactions moved haltingly inland from Calcutta, Bombay, and Madras, drawing

---

[19] Nevertheless, Britain currently has the highest level of 'intermarriage' in Europe. See Hyam, *Empire and Sexuality*; and Henriques, *Children*.

Indian people from each region to Britain at different rates. Christian Indians and people of mixed Indian–European descent were among the first and most frequent travellers. In contrast, throughout this period, high-caste Hindus found the journey threatening to their purity and the relatively few orthodox people who undertook it faced hardships, particularly when preparing food according to religious injunctions. Many more members of minority communities with transregional cultural frameworks, including Muslims and Parsis, were willing to go, although they also had to make choices about how much their sartorial, dietary, and other religious practices would separate them from Britons. For Indian seamen and servants, the economic opportunities promised by working their way to and in Britain usually outweighed religious considerations, and many chose or were compelled to adopt British names, dress, and diet.

Indian settlers and travellers lived in a specific historical moment which shaped their experiences. Rejecting presumptions that cultural constructs like race, gender, class, and ethnicity were static, this book reveals major historical shifts in these, as felt and shaped by Indians in Britain. There was no indigenous Indian term that corresponds to 'race' as used today; Indian authors in Persian and Urdu used *qaum* (from 'to stand', meaning 'a people') and jati (from 'birth', meaning 'genus', often translated as 'caste' or 'sub-caste') to describe groups with a common identity. Substantial scholarship—most recently that of Sudipta Sen—has traced the ways that British territorial assertions in India interacted with British theorizations of race during the formative decades following 1757.[20] For many eighteenth- and early-nineteenth-century Britons, as Kathleen Wilson explains, ' "Race", . . . like gender and ethnicity, was a historically contingent construction that did not describe empirical, static or absolute conditions in societies, but positional relationships made and unmade in historical circumstances and manipulated in the pursuit of power . . . [race] was identified and signified through religion, custom, language, climate, aesthetics and historical time, as much as physiognomy and biology.'[21]

[20] See Sen, *Distant Sovereignty*, and Travers, 'Contested Notions ' (Ph.D., 1998).

[21] Wilson, *Island Race*, p. 11. See also Bayly, *Imperial*; Ballantyne, *Orientalism*; Harrison, *Climates*; Rich, *Race*.

Since Indians in Britain who had the means and who so chose could adapt to British norms, that is 'transculturate' or 'Anglicize' themselves in all these categories (except physiognomy and biology)—this left them some room to reshape their identities there. By the mid nineteenth century, however, the scope for Indians to affect British attitudes on race and India diminished considerably.

The term 'Black' also meant different things to Britons in different times. The quite dissimilar dimensions of the European slave trade in Africa and Asia and their separate colonial histories meant that most Indians and Africans had varying experiences in Britain during the period covered in this book. Certainly, there were times when individuals and groups in Britain conflated the two as 'Black'.[22] Significantly, many of those in British society most dismissive of, or hostile to, Indians and Africans collectively were those Britons who had experience in the colonies and who retained their colonial attitudes when they returned to Britain.[23] There were also times and places where working-class or indigent Africans and Indians came together. Yet, based on their words and actions, most Indians and Africans in Britain regarded their histories and situations as distinct over much of our period. Given its already vast scope, in this book Africans will thus appear primarily for comparison or when closely identified with Indians.

Colonialism was not hegemonic or dichotomous between colonizer and colonized. Rather, there were multiple sites of contestation and cooperation as well as inconsistencies and contradictions among both Britons and Indians. Further, patterns of exchange and knowledge production were asymmetrical and occurred differently in Britain and India, and shifted over time. As such, this book engages in debates

[22] E.g., *Public Advertiser* 5/1/1786 4c, 7/1/1786 2b and 4b, 9/1/1786 3b, 10/1/1786 4c, 12/1/1786 4d, 16/1/1786 4d, 19/1/1786 3b; *Morning Chronicle* 28/1/1786 1c.

[23] In particular, British slave owners largely identified African, African Caribbean, and other non-White peoples as sub-human commodities. Edward Long's three volume *History of Jamaica* (1774) stands as a particularly powerful assertion of this colonial position; the influence of this work on the British populace in England, however, has sometimes been overstated as the prevailing—rather than just one contending—voice. See Barker, *African Link*; Bolt, *Victorian Attitudes*; Myers, *Reconstructing*; Rich, *Race*.

about representation that began prior to colonialism and continue to the present.

Knowledge, Representations, and Power

Many of the struggles among Britons and Indians concerned efforts to produce and control knowledge and representations of self and other. During the colonial period, central programmes of British rule were establishing an 'empire of opinion' among Indians, mastery of the Indian 'information order', and enforcement of 'difference' between colonizer and colonized.[24] Many post-colonial scholars have also identified these as essential continuing issues.

Especially from the late eighteenth century, British officials and educators attempted to convince Indians of the superiority and desirability of British culture and rule, and its fundamental distinction from India's alleged traditions of 'Oriental despotism', 'superstition', and current 'decadence'.[25] Indeed, many Indian élites came to regard Anglicization, democracy, and social reform as paths to progress. In India, ever larger numbers of Indians accepted employment or education under the British. By 1857, some 228,000 Indians were enlisted in the Company's armies, and tens of thousands more worked as officials, translators, scribes, seamen, and servants for Britons, while numerous Indian women married or were mistresses of Britons. Nonetheless, these and many other Indians simultaneously resisted British dominance, pursued their own agendas, and sought to reshape British rule according to their own values, although usually from positions of subordination.

The colonial government tried to establish systems of surveillance and control over political and public communication in India. For instance, British indirect rule decreed its monopoly over political intercourse among India's rulers and between them and London. Many

---

[24] See Viswanathan, *Masks*, and Bayly, *Empire*. In 1801, Parliament considered if the many working-class Indians 'brought to London, and, being here corrupted, would on their return . . . carry a bad report of us to Hindostan, [so] the English character would be degraded, and the English empire in the East shaken to its foundations.' Commons debate (25/11/1801), Cobbett, *Parliamentary*, vol. 36, pp. 288–302.

[25] Bayly, *Imperial*, p. 7.

Britons projected their own constructions of Britain into Indian society through state-sponsored or Christian missionary-based educational institutions. European Orientalists attempted to construct images of India for European consumption.

Increasingly, British colonialism explicitly excluded Indians from higher positions of authority. From the late eighteenth century, the Company sought ways to identify and disqualify Indians from its commissioned services. To advance these goals, many British officials tried to discourage Indians from travelling to Britain and so learning directly about it, representing themselves there, and participating in public policy formation in the imperial centre.

Independent Indian knowledge of the limits of British power, and of Britain's internal political, social, and cultural divisions, challenged British efforts to create colonial hegemony. Many Indian envoys and appellants who travelled to Britain did so expressly to bypass British colonial controls and advocate their own cases to the higher authorities there. Once in Britain, Indians explored its society, including forms of government, gender relations, technology, and communication media. Astute Indians learned in Britain how to manipulate the several competing British factions and political and legal authorities in Britain and India against each other. Indian men observed British women in ways not available to them in India. They mastered British sciences—including engineering, medical, and military technologies. They also noted and used British print capitalism to frame and publicize their observations and self-images.

All Indians in Britain made choices about how to present themselves, through their comportment as well as their words. They selected sartorial styles to identify themselves visually and practised dietary customs which shaped their social intercourse with Britons and other Indians. They made their arguments and grievances directly to higher authorities in Britain by testifying before Parliament, law courts, and the Company's stockholders and directors. Indian professors taught in British colleges. Indians of all classes addressed broader British audiences through published books, pamphlets, and newspaper advertisements, using genres and media uncommon in India. A few Indians gave public speeches, and almost all conversed or socialized with Britons. Thus, being present in Britain meant the power to know Britons and address them directly.

Indians also reported their discoveries and assessments about Britain to Indian audiences in writing and orally. Indian emissaries and other visitors explained the complex constitutional powers and practical interactions among often competing political bodies, including the Crown, Parliament, and the Company's directors, in addition to the respective relationships of each of these with various British officials in India. Indian men described their relations with British women and evaluated the condition of British women compared to their own. They advised future visitors about what to enjoy and avoid, and how Indian society should learn from British models and mistakes.

Some scholars who have analysed conflicts over representation, knowledge, and identity have tended to emphasize European agency, as well as the later high colonial period. Edward Said and Mary Pratt, by examining the ways in which Europeans appropriated 'the Orient' and sought to prevent Indians from representing themselves, have done much to demonstrate the power of Western creations of 'the East'.[26] Some critics of imperialism assert that the picture of the colonized which these European Orientalist works exclusively painted convinced even general society in the European home nation to support the colonial process, often against their better interests.[27]

Anglocentric analyses, however, do not sufficiently consider Indian agency and knowledge, tending rather to make them appear mainly as victims and/or objects of scrutiny. As Tanika Sarkar argues:

> Most recent works on cultural developments in the colonial period tend to assume the operations of a single, monolithic colonial discourse with fully hegemonistic capabilities. All that South Asians could possibly do was to either form a secondary, derivative discourse that simply extended the message of the master-text, or refuse and resist its positions and language . . . This position . . . necessarily robs colonized Indians of effective agency and evacuates an especially complicated historical problem of all complexities . . .[28]

---

[26] See Holder, 'Melodrama'; Kamps and Singh, *Travel*; Lowe, *Critical*; Niranjana, 'Translation'; Pratt, *Imperial*; and Said, *Orientalism*.

[27] Compare how Cannadine argues Britons projected their own class categories onto the colonized. Cannadine, *Ornamentalism*.

[28] Sarkar, 'Book', p. 61.

This book reveals some of these complexities by examining many diverse Indian representations and experiences in Britain within their changing historical contexts.

Some recent scholarship has recognized the ways Asians (and Africans) regarded their power to narrate their own experiences in their own terms as a powerful mode of resistance to European cultural domination.[29] This book extends that approach by considering individual Indians and also larger patterns of conflict between Orientalist and Indian self-representations. Conflicts about who could write and teach about India and its cultures were played out between Indians and Britons in Britain as well as India, in the past and also today. Until recently, too, almost all histories of Britain had presupposed its all-White past. Some scholars, however, have begun to recognize the complex roles of Asians and Africans within Britain. They write about multicultural Britain, as Antoinette Burton argues, not as a 'mere pluralizing gesture . . . [but rather to] rematerialize the movement of colonial subjects from the so-called peripheries to the ostensible center . . .'.[30] Yet, there are also strong efforts to suppress that diversity.

After the 1960s, nativist British hostility to immigrants has increased. Part of this agenda is to claim a historically insular all-White England which has come under threat from newly arriving non-White aliens. Enoch Powell's famous 'rivers of blood' speech, the National Front, and the British National Party have all argued a right-wing British view virulently opposed to all non-White immigrants.

Opposing such politically motivated White racist accounts, a growing number of commentators have started writing Britain's 'Black History'. Especially from the 1970s, some committed writers have sought to recuperate the hitherto unrecognized accomplishments and contributions of a distinctive Black community in Britain. Some have sought to demonstrate an essentially distinctive 'Black' experience, historically shared by all non-Whites in Britain, and thus form a

[29] See Ibrahim Abu-Lughod, *Arab*; As-Saffar, *Disorienting*; Bhabha, *Location*; Hasan, 'Resistance'; Lewis, *Muslim*; Said, *Culture*.

[30] Burton, *At the Heart*, pp. 6–7. See also Zastoupil, 'Defining', and Innes, *History*.

unified front of Asians and Africans against White racial prejudice.[31]
As Ron Ramdin argues, Black is 'a "political colour" '.[32] In this contest,
all sides have tried to rewrite British history in light of their own political commitments, often mapping a contemporary sense of race into
the past.

Among recent scholars, Rozina Visram has most extensively documented Asians in Britain. Through painstaking archival research
and interviews with descendants of Indian settlers, she has assembled
an extensive narrative of '400 Years of History', stressing the contributions of many Indians who lived in Britain, particularly the development of their communities from the mid nineteenth century
onwards. Building on her work, this book develops a more chrono-
logically-based analysis, studying how class, race, and gender affected
the lives of diverse Indian peoples over time as they moved between
changing India and Britain during the pre-colonial and early colonial
periods.

The contingent and relational nature of British colonial assertions,
as well as the roles of Indians, are both crucial to understanding the
complexity of the colonial process. Rather than a hegemonic whole,
the empire was not even a single web; it was, as Tony Ballantyne notes,
a 'complex agglomeration of overlapping webs . . .'.[33] Identity was
malleable and contingent, although based on asymmetrical exchanges
and power.

As much as possible, this book studies Indians in Britain in their
own terms. It considers the ways and reasons their identities, experiences, knowledge, and representations all shifted over time and formed larger patterns not visible unless studied in the aggregate. It draws
upon a range of source materials, finding particular intertextual rich-
ness where evidence from one genre or perspective overlays evidence
from others. It builds not so much a single narrative as a broad-based
recognition of how individual travellers and settlers had similarities
with and differences from each other, based on their gender, class, ethnicity, individual circumstances, and historical moment. It recovers

[31] See, for example, Gundara and Duffield, *Essays*, p. 2. In contrast, Scobie
blames Indian seamen for degrading the status of 'Blacks', by which he means
African and African Caribbean peoples. Scobie, *Black Britannia*, p. 64.

[32] Ramdin, *Reimagining*, p. x. See also Gilroy, *'There Ain't'*.

[33] Ballantyne, *Orientalism*, p. 15.

some of the complexity of British history by locating it within the worldwide arena of colonialism. It also broadens the history of India by including Indians who went to Britain, examining their origins, experiences, and effects on Indians in India. Overall, it reveals counterflows that have hitherto been masked by the more visible course of colonialism.

CHAPTER 1

Early Interactions

Indians, Britons, and the Company, 1600s–1750s

Comparative Contexts and Early Arrivals

The small but growing number of English East India Company ships reaching Indian shores from 1608 onwards extended already existing, although still relatively rare, opportunities for Indian employment and travel to Europe. The fact of later British colonial dominance over India should not overshadow ongoing and extensive intra-Asian or intercontinental trade links.[1] Indian seamen and merchants—as well as Arabs, Africans, Persians, and other Asians—had navigated the Indian Ocean for centuries. Portuguese ships had plied sea routes around Africa since the late fifteenth century.[2] Further, around the same time as the English, the Dutch, French, Danes, and other northern European powers arrived. Occasionally, Indians sailed on their ships to Europe.[3] Exchanges between Indians and Britons, we should remember, only gradually became dominant.

Over the 150-year period discussed in this chapter, India, Britain, and the East India Company changed radically. In the early seventeenth century, the Mughal empire was still expanding. English merchants had only begun to sail to India, marry Indian women, form trading partnerships with Indian merchants, and hire Indian seamen,

[1] See Janet Abu-Lughod, *Before European*; Barendse, *Arabian*; Chaudhuri, *Trade*; Dale, *Indian Merchants*; Das Gupta and Pearson, *India*; Furber, *Rival Empires*; Steensgaard, *Carracks*; and Wink, *Al-Hind*.

[2] See Subrahmanyam, *Portuguese Empire*.

[3] For an early traveller to Holland, Ram Singh, see Williams, *Black Hills*, p. 43.

servants, and soldiers. By the mid eighteenth century, the Mughal dynasty remained sovereign only in name, dividing into many warring successor or regional states, each effectively autonomous. Many Indian individuals and groups, including trade diaspora communities like Armenians and Parsis, working-class people, and even scholar-officials and rulers, shifted from the Mughals to more promising employers or partners, including to Europeans trading along their shores.[4]

Over this period, Britain went from a divided island (with some, mostly American, colonies) to a world power, developing complex cultural, economic, and political relations with a range of Asian and African peoples. The East India Company, chartered in 1600 with an English trade monopoly from southern Africa to the Philippines, financed adventures throughout these waters. Company ships also began to bring back Indian travellers and settlers of many classes who then interacted with a populace and state uncertain how to deal with them.[5] English authors and artists created often abstract images of Indians that satisfied local audiences but which did not necessarily reflect lived experiences. Religious identity proved a key element in these years before the concept of the 'nation-state' had fully developed, so Indians often had different receptions depending on whether they were Catholics, Protestants, Parsis, Jews, Muslims, or Hindus. The Crown and Parliament alternately encouraged immigration of outsiders who could advance England economically and discouraged those who might take employment away from current subjects.[6] Indeed, the state remained more concerned about imported Asian merchandise than people. For example, in 1700 Parliament banned the import of Indian printed or painted cloth, seen as threatening to English producers. Consequently, Royal Customs officials sometimes seized the sashes, shawls, and turbans of Indian seamen, claiming them as contraband cloth.[7] While few effective legal restrictions or administrative controls existed over entry into England, from the mid seventeenth century, the East India Company instituted barriers against people leaving England bound for India—even Indians returning home.

---

[4] See Marshall, 'English in Asia', and Lawson, *East India Company*.
[5] See Matar, *Islam in Britain*, and *Turks, Moors, and Englishmen*.
[6] See Bevan, *Development*, pp. 50–67.
[7] E.g., Court Minutes 9/11/1720, 14/12/1720, 22/5/1766, 18/6/1766.

The Company established 'factories' (warehouses staffed by merchants or factors) on India's shores, but this was only a precursor to later colonialism. These factories were at Surat (from 1613), Bombay (from 1668), Masulipatnam (from 1611) which then shifted to Madras (from 1639), and Calcutta (from 1690). Trade, however, fluctuated considerably, depending on conditions both in Asia and Europe. For example over 1620–60 the Company's trade declined, only to rebound following the reconstitution of the Company and English economic recovery after the Stuart Restoration. Rather than the more conventional Anglo-centric view, this book highlights Indian actors in analysing political, economic, social, and cultural interactions that later culminated in colonialism.

Naturally, not all Indians related to Britons identically. Members of trade diaspora communities settled in India proved particularly adept at dealing with the English Company. Mariam, an Armenian from the Mughal imperial court, was one of the first of many Indian wives who travelled to Britain along with their British husbands. Armenian and Parsi merchants particularly profited as intermediaries. Nowroji Rustamji, a Parsi, successfully negotiated directly in London, superseding local Company officials in India; many others would emulate him. Working-class Indians, especially seamen and servants, comprised the largest number of Indians who ventured to Britain. Among these, Indians of part-Portuguese descent, and Muslims, predominated. Their patterns of recruitment in India and lives in Britain reflected asymmetrical negotiations with British employers, fellow workers, and society generally. The lives of these early Indians in Britain demonstrate the contingency of cultural categories like gender, class, and ethnicity, and how they changed over time.

From the Mughal Imperial Court to England and Back

Mariam's life reveals the opportunities afforded by marital links between Indians and Britons, but also the frustration that all too often resulted from divergent personal expectations. Mariam (or, as Britons Anglicized her name, Maria) came from an élite family. Being female and Christian crucially shaped her life. Many Indian wives of Britons had similar experiences, as their gender made them adaptable but also vulnerable in both India and Britain.

Mariam's father, Mubarak Khan, reportedly served Akbar as a high-ranked courtier.[8] Mariam was raised a Christian Armenian, so her mother, and probably Mubarak Khan as well, were of that community which had settled in India and produced several Mughal officials. Although Mubarak Khan died rich, his brothers appropriated his wealth, leaving Mariam relatively dependent and unprotected, her main material inheritance being some jewels. At the Mughal court at Agra in 1609, Jahangir offered her as wife to young William Hawkins (1585?–1613).

This much-travelled English diplomat, merchant, sea-captain, and adventurer represented King James I and the East India Company, which sought a license to trade in India. Hawkins had arrived at Surat in 1608, on the first Company ship to reach India.[9] While the ship returned to England, Hawkins and his entourage journeyed to Agra. Hawkins spoke 'Turki' (Turkish)—a form of the Mughals' original language—so he could communicate independently of his rivals, the Portuguese, already ensconced at court. To honour Hawkins' royal master, Jahangir appointed him as a middle-ranked courtier with an income of some £3,000 annually and the title 'English Khan'.[10]

In addition, Jahangir felt this envoy should have someone trustworthy to manage his household—a wife. Hawkins refused Jahangir's first offer: 'a white Mayden out of his Palace, who would give me all things necessary, with slaves, and [the Emperor] would promise mee she should turne Christian; and by this means my meates and drinkes should be looked unto by them, and I should live without feare [of poisoning]'.[11] In Hawkins' polite refusal, he gave the justification that

---

[8] His son-in-law stated Mubarak Khan's *mansab* (rank) as 1,000, possibly wishing to elevate his bride's status for English readers, but Athar Ali does not accept this high rank. Birdwood and Foster, *Register*, Ali, *Apparatus*. Today's Armenian community claims Mariam with pride. Seth, *History of Armenians*, pp. 96–101.

[9] See Hawkins, *Hawkins' Voyages*; and Rawlinson, *British*.

[10] Mansab rank 400. Birdwood and Foster, *Register*, pp. 65, 97; Ali, *Apparatus*, pp. 49, 53.

[11] Hawkins, *Hawkins' Voyages*, p. 404.

'she was a Moore'. Hawkins correctly assumed Jahangir would respect his alleged custom of only marrying within his own religious community, and that the light skin colour of the proffered bride was not enough. Not to appear ungrateful, however, Hawkins countered that he would accept a Christian-born woman: 'I little thought a Christian's Daughter could bee found'. Jahangir, however, recalled Mariam and offered her to Hawkins. While she might legally have refused this wedding, she did not.

These marriage negotiations highlight the intermediate nature of Armenians, for both Mughals and Britons. Hawkins, like many compatriots, regarded Armenians as 'the Race of the most ancient Christians'. Further, he had essentially pledged that he would accept a Christian woman, should one be available. Consequently, 'seeing she was of so honest a Descent, having passed my word to the King . . . Therefore I tooke her [as wife]'. He thereby also hoped to benefit from her late father's prestige with the Mughal imperial family.

Mariam's wedding occurred in Agra before Christian witnesses but without benefit of clergy, none being available. Indeed, Hawkins' manservant, Nicholas Ufflet, officiated.[12] Later, when the couple encountered an anointed Anglican priest elsewhere in India, that priest proclaimed the sanctified nature of their marriage and wedded them again. From this point until her husband's death, Mariam evidently shifted her allegiance from her natal family to Hawkins. For Hawkins, her submission made this a highly satisfactory marriage: 'for ever after I lived content and without feare, she being willing to goe where I went, and live as I lived'.[13]

Tensions, however, remained between this English envoy, and the Portuguese as well as various hostile Mughal factions. After repeatedly losing Jahangir's favour (including for attending court while drunk), Hawkins determined to return to London. He decided that travelling overland via Persia would be too dangerous, especially for Mariam. This left them reluctantly dependent on the Portuguese. The Portuguese, however, desired to expedite Hawkins' departure, thus removing a rival from India.

---

[12] Danvers, *Letters*, vol. 3, p. 299.
[13] Hawkins, *Hawkins' Voyages*, p. 404.

Yet Mariam's mother and brothers did not want to part from her. They therefore made Hawkins promise he would take her no further than Goa, where they could visit her. Hawkins falsely swore that if he himself left India, he would leave Mariam behind with an endowment. Indeed, to deceive his in-laws Hawkins arranged two different passports from the Portuguese: one permitted him to live in Goa with the same legal protections as a Portuguese subject; the other, which he kept secret, allowed him, Mariam, and his goods to sail to Portugal and then on to Britain. Hawkins asserted that Mariam wished to travel with him, even to Britain.[14] The rise of Empress Nur Jahan's faction at the Mughal court, however, encouraged Hawkins and Mariam to return to Agra, where they resided a while.

Finally, some English Company vessels reached Surat in 1611, two years after their marriage. In order to deceive Mariam's relatives, the couple feigned going to Goa. Mariam's brother escorted them for two days on this misleading journey before returning to Agra, while Hawkins and Mariam hurried instead to Surat. Leaving their investments under local managers, they sailed east to Bantam, then west in 1612 to Britain, touching south Africa. This voyage proved typically deadly. Most of the ship's company and passengers died, including Hawkins.[15] Further, contrary winds drove the ships to Waterford, Ireland, in September 1613, where Mariam buried Hawkins.

Mariam finally reached London early in 1614, but not alone. She travelled with Gabriel Towerson (d. 1623), an English merchant and captain of the ship *Hector*, which had sailed in their fleet from Bantam to Ireland. Soon after Mariam and Towerson reached London, they married in Saint Nicholas Acons Parish Church, on 21 February 1614.[16] Mariam's new husband, Towerson, had spent years in southeast Asia, but his interactions with Asians and Africans were far less sympathetic than Hawkins' had been. This included his relations with his new wife, Mariam. Their first years in London, however, apparently went successfully.

[14] Ibid., p. 413.

[15] PRO, *Calendar*, vol. 2, pp. 346–7.

[16] Parish register, GLRO; and Brigg, *Register*, p. 65. This marriage record is dated 1613, but that must be incorrect since they only reached London early in 1614.

Mariam's two English marriages, which in later centuries might be considered 'inter-racial', did not to our knowledge evoke adverse comment from Britons at that time. Indeed, the year she arrived, the Company's directors considered favourably a request from the Muslim king of Sumatra that he be sent an English gentlewoman as a wife. One English father volunteered his daughter, who boasted 'most excellent parts for music, her needle and good discourse, and also [was] very beautiful and personable'.[17] While most directors favoured this alliance, the Company's religious advisors opposed it, allegedly fearing the jealousy of the king's other wives towards such an accomplished rival.

In London, Mariam and Towerson took their complex financial affairs before the Company's directors.[18] In particular, Hawkins had borrowed £300 from his brother, Charles, who now wanted the money back from his widow, Mariam. It was agreed that the directors would arbitrate this dispute and also settle accounts among Hawkins, Mariam, Towerson, and the Company. In these negotiations Mariam made a good impression on the directors. They, 'being charitably affected towards' her, forgave her the debts of her late husband, and moveover gave her £250 'as a token of their love' and in exchange obtained her 'general release' of the Company from all remaining monies that were due Hawkins. Less than a week later, however, Hawkins' servant Nicholas Ufflet (who had presided at her wedding to Hawkins) revealed that Mariam was not destitute, as the directors had supposed, but rather possessed diamonds and other precious stones worth some £6,000. Nevertheless, the Company reconfirmed its agreement and paid Mariam the £250 it had promised. Under English law, a married woman's money came under the control of her husband, in this case Towerson.

During Mariam's stay in London, other people labelled 'Indian' also lived there. Vague and contradictory concepts prevailed about who was 'Indian'.[19] Mariam must have known 'Coree the Indian'

[17] PRO, *Calendar*, vol. 2, pp. 335, 347.

[18] Court Minutes 27/1/1614, 4/2/1614 in PRO, *Calendar*, vol. 2, pp. 273–7.

[19] E.g., Court Minutes 9/1/1607, 10–19/2/1607, 5/6/1607, 23/12/1607 in PRO, *Calendar*, vol. 2, pp. 146–9, 154.

whom her new husband, Towerson, had kidnapped in south Africa and brought to London.[20] She probably also knew a young man from Surat who reached London on 19 August 1614, soon after her. He studied English and Latin, proving particularly noteworthy to the British on account of his desire to convert to Christianity. The directors allowed him £13 annually for expenses and expected him to return to India as 'an instrument in converting some of his nation'. After consultation with the Archbishop of Canterbury, the Lord Mayor, and King James I, this boy was baptized 'Peter' in St Dionis Backchurch on Fenchurch Street (near the Company's headquarters) on 22 December 1616.[21] Peter later returned to India to evangelize, reporting in Latin to his spiritual mentors. Many other young Indian men would go to London for their education over the centuries thereafter.[22] Mariam, as a Christian from birth and an Englishman's wife, apparently entered London society more unremarkably than these converts.

In 1616 Towerson received a commission from the Company to return to India. With him went Mariam, served by English attendants: a 'gentle waiting woman', Mrs Frances Webb; a female companion, Mrs Hudson; and several servants.[23] Towerson hoped his wife's connections would gain him political influence and wealth in India. They arrived in India in 1617, whereupon Towerson's reported arrogance alienated the Englishmen there.[24] In Agra, Mariam's relatives proved less supportive or influential than anticipated. Further, Hawkins' investments in India had diminished during Mariam's absence.

By 1618 tensions between Towerson and Mariam had escalated; he departed to seek his fortune elsewhere. Unwilling or unable to

[20] PRO, *Calendar*, vol. 2, p. 278; Danvers, *Letters*, vol. 2, pp. 330–1; vol. 3, p. 295.

[21] He took the name Peter Pope (perhaps suggesting Catholic sympathies). Court Minutes 19/8/1614, 18/7/1615; Frank Penny, *Church*, pp. 14–15; Neill, *Memoir*, pp. 11–14, 85; Das, 'Early Indian Visitors', pp. 84–5.

[22] E.g., a young man went from Surat to London in 1623. PRO, *Calendar*, vol. 4, p. 142.

[23] PRO, *Calendar*, vol. 3, p. 120. See also Ashley-Brown, *On the Bombay Coast*, p. 64.

[24] Danvers, *Letters*, vol. 4, p. 19; vol. 5, pp. 222, 227; Foster, *English Factories* (1618–21), pp. 16, 19; PRO, *Calendar*, vol. 3, pp. 120, 227.

leave with him, Mariam remained in Agra, attended by her mother and only one of her servants, a young English boy. Towerson left her merely Rs 200, which she soon spent. Towerson sent her no more. By late 1619 she had incurred debts of several hundred rupees, and was reduced to daily petitions to the Company's agents in Agra for aid, which they declined. As these agents reported, 'whereupon [Mariam] railed upon her husband and [his] nation . . . which is no small discredit to our nation'.[25] These Company men recommended that the directors induce Towerson to send his wife an allowance, if only so that she and her mother should not 'breed much trouble to your factors at Agra and the court with their exclamations . . . [causing] expence, trouble, and scandal' to the Company. Indeed, Mariam continued for years to complain to the English and others against her husband. Unfortunately, we do not know her final end, although her family continued its connections with other Europeans in India.[26]

As for Towerson, after returning to Britain late in 1619 he went to Amboyna as the Company's principal merchant.[27] The Dutch, however, charged him with criminal conspiracy, torturing and executing him in 1623, along with nine other Englishmen, one Portuguese, and nine Japanese employees of the Company. Learning of this massacre, the directors paid the money owing to the late Towerson to his brother, rather than to Mariam.[28]

While in England, Mariam had entered British society relatively easily, negotiating for herself an honoured place there, aided by her Christianity and class status. She undoubtedly had some voice in the British public sphere and learned much about life there, which she subsequently recounted to relatives and friends in India. Yet, she could evidently sustain little independence. Like many wives, she seems to have been caught between obligations to her English husbands and to

[25] Foster, *English Factories* (1618–21), pp. 155, 168–9, 184, 327.

[26] Mariam's mother reportedly married a Dutchman and her aunt was courted by a Portuguese merchant. Danvers, *Letters*, vol. 5, p. 121n; PRO, *Calendar*, vol. 3, p. 18; Foster, *English Factories* (1618–21), p. 89n.

[27] Foster, *English Factories* (1618–21), p. 216.

[28] PRO, *Calendar*, vol. 4, p. 437. John Dryden made Mariam the heroine, 'Ysabinda', and Towerson the victim of Dutch perfidy in his 1673 play 'Amboyna'.

her natal family. Further, she and other Indians necessarily depended on Company ships for transport. No direct evidence has survived about her views on her passage as a wife from the Mughal court to London: her husbands and other Company officials recorded aspects of her life, these observations becoming later a part of what would become the colonial archive. Such asymmetric control over knowledge and transport typically shaped relations between Indians and Britons during these pre-colonial years.

Identities and Rights of Indian Merchants in Britain

The small but growing number of Company ships sailing between India and Britain provided enhanced opportunities for Indian merchants as well. Trade diaspora communities long established in India, including Armenians and Parsis, especially availed themselves of this transport. During the seventeenth century alone, dozens of Armenian merchants based in Surat used Company ships to move merchandise, themselves, and their servants between India and England.[29] Conversely, the Company hoped to use the local knowledge and influence of these Armenians to enhance its trade in India and elsewhere in Asia. Yet, many Company officials also regarded these merchants as rivals, and so began to constrain them and deny them space on their often overcrowded vessels.

To reinforce the Company's shaky monopoly over trade with India, the directors decreed in 1657 that all people leaving England for India must purchase a license or 'permission' from the Company—for the substantial sum of £12. This regulation intended to block European and Asian commercial rivals, but it also inadvertently encompassed all Indians returning home. My compilation of thousands of individual 'permissions' scattered through the Company's records provides extensive evidence about Indians of all classes—including merchants, seamen, and servants—making this passage home.[30]

---

[29] Court Minutes 1/3/1626 to 20/4/1698. See also Gopal, 'Armenian Traders'; Baladouni and Makepeace, *Armenian Merchants*; Ferrier, 'Armenians'.

[30] See Chapter 2. Exempt were Company officials and 'menial servants' (almost all Europeans rather than Asians). This licensing continued for 'natives

In 1688, to establish the rights of Armenians—especially against the hostility of local Company officials in India—the leader of the Armenians in London, Khwaja Panos Kalantar (who died there in 1696), negotiated an arrangement with the directors.[31] This gave Armenians the same rights as Britons: to settle in the Company's enclaves in Asia, to purchase land for their churches there, and to practise their form of Christianity without hindrance. In exchange, Armenians agreed to use only British ships for commerce from Asia to Europe and apply their influence with local rulers to advance the Company. The arrangement helped protect Armenian goods but did not aid the Company as much as the directors desired. Nevertheless, this agreement provided the framework for their relations well into the eighteenth century.[32]

Another small trade diaspora community, the Parsis (Zoroastrians, originally from Persia), also established early commercial relationships with the British in Surat and Bombay.[33] The Rustamji family long served as chief broker to the Company, not only purchasing goods for it from Indian merchants and producers, but also representing it to Mughal officials. In 1716, however, this family came into confrontation with the Company's newly appointed governor of Bombay, William Philips. The family had delivered extensive goods, which the Company's Bombay officials later claimed were of inferior quality, refusing to honour the bonds it had given for them. During this long commercial dispute, in 1721, the governor arrested one brother, Bomanji Rustamji (who had come to negotiate a settlement), and induced Mughal officials in Surat to confine another, Framji Rustamji.

When petitions to Britain did not help, the third brother, Nowroji Rustamji, sailed to London to appeal directly to the directors about the legal and moral injustices of the Bombay government.[34] Nowroji

---

of India' until 1813, when the Company lost its monopoly on trade with India. Court Minutes 17/10/1651, 16/11/1657 to 14/4/1813.

[31] Court Minutes 22/6/1688. See also Lambert, *House of Commons*, vol. 135, pp. 283–4; and *Hansard*, series 3, vol. 125, pp. 518–21.

[32] Court Minutes 10/10/1733, 4/12/1754. See also Baladouni and Makepeace, *Armenian Merchants*, pp. 131–2, 190–2.

[33] See White, *Competition*, especially pp. 70–81, 95n37, and Hinnells, *Zoroastrians*.

[34] Court Minutes 21/2/1721, 3/4/1723, 5/7/1723.

brought his wife and children, a dozen Parsi servants, plus Indian goods, to sell there. Soon after his arrival early in 1724, he personally presented his case to the directors, which they agreed to consider. The English climate proved unhealthy for Nowroji, however, and London being far more expensive than he anticipated, he soon ran out of cash. He thus had to petition the directors to advance him £5,000, with his goods as security. After considerable negotiations the directors agreed to loan Nowroji £2,000 and also ordered his brothers released.[35]

By November 1724 the directors proposed their solution: four arbitrators from among their own number would decide the case. Nowroji was to select two, the directors the others. Nowroji agreed.[36] Early in 1725, these arbitrators recognized the legally binding force of contracts and thus found in favour of Nowroji: the Company had accepted the goods and, regardless of their quality, it must honour its bonds given in payment.[37] The directors therefore paid the money due his family, Rs 513,427 (equal to £57,753) plus interest of another Rs 54,213. They further promised to help him sell his goods in Britain. Nowroji thus successfully overrode the Bombay governor through his negotiations in London.

Nowroji received one instalment of £14,625 in London. With this money he purchased British-made merchandise that he knew would sell in India: weapons (16 brass cannon, 10 lead sheets for bullets, 720 knives, and 100 sword blades) plus mechanical equipment (11 clocks) and distilling equipment (10 copper pots, 12 pewter distilling worms, 3 small stills) in addition to personal clothing, liquor, and other provisions.[38] Further, the Company's directors ordered the award of robes of honour (*saropa*, literally 'head to foot') and a horse to the Rustamji brothers, plus tax exemption for Nowroji's houses in Bombay. The Bombay government reluctantly obeyed.

Meanwhile, both the Bombay governor's agents and Commodore Thomas Matthews, the Royal Navy commander who had conveyed Nowroji to London, brought lawsuits against him there. Threatened

[35] Court Minutes 13/5/1724 to 14/10/1724; Committee of Correspondence, Reports 9/6/1724, 7/7/1724, BL.

[36] Court Minutes 18/11/1724.

[37] Court Minutes 18/1/1725.

[38] Court Minutes 27/1/1725, 5–10/2/1725; Committee of Correspondence, Memoranda (1725–30), f. 9, BL.

with arrest, Nowroji appealed to the directors to guarantee bail for him, which they did and they recommended their lawyer to him as well. Nowroji won these lawsuits and returned to Bombay in triumph.[39] While the family was not restored to its position as Broker to the Company, Nowroji rose to be a prominent member of the Parsi community.

Nowroji thus set the pattern that many other Indian merchants, rulers, and employees would attempt to emulate, rarely so successfully. Despite his religious and ethnic differences from the British, he obtained a fair hearing and justice in London, both from the directors and from British law courts. Further, he and his entourage undoubtedly recounted back in India much about how law, politics, and life functioned in Britain. The Company was not a monolith, its directors and stockholders were composed of rival factions that might be manipulated by Indians there to overrule Company officials in India. Further, Nowroji's class and wealth privileged him in Britain in ways not available to many other Indians there. Over time, however, the growth of British colonialism made it harder for Indians to gain redress in London. Yet British ideological assertions that their administration guaranteed the rule of law to Indians under its authority continued to convince many Indians over the centuries that if they, like Nowroji, could only reach London, injustices suffered at the hands of Company officials in India would be rectified.

Indian Sailors and Lascars Make the Passage

Throughout the period covered in this book, more Indian seamen than any other class went to Britain, but their relations with British authorities remained particularly contested. Many Indian seamen had prior experience of long voyages to distant, unknown lands and so agreed to work on Company ships bound not only for coastal trade in Asia but also west to Britain. Yet their labour was initially very costly for the British. Indian seamen continually struggled with British captains and other authorities over wages, terms of employment, and treatment. Once in Britain, they interacted with British society in

[39] Court Minutes 19/2/1725, 12/3/1725, 12/1/1726, 9/2/1726.

complex ways, some marrying and settling but most visiting for a few months, often making this journey several times in a lifetime.

Trade was the lifeblood of the expanding British world system and only Indian maritime labour made British imports from India possible. There remained a constant shortage of European seamen in India. Asia's reported wealth and sensuality, which induced many European men to undertake the voyage, led large numbers to desert upon arrival there. Many others died aboard due to disease, accident, fights, or battles. The British Royal Navy remained desperate for experienced seamen and therefore conscripted ('impressed') merchant seamen on a vast scale. Consequently, British captains necessarily recruited large numbers of Indian seamen for the return voyage to Britain.

As the Company entered the ongoing networks of trade in the Indian Ocean, its ships accepted the two long-established modes of hiring Indians either as sailors or as lascars. Some Indians signed on as individual sailors, contracting personally with shipowners, as was the practice in Europe. But most followed the more widespread custom of joining maritime labour gangs, hired as a block. When employed in this second mode, they were customarily termed lascars (from *lashkar*, or *khalasi*, earlier meaning 'a group of armed men, an army', or, more specifically, 'the crew attached to an artillery piece'). Lascar referred to their terms of employment rather than ethnicity, so men with very diverse religious, regional, and caste backgrounds often worked in a single maritime labour gang. Despite their diversity, lascars on a voyage seem generally to have bonded with each other.

Seamen seeking work as lascars went first to a maritime labour contractor: a *ghat serang* (literally 'dock or landing head man', sometimes termed *seer* or 'chief' serang). Since shipping into and out of Indian ports in those days of wind-powered sailing vessels depended on the monsoons, employment remained highly seasonal. Consequently, between seasons lascars depended for food, housing, and credit from ghat serangs, which they more than repaid from future wages. They thus provided the ghat serang with control over the supply of lascar labour at times of peak demand when he could extract the most from desperate captains fearful of missing the sailing season.[40]

---

[40] Intermediary labour recruiters were not unique to the Indian Ocean. In Europe, 'crimps' specialized in recruiting seamen (including through coercion

The ghat serang negotiated a corporate contract with each captain for a pre-assembled lascar crew for the voyage (or for loading or unloading a ship in port). While captains resented their dependence and the high wages they necessarily paid, the Company recognized the right of designated ghat serangs as official labour contractors. For example, in 1699 the Company declared that, in Bengal, 'Serang Doud . . . shall be our Serang to furnish our ships with Lascars when there is occasion', contingent on his continued good behaviour.[41] The position of ghat serang remained an inheritable proprietary right at least through the eighteenth century.[42]

Ghat serangs also supplied Indian petty officers. As 'headman', a serang commanded the lascars on each ship. Earlier in the Indian Ocean, the serang was ship's navigator, but on European vessels he served as paymaster and boatswain: the intermediary who conveyed orders from European officers to the lascar crew and who also represented the lascars before the officers. He was assisted by one or more tindals (*tandail* or *tandel,* 'the head of a *tanda* or body of men', 'a gang boss').[43]

Contracts negotiated between the ghat serang and the captain for a passage to Britain often ran for six or more months. Customarily, half the contracted wages had to be paid in advance by captains, from which the lascars repaid debts they owed the ghat serang. The ghat serang also received a fee from the captain, pro-rated for the number and alleged skills of lascars, tindals, and serang whom he supplied. On arrival in Britain, the captain gave his ship's serang the remainder of the contracted wages due to the lascars, which the serang then distributed, minus his fees. The serang also conveyed wages due to deceased lascars back to their relatives in India.

Lascars and their petty officers generally had salaries quite comparable with other Indians and Britons of their class. Lascar salaries ranged considerably over time and specific conditions, but were roughly 15–22 shillings monthly (plus provisions) in the early seventeenth

---

or deception). The difference lay in the continued corporate contracts with lascars as opposed to sailors, either European or Indian.

[41] Declaration December 1699, HMS 36, f. 450.

[42] See Chapter 2.

[43] See Das Gupta and Pearson, *India*, p. 15.

century. Indeed, Company officials in India complained about these excessively high payments. For example, in 1637–8, an English official at Masulipatnam wrote of the need to hire 'these country people at extraordinary great wages to sayle in our ships', due to the shortage of European sailors.[44] Further, captains and Company officials perceived Indian seamen as generally less productive: weaker and less willing to fight an enemy than Britons. Yet the rising demand for lascars lifted their wages to 23–30 shillings during the mid eighteenth century.[45] Indian petty officers had appropriately higher wages: 28–40 shillings monthly for serangs (in the mid eighteenth century), slightly less for tindals; serangs and tindals also collected fees from their lascars. For comparison, Indian soldiers (*sepoys*) apparently received less than lascars, in the late eighteenth century only 6–9 rupees (roughly 12–18 shillings) monthly. Army petty officers (*naiks* and *havildars*) received 16–20 rupees (roughly 32–40 shillings) monthly.[46] Under the British, however, sepoys usually had continuous employment, while lascars worked only seasonally.

The wages paid to British sailors on these same Asia-bound ships rose from 8–9 shillings monthly in the early seventeenth century (less than lascars) to 30–45 shillings by the mid eighteenth century (more than lascars), depending on their experience and level of skill.[47] Thus, there was a marked shift in respective wage levels between lascars and British seamen. In calculating relative costs to shipowners of lascars versus British or Indian sailors, however, owners had to pay the additional expenses of maintenance in Britain and passage home of lascars but not Indians or Britons who contracted as sailors (see below).

Not surprisingly, labour relations between Indian (and also non-Indian) seamen and British captains frequently proved acrimonious. Storms and contrary winds, inadequate and unhealthy food, inevitable shortages and spoilage of water, and rampant disease in confined

---

[44] Foster, *English Factories* (1634–6), pp. 30, 45, 50.

[45] Wages are cited in various currencies of fluctuating values. Thus, these are only estimates. Foster, *English Factories* (1634–6), pp. 186–7, 280. See, for example, Court Minutes 14/4/1757 and L/MAR/B/series, *passim*, BL.

[46] E.g., Bengal Secret and Military Consultation 25/8/1777; Infantry Establishment and Bengal Military Consultation 17/3/1779, NAI.

[47] Chaudhuri, *English East India Company*, p. 105.

quarters combined with hostile naval and pirate ships to make life on board these relatively tiny and fragile vessels hellish for all. During the Company's first twenty years, less than half its ships ever returned from Asia; 160 Company ships sank or were captured between 1700 and 1818.[48] While officers and passengers suffered much, the rigid discipline and inevitable class and personal conflicts during long voyages made life for all seamen extremely brutal. In the case of Indian seamen, linguistic and other cultural differences between them and their British officers often exacerbated these confrontations.

Under such conditions, the serang also served as shop-steward, representing the lascars against the captain. Given the inherently conflicted relationship between captains and their crews, labour disputes frequently oppressed the lascars and troubled the directors.[49] The time of disembarkation and final 'paying off' in Britain, when the contradictory expectations of the crew and owners culminated, often proved one of confrontation. Many serangs and their lascars turned to the directors, British law courts, or other British authorities for redress of grievances inflicted by their British captains. Often, the directors intervened to obtain for lascars promised but undelivered wages or provisions. Petitions have survived from serangs and lascars of the ships: *St George* (1667–8), *Anna* (1699–1700), *Scipio* (1705–6), *Duchess* (1706), *St George* (1712–13), *Stringer* (1713), *Mermaid* (1713), *Nathaniel* (1714), *Torerie* (1721), *Tartar Galley* (1721), *Bedford* (1735), *Princess of Wales* (1741), *Heathcote* (1741), *Beaufort* (1742), and *Syren* (1757).[50]

The first of these many examples, the *St George*, which reached London from Surat late in 1667, stands particularly well documented. Typically, Captain Lord had on departure from India supplemented his diminished European crew with Indians: a serang, a tindal, and eight lascars. On disembarking in London, the serang and the tindal complained to the directors that Lord had denied the wages due to them and had also attempted to sell them into slavery and shipment to America. The directors immediately created a committee of

[48] Ibid., p. 91.
[49] Cases also arose on non-Company ships which sailed under its license. Letter of James Hungerford, 24/10/1713, SP/34/22, ff. 76–7, PRO.
[50] Court Minutes 19/11/1679 to 13/10/1742; Dispatches to Bengal, 11/11/1757, E/4/616(I), 633, para 62, BL.

its leading members to investigate.[51] Two days later, this committee reported that, while slightly exaggerated, the complaint by the serang had substance. An alehouse keeper in Shadwell had sold two of the lascars to Captain Tilman of the ship *Constant Friendship*, which had already left London on its voyage to Virginia. The committee dispatched an urgent message to the Royal Collector of Customs at the Downs, off the Kent coast, to forbid the ship its final clearance to sail. When Tilman refused to relinquish these men without reimbursement for his purchase price, the Company repaid him. It also purchased clothes, food, and lodging for all of the lascars during their time in London, and arranged for them to be employed on one of its ships, the aptly named *Return*, sailing back to Surat that spring. Ever careful of its own balance sheet, the Company charged Captain Lord £42 3s. 8d., which it had laid out to redeem and maintain these lascars.[52] Complaints by serangs against their captains would continue over the centuries to come.

From the mid seventeenth century onwards, the labour market for Asian seamen in Britain was legally suppressed by Parliament. The British mercantilist Navigation Acts, particularly those passed from 1660 on, privileged those ships defined in law as British.[53] Non-British ships were excluded entirely from certain kinds of trade with Britain and suffered higher tariffs on other designated commodities. For most of this period, the Acts defined as British only those ships with a crew at least three-quarters British—as well as being British-built, British-owned, and British-captained. The Royal Customs office tried to monitor all incoming and outgoing ships.[54]

Through their constructions of ethnic categories, these Acts profoundly and particularly affected Asian seamen by defining them as 'non-British'. In contrast, African and Caribbean seamen could be classed as British. The Royal Navy justified this as necessary to produce a pool of experienced and trustworthy merchant seamen ready for conscription—men the navy considered worthy fighters. The navy

[51] Court Minutes 31/12/1667.

[52] E.g., Court Minutes 2–15/1/1668, 22/2/1668, 27/3/1668, 13–27/11/1713.

[53] The most crucial was Act 12, Car. 2, c. 18 (1660). Parliament periodically modified these acts until largely repealing them in 1849 and 1854.

[54] E.g., Court Minutes 26/8/1720.

generally regarded Asian seamen as lacking sufficient physical and moral strength to plunge themselves into battle; in contrast, African-descended sailors reputedly embodied these qualities, as did British seamen, of course. In practice, the navy impressed and hired substantial numbers of Indians, although this reflected its frequent desperation for manpower rather than its preference. Thus, for example, in 1749 at the end of the War of Austrian Succession, the navy discharged and consigned to the Company for repatriation fifty-six Indian seamen who had survived its service.[55]

The Navigation Acts thus created an unintended surplus of unemployable Indian seamen in Britain. Ships arriving from Asia were excused from the requirement of three-quarters British crew since the government recognized the necessity of hiring Asian seamen there for the voyage home. Yet, on leaving Britain, these Acts precluded ships which wished to be classed as British from employing Asians above one-quarter of the crew.[56] Indeed, the Company's directors periodically instructed its outgoing ships to have all-British crews, thereby minimizing dependence on lascars.[57]

The directors and other British authorities struggled henceforth with the consequent perennial problem of growing numbers of stranded and unwanted Indian seamen in their midst. While some owners made provision for the lascars their ships brought to Britain, others did not, simply discharging them into British society. Throughout the period covered in this book, reports repeatedly reached the directors about Indian seamen 'daily strowling about [London's] Streets, and begging'.[58] In what was described by British authorities as an act of lunacy, but might have been a desecration of symbols of British world power, an armed lascar entered St Paul's cathedral in 1679. He broke away the orb and sceptre from a statue of Queen Anne and defaced the symbols of the four quarters of the globe over which Britain ruled, before he was subdued.[59] Most lascar resistance was less overt.

[55] Court Minutes 1–8/11/1749, 6/12/1749.

[56] In war, this was relaxed to require only a quarter of the crew need be British. E.g., Act 13, Geo. 2, c. 3 (1740).

[57] E.g., Court Resolution 8/11/1671.

[58] Court Minutes 24/11/1714. See also Court Minutes 23/12/1713, 17/10/1718.

[59] *Annual Register* 12–17/9/1769, Chronicle, p. 131.

The directors largely accepted paternalistic responsibility for these men, motivated only in part by a sense of humane justice due them. They also feared harm to their image in British official and public opinion, which regarded such indigent Indians as the Company's moral obligation. Thus, the directors intervened to repatriate lascars, on occasion having to bail them out of British jails first.[60] Nevertheless, out of deference to the Company's profits, the directors sought the lowest reasonable expense in discharging this burden. Generally, in accord with the Navigation Acts, they arranged for lascars to travel back to India free as passengers—at the cheapest cost.

Over time, the financial obligations of the Company toward these lascars proved considerable. At the end of the seventeenth century, for example, the directors allotted 6 pence daily per man, plus return passage of £4-6 for each lascar and £10 for each serang.[61] Since this was roughly equivalent to the wages already paid them for the voyage in, it doubled the cost of employing a lascar. The Company regularly charged these expenses to the owners of the ships which had brought those particular lascars to Britain, when they could be identified.[62] Since owners of arriving ships were liable for this fixed cost, they had no financial incentive to give the lascars they discharged any clothing or food, but rather often just set them loose in Britain, at best with the pay owing them. Until the end of the eighteenth century, no regular system existed for housing or feeding these Asians awaiting passage home; rather it was arranged on a case-by-case basis, if at all.

In 1689, the directors tried an innovation to save this passage money. They ordered lascars to work on their voyage home, not for wages—since the Navigation Acts largely forbade employment—but simply to cover their costs.[63] Serangs made this impossible by (quite reasonably) objecting to work without pay in violation of the terms of the agreement they had contracted before leaving India. In 1693, for example, Serang Pulsetty on behalf of his five lascars and Mahmood Hussan on behalf of his seven argued successfully against this

[60] E.g., Court Minutes 17/11/1749.

[61] The Company also allotted £10 each for European soldiers. E.g., Court Minutes 28/9/1688, 17/2/1693, 23/6/1693.

[62] Court Minutes 18/11/1685, 9/11/1687, 21/12/1691, 15/3/1694, 4/4/1700.

[63] Court Minutes 24/3/1689.

non-contractual requirement, demanding either payment of wages or free passage as passengers.[64] This 1689 experiment died in the face of objections by serangs. Nevertheless, in practise many captains evidently forced lascars to work—despite officially being passengers with their passages prepaid.[65]

Serangs also learned how to put political and moral pressure on the directors. On at least four occasions early in the eighteenth century, serangs sent petitions not only to the directors but also to the British royal family. These included the serang of the *Montague* who petitioned Queen Anne's husband, Prince George, in 1706; the serangs of the *Mermaid* and *St George* who petitioned Queen Anne in 1713; and the serang of the *Torerie* who petitioned King George I in 1721.[66] Their faith in the authority of the Crown over the directors seems indeed to have helped draw attention to their cases, since in each instance officials in the royal establishment wrote to the directors demanding an explanation. On the other hand, so 'clamorous' was Ghulam Mahmud, serang of the *St George* who petitioned Queen Anne in 1713, that, although he succeeded in his case in Britain, the directors blacklisted him and his tindals, ordering Company's officials in India never to employ them again.[67]

During the seventeenth century, the frequent lack of an explicit contract between the serang and the captain often led to strong differences between them as to the terms of employment. After a particularly bitter disagreement between the serang and the captain of the *Montagu* in 1706, the directors attempted decisively to solve this problem. To avoid in future inciting the 'clamorous temper' of the serangs, the directors ordered each of its port officials in India to require a written labour contract before a ship could leave. The captain and the lascars were all to appear in person and sign an 'equitable' agreement, countersigned by the Company's local agent, copies of which were kept by the

[64] Court Minutes 1/2/1693, 29/3/1693.

[65] Act 55 Geo. 3, c. 116 (1814–15). PP, Returns (Commons), 1814–15, vol. 3, paper 471, pp. 217–29.

[66] Court Minutes 19/4/1706, 11/12/1706, 21/1/1713, 23/10/1713, 4/11/1713, 10–15/2/1721.

[67] Court Minutes 2–21/1/1713.

serang, the captain, and local Company official, with yet another copy sent to Britain.[68]

In practice, the contracted amount due to lascars shrank at the time of payout due to various deductions. These began even before the voyage. The ghat serang normally took as his share about 20% of the lascar's entire salary, plus any loans or provisions he had advanced. The ghat serang's accountant deducted an additional fee (usually one anna per rupee or 6.25%) for himself. During the voyage, ship serangs appear to have regularly charged lascars under them customary and occasional fees, including fines for alleged violations of discipline and payments for clothing and other supplies. Captains likewise levied fines for sundry alleged infractions and also charged highly for required or optional clothing and supplies from the ship's store. Further, the official British tariffs on all seamen included fees to Greenwich Hospital (for disabled seamen); by the late eighteenth century, lascars had 1 shilling monthly deducted by the Merchant Shipping Office in London and another fee taken by the navy agent.[69] In all, of the contracted salary due on disembarkation in Britain, lascars often received less than half. Nevertheless, what they received could be a substantial sum for a working-class man at the time. For example, account books from 1693 show some serangs receiving in London £15 each and lascars £4.[70]

Once in Britain, most Indian seamen determined to seek entertainment and opportunities. Like many seamen around the world, many lascars often quickly spent their pay and fell into destitution. Others, however, found employment, married, and settled in Britain. In 1614, dwelling in London were three 'Indian' seamen (so designated despite their Europeanized names, Salvador, Samuel Mounar, and Antony Deleber).[71] This pre-dated the Navigation Acts so they engaged to work on a Company ship bound for the East Indies. What brought

---

[68] Letter Book from Managers 7/2/1706, E/3/96, BL.

[69] *Times* 9/12/1814 3d; *Morning Chronicle* 30/11/1785, 1/12/1785.

[70] E.g., Court Minutes 29/3/1693. But payments varied widely, see L/MAR/B/series, *passim*, BL.

[71] The exact origins of these men are unclear, but their Portuguese-style names may indicate they came from western India. PRO, *Calendar*, vol. 2, p. 275.

them into the official record was their request to take their English wives back with them. The directors refused, but not because of what later Britons might term the 'inter-racial' quality of their marriages. Rather, the directors refused on grounds of safety, considering it unfitting 'for such women to go among so many unruly sailors' for such a long voyage. The directors instead arranged for part of these men's wages to go to their wives during their absence, thus recognizing their marriages as legitimate and holding these Indian seamen financially responsible for their English wives. Marriages in Britain between Indian men and British women remained frequent and Indian sailors became a visible feature of British society, particularly, but not exclusively, in the dock areas of east London.[72] Indian seamen who failed or simply wished to return home relied increasingly on the directors to provide them basic maintenance and free passage back to India.

Indian seamen sailing to Britain thus endured not only the hardships common to the working classes in their age but also the everpresent dangers of the sea. Yet they commanded relatively high wages, retained much of their customary form of recruitment and collective service, and occasionally secured their rights in the face of hostile British authorities. A few saved or earned enough to pay their own passage home, as did eight lascars in 1744.[73] Many evidently returned to India with materially little or nothing to show for their long labours, although they had learned much about Britain. They thus knew better what to expect when they approached the ghat serang for future voyages. Nevertheless, many of the economic and legal forces and constraints on them and other Indians in Britain were beyond their control.

Indian Servants and Slaves Working in Britain

Like seamen, Indians who sought—or at least accepted—work as servants found the arrival of the British meant new opportunities for employment, though not always to their long-term advantage. Indian

[72] For example, in 1697, some Asian seamen joined the crowds watching the public execution of pirates at Wapping Dock. Das, 'Early Indian Visitors', p. 84. See also Lorimer, *Colour*; and Wheeler, *Complexion*.
[73] Court Minutes 20/2/1744.

servants who sailed to Britain were distanced from family and community; unlike lascars, they usually laboured isolated from other Indians. Yet a growing number found it a relatively attractive option, compared to their limited prospects in India. For slaves, there was obviously less choice, although they could affect their situation by co-operating or resisting on their passage to Britain. Yet, for slaves willing to adapt themselves to British culture and religion, emancipation was possible there. Overall, the relative rarity of Indian servants in Britain during this early period, and their unusual (for Britain) distinctive Indian characteristics, often added to their value in the eyes of their employers or masters. Their exotic identities tended to be highlighted in formal occasions, like paintings or parties, while in mundane settings their masters and the surrounding society pressurized them to Anglicize. Yet, even when Anglicized, they stood out in different degrees from Britons of their class, with both advantages and disadvantages.

Indian servants and slaves were unusual enough in seventeenth century Britain to often provide a particular cachet to their master's household.[74] In 1630, William Feilding, first Earl of Denbigh (1582–1643), went to India representing Charles I. On Denbigh's return in 1633, he brought with him at least one Indian servant, as well as various other souvenirs.[75] He then commissioned Anthony Van Dyck to paint a joint portrait of him and his (unnamed) Indian servant (see Image 1).

The painting highlights Denbigh's oriental experiences, but in complex ways. Although Van Dyck painted the figures from life in England, he created for them an Indian setting—not very accurately. Denbigh's own jacket and pajamas vaguely imitate an Indian gentleman's clothing. Denbigh, according to his family's oral tradition, had become totally lost in an Indian jungle until his servant rescued him by directing his safe return.[76] This portrait thus not only shows Denbigh as semi-orientalized in dress but also disoriented in location, needing an Indian's knowledge in order to proceed. While Van Dyck foregrounded and highlighted the patron, he also painted the young Indian with agency, wearing an incongruously elaborate turban and

[74] Africans also appeared as 'exotic' ornaments in élite British households and public occasions. See Fryer, *Staying Power*.

[75] PRO, *Calendar*, vol. 7, p. xliii.

[76] Feilding, *Royalist Father*, p. 77.

robe for his station in life.[77] This young Indian servant, after living about two years in Britain and adding lustre to the earl's household and status, sailed home with much to recount about Britain.[78]

Other British aristocrats likewise used Indians to distinguish themselves, sometimes with only limited references to the 'orient'. Around 1674, Lady Charlotte Fitzroy was painted by Peter Lely being served by an Indian, evidently done from life (see Image 2). Yet, in the vaguely classical setting, neither the servant's costume nor the frieze in the background marks him as Indian. Lady Charlotte was apparently not claiming any 'oriental' accomplishments for herself but rather displaying her possession of a rare and valuable servant who was Indian by birth if not dress. Further, Lely's careful delineation of the Indian's face reveals him as having character, rather than as an abstract stereotype, even if he remained in an anonymous serving role.[79]

In contrast, British use of Indians took a more crude form when, in 1683, Charles II sought to add distinction to his court through combining the oriental and the grotesque. He commanded the East India Company to provide him with 'one Male, and two Female Blacks, but they must be Dwarfs, and of the least size that you can procure'.[80] Thus, in this period, some English aristocrats evidently recognized Indian servants as individuals whose attending presence added to their status—with or without strong associations with India—while others regarded them as simply rare objects indicative of the exotic.

Over time, increasing numbers of middle-class Britons imitated the aristocracy by using Indian servants and slaves to attend or ornament their households. Not all Indians cooperated. An Indian from Madras had been enslaved in his early teens, brought to Britain around 1720 by Captain Dawes, and then given to Mrs Elizabeth Turner, who called him Julian. He reportedly refused to learn English or become Christian. Using him to display her possession of the 'exotic', Mrs Turner made him dance and sing in 'Indian style' before her guests

---

[77] National Gallery, London NG5633. See Martin, *Flemish School*, pp. 52–5. For its engraving by H.T. Ryall, see Foster, *English Factories* (1630–3), frontispiece.

[78] Court Minutes 18/2/1635.

[79] See Steward, *New Child*, pp. 38, 84.

[80] Court Letters 4/5/1683, cited in Hedges, *Diary*, vol. 2, p. ccclvii.

at parties. Although Mrs Turner denied awareness of his discontent, he rebelled by stealing 20 guineas and setting fire to her house (on 8 August 1724).[81] In prison, awaiting execution for theft and arson, he accepted Christianity and was baptized 'John', allegedly in the vain hope it would lead to his release. He was hanged at Tyburn.

In other cases, Indian slaves who converted to Christianity did receive liberation. From the seventeenth century, increasing numbers of Britons believed that slavery was incompatible with being Christian and living in Britain. Yet the British legal system did not stop the export of slaves from Britain until the late eighteenth century; slavery within Britain continued in individual cases into the nineteenth century (see Chapter 6).

The Company both participated in slaving overseas and sometimes supported emancipation in Britain. The Company's strategically located base at St Helena served the brutal trans-Atlantic slave trade. The Company purchased, transported, and sold Asian and African slaves throughout Asia, albeit on a far smaller scale than other British merchants did in the Atlantic world.[82] Well into the nineteenth century, despite pressure from Parliament and the abolition of slavery in 1833, the Company proved reluctant to stop slavery as practised within parts of Indian society.[83]

Nevertheless, the majority of the Company's directors and shareholders personally believed in the liberating virtues of Christianity and British culture. For example, in 1670 the directors ordered the emancipation of any slave at St Helena who converted and then proved over a seven-year trial period to be a zealous Christian.[84] The Company also occasionally rescued and restored Indians who came to Britain as free

[81] OBP 14/10/1724, www.oldbaileyonline.org, ref. t17241014–79; Hayward, *Lives*, pp. 175–7.

[82] E.g., Court Minutes 13/1/1671.

[83] The 1833 Charter Renewal Act (Clause 88) required the directors to abolish slavery in India, but this was not effected until the Government of India Act 5 of 1843. See *Times* 31/7/1829 2f, 30/7/1836 4a, 21/12/1847 5a. See also Adam, *Slavery*; Banaji, *Slavery*; British and Foreign Anti-Slavery Society, *Slavery*; Indrani Chatterjee, *Gender, Slavery*; Chattopadhyay, *Slavery*; and Peggs, *Slavery*.

[84] Court Minutes 7/12/1670.

servants (or, as discussed above, sailors) and were thereafter enslaved. In 1737, for example, a letter 'from a Black Fellow born in Bengal called Pompey, and brought to Britain by Captain Benfield, and since a servant to Major Woodford at Virginia who now detains him as a Slave' led to an investigation and intervention by the Company to return him to India.[85] Yet, many among the Company's shareholders and directors themselves owned slaves in Britain and elsewhere.

Becoming Christian might emancipate slaves, but emancipation could expose them to hardships all too common to the poor in Britain. A ten-year-old Indian came to London from Bengal around 1741 as the slave of Mr Suthern Davies, who passed her on to a relative, Mrs Ann Suthern. The slave converted into the Church of England: she was christened 'Catherine Bengall' at St James, Westminster, on 26 November 1745.[86] Emancipated by this, she left Mrs Suthern's household (either voluntarily or perforce) and lodged at the *Ship* tavern. Her ongoing sexual relationship with William Lloyd, however, left her pregnant and destitute. When her pregnancy became evident in July 1746, she had to appear before the local magistrate, who admitted her to the workhouse of the parish of St Martin in the Fields, where she resided.[87] There she gave birth to a son, christened with the father's name, William, on 22 September 1746. Like so many women of her class, Indian and British, she and her son then disappeared from surviving British records, either due to death or merger into British society.

Even in the seventeenth century, a small pool of Indian labour had emerged in Britain. Some clearly adapted themselves to British values and entered society there. Since many took English names and converted (at least nominally) to Anglican Christianity, indication of their Indian origins only occasionally appeared in parish and legal records, or newspapers, often through the qualifier 'the Indian' or 'the East Indian'.[88] Thus, James 'the Indian' worked for James Duppa, a beer

---

[85] Court Minutes 31/8/1737.

[86] Baptism 26/11/1745, St James, Westminster, WAC.

[87] Testimony of Catherine Bengall of St Martin-in-the-Fields, 23/7/1746, in Barber, *Celebrating*, vol. 2, pp. 25–34.

[88] See WAC, Baptisms Index; successful prosecution by Augustine Darosario of Bengal against Anne Howard, for theft, 26/2/1746, www.oldbaileyonline.org, Ref: t17460226-1; Visram, *Asians*, pp. 2, 9.

brewer, in London, died in September 1618, and was buried in the parish church of St Botolph without Aldgate.[89] His Indian origin and continuing identity did not prevent him from being accepted as a member of the Church of England and buried with honour.

Nonetheless, quite apart from any exotic appeal, these servants' Indian identity occasionally marked them as different from the working people around them, for better or worse. On one hand, they could turn to the Company's directors, who accepted special responsibility to provide them succour and relief, much as a English parish would for any established resident within it. Thus, 'John, the Indian', worked as a weaver in England in 1609—suggesting that artisans from India participated in the British cloth industry. Unfortunately, John lost his thumb through an accident, disabling him for his craft. Consequently, the directors granted his request for employment at the Company docks, where he was still able to work.[90] The directors also provided clothing and maintenance for various other Indians in Britain as well, but usually required them to work in exchange.[91]

When Indian slaves or servants left their masters or employers, however, their Indian identity made it more difficult for them to escape. Returning home independently required the purchase of a £12 'permission' from the directors in addition to the £4–9 passage fare, both very difficult for a runaway servant or slave to manage.[92] Furthermore, from the seventeenth century onwards, English newspapers began to carry advertisements calling for the return of self-liberated Indian slaves or servants.[93] Such descriptions typically identified them as Indian in complexion, but their clothing tended to be European in style, suggesting their Anglicization. For example, in July 1702, an employer sought the return of an

> Indian Black Servant: Went away from his master's house in Drury-Lane upon Monday . . . and has been since seen at Hampstead, Highgate, and

[89] Forbes, *Chronicle*, pp. 3–4.

[90] Since the first Company fleet only returned from India that year, John may have come by another means or from elsewhere in Asia. PRO, *Calendar*, vol. 2, pp. 192–3.

[91] E.g., PRO, *Calendar*, vol. 6, pp. 193–4, 201; vol. 7, pp. 412, 438, 536.

[92] Yet, in 1685, a 'black servant' purchased his passage home to South East Asia and had £10 savings. Court Minutes 7/10/1685.

[93] See Visram, *Asians*, p. 13.

Tottenham-Court, an Indian black boy with long hair, about 15 years of age, speaks very good English; he went away in a brown fustian frock, a blue waistcoat, and scarlet shag breeches, and is called by the name of Morat: Whoever brings him to, or gives notice of him, so as he may be brought to Mr Pain's House in Prince's Court, Westminster, shall have a guinea reward, and the boy shall be kindly received.[94]

Such advertisements were common for British runaways as well, suggesting that class, not necessarily ethnic, conflict, impelled them to flee, but their Indian identity made them stand out once they had done so.

Thus, servants from India held many roles in Britain. Given the cost of their transportation to and from Britain, they were by no means inexpensive labour. Some found that their Indian identity enhanced their value to their masters by distinguishing them from British servants, albeit at the cost of occasionally being treated as oriental ornaments. For a few, particularly Indian slaves, there were possibilities for upward mobility if they adapted to British culture and religion. Nor were their roles fixed. Sometimes a man might work as a sailor or lascar on the voyage in, and then as a servant once in Britain or on the return voyage.[95] The growth of British colonialism in India from the mid eighteenth century onwards, the concomitant shifts in British concepts of race, and the changes over time in class relations within Britain all affected the lives of Indian servants and slaves there.

The First 150 Years

Prior to the 1750s, even before the British established colonial rule over Indians, complex asymmetries developed in the relations among these peoples. Over this period, Britons and Indians shifted their identifications of themselves and others. Britain was beginning its transformation into a nation-state that would soon start an empire in Asia. Mughal imperial rule expanded, but then India began to revert to strong region-based polities. As Britons and Indians entered each others' lands at about the same time, their interactions affected each other unequally.

[94] *Flying Post* 11–14/7/1702, cited in Scott, *Every One*, pp. 231–2.
[95] E.g., Court Minutes 3/11/1669.

Most Britons who reached India sought trade and fortune, but they often came at the sufferance of Indian regional rulers or Mughal officials. Yet, in India they took wives, began commercial partnerships, hired seamen and servants, and bought slaves. Conversely, most Indians who ventured to Britain went as dependants of Britons, if only because the ships that regularly made the passage from India to Britain were British-owned and commanded, although often partly Indian crewed. Even wealthy Indian merchants in Britain had to seek permission from the Company to return to their homeland.

Living in Britain, each Indian had to negotiate his or her identity and relationship with the host culture, one that was as yet relatively unfamiliar with Indians. Britons on occasion included as 'Indian' people from Africa or South East Asia. Religious affiliation as Christian (or not), gender, and class strongly determined an Indian's status and experiences in Britain. Conversion to Anglican Christianity could bring emancipation from slavery and/or acceptance into a parish and with it basic social supports during life as well as an honoured burial after death. Women appeared more transmutable than men. In Britain, Indian slaves, servants, and seamen often had more in common with their British peers than with wealthy Indians there. Thus, in the period prior to the establishment of colonialism, Indians had some scope to reshape their identities within British society.

Those who returned to India took with themselves a wider knowledge of Britain, its people, and society. Certainly, many Indians took employment or made the passage to Britain only to be disappointed in their lives there. Given available evidence, however, we cannot recover how much the knowledge produced by these Britain-returned Indians spread through Indian society.

Particularly for this early period, our knowledge of Indians in Britain comes primarily through a careful reading of British records, often against the grain. Most Indian self-representations appear only indirectly. Over time, however, with the coming of British colonial rule over increasing parts of India, the number of Indians who made the journey to Britain would expand—as does our knowledge of their voices. Thus, paradoxically, colonialism brought greater access for Indians to the public sphere in metropolitan Britain.

CHAPTER 2

Indians in Britain as British Colonial Conquests Begin

1750s–1790s

Early Colonial India and Britain

From the mid eighteenth century, the movement of Indians to Britain expanded significantly in number and diversity, reflecting rapidly shifting conditions in each locale. Increasingly, Indian servants and seamen negotiated employment on the passage to Britain and in its changing society. As Indian merchants and rulers struggled with various competing officials of the Company, some went or sent Indian agents to Britain. In various ways, these people could shape their identities and roles there, either by influencing what being Indian meant for Britons or by Anglicizing. Many represented themselves in the public sphere, including through direct testimony to Parliament, the directors, law courts, and other authorities. Some gained redress of grievances or influenced colonial policy; all faced some degree of British surveillance and control. Their experiences of Britain, and the information they brought back to India, varied considerably by class, religion, and gender. In the absence of relevant political, diplomatic, or legal precedents for relations between Indian and British peoples and polities, all parties improvised practises and advanced competing principles during this early transition to colonialism.

Britain itself underwent rapid and conflict-ridden changes during this period, several centring on the Company. Long world wars, especially against the French—in Europe, India, and other colonies—both strained Britain and forged its nation-statehood. The Company's vast annexations in India—and Britain's territorial gains and losses in the Americas—particularly intensified the debate about Britain as an empire. Indeed, the Company's costly wars rocked its administration and drove it into debt and discredit in Britain, bringing further ten-

sions with the British state and public. The Company's import of Indian goods—which were often re-exported to the European continent,
Africa, or the Americas—reoriented Britain's developing economy
and inadvertently created a body of unemployed Indian seamen there.
Political bargaining between Members of Parliament and stockholders and directors of the Company produced military and financial
support for the Company but also greater parliamentary control.[1]

The 1773 Regulating Act restructured the Company's administration in India, including making the governors of Bombay and Madras
subordinate to the governor-general in Bengal. The 1784 India Act
created the 'Board of Control' through which the British government
supervised the Company's political policies. The many Parliamentary
Secret and Select Committee hearings, the attacks on Robert Clive,
and the impeachment in the Commons and seven-year trial of Warren
Hastings in the House of Lords (1788–95), all reflected British factional and ideological discord, in which Indian merchants and representatives participated. Returning British 'nabobs' imported Indian
treasure and servants, raising further moral controversies and social
strains.[2] Bitter public and political arguments raged about Britain's
central role in the slave trade; yet slaves in Britain occasionally achieved emancipation in advance of their fellows in India and elsewhere.
British assessments of themselves and others tended to highlight the
often more changeable categories of religion, language, class, and comportment rather than biological race, although this was changing in
the colonies. British literature and art reflected all these concerns,
although they did not necessarily depict accurately the lived experience
of the small but growing number of Indians in Britain.

Over the late eighteenth century India also underwent fundamental
changes, with the Company central to many of them. Various disaf-
fected governors (nominally subordinate to the Mughal emperor),
emergent warlords, and European companies fought for power as
autonomous regional rulers; of these, the English East India Company expanded most aggressively. The Company allied with dynamic
Indian social groups and individuals, although their interests often

[1] See Bowen, *Revenue.*

[2] See Heiton, *Castes*, pp. 158–71; Holzman, *Nabobs*; Lawson and Phillips,
'"Our Execrable Banditti'''; Marshall, *East Indian Fortunes*; Spear, *Nabobs*;
Thompson, *Intrigues.*

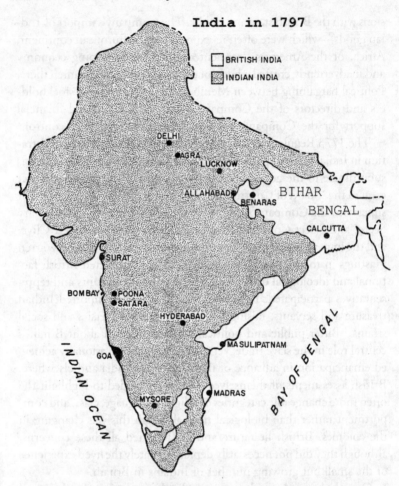

Map 1: India in 1797.

clashed. Indian merchants supplied the goods that the Company exported to Britain, but contended for a share of the profits. Indian seamen worked the ships that transported these goods, but not without frequent disputes over their rights and working conditions. Indian officials and servants took employment under Company officials, often with deep differences over conflicting expectations. Some Indian rulers or claimants to rule allied with the Company, seeking to use its armies of Indian soldiers trained as sepoys under British officers. But

Company officials confiscated the treasuries of many Indian rulers and annexed their vast territories, bringing millions of Indians under Company rule. Most strikingly, the nawab of the rich provinces of Bengal and Bihar lost the battle of Plassey in 1757, bringing these lands (three times the size of England) suddenly under the Company's power through a series of puppet successors.

Following further fighting in 1764, the Company extended military control over much of north India, including over the Mughal emperor, a still-powerful political and cultural symbol. The Company's base at Bombay dealt less effectively against the surrounding Maratha powers during this period. In south India, the Company struggled desperately in a series of wars against Tipu Sultan of Mysore (r. 1782–99). From this context of expanding Company rule, many Indian servants, seamen, merchants, political agents, diplomats, and noblemen ventured to Britain.

Indian Servants and Slaves

With expanding British imperialism of the late eighteenth century, Indian servants (including slaves) changed from a relative rarity to a distinctive presence in Britain. Their numbers grew markedly and their particular composition and condition differentiated them from the general working-class populations of both Britain and India. Their isolation from India and their economic dependence on British empployers or owners put pressure on them to accept British-style names, dress, deportment, and (at least nominal) Christianity.[3] Such Anglicization brought a degree of acceptance, and for slaves possible emancipation, at the cost of covering up their natal culture. Over time, their collective presence came to appear a 'problem' for British authorities but British efforts to regulate and control them had mixed results.

[3] In the relatively fewer instances where Indian servants served élite Indians in Britain, this pressure to Anglicize was somewhat less. Significantly, most élite Indians in Britain (including merchants, diplomats, royalty, and scholars) employed servants from their own communities, in part so religious dietary strictures could be satisfied but also apparently out of cultural solidarity. For discussion of 'cross-dressing' and the 'appropriation' of the colonizer's clothing by the colonized as resistance and empowerment, see Tobin, *Picturing*, pp. 22ff.

In India, Britons now hired ever larger numbers of Indian servants and purchased ever more slaves. British servants were very costly to import and had high mortality rates there, while Indian servants were inexpensive and abundant. Thus, imitating élite Indian households, newly-rich Britons adopted with increasing assurance the trappings of wealth by establishing households containing a vast array of servant specialists. Even middle-level British officials hired dozens of servants including: gardeners and night-soil removers, horse-grooms and palanquin carriers, heralds and messengers, cooks and table attendants, hooka-tenders and body servants, armed guards and clerks, translators and language teachers, as well as lady's maids, nursemaids (ayahs), and concubines.

Britons returning home often brought some Indian servants to attend them or their children on the voyage and to continue their lifestyle acquired in India. The most prominent and controversial newly rich Britons entered society as 'nabobs', with Indian attendants marking their newly elevated status. In selecting Indian servants to bring along, Britons sought peoples with whom they were familiar or who had previous experience of the voyage or special skills. On moving to Britain, Indian servants, however, were no longer cheap labour.

Despite widespread impoverishment in India (in part exacerbated by the transition to British rule), not all Indian servants were willing to move to Britain: the passage alone had high mortality rates. Given the length of the journey, return home in less than a year was impossible. Having survived this, most servants would remain away many years, sometimes settling in Britain. In Britain, most Indian servants worked singly in British households, isolated from other Indians and thus under particularly strong pressure from their masters and British society around them to Anglicize.

One particularly noteworthy Indian who worked his way up from a camp follower to subaltern officer in India, before settling and marrying in Ireland in 1783 was Sake Dean Mahomed (1759–1851) of Patna.[4] In 1794, he wrote and published his autobiographical travel narrative in English. He later moved to England where he worked as a servant, restauranteur, and then flourished as a practitioner of Indian medicine: 'the Shampooing Surgeon'.

---

[4] For his own writings and a biography, see Fisher, *First Indian Author*.

The special relationship of Indian servants in Britain to the Company distinguished them from British men and women of their class. Under prevailing British poor laws, the parish in which an indigent resided had responsibility for rudimentary social support. For indigent Indians not accepted into a parish, the Company was responsible. Many Indian servants who had been abused or abandoned by their British (or Indian) masters therefore appealed successfully to the directors for investigation of their complaints, maintenance in Britain, and free passage home (with the master, if identified, liable for reimbursement to the Company for these costs).

The Company's archive of surveillance and control over Indian servants in Britain reveals their composition. As we saw, from 1657 the directors required all people, including 'Black servants', leaving Britain for India to purchase its 'permission' for £12. These permission records enable us to identify thousands of Indian servants—at least in fragmentary ways. Many appear only with the identity male or female 'Black servant' rather than by name, or else by a single name like 'Mary, a Black maidservant'. This imprecision reveals how little attention British authorities paid the individuality of working-class Indians. These records became even less complete by the late eighteenth century, as the number of such Indian servants overwhelmed the Company's controls; in 1813, the directors abandoned this increasingly futile requirement of a permission for 'natives of India' when the Company lost its monopoly over trade with India.[5] We can compile from these thousands of fragments incomparable evidence about the changing patterns of the lives of these men and women servants. Chart 1 suggests—but underestimates—the magnitude of Indian servants leaving Britain from the period when these records were most comprehensive. Since this chart tracks only officially reported departures from Britain that can be documented today, it undercounts the number who actu-ally left Britain due to the smuggling out of Indians, the incompleteness of the Company's controls and records, the substantial numbers of Indian deaths there, and Indians settling in Britain. Nonetheless, the chart indicates a slow and relatively steady increase in the number of servants until 1757, with significantly more rapid growth thereafter, mirroring the Company's subsequent expansion.

[5] Court Minutes 14/4/1813.

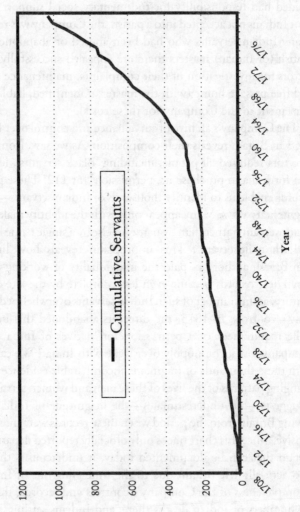

Chart 1: Cumulative Servants by Year, 1708–79.

By 1779, over 1,000 'Black servants' had officially departed Britain for India. This was more than a tenfold increase (although from a low base), from an average of only about four servants annually for the first decade of this period to an average of forty-four during its last decade.

Analysing further, Chart 2 largely reflects the relative level of activity in each of the Company's presidencies.[6]

In the early eighteenth century, the Coromandal coast (with Madras as the emergent main base) showed slightly more extensive employment of Indian servants. By the mid eighteenth century, and increasingly thereafter, Bengal surpassed it, particularly following the political transformation after 1757. The western Indian ports of Bombay and Surat lagged throughout this period.

These officially reported figures also give us evidence about the changing composition of these Indian servants by sex. Chart 3 indicates that Indian women servants slightly outnumbered men until the mid-eighteenth century, when males caught up; gender parity would continue thereafter.

Using these officially reported figures in a different way, we can see the recorded identities of servants as a whole for the eighteenth century.

Table 1: Servants Leaving Britain for India, 1708–91

n/%	Male	Female	Total
All European	367/40%	366/40%	733/80%
British	302/33%	285/31%	587/64%
Portuguese	65/7%	81/9%	146/16%
Muslim	39/2%	6/1%	45/5%
Hindu	3/0%	0/0%	3/0%
Other/Unknown	40/4%	95/10%	135/15%
Total	409/49%	372/51%	916/100%

The vast majority (80 per cent) of these Indian servants leaving Britain over the 1708–91 period appear in these official Company records with European or Europeanized names (either British or Portuguese). Some were of part European descent, with their European name

[6] Since Company officials compiled all these records in London, they differ from the records considered in Chapter 6, which were compiled separately by each Presidency, following different local practises and unevenly preserved.

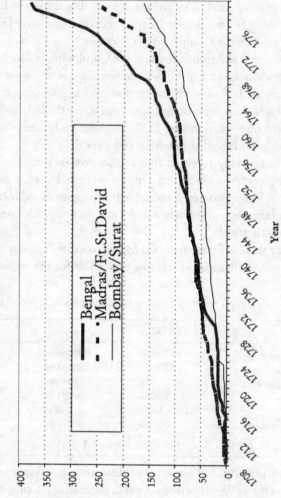

Chart 2: Servants by Presidency, Cumulative, 1708–79.

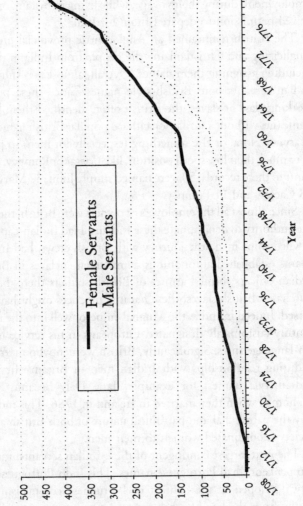

Chart 3: Servants by Gender, 1708–79.

coming from their patrilineage. Others had either adopted, or had thrust upon them, names (and other cultural features) that the British found recognizable and acceptable. This might occur at the time of employment, during their voyage, while living in Britain, or as they received permission to depart Britain for India.

The British maintained an Anglocentric provincial proclivity for Anglicizing and Christianizing the people from India in their midst, including assigning them names. Overall, almost two-thirds of these Indian servants bore British-style names. Since these people were working-class or slaves, the British often identified them by a single name (i.e. without a surname): either a popular British name like John, Mary, or Flora, or else something (especially for men) so pretentious as to mock their low social position, like Caesar or Pompey. Of the servants in these records, 50 were named simply John, 37 Mary, 25 Flora, 18 Caesar, and 11 Pompey.

Since almost all the employers or owners were British, they assumed the authority to denominate these Indians. Had Indian-captained and -owned ships made the journey with British crews, had Indian merchants established autonomous commercial enclaves in Britain, had Indian officers formed armies of British soldiers there, had Indians purchased British slaves, these naming practices might have been reversed. Indeed in India, the Mughal emperor well into the nineteenth century customarily designated Europeans in his service using Persian-language titles. Significantly, British women who married or had enduring relationships with Indian men in Britain often accepted Indian-style names; for example, Jane Daly became Mrs Dean Mahomed when they married in Ireland in 1786. This indicates one way the patriarchal and patrilineal nature of both British and Indian society subordinated women to their men.

The next largest contingent of these Indian servants, totaling 146 (16 per cent), had Portuguese names. This Indo-Portuguese community developed in the context of Portuguese colonialism in India, dating from the late fifteenth century. Over time, many Portuguese (mainly male) settlers in India married Indian women, and raised their descendants as Catholic, giving them Portuguese surnames, probably including the two servants named Pedro de Cruz and Maria de Lobo. The 35 servants simply designated Maria are also likely to have had a

Portuguese identity, possibly due to conversion.[7] Many of these Portuguese-associated Indian people regarded the newly arriving British as potential employers, particularly since the Portuguese empire in Asia declined from the early seventeenth century, reducing the number of servants it employed. Conversely, these servants' European culture and skills evidently made them particularly attractive for Britons to hire. People from India with Portuguese names comprised a continuing proportion of the servants (and sailors) who journeyed to Britain well into the nineteenth century (see Part III).

Only relatively few Indian servants continued to bear Indian names at the time of leaving Britain. Of this small number, many more had Muslim than Hindu names, suggesting the diversity of these people. Included among the 'other' Indians was 'a Jew Servant, David Garcia' who returned to India in 1765.[8] A much larger proportion appears in these records only identified by sex, e.g., 'Black female maid servant' or 'native man', with their names 'unknown'.

We can also use British fictional and artistic sources to consider the mixed images of Indian servants in Britain during this period. Many appeared in English literature, usually as supporting figures for immorally rich British 'nabobs' on whom the central attention, and often ridicule, fell.[9] Thus, the culturally negative valuation of 'India' was conveyed through British colonizers, with Indian servants among the exotic objects they brought back to Britain. Similarly, some British artists also used stereotypical images of Indians to convey messages about oriental wealth, knowledge, and sexuality that were morally corrupting Britons.[10] This fiction and painting thus inform us about abstract images of Indians but tell us little about actual Indians in Britain.

In contrast, various other British portraits from this period (like those discussed in Chapter 1) display Indian servants in Britain,

[7] Yet Armenian Mariam used Maria as her Europeanized name; see Chapter 1.

[8] Court Minutes 27/3/1765.

[9] E.g., plays Foote, *Nabob* (1772) and Kelly, *Romance*. See also *Public Advertiser* 31/7/1783 3a.

[10] For example, William Hogarth included caricatured dark-complexioned servants, sometimes wearing Indian costume, in his 'Marriage a-la-mode' series (1745). See Cowley, *Hogarth's Marriage*, and Dabydeen, *Hogarth's Blacks*.

painted from life. These paintings reveal these Indians as individuals, although the captions conventionally specified their servant status rather than their names. While these people stand as attendants in subordinate and supportive roles towards their British masters, the artist often portrays them with personalities and agency, adorned with jewelry. Significantly, many of these Indian servants wear European-style dress rather than distinctively Indian clothing that would highlight their oriental origin. Evidently they were included in the family portrait not necessarily because the patron wished to proclaim his possession of a costly exotic object, but because these servants were members of his household who needed to be included in portrayals of it.

For example, the favoured Bengali maidservant of Edward Holden Cruttenden appears in a group portrait by Sir Joshua Reynolds (Image 3). She was evidently one of three Indian women, called Rebecca, Patty, and Sophia, whom Cruttenden's family brought back to Britain; Cruttenden returned them (along with Indian manservant Caesar) to Calcutta in 1759.[11] Reynolds (who owned East India Company stock, involved himself in Indian affairs in Britain, but had never gone to India) apparently painted her from life. She wears jewelry and, although looking modestly downward, stands central in the social space of the children whom she serves yet supervises and protects; indeed, she reportedly saved their lives during an insurrection in India.[12] Cruttenden did not feel the need to dress her in Indian-style costume nor name her or his children in the caption: 'Children of Edward Holden Cruttenden and Ayah'. In contrast, the many British paintings of Indian servants that were painted in India almost invariably depict them wearing Indian-style clothes.

A later Reynolds group portrait similarly depicts another Indian maidservant (Image 4). This Indian was probably named Bolah, one of the servants who went to Britain along with her master, George Clive (brother of Robert Clive), and was returned to India by him in 1766.[13] She appears with a distinct personality, adorned with gold and

[11] Court Minutes 19/4/1759, 28/11/1759.

[12] Steward, *New Child*, pp. 39, 85.

[13] Court Minutes 15/10/1766. See Nicholas Penny, *Reynolds*, pp. 216–17; Leslie and Taylor, *Life*, vol. 2, 454ff; Steward, *New Child*, p. 114.

ivory jewellery, including a necklace indicating her married status. She has a modest supporting role, yet one central to the social space of the family. Her clothing could be Indian but is not highlighted as such. In contrast, Clive's daughter is shown wearing Indian costume, explicitly alluding to his career and source of wealth. None of the three women is named in the caption. These artistic representations suggest the complex roles of Indian domestic servants in British households.

Some Indian servants, however, were distinguished by their uniquely oriental skills, unmatched by Britons. A number of Indian expert animal trainers accompanied rare Asian creatures to London. While British accounts focused mainly on the Indian beast, we are more interested in their keepers. Indian notables and the Company officials had long curried favour in Britain through presents of the rare and outlandish from Asia. Nawab Mir Jafar Ali Khan (r. 1757–60, 1763–5) was installed by Robert Clive as ruler of Bengal but he determined to establish a direct relationship with the British king. Mir Jafar's offering to George III was a rare syagush (from the Persian *siayah gosh*, 'black ear') or caracal from central Asia. To convey this fierce and yet delicate feline safely from Bengal to London, Mir Jafar deputed Abdullah, from his own household.

Abdullah escorted the animal to London in 1759. King George then deputed his minister, William Pitt, to arrange not only for the installation of the animal in the Tower of London's menagerie but also for the honoured treatment of Abdullah, paid by the royal treasury. The Royal Keeper of the Beasts in the Tower accepted this addition to the collection, and personally guided Abdullah around London. The directors instructed Clive: 'As Mr Pitt has very strenuously interested himself in favour of this poor fellow and paid Captain Quick thirty guineas in full for his passage, diet, liquours, and accommodation, you are to make an enquiry upon his arrival whether he has been used well in the voyage or otherwise . . .'.[14] In addition to providing Abdullah a relatively luxurious passage, Pitt also presented him with a handsome gratuity of fifty guineas (Rs 525).[15] As a skilled representative of the

[14] Court to Bengal 1/4/1760, Letters to Bengal, E/4/617, BL.
[15] Court Minutes 12/3/1760. Wood to Directors 18/3/1760 and Lord Chamberlain's Office to James 10/6/1760, Letters from Bengal, E/4/42, ff. 47, 92, BL. *Annual Register* (1759), Chronicle, p. 119b.

nawab, Abdullah gained much materially, and in terms of knowledge about London from his year there.

Indian attendants also accompanied rare creatures on behalf of British employers. For example, a Muslim expert animal-trainer from Bengal made multiple trips to Britain, using the Anglicized name John Morgan there. On his third visit, in 1764, he arrived with a Muslim assistant and a cheetah, part of the entourage of Sir George Pigot, retiring Governor of Madras, that included six Indian servants. Pigot presented the cheetah to George III. In Windsor Great Park (30 June 1764), they had Morgan set the cheetah against an English stag. After three attacks failed, the cheetah broke away and killed a fallow deer. Newspapers reported: 'While it was devouring its prey, the Indian attendants caught it, covered its head with a hood, put on its collar and secured it'.[16] George Stubbs recorded the event but also the agency and personalities of Morgan and his assistant through careful delineation of their features (Image 5). Here, their oriental clothing reiterates the exoticness of the cheetah (which apparently ended up in the Tower).[17]

Before Morgan returned to India, he was robbed in a 'bawdy-house' in Rosemary Lane, near Kew Garden, where he and a Muslim fellow-servant were spending the night (30 October 1764). Morgan swore on the Quran that the tavern-keepers, the Ryan family, forcibly stole his 'silver shoe-buckles, value 10 shillings, a pair of cotton stockings, value 1 shilling, one silk purse, value 2 pence, one linen purse, value 1 pence, one piece of silver coin, called a rupee, value 2 shillings, two pieces of coin called Fernams, value 1 penny, five guineas, and fourteen shillings'.[18] The court believed Morgan, convicted the Ryans, and

[16] Archer, *India and British*, p. 413; Clutton, 'Cheetah'; Tate Gallery, *George Stubbs*, pp. 79–80; Basil Taylor, 'George Stubbs's Painting'.

[17] Stubbs painted it or another cheetah in 1788. Other Indians and Britons in India would continue this practise. For example, in 1763 and 1764, the king received elephants from British sea-officers, each accompanied by two Indian keepers. By 1800, the Tower's Royal Menagerie included a spotted black leopard from Governor-General Warren Hastings; a royal tiger from Governor of Madras Lord McCartney; and a lion from Governor of Bombay William Hornby. See Anonymous, *Historical Description*, p. 14; Bennett, *Tower Menagerie*, pp. 57–60, 68, 174–6; Pennant, *Synopsis*; Court Minutes 21–8/9/1763, 23/12/1763, 31/10/1764.

[18] OBP (27/2/1765), ref.: t17650227-5, Oldbaileyonline.org

restored his valuable apparel and cash (worth some £7). He returned with Pigot's other servants to India that spring. Such Indian animal trainers thus served a specialist role: conveying valuable animals from India and instructing British zookeepers in their care and feeding. They also returned to India conveying colourful personal accounts of Britain to their peers.

The growing number of Indian servants present in Britain eventually caused the Company's directors to seek to control their departure from India bound for Britain. The directors became particularly concerned about Indians who might become indigent in Britain since the British government held the Company responsible for their expenses and return passage. Each Indian in Britain during this period cost the Company about 2s. per day plus at least £15 for the cheapest passage back. The directors determined that masters who brought these servants must have an economic incentive to retain control over them and to return them to India quickly at no expense to the Company. They instituted in 1769 a system of substantial bonds (£50 later £100) officially required from all masters before any Indian servant could be taken from India. While ever larger numbers of Indian servants nevertheless entered Britain, this bonding system significantly altered their conditions of service thereafter (see Chapter 6).

Indian Seamen: Lascars and Sailors

The number of Indian seamen voyaging to Britain also rose significantly during the late eighteenth century, reflecting and enabling the burgeoning British world trade. Indeed, seamen (both lascars who contracted collectively as a unit and sailors who signed on individually) comprised the largest proportion of working-class Indians in Britain. Yet, the composition and marketability of the skills of seamen varied from servants, as did their relationship to British society. About half of Indian servants were women, while all seamen were men, therefore subject to differing gender norms in Britain. Servants could work in Britain and on the passage home but Indian lascars were largely barred from their profession once they reached Britain. Unlike most servants who came as individuals, seamen generally worked and lived in groups. This provided them with a corporate identity, and diminished (but did not eliminate) the pressure to adopt the British cultural practices of their employers. Further, most seamen had relatively less experience of Britain, remaining in ports and only between the seasonal arrival and departure of Company ships. However, some determined to establish themselves in London or elsewhere in Britain rather than soon return to India. British authorities came to regard the growing presence of seamen, even more than servants, as a 'problem', an apparently alien, undisciplined, and expensive presence in their midst. British authorities in India also struggled to gain control over this maritime labour force.

The fullest records about Indian seamen in Britain come from the permissions granted by the directors for departure to India (which loosely applied to Indian seamen, although there was no £12 fee required). Chart 4 shows their growing numbers for the period when the Company's officials were the most thorough; prior to that, they seem not to have kept much track of them, subsequently, their numbers rose to be so many that they largely gave up recording every crew.

Throughout this 1740–68 period, a mean average of over 40 lascars departed Britain annually, with a peak of 138 in 1760. Many more, of course, arrived but never departed, either settling or dying in Britain, or escaped official notice. By the early nineteenth century, roughly a thousand Asian seamen arrived annually (see Chapter 4).

Although lascars often received harsh and exploitative treatment in Britain, they had some recourse to British authorities for redress, even against Britons. For example, in 1785, Sawney Clough, a lascar, claimed that a Royal Navy seaman, Patrick Coffield, had assaulted and robbed him of four shillings and some clothing. The lascar also claimed that Coffield had called him a 'black bugger', combining racial and sexual slurs. The Old Bailey court found for the lascar, sentencing the Royal Navy seaman to be executed for these crimes.[19] In various cases, serangs, lascars, the navy agent, or self-appointed British advocates went to court in order to extract wages due to lascars from defaulting employers. In 1785, for example, a jury awarded four lascars each £20 10s. in wages from their shipowners.[20] Thus, in at least some instances,

---

[19] OBP, number 7, part 7 (14/9/1785), pp. 1067–8, case no. 813.
[20] *Morning Chronicle* 30/11/1785, 1/12/1785. For other cases see Court Minutes 25/2/1761, 20/6/1764.

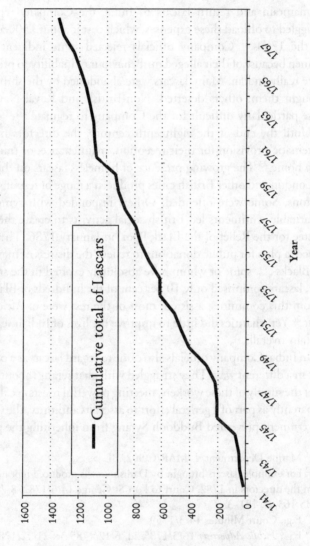

Chart 4: Cumulative Total of Lascars, 1741–8.

lascars found that British law supported them, although individual Britons wronged them.

While the directors recognized their moral and legal responsibility to maintain and return lascars to India, the Company repeatedly struggled to offload these expenses, which cost it about £500 annually by the 1780s.[21] Company officials rejected some indigent Indian seamen because of their alleged misbehaviour or inability to prove they were really Indian. Many lascars were abandoned by the ships which brought them; others deserted. Non-British and Royal Navy ships were particularly difficult for the Company to regulate.[22]

Until the end of the eighteenth century, the directors made no systematic provision for their reception, maintenance, or transportation home.[23] The growing presence of homeless lascars on the streets of London and other British cities produced a range of responses from Britons. Some were offended. Others responded with sympathy.[24] Charitable sentiments led British social activists to create the 'Committee for the Relief of the Black Poor' in January 1786. They established 'a plan for public donations to relieve the distress of many Asiatic Blacks . . . some of whom have absolutely expired in the streets.'[25] Yet, lascars comprised only 10 per cent of the hundreds of Black poor whom this committee assisted; most of the rest were of African descent.[26] Yet, charities did little to improve the lives of Indian seamen in Britain overall.

In India, Company officials also came to regard lascars as a problem, but in a different way. They struggled with ghat serangs about control over the supply of these workers, meeting powerful resistance. In 1780, apparently as part of a general effort to assert its authority, the Calcutta government prevented Buddooh Syrang from inheriting the position

[21] Marine Department, L/MAR/C.902, BL.

[22] For example, lascars brought by Danish vessels produced repeated letters from the directors in 1782. Court to Fort St George 14/6/1782, 8/7/1782 in HMS 163, ff. 181–3.

[23] E.g., Court Minutes 14/3/1759.

[24] E.g., *Public Advertiser* 16/3/1785 2d, 6/12/1785 3c, 21/12/1785 1c.

[25] *Public Advertiser* 5/1/1786 4c, 12/1/1786 4d, 3/1/1787 4b; *Morning Chronicle* 28/1/1786 1c.

[26] The committee's ill-fated scheme to establish a colony in Sierra Leone included a few Indians. See Braidwood, *Black Poor*.

of ghat serang. He protested to London that 'his late Father had served the Company in providing and training Lascars for the Shipping and Train of Artillery in Bengal' but Calcutta authorities had appointed someone else to that 'office'.[27] Buddooh therefore argued he had been illegally deprived of his property rights, and petitioned the directors to order restoration of his father's legacy. The directors recognized the principle that the post was property which should be inherited and ordered an investigation (although it is not clear if they ultimately installed him in the post).

About this time, Calcutta authorities also supported an appeal by European ship captains and merchants to replace the ghat serangs with a British official as sole supplier and regulator of lascar labour, so vitally needed by British shipping. In 1783, these Europeans petitioned the governor-general to appoint a British Registrar of Lascars and also to fix wage rates.[28] Making their argument (but not telling the full story), they wrote of the 'great hardships, delays, hindrances, difficulties, and an unnecessary expense in the procuring proper Seafaring Men' due 'to a certain Person called a Seer ["chief"] Sarang, from whose Impositions both they and the said Seafaring Men are subjected to grievous and heavy losses'. The merchants continued that before the ghat serang would supply lascars, he demanded three months' wages in advance, much of which he kept himself (they neglected to add that the ghat serang usually advanced money to lascars awaiting employment). Further, he did not supply all the men until the very last moment before sailing, when desperate captains had to accept whatever low quality and inexperienced men he provided: 'the said Seer Serang does frequently instead of able Seamen put on board . . . men kidnapped or forcibly impressed and altogether unused to the sea and unacquainted with the Business of a Seamen.' Finally, the merchants set out the monthly wages that they wanted the government to fix by regulation.

These proposed wages were approximately the current rate for serangs, but only about half for lascars.[29] While the merchants thus

[27] Court Minutes 15/3/1780; see also 18/7/1764.

[28] Petition to the Governor-General from the Principal Merchants and Ship Owners of Calcutta, 19/2/1783, HMS 190, ff. 65–103.

[29] Lascars would also receive *batta* (supplement) of Rs 10 monthly, if not provisioned by the owners. See, for example, Court Minutes 14/4/1757 and Marine Department, L/MAR/B/series, BL.

Table 2: Proposed Pay Regulations

(in sicca Rs)	During peace	During war
Serang	15	20
1st Tindal	12	15
2nd Tindal	10	12
1st Lascars	6	7
2nd Lascars	4	5

ostensibly argued for a more bureaucratic and efficient process, they really meant one under British, not Indian, control.

A few months later, the Bengal government indeed passed a regulation that attempted to enforce all that these merchants requested.[30] This established a British 'Marine Register Officer' (on the model prevailing in Britain) who would replace the ghat serang. All Indian seamen would pay 1 Anna per Rupee (6.25 per cent) of their wages plus a 1 Rupee fee to be listed in his books. The officer would also find an 'abode' for the seamen awaiting assignment. He would hold exclusive authority to supply seamen to all ships, delivering them as requested by captains on twelve days' notice.

Soon after this system was imposed, the merchants found to their horror that it failed to deliver the expected results. The ghat serangs held such power that they prevented the Marine Register Officer from supplying lascars. Within a year, the European merchants of Calcutta again petitioned the Company, begging the revocation of this regulation and the return to the old system.

Repeated efforts over the next half century by British merchants and shipowners to gain control over this vital supply of lascar labour similarly failed. When British employers offered wages that were too low, lascars refused to work.[31] In 1790, applicants for the post of Marine Register Officer promised to deliver all that the European merchants

[30] 'Rule, Ordinance and Regulation for Ascertaining and fixing the Wages to be Paid to the Native Seafaring Men belonging to the Port of Calcutta', registered with the Supreme Court of Calcutta 7/7/1783, in HMS 190, ff. 65–103.

[31] Home Public Consultation 29/2/1795, no. 33 and 15/5/1797, no. 18, NAI.

had sought in their earlier petition, to no avail.[32] The Calcutta government ordered a Committee on the State of Marine to investigate and report about the power and alleged abuses of ghat serangs. Yet, in 1793, the superintendent of police in Calcutta reiterated these same accusations about 'the rapacity and villainy of Ghaut Serangs' who used their labour monopoly to supply insufficient numbers of inexperienced Indians at exorbitant wages on the eve of sailing, whom European captains perforce accepted rather than miss the season.[33] Further, British merchants accused lascars of wholesale arson: taking wage advances and then torching their ship so that they could abscond.[34] When one British captain resorted in 1798 to kidnapping and sailing off with lascars who had only agreed to load his ship in port, virtually all lascars boycotted such work on British-bound ships, despite the governor-general's repeated public assurances that such offending captains would be punished.[35] Indeed, until the mid nineteenth century lascars and ghat serangs largely resisted repeated efforts by British merchants to gain control over this maritime labour supply, so essential to the Anglocentric world system (see Part III).

From Sailor to Gentleman and Back to Subaltern

The writings of Emin (1726–1809) provide rare first-person accounts by a man who worked as a sailor from Calcutta to London, then as a manual labourer, servant-student, and clerk there. While in Britain, he learned how to represent himself autobiographically in English. Ultimately, however, his dramatic upward mobility to gentleman officer in England could not be sustained in colonial Bengal, where local British authorities relegated him to marginal subaltern officer status.[36]

[32] Home Public Consultation 6/10/1790, nos 15–17, NAI.

[33] Home Public Consultation 22/11/1793, no. 3, NAI.

[34] Home Public Consultation 4/2/1800, no. 22, NAI and numerous cases in *Calcutta Monthly Journal.*

[35] Home Public Consultation 28/6/1799, no. 7, 16/8/1798, no. 22, and 26/11/1798, no. 7, NAI.

[36] Research into Emin's life by his descendant, Amy Apcar, published in her edition of his book, has added considerably to our understanding of Emin. See

Armenian intermediaries (including Mariam and many merchants)
had adapted to expanding British maritime networks. Although Emin
spent most of his life (over forty years) in Calcutta, settling as a youth
and dying there, he was born in Hamadan, Iran. He followed his father
to Bengal in 1744, joining the other 3,000–4,000 Armenians there,
manoeuvring dangerously among various European and Indian regional powers.[37]

In Calcutta in 1746, several European Companies were in conten-
tion. Emin's own merchant father lost two ships when Commodore
Griffin of the Royal Navy seized them, claiming that, although flying
Dutch flags, they were really French-owned. His family's lawsuit
against Griffin ultimately failed, despite the support of the Nawab of
Bengal and also the Company, in both Calcutta and London.[38]

In 1746, Emin's father offered him the options of learning Portuguese, French, or English. He presciently selected the last, studying
for two years at Mr Parrent's English school in Calcutta's Old Court
House. Emin then determined to venture to Britain and improve himself there, convincing another young Armenian to join him.

Despite his family's opposition, Emin secretly sought work on a
British ship, but he and his friend found it frustratingly difficult. Instead of joining a ghat serang's crew, they asked British captains directly. The captains whom they approached in 1750 rejected them as unfit
to be seamen. Even when Emin promised to shorten his long Armenian robe and abandon his turban, his inexperience reduced his
apparent value.[39] Indeed, in February 1751, near the end of the next
sailing season, the third captain they appealed to, Thomas Fea of the

---

also Hewlett, 'Armenian'; Ioannisian, *Iosif Emin*; Aslanyan, 'Hovsep Emine'.
Khashmanean has translated his autobiography into Armenian: *Hovsep Emini*.
Emin has become an Armenian national hero, with a street named after him in
Yerevan, Armenia.

[37] Letters to Bengal 3/12/1755, 3/3/1758, E/4/616, BL.

[38] Later, while Emin was himself in London, he went to the King's Bench to
support his father's case, only to hear Armenians abused for trading with the
enemy. Emin, *Life* (pagination hereinafter from 1918 edition), pp. 16–17;
Lambert, *House of Commons*, vol. 135, Select Committee Report 1, p. 140; NAI,
Fort William, vol. 1, pp. xxv–xxvii; Court Minutes 10/1/1751 to 6/12/1752.

[39] Emin, *Life*, pp. 19–22.

Walpole, also initially rejected them. Only after Emin and his friend paid a gratuity to the Captain's *sircar* (accountant) were they able to sign on as seamen, to the dismay of some of the ship's British officers. His monthly wage was only fifteen shillings, much less than a skilled lascar or British seaman. Indeed, at first Emin could only do the manual labour of loading the cargo of rice, saltpetre, redwood, and turmeric, as well as cleaning the ship. Gradually, over the course of the voyage, he started to learn the ropes.

Emin articulated his consciousness of being an outsider to both maritime life and the majority European crew. Significantly, his account of this voyage omitted mentioning the tindal and six lascars whom the *Walpole* also hired in Calcutta.[40] He did record complaints from European sailors that Asians were taking work away from them (complaints that persisted into the twentieth century).[41] When a non-British European seaman 'gave Emin abusive language', Emin

> ... losing no time, brought the poor man down (although three times as big as himself) with a single slap on the left side of his face ... [T]he combatant ... was carried to his hammock, and could not come on the deck for some days. What happened then? the honest English mariners jumped up, and hallooed with loud voices, David has conquered the great Goliath! ... all of them shaking hands with [Emin] in turns.[42]

Emin thus associated himself forcefully and rhetorically with Englishmen against non-Britons. Similarly, European seamen made Emin and his Armenian companion eat separately, until their superior cooking and gifts of liquour allowance won them a shared place. Emin made a recurrent theme in his autobiographical accounts of how his personal courage and willingness to adapt to British values would (and should) earn him the admiration of British audiences.

After a perilous voyage, they reached London in August 1751. Emin and his Armenian friend hesitated to enter British society. For an additional ten days, they worked unloading the ship (at a shilling per day, double his salary as a seaman), living and dining aboard. Finally, they disembarked and were paid: Emin received 4 pounds

[40] Log of *Walpole* L/MAR/B/293H, BL.
[41] See Dixon, 'Lascars', and Tabili, 'Construction'.
[42] Emin, *Life*, pp. xxxi–xxxii.

11 shillings 4 pence minus the required Greenwich Hospital fee of 3 shillings 2 pence and his debt to the ship's store of 7 shillings 6 pence.[43]

The cosmopolitan nature of London, particularly around its docks, provided his first means of entry. Emin noted how British women particularly sympathized with his plight. He initially stayed in a lodging house in Wapping run by a Swede and his English wife, which charged one shilling weekly. He especially noted the kindness of the house maidservant: 'the beautiful Sally, lately married to a sailor who was gone to sea'.[44] Emin considered Sally 'like to an angel', and admitted to being 'in love' with her, but simultaneously admired her faithfulness to her absent husband and regarded her 'with as much affection as a brother to a sister'. Further, British landladies also displayed special fondness for him. Although Emin initially depended on the patronage of an Armenian jewel-merchant, Stephan Cogigian, and occasionally had contact with other Armenians in London, he did not settle among them.[45] Rather, he chose social situations where he was the only Armenian present. He largely adapted himself to British sartorial norms and also Anglicized his name from 'Ameen son of Hovsep' to 'Joseph Emin', to make it easier for Britons to recognize and pronounce.[46]

Over the next three years, Emin struggled in London. He studied at Mr Middleton's Academy for boys in Bishopsgate but, unable to pay his fees, left. He did unskilled manual labour for a bricklayer in Drury Lane and a grocer in the City. In desperation, he signed indentures for a Jamaica plantation (which he then repudiated). After returning briefly to Middleton's Academy as a servant-student, he then worked as a load carrier, but this caused him serious injury. Next, he served as a law clerk copying cases. Unlike most Indians in Britain, Emin's own family eventually offered to pay his passage to Calcutta. Yet he refused to leave Britain in failure.[47]

---

[43] Receipt Book of *Walpole* L/MAR/B/293FF, BL.

[44] Emin, *Life*, pp. 29–31.

[45] Memorial of Stephen Cogigian, Court Minutes 4/12/1754; see also Court Minutes 27/5/1752, 29/11/1752, 6/12/1752, 4–11/12/1754.

[46] *Gentleman's Magazine*, 37 (January 1767), pp. 3–7. Emin, *Life*, p. 111.

[47] Emin, *Life*, pp. 16, 31, 47.

Emin found that many Britons with whom he dealt had few preconceptions about his ethnicity or much awareness of Asia generally.
One potential employer cursed Emin for being a Frenchman. When
Emin denied being French and began to explain what being an Armenian meant, the man identified him as German. Finally, the man employed Emin, concluding 'Well, well, Germans and Armenians are
all alike, as long as you are not a Frenchman'.[48] Thus, within Britain,
Emin had some scope to negotiate his particular identity among the
range of aliens whom Britons ranked hierarchically. Being a non-
Catholic Christian privileged him over some Catholic Europeans,
such as Irish and Frenchmen. Indeed, he broke with his former Armenian patron in London, Stephen Cogigian, when the latter converted
to Catholicism. Emin denounced him (using striking epithets that
conflated Catholics and Jews through a Shakespearean reference), as
a 'papist . . . turncoat . . . [as greedy as] Shylock the avaricious Jew in
the Merchant of Venice'.[49]

Emin's opportunity to rise in status derived from his self-identification as an Armenian patriot. In 1755, while strolling in St James
Park, Emin met Edmund Burke (1729–97), then a struggling law
student. They became enduring friends, Burke regarding Emin as a
'Gentleman' despite his poverty. Emin copied out Burke's work as he
wrote it, including his essay 'On the Sublime and Beautiful' and
Vindications of Natural Society (1756). Although three years younger,
Burke guided Emin's education like a 'dear uncle' and they held long
political discussions, as well as played chess and drank together.[50] This
warmth lasted even as Burke entered Parliament and rose to become
one of its leading lights. Burke later sheltered other Indians (including
Hanumantrao, see below), and took the foremost role in the impeachment and trial of Warren Hastings in Parliament for abuses of Indian's
human and political rights.[51] Emin, from his first encounter with

[48] Ibid., *Life*, p. 34.

[49] Ibid., *Life*, pp. 32, 37.

[50] Burke to Emin, *ca.* 7/8/1757 and 29/3/1789 in Burke, *Correspondence*,
vol. 1, pp. 120–2; vol. 5, pp. 455–7; Emin, *Life*, p. 51; Lock, *Edmund Burke*,
vol. 1, p. 82.

[51] Further, a relative, William Burke, had an Indian body-servant, Tombee,
who lived with them at Beaconsfield and was William's main heir. Magnus,

Burke, found that Armenian patriotic sentiments and a claim of an in-
domitable quest for liberty for his oppressed people gained him British
respect and continued sponsorship.

Emin's entrée to his first powerful patron, Hugh Smithson, Duke
of Northumberland (1714–86), also came from a chance meeting in
1755 with a man whom he recognized as a fellow Armenian. As Emin
recounted:

> one morning [Emin] . . . met a young man in a Turkish habit, and [had]
> the curiosity to speak to him in that language, as he found him to be an
> Armenian; both parties were glad to see each other. Emin after inquiry, was
> informed that the man had been sent over with an Arabian horse, as a
> groom, by the English merchants of Aleppo, for . . . Northumberland.[52]

This immediate bonding suggests how networks of Asians in Britain
could quickly develop. Nevertheless, these bonds did not always trans-
cend class differences. Emin regarded himself as superior in status and
education to the groom, refusing to eat at his table with the footmen,
but rather among the duke's upper retainers.

The Duke elicited Emin's story of his militant ambitions, encouraged him in 1756 to write an autobiographical letter, and then circulated this among 300 of the British élite.[53] As Emin represented
himself, he had only moved to Britain for military training on behalf
of his persecuted people. He stressed his non-Catholic Christianity which the British shared. Further, he and Britons both struggled
against Muslims and other non-Christians, whom he described as
'wild and barbarous nations'.[54] Nevertheless, he accepted the superiority of British military technology:

> [In 1744 in Calcutta] . . . I saw the Fort of the Europeans and the Soldiers
> Exercise, and the Shipping and that they were dextrous and perfect in all
> things, then I grieved with myself, for my Religion and my Country, that
> we were in Slavery and Ignorance like Jews Vagabonds upon Earth . . . but
> I resolved I would go to Europe to learn Art Military and other Sciences

---

Edmund Burke, p. 288; William Burke, Will (13/10/1795) in Wecter, *Edmund Burke*, p. 94.

[52] Emin, *Life*, p. 54.

[53] Ibid., p. 55; Montagu, *Elizabeth*, vol. 2, p. 101.

[54] Emin, *Life*, pp. xxix, xxxii, 431.

to assist that Art . . . I came to England with much labour . . . I was first a Scholar, and when my Money was gone . . . I went into the Street to work for my Bread, for I could not bear to go wagging a Tail at Peoples doors for a bit of Meat . . . I . . . paid out of my Wages to learn Geometry, and to complete my Writing, and just to begin a little French, but because my Lord I almost starved myself to pay for this and carried Burthens more than my Strength, I hurted myself and could not work any longer, so that I was in dispair . . . but a Friend put me to write with one Mr Webster an Attorney in Cheapside which for a little time got Bread . . . I am afraid I am too troublesome in my Accounts to your Lordship but we people of Asia can't say little and a great deal like Scholars. Now I met by chance some Gentlemen who encouraged me, and gave me Books to read and advised me to kiss Colo[nel] Dingley's hands and shew my business to him, he was a brave Soldier, took me by the hand, spoke to his own Serjeant an Honest Man to teach me Manual Exercise and gave me Bland's [Treatise of] Military Discipline and promised to help me to learn Gunnery and Fortification; but I was again unfortuned, for when light just began to come to my Eyes he died, and I was like before except that I knew a little of Manual Exercise and read some of the Roman History . . . [I]f I must return [to India] after four years Slavery and Misery to the same Ignorance without doing any good would break my heart . . .[55]

Touched by Emin's appeal, Northumberland and others gave support; the royal Duke of Cumberland enrolled Emin as a cadet in the royal military academy at Woolwich. Lord George Lyttleton also apparently commissioned artist Arthur Pond to paint Emin as a gentleman officer (Image 6).[56]

Subsequent autobiographical letters from Emin to various British élites have also survived.[57] In them, Emin consistently revealed himself as a self-reflective individual, aware of how others regarded him, and aspiring to reshape their perceptions of Asians and himself. British contemporaries described Emin as an enlightened leader of his oppressed people, elevating him to the aristocracy, noting his intellect, his squint, but not his somewhat swarthy skin colour: 'This Prince,

[55] Emin to Northumberland, 1756, in Emin, *Life*, pp. 58–60.

[56] Once owned by Hagley Hall, this painting was apparently destroyed by fire in 1925. Personal communication from Lord Cobham, 5/7/2002.

[57] E.g., letters to and from Emin in Montagu Manuscripts MO 714, 937, 938, 1328, 1511, 1575, 4367, Huntington Library; Davis, *Good*, pp. 288–90.

Image 6: Portrait of Emin, attributed to Arthur Pond, 1756/8.

while in *England*, was known by the name of *Imene*. His person was of the middle size, had a slight cast in his eyes, of a sprightly disposition, very intelligent and entertaining in his conversation, and exceedingly fond of discoursing on the sciences . . .'[58]

Emin's British patrons included numerous élite women who regarded his cause as a romantic quest. Among them, Lady Yarmouth

[58] Letter to the Editor, *Gentleman's Magazine*, 36 (1766) Supplement, pp. 583–4. See also *Gentleman's Magazine*, 37 (January 1767), pp. 3–7 and *Annual Register* (1767) Chronicle, pp. 204–10.

sponsored his correspondence, and then meeting, with William Pitt (later Earl of Chatham).[59] In particular, Elizabeth Robinson Montagu (1720–1800), a leading literary figure six years his senior, made herself his champion in high society. Emin regularly addressed her as 'My Queen of Sheba', both showing her respect and simultaneously identifying her with eastern culture.[60] He identified himself in the male role, as inspired by his patroness, yet never aspiring to possess her: 'Your Persian Slave whom you have been pleased to honour with the Title of a Hero'. Thus, Emin's recorded interactions with various European women remained platonic, in contrast with many fellow Asians in Britain who married or cohabited with British women.

In all, Emin served five years as a gentleman officer attached to the British and Prussian royal armies, occasionally campaigning on the continent against the French during the Seven Years War. Then, for ten years (1759–69), Emin fought for Armenians living under Ottoman and Russian rule.[61] Emin claimed he once led 18,000 Armenian mountaineers into battle. As with so many other Armenian liberation struggles, however, his efforts proved bloody but futile. He returned to Calcutta via Basra in 1770.

Next, Emin sought a commission in the Company's Bengal Army but he confronted stronger ethnic barriers than in London. By current Company procedures, Catholics and non-Europeans could not be commissioned officers except by special dispensation.[62] Thus, despite Emin's powerful supporters in England, his prestigious military training at Woolwich, and his considerable battlefield experience, his ethnic identity put him outside the British power structure in Calcutta. The Bengal Army gave him the most marginal subaltern officer's rank: brevet *risaldar* of Turksowars (temporary appointment as ensign, the

[59] Montagu to her husband March 1758 in Emin, *Life*, pp. 91–2.

[60] Emin to Montagu 14/9/1757, 7/8/1785, in Emin, *Life*, pp. 80, 486; Emin to Montagu 10/5/1757 and Montagu to her husband 1757 in Montagu, *Elizabeth*, vol. 2, pp. 102, 107–8; Jones to Macpherson 6/5/1786, in Jones, *Memoirs*, pp. xxi–xxiii, 277.

[61] Emin, *Life*, pp. 133–61, 168–423.

[62] French officers and men of mixed ancestry faced similar barriers to regular careers in the Bengal Army. See Llewlyn-Jones, *Very Ingenious*, and Alam and Alavi, *European Experience*.

lowest rank among officers, in the irregular cavalry), although at an officer's pay of Rs 300 monthly (60 times his seaman's wage).[63]

Emin appealed to his powerful patrons, the dukes of Northumberland and Cumberland, to have him officially nationalized as British, and therefore able to gain an officer's commission. They confessed their inability to arrange this from London.[64] Burke lamented that 'a man once countenanced by the first people of this kingdom as well as of Germany, should . . . pass his life in misery and contempt in an English settlement. I know many think him an impostor, but I can bear witness to the truth of what he asserted . . .'.[65] After two years of thankless military employment, Emin lost active service status in 1772 when Governor Hastings demobilized the Bengal Army's irregular cavalry.

Still seeking martial distinction and advancement, Emin took leave and journeyed as a volunteer officer to support an unsuccessful British expedition at Basra (March 1775).[66] On his return, Emin was retired to the Third European Invalid unit in Calcutta. Yet, due to his anomalous status, he had to petition the Company for twenty-five years before he received his monthly pension of Rs 91 and back pay.[67] He spent the remainder of his life largely among the struggling Armenian community in Bengal.

Yet, Emin also related himself to British audiences by writing his autobiography in English. Emin sent drafts of his work to Mrs Montagu and Warren Hastings in London and 'My guardian Angel' Sir William Jones (1746-94) in Calcutta, requesting them to recruit

---

[63] General Return of the Troops (1770–8), NAI. Hodson, *List*, vol. 2, p. 137. Emin, *Life*, pp. 439, 483. This salary included batta.

[64] Northumberland to Emin 17/5/1771 in Emin, *Life*, pp. 440–1.

[65] Burke to Stewart 30/10/1772 in Burke, *Correspondence*, vol. 2, pp. 359–60.

[66] Emin to Hastings 3/3/1774, Warren Hastings, General Correspondence, ADD 29134, ff. 322–3, BL. See also Al-Najjar *et al.*, *Bussorah*, vol. 1, p. 325. While still in Iran (around 1777), Emin had an arranged marriage with Thangoom Khatoon (1748–1843), a member of the Armenian community of Isfahan. Emin, *Life*, pp. 441–77, 514. She eventually returned to Isfahan, retaining her late husband's pension. Petition of Thangoom Emin, Board Collections F/4/1511 no 59571; Letter to India (Political) 4/11/1835, draft 602/1835, E/4/746, f. 8, BL.

[67] Emin, *Life*, pp. 479, 483, 513.

subscribers (at two guineas each) and also for their advice on revisions.[68] In response, Mrs Montagu complimented him on how well he retained his English diction. In Calcutta, Jones less sympathetically urged Emin to 'strike out every passage that may favour of self-approbation . . . [D]iscard forever the Asiatick style of panegyrick, to which you are too much addicted . . . [T]he Asiatick style . . . is utterly repugnant to English manners, which you prefer, I know . . . .'.[69] Nevertheless, Jones himself 'corrected only those errors in language and orthography, which were unavoidable in an English work written by a native of Hamadan . . .'.

Thus sponsored by Britons, in 1792 at age 66, Emin published his 640 page book in London: *The Life and Adventures of Joseph Emin, An Armenian, Written in English by Himself.*[70] Throughout this book, Emin sought to make his identity comprehensible and respectable to Britons, yet he located himself as an aspiring outsider to their culture. He consistently ascribed his self-alleged literary inadequacies to his 'wild Asiatic temper'.[71] As Emin explained to Mrs Montagu: 'I . . . cannot avoid mixing an Asiatic tincture in my writing, I indeavour much to naturalize my sentiments to the English'.[72] The autobiographical genre that he selected shaped his enterprise in distinctive ways, different from how genres produced by Asian cultures would have done. He was certainly multilingual in Armenian, Persian, Turkish, English, French, and Portuguese, and probably Bengali as well. He would have been familiar with indigenous Asian literary forms of history and travel writing current in India, but little in his book reflected those.

---

[68] Emin to Hastings 15/1/1789, Warren Hastings, General Correspondence, ADD 29171, f. 255, BL. *Calcutta Gazette*, 1/1/1789; Emin to Montagu 15/1/1789 and 15/8/1791 in Emin, *Life*, pp. 489–96.

[69] Jones to Emin 10/8/1788 in Emin, *Life*, pp. xix–xx.

[70] Emin paid £50 for publication costs, far cheaper than he could have arranged in Calcutta. My analysis of the list of the 73 subscribers to this book indicates 80 per cent were European (including 5 European women) and the remainder Asians. Emin advertised its sale in English newspapers in Calcutta as well. Emin, *Life*, p. 489.

[71] E.g., Emin, *Life*, pp. xxix–xxx, 2, 41.

[72] Emin to Montagu 15/8/1791, in Emin, *Life*, pp. 493–6.

Despite articulating his own account of his life through his book, Emin never gained the recognition in Bengal or Britain that he believed he deserved. Nor could he gain enough financial support to bring his son to Britain for education there as he hoped. Like other Armenians in India, he sought to use British institutions to advance himself but found the colonial context confining, although life in London held more promise.

Armenian Merchants from Bengal in London

With expanding British territorial and economic assertions in India, commerce—and tensions—increased significantly between Indian merchants and British officials. The power relationships in India disadvantaged these merchants, but some successfully invoked higher authorities in Britain—as had Nowroji Rustamji earlier. In particular, two Armenians of Bengal, Khwaja Gregore Cojamaul and Khwaja Johannes Padre Rafael, who had been trapped between rival factions within the Bengal government, set off for London to represent themselves there just before Emin returned to Calcutta. From 1769 until 1777, they personally brought claims for unjust imprisonment against Harry Verelst (Governor of Bengal, 1767–9, d.1785) before the Company's directors, British newspapers, London law courts, and Parliament. They had the backing of their former commercial associate and ex-Company official, William Bolts (1735–1808). Their cases indicate the factional nature of British politics: Verelst was a protégé of Robert Clive, while Bolts allied himself with Clive's many enemies. The actions of these Armenians also indicate how people from India could directly enter the British public sphere, availing themselves of British legal and political institutions and parties in order ultimately to obtain justice denied in India.

As context, Governor Verelst, having dismissed Bolts, a Dutchman, from the Company's administration, desired to drive him out of India.[73] Lacking any legal way to do so, Verelst determined to ruin Bolts financially by suddenly terminating his commercial ventures in

---

[73] See Bolts, *Considerations*, and Verelst, *View*. See also Kumkum Chatterjee, *Merchants*; Hallward, *William Bolts*; Kuiters, 'Law '; Sudipta Sen, *Empire*, pp. 64ff; Sutherland, *East India Company*, p. 220.

north India. In 1768, Verelst thus requested two of the Company's subordinate allies, the Raja of Benares and the Nawab of Awadh, to seize Cojamaul and Rafael (among others) as agents of Bolts.[74]

Evidence later demonstrated that these Armenians (originally from Isfahan but long established with their families in Bengal) were in fact independent merchants with a licence to trade from the Company. They had partnerships with many Britons, rather than being employees of Bolts, although they did indeed have close commercial links with him.[75] The Benares and Awadh rulers arrested these merchants, then turned them over to the nominally independent, but actually dependent, Nawab of Bengal. These abrupt arrests did considerable damage to their finances. Yet, they were eventually released months later with formal charges never having been filed against them. Further, Verelst issued orders forbidding any Armenian or Portuguese merchant based in Calcutta from trading outside the Company's territories.[76] This threatened the livelihood of both communities and contradicted the 1688 agreement between the Company and Armenians (see Chapter 1).

After reaching London in August 1769, Cojamaul and Rafael first petitioned the directors. When told to go back to the Calcutta courts, they successfully argued that they could legally appeal directly in London since they could not obtain a fair hearing in Bengal, either from the Nawab or the Company. They, and Bolts, received political support from the anti-Clive faction in the Company and Parliament. The directors wrote with annoyance to Calcutta, mainly upset that they had been presented with such a politically embarrassing situation in London: 'we hope the allegations in their memorial are not well founded, [but] you should have endeavored to have accommodated this affair in Bengal, as their appearance here in a clamorous manner may prove prejudicial to our affairs and is very unpleasing.'[77] The majority of the directors backed Verelst and rejected their appeals.[78]

[74] *CPC*, vol. 2., pp. 246, 261; Lambert, *House of Commons*, vol. 135, pp. 272–3.

[75] Lambert, *House of Commons*, vol. 135, pp. 277–80.

[76] Court Minutes 4/12/1754, 26/2/1773.

[77] NAI, *Fort William*, vol. 6, p. 32.

[78] Court Minutes 14/9/1769; Letter from Court 30/6/1769 in NAI, *Fort William*, vol. 5, pp. 222–9; Letter to Bengal 23/3/1770, E/4/620, BL.

Accusing Verelst personally for his illegal actions while governor, Cojamaul and Rafael filed separate cases in the Court of Chancery and the Court of Common Pleas. Over the years, their cases also went through the Court of Exchequer and the House of Lords. Cojamaul and Rafael received sympathetic attention in popular London newspapers. They also petitioned the House of Commons, which held hearings into their case in 1772 as part of its larger investigations into the Company's actions in India generally. Giving direct testimony to a Parliamentary Committee, Cojamaul and Rafael explained the oppressions that they, as well as the entire Armenian and Portuguese communities, had suffered from Company officials.[79]

Finally, after six years of petitions, testimony, and lawsuits, Rafael won an award of £5,000 damages plus full costs (reduced to £4,000 plus costs after a retrial) while Cojamaul won £4,000 damages plus costs (reduced to £3,200).[80] The Company's directors, however, reimbursed Verelst for his losses in exchange for his dropping his own lawsuit against the Company.[81] Rafael used his seven years in London to study English; he even composed and presented to the Company 'a dictionary, grammar, and dialogue in the Hindustan language (commonly called Moors) and that of English, believing it may be useful to Mankind and the Company's servants'.[82] These two Armenians remained in Britain for some time, and then moved to other parts of Europe.[83]

These merchants found that they could have a voice in British public discourse. To the extent that their testimony impressed British legislators, they helped shape the 1773 Regulating Act. British law courts eventually found in their favour. In part, their success in Britain

[79] Second Report, in Lambert, *House of Commons*, vol. 135, pp. 263–96.

[80] *Annual Register* (1774) Chronicle, pp. 170–1; *Annual Register* (1776) Chronicle, p. 120; Court Minutes 29/11/1775, 19/11/1777. In 1777, another Armenian whom Verelst had imprisoned, Khwaja Wuscan Estephan (who did not go to Europe), also won his case, receiving £2,500 plus costs of £108 10s.

[81] Court Minutes 11/3/1772, 27/6/1776; *Annual Register* (1776) Chronicle, p. 153.

[82] Court Minutes 27/6/1776, 3/7/1776.

[83] See Hallward, *William Bolts*, pp. 135ff; Kuiters, 'Law', p. 13; Seth, *History of Armenians*, pp. 261–2.

depended on the support of powerful political factions there who sought evidence and allies against mutual British enemies. Merchants, however, were not the only Indians who entered the political sphere in London.

Indian Envoys from the Mughal Empire

From the mid eighteenth century, a small but growing number of Indian royalty, also frustrated by Company officials in India, similarly sought to supersede them by establishing a direct presence in London. As part of the Company's colonial system of surveillance and control, it tried to master the Indian 'information order', both in territories under its direct rule and also among the rulers it had indirectly subordinated.[84] This included eventually establishing a British political agent ('Resident') at each key Indian court. Residents gradually monopolized political communication, isolating rulers from each other and from London. Some Indian rulers bypassed such controls: sending to Britain Indian intermediaries (particularly those with experience dealing with Britons), or trusted courtiers, or going themselves. Once there, these men began slowly to learn about complex British political processes—especially the shifting and contested relationships among Crown, Parliament, Board of Control, directors, and Company stockholders. They sought to shape British colonial policies by communicating with the king, testifying before Parliament, negotiating with the directors, and lobbying influential Britons. By representing India directly, they struggled against growing colonialism supported by and supporting 'Orientalism'—constructions of 'the Orient' by Europeans. During this early period, the Company's authorities in London often had little knowledge about these Indian agents, diplomats, and royalty in their midst, nor had they developed legal precedents to manage them.

The distinctive knowledge these Indian representatives gained about British politics, society, and culture informed Indian society, albeit only unevenly. Their position as Indian political agents contrasted their perspective, and the information they brought back, from those of either Britons or Indian seamen or servants, who also spread

[84] See Bayly, *Empire*, and Fisher, *Indirect Rule*.

accounts about Britain. Yet, the oral reports and writings of these Indian envoys about their experiences in Britain did not circulate widely in India.

Competing and relatively isolated Indian rulers never created a centralized archive that would enable them collectively to accumulate the hard-earned intelligence gained by these missions—or coordinate their responses to spreading British colonialism. Only occasionally do we find later envoys referring to the knowledge produced by their precursors. Thus, most Indian envoys and royalty reached Britain largely unprepared for what they would encounter, rather having to learn afresh for themselves. This also disadvantaged Indians in dealing with the British in both India and Britain.

To explore the goals of these representatives and royalty, their experiences in Britain, and the consequences of their efforts, let us consider three contrasting early Indian missions: the first sent by the Mughal emperor in 1766; the next delegated by an aspiring peshwa of the Marathas in 1780; and the third undertaken personally by an heir to the deposed Nawab of Broach in 1794. They respectively represented what would become the three broad trends in such missions to supersede Company officials in India by intervening in London: rulers (including nominal rulers) seeking political advantage; would-be rulers seeking installation; and deposed rulers or their heirs seeking pension enhancements.

Mughal emperors had for much of the eighteenth century been palace prisoners of various Indian warlords. The 1764 battle of Buxar brought Emperor Shah Alam II temporarily into the Company's custody. Using established Mughal protocols, he sought to establish personal and diplomatic bonds with the British monarch, thereby obtaining a British army to restore him to power. He wrote to King George III in Persian, addressing him as 'sovereign of the land of friendship, my brother, dear to me as life, whom may the Almighty assist and support'. The emperor explained his situation:

> [due to] the ingratitude, treachery, infidelity, and arrogance of the Nobles of Hindostan . . . the empire has been reduced to a state of confusion and disorder . . . I attribute it to your royal favour and friendship and brotherly love that I am now established with the English gentlemen [of the Company] in the fort of Allahabad and I earnestly request that your

Majesty will send to Calcutta 5 or 6,000 young men practiced in war
[who] . . . may carry me to Shahjehanabad [Delhi], my capital, and firmly
seat me on the throne of the Hindostan Empire, which is my undoubted
right . . . Your Majesty's restoring me to my right will cause your name to
be celebrated till the destruction of the world in every part of the habitable
earth, and I shall be obliged to you as long as I live. . . .

    P.S. As it is customary in this country to send with a letter something
by way of present [*nazr*], I shall therefore send a few trifles for you my
Brother and your royal consort my Sister. They will arrive hereafter and I
hope from your friendship that you will be kind enough to accept them.[85]

Under Mughal political theory, acceptance by George III of the proffered nazr (Rs 100,000 and other gifts) would make the emperor his
dependant, whom he was morally bound to protect. The British recognized the emperor's sovereignty, although his power was more
nominal than actual, so his right to send a diplomatic mission to London could not be officially denied. The emperor appointed a Briton,
Captain Archibald Swinton (1731–1804), to head his embassy;
Swinton resigned the Company's service to accept.[86]

    The emperor also appointed Shaikh I'tisam al-Din (1730–1800) as
the mission's expert in both Persian diplomacy and dealing with the
British, granting him the honourific Mirza ('prince'). I'tisam al-Din
(born in Nadia, Bengal, putatively descended from the Prophet
Muhammad) initially trained as a scholar-official under the Nawabs
of Bengal. However, he had long served Britons. Thus, while he respected the emperor's authority, he did not have established ties to the
imperial court. When he accepted this imperial mission, he received
Rs 4,000 for his future efforts and expenses, which both proved much
more onerous than he anticipated.

    This mission encountered opposition and delay from its inception.
High Company officials in Calcutta wished to prevent the emperor's envoys from establishing any direct relationship with the British king or intervening into politics in London. Thus, the Calcutta
government delayed the emperor's letter from reaching the envoys.

[85] Shah Alam to King of Great Britain, Sutton Court Collection, MSS EUR
F.128/111, ff. 100–2, BL. See also Buckler, *Legitimacy*.
[86] Shitab Roy to Md. Reza Khan 19/6/1765, Sutton Court Collection, MSS
EUR F.128/111, f. 37, BL; Evan Cotton, *Journals*, pp. 121–8.

Further, the Mughal treasury had difficulty amassing the promised Rs 100,000 nazr. Finally, after a year of waiting, I'tisam al-Din, his servant, Muhammad Muqim, and Swinton sailed on a French ship from Calcutta in January 1766.[87]

After the imperial mission finally reached Britain, it foundered. Like many other British agents hired by Indian rulers, Swinton showed little commitment to the emperor. I'tisam al-Din criticized Swinton for this and his negative attitudes toward Islam. Nor would George III or Parliament intervene in the Company's relations with the Mughal emperor.

I'tisam al-Din, like all Indians in Britain, made choices about his deportment, including his dress and diet, which affected his social relations. He decided to retain his customary turban, shawl, and Hindustani robe, which attracted admiring attention. The British public regarded him as a nobleman, particularly, he reported, compared to the many lascars with whom they were more familiar. Indeed, he accused Swinton of exaggerating his status to that of royalty, thus elevating Swinton's own standing as his companion. I'tisam al-Din also observed Muslim halal dietary practices. Since Swinton ridiculed these restrictions as superstitious, and allegedly arranged to frustrate them, I'tisam al-Din often suffered privation. He also did not learn English during his stay, which kept him particularly dependent on Swinton.

I'tisam al-Din also grew increasingly frustrated at his own inability to advance the emperor's cause; he was only an assistant to Swinton, not able to manoeuvre effectively on his own within the British political system. Swinton settled into prosperous retirement in Scotland, going to London mainly to join in the attacks on Robert Clive. I'tisam al-Din claimed the emperor's letter never arrived and that Clive personally presented the imperial gifts to the king in his own name. In fact, the emperor's letter did reach the British king, but not the Rs 100,000 nazr (which was never satisfactorily accounted for by the Company).[88] Thus, this mission failed in its overly-ambitious goal:

[87] Letter to Court 29/1/1766 in NAI, *Fort William*, vol. 4, p. 371. I'tisam al-Din, giving the date 11 Shaban 1180, seems to be off by one year. Swinton Letters, MSS EUR F.128/56, BL.

[88] George III, *Correspondence*, vol. 1, pp. 443–6; Letter to Bengal 20/11/1767, E/4/618, vol. 3, f. 811, BL.

inducing King George to send a British army to restore the emperor and override the Company's Bengal government.

While the mission struggled in Britain, the emperor futilely remained in expectation of success. Yet, he received no response to his letter or nazr, despite his repeated queries about them.[89] This was all the more frustrating since the emperor knew his nominal subordinate, the Nawab of the Carnatic (Arcot), had recently received a formal letter from the British king.[90] The emperor thus misunderstood British political realities.

Finally, I'tisam al-Din and his servant returned in 1769 with little to show in political terms but with much information about Britain, its people, and its politics.[91] He once again took service with British officials, including negotiating on their behalf with the Marathas in 1775. In addition to his oral accounts of Britain that he passed on to his peers, he wrote in 1784/5 among the earliest written accounts by an Indian about Britain, an extensive Persian-language narrative of his trip: 'Shigrif-namah-i Wilayat' (Wonder-book of Europe).[92]

I'tisam al-Din explained to his Indian listeners and readers his perceptions of Britain, laying out many themes that later Indians travellers would reiterate. Like many later Asian males in Britain, he drew particular attention to the striking sexuality blatant there, as contrasted with India.[93] He recorded the very suggestive words and behaviour of British market women on the street towards him, including their bantering requests for a kiss. He watched closely as lovers flirted immodestly in St James Park 'like peacocks', without fear of civic authorities. He also noted Britain's generous care of the illegitimate children that illicit lovers engendered.

In an exchange that would recur with later Indians, he claimed his hosts urged him to marry a British woman and settle there as a professor of Persian. He declined this abstract offer, saying that élite

---

[89] Letter to Court 17/2/1769, E/4/28, ff. 268–9, BL.

[90] Court Minutes 7/7/1762.

[91] Court Minutes 12/1/1768.

[92] His Persian manuscript is OR 200, BL. For a full translation (via Bengali) see I'tisam al-Daula, *Wonders*, tr. Haq. Mohammad Tavakoli-Targhi is currently working on a definitive translation. For I'tisam al-Din's family history, see Sadrul Ola, *History*. See also Gulfishan Khan, *Indian Muslim*, pp. 72–8.

[93] C.f., Tavakoli-Targhi, 'Imagining'.

British women would not have him and he would not accept a lower-class wife. Indeed, many such 'interracial' marriages occurred in this period, without much adverse notice by British society. .

Among the other attractions of London, I'tisam al-Din highlighted those which appeared to validate his own culture. At Vauxhall pleasure gardens, he commented approvingly on a realistic painting by Francis Hayman of 'Lord Clive Meeting Mir Jafar' (1761–2). Visiting Oxford, he compared 'Orientalist' William Jones' expertise in Persian un-favourably with his own. He also recorded his debates with Christian religious authorities that ended in their defeat before his own advocacy of Islam, and defence of polygamy. Yet, he recognized the greater British industriousness and their comparatively more effective and less vainglorious political and military leadership. He also lauded the widely and inexpensively available printed books and pamphlets, a medium largely unavailable in India at this time. While he often des-cribed himself and other Indians (including an Indo-Portuguese fellow-passenger) as 'black' (*siyah*) in complexion compared to Bri-tons, he recorded no sense of racial or cultural inferiority, as would some later nineteenth-century Indians.

The rich knowledge that I'tisam al-Din brought back about the political and social conditions in Britain disseminated in India, but not widely. His book remained in manuscript until first published in partial translation in London in 1827.[94] Nevertheless, his experience apparently informed some later emissaries, including Hanumantrao (see below) and Karim Khan (see Chapter 7), who cited evidence from his book.

Representing a Would-be Ruler

Former and would-be Peshwa Raghunathrao (1734–84) sent Indian ambassadors to Britain in 1780. Like the emperor, Raghunathrao sought thereby to overrule Company authorities in India. While his representatives participated in high-level debate in London over British policy in India, they failed to reinstate Raghunathrao as peshwa.

[94] In 1827, James Edward Alexander, assisted by Munshi Shumsher Khan, incompletely translated this manuscript into Urdu and English, published as I'tisam al-Din, *Shigurf Namah-i Velaet*.

For a century, Raghunathrao's Chitpavan Brahmin family had used their hereditary office of peshwa to lead the Maratha Confederacy. Raghunathrao, personally ousted as peshwa by rival family members and Maratha enemies, had turned to the British.[95] In 1775, he negotiated a treaty with the nearby Company's Bombay government which recognized him as peshwa and promised 2,500 troops in exchange for Raghunathrao's territorial cessions, Rs 600,000 bond, and future annual payments of Rs 1,875,000. This alliance comprised the first major intervention by the Company's Bombay government into regional politics. However, competing Maratha powers repeatedly defeated their joint forces. Further, Governor-General Warren Hastings overruled the Bombay governor, unilaterally annulling this treaty. Nevertheless, the governor intermittently supported Raghunathrao financially and militarily, in the face of opposition from both most Marathas and also Hastings.

In the midst of these multi-sided struggles, Raghunathrao sought backing from Europe through diplomacy. He wrote to the British king in 1776, requesting him to overrule the governor-general. Although the Bombay government forwarded this letter to London, it produced promising reports but no substantial results.[96]

Next, Raghunathrao determined to deploy an Indian envoy to Britain. He probably knew about I'tisam al-Din's earlier mission, since that London-returned envoy had recently moved among the Maratha powers, negotiating on behalf of the Company. Instead of a Briton like Swinton to head his mission, Raghunathrao selected as his ambassador a loyal fellow Brahmin, Hanumantrao of Rajapur.

Hanumantrao, however, did not know English or apparently have much experience dealing with Britons. Raghunathrao was evidently aware of the Parsi community's long experience with Britons, and

[95] See Gaikwad, 'Life' (Ph.D. 1970); Forrest, *Selections*, vol. 1, part 2; Duff, *History*, vol. 2, pp. 116–337; Gordon, *Marathas*, pp. 154–73.

[96] In his letter, Raghunathrao expressed surprise at the dissention among the Company's officials in India. His vakeel in Calcutta inaccurately reported this letter's success in London. Raghunathrao further sent appeals to the Portuguese queen and viceroy and also the French. See Divekar, 'Raghunathrao' (M.A., 1933), ff. 409–35; Gaikwad, 'Life', ff. 511–78; Parasnis, 'Original'; and Pissulencar, 'Some Unknown Dealings'.

perhaps even Nowroji Rustamji's successful mission to London a half-century earlier. He therefore appointed as Hanumantrao's assistant a Parsi, Maniar Ratanji—accompanied by his son, Cursetji Maniar.

Raghunathrao entrusted his ambassador with a letter he composed in November 1778, addressing the British king:

> . . . being satisfied, both from experience and report, of the good faith of the English, and considering their interests as inseparably united with his own, he had, at a time of great difficulty and danger, committed himself to them with the utmost confidence [by the 1775 Treaty, but now] his endeavors in the public service had been impeded and defeated by a prevailing spirit of avarice and ambition [within the Company's Government]. Since all he has to communicate on this subject could not be confined to the narrow limits of a Letter; he had therefore commissioned three Persons, on whose fidelity and ability he could entirely rely, to repair to England, and explain his sentiments *viva voce*. That he flattered himself, the object of their mission being of the last [i.e. highest] importance, it would be speedily investigated and decided upon.[97]

Like the Mughal emperor, Raghunathrao thus appealed to George III as a fellow monarch, seeking diplomatic recognition, a political alliance, supersession of British officials in India, and military support.

In 1780, the mission made its way slowly to Europe via the Persian Gulf. Hanumantrao endured hardship by scrupulously eating only food prepared by himself under conditions of strict Brahmanic ritual purity.[98] Like I'tisam al-Din, he also continued to wear his customary dress.

Reaching England early in 1781, they went first to the Crown's foreign office, which was unsure if Raghunathrao was entitled to be an ambassador, referred them to the directors, but retained an interest in their mission. The directors officially accepted Raghunathrao's letter. Not knowing what to do with these putative ambassadors, however, the directors sent them off to Islington while they deliberated.[99]

This dismissive behaviour offended the envoys and their growing number of British supporters as well. Their appeal against Hastings

[97] HMS 149, ff. 459, 463, 467–8.

[98] Despite evidence of high born Hindus travelling overseas, the prescriptive shastras warned against the pollution entailed. See Basham, 'Notes'.

[99] Court Minutes 22/2/1781.

interested several political leaders, including Edmund Burke and Charles William Boughton Rouse (1747–1821). Revealing the factionalism of British politics, Harry Verelst (the protégé of Clive who had been earlier successfully sued by Cojamaul and Rafael) also supported this Maratha mission. These British allies used their influence with Secretary of State Wills Hill, Earl of Hillsborough, and other powerful men to induce the directors to adopt a more gracious attitude.[100] Burke also provided his greenhouse at Beaconsfield for Hanumantrao to live in, and thus prepare his food and bathe in the pure isolation that he required on pain of excommunication.

Hanumantrao came to the attention of Parliament not only as emissary but also as an expert who could represent India and its people directly. The Parliamentary Committee investigating Hastings invited Hanumantrao as a witness (just as an opposing faction had invited Cojamaul and Rafael to testify nine years earlier). This committee proclaimed Hanumantrao 'the most authentic Source of Information, concerning the Usages and Religion of the Hindoos'.[101] Accompanied by his Parsi companions, Hanumantrao testified (26 February 1781), translated by Rouse, a member of the committee. He gave lengthy explanations about the system of 'cast', describing the religiously, socially, and judicially privileged position of Brahmins, including himself, following very closely the models prescribed in the *dharmashastra*. His testimony particularly condemned Hastings and the Calcutta Supreme Court for the public hanging of Brahmin Nandakumar in 1775. These Parliamentary investigations resulted in the 1781 Bengal Judicature Act, and contributed to Pitt's 1784 India Act, and then the impeachment and trial of Hastings by Parliament, in which Hanumantrao's patron, Burke, took a leading role.

Hanumantrao's testimony about the cultural meanings of his high Brahmanic rank also enhanced the status of himself and his mission. Further, Burke and most other Britons clearly favoured him over his Parsi assistants because of British unequal images of their respective communities and/or based on their individual personalities. Indeed, a British acquaintance called Maniar 'one of the most quarrelsome,

---

[100] Burke to Hillsborough 12/7/1781 in Burke, *Correspondence*, vol. 4, pp. 356–8; Marshall, 'Edmund Burke'.

[101] Lambert, *House of Commons*, vol. 138, pp. 39–40.

troublesome, provoking men I ever met with' but Hanumantrao 'a peaceable and reasonable creature'.[102]

Following Hanumantrao's testimony before Parliament, the emissaries received further attentions from the directors. They provided house rental and maintenance allowance for the envoys. Not until 15 June 1781, however, did the directors have a letter of reply to Raghunathrao prepared.[103] This was quite vague in its assurances, since the directors had only uncertain and outdated information about the complex and constantly shifting conflicts among Maratha powers and between them and the Company. On 6 July, the directors summoned the emissaries to receive this sealed reply.

While the two Parsis appeared before the directors, Hanumantrao did not, perhaps tactfully absenting himself from what would be a painful confrontation. The Parsis unsuccessfully asserted their right to know the contents of this sealed letter and also to obtain answers to the issues they had raised verbally. The directors regarded Maniar as 'making some unreasonable Demands, and delivering himself with much Impropriety . . . the Court being much displeased with his Behaviour, agreed not to receive the Agents again without an Apology . . . and resolved that all future assistance should be withdrawn if they do not proceed on their Journey within the Space of eight days'.[104] As Maniar described this confrontation: 'This Treatment [by the directors] threw [him], who was there with his Son, into some heat, in which he used some expressions, not the most measured. The directors put them out of the Room, after telling them . . . that they were eating the Company's bread; and that if they did not depart in a few days, their allowance would be stopped.'[105] The emissaries, however, attempted to defend their dignity and refused to leave.

Once again, Burke intervened with His Majesty's government. He requested Hillsborough counteract 'the late rude and abrupt order for their departure' by the directors. While Burke did not excuse the conduct of Maniar, calling it 'something mysterious and unaccountable', nevertheless he feared the Company's behaviour was—

[102] Richie to Court, Miscellaneous Letters Received, 69, ff. 86, 101, 113, BL.

[103] Court Minutes 2/3/1781, 15/6/1781.

[104] Court Minutes 6/7/1781.

[105] Burke to Hillsborough 12/7/1781 in Burke, *Correspondence*, vol. 4, pp. 356–8.

a great, and I conceive a very needless insult . . . all taken together [it] will hardly furnish in the East the most favourable Idea of our national Character or of our Conduct towards a people who are to be, as hitherto they have been, the main supports of the power and greatness of this Nation . . . [There is] no reason why they should be treated in a manner unworthy of ourselves, and unbecoming to their Commission, since they are undoubtedly sent by an Ally of this Country, late a Sovereign Prince of extensive Dominions and by whose Grant the Company are possessed of Territories of very great Value.[106]

Further, Burke urged that the directors do more to satisfy the honour of these representatives and their Indian master:

to impress them with an Idea of the National Hospitality, and to send them away in good humour . . . they ought certainly to be clad new, and in a handsome manner, and according to the useage of the East, to be sent off with presents. Trifles would serve, and I am sure I could point out such, as would be perfectly grateful to them, and send them off in good humour, at an expence of not more than £150 . . .

Burke's sentiments were shared by many influential men.

In response to such pressure, and facing an incipient General Court of Proprietors meeting which some stockholders threatened to summon over this affair, the directors granted the envoys £800 for their travelling expenses. They retorted that this was inadequate. The directors raised it by another £200 to a round £1,000, but in return demanded that they set off by 1 August at the latest.[107]

The emissaries still made no preparation to leave, insisting that they also receive a letter from the king. The directors then requested that Hillsborough write formally as well.[108] Thus on 31 July Hillsborough composed a formal letter to Raghunathrao which he presented to the mission unsealed:

Illustrious Sir, I should think myself very unworthy of the Honor you have done me by Your Letter, if I omitted to express to You in writing the high sense I entertain of it. It is for this Reason that I deliver this Letter to the Three Persons you have sent into this Kingdom. The king, my Royal Master, having long since delegated the Care of East India Affairs for this

[106] Ibid.

[107] Court Minutes 25/7/1781; Burke to Udny 3/8/1781 in Burke, *Correspondence*, vol. 4, pp. 361–2.

[108] Mitchell letter 26/7/1781, HMS 153, ff. 371–2.

Country, to the East India Company, those Persons were immediately referred to the Principal directors of that Company, to hold Conference with
them upon such matters as they had in Charge from You, and I understand
they have conferred with the Principal directors accordingly.[109]

Further, Burke also interested King George III personally in these
envoys. That monarch ordered his government to give them presents
worth £267 15s., declaring, 'Nothing can be more shameful than the
conduct of the East India directors toward the Agents from Ragobar
[Raghunathrao].'[110]

When the envoys still refused to leave until more was paid, the
directors awarded yet another £200 on 15 August 1781.[111] They finally left, but at Venice the mission split irreconcilably as 'the Bramin
protested against going in the same ship with [Maniar,] such a furious
madman.'[112] Maniar and his son returned to Bombay by one route,
while Hanumantrao went another. They and the letters from the
Company and Crown reached Raghunathrao in late 1782, with eleven
boxes of presents from King George arriving subsequently.[113]

Raghunathrao recognized all the efforts on his behalf that Burke
had made, writing him a letter of thanks. Burke replied graciously,
seeking to compensate for the cold reception Raghunathrao's agents
had received, and promising to make better arrangements for any
future Brahmin emissaries: 'The sufferings this Gentleman underwent at first was owing to the ignorance not to the unkindness of this
Nation. Hunment Row is a faithful and able Servant of yours. And
Manuar Parsi and his Son used every exertion to second him. If your
affairs have not succeeded to your wishes it is no fault of theirs.'[114]

[109] Hillsborough to Ragonath Row 31/7/1781 and Receipt, HMS 153,
ff. 379, 387–91.

[110] George III, *Correspondence*, vol. 5, pp. 260–1.

[111] Court Minutes 15/8/1781; Letter from Court 25/1/1782 in NAI, *Fort
William*, vol. 9, p. 7.

[112] Richie to Court, Miscellaneous Letters Received, 69, ff. 86, 101, 113;
Burke to Molini 11/9/1781, in Burke, *Correspondence*, vol. 4, pp. 371–2; Court
Minutes 7/9/1781, 28/11/1781.

[113] Raghunath Rao to Court 16/1/1783, *CPC*, vol. 6, p. 243; Court Minutes
8/5/1782.

[114] Burke to Ragunath Rao August 1781, in Burke, *Correspondence*, vol. 4,
pp. 367–8.

Indeed, the mission and Raghunathrao's political careers both failed to live up to his expectations. Nevertheless, he continued to hope for King George III's support, writing him another letter in 1783, asking for 10,000 troops and an enhanced pension.[115]

Such diplomacy, however, could not restore Raghunathrao to power. Under its 1783–4 Treaty of Salbai with Raghunathrao's Maratha enemies, the Company surrendered him, but with the provision that he be allowed to retire under Maratha custody with a pension of Rs 300,000 annually. Although he died soon afterwards, his son, Baji Rao II, succeeded to the office of peshwa in 1795.

Despite the failure of Raghunathrao's diplomatic initiative to establish himself as a ruler under British protection, this mission nevertheless remained a significant event in local tradition. Indeed, a century later, the precedent of Hanumantrao's visit still served as justification for other Brahmins making the voyage without automatic excommunication.[116] Further, it gained Indian rulers in the region valuable information about Britain, especially highlighting the divisions within British politics and the Company. Many other diplomatic and political missions from western India would follow, although we cannot know the extent to which they were informed by earlier accounts.

Indian Diplomats and 'Royalty' in Britain

Even decades after losing their territories, the descendants of former rulers could sometimes convince British authorities in London that they were morally entitled to pensions and honours, particularly when supported by legally binding treaties. In contrast, many British officials in India regarded the descendants of former rulers as expensive nuisances. In January 1794, Mirza Odudeen Khan (d.1814) reached London representing himself and five brothers, sons of the late Nawab of Broach—whom the Company had deposed in 1772.[117] At that

---

[115] Parasnis, 'Original'.

[116] After returning, Hanumantrao reportedly purified himself by passing through a pure gold *yoni* (symbolizing rebirth). Parasnis, 'Original', pp. 94–5. See also Standing Committee on the Hindu Sea-Voyage Question, *Hindu Sea-Voyage*, pp. 36–7.

[117] He himself used Odudeen as his name although some called him 'Ahid al-Din Khan. Court Minutes 5/2/1794; Personal Records O/6/8, ff. 53–4, BL. See also Bombay, Public and Secret and Political Diaries, 1794–1816, MSA.

point, only three of the brothers received any pensions from the Company whatsoever (Rs 6 or 8 monthly). After repeated fruitless appeals to Bombay, the family finally pooled its resources and sent Mirza Odudeen to London (accompanied by a secretary, Mustapha Khan, and a servant, Adun Mahomet). There, he demanded twenty years' back income, totaling Rs 180,000,000, in addition to Rs 900,000 annually thereafter.

Since Mirza arrived in London unannounced, the directors had no information whether he was the man he claimed to be, and, if so, either what being an heir to the Nawab of Broach meant or how legitimate his extravagant claims were. They made inquiries in London among their former officials who had served in Bombay.[118] They sent representatives to interview him in person. They commissioned research in the Company's records about this family. They also sent a letter to Bombay asking for clarification. The Bombay governor, however, knowing about the Broach mission, had already dispatched a letter of explanation, which arrived a week after the directors' inquiry was written.

While all this was going on, Mirza tried to secure political support and also adapt life in London to his own expectations. He hired a Briton, Henry Frederick Thompson, to advise him. A growing number of British lawyers, politicians, and other entrepreneurs worked for Indian notables as agents (either when these Indians came to Britain or stayed in India), often promising more success than they could deliver but usually taking fat fees. They generally differed from Indian agents in Britain in terms of their commitment to their clients and also their orientations towards India and Britain.

As Ramzan 1208 Hijri (22 March–20 April 1794 CE) approached, Mirza requested the directors to supply him and his suite with the foodstuffs he required for each night's post-sunset feast during his observance of this month of daylight fasting.[119] These the directors provided as best they could. They also, three months after his arrival, made arrangements for his 'proper Accommodation', including providing a daily allowance of three guineas (Rs 32) plus a carriage.

---

[118] Court Minutes 12–26/2/1794.
[119] Court Minutes 26/3/1794.

The next month, however, the directors decided that his continued presence would only bring them further expense and trouble. They offered him and his party free passage home, plus a grant of £100 to purchase the equipage needed for the voyage. Should he not accept these offers and depart forthwith, the directors informed him in person that they would 'be under the necessity of withdrawing all further allowance, and of finally rejecting every sort of application from him in future'.[120] They also cut his allowance in half and withdrew his carriage.

The directors, however, also instructed the Bombay government to investigate him further. If his claims proved valid, they were to provide him with a pension of Rs 2,400 annually and the house in Surat that he claimed. Further, if any of his five brothers could prove their rights, they and their children were to receive an equivalent pension.

Mirza did not take his dismissal well. He again personally confronted the directors, explicitly stating that he wanted to settle in England and receive his pension there. When the directors repeated their threat that he must leave immediately or lose all they had promised and all future support, he contemptuously rejected their offer as 'a miserable pittance' and also resented their condescending tone. He wrote a detailed letter of bitter protest.[121] In impassioned terms, Mirza refuted the directors' implication that he was a petitioner seeking favours or compassion, asserting instead that his family were justly claming their legal and moral rights and redress for 'the manifest oppressions and notorious Injuries . . . received from the Company . . . [He] demand[ed] . . . the payment of [the Company's] enormous debt [to his family], contracted by avarice, prosecuted by rapine, and maintained by cruelty, violence, and injustice.' He cited the Company's equally unjust and disgraceful treatment of the heirs of the nawab of the Carnatic. He vowed to shame the directors before the British 'Public' by claiming his rights to shelter in a London poor house: 'We shall be transferred from the hands of oppression to those of the overseers of the Poor; who will with wonder receive into their House,

---

[120] Court Minutes 16/4/1794, 30/5/1794.

[121] Court Minutes 3/6/1794; Minutes of Committee of Correspondence 3/6/1794.

People once supported by your beneficence . . . [but now], as the pulse of avarice and self conviction actuated your minds, . . . destitute of Bread, and driven with ignominy from your Court.'

Apprehensive about the political implications of these assertions, the directors referred this matter to the Board of Control, asking for advice about how 'to compel him to embark for India'.[122] Before the board could decide what to do, Mirza reconsidered, accepted the directors' terms, and boarded ship with his party plus an English servant, Henry Monmouth. In parting, he appointed Thompson as his legal agent and then wrote an seemingly ironic letter to the directors 'expressing his thanks to the Court for their kindness to him during his residence in London'.[123] On his return, he arranged that his brothers each received the Rs 2,400 promised. They each gave him part of these pensions because 'he [had] expended a large sum and undertaken great trouble for their joint behalf, by his proceeding to England where his representations . . . procured . . . that increased allowance . . . .'.[124]

He did not remain long in Bombay, however. After arriving in December 1794, he collected one of his brothers and set off again for Europe.[125] In April 1795, he wrote to the directors from Salonica (Greece), intimating that he was about to revisit London. The directors offered 400 guineas (Rs 4,200) if he swore never to approach them again. He seems to have accepted this arrangement.[126] In 1809, the directors raised the pensions to this family and made them hereditary, since they belatedly recognized that some ancestral property had in fact been illegally seized in 1772, as Mirza had claimed. This family continued to receive this allowance long thereafter.[127] Thus, after receiving only rebuffs from Company officials in India, this family gained

[122] Board Letter Books, Draft Dispatches 23–30/5/1794, F/3/57, ff. 115–21, BL.

[123] Court Minutes 11/6/1794, 10/9/1794.

[124] The Governor of Bombay later declared these pensions would remain only for three generations. Bombay, Political Diary (1794–1807) nos 112–97, MSA.

[125] Log of Sir Edward Hughes, L/MAR/B/354C, BL.

[126] Court Minutes 22/4/1795.

[127] These pensions continued but remained contested, within the family and between it and the Company. In 1874, for example, fourteen descendants received pensions totaling Rs 4,500. Bombay, Political and Secret Diaries, *passim*,

much financially from its mission to Britain—although not everything it demanded.

Over this period, various other Indian missions reached London. A putative south Indian raja (whom the directors never fully identified) briefly visited in 1785.[128] As a result of these experiences, the directors became wary of all Indian dignitaries who reached London unannounced and unknown to them. As scholar-official Abu Talib noted around 1800: 'When I first arrived in England, several of the directors imagined that I had been sent as an agent by some of the Princes of India, to complain against their servants. They were therefore, for some time very distrustful, and reserved in their conduct; but after they were convinced of their error, they received me kindly, and paid me much attention.'[129] Yet, in the British public sphere, Abu Talib himself passed as 'the Persian Prince' (see Chapter 3).

Over the decades that followed, dozens of Indian political agents, diplomats, and noblemen and women would journey to Britain. Being Indian 'royalty' continued to hold a cachet in society there. Some Indian agents gained much. Yet they increasingly faced British authorities with growing experience in identifying and managing them and a British public ever more familiar with Indians as the colonized.

Early Effects of Colonialism

During the late eighteenth century, the growing number and diversity of Indians going to Britain, and their changing experiences there, reflected the rapid early expansion of Company trade and rule in India. Yet, the British establishment and British colonialism were neither monolithic nor hegemonic. Thus, Indian travellers and settlers in Britain could negotiate roles and relationships that might benefit them despite the inequities of power they faced. Further, they often proved able to represent themselves in Britain and bring back to India firsthand knowledge of it, mostly oral but increasingly written.

What it was to be Indian in Britain had changed over time. The 'exotic oriental' identities of some Indian women and men servants

---

MSA; Government of India, *Gazetteer of the Bombay Presidency*, vol. 2, pp. 471–2.

[128] *Times* 12/10/1785 2c.

[129] Abu Talib, *Masir* (reprint), p. 151.

and slaves may have added to their attractiveness for their British employers and distinguished them from their British fellow servants. But that appeal diminished as their numbers rose and India became a subordinated colony. Indian seaman signed on to sail British ships, working to preserve their own structures of recruitment and service. Yet, their labour, vital for shipping from India to Britain, had little value once they arrived. Some Indian merchants profited as intermediaries and brokers from the Company's commerce. While they might face injustice in India, in London they sometimes gained a more sympathetic hearing from British law courts and opposition political factions. A few Indian rulers tried to draw authorities in London into supporting them through diplomatic or political missions. Each of these Indian individuals and groups sought to gain from their venture to Britain, but often had to adjust to the host culture and endure disappointments there.

By the end of the eighteenth century, the force of British colonialism further altered most of these relationships to the detriment of Indians. To most directors and other British authorities, indigent Indian servants and seamen began to appear as social problems, dissident Indian merchants, envoys, and noblemen as political and/or legal ones. In response, the Company gradually developed policies to manage the activities of Indians in London, but with mixed results. As conditions in India and Britain changed over time, so too did the experiences and agency of Indians who made the journey.

CHAPTER 3

Indian Scholars and Teachers during Early Colonialism

Shifting Cultures of Colonial Rule

Between the 1790s and 1820s, various Indian social classes perforce contended in distinctive ways with expanding British colonialism and its ever more confident Anglicized values and personnel. During this period the Company defeated virtually all opposing rulers, annexed 644,000 square kilometers into its direct administration, and extended its indirect rule over almost all the rest. Increasing numbers of Indian scholar-officials, seamen, wives and children of Europeans, servants, diplomats, envoys, and noblemen now travelled to Britain, negotiating there with the local society over their respective roles and relationships. Common patterns run through the experiences of each, but there were also striking differences based on class, ethnicity, and gender. While subsequent chapters in Part Two consider these others, here we examine men strongly identified with the former dominant political culture: Indian scholar-officials embodying Persian literature, Islamic sciences, and Mughal administrative technologies. These highly trained teachers, authors, and administrators had held respect and influence even during Mughal decline over the eighteenth century; they continued to instruct, write, and administer as service élites in various regional successor states. Britons in India initially employed them and studied their expertise, while not necessarily accepting their cultural values.[1] From the late eighteenth century, however, these scholar-officials began to lose out to British colonial officials and professors, who made them mere clerks and

---

[1] See Cohn, *Colonialism*, and Marshall, 'Indian Officials'.

language tutors. British 'Orientalists' largely appropriated their cultural authority while British 'Anglicizers' devalued it.

Indian scholar-officials nonetheless had some agency in these transitions. Many sought to maintain their positions by working for the British, as they had for earlier rulers. Not necessarily enamoured of British rule per se, they found it an opportune haven from the insecurities of service to embattled Indian dynasties. Consequently, they desired to instruct their new British employers in the superiority of their own cultural values and techniques of administration, including by venturing to Britain to do so.[2] These educated men—like most other Indians—usually made this journey as dependents, employed or guided by Britons.

Once there, they attempted to establish themselves as teachers with Britons as their pupils. I'tisam al-Din went in 1766–8 as an expert in Persian diplomacy, representing the Mughal emperor (see Chapter 2). He was followed by Persian language teachers—Munshi Isma'il in 1772 (who accompanied Claude Russell), Mir Muhammad Husain ibn Abdul 'Azim Isfahani in 1775–6 (d.1790, who went with Elliot), and Munshi Muhammad Sami around 1785 (who accompanied Sir John D'Oyly). Mirza Abu Talib Khan Isfahani (1752–1806) ventured to Britain in 1799–1802 (initially accompanying Captain David Richardson), intending to establish a government-sponsored Persian-language training institute there under his own direction. Four of these Indian scholars wrote books (in Persian or Arabic) about their experiences of—and moral judgments about—British faults, as well as accomplishments, for the edification of Indian and British readers.[3] Abu Talib's published articles and books had especially wide

---

[2] Bayly denotes this 'old patriotism'. Such attitudes contrasted with the trend followed by some Hindu or Muslim 'reformist' movements, which turned inward, seeking to ascribe the causes of British expansion to their own culture's lapses. Bayly, *Origins*, pp. 58–9.

[3] See Khan, 'Masir Talibi fi Bilad Afranji', Persian ADD 8145–7, BL (my pagination is from the Persian reprint edited by Khadive-Jam); Mir Muhammad Husain, 'Risalah-i Ahwal-i Mulk-i Farang', K.R. Cama Oriental Research Library, Bombay and Maulana Azad Library, Aligarh. For biographical information see *CPC*, vol. 9, pp. 196–7; Digby, 'Eighteenth Century Narrative'; Kabir, *Mirza Abu Talib Khan*; Gulfishan Khan, *Indian Muslim*; Llewellyn-Jones, 'Indian Travellers'; Rizvi, *Socio-Intellectual History*, vol. 2, pp. 230–3; Sankhdher, 'Mirza Abu Talib Khan'.

audiences in India and Europe.[4] Having returned, these travellers also located themselves above their peers in India due to their knowledge and experience of Britain.

Most but not all of the scholar-administrators going to Britain were Muslim. A Bengali Hindu by birth, Goneshamdass, served as Persian translator to Colonel Graham. He travelled to England and testified in English before Parliament in 1773 as an expert on Islamic and Hindu legal practices as they related to British colonial courts.[5] Subsequently, he became confidential munshi to Sir Elijah Impey, newly-appointed Chief Justice of the Calcutta Supreme Court, and deposed in his defence against accusations that Impey had wrongly executed Nandakumar. A man who moved among cultures, he converted to Christianity as Robert Goneshamdass, and retired on a pension from Impey.

Indian teachers found eager British students of their languages and cultures, particularly among the many Britons preparing to go out to India to conquer, rule, or trade. Among others, in 1777, Monshee Mahomet Saeed of Bengal advertised in London newspapers for British paying pupils to whom he could teach 'Persian and Arabick' languages.[6] Abu Talib gave private tuitions in Persian during his years in Britain. Mirza Mohammed Fitrut of Lucknow (who accompanied Sir John Murray to Britain in 1797), advertised himself in 1801 as teacher of 'the true Court Persian Tongue, and also the Arabic and Hindostannee Languages, as Pronounced in the Country'—skills a cultured Briton going to India should desire.[7]

These scholars generally did not approach British culture with a sense of inferiority, particularly during the late eighteenth century—while the British drive for cultural hegemony over India was only incipient. Many admitted their own society's less advanced knowledge of certain physical sciences and technology—including medicine,

---

[4] See Fisher, 'Representing "His" Women'.

[5] Lambert, *House of Commons*, vol. 135, pp. 546–9; vol. 138, p. 124; Impey, *Memoirs*, p. 237.

[6] *Public Advertiser* 5/11/1777.

[7] Returning to Calcutta and attached to Fort William College (1803–5), Mirza Fitrut translated the four Christian Gospels into Hindustani. *European Magazine* 39 (January–June 1801), pp. 7–8; Home Political Consultation 15/5/1797, no. 50, Home Miscellaneous, vol. 559, ff. 297–301, 405, NAI.

military sciences, and print-publishing. Yet most such early travellers remained staunch advocates of their own religion and customs. Islamic monotheism assailed Christian doctrines like the trinity. Insistence on halal meat and/or avoiding alcohol challenged British habits. Indian dress distinguished them from the host society. These men's own accounts of such confrontations almost invariably demonstrated to their Indian readers how they, and the truth of their religion and values, had triumphed (British versions of these confrontations usually recorded the reverse).[8] In other cases, however, the traveller or settler accepted, or even revelled in, British drink and food (usually pork aside). For example, Abu Talib cited the Persian poet Hafiz as legitimating his imbibing.

Significantly, religion was often coupled with their attitudes towards, and relationships with, women. These men repeatedly noted their strikingly free access to British women of all classes, so amazingly different from the prevalent practice in India. Indian writers (like British travellers and officials) assessed the local society based on their valuation of the status of women there. Several commented upon the many unmarried but cohabiting couples and the vast number of prostitutes (*fahisha*) they observed on London's streets.[9] Writing as males, they often felt both empowered and threatened, both titillated and repulsed, by the liberties displayed by British women towards them in Britain. In contrast, in India they generally confined their womenfolk from non-related males, both Indian and British. Likewise, the few British women present in India remained largely outside the personal experience of Indian men (except Indian male servants). Most Indian scholars (like Indian seamen and servants) who settled in Britain married British women in parish churches, and therefore legally had to convert (at least nominally) to Anglican Christianity.

Other major cultural confrontations with Britons centred on control over Persianate knowledge. For many Indian scholars, securing a professorial position of authority in Britain appeared an attractive and lucrative vocation. They appreciated in Britons respectful emulation,

[8] Bayly identifies Abu Talib with 'that tradition of rational observation of peoples and faiths which we have called spiritual anthropology.' Bayly, *Empire*, pp. 86–7.

[9] Khan, *Masir*, p. 272.

but not appropriation of their expertise by the unworthy. Indians scrutinizing British libraries were impressed by the vast, and growing, collections of oriental books and manuscripts showcased there.[10] They did not regard this as looting Indian knowledge but rather as laudable appreciation of their literature by British scholars. Nevertheless, these Indian educators decried the poor quality instruction in Persian language offered by British self-professed experts, calling them 'false teachers', incompetents who were outrageously charging for each useless 90 minute lesson a guinea-and-a-half (Rs 16, equivalent to a month's pay for a British workingman or Indian lascar).[11]

In contrast, these Indian scholars asserted that they themselves exclusively offered accurate and authentic language and cultural training. Several denigrated the Persian language skills of Orientalist scholars like Sir William Jones; Abu Talib wrote:

> Whenever I was applied to by any [British] person for instruction in the Persian language who had previously studied [Jones'] grammar, I found it much more difficult to correct the bad pronunciation he had acquired, and the errors he had adopted, than it was to instruct a person who had never before seen the Persian alphabet. Such books are now so numerous in London, that, in a short time, it will be difficult to discriminate or separate them from works of real value.[12]

Nevertheless, he graciously excused Jones personally for his immature efforts, continuing:

> Far be it from me to depreciate the transcendent abilities and angelic character of Sir William Jones; but his Persian Grammar, having been written when he was a young man, and previous to his having acquired any experience in Hindoostan, is, in many places, very defective; and it is much to be regretted that his public avocations, and other studies, did not permit him to revise it, after he had been some years in India.

[10] E.g., Khan, *Masir*, p. 116.

[11] For advertisements by putative British Persian language teachers, and their fees, see *Times* 10/1/1792 4b, 16/4/1796 1c, 27/6/1796 1c, 14/3/1797 1b; *Morning Herald and Daily Advertiser* 26/1/1784 1b; *Morning Chronicle*, 29/3/1800 4a; *European Magazine*, 43 (January–June 1803), p. 3; College Committee Minutes, J/2/12, f. 165, BL; London Oriental Institution, *Annual Reports*.

[12] Khan, *Masir*, tr. Stewart (1814), pp. 173–4.

In particular, Abu Talib recalled how he had saved one eager pupil from the errors of ill-informed British teachers:

> . . . an amiable young man, Mr [George] Swinton; and I agreed, that, if he would attend me at *eight* o'clock in the morning, I would instruct him. As he was full of ardour, and delighted with the subject, he frequently forsook his breakfast, to come to my house in time. Thanks be to God, that my efforts were crowned with success! and that he having escaped the instructions of *self-taught* masters, has acquired such a knowledge of the principles of the language, as so correct an idea of its idiom and pronunciation, that I have no doubt, after a few years' residence in India, he will attain to such a degree of excellence as has not yet been acquired by any other Englishman![13]

Europeans who presumed inappropriately to claim expertise needed to be humbled.

The force of colonialism, however, altered these Indian scholar-officials' relationship to Britons, demoting them and their Persianate knowledge. This occurred more rapidly in India than in Britain. In India, as British rule expanded, Indian officials and teachers lost out to Britons in state-sponsored institutions.[14] In 1800, Governor-General Richard Wellesley established Fort William College in Calcutta where recently arrived British civil servants would study Persian, Hindustani, and other Indian languages. Its top faculty were British Orientalists, while Indian tutors only assisted them, and British students, as paid subordinates. Thus, Sisir Das notes, 'the teacher–taught relation with which the Indian teachers were familiar did not exist in the College of Fort William. It was a new relationship, that of *Sahibs*

[13] Ibid., p. 101; see also, p. 92.

[14] Historians have conventionally contrasted the administrations of governors-general Warren Hastings (1772–85), which drew upon this traditional service élite to advance British goals, and Cornwallis (1785–93), which discounted them and relied more on British officials. Yet, Cornwallis was a longtime patron of Abu Talib in Calcutta and Ireland. For example, in Britain Cornwallis promised Abu Talib the post of Company political agent in Hyderabad. This offer was, however, withdrawn when the Government of India found it 'advisable to transfer the appointment to an English officer' instead. See Kirkpatrick to Kennaway, 20/7/1791, cited in Bayly, *Empire*, p. 86n.128. See also Zastoupil and Moir, *Great Indian Education*.

and *Munshis*, that of European officers and their servants'.[15] Yet, even this Orientalist use of Indian languages subsequently diminished due to a growing stress on English-based education administration; in 1830, Fort William College largely closed.[16] The eventual predominance of Anglicist over Orientalist emphasis in India was generally marked by Thomas Macaulay's 1835 Minute on Education. This often-quoted policy statement downgraded reliance on Persian in favour of educational and administrative systems based on English, for both Britons and Indians. Indeed, the official language of the Company's administration, which had been Persian, became English in 1837.[17]

In Britain, these processes followed a somewhat different trajectory. Some Indian scholars moved in the highest social circles in Britain, socializing with the aristocracy and holding positions of respect in society; others established themselves in the British middle class. On their return to India, however, they found themselves relegated to the status of clerks or hired tutors. For example, Abu Talib enjoyed several splendid London 'seasons', as the celebrated 'Persian Prince', familiar guest of the Duchess of Devonshire in particular. Yet, a Bengal infantry captain, Thomas Williamson, who sailed on the same ship, ridiculed Abu Talib as a pompous fraud whose pretentious boasts about his intimate relations with British aristocratic women could not possibly have been true. Williamson erroneously asserted that Abu Talib must have been deceived in London by low women, being unable to distinguish them from true British ladies. Williamson also belittled his poetry as a 'labyrinth of poetical absurdity, so delectable among Asiatics'.[18] Indeed, after his return, Abu Talib never received appointment to offices promised him in Britain.

[15] Das, *Sahibs*, p. 108. See also Kopf, *British Orientalism*; and Cohn, *Colonialism*, pp. 49ff.

[16] Yet, in 1812, the Company opened Fort St George College, in Madras, for training Britons in south Indian languages and also law. Fort William College remained as an examination centre.

[17] Government of India Act 29 of 1837. Chapter 9 examines early Anglicized Indian officials.

[18] Williamson advocated 'interracial' sexual relations between British men and Indian women, and apparently did not find relations between Indian men and lower-class British women offensive, but those with upper-class British women unthinkable. Williamson, *East India*, vol. 1, pp. 503–9.

Gradually over the early nineteenth century, British Orientalists took control over Indian language teaching in Britain. They codified these languages following European epistemologies and pedagogies. Yet, even among the leading British scholars, few composed original works in Persian or other Indian languages, largely confining themselves to translation into English, or selecting phrases or paragraphs for dictionaries, grammars, and textbooks as teaching aids for Anglophone students. In contrast, Indians composed new books in these languages, using traditional genres or adapting European ones.[19] But even when Indians wrote these texts, Britons often took over editorial reshaping for publication. Such Orientalists were often far less expert, especially in the idiomatic and spoken forms of these languages, but, being British, took over.

Eventually, advocates of Anglicist policies largely prevailed over Orientalists in Britain as well. The Company's directors made learning Indian languages only a secondary consideration for young Britons newly appointed as its officials and officers. Rather, they should primarily receive the education they needed above all: moral training in British Christian values, fully available only in Britain. So that these youths should not be—or at least not appear—totally ignorant of Indian languages on arrival in India, they should simultaneously study introductory Persian, Hindustani, Arabic, Bengali, and/or Sanskrit.[20] The directors therefore created two colleges in Britain: one in 1806 for civil servants (originally in Hertford Castle, then moved to a nearby purpose-built facility) at Haileybury, and one in 1809 for military cadets at Addiscombe (south of London). They simultaneously ordered Fort William College in Calcutta (which had proven quite expensive due to the salaries paid to British Orientalist professors) to be reduced in size and cost, and most of its functions shifted to these two colleges in Britain.

Appointments to the faculty of the two colleges were contested for decades. British scholars, mostly veterans of the Company's service in India, argued that they had the moral right to be handsomely

---

[19] Cole notes most Persian writers accepted Western categories even for their critiques of the West. Cole, 'Invisible Occidentalism'.

[20] The college emphasized 'classical' Indian languages, Persian and Sanskrit, over regional vernaculars. Report Plan for the College 26/10/1804, J/2/1, BL.

employed to import Oriental language training. Even British Orient-alists, however, recognized that only Indian teachers could pro-vide 'that idiomatical accuracy (which never can be attained by any foreigner) so essential to such works.'[21] Hence, four Indians received permanent faculty positions at these colleges. Two had travelled to Britain independently and, once there, applied for the posts; two were recruited in India by the Company.

Continuing faculty, experts in Persian, Arabic, and/or Hindustani languages and literatures, these four teachers provided formative training about their Indian cultures to thousands of young British civil servants and military officers until 1823. They constituted the first direct experience of Indians and Indian cultures for most such Britons. Three took British wives (usually of lower social status than them-selves), thus demonstrating how their male gender and professional class standing overcame their difference by 'race' in British society at the time. To marry these women, they had to become at least nomi-nally Anglican; two were buried in Anglican parish churchyards. At least one accepted British students into his home as paying boarders.

These Indian faculty apparently regarded themselves as bestowing a service on their British students by teaching them the language and culture appropriate to administrators and officers in India. They wrote and translated texts on 'oriental' subjects, generating grammars and other teaching aids. These men enjoyed far superior salaries to what they would have received teaching languages in India, took positions of authority over their British students, and also held the status of scho-lar, professional, and gentleman in British society. Yet, they taught Indian languages in institutions in Britain, designed and run by Bri-tons, using British codifications and pedagogy, to British students who were preparing to conquer and rule ever larger parts of India.

Further, both colleges placed these Indians under the adminis-trative authority of British faculty who defined and then gradually marginalized their expertise. By the 1830s, college policy rejected em-ploying Indians as faculty members in future. Further, their former pupils, once in India, largely reversed the social examples demonstra-ted by their Indian professors: in India they 'feminized' men of their teachers' social class, and tried to enforce rigid barriers against Indian

[21] Jonathan Scott, *Observations*, p. 10.

men's social and sexual relations with European women.[22] Thus, these four teachers had complex agency—as members of British society and as professors of their own culture and languages—in the construction of British knowledge and rule over India.

Indian Faculty at Haileybury

The first Indian to join the faculty at the Company's civil service college at Haileybury, Sheth Ghoolam Hyder (1776–1823, born in Darbhanga, Bihar), journeyed of his own accord to London, seeking employment teaching Persian.[23] Having heard of newly opened Haileybury College, he directly applied in August 1806 'as Persian Writing Master'.[24] To demonstrate his abilities, he enclosed with his unsolicited application a sample of his calligraphy, using Persian verses as his text. Although the college deemed his English barely adequate for the position, he was appointed within days. Ghoolam Hyder received an annual salary of £200, equivalent to salaries of European junior faculty at Haileybury.[25] It was also towards the top of the scale paid to munshis working at Fort William College, which ranged from £36 to £240 annually (but far less than the £1,800 to £3,200 paid British professors of Hindustani, Persian, or Arabic there).[26] After he settled down, he returned his Indian servant to India and hired British ones.[27] As indicated in a contemporary image, he instructed his students wearing his turban and traditional robes, even as they wore traditional British academic caps and gowns (Image 7).

Ghoolam Hyder served as assistant to the professor of Persian, Captain Charles Stewart (1764–1837), newly appointed at £500

[22] See Sinha, *Colonial Masculinity.*

[23] He may have gone to Britain to secure the release of his uncle, confined for life at Prince of Wales Island. Court Minutes 23/12/1806.

[24] Letter of Ghoolam Hyder 15/8/1806, College Committee References, J/1/21, ff. 456–7, BL.

[25] Organization of the Home Establishment, L/AG/30/12, BL.

[26] Bengal Public Consultations 4/9/1808, no. 29, NAI; Letter from Bengal 8/2/1808, BL; Gilchrist letter 15/6/1803, HMS 559, ff. 257–60; Das, *Sahibs*, p. 12.

[27] Court Minutes 27/5/1807.

Image 7: Detail of picture of Haileybury by Thomas Medland, *c.* 1808, showing Ghoolam Hyder and two students.

annually. These two comprised the first appointees in 'the Muham-madan Division' (which included Hindustani and Arabic as well)— as opposed to the 'Hindoo Division' (Sanskrit and Bengali).[28] Such linguistic alignments reflected British colonial sociologies that linked language, religion, and ethnicity. Further, while numerous Muslim scholars travelled to Britain, very few educated Hindu ones did; the 'Hindoo Division' remained exclusively in British hands.

In his pedagogy, Ghoolam Hyder served much as a munshi would in Fort William College (or as a 'native drill-master' would at a West-ern university in the twenty-first century); indeed, Hyder was occa-sionally titled in official documents as 'the Munshi'. Under his direction, Haileybury students copied 'Select passages' in Persio-Arabic characters, which had been 'engraved upon several copper

[28] For British conceptions of Sanskrit and Hinduism, see Trautmann, *Aryans.*

plates of the same size, so that they may be used separately, or bound up together . . .'.[29] He also drilled and corrected their pronunciation. In addition, the Company authorities asked Hyder—'at such periods as would not interfere with his Duties at the College'—to teach 'Persian Writing' to the pupils in the preparatory school associated with Haileybury.[30] Even as Hyder joined the faculty, the directors were seeking to recruit language teachers directly from India.

First, the directors sent an invitation in May 1806 to Abu Talib, proposing that he return to England. They wrote: 'A Moonshee of the name of Abu Talib who was some time ago in this Country, then offered his Services to be employed in this way; if he is now resident in Bengal and wishes to be appointed to the College here, we shall be desirous of engaging him for that purpose as we have received a favourable account of his qualifications'.[31] Unfortunately, Abu Talib had died in December 1806, a few days before the message could reach him.[32] The directors then ordered Fort William College to recruit (at the lowest possible salaries acceptable, they insisted) one Persian and one Hindustani munshi; they simultaneously slashed Fort William College's budget.

Even with these cutbacks among the Indian staff at Fort William College, attracting learned men to leave their families and teach in England proved difficult. Abu Talib's narrative of his trip to Britain, and therefore his proposed salary and plans for an institute under his direction, were well known to his peers.[33] After much effort, the Company finally found two qualified men. Moolvey Meer Abdool Alee of

[29] College Committee Minutes 1/10/1806.

[30] This largely autonomous school, established in 1805, was designed to feed students into the College. College Committee Minutes 9/3/1808.

[31] Public letter to Bengal 31/5/1806, Board Collections F/4/212, no. 4732, BL.

[32] Letter from Baillie 19/12/1806, Bengal Political Consultations 1/1/1807, no. 99, NAI. See also Extract, Political Letter from Bengal 26/2/1807 in Board Collections F/4/212, no. 4732, BL.

[33] In addition to Abu Talib circulating his manuscript among his peers, the *Calcutta Gazette* serialized selective translation in its Supplement (September 1807–February 1808). In 1812, the Company commissioned his son and a colleague to edit and publish the Persian text at Fort William College. See Extract Public Letter from Bengal 9/5/1812, Board Collections F/4/384, no. 9741, BL; Home Miscellaneous, vol. 562, ff. 18–19, NAI.

Benaras had already worked for Fort William College as a munshi in the Persian department since about 1801, but he also qualified to teach Hindustani.[34] Moolvey Mirza Khaleel of Lucknow qualified to teach those two languages plus Arabic. Both were persuaded to accept these appointments, but only at exactly the same substantial annual salary Abu Talib had proposed for himself: £600 plus expenses (including free passage to and from England). This was more than double the highest salary paid a munshi at Fort William College. Indeed, Hailey-bury authorities complained that this created an 'unpleasant situation' since their salary exceeded by £100 (20 per cent) that of the highest paid British professors there (including Thomas Malthus and their direct supervisor, Stewart).[35] These two men made their way separately to England in 1807 and 1808 respectively, each attended by a Muslim servant.[36]

On their arrival, they received appointments as assistant professors, higher in status than 'writing master' Ghoolam Hyder (and more than three times his salary). They were also his social superiors, in India as well as in Britain. They taught the rudiments of Persian, Hindustani, and Arabic to some 130 students each year.[37] Along with British professors, they read out, glossed, and parsed selections, and dictated translations to their students, who memorized their words. Thus, Abdool Alee and Mirza Khaleel were comparable to the highest British faculty at the college, rather than munshis—in duties and salary, if not in rank and administrative responsibilities.

Despite their relatively high incomes, they repeatedly asserted their compensation was inadequate to maintain their appropriate status,

[34] Public Letter from Bengal 8/2/1808, Board Collections F/4/259, no. 5665, BL.

[35] Memorandum on the Present State of the Oriental Department at the College, Extract Public Letter to Bengal 7/9/1808, J/1/35, f. 267, BL; Organization of the Home Establishment L/AG/30/12, ff. 594–601, BL; Home Miscellaneous, vol. 560 ff. 337–9, 380–5; vol. 561, ff. 31–2, NAI.

[36] See L/MAR/B/117H and L/MAR/B/296D, BL; Extract Letters from Bengal 14[24]/7/1807, 25/9/1807, Board Collections F/4/259, no. 5665, BL; Letter to Bengal 21/5/1806, J/1/35, BL.

[37] E.g., in 1817, the Persian class had 71 students per term, Hindustani 55, and Arabic 10, totaling 136; Sanskrit had 16 and Bengali 34, totaling 50. Stewart letter 13/3/1817, College Committee References, J/1/32 1817, ff. 233–5, BL.

England proving more costly than they anticipated. They wrote (in the third person): 'from the great expense of living in this country, they are not able to make any provision for their families and relations in India, an object they had entirely in view, at the time of engaging for the Company's service in England.'[38] They further felt betrayed when the government deducted 10 per cent of their salaries as income tax, levied due to the Anglo-French wars: 'Encouraged by the Liberal offers made to us by the Hon'ble Company, we were induced to leave our homes and undertake a long and disagreeable journey, any deduction from our salaries must therefore be a source of much uneasiness and distress.' Their petitions to the government for exemption as 'foreigners', and on the grounds that the tax was 'unknown to them at the time of their engagement by the Bengal Government', failed. Further, they were surprised by sundry deductions, including stamp duties. Nevertheless, they negotiated from the College £25 house rent plus £5 tax rebate plus £15 for furniture rental annually, in addition to their £600 salary. Having secured their services, the directors proved willing to enhance their pay and benefits rather than lose them or threaten their prestige as college faculty.

While they socialized with each other, they also entered deeply (albeit to different degrees) into British society. They accepted British models for teaching their languages, and also assumed British social roles for themselves as middle-class professionals. Thus, their social position in England and their personal relations with Britons there contrast strikingly with those of mere hired tutors, a status which many of their peers at Fort William College had to endure.

In December 1808, within eight months of his arrival in Haileybury, Moolvey Abdool Alee married a woman whom the college authorities regarded as 'tho not of the first rank in society . . . [of] the utmost respectability . . .'.[39] His title became her last name: Elizabeth Moolvey. To establish himself and his wife in the style he felt commensurate with his professional status, he stopped sending money home to his family in India, who protested in vain. He purchased a horse and chaise. He

---

[38] Petitions of Abdool Alee and Mirza Kheleel, College Committee References, J/1/24, ff. 451, 483–7, BL.

[39] Dalman to Batten 9/9/1815, College Committee References, J/1/30, BL.

left the house which the college had arranged for him to rent and moved into an expensive, recently constructed residence near the college. He justified his new quarters as adding to his value to the college: 'wishing to render himself as useful as possible to his Hon'ble employers, he resolved to take up his residence in the vicinity of the College by which means the Students might have access to him at all times; this object has been fully realized, as a day never passes that some of the Students do not call to consult with him or to read some book which may be too difficult for the class at large'.[40] Thus, his British students became callers at his home, coming to seek guidance and advanced instruction.

Though only a tenant, Abdool Alee expended considerable sums (totalling £125) improving his house and ensuring domestic seclusion by 'enclosing the Garden and securing the Premises' with a compound wall. He purchased 'some additional but requisite furniture' for £75 more. Fearing that he would be turned out when the builder sold the property, he asked the college to purchase and allot the house to him, or to rent it on a seven-year renewable lease, but in vain. Having sunk so much money into the house, he could not leave even when it proved unhealthy. According to his doctor, they had moved into the 'new built house before it was dry; and the situation is such that it is scarcely possible for to make it dry; for, after a heavy rain, the water rises a foot high in the kitchen (from land springs). I have seen the water hang like heavy dew on the inside of the walls.'[41] All this expense was more than Abdool Alee could afford: 'his Creditors are very clamorous and give him much trouble.'[42] In desperation, he successfully asked the college for an advance of £200, offering the security of his worldly possessions 'valued at nearly £1000'. Further, he pledged 'never again to trouble the Hon'ble Company with his Pecuniary concerns, having acquired sufficient experience to enable him hereafter to suit his expenses to his

[40] Petition in Persian (with English translation) from Abdool Alee 20/12/1810, College Committee References, J/1/26, ff. 314–16, BL. See also Abdool Alee letter, in Stewart, *Original Persian*, pp. 84–6.

[41] James letter 22/12/1812, College Committee References, J/1/27, f. 243, BL.

[42] Petitions of Abdool Alee, March 1811 and 19/4/1811, College Committee References, J/1/26, ff. 345–6, 357–8, BL.

Income.' The college clearly felt a patronizing responsibility to sustain the dignity of its faculty with such financial support.

In June 1811, only two months after taking this advance, Abdool Alee fell fatally ill with a paralytic affliction. Despite the protests of his attending local doctor, he travelled to London, where he placed himself under the care of a proficient in the Indian medical steam-bath treatment.[43] Nonetheless, after more than a year of agonizing illness, he expired (October 1812) deeply in debt.[44] In accordance with 'the dying hope of the poor man that no stain might rest on his memory on account of his debts', the college paid for his burial at the Anglican parochial churchyard in Hertford 'but with all the economy that decency will admit'.[45] His widow, Elizabeth Moolvey, had to watch their costly house given up and all their possessions sold at auction to partially pay off their creditors. The college gave an extra £100 in salary plus a 'gratuity' of £20 for mourning clothes and 'immediate relief'.[46] She began a small school which, while initially promising, soon lost the few students it attracted. Ill with breast cancer, she petitioned the Company a few years later that she was 'now reduced to absolute want . . . [a] truly wretched situation'.[47] The college granted her an annual pension of £25 until her death, decades later.[48]

As a 'writing master', Ghoolam Hyder earned less than the other Indian faculty. Yet he too sought to maintain himself appropriately for his professional status, send money to his family in India, and save for his return there. But he found his salary 'barely sufficient to cover his expences in England' and inadequate for his other goals; in 1808 he wrote a formal Persian petition asking for a salary increase.[49] The

---

[43] Probably 'shampooing surgeon' Dean Mahomed. See Fisher, *First Indian Author.*

[44] Obituary of Moolvey Meer Abdool Alee, *Times* 21/10/1812 4b.

[45] Henley letter 6/11/1812, College Committee References, J/1/27, ff. 224–5, BL.

[46] Petition of Elizabeth Moolvey 6/11/1812, College Committee References, J/1/30, ff. 226–7, BL.

[47] Batten letter September 1815 and Memorial of Elizabeth Moulvey 5/7/1815, College Committee References, J/1/30, ff. 438–44, BL.

[48] College Committee Report 1/11/1815, J/1/38, f. 338, BL; General Register of Pensions, L/AG/21/6/1–2, BL.

[49] Persian Petition of Ghoolam Hyder 16/8/1808, College Committee References, J/1/23, ff. 391–3, BL.

Company did not approve his request, but it did grant him retroactively an additional £40 annual house rent subsidy.

Part of Hyder's financial need came from his effort to maintain two families. He had left a wife and two children in India (yet another wife there had died) to whom he continued to send remittances. In 1810 he also married an Englishwoman, Rose Slocomb (1790–1844), daughter of William Grant Slocomb, 'who for thirty years was Master of the Green Coat School' (an Anglican charity school for young boys in Hertford). As Hyder explained: 'your petitioner finding it impossible to exist without female society, was induced (conformably to the Mohammedan Law) to marry a second time.'[50] They wed in Anglican Saint Botolph's Church, Bishopsgate, London, and eventually had at least six children.[51] Rose stood in the eyes of Hyder's British colleagues as his social inferior, his immediate supervisor commenting: 'She had no family and was *not* recommended by the College.'[52] They lived not in the college, but in a rented house in nearby Hertford.

Hyder's students found his Muslim and bigamous identity amusing, in a sympathetic way. Even in a satirical doggerel poem (which likewise pokes fun at another foreigner, the Frenchman teaching that language) there is no hint of concern about 'interracial sex'. Rather, it is Hyder who is to be pitied for his excessive domestic burdens, inadequate British wife, and dark-skinned Indian children:

> . . . How oft alas! poor Hyder's looks express'd,
> He wished his wife at Mecca or Modena,
> And often too, his trembling lips confess'd
> His great regret, that he had ever seen her,
> For though she was exceedingly well drest,
> And always very modest in demeanour,

[50] Petition of Ghoolam Hyder 31/10/1811, College Committee References, J/1/26, ff. 367–8, BL.

[51] He contracted a marriage license, and posted a bond for £200, to guarantee the legitimacy of the wedding. The first child, who died, was conceived just before or after marriage, born no later than October 1810. Other children were: John Master (born 6/8/1811); Sulivan alias Sulman (born 21/7/1812); Mary (born 7/11/1813); Emma (born 15/3/1818); and a non-surviving child (born c.12/1823). Hertford Local Library and Archives.

[52] Stewart to Principal 8/6/1823, College Committee References, J/1/38, f. 331, BL.

Her drinking wine, and eating of pork sausages,
Appeared to him, as very great monstrosities!

Lucky that Hyder's prophet did allow,
His faithful followers, to be well supplied
With wives, for Hyder, ere he left Lucknow,
Had married three [*sic*], tho' one of them had died,
But if from grief or want, I do not know,
That is a question, which I can't decide,
His English wife, was hardest to controul,
Because she had th' advantage of a soul!

. . . The Students having heard of this plurality,
Used so to plague this poor unhappy Moor,
About his Indian wives, that in reality,
'Twas more than he, could very well endure,
For though it was against all due formality,
Or what in Hindoostan, is called *dustoor* [custom],
Still he was forced, full often to describe,
Both males and females, of the Hyder tribe!

Lovewell [a fictional student, the central subject of this poem's satire]
    would say, 'come Hyder tell us how,
'That charming wife of your's, your English rib is,
'When did you last, get tidings from Lucknow,
'About your children, and your Indian *bebees* [wives]?
'What are they like to, are they black or no?
'And are they handsome Hyder, as your *jib* [?] is?'
Hyder scarce knowing, if to speak or not,
Would answer him, *hah! Sahib, khoob surut [very handsome], got!*[53]

To add to Hyder's difficulties, late in 1811 he became quite ill, unable to teach and incurred 'a considerable debt to the Surgeon and Apothecary who attended him.' The Company respected his need and increased his salary by 25 per cent, to £250 (plus the £40 rental subsidy).[54] Hyder's troubles, however, did not end. In 1812 his landlord died; the new owners intended to sell the house and notified him to

[53] Anonymous, *Life*, pp. 58–60.
[54] Petition of Ghoolam Hyder 31/10/1811, College Committee References, J/1/26, ff. 337, 367–8, BL.

vacate. Moving presented a particular problem for the ailing Hyder. He had been living in the Parish of All Saints, Hertford, from before his marriage. Under extant Poor Laws, each parish was responsible for maintaining residents who become destitute. Were such a resident to settle in another parish, the responsibility would shift there. Thus, no other parish would accept him, yet he could find no suitable home in All Saints that he could afford. Hyder thus proposed an augmented house rental subsidy of £50, plus a guarantee from the directors that they would reimburse the new parish for 'any charge, in the contingency that either the Moonshee, or his Family, should need Parochial relief.'[55] In return, Hyder offered: 'your Petitioner will for ever pray for the Prosperity of the East India Company.' While the directors enhanced his rental subsidy as requested, they refused to guarantee his family's possible welfare costs.[56] Thus, barred from other parishes, Hyder had to move his family to 'a very bad and disagreeable House in the Parish of All Saints where his Children were born'.[57] At the same time, he renewed his request for another £50 salary increment, promising, if granted, 'however long he may continue in this Country, he will not trouble them [the Company] for any further increase.' Eventually, the college arranged to rent another house for him and his growing family, but at his expense. To enable him to afford the rent, the Company made a final salary increase to £350 annually, plus the £50 subsidy.[58] Thus, the directors assumed the role of patron and protector, raising his salary (within limits) to reflect their appreciation of his worth and the need to sustain his respectability and, by reflection, that of the college.

For the next decade, despite continuing illness, Hyder taught Persian orthography. But he also incurred mounting debts. There were openings in the faculty but he was not promoted; Britons superseded him. When he died (May 1823), he left four surviving

[55] Henley letter 16/9/1812, College Committee References, J/1/27, ff. 211–13, BL.

[56] College Committee Minutes 23–6/9/1812.

[57] Petition of Ghoolam Hyder June 1813, College Committee References, J/1/28, ff. 356–7, BL.

[58] College Committee Minutes 18–21/8/1813. The Hyder family may also have moved to St Andrews Parish.

children and his wife, three months pregnant, ill with cancer in her leg, and deeply in debt.[59] Out of their respect for him, Hyder's students spontaneously subscribed £15 for gravestones.[60] His immediate supervisor, Stewart, personally purchased for the family from the public auction £45 worth of their possessions, and urged Haileybury's principal to continue his salary to the end of the quarter. Stewart also enrolled Hyder's two sons in the First Church Hospital (a charity home) and had his two daughters trained as domestic servants, at a cost to the college of £100 annually.[61] The widow, Rose Hyder, received from the Company an annual pension of £40; each child received a pension of £15 until maturity.[62] Nevertheless, she had barely sufficient income to maintain a middle-class lifestyle, as appropriate to her late husband's status. She rented a small house at £20 annually, leaving her just over a shilling per day for all her other expenses. Since a soldier or labourer earned only about that much, she could certainly survive on this pension, but sustaining gentility was difficult.[63] One son, John Master Hyder, died at age 16; a daughter, Emma Hyder, at age 10. The college paid £15 and £5 19s. 8d. respectively for their funerals.[64]

The surviving son, Sullivan (a.k.a. Sulman) Law Hyder, found difficulty establishing himself in Britain. For five years, the Company

[59] Petition of Rose Hyder 28/5/1823 and Stewart letter 31/7/1823, College Committee References, J/1/38, ff. 325, 571–2, BL. Admonition and Allegation Ghoolam Hyder of St Andrews Parish, Hertford, 27/5/1823, H23/1319, Hertford Local Library and Archives.

[60] Stewart letter 15/9/1823, College Committee References, J/1/38, ff. 585–6, BL.

[61] Stewart letter 13/5/1823, College Committee References, J/1/38, f. 329, BL.

[62] Stewart letter 30/5/1823, College Committee References, J/1/38, f. 333, Organization of the Home Establishment L/AG/30/12, f. 603, BL; Court Minutes 4/6/1823, 23/7/1823.

[63] Her parish, Saint John and All Saints, Hertford, apparently accepted the family as parishioners, but only after it rebaptized (4/2/1824) all four surviving children. She lived until 1844 with her unmarried daughter, Mary. 1841 Census HO 107/447: All Saints, Church Lane. National Register of Deaths, March Quarter, 1844, Family Record Centre. See also Boot, 'Real Incomes'.

[64] College Committee Minutes 2/6/1827; Correspondence Committee Minutes 16/!/1827.

apprenticed him to printer Richard Watts, famous for producing Oriental language books. Although Sulman 'learned his business well, and is capable of earning his bread by that trade', the Company's officials saw no career for him in England and disapproved of his lifestyle: 'he has formed connections and fallen into habits in London, which are unfavourable to his morals and industry and may involve him in ruin . . .'. Consequently, when he was 19, the Company gave him £20 and paid his passage 'to Bengal, his Father's Native Country', 'where Mr Watts thinks he can place him advantageously with some friends of his who are printers in Calcutta.'[65] Soon after his arrival, he married Amelia Botellho, an illiterate woman, probably of mixed Indian and European descent—like Sullivan Hyder himself.[66]

The other assistant professor, Mirza Khaleel, in contrast to all his Indian colleagues, remained a strict Muslim. He was the son of Haji Kerbala Muhammad Tehrani, a Shi'ite merchant associated with the ruling Awadh dynasty.[67] During Khaleel's voyage to England, and throughout his stay, he remained aloof from British society, including eating apart.[68] Further, unlike his colleagues, he never married in England. Yet he too repeatedly asserted that the cost of food was astonishingly high, and that the quality of the housing he could afford was inadequate to his social standing.[69] After a year in England, Khaleel, who had been regularly remitting half his salary to his wife and family in India, stopped doing so despite their bitter appeals.[70]

Following eleven years of employment at the college, he resigned suddenly in the middle of the 1819 term, after what he called an

[65] College Committee Minutes 18/5/1831; Court Minutes 18/5/1831; Shipping Committee Minutes 1/6/1831.

[66] Wedding 11/5/1833, Quarterly Ecclesiastical Returns for the Archdeaconry of Calcutta, N/1/36, f.46, BL.

[67] Mirza Khaleel Arzee, in Stewart, *Original Persian*, pp. 86–7, 90–5.

[68] William Hickey, autobiographical manuscript, MSS EUR G.118, BL.

[69] Henley letters 25/4/1808, 4/10/1808, Mirza Khaleel letters 20/9/1809, 14/6/1810, Stewart letter 27/9/1809, College Committee References J/1/23, ff. 345–6, 396–7; J/1/24, ff. 481–2, 485; J/1/25, ff. 409–10, BL.

[70] Extract Public Letter to Bengal 21/4/1809, College Committee References, J/1/25, ff. 368–71, BL; Court Minutes 25/11/1812, 22/12/1812; Home Miscellaneous, vol. 560, ff. 125–8, 459–60; vol. 561, ff. 85–6, 125–8, 459–60; vol. 562, ff. 83, 120–1, NAI.

'unfortunate event'. The incident, suppressed by college authorities, apparently was an assault on him by a Briton.[71] The Company agreed to pay Khaleel a pension of £360 annually for life, plus purchased his equipage and passage back to India.[72] Although he originally intended a three-year journey via the Islamic holy lands, he apparently remained in England until 1826. He evidently earned enough to live on (probably by teaching Indian languages) and returned to Lucknow with seven years' pension saved—£2,500 cash.[73]

The language training imparted to Haileybury students by these three Indian faculty, and by their British supervisors, tended to be limited. Until 1814, students had no examination in these languages, which mitigated against serious study by most. Thereafter, to force their attention, an outside Visitor, Sir Charles Wilkins, examined the students (and, indirectly, the faculty). As had become customary for British school examinations in Latin and Greek, this test required students to 'write the character in a fair and legible hand, [have] thorough acquaintance with terms of grammar [and] reading, translating, and parsing an easy passage.'[74] Yet, while some students individually learned much from their instructors, the system of education in Indian languages generally tended to be relatively impractical and a subject of little consequence.[75] It also differed significantly from the ways these languages were traditionally taught in India.

Most British attitudes increasingly disparaged Indians generally, and these faculty particularly. As Stewart asserted in 1816: 'such is the prejudice of Young Men against the Tuition of a Native of India, that only the few steady ones derive any benefit from his Lectures . . .'.[76]

---

[71] A Briton was found guilty and imprisoned for an assault on one of the Indian faculty. Mirza Khaleel letter (from London) 20/10/1819, Stewart letter 31/7/1823, College Committee References J/1/35, ff. 271–2; J/1/38, ff. 571–2, BL; Schofield, 'Foundation' (M.A., 1985), p. 71.

[72] Mirza Khaleel letters 20/10/1819 and 17/4/1820, College Committee References J/1/35, ff. 271–2, 304–5, BL; Correspondence Committee Minutes 16/8/1820; Home Miscellaneous, vol. 566, ff. 219–20, 349–51, NAI.

[73] Court Minutes 4/4/1826, 3/5/1826, 3/3/1830.

[74] College Committee Minutes 15/2/1814.

[75] Stewart and Hamilton letter 26/11/1813, Read letter 8/8/1814, College Committee References J/1/27, ff. 376–8, J/1/29, ff. 478–82.

[76] Stewart letter 7/4/1816, College Committee References, J/1/31, f. 213, BL.

He contended that these Indian faculty were incapable of attending class regularly without discipline from a Briton: 'it is a very disagreeable part of my duty to enforce due attendance on [Mirza Khaleel] and the Persian Writing Master [Ghoolam Hyder.]' Recognizing the widespread prejudice against Indians, the chairman of the directors enjoined the Haileybury graduating class of 1817 (evidently in the presence of these Indian faculty) to refrain paternalistically from discrimination against the Indian 'race':

> He cautioned them on their arrival in India from being prejudiced against the Natives from difference of Color, of Language, of manners and customs and also against letting their minds be prepossessed by the reports which of late years had been industriously circulated in [Britain] to their prejudice. That from his own experience during a residence of many years among them he knew them to be a mild, inoffensive, well-disposed, benevolent race of Men, and earnestly recommended that they should on all occasions be treated with humanity and kindness.[77]

Thus, the positions of these three men as permanent faculty at the college and as respectable professionals in British society confronted growing British sentiment against Indians as the inferior colonized. Similar patterns developed at the Company's other college.

Addiscombe's Indian Professor

A few years after the Company established Haileybury for its civil servants, it opened for its cadets a Military Seminary at Addiscombe.[78] Meer Hassan Ali of Lucknow, a well-born scholar and former official for the Company and the nawab of Awadh, had come on his own to England in September 1809, seeking employment as a teacher of Persian, Arabic, Hindustani, and/or Bengali.[79] He applied first to Haileybury but that college believed it had enough Indian professors. Then he applied to the newly-opened Addiscombe College. In May 1810 he joined that faculty (initially paid £250 annually, raised to £400 in

[77] College Committee Minutes 4/12/1817.
[78] The Company allowed only Britons to attend, despite a request from a Persian to do so. Miscellaneous Letters Received 14–29/5/1817, E/1/253, BL; Correspondence Committee Minutes 28/5/1817.
[79] Court Minutes 13/9/1809, 17/10/1809. Dorsetshire Log, L/MAR/B/13, BL.

1811) as Assistant to the Professor of Oriental Literature, John Shakespear.[80] Hassan Ali's duties were 'teaching the Cadets to write, and the proper pronunciation of the Hindostanni and Persian Languages' (its pronunciation being something Shakespear knew little about).[81] He also taught Devanagari and Persian orthography. College authorities addressed him variously by his official title, 'Assistant to the Professor', and the more 'native' title, 'Persian Moonshee', like Ghoolam Hyder.[82]

Addiscombe cadets were even less interested in Indian languages than Haileybury students. This made Hassan Ali's teaching a particular burden. Both he and Shakespear complained repeatedly about 'the general disinclination and inattention of the Cadets to the Study of Hindustanie'.[83] To ensure greater attention, Addiscombe established a required examination in this subject in 1810, with the Visitor, Wilkins, testing the quality of the language training.[84] In 1814, the seminary directed Hassan Ali to provide extra tutorials, twice or thrice each week. The goal was that students should have: '[the ability] to write the two Characters in which the Hindustani is usually expressed [Persian and Devanagari] in a fair and legible hand; an acquaintance with the terms of Grammar as expressed in the Hindustani Language; a competent knowledge of the rudiments of the Language as expressed in Mr Shakespear's Grammar; the ability to read, translate, and parse some easy passage in Hindustani [and] to repeat from memory some easy dialogue as introductory to the habit of conversing in the Language.'[85] Even this basic knowledge was too much for many cadets.

[80] Scott, *Observations*, pp. ii, 7. Meer Hassan Ali Memorial n.d., College Committee References J/1/27, ff. 218–19, BL; College Committee Minutes 6/11/1812, 21/10/1813; Court Minutes 16/5/1810, 20/6/1810, 26/9/1810; Seminary Committee Reports 15/5/1810, 6/11/1811, L/MIL/1/9–10, BL.

[81] Lutfullah wrote that on 30/5/1844 he met 'John Shakespear, the author of the Hindustani Dictionary . . . But, alas! I found that he could not understand me, nor could he utter a word in that language in which he had composed several very useful books.' Lutfullah, *Autobiography*, p. 412.

[82] College Committee Minutes 24/9/1813.

[83] College Committee Minutes 5/9/1810. See Vibart, *Addiscombe*, p. 41.

[84] College Committee Minutes 7/11/1810; Seminary Committee Reports 6/11/1811, 23/11/1814, L/MIL/1/10, BL; East India College, *Directions*, Act 53 Geo. 3, c. 155, section 44.

[85] Seminary Committee Reports 6/7/1814, L/MIL/1/10, BL.

During his six years on the Addiscombe faculty, Hassan Ali established himself in local society. He took students into his home as lodgers.[86] Yet two of these students, whose parents were in distant Ireland, proved so highly disruptive 'in their uncontrol'd pursuits' that they left and moved into private lodgings in Croydon, where they were even more troublesome to the town authorities.[87] Indeed, Haileybury students also frequently 'rioted'.[88] Although Hassan Ali was relatively isolated as the only Indian at Addiscombe, he and the Indian faculty at Haileybury met occasionally, forming a support group; he witnessed Ghoolam Hyder's wedding, for example.[89]

Hassan Ali sought advancement of himself and his students through composing learning aids. He argued his status as a native speaker ensured the superiority of his pedagogy over that of Britons. Yet, he perforce had to appeal to more established British orientalist scholars to authenticate his work. He completed in 1812 a 150-page *Grammar of the Hindoostanie Language*, which he described as:

> being the first work of the kind ever attempted by a Native of India, which contains also many useful additions, I have also corrected several material Errors that are to be found in works of a similar kind in English, I humbly beg leave to solicit your patronage towards the publication of this my work, referring (if need be) its merits to be tried by any of the Oriental Scholars at your Civil College, or by Dr Gilchrist, an eminent Writer on the Subject. The book consists of 3 parts; 1st containing the Hindoustanie as taught in India by the Natives; the 2nd, that Grammar reduced to the English scale, and accompanied as far as possible to the Rules of Grammar received in this Country; and the 3rd containing a selection of Vocables, Dialogues, and Exercises very useful to Hindoustanie Scholars when beginning to read or write the Language . . .[90]

Even before it was completed, the college committee recommended that Hassan Ali be granted 'an advance of £100 towards enabling him

[86] Vibart, *Addiscombe*, pp. 41–2.

[87] College Committee Minutes 24/9/1813.

[88] There were major student riots at Haileybury in 1808, 1809, 1811, 1815, 1817. See Schofield, 'Foundation' (M.A., 1985), p. 105.

[89] Wedding license, Guildhall Library.

[90] Stewart and Hamilton Letter November 1813, College Committee References J/1/27, ff. 374–6, BL.

to defray the expense of printing and publishing' this Grammar, 'as a mark of the Committee's approbation of his endeavours'.[91] In general, language teachers at Addiscombe and Haileybury, including Hassan Ali's supervisor, Shakespear, greatly enhanced their incomes by publishing text books and requiring their students to purchase them. Indeed, Shakespear had just published a very similar grammar.[92]

When Hassan Ali completed his *Grammar*, the directors sent it for assessment by orientalists Charles Stewart and Alexander Hamilton. On the whole, they were patronizing of his efforts and unimpressed by his work:

> It must be premised that Husun Aly has attempted one of the most difficult undertakings in Literary acquirements, viz. that of translating from his own into a Foreign language, and therefore it could not but be expected that a person who has resided but a few years in this country should in some measure fail in explaining in English the intricacies of Oriental Grammar, in the attempt he has however manifested a very considerable acquaintance with the English language and an extensive knowledge of the Hindoostany, but as Doctor Gilchrist had many years ago completely sifted that dialect, and left scarcely any thing new to be explained, all that was required was an abridgement of that Gentleman's quarto grammar, in the Oriental and English characters.[93] In this particular Husun Aly has been anticipated by a recent publication [Shakespear's *Grammar*], we are therefore of opinion that the utility of Printing his book would not be adequate to the trouble and expense but take the liberty of suggesting that the author should be distinguished by the Hon'ble Company with some mark of their favour and that the Book be deposited in their Library as a Literary curiosity.

> P.S. The hand writing both Persian and English is his own.[94]

They thus asserted that John Borthwick Gilchrist had already exhaustively mastered Hindustani and also that a native speaker's fluency and

---

[91] College Committee Minutes 26/11/1813.

[92] John Shakespear, *Grammar*.

[93] Gilchrist, *Dictionary*.

[94] Stewart and Hamilton Letter November 1813, College Committee References J/1/27, ff. 374–6, BL. Stewart reproduced Hassan Ali's letter of thanks for the £100, but Stewart glosses this as sarcastic since the amount was so small. Stewart, *Original Persian*, pp. 72–4.

calligraphy were less significant than his alleged inadequate control over English-language grammatical explanations.

Following Abdool Alee's death in 1812, Hassan Ali applied for his position as Assistant Professor of Oriental Literature at Haileybury, offering to teach Persian, Arabic, and Hindustani.[95] To bolster his application, Hassan Ali argued that Arabic 'on account of its difficulty requires to be taught, by a duly qualified Native'.[96] He further cited his years of satisfactory service at Addiscombe. He obtained warm testimonials from his friends Mirza Khaleel and Ghoolam Hyder, currently at Haileybury. Both testified not only to his abilities, but also to his high birth and accomplishments: 'descended from a Noble Family . . . the Grandson of the Nawaub Birem Khan (peace be unto him) . . . proficient in the Arabic, Persian, and Hindoostanee Languages, and in his Style of writing has not his equal in this Kingdom.'[97] Should his request for appointment not be approved, Hassan Ali threatened to resign from Addiscombe and return to India 'by the first Fleet'.[98] He did not get the desired appointment; nor did he resign until four years later.

At Addiscombe, Hassan Ali continued his writing. He translated the Gospel of St Matthew into Hindustani, which he presented to the Company and received a £50 gratuity.[99] His apparent collaborator in this work was a pious Anglican Englishwoman, Biddy Timms.

Hassan Ali finally resigned from Addiscombe in 1816 on the grounds of chronic ill health (asthma). For his six years' service he received an annual pension from the Company of £120 plus £205 for his sea passage, and also free transportation via Calcutta to his home,

[95] Maynard letter 23/10/1812, College Committee References J/1/27, ff. 220–9, BL. See also College Committee References J/1/25, ff. 447–8, BL; Court Minutes 2/12/1812.

[96] Meer Hasun Ali Petition 14/1/1814, College Committee References J/1/27, ff. 186–8, BL.

[97] Mirza Khaleel and Gholam Hyder Memorial 17/10/1812, College Committee References J/1/27, ff. 214–17, BL.

[98] Meer Hassan Ali Petition 27/11/1812, College Committee References J/1/27, ff. 241–2.

[99] Meer Hasun Ali, 'Gospel of St Matthew translated into Hindoostanee' ISL 3063, BL; Vibart, *Addiscombe*, p. 42.

Lucknow.[100] Just before his departure, he married a Miss Timms (March 1817 in St James Parish Church, Westminster), and they travelled to Lucknow together.[101] He and his wife lived in north India for a dozen years, both in Lucknow and, when exiled from that court, in the employ of the Company at Kanauj.[102] Following his English wife's separation from him and return to England, she published an epistolary book about her life as a Christian wife in a leading Muslim family: Mrs Meer Hassan Ali, *Observations on the Mussulmauns of India*.[103] Hassan Ali subsequently married women of his own class and had descendants who served the Company.

After Hassan Ali's departure from Addiscombe, its headmaster assured the directors that he need not be replaced: 'necessity no longer exists as the publication of Mr Shakespear's Hindustani Grammar and Lexicon will so much facilitate the Studies in that Department that another Assistant Teacher will not be wanted.'[104] Four years later, when the Addiscombe authorities reversed themselves and sought an assistant for Shakespear, they recommended 'an European who has been habituated to application and labour . . . as the habits and general health of an Indian (in this country) are not suited to the

[100] 'Memorandum relative to Mirza Khuleel', College Committee References J/1/35, ff. 273–6, BL; Seminary Committee Reports 3/4/1816, 12/12/1816, L/MIL/1/11, BL.

[101] Bishop of London, Marriage Allegations 22/3/1817 and Diocese of London, Marriage Bond 22/3/1817, WAC. St James Parish, Westminster (Piccadilly) 27/3/1817, Guildhall Library. Court Minutes 23/4/1817.

[102] Foreign Political Consultation 14/10/1831, nos 40–1 and Foreign Secret Consultations 30/4/1830 nos 49–50, 3/4/1830, nos 14–18, 24/4/1834, nos 46–8, NAI.

[103] Mrs Meer Hassan Ali returned to England but received no support from the directors, who even rejected her request that they stand as patrons of her book. She presented them a copy anyway: see handwritten slip bound in Mrs Meer Hassan Ali, *Observations*, in IOL. Court to Mrs Meer Hassan Ali, 14/5/1832, Miscellanies Sent, E/1/268, f. 1095, BL; Court Minutes 16/11/1831. Karim Khan, who was in London when she published, critiqued her assertions about gender. *Siyahatnama*, pp. 277–8.

[104] Andrew letter (read) 12/12/1816, Military Seminary Committee Report, L/MIL/1/11, no. 26A, BL.

labours of the [Military] Seminary.'[105] They suggested thereby that all Indians were morally and physically inadequate for the position. Thereafter, training in Indian languages at Addiscombe was conducted by often notoriously incompetent British professors.[106]

The Company's Termination of Indian Academics

From 1823, with the death of two and the resignation of the two other Indian faculty, British Orientalists excluded Indian scholars from these college faculties. The positions initially went vacant. Then, when increased numbers of students made the colleges fill them, they appointed Britons, with only one exception (discussed below). The college authorities had decided that the alleged disruption these Muslim Indian men had on a student's moral education outweighed their linguistic advantages as 'native speakers'. The Visitor at both colleges, Wilkins, asserted: 'The Natives however are but of little consequence . . . for whatever may be their Abilities, the Listlessness and Indifference, peculiar to the Asiatick Character, render them incapable of making the Exertions necessary in a Teacher for maintaining due order and authority in the Class and conquering the tedium of teaching the dull and reluctant Pupil, as well as the clever and willing.'[107] This reflected the increasingly disparaging colonial attitudes towards Indians generally.

It was British ideology rather than the lack of Indian scholars that prevented their further employment. In 1823, for example, Mirza Abdullah wrote from London 'offering his services in teaching the Persian languages at the Company's Seminary at Addiscombe.'[108] A veteran of the Company's Custom Service in Bengal for two decades, he had travelled to Britain three years earlier to advance his career.[109]

[105] Letter from Andrew, enclosing one from Shakespear, 25/4/1821, Military Seminary Committee Report, L/MIL/1/12, no. 40, BL.

[106] See Vibart, *Addiscombe*, pp. 71ff, 216–18.

[107] Wilkins 'Report', College Committee Reports, J/1/19, ff. 464–5, BL.

[108] Court Minutes 1/4/1823.

[109] Court Minutes 19–26/1/1821.

A year after his arrival, he had converted to Christianity, taking the name Daniel Abdullah, married a Briton, Mary Callesteur, and then had a daughter with her: Mariam Julia Clementine Abdullah.[110] The directors, however, repeatedly rejected his various applications for employment in Britain (and in India), but offered him a free passage home. Finally, claiming destitution, he apparently accepted this offer and left Britain.[111]

In 1826, the college authorities asserted four major objections to Indian faculty, each reflecting growing British imperialist and Anglicist attitudes.[112] 'First the difference in religion, dress, customs, and manners, which has a tendency to lessen that respect on the part of the pupil towards his teachers which is indispensable to the former's improvement.' Second, they presupposed all Indians incapable of mastering proper English (in the face of much evidence to the contrary): 'The total ignorance of the English language on the part of the Native Indian and Persian teachers . . . deprives them of the power of being useful to beginners (which all the Students necessarily are) in the study of Persian and Hindostanee.'[113] Third, they claimed Indians living in Britain had proved socially deviant: 'The too frequently observed irregularity, or rather immorality, of conduct in Mussulmans residing in this Country, which may be productive of the greatest inconvenience, if not the most injurious effects as to the discipline of the College.' Finally, these authorities claimed Indians naturally lacked financial responsibility, so they pestered the directors for increased income and left their British widows and children indigent: 'The inconvenience and embarrassment to which the Court of Directors are subjected, by the . . . constantly recurring demands of Individuals of this class, arising from their habitual improvidence, and more especially by the pretensions of the family, which, in the event of death will generally be left in a destitute condition, or dependents upon the bounty of the Company.' In short, they concluded, Indians

[110] They settled on Firth Street in Westminster. Marriage certificate 25/4/1821 and Baptismal record 20/7/1822, St Anne, Soho, WAC.

[111] Court Minutes 21/5/1823, 13/6/1823.

[112] Edmonstone and Baillie Memorandum (read) 19/7/1826, College Committee Reports J/2/5, ff. 279–85.

[113] For this sentiment see also Letter to the Editor, *Times* 21/10/1825 4a.

had proven incapable of the standards required of a faculty member at Haileybury and Addiscombe.

Yet, British faculty also recognized that they could not offer quality language instruction without some kind of a native speaker. They admitted that the 'attachment of some learned Asiatics to the college is not only conductive to the credit and respectability of the institution, but also essential to the accomplishment of one of its declared objects, the attainment of a high degree of proficiency in a few of the languages of the East.'[114] They acknowledged the evident decline 'both of pronunciation and classical attainment between the earlier Students at the college, and those of a more recent period.' They dealt with this dilemma by appointing in 1826 Mirza Muhammed Ibrahim (*c.* 1800–57), an Iranian scholar who had come to London seeking employment. He was a native Persian speaker, but allegedly embodied none of the objections inherent in many British minds against Indians.

Yet, college authorities believed that, as an Iranian, Muhammed Ibrahim presented other significant shortcomings. He knew Arabic and the Persian of Iran well, but nothing about Indian languages:

> the Persian, which he must be supposed to write and to speak with the utmost purity and correctness, is nevertheless by no means either the written or colloquial Persian of men of business or even of education and science in India, and is further unquestionably different, both in idiom and pronunciation, from that at present taught in the college; so that the students, alternately engaged with their English and Persian instructors, might receive lessons from each counteracting the efforts of the other and thus in the end be deprived of any permanent advantage from either . . . the apparent improvement in Persian pronunciation which might be derived from the labors of a Native Persian in the college, would probably fail to render the English Students more intelligible by the Natives of India on his first arrival in that Country, than he may become under his present [British] Instructors.[115]

Further, he had 'total ignorance of [Hindustani] the great colloquial language, and indeed of all the other languages of India.' Nevertheless,

[114] Edmonstone and Baillie Memorandum (read) 19/7/1826, College Committee Reports J/2/5, ff. 279–85.
[115] Ibid.

given the alternative of no native speakers on the faculty, he was better than nothing and knew Persian 'unquestionably superior ... to the Person formerly employed in the college (a Native of Bengal) [Mirza Khaleel].' Haileybury's students did not require much Persian training anyway: 'all that can be expected during the short term of residence at the college is merely an elementary knowledge . . . .'.

To further recommend Muhammed Ibrahim personally, he had made good progress in Anglicizing himself. He 'has adopted the European Costume for the avowed purpose of acquiring knowledge, and rendering himself useful in this Country without attracting public observation which might interfere with those objects'. Additionally, 'he would not object to [eating in] Commons with the English Professors and Teachers, an objection which was always made by the Mussulman Natives of India, and attended probably with inconvenience and additional expense.' Moreover, he 'has commenced and made some progress in the study of the English language.' Finally, he appeared a 'young man of agreeable manners, correct demeanor, and studious habits.' Thus, the college appointed him (at £400, plus £50 rental subsidy) as Assistant to the Professor of Arabic and Persian, Reverend Henry George Keene.[116] He remained on the faculty eighteen years until his retirement in 1844, when he returned to Iran.[117]

After Muhammed Ibrahim's retirement, no further Asians were appointed to the Company's colleges. Indeed, there were complaints by Anglicist college authorities that 'too much time and attention are devoted to oriental Study.'[118] Indians who applied were rejected. For example, in the 1850s, Hafiz Ludroo Islam Khan and P. Joyaloo Naidoo independently travelled to London and then futilely offered their services to Haileybury and Addiscombe, the former as would-be Professor of Hindustani and Persian, the latter of Telugu and Tamil.[119] As we will see in Chapter 10, other Indian scholars also taught in Britain privately or at other institutions.

[116] Court Minutes 2/8/1826, 1/8/1827; Organization of the Home Establishment L/AG/30/12, ff. 594–601, BL.
[117] See Fisher, 'Persian Professor'.
[118] Memorandum on Haileybury Studies, Oriental Department (*c.* 1844), MSS EUR F.303/445, BL.
[119] Court Minutes 29/3/1854, 5/4/1854, 14–20/3/1855.

Indian Educators in
Early-Nineteenth-Century Britain

Many Indian scholar-officials sought to educate Britons about the linguistic knowledge and Mughal high culture they embodied. In India, they vainly struggled to maintain their élite standing in the Company's administration, as they had under earlier rulers. In Britain they advanced themselves, sometimes achieving positions of social and professional standing. Four secured continuing appointments on the faculty of the Company's colleges. There, they taught thousands of British future civil officials and military officers both Indian languages and, by example, about Indians as respected authorities. Their British wives and children also demonstrated that 'mixed' marriages and descent were acceptable in Britain. Their careers contrasted with men of their class in India.

These Indian scholars tried to negotiate their way through British society. Despite the growing British stress on ethnicity as determining social identity in the metropole (as it had been established earlier in the colonies), the gender and class status enjoyed in British society by these Indian men elevated them over their British wives. Their positions within these educational institutions also placed them above their British pupils, not as hired servants like munshis in India, but as faculty with titular and pedagogic authority over them.

Yet, each of these four Indian teachers struggled, often unsuccessfully, to sustain their professional and social status in Britain. Two died deeply in debt, having exceeded their substantial salaries in an effort to sustain their social standing. The other two resigned prematurely after career frustrations and setbacks. Indian applicants for their positions met only with rejection based on their Indian and Muslim identities and on British assertions of control over lucrative positions in the Company's colleges.

Over time Britons appropriated and degraded knowledge of Indian languages and cultures. In the creation of British colonial knowledge about India, these Indian faculty had complex roles. Even at the height of British imperial expansion across India, British Orientalists recognized the superior abilities of Indian 'native speakers' in aspects of language training. Yet Anglicists increasingly discounted the importance of those abilities and elevated British and Christian moral training over them.

As we will see, despite these attitudes the private market for 'oriental' language teaching persisted in Britain, where some Indians managed to find employment. Especially from the mid nineteenth century, various institutions came to appreciate the abilities of Indian native speakers, and the need for their skills, which meant employment for them in Britain. Working-class Indians also found employment under Britons.

CHAPTER 4

Indian Seamen and the Company

Patterns of Recruitment and Service
of Lascars

B etween the 1790s and 1834, many thousand Indian seamen accepted employment on the long voyage to Britain, voluntarily entering a world of severe hardships and expected rewards.[1] Changing worldwide economic forces and British laws shaped the demand for their labour and the conditions under which they functioned. During this period British authorities in India and Britain repeatedly failed to secure control over this maritime labour force, despite the central role of shipping in the Anglo-centric world economy. Rather, ghat serangs in India's major ports continued to recruit lascars and supply them in labour gangs to British captains, replacements needed on account of the death, desertion, or conscription of their European crews. Salaries offered by British ships to lascars were favourable compared to other working-class people, such as sepoys, and were far superior to those of Indian coastal fishermen or agricultural labourers. Yet over this period a lascar's pay slipped below that of a European seaman, in part because of their costs to their employers once in Britain.

Lascars continued to sail under the direct command of Indian petty officers: serangs and tindals. Many were former lascars themselves, having risen with increased expertise. Since many serangs and lascars had the experience of multiple trips to Britain to guide them, they

---

[1] For discussion of lascars versus sailors, collectively called seamen, see Chapter 1. See also *Times*, 9/12/1814 3d and *Calcutta Monthly Journal*, *passim*, for evidence about ineffective British efforts to control lascar labour supply. For the role of sailors generally, see Land, 'Domesticating' (Ph.D., 1999) and 'Customs'.

knew what to expect on the voyage and arrival, and evidently found this employment more desirable than available alternatives. However, this was never an easy or safe occupation.

Many British officers treated lascars brutally. Such brutality stands clearly revealed, for instance, in the memoirs of Captain Robert East-wick, who spent his career (1792–1825) mostly on ships in Asia.[2] He considered lascars as virtual animals, easily panicked, useless in a crisis, and not worth saving in a wreck. On one voyage from England to India in 1810, his ship, the *Elizabeth*, carried 320 lascars (mostly passengers being returned home). When this ship sank off Dunkirk, Eastwick remorselessly used an oar to beat off as many lascars as he could, so that the lifeboat in which he saved himself would not swamp. Of the lascars aboard, 310 died in the wintry waters (along with many Europeans and 8 Indian female servants). To some Britons, including men like Eastwick, lascars were not individuals but a collective mass.

Despite such captains, thousands of lascars responded to the need for their labour by sailing British ships from India to Britain. The Government of India increasingly tried to regulate their wages and employment conditions. It specified the type and amount of clothing, bedding, and rations (including Indian spices) issued them, as well as the volume of space allotted to each seaman for sleeping, and ordered that a surgeon and specified medicines must be aboard. As the Company's own inspectors reported, however, these regulations were often not fulfilled.

Once in Britain, they encountered a variety of receptions from the British public and authorities, ranging from supportive to violent. Until 1834 (when this chapter concludes), the Company legally had responsibility for maintaining Indian seamen, which it carried out inconsistently. While most left after only a few months, some established themselves there for years, or the rest of their lives. British laws barred most lascars from working the return passage, making them sail to India unpaid. Thus, Indian seamen interacted in complex ways with a variety of British men and women, sometimes in conflict, other times in partnership, but always within the context of developing British colonialism in Asia.

[2] Eastwick, *Master Mariner*, pp. 262–82; *Times*, 1/1/1811 4d–e.

The Changing Demand for Lascars

Lascars were not cheap labour. Indeed, the directors consistently discouraged their captains from employing lascars, who cost them much money, effort, and frustration. Parliament also discouraged their employment.[3] However, high European mortality rates in Asia and the continuing Anglo-French wars (until 1815) reduced the number of European sailors available for the return voyage to Britain. Indian lascars, responding to this increased demand, arrived in Britain in ever larger numbers over the first decade of the nineteenth century. Thereafter, periodic global economic downturns and the Navy's largescale demobilization of British seamen reduced the demand for lascars, although it finally rose again towards the mid nineteenth century.

Even at times of peak demand, the directors only reluctantly recognized the necessity of hiring lascars. To keep down the number arriving in Britain, the Company wanted as large a pool of British seamen on its outgoing ships as possible, to compensate for their expected losses. Thus, for example in 1808, the directors reiterated that all their outbound ships must have entirely British crews—even though they were allowed one-quarter non-British crews under the Navigation Acts.[4]

Reconstructing accurate numbers for Asian seamen who survived to reach Britain is difficult. Chapter 2 showed how the directors attempted, during the mid eighteenth century, to monitor all lascars returning to India (as a byproduct of their primary desire to control access by Europeans to India). Periodically thereafter, the directors or Parliament ordered compilations of statistics about lascars, but no systematic accounting was maintained. These compilations followed varying principles and categorizations (e.g., occasionally including Chinese and other Asians). Nevertheless, supplemented with informed estimates by British writers of the time, the figures in Table 3 permit an understanding of the scale of lascar presence in Britain.

[3] In 1802, Parliament officially prohibited lascars from serving on ships west of the Cape of Good Hope (Act 42 Geo. 3, c. 61)—although this act was not fully enforced.

[4] Lascar Papers, vol. 1, f. 24. In later years, with increasing shortages of British seamen, the directors allowed up to a quarter of the crew on outgoing—vessels to be Indians, which still made them legally British ships.

Table 3: Asian Seamen Arriving in Britain, 1803–1850s[5]

Year	Reported number
1803	224
1804	471
1805	603
1806	538
1807	1,278
1808	1,110
1809	965
1810	1,403
1811	929
1812	1,193
1813	1,336
1814–15*	1,000–1,100
1821–2	509
1855*	3–3,600

* estimates

The years 1803–13 show a total of 10,050, rising from an annual average of 348 (1803–4) to 1,265 (1812–13), with an overall a mean average of 912. Thereafter the reported numbers fell, only to rise again in mid century.

This considerable fluctuation suggests the inconsistent demand for lascars, with powerful effects on their careers—but due to forces largely outside their control. In 1813, Parliament ended the Company's monopoly over trade with India. This meant entry into the trade of larger numbers of private ships, which operated outside the Company's purview, as did their lascars. Further, trade between India and Britain varied significantly, along with the supply of British seamen for merchant ships. Since British captains in India primarily hired lascars as replacements for European seamen, the demand varied directly with

[5] The shipping season covered parts of two calendar years, so some differences between years may not be significant. To 1822, they are based on Lascar Papers and PP, Returns (Commons), 1823, vol. 17, paper 491, pp. 149–56. In 1855, Colonel Hughes estimated 10,000–12,000 lascars served the British merchant fleet, with 5,000–6,000 reaching Britain annually, of whom 3,000-3,600 were Indian. Cited in Visram, *Ayahs*, p. 52.

the volume of trade and inversely with the supply of Britons, but imperfectly so since a range of other factors intervened. Nor was demand in Britain necessarily correlated with supply from India. The mid 1820s, for example, saw a severe shortage of British sailors available for India-bound ships, but the number of lascars hired to go to Britain also declined significantly.[6]

Over this period, lascars continued to serve in substantial labour gangs, which comprised much of their ship's crew, rather than as scattered individuals. In 1813, for example, only 32 ships arriving in Britain reported lascars aboard. Their proportion of lascars ranged from 20 per cent to over 50 per cent of the crew. The average size of a lascar gang was 34—the largest being 56 and the smallest 16. Overall, of the 3,311 total seamen aboard these 32 ships, about 30 per cent were lascars.[7]

In contrast, during the year July 1821–June 1822, only 7 of the 197 ships arriving in London from India had lascars aboard (in addition, Liverpool, Hull, and Greenock/Glasgow had 22 ships arriving, none with lascars reported). This was only 22 per cent of the number of ships arriving with lascars in 1813. On these 7 ships, however, lascars still comprised large labour gangs: 110, 107, 86, 72, 66, 38, and 30 lascars respectively (there were only 91 British and 21 'other foreign' sailors on these ships).[8] That equals 509 lascars, less than 5 per cent of the total seamen arriving, compared to 10,000 Britons and 1,000 'foreigners' (some of whom may have been Indian sailors). This was a much smaller proportion of the total manpower and less than half the absolute number of lascars of 1813. Yet, ships on this intercontinental trade had grown larger; the average size of a lascar crew was 73 men, over double that of 1813. Thus, relatively fewer ships carried virtually all of the incoming lascars in larger crews than earlier.

The floating population of lascars proved difficult for the British, like other state authorities, to control or even identify. Like the British, only rarely can we discover the origins of the lascars in a crew, although

[6] Shipping Committee Minutes 7/1/1825, 20/4/1825, 22/11/1825, 26/7/1826.

[7] Lascar Papers, vol. 1, f. 124.

[8] PP, Returns (Commons), 1823, vol. 17, paper 491, pp. 149–56.

when we can, patterns of service become evident. For example, the records of the ship *Hercules* (sailing from Calcutta to Britain in 1818) preserve the self-reported origins of its serang, tindals, lascars, and ship's servants and sepoys.[9] Map 2 demonstrates that this nominally 'Indian' crew of 50 included: 6 lascars from southeast Asia; a tindal, 2 lascars, and a servant from the Arabian Peninsula (plus a servant from Mauritius); in addition to 39 men from India. While most of those from India came from Bengal Presidency, 15 (including Serang Baxo) had origins along India's southern or western coasts.

The geographic diversity of the serang and tindals, and between them and the other crew members, highlight how the ghat serang assembled them *ad hoc*. Unlike Indian labour gangs in factories or indentured labourers, whom headmen often recruited from their own home village or region, these maritime workers came together through their employment, and forged bonds during their passage. Their subsequent solidarity in Britain as mutually supportive shipmates suggests how powerful that experience was, often transcending regional or ethnic identities (as discussed below).

Towards the mid nineteenth century, trade between India and Britain expanded rapidly, so larger numbers of lascars arrived. According to official figures, the volume of exports from India to Britain more than tripled between 1835 and 1850, while the volume of exports from Britain to India more than doubled.[10] Since the Company stopped keeping track of lascars, it is impossible to reconstruct their numbers precisely. We can, however, gain a rough idea of the increase by using

[9] Note: one servant gave Cheran Chupah [*sic*] as his birthplace, which cannot be identified. Further, Mauritius is located further south than indicated. In addition, the six seaconnies (helmsmen) came from Penang, Malinga, Malacca, and three from Manila, while the captain, two officers, gunner, and carpenter were all Europeans. Home Miscellaneous, vol. 253, ff. 135–8, NAI. Confirming these patterns, similarly diverse lascar crews are found for other ships in Home Miscellaneous, vol. 253, ff. 203–6, vol. 425, ff. 6–8, NAI. See also Balachandran, 'Circulation'.

[10] British exports to India rose from 108,870 tons (1834–5) to 252,153 tons (1849–50) while British imports from India rose from 83,776 to 280,897 tons. Lords Debate 2/4/1852, Commons Debate 19/4/1852 in *Hansard*, series 3, vol. 120, pp. 546–80, 806–68.

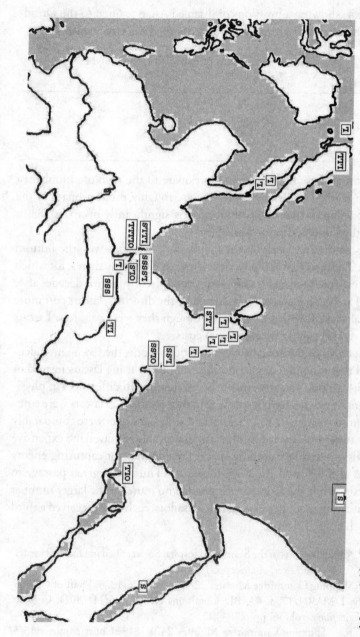

Map 2: Self-Reported Origins of the Serang/Tindals (O), Lascars (L), and Ship's Servants and Sepoys (S) of the *Hercules*, sailing from Calcutta to England, 1818.

Table 4, showing admissions of disabled Asian seamen to the Dreadnought Seamen's Hospital—a hulk moored off Greenwich.[11]

Table 4: Admissions of Asians to Dreadnought
Seamen's Hospital, 1820s–1860s

1821–30	71
1831–40	422
1841–50	553
1851–60	1,269

Assuming these figures are proportionate to the absolute number of Asian seamen in Britain (and they are roughly proportionate to the trade volume) then their number grew significantly over the 1830s, and then doubled over the 1850s.

A continuing factor in the Company's decisions was 'the bottom line'. The directors and proprietors owned Company shares, for which they expected to receive annual dividends (set by law for decades after 1793 at 10.5 per cent). As evaluated by the directors, lascars cost more overall than British seamen, even though they were paid less. Lascars also carried higher non-financial costs.

In terms of the actual voyage to Britain alone, the Company calculated that it neither gained nor lost money by using lascars instead of British sailors. The directors believed that due to differences in physical and moral strength (especially in cold weather), 3 lascars were equivalent in manpower to 2 Europeans, so lascar wages were comparably only two-thirds that of European.[12] Lascars also received less expensive provisions and less sleeping space. Prize money for capturing enemy ships also followed the wage formula.[13] Thus, on a given passage to Britain, while the Company expended no more on the larger number of lascars than for better paid British sailors, each lascar received a third less than each Briton.

[11] Annual Reports of the Seamen's Hospital Society cited in Dixon, 'Lascars', p. 269. See also Salter, *Asiatic*, pp. 126–42.
[12] Shipping Committee Minutes 22/2/1804, 18/6/1828; Draft of Charter-Party, L/MAR/1/17, f. 43, BL; Commons Debate (25/11/1801), Cobbett, *Parliamentary*, vol. 36, pp. 288–302.
[13] E.g., Shipping Committee Minutes 24/9/1813; Court Minutes 13/8/1823.

After the lascars reached Britain, they entailed substantial financial, logistical, and political costs for the Company. Its average expenditure for maintaining each lascar in Britain and returning him to India was £37 (for 1803–13). Of this, clothing averaged 10 per cent, food and lodging 32 per cent, medicine 4 per cent, and passage home 54 per cent.[14] This expenditure was much more than the entire wage paid a lascar for the voyage (roughly a shilling per day on the passage in; most lascars were unpaid returning home). Employing British or Indian sailors carried no such expense following the end of their contract.

Many private merchant and Royal Navy vessels also brought Indian seamen to Britain, for whom the Company often found itself subsequently responsible. To recover its costs from private shipowners, from 1811 to 1828 the Company instituted a system of bonds: ships leaving India had to pledge money to cover the future costs of maintaining and returning their lascars.[15] Nevertheless, the directors calculated for 1815–25 that they still paid £9,075 for Indian seamen brought on private ships. Further, the directors also took financial responsibility for Indian seamen captured by hostile warships, or shipwrecked or abandoned on the European continent, in Ireland, or in the Americas.[16]

The Royal Navy officially argued that Indian seamen were physically and morally unsuited to combat. Nonetheless, the Navy in fact conscripted or recruited hundreds, especially during wartime. When they were disabled or demobilized in Britain, the Navy sent them to the Company for return to India.[17] In 1814 alone, the Company transported to India well over a hundred Indians discharged from Navy ships. Even the Royal Army recruited some Indians in Britain, particularly in 1804 for its 'African Corps'.[18] The directors, however, could usually extract reimbursement from the government for maintaining and returning such discharged Indians.

[14] Lascar Papers, vol. 1, f. 120.

[15] Shipping Committee Minutes 27/4/1831, 4/5/1831.

[16] Court Minutes 26/7/1797, 9/7/1799, 11/2/1800; Shipping Committee Minutes 19/5/1813, 5–17/11/1813, 8/6/1814, 6/7/1814, 3–10/8/1814.

[17] Court Minutes 27/5/1807; Shipping Committee Minutes 21/8/1813 to 11/1/1826.

[18] Court Minutes 30/12/1803; Shipping Committee Minutes 23/12/1803, 4/1/1804, 1/2/1832.

In addition to financial costs, Indian seamen in Britain presented the directors with what they considered endless political and moral embarrassments. Increasing numbers of evidently penurious Indians appeared throughout Britain. Many offended the British public by begging, petty-theft, street-peddling, or their very presence. Various 'riots' broke out where lascars congregated, as when armed Indian and Chinese seamen fought a 'desperate affray' with swords, knives, and bludgeons at Stepney (in London) in 1785.[19] Directors spent much time trying to control lascars, and defend themselves against various political and public allegations concerning these men. Efforts by the Company in 1805 to bind lascars to leave quickly and obediently by having them sign contracts to do so before they embarked from India proved of little use.[20]

While most Indian seamen remained together in London's dock-lands, a significant number entered British towns and the countryside. Sometimes they succeeded in establishing themselves, and thus were not perceived as 'problems' by British authorities. When less success-ful, they sometimes generated unfavourable public or official notice as 'infesting the streets in the metropolis and wandering about the Coun-try'.[21] Magistrates and Poor House administrators wrote to the direc-tors from all over Britain, seeking reimbursement for maintaining indigent Indians and requesting instructions for their disposal. For 1804–14 alone, impoverished Indian seamen appeared in Alnwick (Northumberland), Chelmsford (Essex), Cork (Ireland), Dartford (Kent), Durham (Durham), Exeter (Devon), Leicester (Leicester-shire), Lewes (Sussex), Lincoln (Lincolnshire), Liverpool (Mersey-side), Maidenhead (Windsor), Maidstone (Kent), Plymouth (Plymouth), Portsmouth (Portsmouth), St Albans (Hertfordshire), Shepperton (Surrey), Symington (Ayrshire), and Winchester (Hamp-shire).[22] Indians who approached the directors (or were sent there by local authorities), even after a decade in Britain, received maintenance and free passage home.[23]

[19] *Annual Register* (1784–5), 27, Chronicle, pp. 242–3.

[20] Court Minutes 10/7/1805.

[21] Court Minutes 31/10/1798; Commons debate (25/11/1801), Cobbett, *Parliamentary*, vol. 36, pp. 288–302.

[22] Shipping Committee Minutes 29/10/1813 to 14/3/1821.

[23] Shipping Committee Minutes 5/1/1825 to 4/6/1828.

Itinerant Indians in Britain's interior occasionally generated sympathetic (if patronizing) attention in literature and art. Mary Darby Robinson (1758–1800), for example, wrote a deeply compassionate poem about a homeless young lascar wandering the British countryside.[24] Cruelly and unjustly turned away from church and sheltering home, this Indian died tragically at the hands of a misguided Briton. The famous 1841 painting by William Mulready (1786–1863), 'Train Up a Child in the Way He Should Go; and When He Is Old He Will Not Depart from It', depicts three indigent lascars deep in Britain (Image 8). Two supporting British women encourage a young British boy to overcome fear of these dark aliens and practise charity toward them as lesser beings.[25] These fictional and artistic creations cannot tell us about individual Indians, but they do indicate that Britons expected lascars to be present in the British countryside and viewed them as the proper objects of British alms.

The sizeable and widespread lascar population in Britain had negative moral and political implications for the directors. First, most directors remained concerned about the Company's image in Britain. Further, the directors themselves as individuals were often public figures, with personal standing to protect. They had invested much money and effort gaining their directorships. Reputedly indigent and/or riotous Indians on London's streets or elsewhere in Britain seemed to them, and the British public, detrimental to the Company's and Directors' reputations. Second, many directors, especially devout Christians, desired to give charitably to the impoverished and non-Christians; the largest number of Indian 'poor benighted heathen' in their presence were lascars. Third, the British government expected the Company to take responsibility for all needy Indians in Britain, just as each Anglican parish was responsible under prevailing Poor Laws to care for indigents domiciled in it. These expectations were, for much of this period, enforced by law. Despite the desires of the directors, substantial numbers of lascars continued to reach and remain in Britain. We can best consider their changing roles chronologically.

[24] Robinson, *Poetical*, vol. 2, pp. 133–47. See also Robinson, *Memoirs*.

[25] This painting has evoked widely different interpretations, at the time and thereafter, see: Stullybrass, 'Marx'; Pointon, *Mulready*, pp. 18, 102; Heleniak, *William Mulready*, pp. 98–106, 215–16.

Lascars Prior to the Depot System

Until the late eighteenth century, provision for lascars arriving in Britain varied considerably since individual shipowners largely had direct responsibility for them. Throughout most of its history, the Company leased rather than owned most of its merchant ships. Up to 1795, the Company allowed in such leases £1 per ton to the owners for the costs of maintenance in Britain and return of their lascars.[26] Many owners, however, kept the money but failed to provide adequately for their lascars. In addition, foreign and private shipowners, not under the Company's control, evaded responsibility for them.

The period following the lascars' arrival was often one of confrontation with their employers. Some stayed aboard and unloaded their ships, receiving extra pay for this.[27] Such work, however, placed them in conflict with British stevedores. Frequently, lascars disembarked and appealed under the leadership of their serang directly to British authorities for redress of grievances.[28] British authorities sometimes regarded such acts as desertion and riot, arresting the serang 'ringleader' to suppress the rest.[29] Other times, depending on the particular circumstances and how effectively serangs represented their cases, British authorities—including the directors, naval agent, municipal officials, and law courts—might consider and act on their complaints.[30] For example, in 1813–14, the naval agent in London reportedly collected £262 10s. in fees deducted from lascars' pay (at 1 shilling per month each), but collected for lascars £1,571 in disputed wages from shipowners.[31] To some extent, therefore, lascars had agency in gaining compensation for provable breaches of contract or regulations by shipowners.

Customarily, lascars only received their pay weeks after reaching port. To survive or entertain themselves for those weeks, many sold their possessions, including their bedding and clothing. Further, since most ships arrived from India in fall and departed in spring, virtually

[26] Lascar Papers, vol. 1, ff. 33ff.
[27] Emin, *Life* (1794), p. 51.
[28] E.g., Court Minutes 3/1/1798.
[29] E.g., *Times*, 23/9/1796 3d.
[30] Court Minutes 26/5/1802, 21/7/1802, 16/7/1806; HMS 501, ff. 1–93.
[31] *Statesman*, 21/7/1813; *Times*, 9/12/1814 3d; Shipping Committee Minutes 22/7/1813.

all lascars had to endure a cold winter in Britain (colder than today due to the 'Little Ice Age' then gripping Europe).[32]

All these factors led to repeated British public complaints against the directors for failing in their moral duty towards obviously destitute and occasionally 'riotous' Indians increasingly present in Britain.[33] In 1786, a private charity paid bakers to provide a loaf of bread per day to each indigent lascar on London's streets; the ill-fated Sierra Leone scheme of that time included Indian lascars among its doomed colonists.[34] Other private charitable initiatives would follow.

The directors sought to defend themselves against charges of neglect, particularly every twenty years when the Company's charter was being considered by Parliament for termination or renewal, as in 1793. Repeatedly in 1792, for example, directors publicly asserted that the Indian 'poor wretches' on London's streets were mostly lascars dumped by non-British ships.[35] The directors added, while neither legally nor morally required to do so, they would nonetheless, at great expense, provide free housing, food, clothing, and passage to India to any who applied. The continued presence in the streets of such mendicants, the directors unconvincingly concluded, was therefore solely because these lascars had decided not to seek such aid. Simultaneously, the directors requested the British government to pressurize foreign governments, and also the Royal Navy, to cooperate by halting their practice of bringing lascars to Britain.[36]

The directors' arguments neither stopped the influx of lascars nor convinced the British public that the Company was not responsible for them. Since shipowners had proved hard to hold accountable, from the late eighteenth century the Company itself began to arrange the maintenance and return of lascars.[37] To recoup these expenses, the

[32] E.g., *Times*, 23/3/1799 2d.

[33] E.g., *Times*, 16/3/1785 2d–3a; *Public Advertiser* 21/12/1785 1c, 10/1/1786 4c.

[34] Braidwood, *Black Poor*, pp. 32ff.

[35] *Times*, 10/3/1792 3a, 9/4/1792 2c; *Public Advertiser*, 7/1/1786 2b.

[36] This had been an issue for many years. E.g., Court Minutes 29/3/1786, 30/11/1787, 31/10/1798. See also Murray to Dundas 13/4/1790, ADD 42,073, Hamilton and Greville Papers, vol. 6, f. 77 (I thank Robert Travers for this reference).

[37] Court Minutes 15/2/1786.

directors assessed each owner who leased a ship to them at £5 per ton. Since not all ships brought lascars, this was a burden not proportionate to the responsibility. Consequently, the directors soon shifted to an arrangement where they charged owners for each lascar individually.

Further, 'country ships' (which sailed from India under license from the Company but not under its lease) increased over the late eighteenth century, bringing additional lascars outside the Company's direct control.[38] In theory, their shipowners had to take care of them (or pay the Company a flat fee to do so, £14 per man in 1802, although the figure varied over time) plus return them to India. Particularly for ships dismissing lascars outside London, however, the Company often had difficulty assigning financial liability. Since owners begrudged this expense, some simply discharged their lascars into British society, knowing the directors would ultimately have to take care of them, if anyone did. Private shipowners reported 'desertion' rates of lascars in Britain of 10–20 per cent.[39] Some lascars (especially those who had deserted) refused to name the ship on which they arrived; consequently, their employers could not be assessed for maintaining and returning them to India. For the directors, identifying the owner of each ship that brought each lascar, and extracting money from that owner, remained an ongoing and frustrating expense.

Establishing the Contract Depot System (1797–1813)

By the late eighteenth century, the directors determined to solve the 'problems' of their lack of control over the increasing numbers of Indian seamen in Britain and the haphazard arrangements for their maintenance. The Company contracted with private lodging-keepers in London to feed, clothe, shelter, and manage these men at fixed rates per capita. For most of this period, the rate varied between 1 shilling and 1 shilling 8 pence each per day, which could total a substantial sum, given the number of men and the length of their stay.[40]

The first two contractors were in Shoreditch, north of the City of

[38] Benjamin, 'British and Indian Sailors'.
[39] HMS 501, ff. 1–93; Commons Debate (25/11/1801), Cobbett, *Parliamentary*, vol. 36, pp. 301–2.
[40] Court Minutes 9/10/1799.

London: Ms Susannah Smetza in Kingsland Road (contracts from 1797–1801) and Mr Coates in Hackney Road (1798–1802).[41] The distance of these lodgings from London's docks and the limited facilities available there meant, however, that many lascars made their own arrangements. Nevertheless, those lascars who did stay in Shoreditch incurred the hostility of the neighbourhood: local magistrates complained to the directors about the 'nuisance' that large numbers of lascars in their midst created.[42]

The Directors next contracted with two men in Shadwell, much more convenient to London's docks: John Anthony (contracts 1799–1804) and Abraham Gole and son (1802 onward). Indeed, Gole constructed a purpose-built depot off the Ratcliffe Highway and soon took the entire contract for housing and feeding lascars.[43] He and (after his death in 1819) his son, Abraham Gole, Junior (b. 1777), would retain this exclusive contract until 1834.

The Company paid contractors a considerable amount for lascars: over the 1803–13 period alone, £169,795 for food, maintenance, medicine, and clothing (plus £200,692 for passage money to Asia).[44] Gole was the largest contractor; the Company paid him £117,958 to lodge and feed these men over this period. Since lascars arrived seasonally, Gole's quarterly income varied widely. For the five peak months of the 1813–14 season alone, he received £13,804.[45] In addition, during 1803–13, the Company paid £37,043 for clothing and bedding— mainly to Miss Mary Base (who held these contracts for at least thirty years).[46] As medical superintendent, in 1798 the Company appointed William Docker. After his death in 1807, his assistant and brother, Hilton Docker, took over this contract (agreeing to pay his brother's widow half his net income from it).[47] When Hilton Docker retired in 1815, he nominated a successor, Thomas Barker (an off-duty army

[41] Lascar Papers, vol. 1, ff. 33–8.

[42] Court Minutes 12/8/1801.

[43] Gole had worked in India and could speak some Hindustani. *Times*, 4/9/1801 2c, 22/10/1806 2c.

[44] Lascar Papers, vol. 1, f. 120.

[45] Shipping Committee Minutes 18/8/1813, 16/9/1813, 13/10/1813, 17/11/1813, 31/12/1813.

[46] See bills in Shipping Committee Minutes, 1803–34, *passim*.

[47] Shipping Committee Minutes 10/7/1816.

surgeon, who may have compensated Docker for the nomination).[48] So lucrative was this appointment, however, that a heated battle arose before the post went on a close vote to another man, Thomas Hyslop (who held it 1816–34).[49] The directors also contracted with a resident surgeon to meet at Gravesend (near the Thames mouth) each ship carrying Asian seamen inbound or outbound, whether chartered by the Company or not. William Hunter received this appointment in 1801.[50] In 1812, Adam Park, a board certified surgeon, gained this contract and held it until 1836 at least, billing the directors for hundreds of pounds annually.[51] The Company paid £14,793 for medicine and treatment over the 1803–13 period.

For most lascars, arrival in Britain meant dealing directly with these contractors, who each sought to profit from them. When ships first reached the Thames, the serangs and ship captains reported to the resident surgeon about the condition of each lascar, in terms of health and clothing. This surgeon also examined the men and reported his findings weekly to the shipping committee of the directors, billing quarterly on a per capita basis. The resident surgeon summoned the port's master attendant to investigate any ship carrying lascars whose condition was particularly bad.[52] The surgeon's detailed records provide graphic evidence of how harsh life aboard was for lascars, including death rates of 30–40 per cent on some ships.[53]

The resident surgeon also examined lascars leaving for Asia as passengers or crew. He noted that the death and disease rates were generally even higher among lascars leaving England than those arriving, over 50 per cent died on some voyages to India.[54] In the nineteenth century, as British medical theories of the 'body', and of the 'Asian body' as opposed to the 'European body', shifted, so did explanations

---

[48] Lascar Papers, vol. 1, f. 57. Shipping Committee Minutes 25/10/1815, 1/11/1815.

[49] Shipping Committee Minutes 19/6/1816, 12–17/7/1816.

[50] Hunter, *Essay*.

[51] Shipping Committee Minutes 20/2/1812 and *passim*; Lascar Papers, vols 1–2, *passim*.

[52] Shipping Committee Minutes 22/3/1814.

[53] Hunter, *Essay*; HMS 501, ff. 1–93.

[54] Hunter, *Essay*; Lascar Papers, vol. 1, ff. 90–4.

by these surgeons and other commentators for the high death rates among lascars.[55] Gradually, the British idea of Indians as biologically different from Europeans replaced specific environmental explanations.[56] In 1804, the resident surgeon attributed high lascar death rates on leaving London largely to a diet there too rich in 'animal food' (i.e. meat), for which he felt lascars were constitutionally unsuited.[57] Conditions in the depot can also explain why lascars often left more ill than they arrived.

Under the contract arrangement, when their ship reached harbour, lascars disembarked to be transported from the dockyard to Gole's depot in his cart. Gole charged the Company 2s. per man for this. Those lascars who arrived at ports other than London were customarily sent by the Company's local agents to Gole's depot, often by public coach. No one, however, had authority to force lascars to go to this depot or remain in it. The directors rather relied on the shelter's food, clothing, and camaraderie to attract and hold lascars.

Yet, the interests of the contractors, directors, and lascars inherently clashed. Gole (like the other contractors) needed to keep his costs down in order to profit from the lascars. Yet, since their public outbursts of resistance or violence drew unwanted official or philanthropic attention, he also had an incentive to secure cooperation or submission from them. As contractor, he received from the directors a fixed amount per lascar in his charge, for most of this period: 1 shilling 6 pence board and lodging plus 2 pence tobacco per man per day. As prices rose he requested increases in this rate, for example repeatedly in June 1813.[58] The directors responded by rhetorically asking how much was paid by the government for each prisoner of war: less than half what Gole received. Consequently, by comparing the treatment of lascars to war prisoners, they justified their rejection of his requests. Gole therefore apparently reduced the quality of the food he provided.

Yet, Gole regularly reported that he supplied lascars with all that he had contracted for, which was more than adequate. Lascars received candles at 4 p.m. each day and fuel for their heating and cooking fires.

[55] See Harrison, *Climates.*
[56] See Metcalf, *Ideologies.*
[57] Hunter, *Essay,* pp. 1, 9–10.
[58] Shipping Committee Minutes 2–23/6/1813.

Each morning at 8, Gole's men distributed the day's foodstuffs, reportedly: 'Each man one pound of rice with sugar, tea, pepper, salt and
onions also an unlimited allowance of vegetables and potatoes, every
day; every second day, three quarters of a pound of mutton; and each
intervening day, two or three red herrings according to the size.'[59]
Indeed, Gole, supported by Docker, claimed that he supplied such a
superabundance of food that the lascars profited from it: 'The men
save large portions of the allowance of fish to take with them to
sea . . . [the] Natives [*sic*] sell the tea, sugar and tobacco . . .'.

Similarly, the contracting surgeon, Docker, had interests which
conflicted with those of the directors and lascars. On one hand, he
often stood as advocate to the directors on behalf of the ill, injured, or
mistreated lascars he attended. Yet, his advice usually meant additional
costs to the directors.[60] Docker also issued clothing to each man who
entered the depot in need of it, for which the Company paid. At least
according to the official bills the directors received, each had: '[a] Blue
Jacket lined throughout with Flannel, Blue Trowsers lined throughout with Flannel, Guernsey Frock, Shoes, Stocking and Cap.'[61] Since
these were very saleable commodities, Docker insisted that he, and not
the serangs, should control clothing distribution.

British critics of the depot questioned the quality and quantity of
the clothing actually supplied, citing visual evidence that many of the
lascars were very poorly dressed.[62] Docker responded that lascars often
immediately pawned or sold this clothing in order to raise cash for
their drinking, buying sex, and other immoral habits.[63] Indeed, much
clothing intended for the lascars ended up in the open market, whether
by the lascar's agency or that of the contractors, or a combination; the
Company futilely requested that Parliament make illegal the possession of clothing identified with its markings. Docker therefore refused
to issue a second set of clothing, even to lascars who appeared virtually
naked. He further justified himself by explaining that Chinese seamen
at the depot were always well-dressed, but Indians and Malays were
not, although they all received the same clothing allowance; hence, it

[59] Lascar Papers, vol. 1, ff. 76–86, 104–11.
[60] Shipping Committee Minutes 9/12/1803.
[61] Lascar Papers, vol. 1, ff. 76–86, 122.
[62] Shipping Committee Minutes 4/12/1816.
[63] Lascar Papers, vol. 1, ff. 31–2, 61–8, 76–86.

was their ethnic proclivities that kept Indians so evidently ill-clothed. Lascars were also supposed to have brought their bedding from their ships, but this rarely occurred in practice; shipowners and Docker alleged that lascars sold it, while lascars asserted that captains prevented them from removing it when they disembarked. As a result, many lascars went without.

On their part, the directors regularly pressurized the contractors to keep their costs down and productivity up. Thus, for example, the directors questioned Docker's 'unreasonable' medical bill for October 1809: £224 9s.[64] Simultaneously, however, they also interrogated him about the high mortality rate among the lascars that month. Docker justified his charges and also the high death rate as due to the generally 'bad constitution' of lascars, weakened by the long voyage, who succumbed to the harsh London winter; a lascar crew's desire to remain together in the depot, which meant the diseased could not be isolated from their shipmates, therefore spreading contagion among them; and lascars' weakness for the sensual temptations that surrounded the depot, 'almost all of them give way to every excess in drinking, and debauchery, and contract to a violent degree those diseases (particularly venereal) which such habits are calculated to produce . . .'. Indeed, he concluded in self-praise, 'if there was any relaxation in my exertions very few men could escape disease, and great mortality would be the consequence.' Due to his efforts, 'only eight in the whole house died' over the preceding year.

The mortality rate rose considerably the next year. Docker explained that 1810's higher death rate was 'principally [among] those that never have been in England before' and he reiterated that 'the idle, inactive, debauched lives the men lead immediately on coming on shore' had proved deadly. He therefore built a rope-works at the depot that would keep them productively active.[65] This experiment in make-work failed since the lascars showed no interest in it without pay; Docker also concluded they had proved constitutionally inadequate for rope-making.

It is clear that, especially at peak times, this depot could not contain all the lascars. Many lodged in private rooming houses in the vicinity. The interactions between the large number of lascars and the

[64] Lascar Papers, vol. 1, ff. 25–6.
[65] Docker letter 10/3/1810, Lascar Papers, vol. 1, ff. 27, 53.

surrounding community of Shadwell was complex and often fraught with conflicts as well as cooperation.

Lascar Life in London's Docklands during the Early Nineteenth Century

For the nearly 1,000 Asian seamen who arrived annually during the early nineteenth century, Gole's depot was their base, but not the limit of their activities. Further, the lascars housed at the depot had no official occupation or income. They could come and go during the day, or leave for weeks or years together. Their bonds with each other, and their clashes, reflected their identities and situation. As in many ports, interactions between seamen and the local residents often involved commerce as well as strife.

Throughout this period, informal communities and economies grew up around these Asian seamen. With their wages in hand after a long, dangerous, and harsh voyage, many seamen sought entertainment. Their wages attracted tavernkeepers, pawnbrokers, and sharpers who practised separating seamen from their money. Sex workers, including British and African Caribbean women, reportedly specialized in entertaining seamen (no evidence has emerged that Indian women joined them during this period). The local constabulary and magistrates tried, often in vain, to discipline the lascars and the informal service industry they supported, but the judicial system was not solely hostile to them.

Analysing the dozen cases involving lascars that appeared in Old Bailey Court (1785–1832), Table 5 shows the kinds of crimes, and the kinds of judgments by British authorities, that involved lascars in London during this period.[66] Of these cases, 7 involved charges of robbery, 2 assault, 1 manslaughter, 1 sodomy, and 1 false accusation of murder. As one would expect, much of the crime was committed between lascars and other Asian seamen but some cases pitted Indians against Britons. Although a limited number and a small proportion of

---

[66] The Old Bailey was only one of many London courts but, by using a consistent body of cases, we can explore patterns. OBP, *passim*. See also *Asiatic Journal and Monthly Register*, 1 (1816), p. 98 and Myers, *Reconstructing*, pp. 85–6, 104–17.

Table 5: Criminal Cases in London's Old Bailey Court,
1785–1832

Year	Victim	Accused	Alleged Crime	Sentence
1785	lascar	British Royal Navy seaman	Theft	Death
1808	lascar	Malay sailors	Manslaughter	1 year imprisonment
1814	British boot-maker	2 lascars	Theft	Not guilty
1814	none	lascar	'Unnatural act' [sodomy]	Death
1815	serang	lascar	Theft	7 years transportation
1815	British ship-captain	serang	False accusation of murder	2 years imprisonment
1816	British haberdasher	lascar	Theft	Not guilty
1822	lascar	lascar	Theft	Not guilty
1823	British ship-owner	lascar	Theft	Not guilty
1824	British rooming house clerk	lascar	Theft	Death
1831	lascar	Portuguese sailors	Assault	Death
1832	lascar	lascar	Assault	Not guilty

crime in London, these cases reveal the balance of judgments for and
against lascars.

Overall, this court evidently not only attended to lascar victims (6
of the 12 cases), it was not necessarily hostile to lascar accused. Of the
10 lascars accused, half were found not guilty (of those judged guilty,
3 received death sentences, 1 was imprisoned, and 1 transported). In
3 of the theft cases, the lascar accused even admitted taking or possessing the stolen item, but denied he had actually committed theft; all

were judged not guilty. For example, in January 1814, the police arrested two lascars, Sack Mahomet and Mandane, for attempting to sell a stolen pair of boots, worth 34 shillings.[67] Although the boot-maker, Francis Brown, identified the footwear as stolen from his shop at 72 Ratcliffe Highway, Sack Mahomet pleaded ignorance: 'I was going along Rosemary-lane, a white man gave me them boots to sell; he said he would give me something if I would sell them. I do not know the man, nor where he lived.' The jury found these lascars not guilty. Indeed, the court acquitted lascars accused by Britons in 3 of 5 cases. Overall, in cases where Indians opposed Britons, Indians 'won' twice as often.

Evidently, class could prove more decisive than ethnicity. Where a lascar accused a British seaman of theft, that Briton was found guilty and sentenced to death. Where a serang accused a British ship captain of murder, however, the court heard the case but believed the captain and imprisoned the serang for giving false testimony. In two cases, the British mistress of a lascar testified in his favour, once successfully, once not. Thus, these women did not necessarily lose credibility by openly discussing their out-of-wedlock sexual relations with lascars. Even these dozen cases therefore reveal complex interactions, where the outcome of the trial was not automatically determined by the identity of the victim or accused, although these were certainly factors in the judgment.

On a daily basis, Gole, Docker, and the depot staff (six European employees, later reduced to two) struggled to control hundreds of Asian seamen, with limited success. A tall compound wall surrounded the depot, separating the seamen within from the surrounding neighbourhood. A locking gate enabled Gole's staff to exercise some surveillance and control over entry and egress—when they devoted resources to doing so, but that cost Gole money and was apparently rarely done during the day. At times when fights erupted within the depot, Gole ordered the gates closed to prevent it from spreading into the surrounding community. Every night at 11 (the legal public-house closing time), Gole sent his men to collect lascars. He then locked the compound gate, excluding the rest—unless the police demanded that

[67] OBP (16/2/1814), pp. 133–4, case 227.

men they had picked up be admitted.[68] These gates reopened at 6 a.m. During the day, lascars could enter or leave freely. The open area inside the wall and outside the barracks was supposed to be swept daily by Gole's British servants. Reflecting British understanding of the potential solidarities and conflicts among ethnicities, the depot initially had separate barracks for Indians, Malays, and Chinese, with Indians by far the largest.

The interior of the barracks remained largely the province of Asian seamen themselves, with little structure or control inserted from the outside. Serangs of each crew exercised authority, including corporal punishment such as whipping and close confinement. Each barracks was divided into rooms, each with a heating stove, with lascars from the same ship generally living in the same room. These lascars organized themselves into cooking and dining groups, ranging in size from 7 to 25, groups apparently reflecting solidarities formed aboard ship as well as ethnic and religious identities.

Bonds among lascar shipmates developed on the voyage which partially overrode religious identities. Lists of names of lascars suggest a single lascar crew might include Muslims, Catholic and Protestant Christians (of part Portuguese or other European descent), Parsis, Armenians, and/or Hindus.[69] However, while on board and then in the depot, members of a crew may have cooked and eaten separately, divided by religious identity.[70] Yet the binding force of the harsh voyage also produced strong solidarities, with evidence of cooperation in religious ceremonies (discussed below).

In contrast, identities like Indian, Chinese, Arab, or Malay apparently remained potent on board ship and in Britain. For example, the same ship might have both lascars and Chinese seamen, although they usually served in separate labour gangs; tensions between them occasionally flared in London. Indeed, there were largescale riots which pitted Indians against other seamen in London's streets. As mentioned

---

[68] Shipping Committee Minutes 29/7/1823.

[69] Even keeping in mind that the name under which a man worked was not necessarily his original name. E.g., Affidavit of James Rowson 7/3/1824, O/1/369, BL.

[70] Emin describes initially eating separately from Europeans, and never mentions dining with the lascars onboard. Emin, *Life* (1794), pp. 44ff.

above, in 1785 groups of Indians fought Chinese.[71] Similarly, in 1806 around the depot, 150 Indians fought 300 Chinese who were supported by some Arab seamen.[72] The alleged causes were an escalating conflict initially generated on the ship *Skelton Castle*, which had sailed to London with 150 lascars and 20 Chinese seamen aboard, and jealousy over some local British women. In London, other Chinese (and Arabs) apparently supported these 20 Chinese seamen against the lascars who had sailed with them. Since most lascars and Arabs were Muslim, and most Chinese seamen were not, this was evidently not a religious conflict.

On a smaller scale, in 1808 three Muslim Malay seamen killed an Indian Muslim lascar, Imambacchus. An Englishwoman, Sarah Williams, testified that she had been living with the victim in a room nearby on Cable Street for the previous month. One night, she took seven shillings from one of the Malay seamen, Glosse, to get drunk and then left the Blue Gate public house (Ratcliffe Highway) with him for sex. The victim arrived just then and caught them. The Malay seaman was joined by a Malay shipmate and a third Malay from another ship. Together, they mortally wounded the lascar. Testifying on behalf of the victim were a Muslim serang and two lascars from the accused's own ship. The jury convicted the Malays of manslaughter. All seven men were boarding in Gole's depot. Though clearly based in sexual rivalry, the sides in the affray were formed around solidarities based on origin that cut across shipmate lines.[73]

Indian lascars also often openly confronted local British inhabitants. For example, in 1803, three lascars armed with cutlasses broke into the City of Carisle public house in Whitechapel, seeking to recover the substantial sum of £150 they claimed that local sex workers there had stolen from them. The landlord had them arrested. The directors bailed them out, paid the damages, and put them aboard an outgoing ship, not to protect the British community from them, but rather the reverse: 'for their better protection from the women of the town'.[74] Élite British fears about the predations of the British poor,

[71] *Annual Register* (1785), 27, Chronicle, pp. 242–3.
[72] *Annual Register* (1806), 48, Chronicle, pp. 450–1; *Times*, 7/10/1806 3 a–b.
[73] OBP (1/6/1808), pp. 280–8, case 395.
[74] *Times*, 6/10/1803 3d.

especially the female British poor, on Asian seamen would recur. In October 1805, lascars took over the streets of Shadwell in a largescale tumult in which 15 people were hospitalized and 19 arrested.[75] A month later, lascars seized the streets east of the Tower of London one Friday night, claiming a sex worker there had robbed one of their members.[76] In 1808, a quarrel between a drunken but armed British sailor and a single lascar brought 400 lascars out of the depot and on to the streets in his support. A passing squad of British militia drove them by bayonet back into the depot, where they barricaded themselves in.[77]

Not all interactions were violent. During the first ten days of the month of Muharram, 1220 Hijri (1–10 April 1805), Shi'ite lascars organized huge religious processions through the streets of Shadwell. A British periodical reported:

> Last Saturday, Monday, Tuesday, and this day, the Lascars of the Mahommedan persuasion, at the east end of town, had a grand religious festival. The first day they went in slow procession along the New-road, St George's in the east, Cannon-street, Ratcliff-highway, Shadwell, and other streets, with drums and tambourines. Part of them were selected, performing pantomimical dances with drawn swords, cutting the air in various directions; then followed four blacks, in long white robes, holding emblematical figures in their hands. Another held a vase, in which was a fire; and a man in a white vestment, treading backwards, threw incense into it; another, with a handkerchief, fanning their faces; when, at every turn of the streets, a group of the same people lifted up their hands and heads to the canopy of Heaven, hymning some passages out of the koran. They conducted themselves with great propriety, although a multitude of people followed them. On Monday and Tuesday they made a visit in solemn procession the same way; and on Thursday another succeeded, which closed their religious revelry, back to their place in Ratcliff-highway. We understand this was a kind of jubilee in honour of the commencement of their new year, and of the translation of Mahommed into Paradise, and imploring him to give peace to the suffering world, and them a safe return to their own country.[78]

[75] *Times*, 15/10/1805 2b.
[76] *Times*, 26/11/1805 2c.
[77] *Annual Register*, (1808), 50, Chronicle, p. 13.
[78] *Annual Register*, (1805), 47, Chronicle, p. 376.

While the description of these processions by the British press is plausible, the reporter's interpretation of their meaning derives from Christian not Islamic theology. This distinctly Shi'ite ritual commemorates the martyred death of Imam Hussain in 680 CE. The response of the British public and press was quizzical but respectful. The staging and tone of this ritual also suggests the cultural self-confidence of these lascars in London. Although in India this Muharram commemoration has frequently been a flash-point of Shi'ite versus Sunni conflict, lascars of both Muslim sects plus many Hindus evidently cooperated in carrying it out in London.

Thus, solidarities and conflicts among many hundreds of unemployed Asian seamen around the depot developed internally and between them and the surrounding British inhabitants. These apparently sometimes united people along ethnic and gender rather than religious or shipmate lines. Further, this large body of seamen in Shadwell increasingly drew the attention of British political and social leaders, particularly at times of heated Parliamentary and public debate over the Company, as when its charter was due to expire in March 1814.

Lascars at the Heart of Controversy (1813–1816)

Tensions around lascars in London especially increased from the fall 1813 season onwards. The particularly large number of Asian seamen arriving that year exacerbated conflicts aboard ship, inside the depot, and with the surrounding British community, all of which drew increased British attention. Several serangs accused their British captains of mistreatment.[79] Within the overcrowded depot, bloody fights erupted, leading to multiple deaths. In September 1813 alone, Malay sailors fought Arabs, killing one; Chinese tongs fought each other, killing three and hospitalizing seventeen; and lascars and Chinese fought as well.[80]

---

[79] Shipping Committee Minutes 22–30/7/1813, 1–26/9/1813, 17/11/1813.

[80] OBP (15/9/1813), pp. 478–9, case 889; Shipping Committee Minutes 15/9/1813; Court Minutes 22/9/1813; *Annual Register* (1813), 55, Chronicle, p. 85. The next season, in October 1814, another fight erupted between Chinese and lascars. Shipping Committee Minutes 5/10/1814.

Many Britons living in Shadwell reacted negatively to this especially large Asian presence among them. With no duties (or wages) during their months in London, Asian seamen took jobs that threatened local workers at a time of great economic hardship in Britain. Irish 'lumpers' (stevedores) fought street battles against Chinese seamen unloading their ships in July 1813 and against Indian lascars in August.[81] Also in August, a British publican had a serang thrown in Marshalsea debtor's prison for owing £24; Gole bailed him out on behalf of the Company.[82] In December, British vandals desecrated the graveyard where lascars buried their dead, disinterring four bodies.[83] Even while this violation occurred, the rector, warden, overseers, and trustees of the local Parish Church of St George collected 192 signatures from their congregation against 'the inconvenience, and Nuisances which arise from the Lascars being accommodated in that Neighbourhood, and that the Property of the Petitioners has been much deteriorated and reduced in value'.[84] The directors responded that the outgoing ships of the season would soon sail, emptying the neighbourhood of lascars and therefore the 'Nuisances'. Indeed, that season, serangs evidently made particularly vigorous efforts to arrange the return passage of the lascars under their command.[85] Rather than keep a lascar who had been convicted of felony in the local jail, the judge sentenced him to be confined in the depot until he could be shipped out at the Company's expense on the next vessel.[86]

To the directors, it was clear that the large numbers of lascars presented insurmountable financial and public-relations problems that the Company was ill equipped to solve but could try to avoid. In negotiating the renewal of its charter in 1813, the Company relinquished its monopoly over trade with India. It consequently requested Parliament legally to 'exonerate the Company from any Charge or risk on account of Lascars brought to this country in private ships' and also to require those private shipowners to pay these costs from a bond

---

[81] Shipping Committee Minutes 14/7/1813, 31/8/1813.
[82] Shipping Committee Minutes 25/8/1813.
[83] Shipping Committee Minutes 8/12/1813.
[84] Shipping Committee Minutes 15/12/1813.
[85] Shipping Committee Minutes 5–19/11/1813.
[86] Shipping Committee Minutes 11/2/1814.

given in India.[87] Since Parliament nevertheless still expected the directors to control and manage lascars, the directors designated some of their leading members to form a 'Lascar Committee'. Gole reported regularly to this committee, providing evidence that would be useful in defending the Company against its critics, especially in Parliament.[88]

Simultaneously, lascars also drew the attention of British Evangelicals and social reformers who sought to ameliorate their condition—spiritual and physical. In spring 1814, Evangelical Christians asserted that hundreds of lascars were attending Anglican churches, where ministers conducted Christian worship services for them in Bengali and Hindustani, as well as English.[89] They also encouraged their young British missionaries to learn Indian languages rapidly. One of their tracts declared optimistically: 'In 3–12 months, you could learn Hindustani . . . The Bengalee, as being nearly allied to the Sanscrit, is allowedly the more difficult language spoken in India; yet in less than four months, a student would be able to read almost any part of the New Testament, and in a few months more begin to compose; and before a twelvemonth expires, hold common conversation.'[90] Since most lascars remained in London for months, and many made 'as many as eight, nine, or ten voyages to England', there would be plenty of time to evangelize among them. The interventions of such missionaries would save these 'pagans', Muslims, and 'Papists' from 'the rapacious [British male] poor, as well as the most abandoned of our abandoned countrywomen. [Lascars] have none, or scarcely any, who will associate with them, but prostitutes, and no house that will receive them, except the public house, and the apartments of the abandoned.'[91] According to these moral reformers, it was British women who preyed upon innocent Indians not, as many Britons would come to believe decades later, innocent White womanhood in danger from sexually predatory Indians.

British social reformers also devoted their particular efforts towards lascars, especially from early 1814 onwards. They alleged (inaccurately

---

[87] Correspondence Committee Minutes 3/12/1813.
[88] Shipping Committee Minutes 30/11/1814.
[89] Anonymous, *Short Address*, p. 14.
[90] Ibid., p. 5.
[91] Ibid., p. 4.

at that point) deaths of about 130 lascars in Gole's depot annually.[92] They sought to use the power of the British government and public opinion to force the Company to improve living conditions for those they portrayed as defenceless Indians living under its authority.

Lascars interacted with these movements in a variety of ways. In January 1814, the serang of the ship *Winchelsea* severely whipped his lascar cook in Gole's depot. Unusually, the cook (whose status was below that of other lascars) went outside the lascar community and appealed for redress from leading British abolitionists and social reformers, including William Allen and Bishop William Wilberforce (the famous leader of the 'Saints' in Parliament).[93] Early in February, Allen and his friends convinced the Company to let them personally inspect the depot, something it had never before officially allowed.[94] Although there were only 200 seamen present at the time, the conditions these reformers found appalled them, and also the British public once they publicized their findings. They immediately founded the 'Society for the Protection of Asiatic Sailors'. Further, they brought policemen into the depot and arrested the *Winchelsea*'s serang. Over the protests of the depot staff that the serang was too ill to move, they hauled him to the Worship Street police station, in distant Shoreditch. Eventually, Docker's and Gole's explanations, and the serang's evident precarious medical condition, convinced the magistrate to release him into their custody. Although this serang was briefly jailed at the time of his trial in April, the charges of assault against him were subsequently dropped, due particularly to Docker's efforts.[95]

Meanwhile, Docker had been working in vain to persuade these reformers that their larger charges were baseless and their interference counterproductive to the welfare of the lascars. He asserted that these reformers mainly threatened the necessary authority of serangs, not that of the Company, Gole, or himself. He maintained that the serangs should be allowed to continue to discipline the lascars since this was the only source of order and security extant within the depot, where British law could not and should not run. He maintained that serangs

[92] Ibid., p. 17.
[93] Allen, *Life*, vol. 1, pp. 140–1.
[94] Shipping Committee Minutes 2/2/1814.
[95] Lascar Papers, vol. 1, ff. 104–11.

did not use excessive force—at least when he was there to moderate it. The cook in question had been justly (albeit admittedly too harshly) punished by his serang for selling new clothes recently provided him and for embezzling provisions issued his shipmates for him to cook. Both widespread practices represented the greatest threats to the health of the lascars and therefore he had to receive exemplary punishment. Thus, Docker argued, a few criminals among the lascars—like this cook—were threatening to destroy the depot's internal governance system by misleading well-meaning but poorly-informed reformers: 'I do not doubt the benevolent intentions of the Gentlemen . . . but I apprehend that their personal ignorance of the Characters of the Native Seamen will make them very liable to be imposed upon particularly as their information is mainly if not entirely collected from the discontented and criminal'.[96] In addition, Docker asserted that the admittedly 'dirty state of the rooms the men live in' was due not to Gole's inattention but to 'the Innate sloth and filthy habits of the Men [which] defy every attempt to remedy.' Thus, as Docker framed it, the issues were the internal autonomy of the lascar community and their inferior natural proclivities that British authority could not reform.[97]

Even as Docker defended the depot, he came under fire from the directors, who formed a subcommittee to inspect it themselves. Protecting the Company's interests, they recommended reforms under their own direction, by appointing their own agent to receive lascar complaints 'without [their] being thrown in such cases into the hands of artful persons' (i.e. the Society).[98] They simultaneously chastised Docker for his excessive fees. In addition, they urged returning lascars to India as quickly as possible. The directors approved the subcommittee's proposed 'Code of Regulations for the Better Protection of Lascars and Asiatic Seamen.'[99] To preclude further interference by outsiders, the depot's gates were closed to unauthorized inspections. These measures, however, failed to end the campaigns by reformers to improve conditions for lascars.

[96] Ibid., ff. 48–50.
[97] Conservative Britons in India at the time made similar arguments against Evangelical, Utilitarian, and other reformers there, for example about sati (abolished after years of debate in 1829). Lascar Papers, vol. 1, ff. 44–5.
[98] Court Minutes 6–22/4/1814, 31/8/1814; Lascar Papers, vol. 1, f. 57.
[99] Court Minutes 16/9/1814.

Following upon these controversies of 1814, the Company's need for lascars rapidly decreased due to the Royal Navy's demobilization (following the end of the French wars), the Company's loss of trade monopoly to India, and the ongoing worldwide economic depression. The directors mistakenly promised Parliament that there would be no further need for lascars at all and the expensive and controversial depot should close. They warned, however, that private ships would continue to bring lascars and therefore Parliament itself should establish 'a strong police to repress the irregularities of the natives [*sic.*], to confine them within proper limits, and to prevent that intercourse between them and the lowest orders of society in this country, for which no endeavours of the Company have hitherto been effectual.'[100] The directors also added a registration fee of 6 shillings per lascar on all private ships leaving India.

Parliament granted part of the directors' request in 1814 (54 George 3, *c.* 134), making private shipowners post a bond on leaving India, at the rate of £5 per ton, and also setting stricter requirements for their care of lascars. Bonds could total well over £6,000 per vessel.[101] As part of this law, however, Parliament also named the directors as 'trustees for the *Asiatic* Sailors, *Lascars* and Natives' of all territories under its charter, which broadened the definition of whom they would have to accept at the depot since the charter extended from south Africa to the Pacific.[102]

While legally bound to protect 'natives' of all territories within its charter, the directors continued to discriminate among them for treatment there. The directors refused to privilege lascars who claimed descent from Indian families of 'respectability . . . influence and Rank in the Native community', but did privilege seamen of European or part European descent, who lived in Gole's own house, received special quality clothing, and enjoyed superior accommodation on the passage home.[103] Further, the directors would not support Indians married to British women who wished to remain in England.[104]

[100] Correspondence Committee Minutes 15/6/1814.
[101] See bonds in O/1/369, BL.
[102] Emphasis in original. Shipping Committee Minutes 30/11/1814; Lascar Papers, vol. 1, f. 59.
[103] Shipping Committee Minutes 2/3/1814 to 5/2/1817.
[104] Shipping Committee Minutes 16/5/1815.

Meanwhile, the Society for the Protection of Asiatic Sailors continued its campaigns. Its leaders took into their homes and provided food (although 'the most frugal and plainest fare') for some nineteen lascars whom, they claimed, had been unjustly expelled from the depot.[105] From these dissidents, the society elicited extensive information on all aspects of lascar service. Docker responded that these men were really paid 'informers' whom 'members of the Society' sent 'occasionally to the Barracks to collect evidence'. Further, Docker asserted that these very men 'have deserted from the ships on which they were embarked, preferring to live under the system they had so much deprecated to returning to their native country; and that the ringleader of them, after having so deserted, has absconded under a charge of felony.'[106] Thus, Docker maintained they had been justly expelled from the depot.

Having obtained no satisfactory response from the directors to their concerns, the society publicized its 'Memorial' of findings in the *Times* attacking the entire lascar system.[107] They accused ghat serangs of kidnapping lascars into ships and appropriating their pay. They charged shipcaptains with mistreating and defrauding lascars. They charged depot authorities with a range of abuses, including embezzlement of clothing and food, permitting cruel and mass beatings by serangs, and causing the high level of deaths of homeless lascars on London's streets.

Two days later, Docker replied at great length to these charges.[108] He explained that the specific deaths which the society cited were not of people properly under his care (one was an African whom the lascars themselves expelled, the others had arrived on a private, not a Company, ship). Docker admitted that between May 1813 and April 1814, 122 lascars (including 31 Chinese) under his authority had died; on one particularly cold day (14 March 1814) 5 died. Docker, however, presented this as a relatively respectable record. He agreed with the reformers that 'the promiscuous intercourse of the Men with abandoned [British] Females is most pernicious to their Health', but retorted that this was not the Company's fault. Overall, Docker maintained

[105] *Times*, 9/12/1814 3d; Correspondence Committee Minutes 25/3/1814.
[106] Lascar Papers, vol. 1, ff. 104–11.
[107] Shipping Committee Minutes 5/10/1814; Allen, *Life*, vol. 1, pp. 140–1; *Times*, 9/12/1814 3d.
[108] Lascar Papers, vol. 1. ff. 76–86, 95–102.

that the breakdown in internal order due to the reformers' interference in the authority of serangs only led to more violence both within the depot and toward the public without.

All this controversy also strengthened the director's desire to be rid of the entire responsibility for lascars, which was costing the Company £13,000 annually. Further, as they wrote Parliament in February 1815, they lacked the police powers to control lascars:

> [these] Evils . . . arise out of the impossibility in this free country of confining those persons within the prescribed limits, and of thereby preventing their intercourse with the dregs of society, which gives the Lascars of vicious dispositions facility in selling their bedding and clothing, and of contracting loathsome disorders . . . and we are compelled to notice that insubordination has been of late much increased by the injudicious though well meant interference of the Society for the Protection of Asiatic Seamen.[109]

Perhaps supportive of the directors' charge that the authority of serangs had weakened, Mahomet Casmet, a serang, had his locked trunk stolen from the depot by a lascar, Nowardin, with the help of four Arab seamen. Incidentally, this case reveals what a serang's possessions might consist of (supporting Docker's assertion that the men hoarded clothing and revealing an import trade in Indian spices): '16 pair of trowsers, value 39 s., 16 shirts value 32 s., 2 brass pots, value 4 s., 140 lbs of spice, value 10 s., and a £5 bank note.' Although the defendant's English mistress, Maria Pearce, testified that he was with her that night in her room on Cornwall Street, the court found him guilty.[110] Here, the court supported the serang against a lascar and his English mistress.

By 1815, some British authorities were less sympathetic to both lascars and serangs in their midst, particularly when their opponent was British. The local constabulary had come to believe that apparently poor lascars begging on the streets were really exploiting charitable Britons and living an easy life through mendacity.[111] The Lord Mayor of London had numerous lascars arrested for theft, and deported on

---

[109] Ibid., ff. 69–75.
[110] OBP (15/2/1815), p. 150, case 284.
[111] PP, Returns (Commons), 1814–15, vol. 3, paper 471, p. 314.

the next outgoing ships.[112] That year as well, a serang in the depot approached the mayor with the charge that his captain had murdered his Indian steward at sea.[113] Although admitting to thrashing the steward, the captain testified, in the midst of this beating, 'When my back was turned, [the steward] fell out of the stern window' and accidentally drowned. The court found the captain innocent but the serang guilty of conspiracy to falsely accuse him. The serang received two years imprisonment; his supporting witness was jailed for one.

In 1815, Parliament created a 'Committee on Lascars and Other Asiatic Seamen' to investigate the entire system of lascar employment.[114] In the midst of their investigations, directors demanded that Gole explain the much publicized death of a 'coloured man' in London's streets.[115] The committee's report, however, for the most part sided with Docker and Gole rather than the society, but did not allow the Company to evade responsibility for lascars in the future. It concluded: 'the treatment of the [lascar] Men on the voyage from India to this country, their food, their clothing and the medical assistance afforded to them, and the protection of them against fraud in the payment of their wages . . . require little improvement.' British reliance on ghat serangs and ship serangs was 'regrettable' but necessary, since no other system could provide and manage the lascars needed. The Committee's unannounced inspection of Gole's depot had revealed overcrowding but the deficiencies in health and cleanliness were, as Docker had maintained, 'owing probably in a great degree to the habits of the Lascars themselves.' The mortality rates were 'peculiarly small', and most deaths were due the lascars' poor adaptation to the British climate and their susceptibility to corrupting immoral habits, mostly with British prostitutes. The committee recommended stronger controls over the lascars, to be exercised by Britons rather than by serangs, in order to keep lascars more closely confined. It regretted that lascars were sent back to India as penniless passengers often forced to work without pay by the captain. It also recommended continuing overall responsibility for lascars with the Company, urging that it establish a more efficient depot, farther from London's centre than Shadwell, and

[112] Shipping Committee Minutes 29/12/1815.
[113] OBP (5/4/1815), pp. 263–4, case 589.
[114] PP, Returns (Commons), 1814–15, vol. 3, paper 471, pp. 217–29.
[115] Shipping Committee Minutes 29/3/1815.

nearer the new East India Docks (completed around 1809) at Blackwall, with a more effective mode for policing the lascars. The goal was 'sufficient authority to enforce the men's return to *India*'.

In 1815, Parliament acted to further discourage the employment of 'Asiatic sailors, Lascars, [and] Natives [of Company territories]' by amending the Navigation Acts.[116] Of all the peoples in all of Britain's colonies, only Asians could not in future be counted as British sailors under these acts. Significantly, this amendment defined its categories differently from other elements in British society of the time: unlike lascars, African and Caribbean sailors from British colonies did count as British. Further, thereafter, the governor of each presidency had to certify a shipowner's declaration that it was 'impossible to procure a crew of British seamen' before that ship could hire a lascar crew in India.[117] This 1815 amendment reflects a growing British antipathy against lascars, including resentment by the directors but also by British sailors fearing them as rivals for employment. Parliament, however, for another twenty years refused to allow the directors to escape responsibility for those lascars who did reach Britain. Further, the economics of maritime labour recruitment in India meant that, although the number of lascars diminished markedly, hundreds would continue to arrive annually on Company and private ships.

The lack of concrete action by the directors for the improvement of the lascars led to new questions in Parliament in April 1816, and a Parliamentary examination of all the relevant documents.[118] The directors reiterated that the British government should establish the new depot, since the Company lacked the police powers to enforce control over the lascars.[119] The directors further declined to build their own new depot as Parliament had recommended.

As a proposed solution to this dilemma, in 1816, the East India Dock Company recommended physically isolating the lascars by confining them to hulks moored in the Thames. This would protect

[116] Act 55, Geo. 3, c. 116. PP, Returns (Commons), 1814–15, vol. 2, paper 281, pp. 587–97.

[117] Act 55, Geo. 3, c. 116, section 8. See Bombay, Political Outward or Order Books for 1818ff for copies of such certificates, MSA.

[118] Commons Debate 25/4/1816, *Hansard*, vol. 33, pp. 1232–4; PP, Returns (Commons), 1816, vol. 10, paper 279, pp. 349–68.

[119] Lascar Papers, vol. 1, ff. 161–70.

Britons living on shore from 'the depravity that attaches to their [lascar] character'.[120] The backers of this plan even approached the Navy to rent one of its old ships. In the end, the plan proved unfeasible. Thus, while both Parliament and the directors agreed that a new depot near the East India Docks would be an improvement, the directors ultimately stuck to their position that the British government should take charge, while Parliament refused but urged the Company to do so.[121] In consequence, Gole's depot remained the prime contractor until 1834.

London's Docklands and the Depot
(1816–1834)

The Shadwell area of London surrounding the depot developed economically and socially over this period. As with many centres of transient seamen life, it functioned out of the control of municipal authorities, not just because of Indians, who were declining in number. For example, in 1817, a local magistrate despaired of removing public houses and prostitutes from Shadwell since their clientele 'consists entirely of foreign sailors, lascars, Chinese, Greeks, and other filthy dirty people of that description' and 'the [British] women of the Town never cohabit with any other people.'[122] Nor could the directors limit their costs. Local jailors charged the Company for the expenses of arrest and maintenance of lascars. Even imprisoned lascars expected and did receive their daily food allowance from the Company.[123]

Part of the resentment of the gentrifying local British community in Shadwell was apparently occasioned by their growing perception that lascars represented a disturbingly foreign culture functioning in their midst. For example, in 1823, Asian seamen carried out an elaborate funeral for one of their number in Britton's burial ground, Church-lane, Whitechapel.[124] These seamen carried the corpse in procession

---

[120] Court Minutes 20/12/1815; Shipping Committee Minutes 29/12/1815, 16/2/1816.

[121] Lascar Papers, vol. 1, ff. 148–9, 156–8.

[122] PP, Returns (Commons), 1817, vol. 7, paper 233, p. 195.

[123] Shipping Committee Minutes 29/9/1815, 1–15/11/1815, 9–14/2/1816.

[124] These were apparently Chinese seamen. *Times*, 17/1/1823 2d.

from Gole's depot, refusing to employ any professional grave-digger or Christian priest. They made prayers and offerings, and stood vigil for several nights. To the local British observers, all this proved inscrutable and threatening.

Another source of resentment by local residents against lascars was the often largescale violence that broke out periodically within or around the depot. These 'affrays' tended during this period to be internecine; for example, Chinese seamen fought among themselves, on a scale that drew particular official notice, in 1816, 1818, 1821, 1822, and 1824.[125] Gole attributed most of the Chinese quarrels to gambling among themselves (while Indians fought, he asserted, usually after drinking together).[126]

While there were intra-ethnic conflicts, there were also solidarities, often based on service under a particular serang. Serangs continued to represent their lascars in labour negotiations about living and working conditions and also stood as paymaster for the lascars serving under them.[127] One serang, Doud Gouber Gash (speaking through a translator), in 1823 described his role as 'an officer looked up to as the father and protector of his men, and appointed by them as the receiver and distributor of their wages, and guardian of their privileges.'[128] This serang, who had made several previous voyages to Britain, led his lascar crew to complain to London's Lord Mayor: he 'handed a long epistle to his Lordship, in which the petitioners described themselves as in a state of starvation, and treated with great cruelty in this free country.' They refused to board the ship leaving for India until they had been paid. The captain admitted that he owed them wages, but asserted they would only run away and squander it; he promised to pay them when they boarded. The *Times* opined that much of the trouble was initiated not by lascars themselves but rather by irresponsible outside agitators: 'For some time past some evil-minded fellows have been using their

[125] Shipping Committee Minutes 13–28/11/1816, 15/4/1818, 16/10/1822, 4/12/1822, 9–16/7/1823, 27/10/1824; Court Minutes 27/6/1821, 4/7/1821.

[126] Shipping Committee Minutes 29/7/1823.

[127] Shipping Committee Minutes, 28–30/6/1815, 12–19/7/1815, 2/8/1815, 1/9/1815, 6–15/12/1815, 19–26/6/1816, 27/5/1818, 8/7/1818, 13–27/1/1819, 2/2/1819.

[128] *Times*, 4/7/1823 3e.

efforts to excite a spirit of insubordination amongst the Lascars, in the East end of the town . . .'.[129] The captain blamed a British professional scribe who worked on behalf of lascars (for a fee, of course): 'a fellow who was in the habit of getting his name written on the walls as a letter-writer, prompted all the applications from the Lascars on the subject of their grievances'. Yet, many serangs had enough experience of Britain and its legal procedures to make a good case on their own.

The overall decline in commerce between India and Britain and rise in unemployed British seamen over this period meant that fewer lascars found work on this passage. For shipowners as well, the decline in commerce meant that their ships were short of cargo. Thus, they were willing to charge the Company ever less to transport lascars back as passengers. At the end of the eighteenth century, the directors had paid less than £12 per lascar.[130] When the number of lascars peaked during the wars in 1813, the going rate had risen to £20 per man (sometimes the conveying ship also charged an additional food allowance of 1 shilling 3 pence per man per day). This could be very big business. In 1813, 3 private ships collectively shipped back 760 lascars.[131] After the wars, however, the charges dropped: in 1814–15 only £18 per man; in 1815 only £16; by 1816 only £10–11; by 1834 only £9.[132] Thus, the 1834 rates were less than half the 1813 charges. With these reduced rates, the captains of the transporting ships apparently reduced the quality of the food and also tried to crowd ever more lascars into the same space.[133] The shipping rates also varied by the class of the person conveyed. For Indian seamen of part Portuguese ancestry, there were additional expenses due to the better food served them. Women servants cost about double the rate for a lascar, due to the separate accommodations necessary.[134] While some lascars could earn wages by helping load the outbound ships, many ended up working the return voyage without pay.

[129] *Times*, 9/12/1823 3d.

[130] Court Minutes 9/10/1799.

[131] This apparently included lascars in their crews. Shipping Committee Minutes 5/10/1813, 12/11/1813.

[132] Shipping Committee Minutes 24/8/1814 to 9/4/1834; Lascar Papers, vol. 1, f. 120.

[133] Shipping Committee Minutes 30/6/1815, 2/7/1816.

[134] Shipping Committee Minutes 24/9/1816, 26/6/1833.

Some lascars, when they saw the conditions offered them, tried to refuse and Gole had to force them back aboard.[135]

As the numbers of lascars shrank over this period, the contractors faced declining incomes. Further, in 1816, Mr Francis Robinson opened a rival depot, located north of London in West Ham, Essex, particularly designed to attract the custom of private shipowners.[136] To meet this competition, Gole reduced his per capita rates by 2d. per day and also cut his charges for conveying lascars from and to their ships by a third.[137] Robinson's depot, however, closed about two years later, apparently due to a combination of declining numbers of lascars, the hostility of local inhabitants to the lascars in their midst, and the more convenient location of Gole's depot.[138] In 1818, Gole pleaded that he had lost money for the previous two years and requested a subsidy from the directors. They replied that he had built the depot as a 'speculation entirely of a private nature' and that therefore he had to bear any losses that his management incurred.[139] The next year, Gole senior died, and his son took over the depot.[140] He tried to reduce his costs even further, which resulted in complaints from lascars about the deteriorating conditions there.[141] Further, Gole junior did not impress the directors as being a very efficient or effective manager.[142] To save expenses, he consolidated the reduced numbers of lascars and Chinese sailors together in one barrack, no longer provided them with different diets, and reduced his British staff from six to two men.[143]

Some of the lascars from private ships stayed not in Gole's depot but in the new lodging house that Francis Robinson opened, this one attached to his home at 72 High Street, Poplar.[144] While this was not a largescale operation, it nevertheless drained clientele from Gole.

[135] Shipping Committee Minutes 15/11/1815.
[136] Shipping Committee Minutes 17/1/1815, 26/6/1816, 31/7/1816, 11/2/1817.
[137] Shipping Committee Minutes 24/1/1816, 7–23/2/1816, 1/3/1816.
[138] Lascar Papers, vol. 1, ff. 171–2.
[139] Court Minutes 6–27/3/1818.
[140] Shipping Committee Minutes 15/9/1819.
[141] Shipping Committee Minutes 13–20/12/1820.
[142] Shipping Committee Minutes 12/1/1821.
[143] Shipping Committee Minutes 29/7/1823.
[144] OBP (7/4/1824), pp. 247–8, case 679.

Further, it was only one of the many private lodging houses for lascars in the Poplar and Limehouse districts, much closer to the East India Docks than Gole's depot.

Continuing the debate over lascar rights as British subjects, Parliament in 1823 (4 George 4, c. 80, section 31) recognized that Asian seamen should not be forcibly confined in the depot or expelled from Britain without due process: 'Asiatic sailors, Lascars, and natives aforesaid may refuse to accept the maintenance to be provided for them under the rules and regulations before referred to, or to return home in the ships or vessels which may be engaged for that purpose.' Yet, if they were convicted of vagrancy, they could be punitively deported by order of a local magistrate. This act also tightened the rules for captains about reporting Asian seamen on arrival in Britain.[145] It established a fine of £10 per unreported man, with a third of the money going to any informer who revealed the infraction, and the rest going towards costs of legal prosecution and maintaining the seaman. This strengthened lascar resistance to Gole's controls over them and also shifted some of the burden of surveillance onto the captains who brought them.

Seeking to recover his profits, Gole began housing and feeding in his depot Indian servants, both male and female (including pregnant ones), at the expense of their British employers (or former employers), while they awaited passage back to India.[146] We have no evidence about the interactions between lascars and these other working class Indians, nor about the effects of having women live in the depot. Over this period, the directors also sent a range of other Indians to live in the depot, including some indigent emissaries (see Chapter 7).[147] Even with these additions, the number of people in the depot continued to decline. In 1825–6, Gole and the other contractors again petitioned the directors for subsidies. While Gole's request failed, the attending surgeon, Hyslop, whose annual income from lascars had dropped over 90 per cent during the decade since his appointment in 1816 (from

[145] Symons, *Law*, pp. 97, 234.

[146] Shipping Committee Minutes 10–16/6/1819, 7/7/1819, 13/10/1819, 27/10/1819.

[147] Miscellaneous Letters Received 11/7/1831, E/1/177, vol. 3, ff. 124–5, BL.

Image 1: Earl of Denbigh and Indian,
by Anthony Van Dyck, *c.* 1633.

Image 2: Lady Charlotte Fitzroy and Indian, by Peter Lely, *c*.1674.

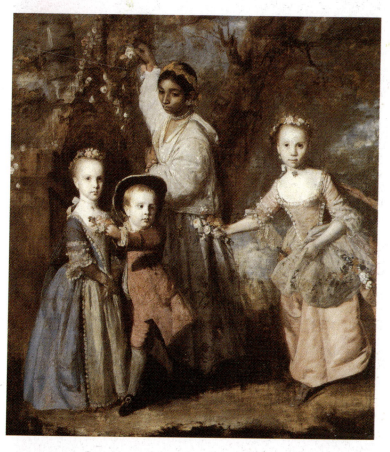

Image 3: Children of Edward Holden Cruttenden and Ayah,
by Joshua Reynolds 1759/62

Image 4:   George Clive, Family, and Ayah, by Sir Joshua Reynolds, 1765/66.

Image 5: Cheeta and Stag with Two Indians, by George Stubbs, 1765.

Image 8: Train Up a Child in the Way He Should Go; and When He Is Old He Will Not Depart from It, by William Mulready, 1841.

Image 11: Portraits of William Hickey, Esq., his favourite black servant, and his dog, by William Thomas, 1819.

Image 24: Sir David Baird Discovering the Body of
Tipu Sultan, preliminary sketch by Wilkie.

£950 to £80), received £300 retrospectively for the previous two years and an annual subsidy of £150 henceforth.[148]

The condition of lascars within and without the depot continued to draw the attentions of social reformers and Parliament. Letters to the newspapers bewailed the number of poor lascars on London's streets.[149] Various reform groups came to investigate the conditions under which lascars lived in Gole's depot. They found very different conditions from what his contract stipulated and what the Company had proclaimed were in effect.[150] They also noted that to enforce their authority, serangs continued to use corporal punishment and confinement of lascars in narrow closets, chaining them to walls or an outdoor pump, and/or imposing ostracism, supported by the other lascars. Yet, most lascars apparently accepted the authority of the serangs and submitted to their discipline.

Among the proliferating philanthropic societies that gave assistance to indigent Indians in this period were, in addition to the Society for the Protection of Asiatic Sailors (discussed above): the Society of Friends of Foreigners in Distress; the Society for the Suppression of Mendicity; the Distressed Sailor's Asylum; the Sailor's Home; the Society for Relief and Instruction of Poor Africans and Asiatics in London; and the Society for the Destitute.[151] Even as these groups criticized Gole's depot and tried to supplant it as the refuge for lascars, they simultaneously solicited donations from the directors.[152] The directors tended not to be very supportive of the efforts and financial solicitations of these various societies, arguing that the Company was already expending large sums on lascars, without the need for intervention by outsiders.

In 1834, Parliament unintentionally but profoundly transformed the experiences of lascars in Britain when it suspended the Company's

[148] Shipping Committee Minutes 26/7/1826, 2–29/8/1826. Finance and Home Committee Minutes 1/3/1836.

[149] E.g., *Times*, 20/3/1834 1d.

[150] Thomas Clarkson described a visit, dating it to 1822 although he may have meant 1814. Clarkson letter 1/11/1842 in Salter, *Asiatic*, pp. 4–5.

[151] Shipping Committee Minutes 19/2/1817 to 23/10/1833; Court Minutes 3–31/10/1821, 7/11/1821.

[152] Shipping Committee Minutes 26/6/1816.

charter to trade in Asia for twenty years. This suspension resulted from
a range of economic and political factors, beyond the plight of lascars
in Britain. Nevertheless, this legally absolved the Company of responsibility for Indians in Britain. The directors therefore terminated the
contract with Gole's depot, leaving lascars and private shipowners to
deal individually with private lodginghouse-keepers. Although Gole
asked for compensation from the Company for his now useless depot,
the directors refused (according to newspaper reports, however, he had
become quite rich from this arrangement despite his protests to the
contrary).[153] While British society and Parliament continued to hold
the directors morally accountable for lascars, especially when indigent,
no centralized system remained for their reception, maintenance, or
control. As we will see in Chapter 10, lascars then formed what would
be known as the Oriental Quarter around London's East India Docks.

Lascar Labour, the Company, and British Society

Over the period covered in this chapter, the number and experiences
of Indian seamen in Britain changed significantly, often due to factors
they could not control. Expanding British administration over India
brought efforts at more official regulation of their recruitment and
conditions of service aboard ship. In Britain, a series of Company policies and Parliamentary acts sought to manage and provide for them.
Yet, despite British efforts to seize control over the recruitment of
maritime labour supply in India, ghat serangs maintained their dominance. Further, arrangements for the reception and maintenance of
lascars in Britain never proved fully satisfactory to any of the parties
involved: the lascars, directors, contractors, and the British public.

Indian seamen were a vital economic factor in British commerce
with India, and the rest of the world. The Company regarded them as
no less costly than British seamen, but found their labour on the
passage to Britain indispensable at times. Once in Britain, however,
Indian seamen mainly represented liabilities for the directors (especially until 1834) and for private shipowners who brought them. For
the most part, these Indian seamen retained their own solidarities and

[153] Court Minutes 5/3/1834.

internal authority structure under serangs, although not without tensions. Conflicts within their number and against other seamen and the surrounding British community were frequent. For the contractors and informal service industry that grew up around these men, they represented economic opportunities as well as risks. Further, British Evangelicals and social reformers sought to reshape their values and behaviour, with much dispute but limited success. Throughout this period, what it meant to be an Indian in Britain shifted, not just for lascars but for other classes as well.

CHAPTER 5

Crossing Identity Boundaries

'Natives of India' in Britain

Especially from the late eighteenth century, people from India confronted Britons with issues of classification, in Britain as well as India. Indian wives and children of British men negotiated places for themselves in British society. Putative Indian noblemen personally presented their claims to largely uninformed British officials. 'Natives of India' sought their rights to support from the Company and free passage home, while the British state and the directors argued over whom that category actually included and excluded. Indeed, shifting official categorizations of diverse peoples from India present in Britain often clashed with both prevalent British cultural categories and the Company's immediate financial interests.

Over this period, British cultural constructions of race and ethnicity shifted at different rates and inconsistently in Britain and India. In the colonies, Britons increasingly tried to separate themselves from 'Blacks', at least officially. Simultaneously, however, many British men consorted with Indian women; some brought them and their children to Britain. The directors then began to exclude such men of part-Indian ancestry from its corps of officials and officers. Across India, the Company's political relations with Indian rulers intensified, but the legal, diplomatic, political, and moral implications of these relationships remained uncertain, especially in Britain. Working-class Indians present in Britain rapidly grew in number, which impelled both the government and the Company's directors to seek to identify and control them. Yet, these authorities often worked at cross-purposes. In these unsettled social, legal, and cultural environments, women and men from India sometimes proved able to shape how they appeared in Britain, more than they could in India.

The status of Indian wives and children in Britain depended on their background, class, and relationship with their men. As we saw in Chapter 1, Mariam gained respect in early-seventeenth-century-Britain, supported by her Christianity, diamonds, and Anglican weddings with prominent Englishmen. Subsequently, many other Indian women and children settlers also achieved recognition and acceptance by British society, with perhaps even an attractiveness due to their exotic ancestry. For those dependent on British men of lower social class, life might be more difficult and uncertain. Some—like many British women and children of the time—were abandoned by their men. In contrast, Indian men in Britain (like the professors in Chapter 3) often had authority over their British wives and mistresses.

Indian men who convinced British society of their nobility might receive a royal welcome. Imperfect communication between India and Britain, inadequate colonial archives, and British presupposition that a man's true class was evident from his comportment and accoutrements, all meant that people of middling status in India could some-times pass as nobility in Britain. Men thus accepted as high-born might convince British authorities that they were entitled to an appropriate income. Thus, travel to Britain could enable a rise in class status, although return to the colony usually meant reversion.

British laws and regulations about who was a 'native of India'—and what that officially entailed—shifted, but not as quickly as public opinion. Place of birth, ancestry (patrilineal or matrilineal), complexion, and culture (religion, language, and/or education) all occasionally defined being 'Indian': people whom the Company would take financial responsibility for housing and returning to India but also whom it would exclude from its commissioned civil and military appointments. As a result, various British authorities frequently expressed frustration in trying to reconcile these conflicting criteria. This proved all the more intense since many Britons at the time presumed that identities were largely fixed, and therefore had difficulties comprehending the differences between law and opinion, and changes in them. People from India therefore occasionally benefited from official contradictions and interstices but also sometimes suffered unexpectedly from them.

Much, but not all, of the agency in these categorizations lay with

British authorities. Yet, Indians had complex influences on Britons with whom they conversed, cohabited, or corresponded. There were often discontinuities between prevailing British attitudes towards India in the abstract and the lived experience of individual Indians in Britain. This chapter traces some of these complexities of identity until the 1830s, when Parliament largely removed from the Company responsibility for the management and control of most Indians in Britain.

Indian Wives and Children

Under spreading British colonialism, the movements of people and their agency were highly gendered. Both Britain and India remained broadly patriarchic. This often empowered Indian men, who predominated and were the large majority among those who made the journey to Britain. Virtually all Indian women and their children went to Britain as dependants.

Indian women (including servants or slaves) and their children usually followed the British men who brought them, scattering into British society. They thus lacked the corporate support available to most Indian seamen or the independent identities of Indian élite men. Most Indian wives and children adopted their British man's surname, class status, and culture, receiving varying levels of acceptance there. Their very assimilation into British society obscured their origins (then, and for us today). While Britons in their immediate social circle might know of their Indian ancestry, this knowledge affected their lives in subtle ways that changed over time, influenced by British attitudes towards India and colonialism and by their individual situations. Nevertheless, especially when Anglicized, elevated by wealth (usually extracted from India), and supported by the British man, these Indian women and children could move into the highest circles, losing much of their 'otherness' within their own lifetime. Indeed, what remained of their Indian identity might distinguish them. If completely abandoned, however, there was little they could do except depend on British charity or petition the directors for passage back to India.

In India, the British presence remained from the beginning predominantly male. Of the relatively few European women present, only an extremely small number were available to Indian men as wives, mistresses, or prostitutes.[1] Increasingly over the nineteenth century, many Britons in India disparaged most Indian men as 'effeminate', particularly those of Bengal.[2] In contrast, British men had sexual relations with significant numbers of Indian women.[3] Among other consequences, these relationships produced children of mixed descent, who became particularly problematic for British moral authority there, although less so in Britain.[4]

Based on much of the growing secondary literature about race, sex, and power within European colonialism, one might expect the British establishment to have excluded people from India, especially those of mixed ancestry, from sexual and social intercourse with Britons. For example, Ann Stoler asserts: '[the] nineteenth century [British establishment had] anxieties around Eurasians, Indos, and mestizos . . . groups seen as "mixed" by blood. They were the "enemy" within, those who might transgress the "interior frontiers" of the nation-state . . . [C]ultural hybridities were seen as subversive and subversion was contagious.'[5]

Yet through the early nineteenth century most people of mixed ancestry experienced such exclusions less in Britain than in the colony. Nor did the establishment in Britain suppress public discourse about such sexual relations there.[6]

Some people of part-Indian descent achieved great prominence in Britain. Amelia Jenkinson, nee Watts, granddaughter of an Indian woman, came to Britain and married (9 February 1769) the Earl of Liverpool. She then died giving birth to his son, Robert Banks Jenkinson

[1] See Arnold, 'European Orphans'.

[2] See Sinha, *Colonial Masculinity*. British 'martial race' theory developed in the late eighteenth century in India. Prior to 1857, however, there were relatively few expressions of British fears about Indian males posing a danger to British women. Sir Walter Scott's 1827 novel, *Surgeon's Daughter*, stands as a rare example of such fears; significantly, Scott had no direct experience of Asia.

[3] See Ghosh, 'Colonial Companions' (Ph.D., 2000).

[4] By the end of the eighteenth century, there were more people of mixed heritage than 'pure' Europeans in India. See Hawes, *Poor Relations*. Added to these were Indian and European men or women in homosexual relationships, rarely with the former on the basis of equal power with the latter.

[5] Stoler, *Race*, p. 52. See also Henriques, *Children*, and Hyam, *Empire*.

[6] See Dyce Sombre, Chapter 8.

(1770–1828), 8th Baronet Hawkesbury, 2nd Earl of Liverpool, who entered Parliament as a Tory in 1790, rising to be prime minister (1812–27, the longest term in that office during the nineteenth century).[7] His peers knew of his part-Indian ancestry, but his wealth and social position made it relatively immaterial. Most people with mixed Indian-British parentage did not rise as high (but another, Dyce Sombre, would be elected to Parliament in 1841, see Chapter 8).

Indian women who settled in Britain, because of their cross-cultural roles, drew the attention of Indian visitors. For example, around 1800 Abu Talib went out of his way to meet two Indians, wives of Anglicized Frenchmen. He later explained to his Indian readers that these Indians had settled in Britain out of devotion to their children, rather than out of love for their European men.[8] One was widely believed to have been a Hindu widow, rescued from concremation as a 'sati' on her husband's funeral pyre, converted to Christianity, and married by Gerard Gustavus Ducarel (1745–?) around 1780. The Ducarel family claimed she was a daughter of the Maharaja of Purnea in Bengal.[9] From her long years in Britain, she had Anglicized, including appearing to Abu Talib's unpractised eye as virtually English: very fair in complexion, fully Anglophone, and displaying British-style dress and deportment. Her teenage children impressed Abu Talib as fully English.

Another woman whom Abu Talib admired was Nur Begum (or Halime Begum, 1770–1853), although her treatment at the hands of her husband left her less privileged than Mrs Ducarel.[10] Nur Begum had been born into a prominent Muslim family of Lucknow. Her sister had already married William Palmer, an affluent banker of mixed British-Indian ancestry. When the French mercenary General Benoit de Boigne (1751–1830) moved to Lucknow, Nur Begum agreed to become his wife (through Islamic rites). Although de Boigne had other Indian wives and mistresses, when he retired as a wealthy man to London in 1797, he brought with him Nur Begum and their two children, Banu (*c.* 1789–1804) and Ali Bakhsh (*c.* 1790–1853). De Boigne renamed her Hélène Bennett. He received British denization

---

[7] Gash, *Lord Liverpool,* p. 10.

[8] Abu Talib, *Masir* (Persian reprint), p. 173.

[9] www.starcourse.org/emd/emdwho.htm

[10] Abu Talib, *Masir* (Persian reprint), pp. 173–5.

(1 January 1798).[11] They socialized with distinguished members of British society, including Edmund Burke and his wife.

De Boigne's ambitions, however, drove him to seek higher social status. He soon contracted a Catholic marriage with Charlotte Louise Eleonore Adelaide d'Osmonde (1781–1866), daughter of exiled and impoverished French nobility. After he promised her and her parents substantial sums, they were married in London's French Chapel (11 June 1798), making fashionable 47 Portland Place their home.[12] They baptized Nur Begum's children as Catholic and christened them Anna and Charles Alexander. De Boigne then moved Nur Begum out of London, first to Enfield and later to Lower Beeding, Sussex, giving her a modest £300 annual allowance.[13] Many prominent members of British society supported Nur Begum, offering to use British law to enforce her rights to de Boigne's vast wealth.[14] She, however, humbly refused their offers and accepted a quiet retirement. The local villagers and her English maidservant showed her respect, although they thought her exotic, as a mysterious 'dark' lady. De Boigne and his new wife eventually established themselves in 1803 at Chambery in Savoy. While de Boigne's and Nur Begum's daughter, Anna, died tragically young in 1804, their son, Charles, succeeded his father as Count de Boigne in 1830.

While the details of the lives of Amelia Jenkinson, Mrs Ducarel, Nur Begum, and their children in England are conspicuous, the general patterns were not unique. Many Indian wives of Europeans who went to Britain were dependent on the continued good-will of their men. Although of mixed Indian-British ancestry, their children often gained the class status of their father. Clearly, the respect that they achieved suggests that some Indian wives and their children could make places for themselves in Britain.

[11] De Boigne, *Memoirs*; Compton, *Particular Account*; Cotton, 'Begum'; Young, *Fountain*.

[12] Young, *Fountain*, p. 191; Family records of de Boigne, personal communication, William Dalrymple, 20/6/2001.

[13] Baldwin, *Story*, pp. 19–22; Boye, *L'Extraordinaire Aventure*, p. 149; Cotton, 'Begum', pp. 91–4; Llewellyn-Jones, *Engaging Scoundrels*, pp. 89–90, 121–2.

[14] Young, *Fountain*, pp. 213–14.

Others, however, fared not so well. Many appealed to the Company for passage home after being abandoned, widowed, or orphaned by the British man who brought them. This was particularly prevalent among working-class families. For example, in 1835, when 'Bridget Peter, a Native of Madras' lost her husband, a British soldier in His Majesty's 1st Foot Regiment, she petitioned the Directors from Chelsea Hospital 'in a state of destitution'.[15] They paid to return her and her three children to India.

In many cases, the British father sent his children to Britain, although the Indian mother did not accompany them.[16] Their status there clearly varied widely. In 1807, Charles Watkins took his 'natural daughter', Sophie, back from Bombay to Britain, but as his British family's maidservant.[17]

In contrast, Lieutenant Colonel James Achilles Kirkpatrick (1764–1805) of the Madras Army was among many Britons who treated some of his Indian children as his heirs.[18] Acceptance of such children of mixed ancestry could be greater in Britain than in the colony. In 1801, Kirkpatrick wrote comparing the opportunities available in Britain and India respectively of two of his Indian sons, an elder one already sent to England and a younger one, Mir Ghulam Ali, Sahib Allum (1801–28), recently born in India to him and Khair al-Nissa, a noblewoman of Hyderabad. For the older one,

> . . . his future happiness . . . [lies in England], rather than his native [land, due to] . . . the illiberal prejudices entertained [in India] against children born of native women, be their colour ever so fair, their conduct ever so correct, or their spirit ever so indisputable.
>
> In point of complexion, my little boy *here*, has greatly the advantage of his Brother in England, being as fair as it is possible to conceive for the offspring by any European female to be, and yet, he would, I have no doubt, be exposed to the same illiberal objections and obloquy, should he ever

[15] Court Minutes 28/7/1835.
[16] For eight wills assigning money to natural children in Europe see Ghosh, 'Colonial Companions' (Ph.D., 2000).
[17] Bombay List of Deposits (1819–20), L/MAR/C/888, BL.
[18] See Dalrymple, *White Mughals*, for a thorough account of Kirkpatrick and his family.

(which I trust he will not) be obliged to seek his misfortunes in manhood, in the country which gave him birth.[19]

Dark skin colour and part-Indian ancestry were thus, as attested by Kirkpatrick, degrading factors in India but less so in Britain.

Indeed, despite the appeals of their mother, Kirkpatrick sent Sahib Allum and their daughter, Nur al-Nissa, Sahiba Begum (1802-89), to Britain in 1805.[20] They were attended by an Indian manservant and lived with his family and then his relatives, the Stracheys. In his will, Kirkpatrick left them £10,000 each. According to his posthumous directions, they were converted and baptized in 1806, becoming William George and Catherine Aurora Kirkpatrick.[21]

Their wealth and connections enabled them to assimilate into British society. In fact, their Indian origin added to their appeal. Catherine, known as Kitty, was widely known as the 'Hindoo Princess' (illustrating the vague concepts held even in educated British society about Indian culture, since she was neither Hindu nor a princess). She was courted by Thomas Carlyle, who described her as possessing £50,000. She was, he added, 'a strangely-complexioned young lady, with soft brown eyes and floods of bronze-red hair, really a pretty-looking, smiling, and amiable, though most foreign bit of magnificence . . . a half-*Begum*; in short, an interesting specimen of the semi-oriental Englishwoman.'[22] According to family tradition, Carlyle was dismissed as her suitor since he appeared (wrongly) to have few prospects in life. Portraits of her in Britain reveal nothing about her Indian background, but rather suggest how Anglicized she had become (Images 9 and

[19] James Kirkpatrick to William Kirkpatrick 6/9/1801, 21/9/1801, Letterbooks of J.A. Kirkpatrick, MSS EUR F.228/55, BL. I thank Durba Ghosh for this reference.

[20] See Kirkpatrick letters 24/7/1802, 1/9/1802, 2/10/1802, 10/12/1802, MSS EUR F.228/57, BL.

[21] Both were baptized 25/3/1806 at Saint Mary, St Marylebone Road.

[22] Carlyle, *Collected Letters*, vol. 3, pp. 81, 166–7, 171–2; Carlyle, *Reminiscences*, pp. 107, 110–11; Conner, *George Chinnery*, pp. 61–5; Dalrymple, *White Mughals*; Elers, *Memoirs*, pp. 179–80, 186–8; Constance Russell, *Rose Goddess*, pp. 1–18; Sanders, *Strachey Family*; Strachey, 'Carlyle'; Strachey, 'Romantic Marriage', pp. 18–29.

Images 9 and 10: Portraits of Catherine Aurora Kirkpatrick,
artist unknown.

10).[23] Indeed, both she and her brother married Britons and died there, leaving children as members of British society.[24] Thus they, like many other women and men of Indian or part-Indian ancestry, negotiated with the Britons around them, their Indian origin being only one of the many factors comprising their identities.

Indians Claiming Nobility in Britain

With the spread of colonialism, Indians claiming noble status increasingly advanced their causes in Britain. Men whose claims had been rejected in India learned that London would consider their appeals from a fresh and largely uninformed, albeit wary, perspective. As we have seen, earlier Indian appellants received mixed responses: merchants Nowroji Rustamji, Cojamaul, and Rafael achieved much through legal and political manoeuvring but diplomats I'tisam al-Din and Hanumantrao gained less; some serangs and lascars secured their rights but others failed. Even into the early nineteenth century, the British government and the Company's directors had only sketchy and obsolete knowledge and limited experience dealing with such people. Instead, authorities in Britain attempted to assess each arrival based on British cultural assumptions about his class. This occasionally led to favourable treatment for Indian noblemen (or claimants to that status) that did not accord with the political desires of the Company's administration in India. Consequently, the directors worked to develop their archive of precedents and of reports and correspondence from India. Nor did Indians always accurately anticipate their reception. All this resulted in complex multi-sided negotiations over the visitor's identity.

---

[23] Compare these portraits to George Chinnery's 'Sahib Allum and Sahiba Begam Kirkpatrick' (*c.* 1804, HSBC Collection), painted before they left India, which shows them in Indian dress. While most Indians painted in India appeared in Indian clothing, many Indians in Britain wore British dress for their portraits.

[24] George married (11/3/1822) Englishwoman Catherine Turner, had three daughters, and died at age 27. Catherine married Englishman Captain John Winslowe Phillips (1802–64) of the élite 7th Hussars, had seven children, and died in 1889. See Censuses, 1841–81, and IGI.

Indians whose entourage, deportment, and claims appeared convincingly noble sometimes received an honoured welcome in Britain. In 1806, Sidi Ali Mahomet Chughai arrived, claiming to be heir to the Nawab of Surat (whom the Company had deposed in 1800).[25] Attended by two servants, Sidi Abdul Rahman and Sidi Mahmoud, he presented a letter of introduction from the Emperor of Morocco, who had just hosted him. The British government, including His Majesty's ministers and the Board of Control, received him, heard his claims, and recommended him to the directors. The directors found no information in the Company's records regarding him, and made no explicit promises, but conveyed him to Bombay in dignity, at their expense. There, that government provided him a house and handsome allowance, until its inquiries embarrassingly disclosed that he was only a cashiered military officer, not nobility at all. The directors then chastised the Bombay government for his inappropriate reception and expense.[26]

Three years later, both London and Madras provided dignified and costly accommodation to Prince Mahomed Hussein Khan, a man with only slightly better credentials than Sidi Ali Mahomet. Mahomed Hussein claimed the province of Cuddapah as a jagir which, because his family had supported the British, they had lost to the Mysore sultans decades earlier. Mahomed Hussein had also made his way across north Africa, acquiring letters of introduction to King George III from the rulers of Egypt, Tunis, Algiers, and Morocco.[27] In 1809, Lord Liverpool (of part-Indian descent as we have seen) met him personally. Accompanied by his secretary, religious advisor, and their servants, Mahomed Hussein apparently also made a strong impression on the British public. A French visitor to London noted:

> There are many native East Indians lately landed. They walk about the town with immense umbrellas, particoloured, red and white, in alternate ribs, and a deep fringe all round . . . These men, who seem to be people of some consequence, are extremely small and meagre. It must seem to them

[25] Court Minutes 8/10/1806; Log of Earl of St Vincent, L/MAR/B/209E, BL.

[26] Bombay to Court, Secret Committee 29/9/1806, L/PS/5/323; Board Collections F/4/355, no. 8299, BL.

[27] Court Minutes 1/11/1809.

as if they were among Patagonians, although the inhabitants of London have no particular claim to size. They are much stared at, but not insulted. An English mob is not that rude unmannerly thing it is generally taken for. It is difficult to conjecture what idea an East Indian may form, beforehand, of the mighty *company* and its august court [of directors]; but I should think they must experience some surprise as he approaches the foot of his sovereign's throne, in Leaden Hall Street.[28]

This Frenchman's account both reflected the public's appreciation of the exotic quality of these men and also ridiculed both the British and the Company.

Although the British government never identified Mahomed Hussein, it ordered the Royal Navy ship *Bucephalus* to convey him and his attendants in state to India. When he reached Madras (May 1810), that government also treated him as royalty, despite its utter ignorance about his case. They reimbursed the *Bucephalus* for its expenses, totaling Pagodas 7,000 (£2,500)—particularly high since 'from the peculiar tenets of his religion they had to provide him a separate table . . .'. Meanwhile, explicitly aware of how Bombay had been chastised a few years earlier for hosting Sidi Ali Mahomet, Madras officials wrote to London for instructions. Meanwhile, they provided him with another Pagodas 1,000 (Rs 3,500) for his immediate expenses and arranged his conveyance over land to Bombay. The official in charge tried to protect himself against accusations of extravagance by explaining '. . . I think the above terms are the easiest on which he can be got rid of.'

As Mahomed Hussein Khan approached Bombay, however, that government cited its reprimand over Sidi Ali Mahomet three years earlier as justification for refusing to receive this putative nobleman before they could investigate. Bombay's extensive inquiries finally discovered he was only the descendant of a Pathan minor official who had served in Cuddapah and then in the Maratha cavalry.[29] He had married into the family of the former nawab of Surat but his wife's early death annulled any claim to that family's property. The Bombay government thus refused him any support, while the Madras government received rebuke from the directors for its expenditures. Once again, the imperfect information available in London led to an embarrassing

[28] Simond, *Journal*, vol. 2, p. 280.
[29] Board Collections F/4/355, no. 8299, BL.

failure to identify a visiting Indian putative nobleman. Yet another man who married a daughter of the former nawab of Surat's family did much better when he went to London decades later, ultimately winning the family's title and vast pension (see Chapter 7).

Although Sidi Ali Mahomet and Mahomed Hussein Khan misled the British with their pretensions, the British continued to take very seriously the claims of similar men. Most British élites believed former rulers were morally owed a life of dignity. Further, the British commitment to the protection of private property sometimes extended to Indians who could demonstrate their rights in British law.

Nawab Faiz Ali Khan Bahadur had claims similar to those of Mahomed Hussein Khan: rights to territories his family once held but that had been seized by the Mysore sultans despite British guarantees in exchange for his support. These claims came from his father, Nawab Hyat Sahib, once governor of the rich province of Bednore, appointed by Tipu Sultan. In 1783, when hard pressed militarily, the Company had determined to seduce Tipu Sultan's commanders into treason; they promised Hyat Sahib personal protection and a large share of Bednore's tax revenues if he would support them.[30] He did so, but the British were subsequently defeated, forcing him to flee. To encourage future defectors and to fulfill its promises, the Company awarded him a pension of Rs 48,000 annually. Since he had lost all his personal property when the Company failed to defend Bednore, he thereafter made a series of claims for reimbursement, as well as increases in his pension. British officials in Bombay did not want to satisfy these, but did not feel justified in rejecting them either, and so tended to ignore his appeals.[31] On his death in 1799, the Bombay government slashed the pension to his family in half, entrusting his widows and young children to the management of a Parsi merchant, Ardaseer Dady.[32] The eldest of his sons, Faiz Ali Khan (b.1786), however, eventually quarrelled with this guardian. The British circulated reports that Faiz Ali had fallen into dissolute ways, which he admitted but blamed his poor upbringing on the irresponsibility of his guardian and, by extension, the British. When Faiz Ali reached maturity, he demanded that

[30] Board Minutes 8/2/1785.
[31] Court Minutes 3/7/1793, 24/8/1796.
[32] Court Minutes 27/7/1808.

the British transfer management of his family's pension and estate from Dady to himself. The Company refused, but then Dady went bankrupt and died in 1810, leaving Faiz Ali even further in debt. Additionally, as Hyat Sahib's widows and younger son died, the Company reduced the family's pension proportionately; indeed, subsequent to each death, it demanded a refund for advances paid against their future pensions.

Faiz Ali, receiving no satisfactory answers from the Bombay government, decided in 1816 to go to London himself to demand justice. When the British refused him permission to go, he applied to send a representative. The Bombay government delayed for three years before giving consent to this. Finally, early in 1819, his envoy, Shaykh Ghulam Muhyi al-Din, reached London with a suite via Cairo, Naples, and Paris, collecting letters of introduction from each of those governments. The directors first refused and then reluctantly agreed to recognize him as accredited agent, but would not pay the ambassador's allowance he demanded. He vowed he would not leave London until Faiz Ali had received justice.[33]

Muhyi al-Din soon learned how the British system worked. He hired London lawyers—Smith, Inglis, and Company—to prosecute his case. These lawyers renewed Hyat Sahib's claim to 120,000 Pagodas (Rs 420,000) of property lost when Bednore fell more than three decades earlier, and demanded the full Rs 48,000 annual pension. The directors agreed to consider minor adjustments in the current pension of Rs 24,000 but refused to recognize Faiz Ali's right to that long-lost property (nevertheless, they ordered their officials in India to investigate, with inconclusive results). The directors proved more sympathetic to his assertion that Bombay had retained Dady as administrator over Faiz Ali's objections and therefore that Dady's financial mismanagement was morally the Company's responsibility.

Muhyi al-Din supplied Faiz Ali with copies of official documents relevant to his case, documents not available in India but in the public domain in London. Further, based on what he learned in London, he informed his master about various authorities in Britain that could override the directors. Using these, Faiz Ali strengthened his cause. He

[33] Court Minutes 20–7/1/1819, 12/2/1819, 3/3/1819; Correspondence Committee Minutes, 12–17/3/1819, 20/8/1819, 1/9/1819.

threatened the directors that: 'Parliament need only to be informed of
my wrongs to immediately order me redress with every suitable satisfaction.'[34] He also stated his right to use British law courts: 'This sum
lawfully due to me I know I can recover of your government in the
Court of Common Pleas in England.' Nevertheless, he added, he
would instead trust to the justice of the directors and only resort to
these other authorities if they refused him.

Meanwhile, Muhyi al-Din (like many other visitors) found life in
London astoundingly expensive. He ran up debts for which he faced
imprisonment. Indeed, a member of his suite, Syed Qamr al-Din,
appealed to the directors that Muhyi al-Din had unjustly fired him
without pay, and volunteered to testify against him in court.[35] To save
Muhyi al-Din from debtor's prison, and also to induce him to leave
London, the Directors advanced him money, conditional on his departing forthwith. Eventually, they give him £3,500 to pay off his
debts and secure passage home, although, over his objections, they intended to deduct this amount from Faiz Ali's pension in £50 monthly
instalments.

While Ghulam Muhyi al-Din suffered humiliation in London, his
mission actually gained much for his master. In May 1819, although
the directors refused to tell Muhyi al-Din in London about this, they
instructed Bombay to grant most of his appeals: to forgive the excess
advances to Faiz Ali's late relatives, to restore the pension to Rs 48,000
(double its current amount), and to pay another Rs 40,000 cash to
cover the expenses of Hyat Sahib's funeral twenty years earlier.[36] Muhyi
al-Din refused to leave Britain, however, until he learned the directors'
decision, either from them or from his employer. He asserted that if
he remained in London for the additional eighteen months necessary
to hear back from India, he would need another £5,000 advance from
the Company. The directors refused to give more. On his part, Faiz Ali
found the Company's compromise offers inadequate, ordering Muhyi
al-Din not to leave without full satisfaction of his claims.

Finally, Muhyi al-Din heard solemn assurances, given to him personally but unofficially by members of the Board of Control and directors, that his master's other claims would be sympathetically dealt

[34] Board Collections F/4/653, no. 17958, BL.
[35] Correspondence Committee Minutes 13/8/1819.
[36] Board Collections F/4/653, no. 17958, BL.

with.[37] Consequently, he returned to Bombay in 1821. Either the board and directors falsely promised Muhyi al-Din more to get rid of him, or else he exaggerated his success to his employer. In any case, Faiz Ali felt betrayed when the expected result never materialized. To add to their difficulties, the ship carrying all the collected correspondence and documents to the governor-general sank in the Bay of Bengal.

After Muhyi al-Din returned to Bombay, he and Faiz Ali continued their struggle for years. They repeated their reminders to the directors that promises made remained unfulfilled. The Bombay government responded to these repeated demands only minimally, forgiving the money that London advanced to Muhyi al-Din in order to get him to leave London.[38]

Informed by Muhyi al-Din, an opposition London newspaper, *The British and Indian Observer*, took up Faiz Ali's cause as another proof of the government's tyranny in India. That newspaper's proprietors wrote to Faiz Ali in 1823, expressing how they 'with horror and indignation have seen the treachery and villainy practiced by the East India Company equally base and ungrateful [both] incompatible with the dignity of men and disgraceful to the honour of the British Nation.'[39] They also solicited his financial support for their newspaper's efforts on his behalf. There had long been in Britain an opposition to the government which sought to use the injustices they apprehended in India for their own domestic British political purposes. Over time, future Indian missions would learn to ally with this opposition to advance their causes as well.

In 1824, after three years of vain waiting, Muhyi al-Din notified the directors that he, and the nawab himself, intended to return to London and resume their campaign. In response to the urgent insistence of directors that this be prevented, the Bombay government replied that they would 'dissuade him from proceeding to England, and will use all our means to discourage the resort of [all] Natives of India to

[37] Miscellaneous Letters Received E/1/139, f. 161; E/1/141, ff. 58, 167, 270, 353–5, 423–5, BL; Court Minutes 19/5/1819 to 31/10/1821; Correspondence Committee Minutes 21/1/1820 to 6/9/1820.

[38] Board Collections F/4/653, no. 17958; Examiner's Office, 9/2/1819, O/6/9, BL.

[39] 'Prospectus for the British and Indian Observer' 11/9/1823, Board Collections F/4/653, no. 26069(2), BL.

England for the purpose of procuring redress'. Nevertheless, Faiz Ali persisted in his intention to go to London himself or send Muhyi al-Din once more.[40]

The Company had mixed feelings about actually forbidding Faiz Ali, or others like him, from going to London. The directors repeatedly expressed their desire to keep Indian diplomats and political agents from bringing their grievances to London. After a landholder from Badowa (near Bareilly) made the journey in 1817 to petition for redress, the directors repeated their instruction that the Indian government 'prevent as far as possible' such journeys of appeal.[41] When this accomplished little, they wrote yet again in 1823: 'The coming of Natives of India to this Country, you would of course always discourage to the extent of your power.'[42] Yet these authorities also recognized that they had no legal way to bar such missions.

In the case of Faiz Ali, the Bombay governor opined that the Company should perhaps agree to let him go, and even pay his pension in England, if only to silence the opposition press and display Faiz Ali's disappointment: 'it is best for [the Company's] reputation to give this man every encouragement consistent with a candid exposition of the hopelessness of his case.'[43] In the end, however, neither Faiz Ali nor Muhyi al-Din made another journey to Britain, but settled for the financial gains from the earlier mission.

In the midst of the negotiations with Faiz Ali, other claimants to Indian nobility arrived in London. In 1821, 'Prince Muly Abdallah ben Zaffer' from Bombay personally approached the directors for support.[44] He, like Sidi Ali and Hussein Ali, had come to London via Morocco; unlike them, he claimed to have been robbed of his property

[40] Miscellaneous Letters Received, E/1/154, ff. 413–14, BL.

[41] Hussein Ali Khan arrived claiming that he had been unjustly deprived of some property in the town of Badowa. The directors refused to decide his case, but they did direct the Bengal government to investigate, something that he would not have obtained had he not come to Britain. Court Minutes 13/1/1818, 4/2/1818; Correspondence Committee Minutes 16–30/1/1818; Personal Records O/6/8, BL.

[42] Board Collections F/4/868, no. 22939(2), BL.

[43] Board Collections F/4/653, no. 26069, BL.

[44] Court Minutes 27/6/1821, 11–17/7/1821.

there. Also unlike them, he only requested a small sum to cover his expenses in Britain and then a free passage home in the style that was appropriate for his noble status. The Company, apparently feeling that it had twice been deceived by similar claimants, repeatedly rejected his several appeals.[45] He seems then to have gone on to Algiers. Thus, the directors had decided not to honour all Indian claimants to royal treatment.

More recognized by the British, but also inscrutable to them, was another Indian dignitary of the Awadh royal dynasty: Nawab Bahadur, Shamshir Khan al-Mulk, Mirza Shah Mir Khan, Fakir al-Daula, Iftikhar (d. 1830). In 1821, Shah Mir independently determined to make the journey from Calcutta to London. He was a distant cousin and in-law of the incumbent Awadh ruler, but from a collateral branch long living in Bengal under British protection.[46] He enjoyed a comfortable pension of Rs 18,000 annually from an endowment entrusted to the Company decades earlier. He set off, accompanied by two wives and many servants, to express general but unspecified grievances about his situation.

The directors found his arrival in London (May 1822) unexpected and puzzling; they never understood what he wanted. The British public, however, immediately desired to view this Indian royalty, and more particularly his royal women. On the whole, both the directors and the British public were disappointed by what they observed, nor did Shah Mir's experiences of Britain live up to his hopes.

As reported in the *Annual Register* under notable events of the year, he was identified (inaccurately) as 'his highness prince Nawab Meer Shaw Khan, son of the King of Delhi'.[47] This journal continued: 'Every attempt, during the voyage, and since his arrival, by [British] gentlemen to see . . . two of the principal ladies of his harem . . . has been abortive. The [British] ladies, who have been admitted, describe them

[45] Miscellaneous Letters Received 13/7/1821, E/1/257, BL; Shipping Committee Minutes 29/6/1821, 11–25/7/1821.

[46] He was a descendant of the Bahu Begum, a widow of a nawab of Awadh, who had left her fortune to the Company and her descendants to its care and protection. One British official reported that Shah Mir had married a daughter of the ruling Awadh nawab.

[47] *Annual Register* (1822), p. 91

as low in stature, pitted with the small-pox, and very uninteresting.'
On his part, Shah Mir and his party anticipated a royal welcome.
When their arrival at east London's Blackwall Docks went initially
unnoticed by the government and directors, they proceeded to the
Plough Tavern to await a welcoming delegation.

The directors finally became aware of his presence and arranged a
reception they considered appropriate to his royal status.[48] They paid
the import duty on his baggage (which duty was usually forgiven by
the Customs in the case of visiting royalty). The directors also dispatched retired Colonel John Baillie, M.P., to serve as official escort.[49]
With the directors' approval, Baillie advanced Shah Mir funds in £100
increments as needed; like the customs duty, they deducted these payments from his pension. Since Shah Mir generally carried a credit on
his account (which was very unusual for pensioned noblemen), the
directors felt comfortable advancing him money.

After submitting his Persian language petition to the directors about
the general injuries he had suffered, Shah Mir agreed to return to Bengal. He does not seem to have demanded any particular changes in his
pension or situation, nor did the directors offer him any. Baillie arranged his departure for November, advancing £500 so he could purchase accoutrements for the trip and paying £700 for his passage and
that of his suite. Shah Mir, however, exhibited what the British began
to regard as somewhat erratic behaviour. He changed his mind about
departing, at the cost of forfeiting half the passage fee, but then succumbed to British pressure and sailed back to India.

On reaching Calcutta, he unpacked and almost immediately boarded
a ship back to England, again accompanied by two wives and many servants, arriving in March 1824.[50] The Bengal government had tried in
vain to prevent this second trip, and knew of no reason for Shah Mir
to undertake it except for 'a disgust conceived towards his native country, and a decided preference for England, operating upon his flighty
and unsettled disposition.'[51]

[48] Court Minutes 31/5/1822 to 18/12/1822; Correspondence Committee
Minutes 3/7/1822 to 20/12/1822.
[49] Hodson, *List*, vol. 1, p. 73.
[50] Correspondence Committee Minutes 3/12/1823, 28/4/1824, 5/5/1824.
[51] Board Collections F/4/868, no. 22939(2), BL.

This time, he had learned as royalty to request exemption from customs duties, which was granted. The directors advanced him £1,000 and assigned Captain Franklin as his escort.[52] Within months, however, Shah Mir had pawned most of his 'Bullion, Jewels, Trinkets and Shawls' for £350 and been incarcerated for debt in the King's Bench prison.[53] One of his servants, Sirk Sadi, who had been with him for a decade, complained of being dismissed without the two years' pay due him (at Rs 10 monthly) and brought suit against him for this, plus his expenses in England and for his return to India, eventually being awarded £163 16s. 10d. by the court.[54]

The directors found Shah Mir's continued presence in London brought only dishonour on them and on him, particularly as he remained in debtor's prison. They tried advancing him money to clear his debts, and when that failed, to withhold money until he would leave Britain. After several months in prison, he finally agreed to go. The Company negotiated payments to his many creditors. He was released in January 1825.[55] He wrote in flowery Persian his gratitude to the directors for securing his liberation.[56]

Once again, however, the directors found it frustratingly difficult to actually get him and his suite on a ship. He expressed strong but contradictory desires to go variously to Constantinople, Mecca, and India. Finally, the combined efforts of a Turkish intermediary living in London, Sadi Ombark Benby, and various British agents of the directors, induced Shah Mir to sail for Egypt, from whence they hoped he would proceed back to India.[57] Instead, he established himself in Alexandria. Both his wives died there, one leaving an infant girl. Shah Mir, over the next five years until his death in May 1830, sank ever more deeply

[52] This was apparently James Franklin (1783–1834) who was on leave at this time. Hodson, *List*, vol. 2, p. 214. Correspondence Committee Minutes 1/9/1824 to 20/4/1825; Court Minutes 28/4/1824.
[53] Miscellaneous Letters Received, E/1/156, vol. 1, ff. 300–2; E/1/160, vol. 1, ff. 140–4, BL.
[54] Court Minutes 18/8/1824.
[55] Court Minutes 14–26/1/1825, 13/4/1825.
[56] Miscellaneous Letters Received E/1/156, vol. 1, ff. 88–91, BL; Correspondence Committee Minutes 2/2/1825.
[57] Court Minutes 10/8/1825; Miscellaneous Letters Received, E/1/156, vol. 1, ff. 343–5, 363, BL.

into what the Company's agents described as violent insanity and religious asceticism.[58]

The example of Shah Mir in Britain suggests the complexity of interactions between Indian noblemen and the British. The directors and British public expected Shah Mir and his wives to meet their notions of the exotic oriental. His wives disappointed in their plainness; Shah Mir only presented the directors with embarrassing and incomprehensible actions. On the part of this Indian nobleman, Britain was clearly attractive enough to visit twice, yet he found British behaviour incomprehensible. His evidently unsettled mental condition may have been brought on by his encounters there, or it may have been the impetus for his travels. Ultimately, he withdrew into a life in Egypt that focused on Islamic piety. His British custodians there could not appreciate what he was doing, but they continued to use his ample pension to provide for his needs, to protect him from the consequences of his violence toward his servants and family members, and to care for his infant daughter. British public opinion was often strikingly sympathetic and tolerant toward unbalanced noblemen (British and Indian).

Over the nineteenth century, negotiations and struggles for control over information by Indian envoys and authorities in London became increasingly asymmetrical (see Chapter 7). Indian envoys, originating from across India, continued to arrive with quite uneven knowledge about what they would encounter in London. They also brought variant levels of skill and resources to manoeuvre within British politics. While some learned from earlier missions, many came woefully unprepared for what they encountered in Britain. In contrast, the directors' experience dealing with a variety of Indian missions accumulated over time, as did their bureaucratic procedures and archive of records, reports, and correspondence from India. All this enabled them to identify and manage successive Indian missions more effectively. Nonetheless, Indian identities and status in Britain remained unsettled and contested, reflecting the actions of both Britons and Indians.

[58] Board Collections F/4/868, no. 22939(2); F/4/912, no. 25727; Miscellaneous Letters Received, E/1/163, vol. 4, ff. 627–8, 632–6, BL; Correspondence Committee Minutes 5/7/1826 to 5/11/1830; Court Minutes 22/12/1829 to 29/9/1830.

Contested Definitions of Indian Identity

British cultural expectations and legal classifications of 'natives of India' both shifted inconsistently over this period, and the interests of various British authorities often differed. In particular, the directors set policies both about exactly whom it would allow into the upper ranks of its employees and also whom it would take financial and moral responsibility for. Yet these policies often clashed with the current British consensus as well as legal definitions set by Parliament. Further, Indians, particularly those on the margins, continually challenged British efforts to define them. As colonialism deepened, however, the scope for Indian agency in this process generally diminished.

From the late eighteenth century, the directors sought increasingly to exclude Indians from its commissioned officers and officials. Yet, who was a 'native of India' remained unclear. In 1791, the directors were compelled by an individual case to articulate their current convictions. In London, a man calling himself John Turing received nomination by a director as a cadet for the Madras Army.[59] The chairman of the Committee of Shipping, however, informed the other directors that Turing 'appears to be a Native of India'. Indeed, he was the Anglicized son of a British official, the former Resident at Ganjam (in Orissa), and a woman from south India. The directors summoned Turing for their own close visual scrutiny and then, having ordered him to step out, immediately and unanimously resolved: 'That no Person, the son of a Native Indian, shall henceforth be appointed by this Court to employment in the Civil, Military, or Marine Service of the Company'.[60] Rejected by the directors as an officer, the next day Turning requested and received their official permission to return to Bengal as 'a Native'.

The timing of this formative 1791 resolution reflected both British desires and fears of the time, but also the immediate need to decide an individual case. The regulation thus articulated the directors' hitherto

[59] Appointments as cadet came by nomination by one of the Company's directors or by the British government. If the possessor of such patronage would not give such an appointment, he might sell it. Indeed, men who themselves had received a cadetship on occasion resold it. Although sales of cadetships were not legal, they were common, and openly advertised in newspapers.

[60] Court Minutes 19–20/4/1791.

implicit beliefs and formally established the Company's policy for the next two decades. Yet, this was not always a clear policy to enforce since no definition of 'native of India' was specified. Nonetheless, as other cases came up, the directors felt compelled to extend this same principle to other high appointments. Only eight months later, the directors voted by ballot to exclude sons of 'Native Indians' from appointments as 'Officers of the Company's [merchant] ships'.[61]

Yet, political influence in individual cases could affect the directors' implementation of this new policy. In March 1792, less than a year after the directors unanimously passed their 1791 resolution against the appointment of 'Natives', a frequent chairman of the directors (six times over 1784–94), William Devaynes nominated a man called Charles Holloway to be an official. Although the directors recognized that he was a 'Native of India', they voted by ballot to suspend their new rule in his case.[62]

Similar imprecision among the directors about how to define identities also came up in a different way, also in December 1791. When faced with one individual's case, the directors considered whether to continue the customary waiver of the £12 permission fee for entry into India for 'European Natives of India' (and if so, who qualified as such). After three weeks of heated discussion, they finally were ready to vote on a motion dealing with part of the issue: 'That the Children born in India of British European parents be permitted to go thither, provided either of their Parents be living and resident in India.'[63] This motion proved so divisive that the directors split exactly. The lot cast to determine the issue fell in the affirmative, so the customary waiving of the permission fee continued for 'European Natives of India' who met this qualification of at least one parent being alive and in India. In contrast, people of solely European descent who did not meet that parental qualification, even if they had been born and/or long resident in India, could only return there with the Company's costly permission, unless employed by the Company, of course.

The directors' overall impulse of the age was to seek to 'purify' its

⁶¹ Court Minutes 9/11/1791.

⁶² Factors determining this exception apparently included Devaynes' influence and that the writership was at Fort Marlborough (in Sumatra). Court Minutes 1/3/1792.

⁶³ Court Minutes 7–22/12/1791.

upper services in other ways as well. In February 1792, the directors resolved: 'That in future no foreigners shall be admitted into the Company's service, as Writer or Cadet.'[64] They did not, however, define 'foreigner', leading to future ambiguity on this definition as well.

As new questions arose from specific cases, the directors continued to extend their exclusion, based on the 1791 principle. In February 1800 Mr Hercules Ross, 'a Native of the Island of Jamaica', presented himself for appointment as Third Mate of an East India ship. The Shipping Committee examined him and reported, 'from the appearance of Mr Ross, the Committee apprehend that both his Parents were not Europeans.' Based on his 'complexion', they turned him down and recommended that the directors again expand the 1791 resolution by excluding 'Persons born in the West India Islands, whose Parents are not Natives of Great Britain or Ireland', which the directors did.[65] The interests of the Company, however, produced inconsistent definitions, and often conflicted with those of the British government.

Returning to the issue of working-class people for whom the Company was legally responsible, we find opposing sets of interests between Parliament and the Company. In the early nineteenth century, reflecting current British policies and cultural categories as well as the government's immediate interests, Parliament specified the range of people for whom the Company was legally responsible and also excluded those people from the category British. These definitions both benefited and disadvantaged people from India, depending on their circumstances. In 1814, Parliament specifically named the directors as 'trustees for the *Asiatic* Sailors, *Lascars* and Natives' from all territories covered in its charter. The Company's solicitor repeatedly advised the directors that, since their charter covered all lands from south Africa east to the Pacific, this act meant they would have to accept legal responsibility in Britain for 'natives' of all those places.[66] Accordingly, directors voted to instruct Gole's depot to accept financial liability for 'all Black Men, navigating ships from India, whether Natives of India, or not', if they were in distress.[67] Subsequently East Africans and even

[64] Court Minutes 9/2/1792.

[65] Court Minutes 19/2/1800.

[66] Shipping Committee Minutes 30/11/1814; Lascar Papers, vol. 1, f. 59.

[67] Shipping Committee Minutes 2/6/1813, 15/12/1813, 25/11/1814, 12/4/1831.

Chinese merchants thus also received food and shelter from the directors.

The next year, Parliament narrowed the definition of British seamen by amending the Navigation Acts legally to exclude from that
category all 'Asiatic sailors, Lascars, [and] Natives [of all Company
territories]'.[68] While West Indians and West Africans from Britain's
colonies thus could count as 'British', East Africans, Indians, and other
Asians could not. One main reason for this exclusion was the desire by
British sailors to eliminate Indians from competition as maritime
labourers following the end of the Napoleonic Wars when the British
navy demobilized and discharged thousands of seamen. These Parliamentary territorial rather than 'racial' distinctions had powerful consequences on people, but failed to conclude the ongoing disputes over
identity faced by the Company.

On their part, the directors hoped to pass onto other bodies the
financial burden for some of the indigent people assigned to it by
Parliament. When in 1815 an African seaman, whose father lived in
Bengal, applied for maintenance and return passage there, Gole initially accepted him into the Company's expense. The directors, however, ordered that he be instead 'sent to the African Society' for their
charity. Only if that Society rejected him would he be allowed back
into the Company's care and cost at the depot.[69] A week later, two
other Africans were expelled from Gole's depot, on the grounds that
they came to Britain on contract terms as British sailors, and also that
they were not destitute.[70]

The Company's policy still was not, however, fully in accord with
the law. In July 1816, on the advice of their lawyer, the directors again
had to broaden their definition, by resolving that all 'Seamen of
Colour . . . whether Africans, Portuguese, or others' who had arrived
from India should be received into the depot and shipped back; physiognomy and region thus both mattered.[71] Yet, the Company's (and
Britain's) classification of peoples remained conflicted, particularly
when the cost of maintaining and returning people was involved.

    [68] Act 55, Geo. 3, *c.* 116. PP, Returns (Commons), 1814–15, vol. 2, paper
281, pp. 587–91 and paper 360, pp. 593–7.
    [69] Shipping Committee Minutes 7/7/1815.
    [70] Shipping Committee Minutes 12–19/7/1815.
·   [71] Shipping Committee Minutes 24/7/1816.

While the directors struggled with identifying which people were entitled to its protection based on Parliament's territorial strictures, they also continued to determine whom they wanted to exclude from Company employment as officials or officers, based on visual and biological criteria. In October 1816, they moved to expand their 1791 resolution to include both ancestry and complexion: 'no person, the grandson of a Native Indian shall henceforward be appointed by this Court to employment in the Civil, Military, or Marine Service of the Company; and that no person whether a Native of Asia, the West Indies, America, or Africa, shall be eligible to employment, whose colour shall appear exceptionable . . .'.[72] The complexity and implications of this resolution, however, meant that, before voting, the directors first referred it to their Committee of Correspondence (the subcommittee which handled particularly vital issues). That Committee was completely divided over this issue.[73] In the meantime, a related issue arose when an Iranian, Mirza Jaafar, came to Britain to improve his English, and then requested permission to study at Addiscombe. The Committee of Correspondence decided that they did not want British military science to be available to non-Britons and they refused him admission.[74] Just a week later, the Committee resumed the long delayed consideration of the proposed expansion of the 1791 resolution. Finally, after more than seven months of deliberation, the committee resolved not to record any opinion at all.[75] This avoidance of the issue, however, did not make it disappear.

By 1819 the directors recognized that their current policy of taking responsibility at Gole's depot for 'all people of Colour' in 'distress' had produced 'great inconvenience' and substantial expense.[76] They therefore revised that policy, requiring that each person seeking support apply to their recently created Lascar Committee in person and be interrogated by its clerk to prove they were actually qualified by being

[72] The Military Seminary Committee, which oversaw the Addiscombe College, had experience scrutinizing cadets, who came from more diverse backgrounds than civil service appointees. Court Minutes 23/10/1816.

[73] Correspondence Committee Minutes 24/1/1817.

[74] Miscellaneous Court Letters 14–29/5/1817, E/1/253, BL; Correspondence Committee Minutes 28/5/1817.

[75] Correspondence Committee Minutes 4/6/1818.

[76] Shipping Committee Minutes 17/12/1819.

both a native of a territory within the Company's charter and also 'in distress'. Should the clerk have any doubts about the man's identity, he should consult a member of the committee for further examination and interrogation, or, lacking that, consult Gole.

This procedure led to disputes with private shipowners who had a financial interest in disqualifying their seamen from inclusion as 'natives of India'. In 1819, the owners of the ship *Cyrus* claimed five of its seamen were natives of Portugal, while the seamen themselves claimed to be natives of India and therefore entitled to maintenance and a free trip home at the ship owner's expense. The Company believed the seamen, not the owners, and billed them for its costs. The owners then demanded proof that the men were indeed 'natives of India'.[77] Rather than citing documentary evidence, the Lascar Committee asserted that they could tell Indians when they examined them, based on 'their appearance and also from the circumstance of their being able, without any difficulty, to speak the language of the Country from whence they stated they came.' Similarly, the committee instructed other private shipowners about the identities of their seamen, based on the committee's own scrutiny alone.[78]

In July 1820 the directors reiterated that all people seeking admission to the depot and passage home must immediately submit to the Shipping Committee for visual inspection and oral interrogation.[79] The next month, however, the Company's solicitor advised them that their current limitations in defining 'Natives of India' were illegal. He explained that even '. . . natives of Manila . . . are Natives of a territory within the limits of the Charter of the East India Company, and are to be provided for as such, under the Act . . . notwithstanding they may be subjects of His Majesty the King of Spain.'[80] The directors thereupon reversed their most recent policy and again broadened the definition of their responsibility to accord with this interpretation of the current law.

Nonetheless, the directors' visual and oral examinations continued to be the basis of their categorization of individuals. A man called John Tobin entered his ship's books on the voyage from India to Britain as

[77] Shipping Committee Minutes 17/11/1819, 1–14/12/1819.
[78] Shipping Committee Minutes 11/11/1818.
[79] Shipping Committee Minutes 12/7/1820.
[80] Shipping Committee Minutes 23/8/1820.

a native Brazilian. After arriving in London, however, he claimed to the Company's Lascar Committee that he was actually 'Asiatic' and therefore legally entitled to maintenance at the depot and free passage to India. The committee interrogated him, and convinced by his ability to speak 'the English and Hindoo [*sic*] languages', supported him and conveyed him home.[81] Thus, a person's status depended not on how he was classified in the ship's or other records, but on how the committee classified his ethnicity based on physical appearance and language abilities.

The directors also publicly disputed with other authorities over who was responsible for whom. In front of London's Lord Mayor in 1820, the Company and the Portuguese consul quarrelled over the identity of one seaman, named Martin Antonio. The directors asserted he was a native of Madeira island, which lay outside its charter and therefore its responsibility. They further declared that they would only pay for 'Portuguese Natives of India not born of European parents who are engaged in navigating Ships belonging to, or in the employ of, the Company, or of Private Merchants trading to India . . . when found in distress in this Country . . . '.[82] Thus parentage, occupation, and condition all were factors. Over subsequent years, the directors engaged in further multisided contests, occasionally resulting in the expulsion from or admission to its depot of seamen whose identities were questioned and then reclassified.[83]

While the Lascar Committee continued to examine seamen, the Military Seminary committee worked to inspect candidates for Company employment as officials or officers. Yet both committees increasingly doubted what they were doing. In November 1821 the latter protested: 'your committee having frequently been called upon to decide upon the nomination of young Men . . . the circumstances of whose birth, combined with their complexion, left [the Committee] in doubt as to the precise extent of the Court's intentions.'[84] Consequently, they pleaded for 'more determinate rules', requesting the Court of directors as a whole 'to establish . . . whether the term "Son

[81] Shipping Committee Minutes 28/2/1821; see also 7/11/1821 to 19/1/1825.
[82] Shipping Committee Minutes 7/4/1820.
[83] Shipping Committee Minutes 17/5/1820 to 8/10/1823.
[84] Seminary Committee Reports 28/11/1821, L/MIL/1/12, BL.

of a Native Indian" shall be construed to limit the exception to young men actually the sons of Natives, or of Native women by European fathers; or to extend the same to descendants of the offspring of such connexions if the Colour of the parties shall exhibit clear signs of such origin, although in a second or third generation.'[85] In short, should complexion and other visible physiological features override distant ancestry?

The directors were divided. They took up consideration of this issue four times in December 1821 and January 1822, but each time postponed coming to any decision. Finally, they moved a series of detailed specifying resolutions that combined issues of gender, 'blood', legitimacy, and education and also specified the documentary evidence to prove the candidate's identity:

(1) That neither the son of a European by a Native woman (that is to say, by a woman whose parents were original native either of Asia, Africa, America, or the West Indies) nor the son of a European woman by an original Native man of any of those Countries, shall henceforth be eligible to an appointment in the Civil, Military, or Maritime, service of the Company.

(2) That it be clearly understood that no description of persons having an equal or a less admixture of *European* blood in him than the persons described in the foregoing Resolution, shall be eligible to an appointment in any of the aforesaid lines of the Company's service.

(3) That neither the son of an European man by a woman whose father was a European but whose mother was an original native of any of the aforesaid countries; nor the son of a European woman by a man one of whose parents was European, and the other an original native of any of those countries, shall be eligible to an appointment in any of the aforesaid lines of the Company's service, unless he shall have been born in Wedlock and shall have been six years at the least regularly educated at some School or Seminary in the United Kingdom of Great Britain; *But* on clear proof being exhibited of such a candidate having been so born in wedlock and so educated, he shall be considered eligible to receive an appointment in any of the aforesaid lines of the Company's service.

(4) That in all cases of doubt when a Candidate is brought forward for

[85] Court Minutes 5/12/1821, 2–16/1/1822.

employment under the last foregoing resolution, the Military Seminary or some other committee before whom such Candidate has to appear, shall require the production of the following Certificates or Proof, vizt.

1) A Certificate or other satisfactory proof of either the grandfather or grandmother of the candidate was born of European parents.

2) A Certificate or other satisfactory proof that one of the parents of the candidate was born of European parents; and that the other was not an original native of Asia, America, or the West Indies.

3) A Certificate or other satisfactory proof of the marriage of the Parents of the Candidate.

4) A Certificate or Certificates from the Schoolmaster or Masters under whom the Candidate has been educated; and in case such Certificates or testimony are not produced, or if produced are not satisfactory, the committee shall use its best discretion under all the circumstances of the case, in passing or rejecting such Candidate.

5) That the same rules as to being born in wedlock, and as to education, that are laid down in the two last foregoing Resolutions, shall be equally applicable to all Candidates for employment, who may be even further removed from native origin, if they exhibit evident signs of such origin.

6) That the foregoing resolutions shall not be construed in any way to infringe on the Resolution of Court of the 9 February 1792, vizt. 'That in future no foreigner shall be admitted into the Company's service, as Writer or Cadet.'

Faced with such specific and controversial delineations, the directors debated extensively and then voted to adjourn without deciding any of these motions. They therefore left their subcommittees in the same dilemma as before.

The Company's inconsistent practices continued in individual cases for years. Two Asian man who arrived in Britain on American ships in 1821 and 1822 respectively received very different treatment. One, who came from India, was not provided for since he was not a native of British but rather princely India and came on an American ship.[86] The other, who came on an American ship from Batavia via Holland, was accepted and sent back at Company expense.[87] Yet, the next year,

---

[86] Shipping Committee Minutes 27/6/1821.
[87] Shipping Committee Minutes 22/5/1822.

a 'Native of India' who came on a French vessel to Bordeaux and then via Hamburg to London was not accepted, excluded not due to nationality but because he came on a 'foreign vessel'.[88] The directors also repeatedly reiterated to its officials in India that all private ships must post a bond to cover the expenses of repatriating all Indian seamen, and that all Indian seamen be notified that they would not receive support if they sailed on non-British vessels.[89] Despite this bond system, in 1822 the Company had to write off almost £6,000 in unreimbursed expenses for maintaining and returning Indian seamen from private ships.[90]

Parliament and the directors also quarreled repeatedly over definitions. In 1823, the directors refused the status of 'native' to seamen of English parents, although born in India.[91] Parliament explicitly repudiated this policy, legislating (4 George 4, *c.* 80, *s.* 27) that 'native of India' included everyone born there, regardless of parentage.[92] Nor were the Company's internal policies consistent. In 1825–6, it decided 'Indo-Britons or Half Castes' could not serve on juries in India, yet they could be appointed as government Veterinary Surgeons.[93]

Over the early nineteenth century, British public opinion increasingly stressed biological 'purity', which official regulations haltingly reflected. The Military Seminary committee, after struggling for nearly seven years, suddenly came to the conclusion in 1827 that the definition of 'native Indian' was 'obvious': '. . . to remove all doubts as to the meaning of the Term "Native Indian" . . . in accordance with its obvious meaning, the exclusion of Persons from the Service under that [1791] Regulation be limited to the offspring of aborigines, that is so say, of Parents of whom either one, or both, are of pure unmixed Native Extraction'.[94] Thus, this committee excluded from appointments all men it considered tainted by full Indian ancestry on either

[88] Shipping Committee Minutes 17/6/1823.

[89] Shipping Committee Minutes 21/3/1820 to 21/9/1825.

[90] Shipping Committee Minutes 14–21/7/1824, 25/8/1826, 6/9/1826.

[91] Shipping Committee Minutes 12/2/1823.

[92] Shipping Committee Minutes 22/9/1824.

[93] Correspondence Committee Minutes 29/6/1825, 30/12/1825, 1/2/1826, 29/12/1826.

[94] Correspondence Committee Minutes 30/10/1827; Court Minutes 31/10/1827, 7/11/1827.

side. Yet, this biological definition for officials and officers contradicted the geographical criteria fixed by the current law set by Parliament to define 'Indians'.

Controversies thus continued. In 1827-8, the owners of the private ship, the *Cornwallis*, refused to pay the costs of returning to India a man named Joseph Delfont. They asserted he was Portuguese, as entered in the ship's records and proved by a certificate from the Bombay police. This, they claimed, made him 'not a native of *British* India' but rather what they called 'a *foreign* Native of India'.[95] The directors retorted that the owners were responsible since the 'man is a Native of India within the meaning of the [1823] Act of Parliament.' Similarly, in 1830, the Company reluctantly paid to send back five 'natives of India' who came to Britain from Manila on a Danish ship.[96] In some cases, the Company and private owners could not agree on responsibility, simply negotiating their respective share of the costs of maintenance and return.[97]

In 1833, Parliament effectively closed the matter for the directors, however. As a byproduct of its suspension of the Company's charter to trade in Asia, Parliament ended its legal responsibility for maintaining and returning Indians in Britain, however defined. It also specified (in section 87) that no 'native' of the Company's territories or 'natural born subject of His Majesty' would be excluded from any appointment in the Indian civil service or army on the basis of religion, place of birth, descent, or colour. Nevertheless, in practice such identities did matter in a man's career. Thus, the question of Indian identity, and what it meant, would continue thereafter, although in different contexts.

Boundaries and Their Limits

Interactions in Britain between people from India and Britons were never equal, but nor were they dichotomous. Much of the initiative for these interactions came from Indians either by their actions or

[95] Shipping Committee Minutes 30/3/1827, 16/4/1828. For a similar case, see Shipping Committee Minutes 10/9/1828.
[96] Court Minutes 14/4/1830. See also Shipping Committee Minutes 6/4/1827.
[97] Shipping Committee Minutes 12/6/1833, 1/8/1833.

presence in Britain. A variety of women and men from India met a range of receptions based on inconsistent and changing cultural constructions and laws about gender, class, and ethnicity. Indian wives and children of British men who went to settle there remained largely dependent on those men for support and class location. Some assimilated into British society and achieved positions of respect, others were abandoned and struggled there, or returned to India. The cultural identities of women usually appeared in both British and Indian eyes more malleable than men.

Over this period in Britain, various Indian noblemen represented themselves, and were identified by British authorities, in differing ways. Indian pensioned noblemen, and claimants to nobility, appreciated the more honoured treatment they received there than in India. Some also regarded access to London as a means to supercede Company officials in India and secure their privileges and rights. Indeed, Faiz Ali gained much financially as a result of his agent's efforts, using evidence from the Company's records, knowledge of British legal and political procedures, and support from the opposition press for his cause. Neither in India nor in Britain did Company officials regard any of these noblemen as practical threats to its rule: even if the British had simply terminated the pensions of Faiz Ali or Shah Mir, these men had no loyal following and were not particularly inspiring figures. Perhaps only indirectly, should other Indian royalty see these cases as instructing them not to trust the British, would there be a possible negative political consequence of this course of action. Yet, ideologically, the British justified their authority over India as bringing the rule of law and, if only to themselves, did not seriously contemplate unilaterally repudiating legal rights. In the case of Faiz Ali, in particular, the British felt morally obliged to his family for their failure to hold Bednore as they had promised, and also for entrusting his finances over his objections to Dady, who had misappropriated his funds. Further, most Britons believed noblemen (Indian as well as British) should enjoy an appropriate lifestyle. The British were also inconsistent about whether they could prevent such missions from leaving India. Indeed, competing British authorities had trouble with legal identifications of Indians generally.

Company definitions of 'Indian' identity were inconsistent and contested, by both individuals and by other authorities. Parliament asserted the broadest geographically-based definition of 'Indian', largely fixing financial responsibility for removing indigents from Britain's streets. Conversely, the directors' immediate financial interest lay in excluding as many destitute people as possible from their depot by constricting the definition of 'Indian'. Simultaneously, however, the directors' cultural values drove them to expand the definition of 'Indian' so as to exclude from its upper services all people of questionable British identity. Various criteria for these opposing exclusions included ancestry, culture, geographic origin, or physical appearance. All these occurred within the context of expanding British colonialism, and efforts by the British state and Company to define and control 'natives' throughout the world.

CHAPTER 6

Indian Servants and Slaves in Early Colonial Britain

Indian Labour in British Domestic and Public Space

From the late eighteenth century, Indian servants (including slaves) entered ever more extensively into the British domestic sphere. Specific Indian communities more readily chose or accepted going for such service to Britain. These servants worked largely cut off from many of the social resources available to them in India and lived constrained by official and informal British controls, subject to class tensions widespread in Britain.[1] Within their overall patterns of employment, the personalities and individual relationships between servants and their masters enabled them different and shifting degrees of agency compared to India.

Their distinctive Indian origin and visible differences from the rest of British society affected their lives in complex ways. Unlike lascars, who usually remained in groups, most servants (like Indian wives and children) had more individual and intimate relations with Britons, particularly with employers in whose homes they lived, and with working-class British women and men who served alongside and sometimes married them. Their circumstances made it more difficult to flee their masters in Britain than in India, where kinship networks, the thinness of British social controls, and neighbouring territories outside British jurisdiction all afforded easier refuge. These personal relations also put great pressure on them to Anglicize, and to assume British deportment

[1] The vast majority of Indian servants worked for European masters; yet, even among those relatively few who worked for élite Indian men or women voyaging to Britain, class conflicts occasionally occurred as well. See Chapter 7.

and culture—dress, language, diet, and Christianity. As British attitudes towards India in the abstract shifted with growing colonialism, so too did the roles that Britons tried to impose on Indian servants. The earlier rarity of Indian servants had identified them with oriental luxury and splendour, and also with the reputedly immoral excesses of British 'nabobs' who returned to 'corrupt' British society. Now, British self-confident colonialism over the late eighteenth and early nineteenth centuries, coupled with increasing numbers of Indian servants in Britain, altered these cultural associations somewhat, making Indians appear to authorities collectively as potential welfare 'problems'. Nevertheless, the lived experience of such servants varied widely, and reflected their individual negotiations—albeit usually from a position of cultural isolation and economic dependence—with their masters and local society.

Even Indian slaves could achieve upward mobility in Britain if they were willing to Anglicize. British anti-slavery sentiment led to the abolition of the slave trade and then slavery itself in 1833. While slavery was mainly associated with Africans, it also affected many Indians. Indeed, domestic slavery continued in India into the 1840s, longer than in Britain's Caribbean colonies. Yet residence in Britain (and conversion to Christianity) could lead to the emancipation of Indian slaves even in the eighteenth century; thus an owner might lose his property rights by taking a slave to Britain.

In contrast to the situation in India, Indian slaves and servants in Britain were not ordinary or cheap labour. Although the purchase price and maintenance cost of a slave might be low and the wages paid free servants no more than those of British ones, Indians entailed expenses not associated with Europeans. These included their transportation costs to Britain, the substantial security bond required before they could leave India (£50 then later £100), and, should they return to India, the £12 'permission' required (until 1813) by the Company, plus passage fare back. Therefore Indian servants needed to possess special value over British ones before their employment in Britain made economic sense. Thus, the context of colonialism, including social, economic, and cultural factors in Britain and India, all affected their condition, place in the labour market, and ability and desire to remain or return home.

Company Efforts to Control Indian Servants

From the late eighteenth century onwards, rising numbers of Indian servants in Britain—correlated with changing British attitudes towards them and India generally—led the Company's directors to seek to control their movement to Britain in more effective ways. In particular, indigent Indian servants increasingly evident in Britain's public spaces after having been abandoned by, or having fled, their British employers came to appear (as did some lascars) a 'problem' for British authorities.[2] Consequently, in 1769 the directors determined to reduce their number in Britain, ensure their employers' accountability for them, and get them quickly out of Britain with no expense to the Company. They therefore required that each employer taking an Indian servant to Britain post a large monetary bond before leaving India, refundable only after that servant's return (or proven death). Revealing their mixed motives, the directors instructed their officials in India:

> It has happened of late years amongst the many Natives of India, who have been sent to England as Servants to Gentlemen or their Families returning home, that several have been forsaken entirely by the Persons in whose Service they engaged, and these poor Creatures from their destitute Circumstance in this distant Land, have Petitioned us for going back at the Company's Expence . . . which not only from the distress of these Indigents, but to prevent reflections on us in this respect from the People of India, we have been induced to grant. In order therefore to remedy these Grievances in future you are hereby directed not to permit any Person whatever on returning to England to take with them a Native of India, without giving Security for every such Native in the Sum of £50—for preventing their being Chargeable to the Company in any manner whatever—And you must send us such Bonds . . . in case of necessity we may put the same in [law] suit here.[3]

The directors professed themselves concerned with the Company's financial burden, its self-projected image among the Indian populace as an all-protecting patron, as well as the dire plight of indigent Indian servants in Britain.

[2] E.g., Court Minutes 10/2/1768.
[3] Court of Directors letter 17/3/1769, NAI, *Fort William*, vol. 5, p. 186.

Nonetheless, many employers evaded giving these bonds and significant numbers of destitute Indians continued to appear unbonded on Britain's streets, in its prisons and workhouses, and on the Company's doorstep. Revealing the limited effectiveness of these controls, the directors repeatedly exhorted their officials in India to extend their exertions.[4] For example, in 1782 they particularly directed attention towards ships of non-British European registry and other notorious evaders of the bond system, in a general effort to reduce the number of Indian servants altogether:

> Notwithstanding our orders that security should be taken for the return of black servants to India yet several have been left destitute here who came to England on foreign ships, or for whom no security had been taken, and the Company thereby have been put to considerable expence. We therefore recommend the discouraging sending of black servants to Europe, but if that cannot be effected, sufficient security must be taken for their maintenance in England, as well as for their return to India, agreeable to the accompanying form of a bond, and it must be certified upon the orders to the commanders for receiving black servants on board of ship that security has been given. And we have come to a resolution that if the commanders shall receive any persons on board the ships without the permission of our Governors and Councils and the certificates before mentioned, they will incur our severest displeasure.[5]

Despite such repeated injunctions, the number of servants rose. Consequently, as a further disincentive to bring Indian servants, the directors in 1807 doubled the bond to £100—five or six times a servant's annual wage.

Despite these elaborate efforts at surveillance and control, many unbonded servants continued to enter Britain undetected. On departing India, captains and employers simply hid Indian servants, boarded them once out of port, or used influence or bribes on officials to overlook them. Some did not even appear in the ship's official logbook. On approaching the British coast, many Britons and their Indian servants left their ships via local fishing vessels or professional smugglers, thus

[4] E.g., Court Minutes 26/2/1773.
[5] Court of Directors letter 12/7/1782, NAI, *Fort William*, vol. 9, pp. 58–9. See also Shipping Committee Minutes 31/7/1816.

evading government customs. Once in Britain, Indian servants faced virtually no official monitoring.[6]

The Company's motive for the bonds was not monetary gain but rather avoiding the costs of caring for and repatriating indigent Indian servants. These bonds usually consisted of cash or interest-bearing East India Company promissory notes deposited by the employer into a presidency treasury. In either case, the depositor customarily received interest (later for cash deposits limited to the first eighteen months), although the capital remained in escrow for at least a year, and usually much more. Many employers evaded this regulation, since the £50 or £100 was a significant amount of capital to tie up, and was often cumbersome to recover. Negating the purpose of the bonds, some masters attempted to recover them before the servant returned home. They asserted that the bonded servant had run away, or joined the Royal Army or Navy, or returned to India unrecorded.[7] Yet, only rarely during this period could a particularly influential employer convince the directors to relinquish the bond prematurely, usually when the master personally guaranteed both that the servant had died or had settled in Britain and he would pay all charges should the servant later decide to return.

As the number of servants abandoned in Britain increased, so too did public protests which lamented such inhumane treatment by irresponsible British masters. For example, in one 1786 newspaper (seventeen years after the bond system began), a Briton publicly chastised British employers (female and male) for the prevalent abuse of Indian servants, Indian women in particular:

Sir,

> When a family return from India, they generally bring over with them one or more female blacks to take care of the children, under a promise to send them back to their native country free of expense.—Many, no doubt, have honesty or humanity enough to keep their word; but the number of those poor wretches who are daily begging for a passage back, proves the generality of those that bring them over leave them to shift for themselves the moment they have no further occasion for their services. Many of them,

---

[6] Act 33 Geo. 3, *c.* 4 (1793, modified repeatedly until 1826) attempted to monitor 'aliens' and 'foreigners' but this evidently did not apply to Indians.

[7] See Shipping Committee Minutes throughout this period.

I am informed, have been in England two or three years; and some of them must for ever remain here, unless the Company will generously give them a passage to India . . .

I am not such a fool . . . as to expect much humanity from a *female adventurer to Bengal*, but the nation has a right to demand common justice from their husbands.—TRUTH.[8]

In reply, another Briton disputed these assertions of inhumanity towards Indian servants, retorting that most of the destitute were 'only' African or Caribbean people, therefore not the Company's concern.[9]

Company authorities used this bonding system to control Indian servants, but later other working-class people as well. Many European soldiers' wives also worked as servants from India, and occasionally were abandoned by their élite employers in Britain, placing a financial burden on the Company to maintain and return them to their husbands in India. In 1797, the directors ordered that 'previous to the wife of a non-commissioned officer or private soldier either in the King's or Company's service being allowed to come to England in attendance upon any passenger, a deposit be made in India to the same amount as that which is deposited respecting Black servants.'[10] This equating of 'Black servants' and European wives reiterated British establishment perceptions equating non-British ethnicity and European female gender for the working classes.

Efforts by the directors through this bonding system to reduce the number of Indian servants in Britain were reinforced by a policy change that facilitated the departure of Indians from Britain. In 1813, Parliament ended the Company's monopoly over trade with India. Subsequently, for 'natives of India' alone, the directors ceased demanding the £12 purchased 'permission' to leave for India that it had originally instituted in 1657.[11] This marked a major change in the emphasis of the Company's efforts to control Indians, from restricting their departure from Britain (through 'permissions') to restricting their entry into Britain (through bonds).

[8] Emphasis in original. *Public Advertiser*, 2/12/1786 2c.

[9] E.g., *Public Advertiser*, 5/12/1786 1d.

[10] Home Public Consultations 5/1/1798 no. 55, Extract Proceedings of Military Department 22/12/1797, NAI; Court Minutes 29/7/1807.

[11] Court Minutes 14/4/1813.

In terms of their conditions of service, whether or not a bond existed undoubtedly affected the relationship between Indian servant and British employer. Such substantial bonds encouraged masters to retain restrictive supervision over their servants. Almost all of the thousands of bonds were eventually redeemed, usually meaning employers satisfied the Company that the servant had returned home or died. These controls by masters would allow servants less opportunity for mobility or finding alternative employment in Britain.

The lack of a bond, however, did not make a servant more vulnerable to deportation. The British government in this period did not have comprehensive checks on immigration, nor any system of official identity papers, nor an effective expulsion mechanism. Masters thus could not use such undocumented status coercively to threaten their servants. Indeed, when unbonded Indians left their masters, the absence of a bond made it more expensive for the Company to deport them to India. Nor did the bonding procedure succeed in protecting all Indian servants from abandonment or maltreatment. A substantial number of bonded but abandoned Indians applied for succour from the directors. Although the Company was later reimbursed out of the bond for their passage home, this usually did not improve the servant's situation.

This bonding requirement did discourage some Britons from bringing servants from India. In 1829, for example, a Briton complained that the bond created a severe financial obstacle for junior officers and other relatively impecunious Britons who nonetheless required an Indian attendant on the voyage home, due to illness for example.[12] Yet, the extent of that discouragement is difficult to quantify. Certainly, the numbers of Indians entering Britain continued to increase, despite the wishes and exertions of the directors. For example, the officially recorded number of servants leaving for Britain from Calcutta alone went up from 39 per season in 1800–2 to 55 per season in 1812–14 to 61 per season in 1817–22 to 71 per season in 1825–9.[13] Therefore,

---

[12] Letter to Editor from 'Madras Subaltern', *Asiatic Journal and Monthly Register*, 27 (January–June 1829), pp. 150–1. For a similar unsuccessful request for smaller bonds, see Bengal, General Proceedings 14/2/1838 no. 58, WBSA.

[13] Figures compiled from 'Lists of Passengers', Home Miscellaneous, vols 250–4, NAI.

this elaborate bonding system only partially achieved its intended goals, but it produced the unintended benefit of extensive evidence for historians studying these working-class Indians.

Profiling Women and Men Servants

These efforts by the Company to control the movement of Indian servants between India and Britain reveal the composition of this class. I have located and compiled records for 1,604 bonded servants between 1792 and 1856. Valuable as they are, these records need to be considered carefully. The British category 'Black servant' itself included a wide array of people, including people of mixed Indian and European descent. While this data set is similar to that used for 'Black servants' in Chapter 2, it also differs in significant ways. The earlier 'permissions' evidence was all compiled in London and thus had more consistent principles of classification (although these shifted over time). In contrast, each presidency compiled its bond records independently, following varying principles. Nor have the bonds survived uniformly for the three presidencies. Of those available, 72 per cent are from Calcutta compared to 22 per cent from Bombay and 6 per cent from Madras, not precisely proportionate to the number of servants from each. There are also many chronological gaps which preclude comparison over time among presidencies or by gender (comparable to the charts in Chapter 2). Further, even the most complete surviving bond registries and passenger lists carried limited information. They always specified the master's name but for the servant, sometimes only position (e.g., 'native servant') or sex (e.g., 'Black maidservant'). Even if given, the servant's name of record might say little about her or his natal identity, since so many laboured under European names. Some diminutive names for servants were used by several communities, like Munnoo (one servant was identified as 'Munnoo a Musilman servant' in 1846; another Munnoo, renamed William Munnew, is discussed extensively below). In addition, Indian names were sometimes ambiguous due to British inconsistent transliterations. In some records, the place, ship, and dates of embarkation appeared; occasionally, the date of return (or death) was added when the bond was redeemed.[14]

[14] Draft of Court of Directors to Fort St George, 8/7/1782, paras 16–17, HMS 163, f. 181.

Nevertheless, these surviving records comprise an incomparably rich source of information for a broad collective profile of these Indian servants. In 1,324 of them, the servant was identifiable by name or sex, as indicated in Table 6.

Table 6: Bonded Servants Leaving India for Britain, 1792–1856[15]

n/%	Male	Female	Total
All European	300/23%	370/28%	670/51%
British	171/13%	217/16%	388/29%
Portuguese	129/10%	153/12%	282/21%
Muslim	195/15%	203/15%	398/30%
Hindu	63/5%	96/7%	159/12%
Parsi	9/1%	0/0%	9/1%
Other/Unknown	31/2%	57/4%	88/7%
Total	598/45%	726/55%	1,324/100%

Overall, a slight majority of servants bore European (i.e. Christian) names. Indians who converted to Christianity, either out of conviction or nominally to suit their European employers, usually adopted such names. Further, people of partial European descent, since it was usually on the father's side, customarily took European names. Some women were Indian or mixed-ancestry wives of British soldiers working their way back to Britain in the service of a higher-ranking European. Almost as many servants bore Portuguese names as British ones, suggesting that the Indo-Portuguese community had well-established patterns of domestic service. Thus, going to Britain for many Indians in service correlated strongly with an European-style name, regardless of their origin.

Yet, this percentage of European-named Indian servants leaving in the early nineteenth century was significantly less than the 80 per cent recorded in the eighteenth century for Indians who had lived in Britain (see Chapter 2). This was unlikely to result from a decrease in supply: the number of servants of partly European descent living in India went up over time, not down, as European men had children with Indian

[15] These figures are from many series in BL, NAI, and WBSA.

women, and as those descendants of mixed descent had children of their own, often keeping the European patrilineal family name. Further, the status of Indians of mixed European and Indian descent generally fell in India from the late eighteenth to the early nineteenth century, as British discrimination reduced them to menial roles like servants.[16]

Within this European-named category, almost all the difference came in British-named servants. This decreased markedly between the proportions evident in the earlier permissions (64 per cent) for servants leaving Britain versus the much smaller percentage (29 per cent) in the later bonds for servants leaving India. In contrast, the proportion of Portuguese-named servants remained more stable between the two data sets (16 per cent and 21 per cent respectively).[17] Various factors can help explain this difference in Anglicization. First, living relatively isolated in Britain evidently impelled servants to Anglicize. Second, this difference might also reflect changing British cultural practices over time: Britons in the later period (employers and/or record keepers) may have been more familiar with and accepting of Indian names, therefore Anglicized them less over time. Finally, British employers might have recruited more widely as time went on, drawing upon less Anglicized Indian servants.

The next largest group after European-named servants, almost a quarter of the total, had male or female Muslim names. Bakhsh (often transliterated Baxo) appeared frequently: 22 men used that name or its forms like Ali Bakhsh. Typical Muslim women's names were Amina and Fatima, with 5 and 9 instances respectively. This large set of Muslim-named male and female servants may also reveal both British preference for them over Hindu servants and/or their greater willingness to sail overseas.

Only 12 per cent of the bonded servants had identifiably Hindu names. This disproportionately small number, compared to the Indian population generally, probably shows both British hiring and renaming practices that discriminated against Hindu identities and/or the reluctance of many Hindus to travel over the 'Black Water'. Roughly

[16] See Hawes, *Poor Relations*.
[17] Even Portuguese-named servants could have their names Anglicized, for example 'a Portuguese servant, William Ross' in 1824.

equal numbers with Hindu names were male (like Rama Samee, Narain, and Lakshman) and female (like Laksme or Lalita Gopi). Some, like 'Rama African' in 1847, evidently had diverse backgrounds.

The small remaining number included a variety of identities. Nine men were Parsi, all sailing from Bombay with either Parsi or British employers. One man from Bombay in 1835, Jacob Levy, was Jewish. Many were identified by their occupation, for example, 65 women were denoted 'Ayah', occasionally with a given name included, like Nancy Ayah (in 1823), or 'Poochiah Mussulmanie Ayah' (in 1835), or Fatima Ayah (in 1840). Other titles included 'Dae' (midwife), 'Syed Junglee Khidmutgar (table attendant)', and 'Sheikh Umeer Tailor'.

Finally, slightly over half (55 per cent) of the entire number of bonded people were female. In all the categories except those with Parsi names, females slightly predominated. This sex ratio was roughly similar in the earlier period (49 per cent male and 51 per cent female).

The time between the bond's deposit and redemption suggests how long that servant spent away from India. Some returned on the next ship home, after only about a year away, others spent considerable time, some the rest of their lives, in service in Britain. Further, these patterns of service changed over time. In the eighteenth century, when Indians servants were rarer and more valued in Britain and transportation slower and riskier, they tended to stay longer. Of 26 bonds redeemed in Calcutta between 1790 and 1800, 8 servants (31 per cent) had remained away for only 1 year, the rest longer, 1 returning after 10 years. Overall, 2–3 years was the average period abroad.[18] In contrast, towards the mid nineteenth century, a greater proportion of servants worked only accompanying their British employers on the voyage, returning to India on the next season's ships. Between 1833 and 1841, 74 servants (76 per cent) returned to Calcutta in a year, 7 returned after 2–3 years away, while 17 remained away longer. Further, to illustrate the slippages in the bonding system after 1834, 3 employers proved able to redeem their bonds although they admitted having lost track of their servants (the employers simply gave personal guarantees that they would cover any future expenses). Conversely, 2 employers who returned their servants and claimed bonds

[18] Home Public Consultations, NAI.

had evidently never actually posted them, their servants having gone unbonded to Britain.[19] Occasionally, we only know that a bond remained as yet unredeemed (meaning this servant had not yet been reported home or dead). This indicated that the servant had been gone at least that long, but might remain away even longer. For Madras, in 1844 there were 34 bonds as yet unredeemed: 1 bond was 43 years old; overall they averaged more than 14 years.[20] When the system of bonding ended in 1857, Bombay still had 7 bonds remaining unredeemed, the oldest deposited 66 years earlier; their average length was 48 years.[21] All this suggests an accumulation of Indian servants in Britain, as their numbers and years of service there mounted, although an increasing percentage returned on the next ship home.

Rich as the information in these records is, we must keep in mind that many more Indian servants entered Britain than appeared in these bonds. Many individuals whom we know about from other sources had no bond recorded. These records thus suggest, but do not fully represent, Indian servants in Britain over this period; other sources from other media supplement these patterns in various ways.

Indian Servants and Slaves and British Rule

The sizable and growing number of Indian servants and slaves who made the voyage to Britain indicate their increasing mobility within the burgeoning British empire. Most free servants apparently had some voice in deciding to seek or accept employment away from India, although economic constraints may have given many of them little other rational choice. While those who were slaves may have been coerced by their masters into making the journey, some slaves nonetheless achieved emancipation due to living in Britain, especially if they were or became Christian and appealed to authorities there on that basis.[22] During this period, life for any slave or working-class person

[19] Compiled from General Proceedings, WBSA.

[20] List of Government Securities 30/4/1844, Madras, L/MAR/C/888.

[21] *Times*, 28–30/11/1857 1b; Court Minutes 25/11/1857.

[22] For example, in 1797, John Rippon of Travancore achieved emancipation simply on the basis that he had lived in Britain, although he had been enslaved

in Britain, Indian or not, could be harsh. As we have seen, Indians there had constraints unique to them, but they could also gain access to sources of redress and self-representation not available to them in India.

After reaching Britain, many Indian servants (as well as seamen) learned and exercised the art of the autobiographical petition to the Company's directors—and to the British public generally. Indians who framed their appeals appropriately, and accepted the directors' patronage, could often obtain freedom from prison or the workhouse, new clothing and adequate food and shelter, the company of fellow Indians of their class, and a free passage back to India. The Company's depot, arranged primarily for seamen, also accepted indigent Indian servants. Thus, in one example out of many, an Indian woman called 'Nanny Jughoo' had come to Britain as a servant with Mr Scott's family. In June 1819, when she and Scott quarrelled, she fled his home one evening and went to the Company's depot for protection and accommodation until her passage back to India could be arranged.[23] The directors were convinced by her appeal to protect her. Scott perforce paid the substantial costs of her maintenance while in England and then her voyage home.

Some Indians found acceptance as members of an Anglican parish, the basis for the limited welfare available in Britain. Official church baptismal, marriage, and death records reported the ever larger number of Indians who converted to Christianity, or were treated as if they had.[24] As we will see for Nabob and Munnoo below, conversion enabled fundamental changes in the relationship between an Indian and the host society.[25] Since most indigent Indians were not legal residents of a parish, however, British society continued to expect the Company to care for them—even between 1834 and 1854 when its charter was suspended.

---

from his youth in Malabar, had allegedly stolen from his several masters in Britain, and had been sold several times over the years in St Helena. Home Public Consultations 1/5/1798 nos. 9–10, 26/6/1798 no. 14, 26/7/1798 no. 5, NAI.

[23] Shipping Committee Minutes 10–16/6/1819, 7/7/1819.

[24] As one example, Hadjee Allee of 61 Boston Place, London, who worked as a cook, had married an Englishwoman, Emma, and had a daughter Sakeena, baptized 26/1/1849. Parish records, St Mary, St Marylebone, Guildhall.

[25] See Viswanathan, *Outside.*

While the directors customarily maintained and returned destitute Indians, they refused to intervene in disputes over wages or living conditions between Indian servants and British (or Indian) masters. They instead referred the disputing parties to British magistrates.[26] Indian servants found that, either as plaintiffs or as defendants, they could sometimes assert their rights in law courts, apparently more so than in India at this time.[27]

Courts thus recorded Indian self-representations, although the nature of such testimony reflects its adversarial context and requires delicate unpacking. The legal status of 'natives of India' remained unclear (as we have seen). Nevertheless, Indians from British India often had the same legal standing in British courts as other British subjects. Indians domiciled in Indian territories outside British rule sometimes had status as 'foreigner', however, which entitled them to a jury of their 'peers', meaning at least half 'foreigners' (not necessarily Indians).[28] Yet, the cultural attitudes of British authorities towards Indians, and towards working-class people generally, affected the application of the law. Some British judges admitted being unable to tell one Indian from another; this led to at least one accused Indian being released, since he could not be definitively identified.[29] British juries also came with their own predispositions towards or against Indians. Court testimony nonetheless provides glimpses of the dress, accouterments, and social status of some Indian servants. In 1795, for example, one Indian servant, Tipoo Saib, accused a 28-year-old Englishwoman, Jane Cartwright, of the theft of his 'metal gilt watch, value 3£, a black silk watch string, value 1d., a stone seal set in base metal, value 1d., and a steel key, value 3d.'[30] He testified:

> I live in Great George-street, Westminster, a servant of Lord MacDonald, the Lord Chief Baron's brother. I was robbed in King-street, Westminster; I met with the prisoner there; I was going home, and . . . she asked me to go with her; I did . . . I was come to our own door, and was ringing the bell,

[26] Correspondence Committee Minutes 14/3/1821; Court Minutes 9/3/1821, 3/11/1824, 10–24/6/1840, 2/7/1840; Miscellaneous Letters Received E/1/257 no. 462, E/1/144 no. 250, BL.

[27] See Ghosh, 'Colonial Companions' (Ph.D., 2000).

[28] See OBP (20/4/1803), p. 295, case 324.

[29] *Times*, 5/3/1840 7c

[30] OBP (16/9/1795), pp. 1093–4, case 414.

standing at the door, and she came aside of me, and I found her hand in my waistcoat pocket, and I put my hand to pull out my watch, and I missed my watch; I ran after her . . .

Cartwright made the counter claim that Tipoo had solicited her, offering a walking stick and money—'he unbuttoned his things, and wanted to be very rude.' When she refused him her body, he falsely accused her of theft. The court accepted Tipoo's word rather than hers and sentenced her to seven years' 'transportation' (deportation) to Australia. This was only one of many court cases that resulted from the extensive social intercourse between working-class Indian and British men and women.[31]

Many judicial judgments apparently favoured property holders, be they Indian or British. Since most Indians were working class, this tended to disadvantage them *vis-à-vis* their employers.[32] Yet, where British employers were accused by Indian employees, the courts often took cognizance and occasionally found for the Indian plaintiffs.[33]

Even when Indians were unable to represent themselves, they could receive a court's judgment. Fetar (*c.* 1812–27) a young Indian slave woman, had been bought in India by Captain Mingnan, allegedly for 100 guineas. In 1826, he posted the requisite bond for her and sent her back to England with his wife, who renamed her Fanny. Mrs Mingnan settled into her mother's home at Greenwich. Over the next six months, Fetar allegedly refused to work, to adjust to the household routine, or to eat or dress according to British custom. Mrs Mingnan and the other servants punished Fetar, with no good results. Matilda Frowd, a fellow servant Fetar's own age, and Hannah Nettleford, the cook, beat her, confined her in a small shed, and soaked her in water, despite her complaints of stomach pains. Fetar finally died. Greenwich authorities brought Mingnan, Frowd, and Nettleford to trial. The testimony of

[31] OBP (3/7/1822), p. 380, case 1009; (16/2/1832), p. 293, case 669.

[32] OBP (12/12/1785), pp. 66–7, case 44; (11/7/1787), pp. 826–31, case 600; (14/9/1785), pp. 1067-68, case 813; (16/9/1795), pp. 986–8, case 375; (14/2/1816), p. 144, case 237. *Annual Register*, (1773), pp. 110–11; *Times*, 3/7/1833 6d, 5/3/1840 7c; Myers, *Reconstructing*, pp. 85–6.

[33] *London Chronicle*, 11–14/10/1800; *Morning Chronicle*, 30/11/1785, 1/12/1785; *Times*, 3/7/1833 6d.

their neighbours about their cruelty to Fetar convinced a jury to find them guilty of manslaughter, despite their denials.[34]

Even more than in the earlier periods, by the late eighteenth century, expanding mechanically-produced and mass-distributed printed newspapers both supported control over working-class Indians and also enhanced their mobility. Some masters used 'runaway' notices to recover possession of their Indian slaves and servants, offering cash rewards for those who caught them, and threatening financial penalties against those who protected them.[35] One advertisement from 1772 stated:

> Run away from his Master Mr Andrew Lucy, THOMAS HORNSEY, a Black, a Native of the Coast of Mallabar, was seen on Monday Evening last at Highgate; has on a brown Livery lined with yellow, the Waistcoat yellow, with yellow and blue Lace mixed, and a new plain hat; is about four Feet nine Inches high, long Hair, well made, likely featured, and speaks English well.
>
> Whoever secures the said Black, and gives Notice to his Master at Epsom; or Mr Underwood, Villiers-Street, York Buildings, Strand, shall be paid Two Guineas. If any Person after this Notice conceals or harbours him, may be assured of a Prosecution being commensed; and any Body that shall prove him to be concealed by any one, shall, besides the above mentioned sum, receive Five Guineas. He is supposed to be either in Highgate, Deptford, or London now, as he is known to have offered himself to several Gentlemen as Servant in those Places.[36]

For a master to offer a large seven-guinea reward to get a servant back testifies to his worth (if not his wages). Further, this servant from Malabar was evidently Anglicized in name, language, and dress.

Some owners used this medium more benevolently, to secure the return home of their Indian slaves. A British woman advertised in 1775:

[34] They absconded and apparently escaped punishment, however. *News*, 27/1/1828 30a–c, cited in Barber, *Celebrating*, p. 35.

[35] See *Daily Advertiser*, 3/3/1775, 26/8/1776, 12/7/1777; *Morning Post and Daily Advertiser*, 11/7/1777; *Morning Chronicle*, 17/2/1795 4c, 6/10/1795 1b. See also Kapur, *Irish Raj*, p. 50; Visram, *Ayahs*; and Fryer, *Staying Power* for many other such advertisements.

[36] *Public Advertiser*, 29/5/1772 4a.

> Any lady going to the East Indies, having occasion for a maid servant may
> be advantageously supplied with one who is lately come from thence; she
> is a Slave Girl, and the mistress who brought her over having no occasion
> for her, will give her over to any Lady to attend her in the passage to India
> and to serve her for three years after the arrival there without wages, pro-
> vided the lady engages at expiration of the Term to give her freedom. She
> is a good servant, perfectly good natured, and talks English well . . .[37]

While designated a 'slave', this Indian woman evidently had entered
into a fixed term of indenture. Thus, the boundary between domestic
slavery and contracted servitude was unclear.

Finally, scores of Indian servants themselves published British newspaper self-advertisements, describing their accomplishments and seeking new employers among the anonymous readership. In such publications, Indian servants proclaimed themselves in the public sphere as
accomplished human beings, worthy of the trust of the reader. An
Indian woman advertised in 1795:

> WANTS PLACE: As a servant to a family going to Bengal, a native of that
> country, where she lived two years with the Lady she is going to leave, who
> brought her to England, and has kept her here for eight years; she does not
> quit her place for any fault, but because it no longer suits the Lady to keep
> her; She can speak French tolerably, having accompanied her mistress to
> France, and remained there twelve months; can dress hair, cook plain
> victuals, make bread, wash well, and will endeavour to make herself useful
> to any lady who may be going to India, or with children. Her mistress with
> whom she still lives till she can otherwise be provided for, will recommend
> her.[38]

This woman boasted ten years' steady employment with the same
British woman, and a range of domestic and linguistic abilities. Britons sailing to India, especially for the first time, might desire her to
guide them in the experiences that lay ahead. In such instances, Indian
servants sought circumstances of employment that they themselves
specified.

[37] *Daily Advertiser*, 1/2/1775.
[38] *Morning Chronicle*, 1/4/1795; see other ads in *Morning Chronicle*, 21/1/
1795 1b, 3/3/1795 4b, 13/3/1795 4a, 8/5/1797 4b, 20/5/1797 1b, 8/1/1798
1b; *Daily Advertiser*, 3/3/1775; *Morning Herald and Daily Advertiser*, 20/5/
1784 3b.

A particularly entrepreneurial Indian settler who worked occasionally as a servant in Britain, Sake Dean Mahomed (1759-1851), used print media extensively.[39] His advertisements for his Indian restaurant in London, 'The Hindostanee Coffee House', extolled its cuisine and ambience. After his restaurant went bankrupt in 1812, he advertised himself as a manservant: 'MAHOMED, late of HINDOSTANEE Coffee House, WANTS a SITUATION, as BUTLER, in a Gentleman's Family, or as Valet to a Single Gentleman; he is perfectly acquainted with marketing, and is capable of conducting the business of a kitchen; has no objections to town or country . . .'[40] Although he failed to find work as a servant, he went on to develop highly successful medical therapies: the innovative 'Indian Medicated Vapour Bath', and 'Shampooing' (from *champi*, 'massage'). He supported his medical practice in Brighton and London through much creative newspaper advertising and several published medical case-books.

After their return to India, servants with experience of Britain had often altered considerably. They certainly described their lives in Britain to their fellow servants, relatives, friends, and perhaps even new employers; such oral accounts spread Indian perceptions of Britain in ways different from British accounts, but are difficult to document today. The skills and lives of such British-returned servants also changed. For example, in the late eighteenth century, a young woman had been recruited from her family in Sylhet by William Robinson, and renamed by him Niobe.[41] Robinson and her father signed a written contract about her terms of service, including a provision by which her father agreed to accept her back into the family should she eventually wish to return. Niobe served Robinson and a friend, Wilkes, on the passage to Britain. There, Robinson apprenticed her for some months to a mantua-maker and milliner. Finally, in 1796, Robinson sent her back to Bengal, bearing knowledge of the latest London fashions and his recommendation: 'She is a good girl, and has behaved pretty well.' She also brought with her 'a good stock of clothes of every sort', in addition to a copy of the written agreement with her father, should she wish to reenter her family. Robinson instructed a friend in Calcutta to give her

[39] See Fisher, *First Indian Author.*
[40] *Times*, 20/4/1813 1c.
[41] Home Public Consultations 3/5/1797, nos 107–8A, NAI.

Rs 500 on her arrival, and either place her with a European lady or pay for her return to Sylhet, as she preferred. Robinson showed somewhat less consideration for two other Indian servants whom he returned to Calcutta: Hannah and Julia. He gave Hannah only Rs 50 'for her assiduous attentions to the children' and arranged that Julia would sail to Calcutta in the service of Miss Pierce. Thus, individual relationships between Indian servants and their employers could vary considerably. To explore in more depth the lived experience of Indian servants in Britain, let us turn to extended studies of two such people, both of whom worked for the same British master over this period.

Emancipation and Back

Both Nabob (*c.* 1770–?) and Munnoo (*c.* 1795–183?) worked for the notorious British lawyer, William Hickey (1749-1827). Hickey's voluminous—and often indiscreet—autobiography, supplemented by other British records, enables us to explore the lives of these men more extensively than most people of their class.[42] For both Nabob and Munnoo, their condition in India and in Britain contrasted markedly, and their sometimes conflicted relationships with their master reveal their agency in both locations. Both men achieved upward mobility in Britain by adapting to British life and culture: through education, by dressing in British-style clothes, and, particularly, by converting to Anglican Christianity. Both achieved the status of free men, although in Nabob's case this was not sustained after his return to India.

As a young boy in Bengal, Nabob had been acquired as a slave by John Lewis Auriol, probably purchased from his family at a time of extreme distress. Auriol held office under the Company (including as Calcutta Police Commissioner). As was common, Auriol named his young slave with the elevated title of a distinguished office, *nawab* ('deputy', meaning governor) that parodied his servitude.[43] Although the name was more associated with the Muslim community, it said

[42] William Hickey's manuscript autobiography is EUR MSS G.118, BL. A version was edited and published by Spencer. Hickey, *Memoirs*.

[43] Interestingly, Hickey was jealous of many of the 'nabobs', or Britons who returned from India excessively rich, whom he met in England. Yet, many people in England regarded Hickey as a 'nabob'.

little with certainty about his birth family. Auriol apparently also taught him functional English, so that he could serve better. When Auriol's friend, William Hickey, was looking for a young servant to accompany him back to England from Calcutta in 1779, Auriol turned Nabob over to Hickey as 'a present'.[44]

Careful reading of Hickey's narrative reveals that Nabob gradually rose in status during their passage to Britain. In India, Nabob was a domestic slave, subject to transfer at his master's whim. Over the long voyage to Britain, Nabob took on a personal identity in Hickey's account. Although Nabob was apparently Hickey's only servant on the journey from India, Hickey in his memoir never mentioned Nabob by name until they left south Africa together, when Hickey first referred to 'my little pet boy, Nabob'.[45] Thereafter, Hickey began more frequently to mention Nabob, demeaningly but fondly. For example, when Hickey asked him to observe and report the weather at sea, Nabob allegedly replied: 'No much ee wind, but too much ee smoke.'[46] Hickey found Nabob's description of fog childishly amusing and worth recording. After reaching Holland, Hickey began to permit Nabob to ride inside the carriage as more of a companion-servant, instead of outside in a more menial position.[47] On landing in England, Hickey even paused on his journey to accommodate Nabob's wants, although Hickey still described these wants in crude terms: 'Nabob complaining of hunger, I stopped that he might appease his craving . . .'.[48] Thus, Hickey's shifting characterizations of Nabob seemed to reflect how the nine-month passage from Calcutta to England together helped Hickey to see Nabob as a person rather than a mere slave. Many other returned British 'nabobs' also came to regard their Indian servants affectionately, as nostalgic reminders of life in India that many other Britons regarded as comically eccentric.[49]

[44] Hickey, *Memoirs*, vol. 3, p. 150.
[45] Ibid., vol. 2, p. 228.
[46] Ibid., p. 232.
[47] Ibid., pp. 238–9.
[48] Ibid., p. 246.
[49] For example, Summud Khan, an Afghan servant, accompanied Captain James Abbott of the Bengal Army across Central Asia and Russia, visiting Britain in 1840. In Britain, both men felt out of place. Summud Khan's reported disorienting encounter in London with Dean Mahomet's 'Indian Bath', reveals

After Hickey reestablished himself with his family in England, he reported that they treated Nabob more as a family favourite than as a working servant. As Hickey recounted, Nabob made himself 'quite at home, [Hickey's sister] Emily having taken a great liking to him. Indeed, he was a little pet with all the ladies, being an interesting-looking, handsome boy.'[50] Hickey used Nabob as an ornament to his own status: 'I dressed him, too, very smart as a husar. As a servant, he was not of the least use to me . . .'. Nevertheless, unlike prior traditions of using Indian servants as exotic symbols of oriental luxury, Hickey dressed Nabob up as a currently fashionable European light-cavalry-man.

During his two years in England, Nabob sought and received 'improvement' in his condition. Hickey's father sent Nabob 'to school to be taught reading and writing, . . . the boy making rapid progress in both. At the end of a few months he expressed a great desire to become a Christian. I therefore, after he was duly instructed, caused him to be baptized at St James's Church.'[51] In Hickey's mind, becoming a Christian automatically emancipated Nabob. This was not, in fact, a legal requirement at this time, which lawyer Hickey must have known.

Marking Nabob's rise in social standing following his conversion and consequent liberation, he began to wear clothes which indicated his status as a free Christian. For example, Hickey had some new clothes custom-made for himself, but then, dissatisfied with them, paid handsomely to have these 'three or four suits of clothes . . . altered to fit my little Bengally', Nabob.[52] Since the style of clothes worn in England marked social status, Nabob would have appeared dressed almost like Hickey himself—lacking the expensive accessories and bearing that marked a real gentleman, however.

While Hickey claimed credit for Nabob's rise in status, Nabob seems not to have accepted it gratefully and submissively as the always egocentric Hickey presumed he would. Rather, on two instances, Nabob

how it had been adapted to British tastes. Abbott, *Narrative*, vol. 2, pp. 230–91. Eastwick describes Summad Khan's later career and retrospective perceptions of Britain. Eastwick, *Glance*, pp. 195–6.

[50] Hickey, *Memoirs*, vol. 3, p. 150.

[51] Ibid., vol. 2, p. 275.

[52] Ibid., p. 281.

displayed strong resistance to Hickey's paternalism. First, while in England, Hickey had borrowed heavily and faced debtors prison, so he hid. To elicit Hickey's refuge, his creditor and a bailiff summoned one of Hickey's father's English servants and offered him a guinea for information of Hickey's whereabouts. This servant indignantly rejected this as disloyal. When Nabob soon thereafter overheard this servant's boasting of his fidelity to Hickey, Nabob reportedly rushed over to the inn where the creditor and bailiff waited. Nabob then offered to accept the reward and bring them to Hickey's distant hiding place. Nabob allegedly asserted that he knew full well that this information would entail Hickey's imprisonment. Hickey reported that the creditor was so shocked at this 'base and unfeeling conduct in the little urchin, knowing as he did full well, the extraordinary and uniform kindness with which he had been treated by me during the voyage, and which had been continued by every one of my family since I had reached England', that he instead beat Nabob and refrained from arresting Hickey. Meanwhile, Hickey paid the debt but did not learn about 'this black rascal's scandalous ingratitude' until after their return to India.[53] While Hickey thus represented his increasingly kind treatment of Nabob over their passage from India to England, he ended his account of their sojourn there with this condemnation of Nabob's greed and inability to appreciate kindness and respond with gratitude. Throughout his life, Hickey clearly misjudged many of his interpersonal relationships, repeatedly reporting betrayals—by people whom he considered friends or lovers—that he found equally unexpected and incomprehensible. Thus, we should not rely on Hickey's interpretation of Nabob's motives.

We can posit that Nabob's perspective on their relationship clearly differed fundamentally from Hickey's. Nabob's reported initiative and eagerness in betraying Hickey to the law and imprisonment may reveal deep resistance to his patronizing master and a newly developed sense of his own agency in Britain. We can speculate that Nabob saw this as a way to escape Hickey's control, and use the guinea reward to begin a new life. This effort by Nabob garnered him instead a beating and diminished standing within Hickey's father's household, which seems to have precluded any further effort by Nabob to leave Hickey's

[53] Ibid., p. 293.

employ and remain in England. Therefore, Nabob's first rejection of Hickey's assumption that he would be grateful and obedient to Hickey's interests must be considered carefully.

The second and more complete instance of Nabob's rejection of Hickey's patronage came after their return to India together in 1783. There, Hickey presumed that Nabob would continue to serve him faithfully, bound not by law any longer but rather by ties of gratitude and financial necessity. Nabob, however, was more autonomous than Hickey expected. On reaching Calcutta, Auriol asked Hickey for his slave back. Hickey found this incredible because he believed Auriol had given Nabob to him completely as 'an absolute and unconditional gift', rather than temporarily as a loan. Hickey further was convinced that he was a far better master for Nabob than Auriol: 'a niggardly, parsimonious fellow in all his pecuniary transactions'.[54] Hickey determined to prove his possession of Nabob by leaving up to him the decision of which master to serve. Hickey explained to Nabob:

> Mr Auriol now desires to have you back, claiming you as his exclusive property. This he undoubtedly has no right to do, nor shall he have you unless you should be desirous of changing masters. Now therefore, what say you? Will you stay with Mrs Hickey and me, or do you prefer going to Mr John Auriol?

To Hickey's dismay, Nabob determined to rejoin Auriol: 'Without a moment's hesitation, and with an exulting smile, he answered he had rather go to Mr Auriol.' Hickey reported himself 'somewhat vexed at so unexpected and unjust claim. . . . Nabob had . . . been treated by myself and the whole of my family with the utmost generosity and kindness, which he repaid with the basest ingratitude . . .'. Hickey's parting admonition to Nabob was that he would be sorry for his choice of masters and to Auriol that 'the boy in question . . . being now a Christian he (Mr Auriol) could no longer be justified, nor would the law permit him, to treat him as a slave.'

Thus, the perception of the master evidently did not always accurately gauge the will of the slave. Nor did Nabob, apparently, elect to remain in England as a free but dependent man by fleeing his master there. Rather Nabob submitted to living in India as a slave, yet he did so under a master of his own choosing.

[54] Ibid., vol. 3, pp. 150–1.

Married and Settled

Another servant of Hickey remained with him for more than twenty-five years, also rising in status over their passage together from India to England. At the end of Hickey's colourful career in Calcutta, he purchased the services of a thirteen-year-old boy called 'Munnoo' (an affectionate diminutive for a male child). Munnoo had already worked since age nine for Hickey: 'a remarkable, smart, good-tempered boy . . . his chief occupation being to make the other servants laugh by his monkey tricks when waiting at table and standing at the back of my chair . . .'.[55] In 1808, Hickey bought or transferred Munnoo from his family in exchange for money: '[Munnoo's] mother, who doted upon the boy, would not for a long time consent to let him go to Europe, until an offer of five hundred sicca Rs [£50] which I made her proved irresistible; she accepted the money and agreed to part with her favourite Munnoo, and a more attached and faithful creature never existed than he proved to me.' While this transaction suggested the sale of Munnoo, Hickey seems to have regarded the boy rather as a servant than a slave, designating him: 'Sirdar ["chief"] bearer', although Munnoo was Hickey's only servant on the voyage.[56]

Hickey apparently smuggled Munnoo, like Nabob, unbonded from India, nor does Munnoo appear in the ship's official logbook.[57] Munnoo's departure from his home proved heart-wrenching. On first sailing, Hickey locked 'the wretched boy' in their cabin: '[Munnoo] fixed himself at the quarter gallery window where he sat looking the very image of despair . . . there he remained as long as the vessel that was rapidly conveying his old friends from him was discernible, leaving the poor fellow in the midst of strangers and in a scene as uncouth as it was novel to him.'[58] While sympathetic in his description of Munnoo's condition from Munnoo's perspective, Hickey clearly asserted his control over him throughout their voyage.

Once in England, Munnoo lived, as Nabob had done, with Hickey's

[55] We should remember that Hickey wrote his memoirs with Munnoo in attendance, so their continuing relationship may have shaped his perspectives on Munnoo favourably. Hickey, *Memoirs*, vol. 4, pp. 376, 398.

[56] Ibid., vol. 4, p. 399.

[57] Journal of Castle Eden, L/MAR/B/296D, BL.

[58] Hickey, *Memoirs*, vol. 4, pp. 405–6.

family. The ageing Hickey treated Munnoo paternalistically, desiring to impress him with England's glory: ' . . . I had anticipated some pleasure from the delight I expected Munnoo would betray upon first beholding the splendid capital of England . . .'.[59] While Hickey may have purchased Munnoo, he came to treat him as a ward, calling him 'my friend', someone who shared Hickey's sense of being an outsider in England due to their mutual domicile in Bengal.

Whatever his legal condition, once in England Munnoo felt free to express some of his own feelings. When Hickey warned his carriage drivers that they were going too fast, Munnoo desired they go even faster: 'my friend Munnoo was exceedingly indignant, saying to me with much earnestness, when I was calling to the boys not to drive at such a rate, "Mud Monakurra mud monakurra! Saheb, kiswastee ni Geldee Jata! bote atcha Geldee Jata!" ' (Hickey's garbled recollection of Munnoo's words probably tells us less about the words Munnoo actually used than Hickey's recollection of Munnoo's intent.) Hickey very loosely translates this for his Anglophone readers as: ' "Don't prevent their going on, it is very pleasant to go fast." '[60] Hickey also made sure they slowed down.

Hickey eventually retired to the late Edmund Burke's village of Beaconsfield, Buckinghamshire. Munnoo was not the first Indian servant who lived there. William Burke (d. 1798), a relative and close companion to Edmund, had brought Tombee ('little brother') with him in 1793 when he came home from India. William Burke's will stated: Tombee 'a native of India [who] did accompany me to this Country thereby losing his Cast privilege and having ever behaved to me with the most dutiful attention, common Justice required I should restore him to his Religion and friends, I desire that the sum of £350 . . . should be applied to the purpose of recovering his Cast and of conveying him to his native country. . . .'[61] Instead, Tombee begged to remain near William's grave rather than return to India, although he later seems to have gone.

In Beaconsfield, Munnoo studied and Anglicized himself, as had Nabob. Hickey credits Munnoo with the full initiative in converting

[59] Ibid., p. 467.
[60] Ibid., pp. 467–8.
[61] See Burke, *Correspondence*, vol. 9, p. 87; Magnus, *Edmund Burke*, p. 288; Wecter, *Edmund Burke*, p. 94.

to the Church of England in 1809: 'my favourite Munnoo, without the least hint or solicitation on my part upon the subject, expressed an earnest desire to be made a Christian. I had upon first coming to Beaconsfield put him to school to be taught to read and write; his schoolmaster, having made the Catechism the first object, probably turned his thoughts that way . . . as the boy was extremely zealous, he soon entitled himself to receive baptism . . .'. Yet it was Hickey who determined 'to anglify his name a little, and therefore instead of Munnoo, I had him designated in the parochial register, "William Munnew".'[62]

While he remained Hickey's servant, Munnew also created his own life and family. Around 1813, Munnew married (or began living with) an Englishwoman, Anne. They had a daughter, christened Anne in 1814 at the Beaconsfield Parish Church.[63] In 1817, Hickey, with Munnew (and probably Munnew's family), moved to London, taking rooms in Westminster.[64] There, in 1819, Hickey commissioned William Thomas to paint a joint portrait of him, Munnew, and Hickey's dog (Image 11).[65] This oil painting suggests the image that Hickey wished to convey about them, their relationships, and context. Hickey was a very experienced sitter, having commissioned many portraits of himself.[66] The caption was demeaning for Munnew, as Hickey's 'favourite black servant'.

Nevertheless, this joint portrait also reflects the eye of the artist, and his assessment of each of his subjects as he saw them, revealed visually to the élite of London when displayed in the Royal Academy Exhibition of 1820.[67] Hickey clearly sits as the proprietor of Munnew, his dog, and his house (which awkwardly is both a library/study and is also open to the English countryside). Hickey has books and papers piled around him, providing his setting and suggesting his professional career as a lawyer, and perhaps as an autobiographer—he had just

[62] Hickey, *Memoirs*, vol. 4, p. 473; *Beaconsfield Parish Register*, 27/2/1809, p.112.

[63] She was christened exactly five years after Munnew. Beaconsfield Parish Church, Baptismal Records, 27/2/1814.

[64] At 19 Manchester Building, Parliament Street. Boyle, *Court Guide* for those years; Westminster Ratebook 1818; Westminster Poll Book 1820, WAC.

[65] See Walker, *Regency*, vol. 1, p. 249; vol. 2, p. 574.

[66] Archer, *India and British*.

[67] Catalogue of the Royal Academy Exhibitions, 1819, no. 245; *Times*, 27/4/1820 3b. The document on the table is curiously blank.

finished writing his memoirs. On the other hand, Hickey, then age seventy, appears quite elderly, and sits holding a limp paper in one hand while the other extends empty. His legs are thin. He is centred in the composition and yet is partly shadowed. Hickey inattentively looks vaguely in front of him.

In clear contrast, Munnew (age twenty-four) and the terrier both display youthful movement and action, full of vigour and energy, on strong legs. It is Munnew who provides direction, illuminated by the English sun, and pointing levelly outward into the open countryside (or India). Glancing down, he guides Hickey which way to look, although Hickey seems to be unaware of this. The terrier devotes his attention to Munnew not Hickey. Munnew's skin colour, hair, and other features clearly distinguish him as Indian. Yet Munnew has dressed not in oriental or servant's garb but rather in the clothes of a British gentleman (or gentleman's gentleman), complete with stylish cravat and waistcoat, much as Nabob seems to have done, plus gold watch-fob and other jewelry. Overall, this painting contrasts sharply with earlier portrayals of Indian servants as oriental ornaments and/or subordinated to their British masters.

Thereafter, Hickey, Munnew, and Munnew's growing family moved to Richmond, Surrey around 1820. There, Munnew and Anne christened their newborn son, William.[68] Hickey returned to London sometime before his death in February 1827.[69] Around then, Munnew rose from servant to 'licenced victualler', before he himself died in the 1830s. His family settled in Westminster. His eldest son, William, became a skilled pianoforte-tuner and maker. In 1840, he married Elizabeth Mills (1816–?), the daughter of a Kent horse dealer, soon after the birth of their son, William, the first of at least ten children.[70]

---

[68] William Munnew born 10/12/1820; christened 5/1/1821, St Mary Magdaline, Richmond, Surrey, IGI.

[69] Burial certificate, St John Evangelist, Smith Square, 10/2/1827, WAC.

[70] They lived at 93 Norton Street and then settled for many years at 41 Foley Street. Marriage certificate 7/6/1840, Trinity Church, St Marylebone. While living there, they had William (born 9/9/1839, christened 11/7/1841), Elizabeth (born 17/6/1841, christened 11/7/1841), Mary Ann (born 1843), Emily (christened 14/11/1845), George (christened 14/11/1845), another Elizabeth and Grace (c. 1846), James (born 7/5/1846, christened 29/6/1847), Arthur

The family had merged into British society, associated neither by name or deportment with India. This was a long way from Munnoo's birth in Calcutta and life there. Like so many other Indian slaves and servants, Munnoo found that Anglicization and marriage with a British woman proved ways of settling successfully in Britain.

Service and Slavery in India and Britain

The composition, contexts, and agency of Indian servants and slaves changed over time and as they moved between India and Britain, albeit in unequal relationships with their masters. As with most working-class people of that time, evidence about them and their perspectives must be carefully reconstructed, often reading sources against the grain. Nonetheless, quantitative patterns and individual studies suggest how they were distinct from other working-class people in both India and Britain.

Not all Indian communities were equally willing to serve on the passage to and in Britain. Disproportionate numbers had or adopted European-style identities for this work. A substantial number had part Portuguese ancestry or cultural associations; many perforce Anglicized. Relatively more Muslims than Hindus apparently undertook such service. All these patterns changed from the earlier period as British and Indian employment preferences and cultural values shifted.

Once in Britain, these Indian servants and slaves laboured under constraints not faced by Britons of their class, but also had distinctive opportunities. They stood out visually for their features, but, compared to the earlier periods, British culture generally regarded them as less symbolic of rare oriental splendour or the excessive luxury and corruption entering Britain along with the British 'nabobs'. The indigent among them became perceived by British authorities as a growing

---

(born 1848, died 1923 in Tasmania), and Frederick John (born 17/8/1852, christened 10/5/1857). Eventually William left London, remarried, and settled at 16 McKerrell Road Camberwell, Surrey. William Munnew married Mary Ann Collier 6/1/1872, St Mary Spitalfields or Wheeler Chapel Spitalfields. Elizabeth Munnew married George Freston 15/10/1866, St Anne, Soho, Westminster. See 1851–81 Census, IGI, GLRO.

welfare 'problem'. Efforts to regulate them and reduce their numbers, most notably through the Company's system of bonds, had mixed results but seem to have encouraged their employers' surveillance and control over them. Nevertheless, we should not overlook the many Indians who died in Britain from neglect or cruelty by their masters, unfavourable climate, unaccustomed diseases, and unpalatable food.

Nevertheless, some opportunities for such Indians who came to Britain evidently improved over what was available to them in India. Certainly, self-representations by lower-class Indians in public discourse came more easily through the more widespread British print media. British law courts sometimes recognized their rights. Accepting Anglican Christianity could obtain freedom from slavery. Marriage with a Briton enabled some assimilation into the host society. Further, when Indian servants in Britain became destitute, most secured from the directors shelter, food, and clothing, as well as free passage home. Those who returned after one or many years away brought back new experiences and skills with them. Overall, these quantitative and individual studies reveal aspects of the lived experiences of these Indian servants in India and Britain, working either for Britons or for the growing number of Indian diplomats, political agents, and royalty going to Britain.

CHAPTER 7

Indian Delegations Entering London

Indian Diplomats, Agents, and Royalty in
Colonizing Britain

During the 1830s–50s, spreading British colonialism brought substantially more Indians and Britons into political confrontation in Britain as well as India. By the end of this period, virtually all Indian rulers who fought the British militarily were defeated and either subordinated through indirect rule or else deposed and pensioned off, their lands annexed.[1] But some Indian royalty learned that British rule was not monolithic, especially that they could negotiate in Britain to supersede Company officials in India. They or their trusted Indian envoys argued directly in British political and public arenas for redress of injustices, increases in pensions, and enthronement. In response, British authorities in India and Britain, despite competing interests within them, haltingly developed political theories and coordinated strategies for frustrating Indian diplomats and agents. Nevertheless, the various members of these missions returned to India with extensive direct experience of Britain.

Both the Government of India and the rulers sending delegations to London recognized them as acts of resistance against colonial control. Under colonialism, political knowledge and information were contested commodities. The Company's Residency system of indirect rule sought to monopolize communication among the surviving Indian princely states, and between them and London. Further, Company officials tried to obscure for Indians the policy differences among British authorities. Occasionally, the governor-general deliberately suppressed a rebuff from the directors or Parliament; or else a governor, when overruled by one of the above, avoided informing the

[1] Nepal, which lost in war but retained relative autonomy, was a rare exception.

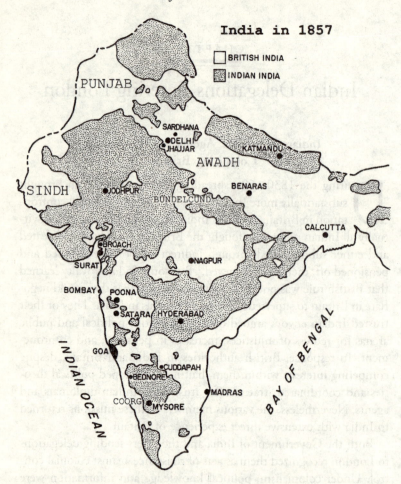

Map 3: Indian India and British India in 1857.

concerned ruler. The English version of a treaty (for readers in Britain) might specify one British entity but the Persian version (for Indian readers) another. Once in London, Indian agents learned first-hand about British politics and could sometimes help compel the Company to open its colonial archive to the British public and therefore to them.

Conversely, these Indian delegations to Britain also demonstrated the continued faith by Indians that London would set right the moral, political, and legal wrongs done by British officials in India. This suggests the power over many Indians of British ideological assertions that Britain bestowed the rule of law on India—despite repeated British colonial violations of that law. Thus, the number and scale of such missions increased significantly over this period, notwithstanding their expense and infrequent success.

Indian delegations varied in their composition, preparedness, and effectiveness. Indian noblemen or claimants to rule personally led some missions. Prior to 1858, British Residents prevented current rulers from making the journey.[2] With rare exceptions, British authorities contested the status of Indian envoys, rejecting their credentials and attempting to classify most of them as political agents without diplomatic standing. Yet, former or would-be rulers stood outside of the Company's political system of indirect rule and therefore could travel, like other British subjects, relatively freely within their British sovereign's domain, including to London. Most Indian deputations were, however, conducted by trusted courtiers or hired experts experienced in dealing with the British. While most British authori ties disparaged such Indian agents, and sought to frustrate them, no laws prevented their residence and political manoeuvring in Britain. All missions included various Indian subordinates and servants whose agendas often diverged from those of their employers; divisions within and between delegations surfaced, based on class, gender, and/or religion. Each member of each embassy thus experienced Britain somewhat differently and returned with unique memories.

In approach and orientation, these Indian diplomats and envoys differed substantially from British agents working for Indian royalty. Indians in Britain were seen as outsiders to British society, even if they settled there for many years. Britons, even if born and raised in India, generally related to Britain as 'home'. Indian representatives usually proved more devoted and loyal to their Indian employers; they often went into debt supporting their cause. European agents usually had more mercenary motives; Parliamentary critics called them 'the

---

[2] E.g., only after Mir Ali Morat had been demoted from Amir of Upper Sindh to simply a large landholder, did the Government of India permit him to go to Britain. FSC 13/7/1844, nos 43–5, 7/10/1848, nos 3–5; FPC 27/3/1852, nos 55–6, 11/7/1856, no. 4, NAI; MSS EUR F.213/53, BL.

greatest curse that could be inflicted on the native princes and chiefs of India . . . the never-failing road to . . . ruin'.[3] Finally, Indians expressed for British audiences different images of India, and for Indian audiences different images of Britain, from those which Britons put forth.

Even during the mid nineteenth century, many Indian envoys arrived woefully unprepared for what they would encounter in Britain. Adhering to more established Indian protocols, some never discovered how to function effectively there. Many anticipated swift justice; others expected their inevitable lengthy struggles. Envoys learned about life and politics there through frustrating personal experience, consultation with other Indians and British supporters, alliances with oppositional British factions, and/or repeated visits. Astute agents developed skilfull tactics of political and legal manoeuvring among (often competing) British bodies, including the Company's directors and proprietors, Parliament and the Board of Control, and British law courts and voters. Those who learned to shift the grounds of their appeals from politics to property rights could sometimes gain much. British officials asserted that their political acts could not be challenged by Indians in British law courts. Yet these authorities were themselves constrained by their ideology, which held that Indians who accepted the British system of law consequently could legitimately claim property rights under that law, even against the British Government of India. Such rights included pensions and titles granted by treaty.

British public responses to these Indian emissaries in their midst remained mixed. Royalty and diplomats usually found Britons in Britain, especially élite Britons, more respectful than those in India. Many Indian noblemen benefited from ingrained British beliefs in the moral right of aristocracy—a category which included descendants of deposed Indian rulers—to a lifestyle appropriate to their birth, in luxury if not power. The British populace, members of Parliament, and even directors as individuals often appreciated the presence of exotic Indian 'princes' (even mere claimants to that status) and ambassadors which enhanced the image of London as cosmopolitan capital. Indians who

---

[3] Commons debates 22/7/1845, 11/7/1848 *Hansard*, series 3, vol. 82, p. 930; vol. 100, pp. 424–5. See also *Bombay Times* 11/9/1839 pp. 578–9, 6/5/1840 p. 292.

articulated informed appeals for British moral justice occasionally thereby gained backers.

The directors came frustratingly to realize that Indian agents in London often caused them embarrassment, cost money and prestige, and occasionally influenced colonial policies in untoward ways. Even with decades of accumulated experience, the directors struggled to prevent Indian missions from arriving and to contain them once there. Nonetheless, given the many hundreds of Indian states into which the British intervened, relatively few—just over thirty—managed to send Indian delegations to London by 1857. This number indicates the Company's capacity to confine to India political intercourse between it and the rulers, rather than conducting it in London. Yet, British officials remained reluctant to forbid Indian missions altogether. Instead, the directors created precedents and policies, including inflicting humiliation and financial exhaustion, to induce Indian embassies to leave London unsatisfied.

The results of these missions also varied widely. Most obtained investigations of their claims, forcing Company officials in India to reconsider cases they had long dismissed. Some missions gained sufficient backing in Parliament or among Company stockholders to make public hitherto confidential Company documents and malfeasance. The most influential among these diplomats and agents caused British politicians in London to warn officials in India to refrain from annexations and other aggressions that had political costs in London. Some deposed dynasties obtained material increases in their pensions through appeals to British law. All faced frustration at their plaintiff position before the Company's bureaucracy and officialdom. None gained all they sought.

By the mid nineteenth century, the British government, directors, and public had moved more solidly behind British colonial expansion and rule, in India and elsewhere. The earlier exotic appeal in Britain of Indian nobility and diplomats, including their secluded womenfolk, faded somewhat. British ideas about Indians as racially different and inferior deepened, fostered by British world economic hegemony and growing colonialist confidence.

Yet, these Indian agents discovered much about Britain firsthand, which they conveyed to audiences in India through their writing and oral reports. A few began to articulate for Indian audiences a more in-clusive understanding of India, and of worldwide colonialism as well. Some married and settled in Britain, merging into society there. Con-versely, several London-returned envoys fought violently against the British in 1857. The experiences of these envoys in Britain thus varied widely and over time, revealing the dynamics of multisided negotia-tions and confrontations between Britons and Indians.

Contrasting Envoys: Eunuch and Savant

In 1831, two divergent missions reached London, suggesting the un-evenness of Indian knowledge of Britain and reception there. Khwajasara ('eunuch') Mahboob Ali Khan and his suite arrived impoverished and poorly prepared, seeking increased pensions for the late nawab of Bun-delcund's widows and his infant son's succession. Lacking resources and unable to escape the directors' constraints, he gained little access to the British public sphere. In contrast, noted scholar and social re-former Raja Rammohun Roy and his suite arrived far better equipped, seeking an increased pension for the Mughal emperor. He manoeu-vred knowledgeably and skilfully in British society and politics. The direct-ors rejected the diplomatic credentials of both delegations, yet even Mahboob gained a new investigation of his cause and Roy secured the promise of much of what he sought.

Mahboob Ali Khan was a dedicated but relatively ill-equipped envoy. In India, widows, even of royal families, often had difficulty gaining a public voice. When the British annexed Bundelcund in 1804, they pensioned the nawab with Rs 400,000 annually. After he died in 1823, his half-brother, Zoolficar Ali Bahadur, inherited the title and pen-sion, with British approval. The widows, Wullayatee Begum, Hoos-seinee Begum, Redjub-oo-Nissa Begum, and Srettee Seloom Begum, received only small stipends from the new nawab and thus felt depriv-ed. They also wanted the late nawab's young son, Ihsan Ali, to inherit with themselves as regents. When they appealed to British authorities in India, the new nawab further confined them physically and finan-cially.

In 1829, these begums appointed Mahboob Ali as their *mukhtar* (agent), supported by a secretary, Shaykh Ameer Allah, and a servant,

Sherif Hassan Ali. After extensive but futile lobbying in Calcutta, these agents determined to directly approach the British monarch, although none knew English or much about Britain.[4] They left India unobstructed by British authorities, ostensibly on Haj to Mecca. In Egypt, they appeared to be respectable subjects of the Government of India who had become destitute; they thus received aid from the Ottoman government, passports from the British consul-general, and passage to Britain from the Company's commercial agents, Biggs Brothers. They deceptively claimed to be going to London only to request passage back to India from the directors.

Reaching London in June 1831, they met the Company's chairman. Much to his surprise, they presented the widows' letter to the king and petition to the directors. While having these Persian documents translated, the chairman sent them to Gole's depot for food and shelter. He also directed Gole to discover who they actually were. Due to Gole's imperfect command of Urdu, he understood their message only vaguely. Finally realizing they were envoys, the directors officially rejected all further communications from them, promising continued food and shelter only if they sailed home (at the Company's expense) immediately.[5]

Nonetheless, the envoys submitted further Persian petitions and documents, from not only the widows but also various local landowners. Thus, in making this long and dangerous journey, they carried the hopes of many Indians for justice. Indeed, Mahboob Ali concluded by requesting the directors to reward him personally for his arduous and loyal service with a tax-free village of his own in perpetuity.

Even as the directors told Mahboob Ali that they would not deal with him, they had their own clerks research the Company's records. They discovered that the local British political agent had dismissed Ihsan Ali as the late nawab's illegitimate son with a 'nautch girl', now long deceased. Further, this agent reported the three widows had no right to inherit. He denied their claims to married *nikah* status, asserting rather they were only 'favoured mistresses': one a Hindu slave,

[4] Miscellaneous Letters Received E/1/176, vol. 2, ff. 437, 439; E/1/177, vol. 3, ff. 124–5, 373–80, 388–96, BL.

[5] Correspondence Committee Reports 3–17/8/1831, D/84; Board Collections F/4/1259, no. 50571, BL.

another an Egyptian who had come to India as the kept-woman of a British officer. Further, the governor-general and the directors themselves had approved the succession.[6]

Nevertheless, Mahboob Ali's appeals induced the directors to order the governor-general to reconsider the case, while the delegation waited in London.[7] The political agent's reply arrived a year later (July 1832), insisting that he had acted properly. The new nawab accused Mahboob Ali of organizing a 'cabal' against him, stealing family jewels to finance the mission, and misleading the widows into this false and futile vendetta against him. He also submitted a testimonial from one widow, Srettee Seloom, repudiating Mahboob Ali's authority to represent her.

The directors, deciding not to overrule their Indian officials, returned Mahboob Ali and his companions to India. There, these agents continued vain appeals to the governor-general. Thus, the mission's long efforts gained the widows a further investigation but no redress, and incidentally the enhanced enmity of the nawab on whom they were dependent. Mahboob Ali and his companions gained little from their arduous voyage except much experience about living in Britain. A eunuch not well-versed in British culture, Mahboob Ali received less respect and support in Britain than better informed and resourceful envoys representing more significant royalty.

In 1831, Raja Rammohun Roy (1772–1833) also reached London, representing Mughal Emperor Muhammad Akbar II (r.1806–37). Roy, who came from a landholding Brahmin family and had prosperously served the Company in his youth, was extensively educated in many languages, including English. A founder of the 'Bengal Renaissance', his debates with both Hindu and Christian religious leaders and his many publications had long made him a prominent public figure, even in London.[8] Roy went to Europe seeking dialogue with wider British audiences and personal exploration of Western culture. He also

---

[6] Miscellaneous Letters Received E/1/177, vol. 3, ff. 381–7, BL.

[7] Board Collections F/4/1456, no. 57386, BL.

[8] For Rammohun Roy, see Banerjee, *Rajah Rammohun Roy's Mission*; Carpenter, *Last Days*; Chanda and Majumdar, eds. *Selections*; Collet, *Life*; Dasgupta, *Rajah Rammohun Roy*; Majumdar, *Raja Rammohun Roy*; Robertson, *Raja Rammohan Ray*; Rammohun Roy, *English Works*; Zastoupil, 'Defining'.

had a broad vision of India, understanding how lack of 'patriotism' had enabled the British conquest.[9] Thus, while Roy accepted the emperor's authority, he regarded himself as representing the honour of all Indians: '. . . I am here [in London] so situated as to be responsible not only to the King of Delhi but to the whole body of my Countrymen for my exertions on his behalf and for their welfare.'[10]

The emperor, however, had commissioned Roy for a less progressive purpose: to increase the imperial pension up to the level specified by the 1805 treaty but long denied by his British captors. In 1828, the emperor bestowed on Roy the titles Raja and *ilchi* ('Ambassador'), giving him 'full and unlimited powers'.[11] The emperor also contracted to pay Roy in perpetuity a percentage of whatever increase in the pension he achieved.[12]

Since the British still nominally recognized the sovereignty of the emperor, his right to send an ambassador was hard for them to contest officially. The emperor, as in his father's 1766 imperial diplomatic mission to London (see Chapter 2), addressed the British king personally as fellow monarch in the letter he entrusted to Roy:

> Sire! My Brother! It is with a mingled feeling of humility and pride that I approach your Majesty with the language of fraternal equality at the very time that the occasion of my addressing your Majesty compels me to consider myself rather as a suppliant at the footstool of your Majesty's throne than as a Monarch entitled to assume the style and claim the privileges of royalty . . . I cannot forget that I am a King only in name . . .[13]

The emperor thus continued to follow traditional Mughal diplomatic protocols and had a more limited vision of India than Roy.

The Government of India rejected Roy's credentials as imperial envoy and strove to prevent him from leaving India. The British Resident in Delhi pressurized the emperor to repudiate Roy, succeeding in

[9] Rammohun Roy, *Exposition*, p. x. For discussion of 'old patriotism' and nationalism see Bayly, *Origins*.
[10] HMS 708, ff. 155–8.
[11] HMS 708, ff. 1–5.
[12] Majumdar, *Raja Rammohun Roy*, pp. 230, 243–5.
[13] Board Collections F/4/1268, no. 50911, BL.

exciting the imperial heir apparent's jealousy against him.[14] Nevertheless, the government recognized it could not legally forbid Roy from
going.

Before leaving India, Roy prepared the emperor's case—including
using some documents obtained illicitly from the Government of
India's own archive. He employed Robert Montgomery Martin (1803–
68) as assistant envoy to analyse these.[15] Martin later claimed, however, that when after four months he realized the documents were 'surreptitiously obtained from the government offices, by bribing the
clerks therein', he resigned in protest.[16] Nonetheless, Roy continued
his embassy.

Roy sailed from Calcutta (November 1830), his suite including his
adopted son, Rajaram Roy; a longtime associate, Ramrotun Mukerjah;
and servants, Ramhurry Dass and Shaikh Baxoo (for the last three Roy
posted Rs 1,000 servant bonds); plus cows to provide fresh milk for
him.[17] During the passage, Roy ate apart from the British passengers,
having his servant cook in his private cabin. However, he reportedly
joined the other passengers after dinner for wine.

After reaching Britain (April 1831), Roy's charisma, tremendous
intellect, and powerful reform programme—expressed through well-
received speeches, sermons, and publications—expanded his strong
British following. Britons largely regarded him as a savant from 'the
East', yet one sympathetic to progressive Christianity, a man from
whom they could derive 'Oriental wisdom' but also someone who
could spread the message of European-style 'modernity' among the
Indian people. Unitarians particularly welcomed him, believing his
religious views resonated with theirs.

Roy experimented with different lifestyles to find one appropriate
to his status. He retained his customary clothing (Image 12). But he
also hired a fashionable coach, with liveried coachman and footman,

[14] Board Collections F/4/1368, no. 54481, BL.

[15] Martin had been the editor of the *Bengal Herald*, one of Roy's newspapers,
but was under deportation orders for criticizing the government. He later became an influential historian.

[16] References of the Revenue, Judicial, and Legislative Committee L/PJ/1/17
f. 3, BL; Majumdar, *Raja Rammohun Roy*, pp. 330–3.

[17] Majumdar, *Raja Rammohun Roy*, p. 336; Collet, *Life*, p. 115.

Image 12: Rajah Rammohun Roy, etching by Annin Smith.

as proper for a 'gentleman of moderate fortune'.[18] Roy hired Stanford Arnot (d.1834, former assistant editor of the *Calcutta Journal*) as his secretary. Arnot apparently convinced Roy to rent for a time extravagant apartments in Cumberland Terrace, Regent's Park. Roy received more invitations from distinguished people than he could possibly accommodate.[19] Among his conversation partners were James Mill and Jeremy Bentham; Bentham proposed nominating Roy for Parliament.[20] Roy attended the coronation of King William IV, seated among the foreign ambassadors in Westminster Abbey.

In London, Roy enhanced his understanding of British politics and ideology. He researched earlier Indian missions—including that of Ghulam Muhyi al-Din (see Chapter 5)—learning tactics and assessing results.[21] Indeed, Roy explicitly contrasted his own insights about 'the character of the local [Indian] Government as well as the nature of the British constitution, and the relation subsisting between them' with his countrymen's vague notions: 'the Natives of India were entirely ignorant of the nature of the government (the popular notion being that the Company was a venerable old lady who sent out her favourite sons successfully to take charge of the Country) . . .'.[22] Yet, his contemporary in London, Mahboob Ali, and also some later envoys arrived (and departed) ill informed about such constitutional relationships. Roy intended to publish a book informing Indians of his discoveries concerning 'the intelligence, riches and power, manners, customs, and especially the female virtue and excellence existing in' Britain.[23] While several others before and after him did write such accounts, Roy's untimely death prevented him from doing so.

Roy did not confine himself to exploring Britain. In preparation for his trip to France, he corresponded with Tallyrand (1754–1838),

[18] James Sutherland in *Indian Gazette* 18/2/1834 cited in Collet, *Life*, p. 128.

[19] E.g., ADD 40856, f. 106; ADD 29747, f. 104; ADD 59655, ff. 140, 142; Frederick Madden Correspondence 6/6/1831, EG 2838, BL.

[20] ADD 33546, f. 506; Elphinstone Papers, F 88/85, BL; Zastoupil, 'Defining', p. 216.

[21] MSS EUR B.399, BL.

[22] HMS 708, ff. 183–202. In 1841, Karim Khan would quote the same popular Indian notion of the Company as an old woman. Karim Khan, *Siyahatnama*, pp. 277–8.

[23] Rammohun Roy, *Exposition*, p. x.

protesting the need for a visa to enter such a free land.[24] He also communicated with French orientalist scholar Garcin de Tassey (1794–1878).[25] In Paris he was very well received, including by King Louis Philippe (r.1830–46). He also planned trips to Austria and Italy.

Nevertheless, many Britons, particularly those with experience in India, refused to recognize Roy as a gentleman. For example, Captain Manleverer, observing Roy at a soirée, exclaimed angrily: 'What is that *black fellow* doing here?'[26] William Thackeray (1811–63, who was born in India) later in his fiction ridiculed both Roy (as the character 'Rummun Loll', a petty merchant claiming royalty) and the British hostesses who fawned on him.[27] Some of this hostility emerged during Roy's ultimately frustrating role as imperial envoy.

The directors attempted initially to deal with Roy's mission as it did others: refused to recognize his accreditation, demanded the emperor communicate only through local authorities in India, and denied Roy knowledge of its deliberations until he ran out of money and departed. Roy had prepared for their stonewalling even before he left India. He held impeccable credentials from the emperor and documented his spurned attempts to correspond through British officials there.

Once in London, Roy negotiated shrewdly, strengthening his hand through his evidence, argumentation, and personal connections among influential Britons. When first writing to the directors, Roy submitted his printed pamphlet detailing and documenting the Mughal's case: *Treaty with the King of Delhi* (London: John Nichols, 1831). But he cannily promised that he had not yet distributed copies, intimating that he could do so to gain public support: 'I mention this fact because I am anxious to bring the whole matter quickly and unostentatiously before the Honourable Court of Directors.'[28] Roy cited specific Government of India regulations proving his case, marking each by hand in a printed manual. Roy insightfully cast his argument in terms of the sanctity of contracts and of private property, bedrocks of British legal and social thinking: '[If the emperor's legal treaty] be not valid and

[24] HMS 708, ff. 289–92, 297, 305–12.

[25] de Tassy, *Rudimens*, Appendix, pp. 30–2.

[26] Collet, *Life*, p. 130.

[27] Thackeray, *Newcomes*, pp. 78–80.

[28] HMS 708, ff. 1–5; Court Minutes 21/6/1831.

obligatory, then no contract can be considered binding, no man's property is secure . . .'.[29] Further, he appealed to the British 'love of justice which breathes through the Acts of Parliament'.

Roy cultivated his friends, especially those on the Board of Control and in Parliament. He was already admired among reformers for his advocacy of the abolition of sati among other measures.[30] Indeed, a Parliamentary Select Committee requested that he, 'as a native' of India, advise them on the upcoming 1833 Company Charter Renewal Bill. Roy published a book compiling his extended advice on colonial policy: *Exposition of the Practical Operation of the Judicial and Revenue Systems of India and of the General Character and Condition of Its Native Inhabitants* (London: Smith, Elder, 1832). When the 1832 Reform Bill passed Parliament, Roy wrote: 'Thank heaven I can now feel proud of being one of your fellow subjects.'[31] The directors therefore decided to make an exception in his case, concluding it would be politic to deal with him rather than have him go to Parliament.

Yet, even as the directors opposed his official purpose, they recognized his personal prestige. They hosted an eighty-person 'family dinner' for him, avoiding officially recognizing him as imperial envoy but showing their respect for him unofficially. There, the chairman toasted that he hoped other 'able and influential' Hindus would emulate Roy by coming to London. Roy ate in their presence, but only rice and water prepared by his own cook.[32]

Despite Roy's social and intellectual advantages, he experienced frustrations that plagued other Indian diplomats and envoys. The directors, after deliberating nearly two years, conceded (February 1833) only a partial increment in the emperor's pension, from its current Rs 1,200,000 annually to Rs 1,500,000. Yet, since the 1805 treaty explicitly promised the emperor the revenues of the Delhi territories, which had risen to Rs 3,000,000, this was an increase only from 40 per cent to 50 per cent of the amount due. Further, to accept this modest increase, the emperor had to relinquish any claim on the rest.

[29] HMS 708, ff. 183–202.
[30] HMS 708, ff. 155–71; Lords debate 1/7/1831, *Hansard*, series 3, vol. 4, pp. 576–8; Board Collections F/4/1268, no. 50911; Miscellaneous Letters Received E/1/178, vol. 4, ff. 22–4, BL.
[31] Roy letter 31/7/1832 in Carpenter, *Last Days*, p. 54.
[32] *Indian Gazette* 8/11/1831; Collet, *Life*, pp. 125–6.

Roy wrote how compromised he felt by his need to plead before the directors, not only on behalf of his imperial master but also in terms of his own self-respect.[33] The directors tried to maintain even in his case their custom of not informing Indian envoys of the outcome of their appeals.[34] Only Roy's warm personal relationship with Charles Grant (1778–1866), president of the Board of Control, convinced the directors to notify him as a 'personal courtesy to himself . . . [since] it is not usual for the Court [of Directors] to enter into any explanation of their decisions.'[35] When he learned how little he had gained, Roy advised the emperor to reject this offer, promising to increase it through further negotiations with Parliament.[36] Nevertheless, Roy's modest success inspired various Indian rulers to try to employ him, send their own Indian representatives, or travel to Britain themselves in emulation.[37] Ultimately, the British never paid even this increase, due to Roy's early death and subsequent disputes between the emperor and governor-general over the money.

Roy faced additional embarrassments. The British banking house in Calcutta which managed his money failed, leaving him without funds. He repeatedly appealed to the directors for a £2,000 loan. They demanded a 'respectable' person as his guarantor. When he offered only his own personal guarantee, they refused the loan.[38] Roy proudly refrained from asking for money from his admiring British supporters, but had to depend upon them for hospitality. Thus, despite his social prominence, publications, and successful public lectures, sermons, and private dialogues, he became despondent and ill over his slighted

[33] HMS 708, ff. 179–82.

[34] Miscellaneous Letters Received E/1/183, vol. 1, ff. 200–1, BL.

[35] Court Minutes 6/3/1833; HMS 708, ff. 317–32; Miscellaneous Letters Received, E/1/181, vol. 3, ff. 303–5, BL. See Philips, *East India Company*, especially pp. 276ff.

[36] Majumdar, *Raja Rammohun Roy*, p. lix.

[37] Royalty who wished to hire or emulate Roy included Baiza Baee of Gwalior, the sons of Tipu Sultan, the nawab of Bengal, and the deposed amirs of Sindh. FPC 21/11/1833, no. 41–53, NAI; Carnac letter 18/8/1836, Broughton Papers MSS EUR F.213/2, BL; *Sumachar Durpan* 28/7/1834, 4/7/1835 in Majumdar, *Raja Rammohun Roy*, p. lviii; Eastwick, *Glance*, pp. 310–37; *Times* 10/12/1835 3a.

[38] Miscellaneous Letters Received, E/1/185, vol. 3, f. 80, BL; Court Minutes 8/5/1833, 30/7/1833.

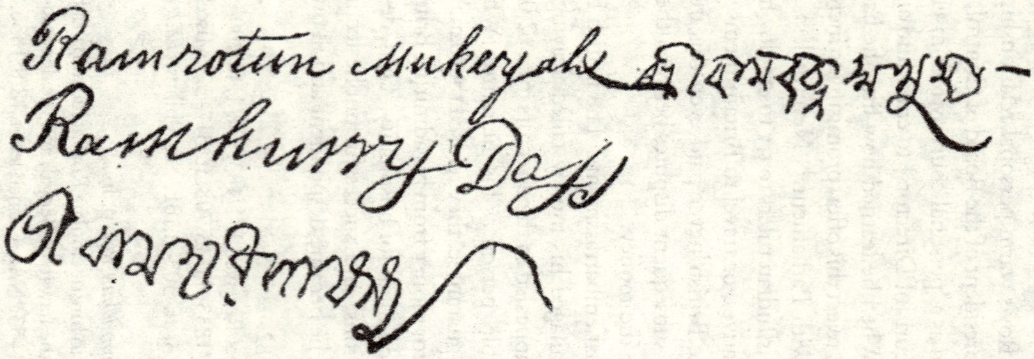

Image 13: Signatures of Ramrotun Mukerjah and Ramhurry Dass.

treatment by the directors, and by his financial difficulties.[39] Further, his secretary, Arnot, demanded large sums from him and later claimed authorship of publications that Roy had dictated to him. On a trip to Bristol, Roy died (27 September 1833). He was much mourned among his supporters and in the British press.[40]

His suite consequently received the sympathies of the British public, government, and even the directors.[41] Ramrotun Mukerjah was an envoy in his own right, presenting a petition from Indian owners of tax free lands (*la-kharaj*) who felt threatened by the Bengal Government's Regulation III of 1828 that empowered local British officials to dispossess them.[42] After Roy's death, Mukerjah received an appointment in the unconvenanted civil service, and became Native Deputy Collector of Murshidabad. Roy's servant Ramhurry Dass returned to India, where the maharaja of Burdwan appointed him head gardener. Shaikh Baxoo had apparently returned earlier. Roy's young adopted son, Rajaram Roy remained in Britain for eight years, adapting himself to British society (see Chapter 8). Thus, Rammohun Roy functioned far more effectively than Mahboob Ali and many other Indian envoys. Yet, even for Roy, the power inequities inherent in colonialism brought much frustration.

From Petitioner to Settler

The interests of the various members of a delegation could diverge while in London. In 1833, Aboo Syed Palowkar (b.1786) arrived from Bombay with his son, Mohammed Ibrahim Palowkar (1811–55), and a suite of servants, claiming long-dispossessed landholdings. While their petition had no realistic chance of success, it reflected their desperate faith in British justice if only they could reach London. Ultimately, their servants themselves appealed to the directors against their

[39] Strachey letter 12/10/1833, Elphinstone Papers F.88/85, BL; Wilson letter 21/12/1833, *Indian Mirror* 15/7/1872 in Collet, *Life*, pp. 144–5.

[40] *Times* 30/9/1833; Strachey letter 12/10/1833, Elphinstone Papers F.88/85; [unnamed newspaper clipping] 12/10/1833, MSS EUR B.399, BL.

[41] Elphinstone Papers F.88/85, BL; Carpenter, *Last Days*, p. 151.

[42] Miscellaneous Letters Received E/1/182, vol. 4, ff. 76–89, BL; Correspondence Committee Minutes 3/10/1832. Collet misidentifies him as Roy's 'cook'. Collet, *Life*, p. 116.

employers, the son married a British woman and settled in London, while the father went home disappointed.

This family claimed origins in Arabia, indeed descent from the Prophet Muhammad, but had acquired its landholdings and title of *deshmulk* ('governor') in 1685, at the peak of Mughal expansion southward.[43] Although these lands lay along the coast at Dabhol in the heart of Maratha territories, the family claimed to hold possession for fifty years, before losing them to the Maratha Peshwa in 1736. The family then fled to Bombay, taking refuge with the Company, while continuing for four generations to try to persuade the Marathas to return the lands. They also assimilated into the local culture, taking the Maratha-style family name: Palowkar.

The Third Anglo-Maratha War (1817–19) replaced Maratha by British rule over the family's claimed lands. British concepts of legal property opened up new possibilities for judicial redress for appellants like the current head of this family, Aboo Syed. For sixteen years, Aboo Syed persisted in submitting documents and arguments to the Bombay government, hiring a British lawyer in Bombay to help him recast his claims in terms those courts would appreciate.[44] He sought not only the restoration of his family's rights, but the arrears of all 'the Rents and Revenues thereof collected during the period of time which your Petitioner and his Ancestors had been wrongfully dispossessed.' Many of the claimed rents and revenues were then going into the Bombay treasury. The Bombay government referred Aboo Syed to local British authorities, who conducted extensive investigations.[45] These confirmed Aboo Syed's original claims but found his family had been dispossessed for over a century, long past the statute of limitations. When finally he asked what further recourse remained, the Bombay government responded that only the Company's directors in London had higher authority than they. Aboo Syed understood this to mean that he should personally venture to London where he would obtain redress.

[43] Much of the following family history comes from 'Petition of Aboo Syed' 17/2/1834, Miscellaneous Letters Received, E/1/186, fol. 60ff; see also Board Collections F/4/1371, no. 54513, BL.

[44] Bombay to Directors 17/5/1833 and Aboo Syed to Governor Bombay 11/8/1832, Board Collections F/4/1371, no. 54513, BL.

[45] Aboo Syed to Malcolm, n.d., Board Collections F/4/1371, no. 54513, BL.

Leaving behind the women and other family members, he brought with him to London his eldest son, Mohammed Ibrahim, three servants, plus a cook. To pay for their passage, he mortgaged his three houses in Bombay. On reaching London in November 1833 (after an eight-month journey via Egypt), they took respectable lodgings at 27 Haberdasher's Street, Shoreditch.[46] Aboo Syed soon took legal advice from William Lyall, Esq. He then submitted his petition to the directors, proposing they overrule the Bombay government.[47] He also borrowed money to sustain his mission, using his expected compensation from the Company as collateral.

The directors quickly repulsed his appeal.[48] Nevertheless, they understood how his hopes had been falsely raised by his over-interpretation of the Bombay government's deference to them: 'he seems to have understood the intimation made to him by the Bombay government as an encouragement to proceed to this country.'[49] Nonetheless, the directors had no intention of undermining the authority of their Bombay government by even hearing Aboo Syed's case and used his increasing financial difficulties in London to induce him to leave: 'the Court are willing to incur a modest expense for defraying the charge of the passage of himself and family back to Bombay.' Aboo Syed, however, persisted. In June, he appealed the directors' rejection, only to have it again rejected.[50] The directors reiterated their proposed payment for his family's return 'provided he avails himself of their offer without loss of time.'[51]

Having learned in London about the Company's subordinate relationship to Parliament, Aboo Syed initiated a new campaign. He submitted his appeal, with all his supporting documents, to the president of the Board of Control, Charles Grant.[52] Unlike Rammohun Roy's

[46] Aboo Syed Petition 23/11/1833, Board Collections F/4/1371, no. 54513, BL.

[47] Court Minutes 27/11/1833, 18–20/12/1833.

[48] Court Minutes 8/1/1834, 19/2/1834, 12/3/1834, 4/4/1834.

[49] Court Minutes 23/4/1834, 14/5/1834.

[50] Court Minutes 11/6/1834.

[51] Court Minutes 14–28/1/1835; Revenue, Judicial, and Legislative Committee Minutes 14/5/1834, 2/7/1834.

[52] Palowkar to Grant 25/8/1834, Revenue, Judicial, and Legislative Committee References, L/PJ/1/18, no. 25, BL.

efforts, his appeal met only polite refusal—Grant's secretary referred him to the directors, urging him to accept their offer of return passage.

Over the months, the mission's financial situation deteriorated. In July 1834 two of Aboo Syed's attendants, Munshi Haji Soolah al-Din (his secretary), and Shaik Sardar Haji (his cook), themselves petitioned the directors that Aboo Syed had stopped paying and even feeding them. Consequently, they had moved out and taken humble lodgings at 10 Crutched Friars Street in the City.[53] The munshi asked the directors for employment in Britain, or else passage home for himself and the cook. The directors refused to interfere in the matter of their wages, but did provide food, clothing, and a place for these two men to live, as well as free passage back to Bombay.[54]

As 1835 began, Aboo Syed appealed again with increasing desperation to both the directors and the Board of Control, not only over his original grievance but also for an additional £600 reimbursement for his expenses coming to England.[55] He pleaded that he was now faced with imprisonment for debt, so he would never be able to leave London.[56] Further, he submitted that, should he return to Bombay not only empty handed but owing for the expenses of his voyage to Britain, he and his family would lose even their remaining heavily mortgaged property. Thus, he offered to exchange his land and revenue claims, which he asserted were worth Rs 300,000, for a modest perpetual pension. Further, he moved into cheaper lodgings at 22 Jewry Street, Aldgate.

After eighteen months (May 1835), Aboo Syed reluctantly agreed to return to Bombay with his plaint unsatisfied. The directors allotted

---

[53] Revenue, Judicial, and Legislative Committee Minutes 2/7/1834, 27/8/1834; Haji addin Salah and Sheik S. Haji to Court 11–12/8/1834, Revenue, Judicial, and Legislative Committee References, L/PJ/1/17, no. 79, BL; Court Minutes 11/6/1834.

[54] Court Minutes 2/7/1834, 20/8/1834; Revenue, Judicial, and Legislative Committee Minutes 2/7/1834, 27/8/1834, 28/1/1835.

[55] Revenue, Judicial, and Legislative Committee Minutes 6/5/1835, 14/7/1835, 12/8/1835; Palowkar to Grant 25/8/1834 Revenue, Judicial, and Legislative Committee References L/PJ/1/18, no. 25, BL.

[56] Palowkar to Court, 21/4/1834, 23/4/1834, 14/5/1834, Revenue, Judicial, and Legislative Committee References L/PJ/1/17, no. 22, BL.

him the 'modest expense' they had promised for his voyage back, but routed him around the Cape of Good Hope. To maintain his status, however, Aboo Syed insisted on travelling back to India via Egypt: 'being much adverse to proceeding by Sea to Bombay by reasons of the many Inconveniences and Privations to which as Mahomedans they would be unavoidably exposed on board an English Ship.' The directors granted him only £300 (£50 less than he claimed necessary).[57] The directors ordered Lyall to purchase tickets for him and his party, insisting 'that no part of the money be paid to Aboo Syed in this Country' lest he delay his departure any further, or use the funds to renew his appeal. In July 1835 all these arrangements had been made, yet Aboo Syed's creditors in London were growing increasingly insistent that the directors pay his debts (some sixteen months overdue) before he depart.

As Aboo Syed prepared to leave, however, his son, Mohammed Ibrahim, disappeared.[58] Although his father unconvincingly denied knowledge of this, he had married a Protestant Irishwoman, Eleanor Deegan, at St Leonard's Church, Shoreditch, the previous 10 February.[59] The directors, however, washed their hands of the matter, arranging that, should Mohammed Ibrahim ever reappear, Lyall would arrange his departure without any further expense to them. Aboo Syed and his remaining party reluctantly boarded ship in August 1835. Aboo Syed never recovered the claimed lands but his family apparently lived as merchants.[60]

Mohammed Ibrahim established himself in Britain. Until his death in 1855, he ran a tobacconist shop.[61] His three sons became respectively merchant's clerk, gas-fitter then electrician, and hatter.[62] This

[57] Court Minutes 1–27/5/1835, 8–22/7/1835; Revenue, Judicial, and Legislative Committee Minutes 28/1/1835, 6/5/1835, 14/7/1835.

[58] Court Minutes 12–19/8/1835; Revenue, Judicial, and Legislative Committee Minutes and Reports 12/8/1835.

[59] St Leonard's Shoreditch 10/2/1835, Guildhall.

[60] East India Yearbook has Sumsoodeen Pallowkar as a Merchant trading from Bendy Bazar Road at least from 1845 to 1866. Personal communication from a descendant, David Wilson, 2/5/2002.

[61] Although he declared bankruptcy in 1834, he apparently recovered, dying as a master tobacconist. *Times* 4/11/1843 3a, 8/11/1843 3a.

[62] However, two sons, William John Fox Palowkar (b. 1836), the clerk, and

family continues in Britain, with some branches taking the surname
Wilson, others keeping Palowkar, but with few family traditions of
their Indian origins.[63]

Ambassadors and Royalty from Awadh

Four Indian missions from the Awadh ruling family went to Britain,
more than from any other dynasty over this period, each with distinct
experiences there. At times the premier Mughal successor state, Awadh
had long and troubled relations with the Company. In 1764 Awadh's
rulers fought the Company but subsequently became its subordinate
ally. They lost huge territories to the Company and gained others,
loaned it Rs 52,000,000, lived under its protection, but also resisted
its controls. This dynasty often found British actions incomprehensible: in 1797–8, the Resident installed and then deposed one ruler,
enthroning instead an uncle who had long lived in exile under British
protection; in 1801 the Company annexed half that ruler's territories;
in 1837 the Resident deposed the late Nasir al-Din Haydar's reputed
son and installed an aged and long-exiled uncle; in 1856, the Company
deposed the incumbent, Wajid Ali Shah, and annexed Awadh. Many
of these actions violated British treaties with Awadh.

In this context, both incumbent rulers and pretenders to the Awadh
throne sought to outmanoeuvre the Resident and each other by directly influencing policy in London. These rival royal relatives evidently
knew about each others' missions, although their mastery of British
politics remained uneven. We saw (in Chapter 5) how Shah Mir Khan
made two feckless visits to Britain (1822–4). Several Awadh rulers
hired European agents but, in 1834, Nasir al-Din (r.1827–37) sent a
diplomatic and scientific delegation including his own kin.[64] In 1837,

---

Mohamed Frederick Palowkar (1848–c.1914), the hatter, both declared bankruptcy, the latter temporarily emigrating to Australia. *Times* 21/1/1865 7e, 15/
11/1880 4d, 20/7/1881 10a, 13/6/1881 13e. See also Visram, *Asians,* pp. 85,
172 and personal communication 18/9/2002.

[63] Jeanne Shirley Palowkar explains '. . . the family now is fair skinned and
blue eyed'. http://familytreemaker.genealogy.com/users/p/a/l/Jeanne-Shirley-
Palowkar/index.html

[64] Fox, *Memories,* pp. 11–13.

Nasir al-Din's cousin, Iqbal al-Daula, went to London to secure his own succession to the Awadh throne. In 1856, the deposed Wajid Ali Shah (r.1847–56) sent his mother, brother, and heir to London seeking to reverse the British annexation of Awadh (see Chapter 10). We consider the 1834 and 1837 delegations here.

Nasir al-Din's 1834 embassy resisted the Resident's efforts to control Awadh's political communications. Diplomatically, this deputation reciprocated for presents and a letter received earlier from King George III.[65] Nasir al-Din sent the British king and queen gifts valued at £80,000, including a portrait of himself, a sword, jewelry, clothes, 26 books, a hookah, chairs, 2 horses, 2 elephants, and 2 buffaloes.[66] Escorting these were European courtiers: Frenchman Colonel A. Du Bois de Jacigny, seconded by Briton Philip Friell. Four Indian animal trainers attended the menagerie.

Nasir al-Din simultaneously sought to acquire direct knowledge of British science. He entrusted this goal to Moomtaroz al-Olama, Moulvee Mahommed Ismael Khan (d. 1837), the son of a high-ranking Awadh judge and the husband of Nasir al-Din's own paternal aunt, Mariam Begum.[67] Nasir al-Din identified him as

> the most learned scholar of this country . . . well versed in mathematics, and acquainted with the astronomy of Ptolemy. He has further obtained a tolerable knowledge of the principles of astronomy as established by the English Philosophers, and was on that account attached to the late Captain [James] Herbert [1791–1833], my astronomer. By his visiting England he will have an opportunity of becoming acquainted with the learned men of London, and will acquire a superior degree of knowledge by ascertaining various minute particulars connected with science, and by seeing the observations of that city and by viewing curious experiments of illustrious Philosophers, so that after his return hither, he may by instructing others spread the knowledge in this country of the sublime science of astronomy.[68]

[65] This was itself a return mission for one sent earlier by Awadh. *Times* 8/7/1823 3b.

[66] Anonymous, *Short Statement*; *Times* 8/8/1835 5d; *Annual Register* (1835), p. 127. See also Llewellyn-Jones, *Engaging Scoundrels*.

[67] Resident Lucknow to Political Secretary 15/11/1837, FPC 13/12/1837, no. 71, NAI.

[68] Board Collections F/4/1548, no. 61872, BL; Hodges, *List*, vol. 2, p. 434.

During the 1830s, increasing numbers of other Indians also decided to visit Britain and master its scientific advances (see Chapter 9).

The Government of India only belatedly realized this embassy's political significance. The Acting Resident in Awadh approved it, as did the governor-general. When the Resident returned, however, he perceived that direct communication with London would enhance Nasir al-Din's status at a delicate time: the Government of India was attempting to coerce him into reforming his administration. The Resident therefore compelled the Awadh ruler to withdraw his accrediting documents and royal letter from the delegation, which had already embarked, until these could be vetted and enclosed in the governor-general's own report to London.[69] Although the diplomats sailed in March 1835, their vital credentials only reached London a year after them.[70] When these did arrive, Friell and Ismael Khan personally presented the Awadh ruler's letter to the British monarch, something the British government disapproved but could not prevent.[71]

Nasir al-Din's letter to King William also elaborated on Ismael Khan's goals: to 'be permitted to kiss the threshold of your Glorious Majesty's Heavenlike Palace and seeing the observatories of those Palaces, visit the most accomplished among the Learned in London . . . It is my intention to erect a College [in Awadh] to learn and teach others the English language and their established Arts and Sciences.'[72] The ruler further requested a British professor for his proposed college, apparently modelled on Delhi English College (established 1828, see Chapter 9).

The mission's European contingent generated continual controversy. Du Bois faced accusations of forgery and fraud even before he left India. Reaching London, he delivered the animals to King William's household, which belatedly discovered that its acceptance of them had undermined government policy against direct communication

[69] Board Collections F/4/1526, no. 60295, BL.

[70] Broughton Papers, MSS EUR F.213/4, ff. 12–13, BL.

[71] PDHC, L/PS/3/106, f. 2; Broughton Papers MSS EUR F.213/2, MSS EUR F.213/4, f. 75; BL.

[72] Board Collections F/4/1526, no. 60295, ff. 73–87, BL.

between Awadh and the British Crown.[73] Further, the directors accused Du Bois of stealing an expensive diamond necklace intended for Queen Adelaide. Ismael Khan claimed Du Bois pilfered £10,000 of the mission's funds. While neither charge was proven, Du Bois departed in disgrace for France and Friell took his place.[74] When the British king refused the rest of the presents, Friell pawned some for £7,500 and started to sell the rest, while the directors demanded possession of them.[75]

Meanwhile, other Indian rulers sent missions bearing similar gifts for the British Crown, each generating political repercussions.[76] Indeed, the Company determined to prevent such delegations wherever possible, instructing its agents in Egypt to deter any which reached there.[77] Governor-general Auckland wrote confidentially, demeaning Asian rulers, exonerating himself, but recognizing the implications of their gifts: '... I am as opposed as you can be to all presents from our dependent native Princes to the King of England. Their minds are childishly wild on these missions and they expect consequences. They know not what, and think, at least, that they may commit follies with impunity. All that are sent from Oude [Awadh], Moorshedabad [Bengal], Nepal, Muscat, were sent before my time.'[78] King William

---

[73] Broughton Papers MSS EUR F.213/4, ff. 13–14, 76, 91–2, BL.

[74] Broughton Papers MSS EUR F.213/5, f. 121, BL; White, *Mirzas Kaiwan Jah,* pp. 37–8. Although White had close connections with Awadh, he is not a reliable source.

[75] Broughton Papers MSS EUR F.213/4, ff. 275–81; MSS EUR F.213/5, f. 121; MSS EUR F.213/6, ff. 4–6, BL.

[76] These included Maharaja Ranjit Singh of Punjab and Junkojee Rao Scindia. FPC 21/11/1834, no. 138, 24/2/1835, no. 71, NAI; Carnac letter 18/8/1836, Broughton Papers MSS EUR F.213/2; MSS EUR F.213/4, ff. 114–20; MSS EUR F.213/5, ff. 32–5, 121, 163; MSS EUR F.213/6, ff. 4–6; Hobhouse letter 30/5/1851, MSS EUR F.213/15; Shepherd letter 31/5/1851, MSS EUR F.213/17; Hobhouse letter 30/5/1851, Elliot letters 10–12/9/1851, MSS EUR F.213/18. *Times* 10/12/1835 3a. For analysis of portraits as presents, see Eaton, 'British Art' (Ph.D., 2001). For further presents from Nepal, see FPC 16/11/1835, no. 46, NAI.

[77] Revenue, Judicial, and Legislative Committee Minutes 4/6/1834.

[78] Broughton Papers MSS EUR F.213/6, f. 158, BL.

insisted on keeping some particularly appealing presents, leaving his discomfited government to negotiate the *quid pro quo*. Since, however, the government wanted to send the Awadh ruler 'a timely reproof', it determined to reject his presents in particular.[79] After two years of wrangling over these gifts (embarrassingly minus the missing necklace and the animals) and their storage and shipping costs, the Company returned them to Awadh.[80]

In London, Mariam Begum (known in London as Princess Moulvee) herself created a small scandal. Her entourage included a slave woman, whom she had acquired thirteen years earlier. During their extended stay, tensions arose between them, which led to her locking the slave in the garden of their Marylebone house 'naked' over a cold March night.[81] Acting on complaints by neighbours, parish authorities broke into the garden, released the woman, and had the police arrest Ismael Khan for 'inhumane cruelty' (authorities thus respected Mariam Begum's purdah). When Ismael Khan appeared in the local police court, 'splendidly attired in the costume of his country', he offered to reimburse the parish, explaining to the magistrate that the woman was insane so his wife had used 'coercion of a mild nature' on her. He was supported by Captains Grindlay and Musgrove (of the Indian Army).[82] The magistrate exonerated him. Parish authorities, themselves finding the woman acting in inexplicable ways, declared her insane and locked her up in the borough asylum.[83] Eventually she apparently returned to Mariam Begum; an Englishwoman remarked upon 'an idiot servant of the Prophet in a little heap in one corner' of Mariam's bedroom in Peone's Hotel just prior to their departure from England.[84]

[79] Broughton Papers MSS EUR F.213/4, f. 66, BL.

[80] FPC 25/7/1836, no. 25–9, NAI; PDHC, L/PS/3/107, f. 69; Court Minutes 16/11/1836, 25/1/1837, 8–22/2/1837, 1–22/3/1837, 5–12/4/1837.

[81] *Times* 14/3/1836 6f.

[82] Robert Melville Grindlay started the East India Agency which served many Indians in London as well as Britons; it became Grindlay's Bank.

[83] *Times* 22/3/1836 3b.

[84] Fox says Mariam implied that she had found this Indian woman in London: the 'idiot . . . with her here she discovered in London, and was very glad to appropriate the little Eastern mystery.' Fox, *Memories*, pp. 11–12.

This incident aside, Ismael Khan and Mariam Begum made a favourable social impression. One distinguished Englishwoman, Caroline Fox (1819–71), provides an extended account, rare about Indian women in London:

> She was seated in great state in the midst of the family circle, talking English with great self possession, inspite of her charming blunders. Her dress was an immense pair of trousers of striped Indian silk, a Cashmere shawl laid over her head, over a close covering of blue and yellow silk, two pairs of remarkable slippers, numbers of anklets and leglets, a great deal of jewelry, and a large blue cloak over all. She was very conversable, showed us her ornaments, wrote her name and title in English and Arabic in my book, and offered to make an egg curry . . . She promised . . . Cashmere shawl [gifts] adding, 'I get them very cheap, five shillings, seven shillings, ten shillings, very good, for I daughter king, duty take I, tell merchants my, make shawls, and I send you' . . . She told us of going to 'the Court of the King of London—He very good man, but he no power.—Parliament all power.— King no give half-penny but call Parliament, make council, council give leave, King give half penny.—For public charity King give one sovereign, poor little shopman, baker-man, fish-man, barter-man also give one sovereign. Poor King!—King Oude [Awadh] he give one thousand rupees, palanquin mans with gold stick, elephants, camels; no ask Parliament.' She and papa talked a little theology: she of course began it. 'I believe but one God, very bad not to think so; you believe Jesus Christ was prophet?' Papa said, 'Not a prophet, but the Son of God.' 'How you think so, God Almighty never marry!' . . . She showed us some magnificent jewelry, immense pearls, diamonds, and emeralds, tied up so carelessly in a dirty handkerchief. Her armlets were very curious, and she had a silver ring on her great toe, which lay in no obscurity before her. Then a number of her superb dresses were displayed, gold and silver tissues, satins, cashmeres, muslins of an almost impossible thinness, which she is going to give away at Mecca.[85]

This description, while condescending, nevertheless portrays Mariam Begum as lively, witty, and intriguingly exotic, and further generally aware of the contrasting constitutional roles of the Awadh and British kings. For years, London society pondered Mariam Begum's behaviour and sought to decipher the limits and connotations of her purdah

---

[85] Fox, *Memories*, pp. 11–13.

practices.[86] Ismael Khan similarly charmed British women with his grace, wealth, and mildly flirtatious Persian poetry.[87]

Ismael Khan continued his mission despite obstacles, particularly those generated by the mission's European contingent. He purchased fifty-four boxes of scientific instruments, texts, and other artifacts. He recruited Professor Felix John Vaughan Seddon (1798–1865, an orientalist scholar of Indian languages and literatures) and a secretary, De Walmer (who carried the model of a multi-shot gun).[88] The embezzlements by Du Bois and Freill, however, forced Ismael Khan to appeal to the directors for a loan; they eventually advanced him £1,000 to induce him to leave.[89] He also apprehended his reception by the Awadh ruler, since the royal presents had been rejected (or stolen). He requested and received from King William and the Board of Control letters extolling his conduct.[90] When he finally sailed for India via Mecca (January 1837), he brought along his acquisitions: Seddon, De Walmer, two shiploads of 'rare and valuable articles', and two British women—one as his wife, and another reportedly intended for Nasir al-Din.[91] After reaching Bombay, however, Ismael Khan died (July 1837), leaving his entourage in disarray.[92]

It is clear from this and other missions that Europeans employed by Indian rulers often had very different personal agendas from Indian diplomats. Du Bois and Friell may have had a better understanding of European society, but they also advanced their own interests more than those of the ruler who paid them. Further, they held very different

---

[86] Britons questioned Karim Khan about her around 1841. Karim Khan, *Siyahatnama*, pp. 277–8.

[87] Fox, *Memories*, pp. 12–13.

[88] See Seddon, *Address*. Seddon died (25/11/1865) in Murshidabad.

[89] FPC 17/4/1837, no. 1, NAI; Hobhouse letter 26/8/1836, Broughton Papers MSS EUR F.213/2, BL; PDHC, L/PS/3/106, ff. 2–3; L/PS/3/107, ff. 7–8, 10, 13, 16; Court Minutes 1/3/1836, 6–12/4/1836, 18/5/1836, 12/10/1836; Political and Military Committee Minutes 5/3/1836, 6/4/1836, 10–16/5/1836.

[90] Broughton Papers, MSS EUR F.213/4, ff. 120, 286, BL.

[91] White, *Mirzas Kaiwan Jah*, pp. 37–8; Miscellaneous Letters Received E/1/187, ff. 33–6; FPC 31/7/1837, nos 3–4, 13/12/1837, no. 71, NAI.

[92] Resident Lucknow to Political Secretary 15/11/1837, FPC 13/12/1837, no. 71, NAI.

social positions from Ismael Khan and Mariam Begum in Europe. The experiences of the mission's Indian servants and slaves were also distinct from those of their masters. For all these Indian travellers and settlers, but in separate ways, class and gender identities affected them powerfully there.

Just as Ismael Khan's mission ended, Nawab Iqbal al-Daula Bahadur (1808–88) went to London to claim the Awadh throne for himself. His father (a younger brother of Nasir al-Din's father) had been passed over for enthronement in 1814; instead, he received a Rs 200,000 annual pension and exile under British protection in Benares. When Iqbal al-Daula's widowed mother died in 1832, Nasir al-Din withdrew this pension from his cousins. Iqbal al-Daula protested, but the Company rejected his plea, saying it was Nasir al-Din's prerogative.[93] Iqbal al-Daula next wrote to the governor-general claiming succession to the Awadh throne himself. This too received no support. In 1837, as Nasir al-Din sickened, Iqbal al-Daula went to Calcutta to renew his claims. When Nasir al-Din finally died, the Resident deposed his putative son, unexpectedly selecting for enthronement Nasir al-Din's (and Iqbal al-Daula's) aged uncle, Muhammad Ali Shah (r.1837–42) who had also been living on a pension under British protection. Iqbal al-Daula then determined to represent his cause personally in the imperial capital.

Iqbal al-Daula arrived in London supported by a suite of Indian retainers, including a younger relative, *munshi* (secretary), *maulvi* (religious scholar), interpreter, cook, and several servants.[94] He also brought a disassembled silver carriage and many costly presents for the coronation of Queen Victoria (r.1837–1901). He would pursue his claims to the Awadh throne or, lacking that, a renewal of his pension, for almost two years in London.[95] He hired lavish apartments and British officers as his escorts. He commissioned cashiered Bengal Army Captain William White to write a book presenting his case in the most colourful

[93] Board Collections F/4/1479, no. 58147, BL; FPC 17/7/1837, nos 100–4, NAI.

[94] PDHC, L/PS/3/106, ff. 26–38; PP, Returns (Commons), 1837–8, vol. 41, papers 599, 660, pp. 381ff.

[95] Political and Military References 20/9/1837 to 29/5/1839, BL; PDHC, L/PS/3/106, ff. 17–20.

and glowing terms, while castigating his enemies, both British and Indian, in the most scurrilous ones: *Prince of Oude, or, The Claim of the Nawaub Ekbal-ood-Dowlah Bahador to the Throne of Oude* (London: William Strange, 1838).[96] The directors, however, refused to recognize him officially. Nevertheless, Iqbal al-Daula received royal honours during his tours of Britain and Ireland.[97] A female admirer surreptitiously sketched him and his suite, displaying their sartorial decisions (Image 14).

Iqbal al-Daula also secured the political support of influential Britons, mainly from the opposition, who used his case against the current government. Most prominent were Viscount Combermere (1773–1865, former Commander-in-Chief in India), Sir William Gore Ousely (1797–1866, former British ambassador to Persia), Winthrop Mackworth Praed (1802–39, Member of Parliament, prominent reform leader, and poet), and future Prime Minister Benjamin Disraeli (1804–81).[98] They, plus strong popular sentiment for him as the 'Awadh king' in their midst, created a political force that only assiduous efforts by government and directors could quell. The president of the Board of Control chided Governor-General Auckland:

> [I] wish that you had not permitted [Iqbal al-Daula Bahadur] to leave Benares—If these *Bahaudoors* are to come to England, they will give infinite trouble, and throw no small suspicion on the wisdom or justice of our Indian government. This man has managed to interest several persons in his favour, and intends to prosecute his claims in Parliament after they shall have been rejected by the Court [of directors]. His arrival has stimulated those connected with Sir Robert Peel's government [dismissed in 1835] to take up the Oude affairs . . . which will make it necessary for me to give an

[96] He lived first in Cornwall Terrace, then, after a brief trip abroad late in 1838, in Sussex Place, Regent's Park. PDHC, L/PS/3/106, ff. 38–42, L/PS/3/107, f. 58; Deposition of Sigmond 6/4/1852 L/L/Box 64 (438); Lushington letter 25/5/1838, Broughton Papers, MSS EUR F.213/3, BL. He also hired Bengal Cavalry Captain Frederick Coventry (1799–1855). Hodson, *List*, vol. 1, p. 395; vol. 4, pp. 455–6.

[97] *Times* 11/9/1838 4e, 14/9/1838 3f, 21/9/1838 4e.

[98] Broughton Papers, MSS EUR F.213/6, ff. 364–6, 388, 416–17; MSS EUR F.213/7, f. 43, BL; Commons debate 11/7/1838, *Hansard*, series 3, vol. 44, pp. 132–3.

Image 14: The Oude Suite (clockwise from top left: Iqbal al-Daula,
his relative, cook, servant, *munshi*, and *maulvi*).
Adapted from H.J., *c*.1838.

account of the transactions at Lucknow, as well as of the treaties existing between you and the state of Oude. I feel some difficulty as to what I shall say on the latter topic, on account of the decision to which we have come in respect to your [1837] Treaty [which London had annulled], as I should not like to make it known that I had the misfortune to differ from you . . . However I shall do my best to fight off the details, and direct attention to that part of the occurrence on which there ought not, and, I think, will not, be a difference of opinion . . . In the meantime I have refused to present the Oude Prince [to the British King], or to take any notice of him; and the same course has been followed by all of us [in Cabinet], except Lord Holland, who returned his card *mistaking him for the Turkish Ambassador*!!![99]

Indeed, in the course of the public and Parliamentary debates on Iqbal al-Daula's claims, the government had to reveal many of the mistakes and illegalities its officials had committed concerning Awadh. This included the governor-general's 1837 treaty with Awadh, which London annulled (although the governor-general 'inadvertently neglected' to inform the Awadh ruler of this embarrassing fact).[100]

Iqbal al-Daula's demands were, however, contested. Stacked against him, his brother Yamin al-Daula in India had long claimed to be older and therefore himself heir.[101] Although Yamin al-Daula's claim had been quickly dismissed by Calcutta, this weakened Iqbal al-Daula's case. Further, the directors were unwilling to reverse their Resident's recent forceful installation of his uncle, Muhammad Ali Shah. Nor did the directors agree to intervene to restore his pension, regarding it as a matter internal to the Awadh ruling family.[102]

Thus, despite his widespread royal reception and powerful political support, Iqbal al-Daula eventually lost his fight for the Awadh throne. He retired to Baghdad where the British later granted him a knighthood and protection until his death there.[103] Compared to life as a

[99] Emphasis in original. Hobhouse letter 9/6/1838, Broughton Papers, MSS EUR F.213/6, ff. 364–6, BL.

[100] FSC 7/8/1837, no. 22, BL; Aitchison, *Treaties*, vol. 1, pp. 162–5.

[101] Broughton Papers, MSS EUR F.213/6, f. 320; Political and Military Committee References 6/6/1838, BL; PDHC, L/PS/3/106, ff. 20–3; L/PS/3/107, ff. 78–9.

[102] PDHC, L/PS/3/107, f. 94.

[103] FPC 25/2/1848, nos 20–2, 18/7/1851, no. 175, NAI. At least one attendant, Suffer Ali, apparently remained in London. *Times* 5/3/1840 7c.

palace prisoner in Benares, he secured high levels of support, honour, and pleasure in London. Ultimately, however, the British government could fend off most assaults by Indian royalty or representatives, at the cost of some credibility and much effort. The largest of these delegations came in 1856, also from Awadh (see Chapter 10).

From the time of Iqbal al-Daula onwards, Indian diplomats and political agents formed a continuous presence in London. Their missions arrived separately, often initially unaware of each other. Their specific goals varied, as did their resources and abilities to function in the British public sphere. Yet, once there, most came together, sharing experiences and ideas, some gradually realizing the scale and extent of British colonialism across India and the world. Their writings and oral reports also began to disseminate such concepts in India.

Missions from Satara and Jhajjar

Rulers in the Maratha confederacy had a long history of deputations to Britain, going back to 1780 (see Chapter 2). When the Maratha ruler of Satara state sent Indian delegations to London in 1838, he and the Bombay governor recognized this as an act of resistance. The governor then deposed the ruler, but his agents continued this cause in London for fifteen years.

The Satara dynasty (descended from Maharaja Shivaji) had for generations been confined by their Peshwas and other nominal subordinates. In 1818, the Company sought to use the family's lingering prestige by releasing and enthroning its current head, Maharaja Pratap Singh (r.1818–39, d.1847), creating Satara state for him. In 1832, Pratap Singh contested the Bombay governor's adverse ruling over their respective jurisdictions, appealing to the directors. They overruled the governor, although he refused to admit this to the maharaja until 1835.[104] The next year, the Bombay government began a secret commission of inquiry into the maharaja. Paid informants provided this commission with extremely unlikely charges that Pratap Singh had conspired with the Portuguese in Goa and the deposed ruler of Nagpur to attack the British, plus he had suborned Indian soldiers in the Bombay Army.

---

[104] Carnac letter 1/2/1832, Broughton Papers, MSS EUR F.213/3, BL. See also Kulkarni, *Sattara Raj*.

The maharaja determined to supersede the Bombay government again. When his European agents in London failed to make progress, he engaged as his ambassador Maulvi Syed Mir Afzul Ali, with Munshi Wasiullah as his secretary. Both were Muslims from Bombay. The maharaja entrusted them with his letter to the directors: '[T]he Bombay government listening or trusting to the misrepresentation of vicious and low people have brought the whole affair into a sad state and occasioned great expense and loss; but their misrepresentations it is hoped will not be noticed by your Hon'ble Court . . . This [Satara] Court has no friendship or intercourse with any other Princes in the country . . . [our] only friendship is with English government . . .'[105] The Maharaja requested the directors to investigate the malfeasance of their Bombay government and overrule it once more.

In selecting his diplomats, Pratap Singh perforce initially looked to men not closely tied to his court. Despite precedents like Hanumantrao and Rammohun Roy, few high-born Hindus wanted to make the perilous journey to Britain, fraught with numerous opportunities for encountering impurities. Further, Mir Afzul Ali declared to British authorities that he was going on pilgrimage to Mecca, as had Mahboob Ali; the Company was reluctant to forbid such religious observances.

Mir Afzul Ali reached London in 1838, immediately inquiring from British supporters and hired counselors how to proceed. They urged quiet lobbying, rather than confronting the directors while negotiations continued in India.[106] This proved a fruitless and costly tactic. The directors adamantly rejected his right to represent the maharaja and accused him of conspiring with the Egyptian pasha and the Russians against Britain.[107] Further, most subsidiary alliance treaties, including Satara's, prohibited communication with 'foreign powers', except through the Resident. The Bombay government interpreted Britain as a 'foreign power', accused Pratap Singh of violating this provision, and moved to dethrone him.

In response, he quickly sent a much more high-powered delegation to London, headed by his relative, Yeswant Rao Rajah Sirkey (1806–?). This ambassador found the voyage to Britain threatening to his

---

[105] PDHC, L/PS/3/107, f. 13; Choksey, *Raja Pratapsinh*, pp. 171–4, 183–6.
[106] PDHC, L/PS/3/106, ff. 80–1.
[107] *Times* 7/7/1840 6b.

purity, but the stakes for his maharaja were so high he persisted.[108] The Bombay government first blocked these envoys from boarding the French ship on which they had booked passage, costing them their £550 unrefundable fare. The envoys finally found an English ship on which to sail in March 1839 (deceptively claiming to be merchants going to Malabar).[109] Meanwhile, the Bombay government reversed its ban on their departure, belatedly realizing it had no legal grounds for doing so. Nevertheless, the maharaja later purchased his own vessel to communicate with Britain without depending on European shipping. As the maharaja's situation deteriorated further, he sent another ambassador in September 1839: his political agent in Bombay, Rungo Bapojee (1804–57/8), whose Chitnavees Purvoe Kayastha Hindu family had long served this dynasty.[110]

That month, the Company deposed Pratap Singh in favour of his brother. The ex-maharaja, exiled from Satara to Benares and stripped of his wealth, persevered in his appeals to the directors. At the peak in 1840, he maintained in London simultaneously four ambassadors, supported by six secretaries and ten servants, which consumed much of his £12,000 annual pension.[111]

A daily account of the private as well as public lives of these envoys in London is preserved in the Urdu personal diary of another Indian ambassador, Karim Khan (b.1811).[112] This envoy arrived in 1840 attended by his secretary, Mahabbat Khan (b.1811), cook, Pir Baksh (b.1811), and servant, Ganda (b.1826). Karim Khan represented his relative, Nawab Hasan Ali Khan, in an appeal to the directors over a

[108] Register of Deposits, Bombay General Treasury, 30/4/1839, L/MAR/C/ 888, BL.

[109] East India Company, *Sattarah Papers*, vol. 1, p. 454; vol. 2, pp. 1077–8.

[110] Basu, *Story*, p. 142.

[111] 1841 Census, 67 Upper Berkeley Street.

[112] His autograph manuscript, apparently given by him to Garcin de Tassey, is now OR 2163, BL. It was published in facsimile, edited by Ibadat Barelvi in 1982. The text itself remains only in Urdu, except for a French translation up to the time of his departure from India: de Tassey, 'Karim'. There is also a paraphrase of parts of Karim Khan's book, published in *Blackwood's Edinburgh Magazine* 54, 336–8 (1843), pp. 453–64, 564–75, 753–65. 1841 Census, 14 Caroline Place, London.

long-running dispute about the family estate of Jhajjar (near Delhi).[113] His Pathan Afghan family had obtained this estate because they backed the British against the Marathas in 1804.

Once the Jhajjar and Satara delegations discovered each other in London, they were 'delighted', although their cordial relations were divided along religious dietary lines.[114] The leading Maratha diplomats were vegetarian so they avoided Karim Khan's food. Karim Khan observed Islamic restrictions so he shared food with Mir Afzul (he also hosted dinners for British supporters, but would not eat their meat). They all met repeatedly, however, sharing tactics, visiting London's noteworthy sites, and attending closely to the directors' repeated and frustrating rebuffs of their respective cases. As earlier delegations had painfully learned, the directors over the years developed containment tactics for dealing with Indian diplomats and envoys: refuse to recognize their credentials, insist that all communication come through British officials in India, and apply financial and other pressures to make the envoys leave London.

Among the Satara ambassadors, Mir Afzul gave up first. He became seriously ill, expended all his funds, and thus faced, in his words, 'actual want and degradation'.[115] Only by borrowing privately from Sir Charles Forbes (1774–1849, a Bombay merchant-banker and long-time supporter of Indian causes), could he manage to pay his debts and the passage money out of Britain in 1840, after two frustrating years.[116]

The remaining Satara ambassadors, despite encountering official rejection, lobbied individual directors, Company shareholders, politicians, and the public. They subsidized the British India Society and its periodical, *Indian Advocate*, as well as other London journals: *British Friend of India* and *Indian Examiner*. They generated enough controversy to cause special Company stockholder's meetings where the directors had openly to defend their dubious policies toward Satara.[117]

[113] Hasan Ali Khan claimed his rights to the estate from his nephew, Faiz Ali Khan, the incumbent ruler. FPC 6/6/1838, no. 15, NAI. According to de Tassey, Karim Khan was the son of Nawab Qa'im Khan and spent two years attached to the governor-general's staff. Introduction to 1982 edition, p. 10.

[114] Karim Khan, *Siyahat*, p. 117 and *passim*.

[115] PDHC, L/PS/3/106, ff. 80–1.

[116] Court Minutes 2/6/1841.

[117] East India Company, *Proceedings*; George Thompson, *Raja of Sattara*.

Their agitation affected British public policy debates. President of the Board of Control Hobhouse and Governor-General Auckland, in their confidential private correspondence, repeatedly exchanged half-serious pleas: Hobhouse urged Auckland to prevent such missions from leaving India, while Auckland desired Hobhouse to stop Parliament from accepting their petitions.[118] Each, however, felt constrained by British law from doing so. Nonetheless, Hobhouse pressured Auckland to refrain from deposing more rulers without strong justification: 'His Highness of Sattara has lost his guddee [throne] . . . and, perhaps, the Guicowar may follow. Each of the dethroned Princes will have Vakeels in England, and I shall have to fight the battles of the deposers in Parliament. I hope, therefore, you will be a little cautious in adopting such measures [depositions] and, if you do adopt them, at least send me over a defensible brief.'[119] We cannot document that such directives from London slowed the pace of annexations and dethronements, since they continued until 1857, albeit with political costs to government.

Lacking the force to reverse the direction of colonialism, the Satara diplomats nevertheless publicized what British officials in India had been doing. In particular, they gained sufficient backing in Parliament to force the directors to publish in 1841 four massive volumes of Company records relevant to Satara.[120] This extensive evidence enabled British politicians and the public to judge the Satara case themselves. This also allowed the ambassadors to read for the first time the records, reports, and correspondence of their opponents; they were shocked to realize their own confidential letters were being intercepted and examined by the Bombay government.

Still, pressure on the envoys mounted. Their personal enemies in Satara used their prolonged absence to dispossess their families, which the Bombay government refused to prevent.[121] By March 1841, they had expended all their funds and had to petition the directors for

[118] Hobhouse to Auckland, various, Broughton Papers, MSS EUR F.213 series, BL.

[119] Hobhouse to Auckland 4/11/1839, Broughton Papers, MSS EUR F.213/7, f. 221, BL.

[120] Hobhouse letter 4/2/1841, Broughton Papers, MSS EUR F.213/8, f. 45, BL. East India Company, *Sattara Papers*.

[121] Home Department, Military Papers, 1–15/6/1840, L/MIL/2/106, BL.

money to continue.[122] The directors rejected their repeated appeals, not wishing to prolong their presence in London. Finally, the directors agreed to loan them £2,500, later raised to £4,000, on condition that they depart forthwith.[123] The Board of Control consented only 'very reluctantly' to this loan, fearing it 'may have an injurious effect as a precedent in India' by encouraging other rulers to send future missions.[124] This was, however, a pattern dating back to the earliest missions: the directors delaying until the agents ran out of funds, but the agents refusing to leave and stop embarrassing the directors before the British public and Parliament until given money to clear their debts and purchase passage home. The Satara agents also asked the directors to guarantee they would not be confined on arrival by the Bombay government; this the directors refused.[125] Nevertheless, in July 1841 part of the mission sailed back via south Africa, the rest via Malta.

Fellow envoy Karim Khan left a few months later, summarizing his similarly fruitless two-year campaign:

> Let it be known that it will amount to sheer meaningless trouble for the powerless to come to England to plead their case and seek justice. If any pain-filled heart thinks: 'I will go there, submitting myself to such distant travel abroad, then perhaps they will show me mercy', this is an absolutely wrong idea. These people with whom you must deal here have neither fear of God nor mercy in their hearts. Your very indigence and need will prevent your gaining access to their favour. But any powerful [Indian] is welcome to make this attempt, only provided that he brings 10,000,000 rupees cash and forty attendants who are proper companions, reliable supporters, civil, and trustworthy people. Then do not even mention your case for a year, but during this period prepare the groundwork for your case using the money you brought . . . Then if you have the Grace of God, you may get a verdict within a year . . .[126]

In Karim Khan's case, the directors finally decided not to intervene in what they considered an intra-familial dispute. But they loaned him

---

[122] Court Minutes 16/3/1841, 13/4/1841.

[123] Court Minutes 11–19/5/1841. In a concession, the directors recovered this money not from the ex-raja's pension but from the state revenues of Satara. East India Company, *Sattara Papers*, vol. 3, p. 83.

[124] PDHC 13/5/1841, L/PS/3/107, ff. 167–8.

[125] Court Minutes 9–25/6/1841.

[126] Karim Khan, *Siyahat*, pp. 283–4.

the £300 he requested to pay his debts and purchase return passage for himself and his suite.[127]

In the case of the Satara ambassadors, the group that travelled via Malta received there more funds and instructions from Pratap Singh, strictly ordering them to continue their work in London. Only Bapojee agreed to do so. He warned his ex-maharaja about how difficult and expensive it had been, and would be in future, to bribe and influence Britons but he returned to London in January 1842 to renew the struggle.[128]

The Longest Among Other Envoys

Despite many obstacles, Bapojee remained a further decade in London, allying with Britons also opposed to official policies, developing his political and communication skills to mobilize much support and publicity in British public discourse, and enhancing his understanding of colonialism and India. On Bapojee's return to London in 1842, the directors immediately informed him that they regarded this as a violation of their loan arrangement, 'nor can [the directors], under such circumstances, in any way regard you as an Agent of the Ex-Raja'.[129] Further, they ignored his complaints about racial insults heaped on him and the ex-maharaja by Company officials aboard ship. Such rejections from the directors, however, did not suppress Bapojee.

Bapojee learned how to agitate for his cause. He lobbied the Company's shareholders unceasingly, leading to special stockholders' meetings about Satara in 1842, 1845, 1847, and 1849.[130] Indeed, Bapojee himself addressed one meeting 'habited in the costume of his country'.[131] He insightfully framed his arguments on moral and legal grounds recognized as sacred by the British establishment: his master had been loyal but the Company arbitrarily accused him of treason on the basis of paid and perjuring informants using forged and incredible evidence

---

[127] FPC 22/2/1843, no. 52, NAI.

[128] Court Minutes 24/1/1842. Choksey, *Raja*, pp. 76–83. 1851 Census, 9 Blandford Place, London.

[129] PDHC, L/PS/3/107, ff. 196–7.

[130] Norris, *Case*; East India Company, *East India Company Debates*; Anonymous, *Raja of Sattara*; Bapojee, *Annexation*, pp. 86–9.

[131] *Times* 23/8/1845 5a.

before a secret tribunal at which he had not been able to represent himself; his master had legal treaties and human rights that the Company violated in deposing, exiling, and confining him; the Company illegally confiscated his master's personal property; his master's household, including pregnant women, were abused by their British guards. Bapojee's extensive efforts led to over thirty questions, petitions, and motions in Parliament in support of his cause, as well as over twenty Parliamentary orders for documents from the directors, and a Parliamentary Commission of Inquiry.[132] Bapojee personally observed sessions of Parliament during these debates.[133] As both his supporters and opponents acknowledged, only his persistent efforts kept the Satara case in British public discourse, while many other Indian rulers, who had also been deposed and their states annexed, received no such attention.[134]

Highlighting Bapojee's achievements by comparison, an unprepared mission arrived in 1845 from the imprisoned amirs of Sindh, protesting their deposition, exile, and confinement by the Company. Although British policy in Sindh remained highly controversial, these envoys—Akhund Habibulla, Diwan Mitharam, and Diwan Dayaram—contributed little to it. They were ill-equipped for what they encountered in Britain, as they acknowledged, being 'Ignorant of England

---

[132] Commons Debates 21/3/1850, 12/8/1850, 18/3/1851, 3/4/1851, *Hansard*, series 3, vol. 109, pp. 1218–19; vol. 113, pp. 1026–8; vol. 115, pp. 124–5, 969–1006; Lords Debates 4/8/1842, 24/6/1844, 8/5/1846, *Hansard*, series 3, vol. 65, pp. 1008–9; vol. 75, pp. 1242–7; vol. 86, pp. 218–19; PP, Returns (Commons), 1843, vol. 38, paper 569, pp. 109ff, vol. 38(I), paper 491, pp. 1ff, 1843, vol. 36, paper 622, pp. 345ff; 1845, vol. 34, paper 419, pp. 433ff; 1846, vol. 31, paper 359, pp. 347ff, paper 465, pp. 351ff, paper 509, pp. 373ff; 1847, vol. 41, paper 291, pp. 45ff, paper 312, pp. 315ff, paper 711, pp. 327ff, Command Paper 875, pp. 339ff; 1847–8, vol. 48, paper 23, pp. 321ff, paper 145, pp. 379ff, paper 247, pp 423ff; 1849, vol. 39, paper 442, pp. 135ff, paper 83, pp. 137ff; 1850, vol. 41, paper 247, pp. 189ff, paper 669, pp. 203ff; 1851, vol. 41, paper 90, pp. 735ff, paper 331, pp. 741ff; 1852–3, vol. 69, paper 437, pp. 535ff, paper 648, pp. 541ff; Court Minutes 27–9/7/1842; Hume, *Rajah of Sattara*; Bapojee, Petition to Lords (24/2/1853) to Commons 2/3/1853.

[133] Commons Debate 31/8/1848, *Hansard*, series 3, vol. 101, pp. 728–49.

[134] Commons Debate 25/6/1847, *Hansard*, series 3, vol. 93, pp. 953–62, 1337.

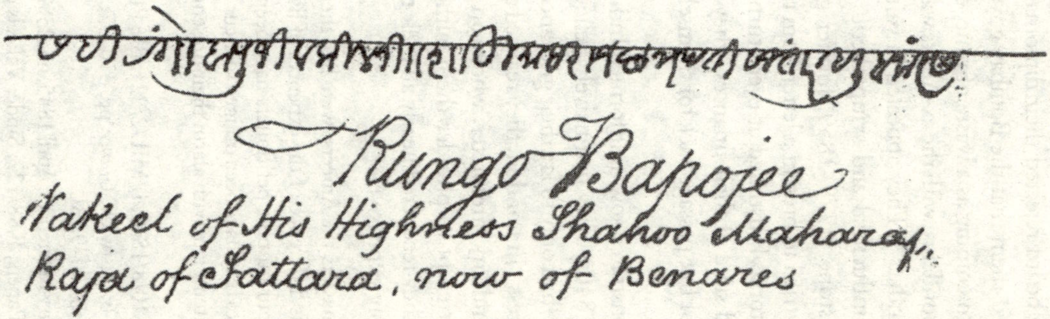

Rungo Bapojee

Wakeel of His Highness Shahoo Maharaj, Raja of Sattara, now of Benares

Image 15: Signature of Rungo Bapojee in Several Languages.

manners and custom, and even of the English language'.[135] Just before
they embarked from Calcutta, they had hired an Indian expert in negotiating with the British, 'through whom they have been obliged to
transact all their business, and make all their disbursements'. As usual,
the directors and the board rejected their diplomatic credentials un-
opened, and reminded them that the Bombay government had tried
to dissuade them from coming as a waste of time, effort, and money.
The mission's correspondence with the ex-Amirs was much delayed by
the Government of India.[136] They appealed in vain to His Majesty's
government and to influential and sympathetic Britons including
Mountstuart Elphinstone (1779–1859, former governor of Bombay).[137] They further tried to present a letter from the wives of the ex-
Amirs to Queen Victoria. Frustrated at every turn, in August 1845,
due to 'the exhausted state of their finances', they gave up and petitioned the directors for free passage back for themselves and their eight
servants.[138]

Their plight demonstrates how uninformed Indian missions might
be, even in the mid 1840s. They had naively believed that once they
reached London they 'had only to lay their grievances at the feet of the
Throne to obtain redress'. In London, they realized almost too late 'the
dishonesty of their [Indian] Interpreter, whom on Saturday last they
detected in a open attempt to plunder them, although through the
activity of the police they recovered nearly all their property'. Further,
London was incredibly expensive:

> Their unfortunate masters the Ameers, were like themselves, quite igno-
> rant of the enormous difference of the expences of living in England and
> in Hindostan . . . Your humble petitioners have been in amazement and
> despair at the expenses they have been obliged to incur . . . [They felt] utter
> helplessness and contemplate with alarm their present position—without

[135] Military Papers 1–10/8/1845, L/MIL/2/221, BL; PDHC, L/PS/3/96, ff.
298–300, 310–11, 325–6; Eastwick, *Glance*, pp. 310–37; *Times* 19/6/1845 3f.
[136] FSC 25/4/1846, nos 60–9, BL.
[137] Political and Military References, April 1845, no. 2352, BL; Sindh, Vakeels
of, letters, Elphinstone Papers, F.88/127; Sinde, Vakeels of, letter 15/8/1845,
Tract 553, appendix, BL; Sindh, Vakeels of, *Translation*.
[138] Court Minutes 16/4/1845, 13/8/1845; Political and Military References,
August 1845, no. 1266, BL.

friends . . . [T]hey dread lest sickness should overtake them and prevent their return to India, their only object therefore is to quit England, and they throw themselves upon the mercy and compassion of your honorable Court [of directors] to provide them with a passage to their Native Country.[139]

The directors were glad to help them leave, although the heated debates on Sindh continued without them.[140]

In contrast, Bapojee's extensive campaigns recruited prominent allies. His most staunch advocate over the years was Joseph Hume (1777–1855), an idealistic Parliamentarian who had made his fortune in India before devoting himself to radical politics.[141] Hume persisted for nearly a decade in articulating Bapojee's arguments. Some House Members were convinced by his speeches, but they were always a minority.

Bapojee also gave financial aid to sympathetic candidates for Parliament. Among these was John Williams (1802–55), elected Member for Macclesfield in 1847. Illustrative of the respect and influence Bapojee held among them, the 'Reformers of Marylebone' seated him at the head-table in the banquet celebrating this election. In the commemorative lithograph, Bapojee appears prominently in Maratha clothing, with a Vaishnavite sectarian emblem on his forehead (Image 16). Since Bapojee observed Hindu dietary restrictions, he apparently did not actually partake of their food or wine.

In addition, Bapojee paid other prominent Britons to support him. Among these, the famous abolitionist and reformer, George Thompson (1804–78), provided moral and rhetorical power for Bapojee's cause and for Indian princes and peoples generally. Thompson helped

[139] Military Papers 1–10/8/1845, L/MIL/2/221, BL.

[140] Despite the failure of these emissaries, the issue of the Sindh annexation continued to be a contested political topic in London. Parliament demanded that all the relevant correspondence be presented for its scrutiny; many Company shareholders openly opposed these annexations. See the many Parliamentary Papers and debates there and in the Courts of Directors and Proprietors on Sindh, 1839–64.

[141] See Hume's correspondence with Hobhouse and Wood in MSS EUR F.213 and EUR F.78/47, BL. See also Chancellor, *Political Life*; Huch and Ziegler, *Joseph Hume*.

Image 16: The Banquet given by the Reformers of Marylebone 1 December 1847 to John Williams to celebrate his return to Parliament for the Borough of Macclesfield, engraved by N. Ploszczynski.

found the British India Association and published articles very favourable to the ex-maharaja in his *British Indian Advocate*.[142] He also made a series of forceful speeches to the Company's stockholders and Parliament.[143] Thompson, however, did not come cheaply. From 1841 to 1847, the ex-maharaja had Bapojee pay him £1,200 annually (a rate half Bapojee's own salary).[144]

In 1842–3 Thompson went to India at the ex-maharaja's expense to consult him personally (and to pursue his other political and financial interests).[145] While in Calcutta, Thompson also gave popular speeches about the need to improve the Government of India and reorganize Calcutta's reformers.[146] He also met there with the agents of the Mughal emperor. Indeed, Thompson travelled to Delhi at the emperor's invitation (and expense). The emperor then appointed Thompson his official ambassador to London (at £1,200 annually, paid a full year in advance, plus all costs) with the titles: Safir al-Daula, Mushir al-Mulk, Bahadur, Musleh Jung ('Envoy of government, Counsellor of State, Hero, Mediator of War').[147] Back in London, Thompson addressed the proprietors on the emperor's behalf, but spoke so abrasively that the Company's chairman rebuked him. Nevertheless, Thompson wrote a glowing article about his speech in his journal, *British Indian Advocate*. Thompson sent this article with a letter extolling his accomplishments to the emperor, and also to fifteen other Indian rulers, suggesting they employ him too. Indeed, at least one (the Awadh ruler) briefly did so.[148] The emperor, after an initial burst of enthusiasm, soon realized in dismay that Thompson was also in the pay of other Indian royalty and had actually accomplished little.[149]

[142] Burleigh, *Reception*. E.g., *British Indian Advocate*, 1/6/1841, p. 42.

[143] George Thompson, *Raja of Sattara*.

[144] Anonymous, *Biographical Sketch*. The *British Indian Advocate* and *Bombay Times* among other newspapers frequently exchanged heated accusations about Thompson's financial gain from his advocacy of Satara.

[145] Thompson travelled with Dwarkanath Tagore, invited and funded by reformers in Calcutta as well as the ex-maharaja. See Kling, *Partner*, pp. 175–8.

[146] George Thompson, *Speeches*.

[147] George Thompson, 'Fragment'; Majumdar, *Raja Rammohun Roy*, p. 284.

[148] Political and Military References, March 1844, no. 3675–6, BL.

[149] Commons debate 11/7/1848, *Hansard*, series 3, vol. 100, pp. 412–14.

The emperor terminated Thompson's employment, but he remained on the Satara payroll for years.

After his return to London, Thompson also renewed his efforts for the ex-maharaja of Satara. In 1845, since Bapojee was diffident about reading his speech to the Company's shareholders in English himself, he selected Thompson to do so.[150] Thompson also drafted in English some of the memorials to the governor-general and the queen, which the ex-Maharaja simply endorsed with his seal. Thompson also passed to Hume a letter stolen from the Government of India's files. Hume quoted it in Parliament to castigate the government. When questioned how they acquired what must have been purloined by 'a fraud, a perjury, or a breach of trust', Thompson claimed that it had mysteriously appeared on his breakfast table.[151] With Bapojee's financial support, Thompson was elected to Parliament in 1847 from Tower Hamlets.[152] With the death of Pratap Singh that year, however, Thompson ceased being paid and stopped working for Satara.[153] As Karl Marx noted ironically in 1853, radical reformers like Hume and Thompson simultaneously supported Indian aristocrats while attacking hereditary privilege in Britain.[154]

Bapojee also appealed to the British public directly, denouncing the Company's injustices against his master and all other Indians. He published a book and many pamphlets advocating his cause.[155] The Satara case appeared repeatedly in British newspapers.[156] In 1846,

[150] Court Minutes 6/10/1847; *Times* 23/8/1845 5a.

[151] Commons debate 18/3/1847, *Hansard*, series 3, vol. 91, pp. 192–6; vol. 93, pp. 953–62.

[152] Coincidentally, many people from Bangladesh settled in this neighbourhood of London during the late twentieth century. George Thompson, *Address*.

[153] Bapojee, *Rajah of Sattara*, p. 33. Thompson, 'Rajah of Sattara'.

[154] Marx, 'The East India Question'.

[155] Among Bapojee's publications were Bapojee, *Annexation of Sattara*; Bapojee, *Letter to the Right Hon. J. C. Herries*; Bapojee, *Letter to the Right Honourable Sir John Cam Hobhouse*; Bapojee, *Rajah of Sattara*; Bapojee, *Statement*; Simha, *Letter*; Vindex, *Dethroned Rajah*. Among those by his supporters were: Jones Brydges, *Case*; Nicholson, *Statement*.

[156] *Times* 1/11/1839 5c–d, 15/2/1840 6d–e, 7/7/1840 6b, 30/7/1842 7a–b, 9/2/1843 5b–c, 10/2/1843 7b–c, 23/8/1845 5a, 25/8/1845 6d; *Sun* 7/11/1850; *Daily News* 7/8/1851.

Bapojee organized a well-attended public meeting in London. There, he claimed to speak for 'the hundred and fifty millions of my fellow-countrymen', asking rhetorically if he should inform them 'that English truth, justice and generosity, in the existence of which they once believed, are but fables, which have deluded them to their subjugation and ruin'.[157] He continued, placing the wrongs done by the British government pejoratively in the broader contexts of slavery and world-wide imperialism:

> The slave-born native of Africa no sooner touches British ground than his chains fall off; he becomes as free as the air he breathes, and knows no other master, under God, than the law. When the free-born, but wronged, Native of India seeks to quit his country to complain, he is hunted, tracked, imprisoned, heavily fined, and the law twisted and tortured to chain him to the earth . . . I am not here relating the conduct of the French in Algiers or in Tahiti; I am not describing the cruelty and tyranny of an emperor of Morocco, nor am I speaking of barbarities perpetuated by savages in New Zealand. I am simply stating what was done in British India to women in travail and peaceable men placed without help in the power of persons acting in the name of the British government, and armed with all its authority.[158]

Thus, like Rammohun Roy a decade earlier, Bapojee invoked British beliefs in their superior justice and rule of law, compared to other powers, even as he articulated his vision of India as a whole.

Bapojee's innovative and persistent attacks on British colonial aggression drew British public attention, but they did not reverse the deposition of Pratap Singh, who died in 1847. Nor, when Pratap Singh's brother and successor as Maharaja died the next year without an heir, could Bapojee stop the annexation of Satara under the 'Doctrine of Lapse'. Nevertheless, Bapojee continued to work for the Satara family and for Indians as a whole.

In 1849, Bapojee decided to expose the extent of British colonialism to all Indian rulers and rally them collectively against it. Based on what he had learned over his years in London, he composed a letter, sending individual copies to the many 'Princes and Chiefs in India'.

[157] Bapojee, *Statement*, p. 2.
[158] Ibid., pp. 11, 23–4.

This warned each of them explicitly against British 'Plots and intrigues', and documented British 'violation of existing treaties'.[159] His letter declared that the British 'Government pretends to be for the benefit of the people of India' but then demonstrated the falsehood of this pretense. He warned each ruler about British *zabar-dasti* ('oppression') and particularly about their annexing of princely states, 'one by one':

> This declaration [the Doctrine of Lapse] is probably not known to your Highness, it behooves you, therefore, to look into your Treaty, and immediately to address the governor-general, to know if . . . you are to be permitted to exercise the right of adoption in conformity with the Law and Custom of the Hindoos, or whether such Law is to be violated and to be henceforth set at naught . . . I address you whether Hindoo or Mussulman, with a view to your own advantage, to prevent the future violation of treaties and the ruin of your families.

He included extracts from printed Parliamentary Papers to document the truth of his warnings.

Despite this letter's collective appeal to all Indian rulers, it expressed 'old patriotism' rather than revolutionary consciousness.[160] It sought to rally Indian princes rather than the Indian people. It called for the constitutional defense of extant treaties and dynasties, not the expulsion of the British. Indeed, it explicitly denied that what he urged was treasonous. Further, Bapojee notified the British authorities about his letter and submitted to them his English translation—long after he had safely sent off the originals to India's rulers. Nevertheless, Bapojee did keenly articulate how the British tried to keep each Indian ruler isolated, ignorant of British aggression in other Indian states. The entire picture was most visible only in London. Although this early effort to rally India's rulers into unity to demand their legal and moral rights had no immediately visible effect, many of the rulers he addressed fought violently in 1857 to drive out the British, motivated by the same colonial injustices that Bapojee warned them about.

Further, Bapojee's time in London made him painfully aware of

---

[159] 'Circular to Princes and Chiefs in India', written 17/9/1849, enclosed in Rungo Bapojee letter 8/11/1849, Broughton Papers, MSS EUR F.213/112, BL. The copy sent to the Maharaja of Mysore fell into British hands. FPC 29/12/1849, nos 165–7, NAI.

[160] See Basu, *Story*, p. 142; Bayly, *Origins*.

how skin-colour and biological race were becoming key factors in colonialism. In 1852, he asserted:

> ... in India ... what is virtue and what is vice, what is innocence and what guilt, what truth, what falsehood, shall be determined by the complexion of the agent; the white man, or Company's servant, being always regarded as the embodiment of virtue and truth, incapable of wrong even in his own showing, and alone worthy of belief—the dark man, or native, held up as the personification of vice and falsehood, to be accused only to be condemned, degraded, vilified, punished, imprisoned at will, tortured, beggared, and all in secret and unheard.[161]

Such explicit accusations suggest both the increasing salience of inherited 'racial' identities in Britain and also Bapojee's deepening understanding of this.[162]

For British authorities in Britain and India, Bapojee's persevering and powerful critiques of public policy remained an embarrassment but not an immediately dangerous threat. He and his British supporters kept the Company's wrongs under public scrutiny. Yet, the government knew that, as long as it held majorities in Parliament and the Court of directors, it could outlast him. Governor-general Dalhousie's 1850 Minute, quoted by Bapojee as revealed in a Parliamentary Paper, stated:

> the withdrawal of Rungo Bapojee from agitation in London, though it would afford relief from a tiresome and useless importunity, cannot be regarded as an object of any moment; and if it were of much more consequence that it is, the object will shortly be obtained without any sacrifice [by the Company] for it is very evident that the means of supporting the agent are no longer forthcoming and that his mission must, of necessity, come to an early end.[163]

Since British authorities could not legally deport Bapojee, they tried to starve him out. Company officials in India indeed put increased pressure on the late Pratap Singh's family which consequently cut off

[161] Bapojee, *Rajah*, p. 13.

[162] Rungo Bapojee had complained in 1842 about slights he had personally received from Britons, and his need 'to bear with resignation the brand of oppression set upon our race and colour grounds'. Bapojee letters 24/1/1842, 12/3/1842, *Sattara Papers*, vol. 2, pp. 1301–2; vol. 3, pp. 28–30.

[163] Governor-General's Minute 7/8/1850, cited in Bapojee, *Rajah*, p. 11.

Bapojee's pay in 1847 and recalled him in July 1850.[164] Bapojee, however, rejected this recall, carrying on for another three years.

Not all missions received the same hostile treatment as Bapojee. In 1850, General Jung Bahadur Rana (1817–77) of Nepal arrived with a large suite to a warm reception.[165] Nepal had fought the Company and lost (1814–16) but subsequently managed to avoid its indirect rule and remain relatively autonomous. Jung Bahadur had recently staged a coup, making himself *de facto* ruler. Before leaving India, Jung Bahadur had applied for and received the approval of the governor-general to be treated as ambassador plenipotentiary. He brought a suite of twenty-five Nepali dignitaries, plus servants, and hired a Briton, Donald Macleod, to escort him.

Jung Bahadur also employed an Indian as a secretary to assist him in his negotiations, someone long-experienced in working with the British, and yet not loyal to them: Mohammed Ali Khan of Rohilkhand. Mohammed Ali had studied in India at British-run Bareilly College and then Roorkee Engineering College.[166] He subsequently entered the Company's engineering service but received degrading appointments as a mere subordinate to less-educated Britons until 1850, when he resigned in disgust.[167]

Since British authorities recognized Jung Bahadur's political power in Nepal, they wanted to impress him with Britain's industrial and military might, thus drawing him into closer alliance. Yet, British authorities still had difficulties identifying his exact status. Indeed, when he arrived, some Britons asserted the man was an imposter. The directors were reduced to surreptitious scrutiny of his finger-ring (given by the Nepal Resident) as proof of his identity.[168] Further, the Board of Control had to ask the directors for the precise English equivalent of the rana's protocol status (since he was ambassador, nominal prime minister, yet also effectively ruler of Nepal).[169] Finally, convinced of

[164] Court Minutes 10/6/1851.

[165] Whelpton, *Jang Bahadur.*

[166] Forbes-Mitchell, *Reminiscences*, pp. 183–93.

[167] Ward, *Our Bones*, pp. 40–9.

[168] Hobhouse letter 28/6/1850 and reply 28/6/1850, Broughton Papers, MSS EUR F.213/18, BL.

[169] Hobhouse letter 20/6/1850, Broughton Papers, MSS EUR F.213/15;

his authenticity, the directors and Board of Control welcomed him, arranged his presentation to Queen Victoria, and hosted dinners for him (aware that he would not actually eat in their presence).[170] While he was being feted, Queen Mother Rani Chanda of the Punjab, wrote him asking for intercession with the British on behalf of her son, Duleep Singh.[171] Jung Bahadur demonstrated to the British his trustworthiness by reporting this overture.

Jung Bahadur had three goals for his mission: to negotiate extended extradition arrangements, to employ British engineers in Nepal, and to gain permission to bypass the Resident in his communications with Britain.[172] The directors rejected all of these, instructing him to negotiate them with the governor-general. In the end, he only gained part of the first of these goals.

While the directors thus deflected Jung Bahadur's political mission as they did those of other envoys, they treated him with much honour. Unlike other Indian envoys whom the British wished would go away, the British tried vainly to persuade Jung Bahadur to remain longer and explore 'the most remarkable of the objects to be found, not only in London, but throughout the country . . . there are still, even in this Capital, a vast variety of exhibitions abounding with curious specimens of our arts and sciences, which you have hitherto been unable to inspect.'[173] Jung Bahadur, indeed, requested that the Company procure and convey to Nepal for him £1,000 worth of advanced machinery and cattle; the directors agreed, supplying horse-powered rice threshing and hulling machinery (although they had to purchase some from their American manufacturers).[174] Jung Bahadur presented his portrait to the directors but left only months after his arrival. He

Political and Military References May 1850, nos 760, 882; July 1850, nos 2083–4, BL.

[170] Court Minutes 30/5/1850; Shepherd letter 28/5/1850, Broughton Papers, MSS EUR F.213/16, BL.

[171] Cavenagh letter 27–8/8/1850, Broughton Papers, MSS EUR F.213/18, BL.

[172] Welpton, *Jang Bahadur*, pp. 100–1.

[173] Hobhouse letter 10/7/1850, Broughton Papers, MSS EUR F.213/18, BL.

[174] Court Minutes 14–21/8/1850, 20/7/1853.

returned to Nepal (via France) impressed enough to support the British militarily and politically during the 1857 conflict.[175] His mission also produced a lengthy, although not always precise, Nepali account of Britain's politics, society, and economy; this manuscript did not circulate widely outside of Jung Bahadur's élite circle, however.[176]

In contrast to Jung Bahadur's mission, Bapojee's appeared to British authorities only an embarrassment. The directors increased their pressure to drive Bapojee out of London. He had expended his funds and personally borrowed heavily in the Satara cause. In 1851, the directors rejected his request that the Company pay his salary. Finally, in 1853, he agreed to leave London and petitioned the directors for £5,000 to cover his debts and passage home; the directors negotiated him down to £2,500 and required he sign a 'written engagement . . . to surrender all supposed claims against the Government of India connected with his Mission to this Country . . . and to refrain from any future agitation here or in India.'[177] Bapojee, compelled by economic necessity, reluctantly agreed; Hume personally paid the final bills due from Bapojee: taxes due the queen.[178]

Before Bapojee left London to return to his wife and family in annexed Satara, however, he briefed another Maratha mission. Dhundu Pant 'Nana Sahib' was the adopted son of exiled Peshwa Baji Rao II (r.1796–1818, d.1853, the son of Raghunathrao discussed in Chapter 2). Yet, the British refused to recognize Dhundu Pant's succession to this title and pension. When Dhundu Pant's hired British representative, Frederick L. Biddle, failed to convince the directors to reverse this policy, Dhundu Pant sent to London a courtier, Raja Piraji Rao Bhonsley (d.1853), a military man, Joala Pershad Risaldar, and two Muslim experts in matters British: Azimullah Khan (c. 1830–58) and Mohammed

[175] Court Minutes 4–25/9/1850, 2/10/1850. See Fisher, *Indirect Rule*, pp. 414–22.
[176] 'Jang Bahadruko Belait-Yatra', translated and analysed in Whelpton, *Jang Bahadur*.
[177] Court Minutes, 21/9/1853 and *passim*.
[178] Court Minutes 1/3/1854; Political and Military Committee Minutes 1/3/1854. British newspapers lamented the departure of this 'Mahratta gentleman'. *Protectionist Paper* reprinted in *Times* 7/12/1853 12d.

Ali Khan (who had recently returned from London with Jung Bahadur's mission).[179] Although Raja Piraji Rao died aboard ship, the rest carried on.[180]

Like Mohammed Ali, Azimullah had long experience with the British in India. He reportedly grew up as a servant, while his widowed mother was an ayah, to a series of British missionaries of the Society for the Propagation of the Gospel in Foreign Parts.[181] They taught him English and French and then employed him as a teacher at their Cawnpore Free School. Dhundu Pant was his student. Azimullah went on to serve as munshi to British generals but, when accused of bribery and dismissed, he entered Dhundu Pant's service in 1851.

This Maratha mission reached Britain in 1853 and learned from Bapojee about how to cultivate influential Britons, and prepare for contests with officialdom. They wore British-style clothing and dined with Britons. Azimullah in particular impressed Britons as having 'gentleman-like style . . . a well bred agreeable person of good intelligence about English matters.'[182] He became a protégé of Lady Lucy Duff Gordon (1821–69), an author and traveller who had married the prime minister's cousin, Sir Alexander Duff Gordon.[183] She educated Azimullah in British culture and politics, believing she had convinced him to relinquish his anti-British sentiments. Although only about ten years older, she signed her letters to him 'your affect. Mother', and he addressed her as 'European Mother' in reply.[184] Additionally, a young British woman in Brighton, 'Miss A.', wrote letters, partly in French,

[179] PDHC 17/8/1857, 9/9/1857, L/PS/3/108.

[180] FPC 24/6/1853, nos 146–8, 26/6/1853, no. 147, NAI; Gordon, *Our India Mission*, pp. 40–9.

[181] Shepherd, *Personal Narrative*, pp. 14, 101; Ward, *Our Bones*, pp. 22–6, 535, 680–1, n.485; Surendra Nath Sen, *Eighteen Fifty-Seven*, pp. 126–9, 368; Misra, *Nana Saheb*, pp. 145, 200–1, 557-60, 574–8.

[182] Anonymous, 'Nana Sahib'; Syed Lutfullah, *Azimullah*, pp. 51–2; Gordon, *Our India Mission*, pp. 40–9; Kaye, *History of the Sepoy War*, vol. 1, pp. 109–11; Trevelyan, *Cawnpore*, p. 44.

[183] Frank, *Lucy Duff Gordon*, pp. 177–81; P. Taylor, *Companion*, pp. 29–31; Ward, *Our Bones*, pp. 40–9, 581, n.193.

[184] Ward, *Our Bones*, pp. 45, 585; Roberts, *Forty One Years*, vol. 1, p. 377; Roberts, *Letters Written*, pp. 120–1; Frank, *Lucy Duff Gordon*, pp. 190–1.

expressing her desire to marry him.[185] Not all Britons accepted Azimullah, however. John Lang (1817–69, a British journalist and lawyer), when introduced to Azimullah as 'the Prince' responded 'Prince indeed! He has changed my plate fifty times in India.'[186] We have earlier seen this same pattern: Britons with experience in India denigrating Indians who were received as royalty in London's salons.

The generally warm social reception received by this delegation contrasted with the cold official one. They submitted Dhundu Pant's documents, which the directors rejected and refused to discuss with them.[187] Frustrated, they left Britain in June 1855. Azimullah travelled via Crimea, where he observed the British and Ottoman armies ineffectively fighting the Russians.[188]

Bapojee, Dhundu Pant, Azimullah, and Mohammed Ali all fought the British in 1857. The first three were never captured and various rumors about them circulated. The British issued a warrant for Bapojee's arrest, with a £50 reward; while Bapojee evaded capture and disappeared, his son was seized and executed.[189] The British accused Dhundu Pant and Azimullah of the 'Cawnpore massacre' of captured Britons. Muhammed Ali Khan served as chief engineer in the Awadh army, but was captured by the British near Lucknow and executed as a spy.[190] Some Indian and Pakistani nationalists, however, have subsequently presented these men as the architects of their respective freedom movements.[191] Thus, long experience in Britain raised these men's awareness of colonialism and sense of patriotism for India.

[185] Ward, *Our Bones*, p. 45; Mowbray Thomson, *Story of Cawnpore*, pp. 53–9; Roberts, *Forty One Years*, vol. 1, pp. 293n, 427–9. These letters produced a range of reactions from hostile to sympathetic. E.g., Toon, *Love Letters*.

[186] Lang, *Wanderings*, pp. 103–19; Keene, *Servant*, pp. 162–3.

[187] Court Minutes 20/7/1853, 3–17/8/1853; Political and Military Committee Minutes 20/7/1853, 17/8/1853.

[188] William Russell, *My Diary*, vol. 1, pp. 165–7.

[189] Basu, *Story*, pp. 341–4. Basu doubts that Bapojee was 'foolish enough' to attack the British, however.

[190] Forbes-Mitchell, *Reminiscences*, pp. 174–83.

[191] E.g., Syed Lutfullah, *Azimullah*, pp. 6, 31; www.vandemataram.com/biographies/patriots/akhan.htm. Basu argues Bapojee 'should be considered the first and pioneer Indian agitator in England, and his failure shows the futility of so-called "constitutional agitation" on the part of Indians for their rights and privileges'. Basu, *Story*, p. 142.

Indian Missions to Britain

Indian diplomatic and political delegations had a range of goals, resources, and results.[192] Some came from Indian royalty who thereby resisted British colonial controls over their political communications by gaining direct access to the public sphere in Britain. Others arrived from would-be Indian rulers seeking enthronement or deposed dynasties seeking enhanced pensions. Going themselves or sending trusted Indian representatives and hired experts in dealing with the British, they sought to advance their causes by manoeuvring among British political and legal authorities and appealing to public opinion.

The level of knowledge about Britain that these envoys arrived with and gained once there varied widely. Most carried false expectations that they would obtain full justice denied them in India, despite the recurrent frustration of earlier missions. In contrast, some brought or developed highly sophisticated understandings of the constitutional and practical relationships among various British political bodies. A few, despite their sojourn in London, apparently returned to India with continued deep misapprehensions about these.

In contrast, British knowledge (and constructions) of Indian politics grew in force over this period. The directors and Government of India, whose experience in dealing with such emissaries also developed over time, accumulated knowledge and policies to suppress, confine, and repulse them. Despite the extent of British political aggression and annexations in India, just over thirty Indian diplomatic and political missions managed to reach London (prior to 1857). This suggests the power of British policies of indirect rule that isolated each Indian state.

The better informed and skillful Indian emissaries used ideological and legal appeals, purchased influence, and allied with opposition parties to mobilize considerable political and/or popular support in London. Many produced knowledge about colonial practises that British

---

[192] This period saw many missions in addition to those discussed in this chapter. For example, Samuldass in 1833 recovered the office and stipend of *desai* of Nerryad apparently as a result of his journey to Britain. Court Minutes 30/10/1833; Miscellaneous Letters Received, E/1/185, vol. 3, f. 147, BL. In 1844, Sayd Hassan and his son arrived in London, having come via Moscow and Berlin, seeking redress against the Punjab government. Court Minutes 13–27/ 11/1844, 4/12/1844; Military and Political Committee Minutes 4/12/1844.

authorities had to struggle to contain. British officials in India were warned by London about the controversies which these delegations from deposed rulers generated, which may have tempered their more extreme actions—although annexations continued apace until 1857.

While the goals of most envoys were limited to the aspirations of their individual employers, some in London expressed a more inclusive, albeit nascent, sense of representing Indians as a whole. Their even limited success in gaining a hearing, direct knowledge of Britain, and occasionally material benefits inspired future delegations with similar grievances. Further, their writings and oral reports informed Indian society, although unevenly, about the true nature of British society, politics, and colonialism. This information differed considerably from that projected by British officials, educators, and missionaries in India.

The social circles formed by the several classes which comprised these diplomatic and political missions thus added to the growing Indian presence in Britain, each with different interests and images. Indian élites consulted about tactics with other Indian and British élites. They also exchanged dinners and celebrations with each other, although the observant among them divided by religious community. They still appeared to many Britons as somewhat exotically attractive, although this would diminish over time. These missions also hired Indian experts in dealing with the British, part of the growing number of Indians who sought and gained extensive knowledge of British culture (discussed in following chapters). Many settled in Britain, while others returned to resist or collaborate with colonialism in India. The servants who attended these missions were part of the growing number of working-class Indian men and women who established themselves, particularly in London's East End, its 'Oriental Quarter'. British authorities increasingly came to see them as 'social problems'. Thus, by the 1830s, these various Indian networks had become an on-going and visible, albeit small, element in British society.

CHAPTER 8

Britain as Site of Pleasure and Advancement

Exploring Britain's Possibilities

From the 1830s, various middle-class and aristocratic Indian men viewed Britain as an accessible site for personal gratification and elevation. In this chapter, we examine the lives of four such men. Unlike Indian envoys, most did not pursue primarily political goals while in Britain but principally personal ones. Each entered British society largely independently, unlike menservants or women who often remained under the control of British employers or patriarchs. Rather, these four men, and others like them, created distinctive places for themselves in British society.

While all reached Britain during the 1830s, their backgrounds and particular roles differed. Rajaram Roy, following the death of his foster father, Raja Rammohun Roy, elected to remain in Britain working for years as a clerk in the Board of Control. Although his British patrons trained him to enter the upper ranks of the civil service that administered India, when he finally returned to Calcutta he found himself ill fitted for life there. Jamh ood-Deen, a son of Tipu Sultan, persuaded the governor-general to release him from palace confinement in India in order to visit Britain. There, he obtained substantial sums from the directors to fund his leisured life as a royal man about town, remaining in Europe until his death. Yusuf Khan, a cavalry officer, chose to tour Britain, exploring its pleasures and people. He returned to India and wrote a book in Urdu, the first of its kind, recounting his adventures and discoveries. David Ochterlony Dyce Sombre, a wealthy man of mixed ancestry, heir to Begum Sombre of Sardhana, settled in Britain, married into the British aristocracy, and had himself elected to Parliament. But he overstepped the bounds of what some in the British social, medical, and legal establishments considered rational and spent the last decade of his life fighting for the recovery of his estate and reputation. Two died in Britain, two returned to recount their experiences to other Indians.

Even at the height of British colonial expansion in India, boundaries and classifications of identity remained relatively negotiable for many Indians in Britain, especially élite men. On arrival, they entered a very different environment from colonized India, where strong racial distancing prevailed. Empowered by their class and gender, élite and middle-class Indian men moved relatively freely within British society, interacting with a range of men and women, through a variety of relationships. At times, each of the four men considered here had power and authority over some Britons, particularly women. Yet they also stood apart from White Britons due to their Indian origins. As Chapter 5 showed, British authorities of this time had not resolved the issue of who exactly was Indian, nor the legal and moral implications of that classification. These four men all crossed cultural boundaries, proving particularly difficult for Britons to define.

Further, since they were all literate, we have more extensive personal accounts by these men than by most other Indians. This enables us to learn about them as distinctive personalities and consider more deeply their critical or laudatory assessments of British society. These men Anglicized themselves to different degrees, yet they did not accept all British assertions of cultural superiority. Each also discovered there were costs to pay for crossing between colony and metropole.

Clerk at the Board of Control

Raja Rammohun Roy had received a generally respectful reception in Britain as a social and religious leader, but simultaneously a more hostile one as envoy of the Mughal emperor. After Roy's death in 1833 his adopted son, Rajaram Roy (b.1817), benefited both from the outpouring of British sympathy and respect for his foster father and from his own adaptation to British cultural norms.

Rajaram Roy's origins are unclear. Rammohun Roy stated that an English friend had found the boy abandoned at the Hardwar festival and entrusted him to Roy.[1] When the Englishman died at sea, Roy

---

[1] Carpenter, *Last Days*, pp. 141–2.

adopted the boy. Critics of Roy asserted that the boy was Roy's own illegitimate child by a Muslim or English mistress.[2] In any case, Roy treated him like a son. Since Roy was busy in London with social, intellectual, and diplomatic engagements, he entrusted the boy to a series of his admirers: Reverend Dawson, heiress Miss Catherine Castle and her maternal aunt, Miss Kiddell, then Reverend Samuel Wood.[3]

After his foster father's death, Rajaram elected to remain in Britain. In 1835, when choosing a career, Rajaram requested employment by the British government. Consequently Sir John Hobhouse, president of the Board of Control, inducted him as an 'extra clerk' on his staff (from August 1835) with £100 as his annual salary.[4] Hobhouse regarded Rajaram's clerkship at the board as a means of his 'acquiring an insight into the mode in which the public business is transacted in England'. Thus trained, Rajaram was supposed to demonstrate the Anglicized model for other Indians to follow: 'it cannot but have a beneficial effect on the natives of India generally . . . to furnish them with the means and motives of rendering themselves capable of assisting, to a much greater extent than at present, in the administration of India.'[5] His moral and technical training proved highly satisfactory to his patron, Hobhouse, who renewed his appointment annually, calling him 'a very superior young fellow', who 'has maintained the best reputation with all those who have had an opportunity of forming a judgement of his character.'[6]

While working for the board, Rajaram socialized with his patron and other élite members of British society. He clearly held his own in aristocratic dinner conversations, once telling a story about his walking tour of Scotland, in which an old Scots peasant woman, on suddenly seeing him, yelled ' "The deil! the deil!" and fled.'[7] This droll story displayed Rajarama's willingness to joke about his own dark complexion, and also aligned his élite audience with him as superior compared

[2] Collet, *Life*, p. 115.

[3] Carpenter, *Last Days*, pp. 81–2; Collet, *Life*, pp. 140–2; S.N. Roy, 'Rajaram'.

[4] Foster, 'India Board'.

[5] Board Minutes 6/8/1835, ff. 460b–61.

[6] Hobhouse letter 9/4/1838, Broughton Papers, MSS EUR F.213/6, ff. 315–16, BL.

[7] Broughton, *Recollections*, vol. 5, p. 68.

to someone quite different: a lower-class, superstitious, uneducated, female, aged, Scot.

In 1836, Hobhouse nominated Rajaram for the Company's civil service in India. The directors, however, almost unanimously objected. The Company's chairman asserted the appointment of rare Anglicized Indians like Rajaram would disgruntle both Britons and more orthodox Indians:

> It is quite certain that at present no considerable number of natives could be entrusted with the higher duties of the service, and the introduction of one or two, while it might excite unpleasant feelings in the minds of the European members of the Service, would, I apprehend, afford little gratification to the Natives, and perhaps might even give rise to no better feeling than that of envy. An isolated appointment it is clear would be likely to be attended with as little ease or comfort to the holder, as of satisfaction to his English associates, or to the great majority of his excluded Native brethren . . . [T]he great mass of Natives can entertain no hope whatever of reaching the higher departments of the Service, and the elevation of an individual who has departed in some degree from the practice and principles of his stricter countrymen would perhaps scarcely be felt as an accomplishment.[8]

Indeed, British public opinion in Calcutta noticed and condemned this proposed appointment.[9] Hobhouse withdrew his nomination and renewed Rajaram's clerkship at the board.

Yet Rajaram's British patrons continued to promise him a high official appointment in India. After eight years in Britain, Rajaram decided to return and accept this. He resigned in 1838, receiving a gratuity of eighteen months' salary (£150) as a reward for his 'diligence' and in memory of his adoptive father.[10] Hobhouse wrote a personal letter to the governor-general requesting he '—take charge of the fortunes of this, otherwise, friendless, creature . . . Indeed I may say that your great patronage cannot be better bestowed than in behalf of

[8] Carnat letter 21/11/1836, Broughton Papers, MSS EUR F.213/2, BL.

[9] See *Calcutta Courier* 17/5/1836 and *Asiatic Journal* December 1836, p. 222. I thank P.T. Nair for providing these references.

[10] Board Minutes 4/8/1835, 6–7/9/1836, 14/8/1837, 26–7/2/1838, 13/3/1838.

my young friend.'[11] As many other Anglicized Indians also discovered, however, returning to India meant losing social status.

The Bengal government, and British society in Calcutta generally, demeaned Rajaram and blighted his prospects for advancement. The much more clearly defined racial separations enforced there between Indians and Britons made him anomalous. Deferring to Hobhouse's strong recommendation, however, the governor-general appointed him as a clerk in the Foreign Office, at a monthly salary of Rs 200 (far more than double his London income). Yet most Britons across India considered him presumptuous; even Hobhouse eventually accepted the governor-general's assessment that: 'Young Ram Roy is a clever fellow, but he was a little spoilt in England . . .'.[12]

In Calcutta, Rajaram attempted the lifestyle of his London friends and also his adoptive father. He lacked the financial resources, however, to sustain this. As Rajaram explained, he was just too generous and his needs outstripped his income: 'I sometimes resolve to be very saving but my resolve after a few months melts away. Indeed with my small means it is difficult to save without being thought stingy and without depriving myself much of the common comforts.'[13] He borrowed heavily from his late father's supporters. When friends of the late David Hare (1775–1842, a reforming educator and backer of Rammohun Roy) raised a subscription for Hare's children, Rajaram felt he was entitled to draw upon this sum to discharge his own personal debts.[14] When one British subscriber objected and charged him in public with 'ingratitude', Rajaram wanted to loose a 'torrent of abuse' on him, but still did not get access to the money.

Finding himself unappreciated in Calcutta, Rajaram wished to return to London. But he could not convince Dwarkanath Tagore (1794–1846) to invite him along when Tagore went to Britain in 1844. Nor

---

[11] Hobhouse letter 9/4/1838, Broughton Papers, MSS EUR F.213/6, ff. 315–16, BL.

[12] Hobhouse letter 26/1/1839, Broughton Papers MSS EUR F.213/7, f. 90, BL. See also letter to Editor, *Calcutta Courier* 26/7/1839, reprinted in *Bombay Times* 10/8/1839 p. 506b–c which notes Rajaram Roy's intermediate position and unsuitable ambition.

[13] Rajaram Roy letter 17/9/1844, MSS EUR C.161, ff. 3–6, BL.

[14] Storm letter 12/8/1844, MSS EUR C.174, BL.

could Rajaram find any other patron to pay for his voyage and finance him as intermediary between Indians and Britons. He described his ambition, and asked for more money from Hare's brother in London:

> I would like to establish myself in London as a petty merchant and an agent in which capacity many of the minor native merchants would gladly assist me. If I fail in my attempt I but return a bad penny to Calcutta to resume my [Government] appointment . . . [H]ere . . . you must succumb to up-starts and humbugs to get your daily bread. Surely with a Govt. situation in London and a little pecuniary assistance from friends, backed by your experience, and trading cautiously and certainly without verging upon speculation or depending upon the throw of a die we ought to get a humble means of maintenance. As a single man I cannot require much, while acti-vity in public life and taking interest in matters connected with Asia might hereafter turn up to some advantage. One thing is certain, I shall be a thou-sand times more happy than I am here and the avocations there will be much more congenial to my feelings than I can possibly expect them to be here. If you can send 100 Rs. or 150 Rs. by return mail you will greatly oblige me . . .[15]

He went on to warn that he had already borrowed money without authorization in Hare's name and that those bills would soon arrive. In short, the remainder of Rajaram's life failed to live up to his years and hopes in Britain.

Rajaram, like so many other Indians who went to Britain, thus en-countered a much reduced standing in India on his return. He found it difficult to reconcile his unequal social positions in Calcutta and London. Some Indian visitors decided to remain in Britain rather than return to India and the relative degradation of life there.

Pensioned Son of Tipu Sultan

While British popular culture demonized Tipu Sultan of Mysore more than any other Indian ruler (prior to 1857), his descendants found honoured acceptance in British society. Many British writers, dra-matists, and painters portrayed Tipu as emblematic not just of ori-ental despotism but also, in his death, of British triumph. Many Indian

[15] Rajaram Roy letter 17/9/1844, MSS EUR C.161, ff. 3–6, BL. See also Rajaram Roy to Janet Hare, cited in Kling, *Partner*, p. 182.

travellers were guided by their British hosts to the war trophies from Tipu's defeat enshrined in Britain.[16]

Tipu's family, however, evoked British sympathies as well as fears. When Tipu was temporarily defeated in 1792, Governor-General Cornwallis took two sons as hostages, a scene which British paintings portrayed touchingly.[17] After Tipu's death in 1799, the governor-general exiled his entire household—including a dozen sons, many wives, and other dependants—to eliminate any possible political threat. Yet the British also allotted them generous pensions. Some of his family were confined at Vellore and later implicated in the 1806 'mutiny' of Indian troops there. The governor-general then removed them to Calcutta. Nevertheless, he simultaneously increased their pensions to demonstrate 'the civilized spirit . . . [and] peculiar character of the [British, through] . . . tender and liberal treatment.'[18]

As the family's number grew over time, these pensions stretched ever thinner to cover their aristocratic pretensions. In 1823, their pleas convinced the Company to increase their stipends yet again. Subsequent appeals, however, met less sympathy. In 1833, the Board of Control retorted: 'The British government cannot take upon itself the burthen of maintaining a constantly and rapidly increasing body of idle and useless pensioners in an undiminishing style of comfort and affluence. The Mysore Stipendiaries must like other persons suffer the inconveniences consequent upon having larger families than they can maintain [and] . . . must train up at least the younger branches of their families to earn a subsistence by useful and honourable exertion.'[19] In response, one of Tipu's younger sons, Shahzada Shaykh Jahangir-i Zaman, Mahomed Jamh ood-Deen (*c.* 1792–1842) determined to resist his slide into obscurity by venturing to London, where he could amuse and advance himself.

Like the other deposed Indian royalty seeking freedom, Jamh ood-Deen had to provide his British keepers with a convincing pretext for

[16] E.g., Nowrojee and Merwanjee, *Journal,* p. 334.

[17] E.g., Robert Home's 'Lord Cornwallis Receiving the Sons of Tipu Sultan' (1792), National Army Museum; Bayly, *Raj,* pp. 154–5.

[18] Minto Minute 19/10/1807, PP Returns (Commons) 1861, vol. 46, paper 44, pp. 107–8.

[19] Board Collections F/4/1531, no. 60579, BL.

release from internment. At age forty-one he claimed: 'I have not enjoyed a perfect state of health, for some months past I am frequently
troubled with anxiety and restlessness of mind', therefore only four
years in England's bracing climate would restore his 'impaired Constitution'.[20] When his British superintendent rejected this, Jamh ood-
Deen appealed personally to Governor-General Bentinck. After two
years' deliberation, Bentinck finally granted permission in 1833 and
provided a letter of introduction to the British king. Jamh ood-Deen
arranged to receive some £2,000 of his annual pension in Britain, while
the remaining Rs 4,500 (£450) would support his extensive household
in India, including eight wives and mistresses, the mother of the senior
of these, his own mother, his estranged adopted son, and seven body-
guards.[21] Early in 1835, he sailed for Britain with only a European
manservant to attend him.

Over the next seven years, Jamh ood-Deen entered British high society as 'the Prince of Mysore', even as he worked with substantial success to convince the directors that they owed him money. His family's
reputation and status, and the governor-general's letter, gained Jamh
ood-Deen a private audience with King William IV, presented by the
president of the Board of Control. He proffered to the British monarch a book narrating his family's history, highlighting his own family's royalty. He also agreed to avoid politics: 'intercourse in any shape
with those parties to whom His Majesty objects'.[22] Jamh ood-Deen
continued to meet with King William and then Queen Victoria, which
firmly established his credentials in British élite society. He also secured the sympathetic support of powerful British politicians and the
French and Belgian monarchs.[23] The lingering notoriety of his father
only added to his prestige.

Like other visiting Indian royalty, Jamh ood-Deen began a campaign to enhance his pension. He employed Captain Grindlay and
British lawyers Allan and Son to pursue his own and his family's cases
before the directors and in British law courts.[24] He argued that by

[20] Board Collections F/4/1523, no. 60155, BL.

[21] Court Minutes 10/6/1835.

[22] Broughton Papers, MSS EUR F.213/4, ff. 42–3; EUR F.213/6, f. 313,
BL.

[23] E.g., Broughton Papers, MSS EUR F.213/6, ff. 287–90, BL.

[24] Court Minutes 19/2/1840 to 13/5/1840; PDHC, L/PS/3/107, ff. 121–2,

treaty, when he had reached age fifteen in 1807, his pension should
have been doubled to £4,800 annually, but less than half that had actually been paid. Therefore he demanded the considerable arrears of
£83,040, and later compound interest on those arrears.[25] After hearing
his arguments for a year, the directors grudgingly acceded to his first
demands for the pension enhancement and arrears, but not the latter
for compound interest.[26]

Funded by these sizeable payments and undiscouraged by the directors' refusal to do more, Jamh ood-Deen continued his campaigns
for the interest and yet a larger pension. These repeated demands, plus
his refusal to return to India, frustrated the Directors and Board of
Control, who could not legally deport him. The president of the board
wrote confidentially to the governor-general in 1837:

> We have *our* grievances also . . . we have the Mysore Prince who, having
> persuaded Lord W. Bentinck to allow him to come to England for his
> health, has turned the journey to account by raising his allowances, and
> now threatens me with an appeal to the H. of Commons, because I will not
> force the Court [of directors] to pay interest on the arrears now granted to
> him. So I say, send us no more missions, and no more Mysore Princes, if
> you please.[27]

A few months later and frequently thereafter, the president privately
directed the governor-general to pressurize 'that wretched fellow'
through his family:

> . . . your Mysore Prince Jamh-ood-Deen is very troublesome and is going
> to bring his case before Parliament. . . . I do wish you would signify to him

---

132, 183, 201; Political and Military References 19/2/1840, no. 497, 4/3/
1840, no. 628, 7/4/1840, no. 772, 5/5/1840, no. 1111, BL.

[25] Court Minutes 25/11/1835 to 27/7/1836; Political and Military Committee Minutes 6–27/4/1842; PDHC, L/PS/3/106, ff. 3–10; Board Collections F/4/1531, no. 60579; Broughton Papers, MSS EUR F.213/3; F 213/4,
ff. 41–2; F 213/8, f. 189; Home Department, Military Papers April 1836,
L/MIL/2/49; Political and Military References 6/6/1838, no. 812, 11/7/1838,
no. 1216, 8/8/1838, no. 1517, 17/10/1838, no. 2110, 16/1/1839, no. 2813,
19/2/1839, no. 3149, 27/1/1841, no. 897, 25/5/1841, no. 2201, 10/7/1841,
no. 2810, April 1842, nos 2101, 2508, BL.

[26] PDHC, L/PS/3/107, ff. 8, 10, 12.

[27] Hobhouse letter 29/3/1837, Broughton Papers, MSS EUR F.213/6, ff. 4–
6, BL.

that unless he returns forthwith you will play the deuce with his wives and mothers of whom he is always talking to me—as if he had as many of the last as the first. You have no notion how very annoying he is, and I repeat my intreaties to you not to tolerate his absence any longer.[28]

Although his initial four-year 'leave' had long expired, in 1841 Jamh ood-Deen arranged for more of his pension to be paid him in London and less to his family in India.[29]

During this time, he lived in fashionable Albany Street with a British maidservant, Rachel Loyd (b.1814).[30] As a wealthy and well-known man-about-town, he socialized with British nobility. He also met frequently with Indian diplomats, agents, and dignitaries, dining with the élite Muslims among them.[31] Indeed, he encouraged other pensioned and confined Indian royalty to visit London, including a younger relative by marriage, Iqbal al-Daula (claimant to the Awadh throne, see Chapter 7).[32] In November 1842, after seven years of this high society life, and still making occasionally successful further claims for augmentation of his pension and that of his brothers, he died while on a pleasure trip to Paris, where he was buried.[33]

His untimely death created yet more difficulties for British authorities, who had to sort out his complex financial affairs. To make things worse for them, Sir Thomas Turton, Registrar and public administrator at Calcutta, embarrassingly had embezzled much of his estate in India. The directors regretted Turton's crimes but argued that since he

[28] Hobhouse letter 30/8/1837, Broughton Papers, MSS EUR F.213/6, ff. 122–3, see also ff. 59, 279, 320; F.213/7, ff. 142, 207, BL.

[29] PDHC, L/PS/3/107, ff. 67, 71–8, 159, 166, 180; Court Minutes 27/1/1841 to 8/9/1841.

[30] 1841 Census, 149 Albany Street; Boyle, *Court Guide* 1841, 1842.

[31] Karim Khan recorded meeting him frequently. *Siyahatnama, passim.*

[32] Broughton Papers, MSS EUR F.213/6, ff. 364–6, 395, 416–17; MSS EUR F.213/7, f. 43, BL.

[33] FPC 5/2/1840, no. 12–14, NAI; *Times* 29/4/1843 1b; Court Minutes 6/4/1842 to 13/9/1843; PDHC, L/PS/3/107, ff. 34–5, 243a; Home Department, Military Papers December 1842, no. 1446, May 1843, no. 3065, November 1842, no. 1157, L/MIL/2/116; Political and Military References September 1843, no. 750, October 1843, nos 928–1055, BL.

had stolen the money in his private, as opposed to public, capacity, they were not responsible.[34] Contrasted with Jamh ood-Deen's restricted life in India, he found mingling with his British and Indian peers in Europe highly gratifying. Although British officialdom found his continued demands frustrating, Jamh ood-Deen's pleasure-filled years and his substantial success in obtaining money from the Company were increasingly emulated by other Indian élites, including other descendants of Tipu Sultan (see Chapter 10). Various middle-class Indians also came to regard London as a site of enjoyment and advancement during this period.

Military Officer and Tourist

Yusuf Khan (*c.* 1803–61), an officer in the cavalry of the Awadh ruler, decided independently to explore British society and amuse himself. His Urdu book, *Tarikh-i Yusufi* (*Yusuf's History*) recalled his encounters with people at all levels of British society, ranging from élites to streetwalkers.[35] Since his main motivation was a desire to see Europe, his journal reads as a tourist account; indeed, he does not mention meeting any other Indians there, confining himself to consideration of the British people and sights.

Yusuf Khan was born into a Sunni Pathan Afghan family that had settled in Hyderabad (Deccan).[36] From age twelve, he searched for a truly fulfilling religious path until he discovered what he called the

[34] Turton embezzled many people's funds. Court Minutes 2/8/1854; PP, Returns (Commons) 1849, vol. 39, paper 417, pp. 391ff; 1850, vol. 19, paper 440, pp. 601ff; 1854–5, vol. 40, paper 248, pp. 437ff.

[35] This book was first published in 1847, edited by Pandit Dharm Narayan; the title page has in English: *Travels in Europe by Yoosoof Khan Kummulposh*, with the rest in Urdu. In 1873, Joseph Johannes brought out a second edition, retitled *Ajaibat-i Farang*. The Mission Printing Press and Nevil Kishore, Lucknow, brought out a 1898 edition. Makkah Books, Lahore, republished this work in 1983 with an Introduction by Tahsin Faruqi, as *Ajaibat-i Farang*. It has never been published in English.

[36] Reid argues unconvincingly that Yusuf Khan was not Indian but rather a Catholic Italian named Delmerich, of the Medici family. Cited in Introduction to 1983 edition, pp. 52–3. See also Llewellyn-Jones, 'Indian Travellers'.

'Sulaimani' religion: 'Having no alternative, I have chosen the Sulaimani religion, which I know is better than the others.'[37] Critics have glossed this doctrine as a combination of deism and hedonism, with Yusuf Khan as its originator and main exponent, but Yusuf Khan presented it as broad humanism.[38] Yusuf Khan's pennames, 'Kambalposh' and its variant, 'Kamalposh', (literally 'blanket-wearer', meaning mendicant), seem to reflect his counter-cultural self-image.

In his mid twenties, Yusuf Khan left Hyderabad. After exploring much of north India, including British-ruled areas and princely states, he settled in Awadh's capital, Lucknow. There he attracted the patronage of a British officer who obtained for him an appointment as *jemadar* (lieutenant) in the cavalry of the ruler, Nasir al-Din Haidar. He then rose to be *subedar* (captain) of the special royal 'Sulaimani Regiment'.[39] Yusuf Khan thus lived outside direct British authority, but he recognized its power.

In Lucknow during the 1830s, Yusuf Khan, like some other men of his class, determined to gain personal access to British culture, which was advancing through military and political assertions across India. He, however, went further than many of his contemporaries: 'I passed my life with ease and gratitude to God. Suddenly I desired to gain the knowledge of the English. With great effort, I mastered it. Then, I mostly read history books and was delighted to see accounts of cities and the nature and customs of nations.'[40] This was the period when British cultural assertions were starting to dominate in many leading educational institutions in India (see Chapter 9).[41]

Yusuf Khan thus prepared himself for visiting Britain, developing a set of expectations about what he would find there, although he would not be limited by them after he arrived.[42] He must also have

---

[37] Yusuf Khan, *Ajaibat*, pp. 133, 158, and elsewhere.

[38] Tahsin Faruqi, Introduction to 1983 edition of Yusuf Khan, *Ajaibat*, pp. 72–4.

[39] The regiment was designated by one of Nasir al-Din's titles. Perhaps this is where Yusuf Khan developed his 'Sulaimani' religion.

[40] Yusuf Khan, *Ajaibat*, p. 98.

[41] See Zastoupil and Moir, *Great Indian Education*. See also Lelyveld, *Aligarh's First*.

[42] See Chatterjee, '500 Years'.

saved sufficient money to support his travels. In 1836 (aged 33) he took a two-year leave of absence to explore British society directly. First, he moved to Calcutta for 5–6 months. From there, he purchased passage to England, sailing in March 1837, via south Africa.

On board, Yusuf Khan enhanced his English language skills while continuing his precise diary in Urdu, recording his impressions of the new lands he encountered. While in south Africa, for example, he noted the 'Cape Coloured,' including their 'beautiful women, neither too dark nor too fair, whose fathers are English and mothers are out-siders.'[43] He admired Muslims living at the Cape, whose women were 'modest and pure', but disdained their religious strictures. Through-out his life, Yusuf Khan delighted in challenging established religious authorities of all communities. He recounted how a Muslim cleric in south Africa chided him, saying 'you are a Muslim, yet you drink wine.' To which he replied: 'Hazrat Paigambar [the Prophet Muham-mad] did not forbid the juice of the grape.'[44]

On reaching England in August 1837, he began his European adven-ture. First, he evaded British Royal Customs by hiring a small boat which, for £5, landed him and an English fellow passenger at a small seaside village, where he spent the night. They then caught a mail coach, which brought him into his first physical contact with an Englishwoman, but he found her, disappointingly, a 'very ugly wo-man . . . fatter than a mountain.'[45] On reaching London, however, he formed a much more favourable impression of British women of all classes: 'strolling along the river were English Sahibs with their wives making a show. What beautiful and elegant women they were, like fairies.'[46] He found his ability to observe even respectable British women in Britain surprising, in contrast to India, where élite Indian women were secluded and where British women also generally remained aloof from Indian men.

Since he intended to spend some time in that city, he rented rooms for £10 per month, sharing the house with a British lodger. He re-counted how he amused the landlord and servants by bathing in the

[43] Yusuf Khan, *Ajaibat*, p. 106.
[44] Ibid., pp. 106–7.
[45] Ibid., pp. 109–10.
[46] Ibid., p. 112.

kitchen instead of the bathroom: 'I became ashamed and could make no answer.'[47] Yet, Yusuf Khan had the self-confidence to record (rather than suppress) this incident, which highlighted his own initial naïveté about British cultural classification of rooms.

While in London, he explored its many attractions. Like many Indian travellers, he described for his Indian readers the most striking tourist sights of London, including Saint Paul's, the British Museum, Westminster Abbey, the Guild Hall, Madam Tussaud's, the Royal Surrey Theatre, a dance hall, the pleasure gardens at Vauxhall, and the Panorama of London in the Coliseum. He also made outings to Greenwich, Woolwich, and the Royal Botanical Gardens at Kew. He often noted cross-cultural encounters. In the British Library, he particularly admired its collections of books in Arabic, Persian, Hebrew, and Greek. He noted that in England there was a demand for language teachers of Persian and Arabic, in neither of which languages Yusuf Khan was himself proficient, alas.[48] At the Tower of London he was especially impressed by weapons and mementos taken in Tipu Sultan's final defeat. At Astley's Theatre, he paid to see an enactment by oriental-costumed British actors of an Iranian Safavid prince defeating Turkmans. This reminded him of the Awadh army in which he had served. He also made a trip to Paris. In each instance, his background made his 'gaze' different from Europeans in the audience: they consumed their own culture; he was an outsider comparing theirs to his own.

While in London, Yusuf Khan debated with authorities of the established Church of England about religious doctrine and performance, including idol worship and morality. Scrutinizing their flaws firsthand, he criticized Britons for hypocrisy: 'those who do not act perfectly should not criticize others.' One conversation-partner, Father Mortimer, 'said "Christianity had been in India for one hundred years, but Hindustani people had not understood the right path." I responded that those people are on the right path for them . . . He rejoined, "what right path, they worship idols." ' Yusuf Khan retorted that Hindus kept idols, but so too did Christians have images. He concluded his account of this debate with his own triumph: 'In truth, they do not know God . . . Hearing this, they were silenced.'[49] He also visited a Jewish

[47] Ibid., p. 114.
[48] Ibid., p. 236.
[49] Ibid., p. 128, see also pp. 131–2.

synagogue, discussing Muslim and Jewish religious and social practices comparatively with a leader of that community. There, he noted
with approval that women sat separately in an upper balcony.

While Yusuf Khan critiqued British cultural and religious customs,
he accepted its political authority over India. He joined the admiring
throng applauding the teenaged Queen Victoria:

> Seeing her face, in my heart arose this prayer: 'O Allah, may her horse come
> near me and she glance at me.' God heard. When her horse came before
> me, it paused and the resplendent visage of the Queen looked so serene like
> the model of divine power. I saluted her. Seeing me, she graciously bestow-
> ed a smile on me. On regarding her, I swelled up with unconfined joy and
> in my heart a prayer arose that, 'Oh God, may this Sultanate never decline
> and always prosper and continue to expand and acquire perfection.'[50]

Among the choices that Indians visiting Britain had to make (and
still have to make) were what sartorial and dietary practises to observe.
Yusuf Khan apparently continued to wear his usual clothes. These distinguished him from the Britons around him, but did not prove sufficiently attention-getting to hamper his movement among them. Since
much informal socializing and politicking in British society took place
commensally, more strictly observant Muslims, Hindus, and Parsis
who eschewed British food often found themselves isolated. Yusuf
Khan, however, did not record any eating or drinking constraints. This
enabled him frequently to dine and drink with a range of British hosts.

As with so many Indian men at the time, Yusuf Khan found his ability to interact with respectable, as well as unknown, British women
utterly new and particularly fascinating. For example, he was startled
when, in the darkness of the Diorama, he inadvertently put his hand
on the shoulder of a woman unknown to him. Although he was ashamed
of himself, he noted none of the Britons around him retaliated. On one
outing with a young British male friend, they entered a coffee house,
and struck up a conversation with 'two beautiful-looking women'.
One attracted him and he offered to share a coffee with her, which she
politely declined, saying 'another time'. He bantered back, 'what confidence is there that we will meet again?'[51]

[50] Ibid., p. 139.
[51] Ibid., p. 136.

Yusuf Khan contrasted his easy social intercourse with British people in Britain with that of his experience in India. As an example,
Colesworthy Grant (1813–80), a British painter then living in Calcutta (who sketched Yusuf Khan as an ethnographic study of a Pathan)
(Image 17), entrusted Yusuf Khan with a letter he had written for his
wife's sisters in London.[52] Yusuf Khan explained:

> I had kept it with me like an amulet . . . They received me with great polite-
> ness . . . This faqir has travelled to many cities but had not met such
> humane people anywhere else. The English who have come to Hindustan
> have a changed nature quite different from these . . . It is sad that people
> of Hindustan do not come to this glorious city so that they can see and
> know with their own eyes the virtues of these people . . .[53]

His report of such easy social intercourse with respectable British women was typical of many Indian male visitors.

Yusuf Khan also explored London's seamier side. On one excursion
into London's night life, Yusuf Khan accompanied British friends to
a crowded cabaret. He described the female performer:

> The master of the house raised a curtain; at once a woman [*randi*, which
> came to mean 'prostitute'], daughter of a fairy came out. The sight of her
> cooled my eyes. She had a wondrous face that would bring shame to the
> moon. Having come out, she came and sat by a table and poured water
> onto her hand and she began to play the twelve glasses. From this sound,
> my heart grew faint. My entire body became an anxious ear in order to hear
> her; my every organ turned into an eager eye in order to see her. Even the
> animals in the jungle would have become submissive and obedient to her.
> I wondered if this was a woman or bewitching fairy.[54]

Yusuf Khan struggled to put into his own cultural framework this
woman's fascinating if (to him) inexplicable behaviour of playing a
crystallophone (musical water-glasses)—then popular in Britain.

Late one night, Yusuf Khan passed through a narrow alley where he
saw a ruffian forcefully grabbing and gagging a woman with a cloth.
Yusuf Khan described how, seeing no policemen around, he joined the

[52] See Mittra, *Life.*
[53] Yusuf Khan, *Ajaibat,* p. 124.
[54] Ibid., pp. 123–4.

Eusuph Khan, Soobadar. A Puthan, Native of Hydrabad. Dekhun.

Image 17: Eusuph Khan, Soobedar, A Pathan, Native of Hydrabad,
Dekkun, by Colesworthy Grant, *c.*1838.

struggle in order to rescue her. He eventually wrestled the man to the ground. Finally, he allowed the thug to flee while he escorted the woman to her house. She and her grateful mother gave Yusuf Khan a drink of liquor, although he declined to give them his name or become intimate with them.[55] In his account, Yusuf Khan thus represented himself acting forcefully and successfully in British public space. His demonstrated power to protect a British woman's honour reversed the usual gendered images in European colonialism, where European men had power and Indian men appeared effeminate or (after 1857) sexually dangerous to European womanhood.

Yusuf Khan also believed Britain could teach India about social responsibility. He took a tour of a charitable shelter for prostitutes and orphans. He compared this humane care with the condition of such people in India: 'If any woman there falls into fornication, she remains in that condition all her life; if any boy becomes an orphan, no one will give him bread or clothing. The English have much better arrangements.'[56]

As it did for many others, however, London proved very costly. Yusuf Khan expended his savings and leave of absence from the Awadh army. He left London in January 1838, seen off by his British, predominantly middle-class, friends. He journeyed via Egypt and Ceylon, then through central India back to Lucknow.

As someone 'England-returned', Yusuf Khan distinguished himself from his countrymen. Unlike many Indians in London at this time, he apparently eschewed meeting them, socializing instead almost exclusively with Britons. Further, his experience of Britain elevated him over his less-travelled friends in India, empowering him to explain authoritatively to them about the relative merits of Britain and India, such as their respective architectural and sartorial styles, as well as their moral systems and practices. While some Indians suggested that he had lost his status as a 'Hindustani' because he had shared food with the British, he retorted that in Europe people kept their religion to themselves and did not eat separately by community.[57] Yusuf Khan particularly contrasted the endless industrious activity of the British, who allowed no

[55] Ibid., pp. 132–3.
[56] Ibid., pp. 134–5.
[57] Ibid., p. 232.

hour of the day to go to waste with the less efficient ways of Indians. He further lauded the productive lives of British women:

> . . . who do not squander time, rather they remain engaged in arts and sciences, in contrast to those of Hindustan, where men only waste their time in worthless matters, having imprisoned their women in the house, keeping them ignorant of the outside. [Indian] women never see anything of the world except the walls of their home or the sky from their courtyard. Every man constantly thinks this purda-bound life appropriate for the chastity of his wife. In truth, they restrain them from knowledge and science.
>
> I think that observing purda is supposed to be for chastity but really a virtuous woman can keep her honour even when seated among one thousand men while an immodest woman, even hidden behind 100,000 curtains, will not refrain from her evil ways . . .[58]

Unlike several earlier travellers, he did not attempt to defend purdah as representing the essence of Indian female virtue.

Further, Yusuf Khan recognized both the dangers and opportunities of British colonial rule. He openly discussed the potential oppression inherent in British colonialism, should the British administration impose the wrong type of policies.[59] Yet he also owed his employment to British patronage. Until his death in 1861, Yusuf Khan reportedly retained his rank as subedar, despite the annexation of Awadh in 1856 and the bloody fighting of 1857.[60]

Yusuf Khan wrote up his travel narrative, intending to publish, but it remained a decade in manuscript, and therefore had somewhat limited readership.[61] Urdu readers gained greater access in 1847 when it was finally published in Delhi. Yusuf Khan's visit and written account compare significantly with those of his contemporaries both for their differences and similarities. In contrast with virtually all earlier written accounts of Britain by Indians, he wrote in Urdu rather than Persian or English. Yusuf Khan was a soldier, while most other Indian

[58] Ibid., p. 247.

[59] Ibid., p. 227.

[60] Introduction to 1983 edition, with Garcin de Tassey as the source, pp. 50–1.

[61] His return was reported in *Janannessan*, 25/7/1838, cited in *Asiatic Journal* (December 1838), Asiatic Intelligence, p. 268a.

writers who visited Britain up to that point were Persian- or English-
literate scholar-administrators. Other Urdu writers would follow him,
however, including envoy Karim Khan (see Chapter 7). Unlike many
Indian diplomats or employees of the British who made this dangerous
and expensive journey, Yusuf Khan evidently had no political or other
formal goal. Rather, he went on his own just to experience Britain's
pleasures and peoples, like numerous other Indian men about London
in his day.[62]

The Begum's Heir in High Society and
Parliament, 1838–1851

David Ochterlony Dyce Sombre (1808–51) had highly diverse origins—biologically and culturally. He was raised from birth as heir by
Farzana Zeb al-Nissa, Begum Sombre (1741/53–1836) ruler of Sardhana. His natural mother, Julianne Reinhard (d.1820), had a French
mother but traced her descent paternally to a German grandfather,
Walter Reinhard (*c.* 1720-78, alias Sombre), and a Muslim grandmother. Dyce Sombre's father, George Alexander Dyce (d.1838), was
the illegitimate son of a Scots officer, Lieutenant David Dyce (1764/
5-90), and an Indian mistress (probably Muslim). Thus, using today's
popular cultural calculation based on 'blood', he was $3/8$ Indian and
$5/8$ European. In contrast, mid-nineteenth century Britons regarded
him variously as Indian or European, depending on whether they
weighed more heavily being born and raised in an Indian princely state
with some Indian ancestors, or having British paternal lineage, some
English-medium education, and being Christian.

Walter Reinhard, the founder of the family fortunes, epitomized
for his British enemies the inverse of European virtues.[63] They condemned him as the infamous mass murderer of 150 helpless British
men, women, and children prisoners at Patna; a turncoat mercenary
who sold his European military skills to many Indian rulers, fleeing at

---

[62] Captain Richmond Shakespear entrusted to Karim Khan's hospitality and
guidance an irregular cavalryman from Rajputana, Fazl Khan (b.1816). Shakespear, 'Personal Narrative' and Karim Khan, *Siyahatnama*, pp. 197ff, 242.

[63] He was variously identified as an Alsatian from Strasbourg, a German from
Trier/Trèves in Rhineland Palatinate, an Austrian from Saltzburg, or a German
Swiss. Keene, *Hindustan*, pp. 16–17; Polier, *Shah Alam*, pp. 93–6; Sharma, *Life*,
pp. 30–2.

crucial moments in defeat but claiming credit for victory.[64] Eventually, he obtained from the Mughal emperor a 240-square-mile jagir at Sardhana (near Meerut), producing and income of Rs 2,500,000 annually. After his death, Reinhard's consort and successor, Begum Sombre (probably a Muslim courtesan purchased as his slave) ruled Sardhana autocratically and virtually autonomously for fifty-eight years and converted to Catholicism.[65] She raised Dyce Sombre surrounded by Catholic, Anglican, Muslim, and Hindu courtiers.

Dyce Sombre grew up moving uneasily among both cultural and social worlds. He briefly studied with John Chamberlain, an evangelical Baptist missionary, and then for four years with Reverend Henry Fisher, an Anglican Church Missionary Society chaplain of St Johns Church in Meerut.[66] He composed poetry in Urdu and Persian but kept a private diary in English (except for occasional literary references and intimate remarks about his sexual partners in Persian). Sardhana courtiers of European, Indian, and mixed ancestry sought to displace him in the Begum's favour and/or buy his influence with her through flattery—in some cases offering him their daughters. His position as the Begum's heir partly privileged him into British social circles, particularly in nearby Meerut Cantonment where Britons enjoyed his generous hospitality, guidance into the world of Indian courtesans and dancers, and incompetent wagering. He usually wore European clothes and regarded himself as European. He joined the Freemasons (where, as 'royal architect', he rose to rank above many British lodge-brothers). His diary recorded his consideration of various British women as potential marriage partners, but none then agreed. His most egalitarian relations were among élite north Indian families of mixed ancestry, like his own.

[64] He worked for many employers including the French and English Companies, Shuja al-Daula, Mir Qasim, the Bharatpur Jats, the Raja of Jaipur, Hafiz Rahmat Khan, Najaf Khan, the Marathas, and the Mughal emperor. Polier, *Shah Alam*, p. 45; NAI, *Fort William*, vol. 4, pp. 132–4, 263, 313–14; Sleeman, *Rambles*, pp. 599–600.

[65] Sleeman, *Rambles*, pp. 567, 600. See, for Begum Sombre: Bacon, *First Impressions*, vol. 2, p. 76; Ghosh, 'Changing'; Heber, *Narrative*, vol. 2, pp. 277–80; Jacquemont, *Letters*, vol. 2, pp. 246–8; Sharma, *Life*. For a colourful account of Dyce Sombre see Shreve, *Indian Heir* and *Dark Legacy*.

[66] Dyce Sombre Papers, D1788/398/2/5–6, Stafford County Record Office.

Dyce Sombre stood heir apparent to a wealthy but doomed state. Begum Sombre's deft defection to the British in 1803 had enabled her to preserve Sardhana's autonomy, but only until her own death in 1836.[67] Before she died, however, she took the following steps: entrusting management of Sardhana to Dyce Sombre; appointing him as a Colonel commanding her army; purchasing from Pope Gregory XVI his knighthood as Chevalier of the Order of Christ; ceding Badshahpur (a personal estate) to him; giving him Rs 3,600,000 cash; and willing him her palaces in Sardhana, Meerut, and Delhi. In all, she left him £800,000 in property and cash. When the British annexed Sardhana in 1836, Dyce Sombre left, setting out across north India to Calcutta.

In Calcutta he confronted gendered issues of ethnicity powerfully. Some European women insulted him to his face, one saying: 'O you blk bgr, if it was not for your money, no European would speak to you.'[68] Others, including governor-general Auckland's sisters, invited him to their official and private functions; he noted: 'the eldest Miss Eden did me the honour to sit near me, & had a few moments' chat.'[69] A British man introduced him to a European prostitute: 'we went to see an European lady, a friend of T[hompson]'s, & he made me shag her; I believe she is the first European I have touched.'[70] These contradictory British responses to him would continue on board his ship to Britain.[71]

On this voyage, he shrank from social contact with British passengers. He felt 'generally speaking, they are all cold, because I am an outcaste, alias an ¹/₂ caste.'[72] To compensate for his sense of insecurity, he periodically flaunted his wealth through excessively generous tips to the captain and crew and extravagant pledges on publicly circulated subscription lists. He also hired European prostitutes in St Helena and London, where his money bought their submission.

After reaching Britain in June 1838, he sued the Company and established himself in high society. The first did him no good, however.

[67] Compton, *Particular*, p. 409.
[68] Diary, 4/7/1837.
[69] Diary, 7–21/2/1837, 2/3/1837, 4/4/1837, 9/5/1837.
[70] Diary, 25/3/1837.
[71] He also made a side-trip to South East Asia and China.
[72] Diary, 26–31/3/1838.

He filed law suits in order to reverse the Sardhana annexation and to recover the Begum's seized personal property. These cases dragged on nearly thirty years, until 1865. The courts finally found the annexation illegal (but not reversible because it was a political decision) and awarded compensation for the confiscation of the Begum's goods (because that was a case of property rights). Dyce Sombre, however, had died fourteen years earlier.

In contrast to these judicial frustrations, Dyce Sombre immediately joined the British social and political élite on the most intimate terms. Since he was somewhat dark in complexion, obese, and frequently unhygienic in his person, his physique does not seem to have been particularly attractive, but his wealth and oriental associations were. He had transferred most of his liquid assets to England, investing in East India Company bonds (worth £440,000, paying 4 per cent) and stocks, plus British government and railway bonds, yielding a princely cash income of £20,000 annually. To establish his credentials in London, he applied for and received a coat of arms (see Image 18) and assumed the title Colonel (as former commander of the Begum's troops and holder of brevets from the French). He further garnered introductions into high society from Britons whom he had known in India, including Viscount Combermere, former commander-in-chief in India.[73]

Only three months after his arrival, Dyce Sombre met Miss Mary Anne Jervis (1812–93), daughter of Viscount St Vincent. She was widely known in select British society as a vivacious woman. She had a much applauded voice and sang in upper-class gatherings, moving elegantly in social circles around the Duke of Wellington and the banker and poet Samuel Rogers. She and Dyce Sombre soon developed a strong mutual interest, exchanging correspondence that reciprocally used the endearment 'My Dearest Friendy'. Dyce Sombre consulted Combermere among others about whether to propose marriage. Despite their advice to the contrary, he did so and she accepted in December 1838, only six months after his arrival in London.

Dyce Sombre expected she would substantially modify her behaviour in accordance with what he considered appropriate for an engaged and then married woman: 'his wife should never go out in a carriage

[73] Affidavit of Combermere 2/3/1844, L/L Box 63 (434), BL.

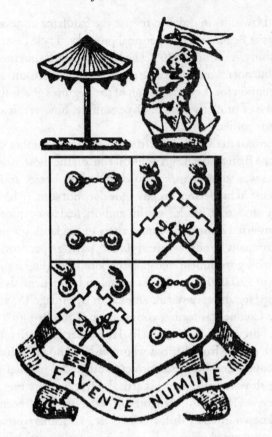

Image 18: Dyce Sombre's Coat of Arms and Motto 'God Willing'.

alone, nor go to the Opera without him.'[74] Dyce Sombre carefully explained these expectations to Miss Jervis and her father, and believed that they understood. She apparently took this as an attractive solicitude, remembering him declaiming: 'No great love could exist without jealousy!'[75]

Clearly her family was highly conscious of Dyce Sombre's ethnicity, yet it did not override his class status. Her father, a former slave owner in Jamaica, had defended slavery in Parliament as necessary

[74] Affidavit of Farr 20/1/1844, L/L Box 63 (434), BL.
[75] Affidavit of Mary Anne Dyce Sombre 25/6/1844, L/L Box 63 (434), BL.

before 'Negroes' could be useful and productive.[76] She described her
father as patronizing to them: he 'was greatly beloved by the slaves on
the Estate—If any of them behaved remarkably well, he would have
them baptised and freed.'[77] St Vincent brought some former slaves to
England; one, Major Jones, became his valet. She described Jones: 'He
was a very smart fellow with his frizzy hair brought up to an enormous
height and cut into the shape of a sugar-loaf . . . all the [British] maids
were in love with him—the Cook especially, who vowed she would
drown herself if he did not marry her—She went to the basin, dipped
her feet in, and came back, saying it was too cold.'[78] For Miss Jervis,
the African valet's hairstyle and the British cook's timidity were both
ridiculous, not due to their respective biological races but rather to the
unsophisticated pretensions of their lower social class. The idea of
(what we would call) 'interracial sex', did not seem frightening to Miss
Jervis, as long as it was between people of the same class. To their
friends, her father described Dyce Sombre as 'a very honourable and
good young man . . . and that there could be nothing against him but
his colour, and that . . . was his Daughter's concern'.[79]

Rather than have a rushed wedding, Miss Jervis requested him to
defer their marriage until the end of the London season. Dyce Sombre,
having business on the continent, reluctantly complied, although averse
to leave his fiancée on her own. Arriving in France, Dyce Sombre
mixed socially with high society including the French king. He also
travelled to Rome, where he arranged a grand funeral mass for the
Begum in 1839.[80] In addition, he commissioned a leading sculptor,
Adamo Tadolini, to create a vast monument to the Begum in the finest
Carrera marble, with inscriptions in Persian, Latin, and English, and
himself shown devotedly at her feet (it stands today in Sardhana Cathedral: Image 19).

In November 1838 Dyce Sombre returned to England and his
fiancée. He tried to enlist the support of St Vincent in curtailing his

[76] Lord St Vincent Speech in Lords 4/6/1833, *Hansard*, series 3, vol. 18,
p. 299.
[77] Foster, 'Notes', ff. 26–27, William Salt Library.
[78] Ibid.
[79] Affidavit of Combermere 2/3/1844, L/L Box 63 (434), BL.
[80] At the Church of San Carlo in Corso, Bishop Wiseman gave the funeral
oration. Sherer, 'Bishop'.

Image 19: D.O. Dyce Sombre (left) on the Begum Sombre's Cenotaph, Sardhana Cathedral, by Adamo Tadolini, 1839–48.

daughter's freedom of movement; when the father supported his daughter instead, Dyce Sombre accused him of alienating her affections and threatened to challenge him to a duel. Their conflicting expectations for her behaviour led to further clashes and to the breaking off of their engagement. Miss Jervis returned almost all his presents and he departed in April 1840 for the continent.[81] The next month, however,

---

[81] Dyce Sombre, *Mr Dyce Sombre's Refutation*, pp. 113–15; Affidavit of Combermere 2/3/1844, L/L Box 63 (434), BL.

she recalled him to London. They resumed the engagement, only to continue to quarrel over her behaviour and also another fundamental principle: they had agreed that all their sons would be raised Catholic like him, and all their daughters as Anglican like her. Dyce Sombre now insisted that if no sons were born, any daughters would be raised Catholic. This led to another rupture of the engagement, only repaired by his concession to her on this hypothetical issue. After obtaining a dispensation from the Anglican and Catholic churches for their marriage and contracting a pre-nuptial settlement which gave her £200,000 in case of his death, they were married on 26 September 1840 in the fashionable Anglican St Georges, Hanover Square, and then privately by Catholic rites.

Their honeymoon towards Italy got no further than Brussels before she became quite ill for eight weeks. It is not clear when he informed her about his many cases of venereal disease. Nevertheless, his constant attendance on her and her inability to move about freely due to her illness seem to have brought out the best in their relationship.

After their return to Britain in December 1840, however, their conflicting expectations resurfaced. During their visits to the country estates of the Duke of Wellington (April 1841), the Marquess of Hastings (May 1841), and the St Vincents themselves (June 1841), Dyce Sombre made an escalating series of public allegations about his wife's immorality: she was an opera singer and therefore a courtesan, had criminal sexual intercourse with men of all classes, and had committed incest with her father. Under pressure from his shocked hosts, he grudgingly withdrew his accusations but clearly did not relinquish them.

That summer, Dyce Sombre stood for Parliament in the Whig Radical (Liberal) interest (Image 20). He had joined the Reform Club in London and wanted political influence to advance his cases against the Company as well as his standing in British society. The Radical party in Sudbury, Suffolk, had solicited candidates at that Club for its two seats; British politician Frederick Villiers agreed and they asked Dyce Sombre to be the constituency's second candidate and campaign financier. Catholics had been emancipated to enter Parliament since 1829 and he possessed sufficient property to stand. It was unclear if people from India qualified as British; indeed, a decade earlier, Jeremy

Image 20: D.O. Dyce Sombre, by Charles Brocky, *c*.1841.

Bentham had reportedly proposed Rammohun Roy as a candidate for Parliament.[82] Although Sudbury had been a safe seat for the Conservatives, there had been local discontent over the government's corn law policy. Further, while some voters—Quakers and teetotalers in particular—voted on principle, most of Sudbury's enfranchised shopkeepers and artisans wanted cash. Dyce Sombre put £3,000 at the campaign's disposal.

Despite the Parliamentary Reform Bill of 1832, Dyce Sombre and Villiers proved able to purchase sufficient votes. Neither ever gave a

---

[82] See Zastoupil, 'Defining Christians'.

speech or even met the voters. They arrived in Sudbury for the first time two days before the election of 29 June 1841, reportedly accompanied by a large, weighty box. The next day, their agents reportedly paid 200 voters £1 each to support their nomination. The following day, about 150 voters entered the Black Boy Inn, received £2 from an unidentified man in an upstairs room, filed out to vote for Dyce Sombre and Villiers, and then entered the Swan Inn across the street, where they received £4 more from another nameless man. Meanwhile, Dyce Sombre and Villiers sat in a downstairs newsroom, where it could be publicly noted that they were not the ones distributing the bribes. The last decisive 10–12 voters reportedly received some £50–60 each.

Both Dyce Sombre and Villiers were elected by narrow majorities. Dyce Sombre received 281 or 50.63 per cent of the 555 votes cast, a seven-vote majority. Suggesting that most voters had no objection to Dyce Sombre personally, Villiers received 284 votes, only three more. Their Conservative opponents, who had likewise no prior connection to the constituency and came down from London's Carleton Club, had only dispensed £2,000.[83]

Dyce Sombre's Parliamentary career, however, proved limited to nine months (August 1841–April 1842). He voted six times but never won. Meanwhile, a petition against his and Villiers' election (among 73 Members of Parliament whose elections were challenged) dragged on. The petition accused Dyce Sombre of being disqualified for election on two grounds: first he 'was not born a subject of this realm, and had never been naturalized, and was therefore incapable of sitting in Parliament' and second, 'on the ground of extensive bribery and treating'.[84] In April 1842, the Election Committee set aside as moot the question of his status as a British subject. They determined the second charge an obvious violation, however, declaring both Dyce Sombre and Villiers, by means of their agents, guilty of 'gross systematic and extensive bribery', and ordering their elections 'controverted'. Proceedings to disenfranchise Sudbury began at the same time, which succeeded in 1844. Thus, Dyce Sombre, Villiers, and the Sudbury voters misjudged the changing values and regulations of British society

[83] PP, Returns (Commons) 1842, vol. 7, pp. 847–942; 1843, vol. 6, pp. 503–89; 1844, vol. 18, pp. 247–561; *Times* 9/4/1842 6e; Barron and Austin, *Report*, pp. 237–62.

[84] Ibid.

328 Counterflows to Colonialism

and the extent to which elections could still be purchased. Around the time Dyce Sombre lost his Parliamentary seat, he also lost the first round of his law suits against the Company.

Dyce Sombre had mixed relations with Indians and Britons in London. He hosted dinners for many élite Indians there and involved them in his pleasures. While they appreciated his generosity, some commented unfavourably on his eccentricities.[85] Similarly, many of the British élite also accepted Dyce Sombre's largesse but his unconventional behaviour made them increasingly uncomfortable. When his personal conflicts with his wife worsened, she collected her relatives and their leading friends. They all pleaded with Dyce Sombre to relinquish his accusations against her, which he refused.[86]

Yet, British property laws favoured him over her. From March 1842 he took control over her father's allowance to her. While he would buy her anything she wished, and constantly showered her with presents, he refused to allow her independent money, claiming that she would use it to buy sex. He secretly followed her when she went out, even in the company of her relatives. He accused her of having lovers hidden about their apartments in the posh Clarendon Hotel, and even introducing them into their bed as he slept.

An extended trip to Scotland and frequent consultations with leading British physicians failed to check Dyce Sombre's accusations and irregular behaviour. He demanded that the famous mesmerist, Dr Elliottson, hypnotize his wife into finding him more attractive; when Elliottson expressed surprise at this unethical request, Dyce Sombre challenged him to a duel. Indeed, Dyce Sombre issued a series of challenges to duels against men he believed had insulted his wife's honour, including doctors who examined her and people they met at social occasions. He attempted to induce her to share his feelings by alleging that British élite women had tried to seduce him; he therefore urged his wife to challenge these women to duels in defence of his honour. He began to threaten her with pistols and knives, vowing to cut off her nose—as was sometimes done to adulterous women in

[85] Karim Khan, *Siyahatnamah* (1982 reprint), pp. 130, 174–5, 192, 229. Dyce Sombre, *Dyce Sombre against Troup*, pp. 306–8, 686.

[86] Lord Chancellor's Judgement 8/8/1844, in Dyce Sombre, *In Lunacy*, pp. 57–92.

India. He asserted that good and evil spirits were battling for his mind; on the orders of an evil spirit, he cast his wife's wedding ring into the fire and shaved off his eyebrows. He sent challenges to Company directors, threatening them with duels. He also appealed to Queen Victoria, promising to entrust his claims against the Company to her.[87] Finally, the physicians attending him convinced his reluctant wife that Dyce Sombre must be restrained, so as not to harm her or himself. In the presence of several eminent doctors and her family, a doctor and two keepers took physical charge of Dyce Sombre (30 March 1843).

At this point in the development of British psychiatry, debate raged over the very nature of madness, as well as its treatment. As a gentleman of means, Dyce Sombre was never in danger of incarceration in an asylum. Nor was he ever actually treated in order to be cured. Rather, over the remainder of his life, he was almost continually being tested by individual or boards of doctors in order to classify him as either sane or, if not sane, the degree to which his lunacy made him a threat to himself, his wife, or his property. At first, he remained in the Clarendon Hotel, separated from his wife, but under the observation of his keepers. He was not allowed to shave himself, but beyond this no personal restraint was imposed upon him. He was allowed to go where he liked, but all dangerous instruments were taken out of his way. This did not prevent him from aiming loaded pistols at his keepers. His doctors examined him repeatedly, noting his various actions and assertions. After two weeks at the Clarendon, they found a more suitable place to confine him: Hanover Lodge in Regent's Park.

Although Dyce Sombre could go out in the company of his warders, he clearly felt a prisoner. For a time, he refused all hot food. He drew up a new will, disinheriting his wife and giving his fortune in trust to the East India Company (with large personal gifts to prominent directors) for a school and other projects in Sardhana. He signed this will 'in the Prison of Hanover Lodge, Regent's Park'.[88] He wrote letters of appeal to the American government. As he later explained to the Russian government: 'by the intrigue of my enemies, I was, under the pretext of being insane, kept under strict watch for four months . . . my

---

[87] Dyce Sombre, *Mr Dyce Sombre's Refutation*, pp. 519–20.

[88] Unattested will dated 10/5/1843 in Dyce Sombre, *Dyce Sombre against Troup*.

things were taken from me, trunks and boxes broken open, sealed letters, packets, letters, and even my will, which is reckoned a sacred thing in all parts of the world, were opened and read, and then given up to persons who may make whatever use they pleased of them.'[89] He identified the spirit tormenting him as a man whom he had fatally imprisoned while managing Sardhana. The Begum herself appeared before him to witness his remarriage with his wife. He envisioned himself conversing with the late George III in a madhouse. In short, his doctors found much to record and report about his well-publicized lunacy case.

A commission of lunacy was drawn up and heard in Hanover Lodge before the lord chancellor and a special jury, attended by a crowded gallery of élite British society and numerous newspaper reporters.[90] Dyce Sombre objected to the proceedings on several grounds. One, holding hearings at 11:00 a.m., before he ordinarily arose, was an insult to his honour. Second, there was a plot against him by his enemy, the East India Company. Third, the hearings should really be aimed at justifying his repudiation of his wife by demonstrating her immorality. Dyce Sombre refused an advocate, preferring to represent himself. While his cross-examination of witnesses made some points that the chancellor recognized as legitimate, his actions generally failed to convince the jury of his sanity.

In his judgment, the lord chancellor summed up the central issues of the case, issues which remained salient until Dyce Sombre's death. First, what was Dyce Sombre: European or 'Asiatic'? If European by 'blood' (as Dyce Sombre insisted, claiming that a majority of his ancestors had at least some European blood) or by education (as several witnesses insisted, primarily based on his four years studying with Reverend Fisher), then, the lord chancellor opined, Dyce Sombre was clearly a lunatic.[91] No sane European would act with his irrational jealousy. However, if he were Indian by blood (as most witnesses asserted, based on the fact that his parents each had some Indian blood)

---

[89] Journal or Report of the Medical Council of St Petersburgh 17/12/1844 in Dyce Sombre, *In Lunacy*, pp. 19–21.

[90] He or his legal cases would appear, usually sympathetically, in more than 120 articles in the *Times* alone.

[91] Dyce Sombre, *Mr Dyce Sombre's Refutation*, p. 19; Affidavit of Combermere 2/3/1844 in Dyce Sombre, *In Lunacy*, pp. 7–10; *Times* 9/8/1844, 2/3/1849.

or by upbringing under Begum Sombre, then were his actions—particularly with regard to his possessive attitudes towards women—normal or abnormal by Indian standards?

On this point, evidence would remain divided. Many Europeans, self-proclaimed experts in oriental cultures, argued that the system of female seclusion prevalent in families of his class indicated an inherent obsessive jealousy. They argued that, given Dyce Sombre's Indian nature, he was being perfectly reasonable, no matter how inappropriate such attitudes were in Europe: 'when [his actions] are interpreted by a reference to Asiatic feelings and modes of thought, [they] are by no means indicative of unsound mind.'[92] Several witnesses questioned the competence of any English jury to comprehend Indian values, so foreign to their experience. In contrast, other European 'experts in Asiatic culture' argued that the normal attitudes of Indians towards their women were essentially similar to those of Europe, and therefore that Dyce Sombre was abnormal in either culture. The Begum's long-time physician, Thomas Drever, wrote 'from his long and intimate acquaintance with the said Dyce Sombre in India and with the natives of India, he is satisfied that neither the education and habits of the said D. O. Dyce Sombre, nor his Eastern parentage, can account for the delusions entertained by the said D. O. Dyce Sombre, but that the same arose from insanity . . .'.[93] The lord chancellor and jury concluded (8 August 1843) that Dyce Sombre (even if Asiatic by blood) had enough European experience to be judged of unsound mind. They declared him lunatic retroactively from 27 October 1842.[94] This led to the order for the establishment of a 'Committee of the Person' as guardian over him.

The second salient issue considered whether Dyce Sombre was a threat to his property. The chancellor heard little evidence that he was, but nevertheless ordered the establishment of a Committee of the

[92] Trevelyan Letter 19/8/1843 in Dyce Sombre, *Mr Dyce Sombre's Refutation*, pp. 8, 13, 256; Dyce Sombre, *In Lunacy*, pp. 12–13, 89–112, Appendix One, pp. 7–10.

[93] Drever Affidavit 24/6/1844, James Martin Affidavit 20/2/1849 in Dyce Sombre, *In Lunacy*, pp. 31–40, 176–8. Drever later publicly defended Dyce Sombre's reputation, even if insane. *Times* 8/8/1856 6e.

[94] This invalidated the above will and other transactions which Dyce Sombre had concluded during the five months prior to his being put under restraint.

Estate to control his money. Thus, while Mrs Dyce Sombre received a handsome annual allowance of £4,000, all his expenses had to be approved by the committee. The chancellor put Dyce Sombre on an allowance of £60 per week (some £3,120 annually) but required him to submit records for every penny. This led to a pattern by Dyce Sombre of disputing bills and demanding receipts down to the cent, even at the cost of much fuss in restaurants and public places. His defenders attributed his minute scrutiny of even tiny charges as a proof of his rationality. His attackers used it, given his vast income and the lavish society in which he moved, to allege his irrationality. Partly convinced of his careful use of his money, the chancellor eventually raised his allowance from his estate to £5,000 per year, about a quarter of its income.

Now officially declared lunatic, Dyce Sombre spent much of the rest of his life trying to get this judgment reversed. As Dyce Sombre wrote in frustration: 'Dead men are never heard, otherwise they would be taken for ghosts; and such is the case with Chancery Lunatics. I am a dead man, according to the existing law.'[95]

Although Hanover Lodge proved not a particularly healthy dwelling place, Dyce Sombre remained there another month, and his further improbable assertions were carefully recorded by his doctors. In order to remove any cause for irritation, he received from the chancellor freedom to travel wherever in Britain he chose, accompanied by a doctor and two keepers. From 9 September 1843, he toured Bath, Bristol, Gloucester, Birmingham, and Liverpool. As long as he behaved normally, as his keepers reported that he did, he was able to move about freely. In Liverpool, he thought to purchase a pleasure yacht for his amusement. Instead, in the middle of the night (21 September 1843), he fled and disappeared. The attendants, aghast at having lost their charge, had the police search the city. They apprehended a tall, dark Indian, who turned out to be the steward of a ship in port. Next, the authorities feared that kidnappers had seized Dyce Sombre for his money, since he had a considerable amount of cash on his person. In reality, Dyce Sombre had escaped to France, where he appeared once again in high society.

[95] Dyce Sombre, *Mr Dyce Sombre's Refutation*, p. 244.

In Paris, and then elsewhere on the continent, Dyce Sombre assembled evidence of his sanity. He took affidavits from his servants, landladies, tradesmen, society companions, and a series of distinguished doctors, all testifying to his perfect sanity. Over the years, he submitted fifty-two such affidavits, from individuals or groups, including from thirty-two medical doctors. Included among these was the Board of Russian Medical Experts, Dyce Sombre having gone to St Petersburg for four months in 1845, his explicit goal being 'to receive a certificate from the medical men of the country, and with that document to return to England and reclaim the remnant of my once brilliant fortune.'[96]

Impressed with this extensive evidence in support of the repeated petitions from Dyce Sombre for a reversal of the lunacy judgment, successive lord chancellors held five exhaustive hearings for supersession of the verdict. In opposition, agents of the Committees of the Person and the Estate gathered affidavits from his acquaintances and servants, attesting to Dyce Sombre's irrationally belligerent behaviour and immoral conduct. One landlady gave two affidavits, one on each side of his lunacy question. Most important for the court, each of the nine medical experts whom the chancellor appointed, in repeated examinations over the years, came unanimously to the same conclusion: Dyce Sombre remained lunatic. Newspapers laid all this out in graphic detail for the British public. The unbridgeably divided opinion among the most distinguished members of the medical profession who specialized in lunacy in Britain and the continent illustrates today, as it did then, the inadequacies of such cultural categories as 'sanity' and 'insanity'.

Also entered into the record were other acts which demonstrated Dyce Sombre's efforts to shape his fate, efforts which British society, and the lord chancellor, found indicative of his unsound mind. Dyce Sombre sought to have the Jockey Club of Paris, where he was a welcome member, hold a formal trial about his wife's immorality. He offered bribes (ranging from £1,500 cash to an annuity of £250 per year) to the wives of the lord chancellor and several of the chancery-appointed medical doctors, as well as Prime Minister Lord John Russell,

<hr>

[96] Dyce Sombre, *In Lunacy*, pp. 19–21.

in exchange for their support for him.[97] He compiled and published
a 591 page book: *Mr Dyce Sombre's Refutation of the Charge of Lunacy
Brought against Him in the Court of Chancery* (Paris; the Author, 1849).

As a proof to the British establishment that their persecution of him
had backfired, Dyce Sombre also published a poem in a newspaper
contrasting English and French women and ridiculing the lord chancellor's efforts to punish him; he sent a copy to the lord chancellor
(which cannot have helped his campaign to prove his sanity):

> A warm French *mistress* now.
>
> I hate your dreary English land,
>   Its clime and hearts so cold;
> Its mercenary altars raised
>   To Mammon and his gold.
>
> I hate your dreary English land—
>   Its scandal, trade and mist—
> Where e'en your women's lips are chilled,
>   However warmly kissed.
>
> Give me the sunny land of Gaul,
>   Its bright wines, its wild blisses;
> Give me the Paris Bacchanals,
>   Dishevelled Locks and Kisses!
>
> Give me French hearts, as light and gay
>   As their own glad champagne;
> Give me those lips that always smile—
>   Those arms that always strain!
>
> Farewell, my lord: when next you have
>   Some spouse a 'madman' made,
> Don't let his keepers take him to
>   The Burlington Arcade!
>
> For me, while France affords a home,
>   *Your* land, I'll ne'er regret it;
> Shall I e'er cross the sea again?
>   Here's wishing—you may get it!
>
>   —Dyce Sombre, Boulogne.[98]

[97] *Times* 8/3/1849 7a.
[98] Newspaper clipping, handwritten on top—'To Lord Lyndhurst', L/L/
Box 64 (438), BL.

In the continuing public arguments over his case, many conflicting British attitudes emerged concerning not only the nature of sanity, but also the relative values of Europe and Asia (especially towards women) and class privilege. While most witnesses concurred over what Dyce Sombre had actually done, high-priced lawyers on each side differed as to their interpretation of these acts: were they excessive or permissible for a man of his class and/or ethnicity? Some newspapers portrayed Mrs Dyce Sombre as a manipulative aristocratic gold-digger who won out over her simple-minded Indian victim.[99] In this view, her gender and class counted against her, while his gender and ethnicity gained some popular support.

In addition to the press keeping debate about his case in British public discourse, Dyce Sombre himself continued to generate much publicity, mostly negative. He openly employed prostitutes in each European city he visited, and frequently got into trouble with the police for his promiscuous solicitation of virtually any nubile unaccompanied woman he saw on the street. In each case, his wealth and social class got him released from confinement. When his obesity, general bad health and frequent cases of venereal disease made him impotent, he hired and trained prostitutes to give him full body massages: 'shampoos'.[100] His inquisitive landlords and landladies observed and report-ed his extraordinary behaviour, further enhancing his unsavoury public reputation as unrestrained by morality or convention.

Throughout the trials, hearings, and rehearings, Mrs Dyce Sombre maintained that she was lovingly loyal to her husband, but that he needed to change his attitudes and behaviour for the protection of himself, herself, and their property. She arranged surprise visits with him, for example in November 1848 during one of his supervised trips to England for further medical examination:

> I sought that interview because I love my said husband and because I longed to see him again [hoping] it might bring him back to what he used to be and revive the former great affection which he entertained for me before he was placed under restraint and which he continued to evince afterwards by several of his letters . . . I hoped if I could bring back his former feelings for me that I might be the means of happily disengaging him

[99] E.g., *Age* 13/2/1852.
[100] Affidavits of Furhberg 8/10/1853 and Amede 8/10/1853, Box 64 (441), vol. 2, pp. 405–8, BL.

from his enemies and my enemies who have for many years been making
a prey of him and causing his destruction both of body and mind. I was
bitterly disappointed . . . When my said husband came into the room I
went up and endeavoured to take hold of his hand and said 'Friendy ain't
you glad to see me' He said 'No' and pushed me away.[101]

Even on the eve of his death, she wrote affectionately to him: 'My
Dearest Friendy, I hear you are ill, and write to say how much I am concerned, and if I can be of any use or comfort to you, I am ready at any
moment to go to you . . . Believe me, yr affectionate, M.A. Dyce
Sombre.'[102] Whatever her feelings, she steadfastly maintained her role
as loving wife.

Dyce Sombre never cleared his name prior to his death. Disease
severely debilitated his body and mind and he finally succumbed to an
infection which spread from his foot. He died in London on 1 July
1851. His body was buried there, but he directed that his heart be
returned to Sardhana and entombed next to the Begum. His wife and
the East India Company conducted long and expensive legal battles
over his estate. If his last will was proven valid, the Company would
inherit. But it was finally set aside, his wife obtaining virtually his entire estate. She then was herself widely celebrated in high society as 'the
Begum', often wearing the oriental clothes Dyce Sombre had given
her, assuming some of her late husband's oriental aura.

The complex case of Dyce Sombre suggests the multiple and often
conflicting ways that gender, class, ethnicity, and normal behaviour
were defined and functioned in Britain during this period. Dyce Sombre's intentions and self-representations often clashed with those of
the various Britons around him. His wealth gained him personal access
to Parliament and aristocratic social circles in Europe, far higher than
the British colonial establishment would allow in India. His identities
as Indian or British, sane or not, remained highly contested. His gender empowered him over his wife, although she eventually succeeded
to his estate and oriental mystique. All this demonstrates the dangers
of simple or static binary characterizations concerning identities, especially under colonialism.

[101] Affidavit of Mary Anne Jarvis 20/2/1849, L/L/ Box 65 (452), BL.
[102] Mrs Dyce Sombre letter 14/6/1851, in Dyce Sombre, *Dyce Sombre against Troup*, p. 990.

Moving in British Society

For increasing numbers of middle- and upper-class Indian men during the 1830s, Britain appeared a place where they could amuse and advance themselves. Some indeed found that their lives there could be enhanced materially from what they experienced in India, including significant pension enhancements there. Several could establish personal connections with influential and sympathetic British élites. All found more easy and familiar social intercourse with Britons of several classes than in India. Their relations with British women, particularly, struck most as gratifyingly different from what was possible in the colony. Life in Britain also brought them intimate knowledge of the new rulers over India, although, unlike the envoys discussed earlier, these men were not primarily on political missions.

Yet there were also real costs to making the journey. Britons never let them forget that they were Indians, although the connotations of that label varied considerably among individuals, classes, genders, and circumstances. While many Britons ascribed exotically attractive associations to Indians, they also tended to regard Indians in the context of colonialism. Two of the men we have examined here remained in Europe until their death. Two returned to India and their subordinate roles there. All adapted somewhat to British values, but never fully accepted all British cultural impositions upon them. In India during this period, many others regarded Anglicization as a way to improve themselves, particularly through employment by the British administration, yet they too found this a complex process of negotiation.

CHAPTER 9

Seeking Honours, Knowledge, Profit, and Justice

Anglicization as Means of Advancement

Over the early nineteenth century, many Indians expected to advance themselves as officials, colleagues, students, or soldiers under the British. Britons had long worked to inculcate the idea that they had made cultural and technological advances worthy of emulation, and that London was the centre of knowledge, justice, profit, and power. Various individuals and families across India responded by submitting their sons to British teachers and Anglicized models of training, expecting the opportunities thus promised for advancement and honour. Indeed, men who could understand English and British culture emerged as intermediaries between the colonial state and the Indian populace, thereby empowering themselves. Yet, this often came at the cost of some alienation from the rest of Indian society. Further, many who worked for the British found their promises unfulfilled, their accomplishments receiving only limited recognition, although somewhat more in Britain than in India.

Indians associated themselves with the British in diverse ways. Young men did so far more than their seniors, and women remained largely excluded from public careers in India and Britain. In the presidency capitals of Bombay and Calcutta, communities like Parsis and élites such as the Bengali bhadralok enhanced their positions within the British administration. In north India, scholar-officials, who had in earlier generations served the Mughals or regional successor states, turned to the British. Some Indians came to believe that conversion to Christianity would bring benefits—spiritual, social, and/or economic. Businessmen looked to the Company for economic opportunities and political influence. Male students saw in British science the path to a salutary future. Hundreds of thousands of Indian soldiers joined the Company's armies.

Especially from the 1830s, growing numbers of these men decided that visiting Britain would enhance their careers, further their education, or obtain them profits, titles, or justice. Each class encountered a different reception. But many Britons' cultural attitudes gradually hardened over this period against Indians, who now came to be regarded as biologically different and inferior. British surveillance over the social intercourse between Indian men and surrounding British society became somewhat more intense. Indians there had to 'prove' their worthiness of respect and their capacity to master English and rigorous Western scientific disciplines. Nonetheless, while there, they entered public discourse, including political debate about British colonial policies. Officials received honours and pay increments. Indian medical students bathed with Britons and studied and probed British bodies, including female bodies, with no evident protest from British authorities; some excelled in direct competition with British students. Wealthy entrepreneurs found receptive audiences. Soldiers with grievances obtained hearings denied them in India.

Some travellers obtained advantages, but virtually none achieved everything they expected. Further, when they returned to India, most faced the even more racially prejudiced colonial establishment there. Indeed, their prominence in Britain sometimes disqualified or limited them for future employment by the British in India. The ability of British ideology to convince Indians that associating with them, especially in Britain, would bring improvement and justice, often in the face of much evidence to the contrary, suggests one power of colonialism.

Parsi Officials and Students

The longstanding and particularly extensive connections between the small Parsi community and the British encouraged movement to Britain (see Chapter 2 for Nowroji Rustamji's 1724–5 visit). From the 1830s, leaders of this community increasingly sent young men to be educated in Britain, attended by Parsi servants.[1] Here we focus on

---

[1] See Hinnells, *Zoroastrians*, p. 81.

three of the same family, who wrote extensively about their experiences there, as representative of the many Parsi men who went during this period.

The Bombay dockyards had been run by the Wadia family for over a century, building ships for the Company, Royal Navy, and private merchants.[2] When engineers in Britain developed steam engines to power oceangoing ships, this family sent three young men to master this new technology. In 1838, first cousins Jehangeer Nowrojee (1821–66) and Hirjeebhoy Merwanjee (1817–83) sailed to Britain for 'improving themselves in the Art of Ship Building'.[3] Their family sent along with them an older Parsi guardian, Dorabjee Muncherjee Navjivora, and two Parsi servants (Image 21). Both cousins had trained and worked in the Bombay dockyard as naval architects in the European mode. Another older cousin, Ardaseer Cursetjee (1808–77), had planned to go to Britain as early as 1835, but illness and responsibilities prevented his departure until September 1839, accompanied by two Parsi servants (Image 22). Also an official at the Bombay dockyard, he went specifically to master the construction and repair of marine steam engines.

At the end of their visits, these men published their travel accounts: Cursetjee wrote *Diary of an Overland Journey from Bombay to England and of a Year's Residence in Great Britain* (London: Henington and Galabin, 1840) and Nowrojee and Merwanjee co-authored *Journal of a Residence of Two Years and a Half in Great Britain* (London: William H. Allen, 1841). They used a British genre, the 'informational travel narrative' for giving 'pleasurable instruction'.[4] Written mainly for Anglophone Indians, these books served many purposes. They demonstrated British society's honoured reception of their authors. They detailed how best to travel to and within Britain, how to select sites to see and what to expect there, specifying the exact prices of various grades of tickets and commodities. The authors occasionally included their own responses as a model for their readers to emulate, whom they presupposed would all be male. They also assessed and

[2] See Ardeshir Wadia, *Scions*.

[3] Court Minutes 25/9/1838.

[4] At this time, Anglophone travel literature in Britain followed two patterns, one more 'experiential' and the other more 'informational'. See Batten, *Pleasurable Instruction*.

Image 21: Hirjibhoy Merwanjee, Jehangir Nowrojee and
Dorabjee Muncherjee, photograph taken by unknown artist
in England, 1840.

critiqued British culture, instructing the Indian élite of Bombay about
British developments that should be imitated or avoided. The three
authors largely concurred in their assessment about Britain, although
they had slightly different experiences there.

Image 22: Ardseer Cursetjee, photograph taken by unknown artist
in England, mid-nineteenth century.

The senior most, Cursetjee, received the attentions of more prominent Britons including Queen Victoria, Prince Albert, various other
members of the British aristocracy, Sir Robert Peele, and many Fellows of the Royal Society. He was elected Member of the Society of
Arts and Sciences. Ardeseer mainly studied to advance his engineering knowledge at Seaward's factory in east London.[5] His book, some

[5] Court Minutes 4/3/1840.

100 pages, covered less ground than that of his younger relatives, whose book was five times longer.

The younger men, Nowrojee and Merwanjee, recorded closer and warmer personal relations with middle-class men and women. They spent their first year in the 'quiet little unobtrusive village' of Egham, near Windsor. There, they studied English and mathematics with the Reverend George Hopkins, and English penmanship and conversation with his brother, Joseph Hopkins, in preparation for their subsequent year-and-a-half of advanced technical education at the Chatham and other Royal Navy and commercial dockyards.[6]

They received cordial welcomes from the directors and the government.[7] Further, Sir Charles Forbes, to whom all three dedicated their books, supplied much advice and guidance about living in British society.[8] During breaks from technical study, they all assiduously sought notable sites around Britain for their further edification: 'we did not go by chance to see this thing or that, but whenever we read a description of places worth seeing, or if any of our friends hinted that it was proper for us to visit certain places, we endeavoured so to do.'[9]

Small diaspora communities like Parsis had long learned to adapt to the surrounding culture, in India and elsewhere. Many Parsis in Bombay had learned English to take advantage of commercial and administrative opportunities that British rule created, but retained distinctive dietary and sartorial customs and spoke Gujarati at home. In Britain, these three studied British technology, society, and culture. But they ate only food prepared in ritually pure ways by their own Parsi servants, although they occasionally served it to Britons and other Indians.[10] This severely constrained their socializing with British

[6] These men were brothers of Captain Hopkins of the *Buckinghamshire*, on which they sailed to England. Court Minutes 4–18/9/1839, 20–7/5/1840, 10/6/1840.

[7] *Times* 19/9/1838 5e.

[8] Nowrojee letter 28/2/1838 in Ardeshir Wadia, *Bombay Dockyard*, p. 307. Another Parsi would write a laudatory biography of Forbes: Ruttonjee Wadia, *Forgotten Friend*. See also 'Balance Sheet of . . . Forbes, Forbes and Co', 31/12/1845, MSS EUR C.549, BL.

[9] Nowrojee and Merwanjee, *Journal*, pp. 90–2.

[10] E.g., Cursetjee, *Diary*, pp. 3, 35; Nowrojee and Merwanjee, *Journal*, pp. 451–2; Broughton, *Recollections*, vol. 5, p. 268.

would-be host families by implying the impurity of their kitchens and homes. The cousins anticipated encountering resistance to their dietary demands but found acquiescence and deference instead: in many of their friends' kitchens and every 'inn and lodging house . . . we and our servants were allowed unmolested to do every thing we required' for such pure food preparation.[11] Thus, these authors recommended to their Parsi readers no compromise in their religious or customary morals or behaviour, but rather indicated that respectable Britons would honour their adherence to these principles and relinquish control even over their domestic space. In contrast, most family kitchens in India remained barred to outsiders.

Further, these men retained their distinguishing 'Parsee costume', including cap and robes (slightly supplemented with warmer undergarments for the British climate) despite the inconvenient but flattering crowds of British gawkers that these attracted. Nowrojee and Merwanjee recorded: our clothing 'collected quite a mob, through which it was difficult to pass to our carriage; we think quite a thousand persons were congregated together.'[12] Later, at the Regent's Park Zoological Gardens, 'we attracted a great number around us from the peculiarity of our dress, and we were objects of very great curiosity to the visitors,—as much so perhaps as the winged and four footed inmates of the place.'[13] While thus made to feel curiosities, they rhetorically reversed the onus by simultaneously making themselves the observers of ill-informed Britons as curiosities: 'It was amusing to hear one call us Chinese; they are Turks says another; no they are Spanish, vociferates a third; thus they were labouring under mistakes, and taking inhabitants of British India for natives of Europe.' The cousins thus took such attention as well-meaning, but also proof of the naïveté of the British public.

Despite Anglicization of many aspects of their lives, these men also consistently retained their strong sense of being Indians, specifically Parsis. They socialized frequently with other Indians in London.[14] In their repeated self-identification as 'natives of India', these authors

[11] Nowrojee and Merwanjee, *Journal,* pp. 76–7.

[12] Ibid., pp. 26–7, 90–2.

[13] Ibid., pp. 34, 428–30.

[14] For example, Karim Khan frequently noted meeting with them. *Siyahatnama, passim.*

called various British customs 'odd' and 'very much to our amusement'.[15] Yet, they also marked themselves off from other Indians by referring to themselves as people of 'our *own country, Persia*', from whence Parsis originally emigrated.[16] Indeed, Cursetjee was shocked at how Anglicized a young Parsi student he met in London in 1840 had become over his six years there: Kaikhushroo Framjee Patuck (1826–51, who died there) was 'so perfect an English child, as to have entirely forgotten our language, and sit talking without a cap, and his servant doing the same.'[17]

These men respected the British monarchy. While describing their approach to the presence of Queen Victoria, they editorialized: 'we, as subjects of the British Crown, felt as much happiness and interest in [her future success] as any [Briton].'[18] They felt they had a shared stake in British imperial progress and supported the East India Company, on whose decisions depended 'the future happiness or the misery of the countless millions of India'.[19] They explained the Company's conquest of India as stemming from justified safeguarding of their mercantile enclaves: '[the British] were compelled, by the necessity of self-defence, to possess themselves of several places in India to protect their property, and were thus forced to become masters of those places . . . and soon led to the acquisition of the interior of Hindoostan.'[20] Indeed, while in Britain, they remained on the Company's payroll, receiving their regular monthly salaries (£4 each for the younger men, £8 for the older) plus substantial monthly supplemental allowances (£15 each, and £30 respectively).[21] Nevertheless, like so many other visitors, their expenses in Britain far exceeded their budgets: 'We have spent a large sum of money upon our maintenance and education, and we humbly hope that our residence in this country has been attended with the desired result.'[22]

[15] Nowrojee and Merwanjee, *Journal*, pp. 36–7, 479–86.

[16] Ibid., p. 226.

[17] Hinnells, *Zoroastrians*, p. 81; Cursetjee, *Diary*, pp. 30–1.

[18] Nowrojee and Merwanjee, *Journal*, p. 322.

[19] Ibid.; p. 35.

[20] Ibid., pp. 342–59.

[21] Court Minutes 19/3/1839 to 7/4/1841; Finance and Home Committee Reports 23–9/1/1840 no. 590, L/F/1/102, ff. 193–4, BL.

[22] Nowrojee and Merwanjee, *Journal*, pp. vii–viii.

While each of these three men admired much about Britain and its accomplishments, particularly in science and technology, they also made insightful and critical assessments of British society. They were all quite disparaging about the British working classes: 'the majority of the lower orders in England are very rude in their manners and behaviour towards strangers, whom they do not like to see in their own country.'[23] The younger cousins particularly noted the cheapest 'pit' area of London's theaters held 'rogues, thieves, and pickpockets' while the lobby held the 'fallen' British women:

> swarms of well-dressed, highly-painted, but unhappy females, who, having lost their virtue, resort, as a means of maintenance, to the saloons of the theatres, and with much wantonness endeavour to draw young men into the snares of vice and misery of which they themselves have been the victims . . . [W]e also think that much of the dissipation, and many of the robberies committed by young men, may be traced to an intimacy with improper females, which commenced within the saloon of the theatre.[24]

They apparently intended to forewarn future Indian men. Hence, while they repeatedly and explicitly denied any prejudice on their part against Britons, they clearly took as fact, not prejudice, that the British lower classes were coarse, xenophobic, and dangerously sexual.

Notwithstanding their praise of Britain's international commercial success and the dynamism of its 'private enterprise', they also repeatedly criticized the excesses of British commercialism.[25] British commodification of everything made people no better than animals: 'money in England can do everything; it makes . . . men assume the appearance of Monkeys.'[26] Cursetjee concurred: 'the shopkeepers and tradesmen of London have generally an unfair practise of speaking against each other in the same line of business, which is the cause of great embarrassment to foreigners, as they cannot have confidence in dealing with such traders.'[27] Nowrojee and Merwanjee attributed the worst practices to 'Jewish' shopkeepers who invested in advertising but

[23] Ibid., pp. 109–10; Cursetjee, *Diary*, p. 65.

[24] Nowrojee and Merwanjee. *Journal*, p. 106.

[25] Ibid., pp. 487–8.

[26] Ibid., p. 109.

[27] Cursetjee, *Diary*, p. 65.

sold shoddy goods (they repeated their anti-Semitic remarks through-out their book).[28] Interestingly, they warned Indian visitors away from British shops that bargained or haggled over prices, recommending only fixed-price shops. Further, the British fetish for profits meant severe strains on family life since men worked excessively long hours away from their wives and children.

Nowrojee and Merwanjee also faulted Britons for misallocating their wealth. For instance, the exorbitant fees paid to ballet dancers as opposed to honest artisans horrified them:

Only think,—one hundred and fifty guineas every night to be paid in England to a woman [Marie Taglioni, 1804–84] to stand for a long time like a goose upon one leg, then to throw one leg straight out, twirl round three or four times with the leg thus extended, to curtsey so low as to nearly seat herself upon the ground, to spring occasionally from one side of the stage to another; all of which jumping about did not, on her part, occupy an hour; and to get more money for *that* hour every evening, than six weav-ers in Spitalfields (who produce beautiful silk for dresses) could earn all of them, working fourteen hours every day, in twelve months![29]

For such wasting of their resources, the British, otherwise a 'clever peo-ple', were 'very foolish indeed'. Significantly, it was not the immodest dress and sexually suggestive behaviour of the dancer (which several other Indian writers censured), but the financial overvaluation of her performance that they particularly criticised.

Like other Indian men, Nowrojee and Merwanjee remarked on the public visibility of even respectable British women, implicitly com-paring it to the general seclusion of élite Indian women. On an early outing in Regent's Park, they 'saw many women, fair and with light hair, many of them appeared to us most beautiful. All of them appear-ed to have mild blue eyes, and very sweet expression of countenance, and we saw more of female beauty in a few hours, than we had ever beheld in all our lives.'[30] Noticeably, these cousins stressed their at-traction to blonde hair and white skin, in implicit contrast to Indian complexions.

[28] Nowrojee and Merwanjee, *Journal,* pp. v, 42, 167, 196–203.
[29] Ibid., pp. 102–4.
[30] Ibid., pp. 30–2.

While they described the physical appearance of no individual British woman with whom they socialized, they included in their book an 'album' of highly sentimental anonymous poems on the theme of loving friendship and the sorrow of parting addressed by such middle- and upper-class women to them, suggesting warm (albeit chaste) relationships.[31] Nowrojee and Merwanjee also described the proper domestic education of young British women to be cultured wives, and the need to emulate such training in India.[32]

Unlike some other Indians in Britain, including Rammohun Roy and Dadabhai Naoroji (1825–1917), Nowrojee and Merwanjee did not perceive the expanding Anglocentric world system as draining India and the other colonized nations of their capital to the advantage of industrial investment within Britain.[33] Rather, they admired Britain's commercial system that enabled them 'to bring cotton from India, thousands of miles, to manufacture it into fine muslin, and to send it back to India and to sell it there *much cheaper* than it can be made there . . .'.[34] They exclaimed: 'Oh, how much do we wish to see something of this kind commenced at Bombay.' Thus, British industrial practices should be emulated in India, not opposed.

In several places, Nowrojee and Merwanjee presented their extended sociological analysis of various British institutions—social, economic, and political. For example, they systematically chronicled the omnibus population in the City of London over the day.[35] They began at 8:45 a.m. with the lowest social class of passengers: 'sober-looking business-like persons, who are principally clerks' in banks, commuting into the City from London's suburbs. At 10:00, a higher class of passengers arrived: 'upper clerks and cashiers of banking houses . . . a little gayer in their attire, a great deal stiffer in their manners, and who seem to think themselves very great men.' Next came the highest class: stockbrokers. Nonetheless, these people were subject to Nowrojee and Merwanjee's recurrent anti-Semitic prejudice:

[31] Ibid., pp. 465–72.
[32] E.g. ibid., pp. 459–60.
[33] Naoroji, *Poverty.*
[34] Nowrojee and Merwanjee, *Journal,* pp. 134–40.
[35] Ibid., p. 42.

smirking, priggish-looking men arriving in great numbers, many of them, if not Jews, looking to have a cross of the Israelite in their blood . . . [S]hould you happen to be in the same Omnibus with them, you can immediately detect them; should an intimate friend get into the Omnibus, they play some quiet practical joke upon him as he passes, either by putting out their feet to cause him to stumble, pulling his coat tail, or some boyish freak to get their hands in for their childish play, when they get to kicking each other's hats to pieces in their room for business.

Nowrojee and Merwanjee's analysis continued throughout the workday, combining their observations and valuations of Britons.[36]

Among other features of British popular culture, Nowrojee and Merwanjee carefully delineated the range of newspapers and other periodicals, describing their manufacturing process, as well as the cost, frequency, readership profile, and political orientation of each. They decried the excesses of inflammatory popular journalism, the consequent unsettling effects on the masses, and also the immoral replacement of religious worship by Sunday newspaper reading. Yet they simultaneously lauded England's freedom of the press (in implicit contrast to British censorship of publications in India). They encouraged the spread of print culture in India, applauding Nowrojee Furdoonjee, a Parsi, for beginning a Bombay Gujarati journal, *Vidya Sagar*.[37]

While admiring British political authorities, these three authors also retained a critical distance over the British subjects of their gaze. While they praised the British Parliament as a model for the rest of the world to follow, they also suggested its flaws in practice. They pointed to the tradition of 'pocket boroughs', through which, they asserted, 'a rich Jew for many years was the owner of so many of these places that he returned six or seven members at least, receiving very large sums of money from those who wished to be returned to Parliament.'[38] The 1832 Reform Act may have officially ended that abuse, but its expansion of the franchise (limited as that extension actually was) also

[36] Another Parsi would a half century later publish his own similar sociology of the London bus and street populations. Malabari, *Indian Eye*. See Burton, *At the Heart*, Chapter 4.

[37] Nowrojee and Merwanjee, *Journal*, pp. 365–84, 464.

[38] Ibid., pp. 167–9.

ensured that 'bribery is more open, more common, and higher sums are given than before . . .'. Nowrojee and Merwanjee also regarded the informal demeanour and clothing of Members of Parliament while in the House to be deplorably beneath the dignity of that office.[39]

In an effort to reshape British cultural categories, Nowrojee and Merwanjee also worked to correct systematic British prejudices against Indians in general and, most galling to themselves, against Parsis in particular. These widespread 'erroneous' beliefs they tactfully blamed on poor information, not malice:

> our knowledge of the English character forbids our attributing wilful mis-representation to any; yet we cannot help regretting that imperfect and inaccurate accounts should have ever appeared before the British public, of the habits and customs of a class of people [the Parsis], who, it has been acknowledged, are the foremost in doing good, by supporting charitable institutions, &c. &c., and who, moreover, are the best and most loyally attached subjects of the British crown.[40]

Conversely, in addressing Indian audiences, all three argued that Britons in Britain were indeed respectful of merit, even in Indians.[41] As proof, they highlighted Cursetjee's own promotion while there. The Company's directors had advertised in London newspapers to fill the post of 'Chief Engineer and Inspector of Machinery' at the Bombay Steam Foundry.[42] Cursetjee applied, submitting that he was uniquely qualified. Part of the specified duties were 'the instructing of natives as engineers', which he could accomplish better than any Briton since he knew them and their languages and customs. After much debate about the precedent of appointing a 'native' to this covenanted office which supervised so many Europeans, the directors awarded it to him.[43]

While many Britons admired what these men had accomplished, the colonial context coloured British assessments of them. For example, the *Times* gave Nowrojee and Merwanjee's book a long but

[39] Ibid., pp. 182–3.
[40] Ibid., pp. 454–5.
[41] Cursetjee, *Diary*, p. 1.
[42] Nowrojee and Merwanjee, *Journal*, pp. 342–59; Cursetjee, *Diary*, pp. 52–3, 57, 93–6.
[43] Court Minutes 11/12/1839, 29/1/1840.

condescending review.[44] The reviewer wondered that 'Asiatics' had actually been capable of writing the chapters on 'Scientific Institutions'. Further, since the book was intended for Indian readers, it provided Britons with authentic and untranslated insights into how 'intelligent' and 'unprejudiced' natives regard Britain. Thus, this review and others patronizingly treated this book not as a serious assessment of British society but rather as a window on Parsi thought and measure of their development: Parsis, while having 'the naïveté of children', were 'almost on a level with Europeans in education and acquirements', compared to less advanced Indian communities.[45]

After their return to Bombay, all three men advanced in their careers. The directors recommended the appointments of Nowrojee and Merwanjee as assistant builders in the Steam Department; the former eventually rose to be Master Builder, the latter Surveyor.[46] Cursetjee long served the British and would eventually make four trips to Britain, dying there in 1877.[47] Many more Parsis would follow them to Britain, as did men from other regions of India.[48]

North Indian Munshis and Persian Secretaries

North India came under British power chronologically later than Bombay or Calcutta but, by the early nineteenth century, British colonialism was influencing career choices there as well. The lives of

[44] *Times* 18/6/1841 8b.

[45] *Blackwood's Edinburgh Magazine* 54, 337 (November 1843), pp. 543, 567–8. See also *Chambers Edinburgh Journal*, *Spectator* 29/5/1841, and *Bombay Times* 21/7/1841, pp. 464–5, and 25/9/1841, p. 622b–d.

[46] Court Minutes 26/8/1840 to 7/4/1841; Ardeshir Wadia, *Bombay Dockyard*, pp. 308–15, 318–21, 330–44.

[47] Darukhanawala, *Parsi Lustre*, vol. 1, pp. 268, 353, 493; Court Minutes 16/10/1851 to 26/10/1853; Ruttonjee Wadia, *Scions*, pp. 52–67.

[48] Among them was Manikjee Cursetjee (b.1808) who lived in Britain 1841–2. Elphinstone Papers, F.88/119, F.88/127, F.88/129; Elphinstone Journal, F.88/16, ff. 330–1; Political and Military References 10/11/1841, no. 335, BL; Broughton, *Recollections*, vol. 6, p. 47. Reform newspapers celebrated him as 'an Indian Prince', while the *Times* derided those and correctly identified him as a customs house official. *Times* 3/11/1841 6b.

Mohan Lal (1812–77) and Mir Shahamat Ali (b.181?) illustrate the opportunities and limitations faced by Anglicized Indian officials in India and Britain. From the beginning of their education at Delhi College, they faced alienation from their communities. This college (founded 1792) was the product of joint efforts by Indian élites, British educators, and the Government of India to disseminate 'modern' education in the Mughal imperial capital. Even the college's initial Persian course of study generated opposition from the most conservative elements in Indian society, including established Islamic and Brahmanic educators and social leaders. When Delhi College added an English course of study in 1828, this heightened the conflict.

Mir Shahamat Ali and Mohan Lal were among the students who first joined this English course. Shahamat Ali explained the difficulties faced by Muslim students:

> Molvies objected either from jealousy or from the excess of prejudice, [and] declared that, by beginning to receive an English education, we had lost our creed; and all the Mussulmans regarded us as infidels, and abstained from eating and drinking with us. The consequence was, that the Mahomedan boys, with the exception of a youth named Hadi Hussein, myself, and one or two others, left the English and returned to the Persian school, and were immediately readmitted into their caste, while we continued for some time to be considered in the light of *Kafirs*.[49]

Yet the attractions of this new Anglicized education, and the employment prospects it brought, convinced some three hundred young men to join the Delhi English College over the next five years.[50]

Mohan Lal's Hindu Kashmiri Pandit family had already made extensive cultural adaptations. For generations they had served the Mughals, assuming some Persianate deportment; his grandfather and father had shifted to service with the British.[51] Further, his father

[49] Shahamat Ali, *Sikhs and Afghans*, pp. vii–ix.

[50] Trevelyan, 'Memoir of Mohan Lal', in Lal, *Travel*, p. xxi. See 'Abdulhaq, *Marhum Dilli Kalij*; Andrews, *Zaka Ullah*; Minault, 'Qiran al-Sa'adain'; Ram, *Qadim Dilli Kalij*. For the context see: Frykenberg, *Delhi*; Narayani Gupta, *Delhi*; Spear, *Twilight*.

[51] His father, Rai Brahm Nath (alias Rae Budh Singh), had served Mountstuart Elphinstone on his diplomatic mission to Peshawar (1808–9). See Hari Gupta,

maintained two families, one with his Pandit wife, the other with a Muslim consort. He had at least one daughter by the latter (reflecting the family's complex identity, this daughter married R. Hodges, a man of mixed ancestry who held subordinate posts in the British administration and remained a long-time associate of Mohan Lal).[52] Indeed, Mohan Lal himself had another more identifiably Kashmiri Brahmin name, Ram Nath, used in his Pandit home.

Despite this family's efforts, they lost their hereditary land grant from the Mughals while Mohan Lal was studying in Delhi College.[53] This forced him to leave after only two years and begin working for British officers. While his official title was *munshi*, Mohan Lal preferred the more Anglicized title 'Persian Secretary'. Over the years, Mohan Lal travelled with Sir Alexander Burnes (1805–41) and other British employers in disguise on covert missions in north-west India, Afghanistan, Central Asia, and Persia, negotiating with various Muslim rulers and peoples there.

The combination in such young men of expertise in Persianate administrative and cultural knowledge plus an Anglicized education made them particularly valued by British officials. Further, Britons believed these men's very alienation from the local community ensured loyalty to the British. Burnes explained: 'I . . . took a Hindoo lad, of Cashmere family, named Mohun Lal, who had been educated at the English Institution at Delhi, as he would assist me in my Persian correspondence, the forms of which amount to a science in the East. His youth and his creed would, I believed, free me from all the danger of his entering into intrigues with the people . . .'[54] While the British

---

Life, pp. 1–5; Lal, *Travel*, p. 229; Sender, *Kashmiri Pandits*; Sharga and Sharga, 'Zutshis'.

[52] Hari Gupta, *Life*, p. 197; FPC 24/12/1832, no. 26, 20/2/1839, no. 38, NAI.

[53] Mohan Lal blamed this confiscation on British administrative 'reforms' but Gupta claims it was the hostility of the jilted Nawab of Ferozepur, whose mistress had become Mohan Lal's stepmother. Lal, *Travel*, p. xx; Hari Gupta, *Life*, p. 3.

[54] Burnes, *Travels*, vol. 1, pp. ix–x, 183. A servant, Ghoolam Husan of Surat, accompanied Captain Sir Alexander Burnes to Britain in 1839. Burnes, *Travels*, vol. 2, pp. 72, 217, 296.

found this alienation valuable, it created difficulties for Mohan Lal and his colleagues.

As instructed by their British teachers, Mohan Lal and Shahamat Ali kept detailed personal diaries in English which they rightly regarded as passports to the attention of the British—indeed, to the favour of the governor-general.[55] Mohan Lal also practised archaeology and ethnography during his travels, in the style of some of his British employers. Mohan Lal, writing from Central Asia in 1833, submitted part of his narrative to the Asiatic Society of Bengal in Calcutta which it published in its *Journal*.[56] On reading his words in print, Mohan Lal then wrote from Kandahar with an autobiographical essay which that *Journal*, as well as the *Delhi Gazette* newspaper, also published.[57] After he reached Calcutta in 1834, conveying reports and papers for his British chief, he read a paper before the Asiatic Society, which it published in its *Proceedings*.[58] He would continue to contribute articles to that Society's *Journal*, including on Greek antiquities that he discovered in Afghanistan.[59] While in Calcutta being trained as a surveyor, Mohan Lal revised his journal and published it as *Travel in the Punjab, Afganistan and Turkistan to Balk, Bokhara and Herat* (Calcutta: the Author, 1834) in the self-promoting popular style of many British official-adventurers on the north-west frontier. The British government rewarded him with a plot of land in Delhi, gifts of surveying instruments, and increased salary.[60]

All this publicity made him well known in the British community as a 'new-model' Indian. As did Dyce Sombre, Dean Mahomet, and other Indians of his social class, Mohan Lal joined the Freemasons.

---

[55] Lal, *Travel*, p. 174; Lal Letter 12/1/1835, Elphinstone Papers F.88/96, BL; Burnes, *Travels*, vol. 2, p. 297.

[56] Lal, 'Letter to Editor' and 'Brief Description of Herat'.

[57] Lal, 'Further Information'.

[58] 'Proceedings', Asiatic Society Meeting 6/8/1834.

[59] Lal, 'Brief Account of Masu'd', 'Description of Uch-Shari'f', 'Account of Kala Bagh', and 'Brief Account of the Origin of the Daud Putras'.

[60] Lal, *Travel*, pp. 226–7; Hari Gupta, *Life*, p. 65. Three decades later the British trained the Indian surveyors known as the 'Pandits', who clandestinely surveyed the lands of Central Asia and Tibet, too dangerous for a Briton to attempt. See Waller, *Pandits*.

Some lodges provided a special arena where Masonic hierarchy super-seded the usual colonial hierarchy based on ethnicity.[61] To further Mohan Lal's moral transformation, a British patron, Charles Edward Trevelyan (1807–86), made arrangements for his protégé to visit England as early as 1832, although he would not make this journey until a dozen years later.[62] This patron explained:

What has given Mohan Lal so decided an advantage over the generality of his countrymen? What is it that has gained for him a willing acknowledg-ment of his personal superiority by the princes of Central Asia, and enables him to enjoy, on terms of equality, the society of European gentlemen? It is simply his knowledge of the English language. Not a critical know-ledge—that he leaves to those philologists in whose estimation languages are desirable objects of acquisition, not so much as a medium of obtaining knowledge, as for their own proper sakes—but such knowledge as enables him to read and understand English books, and to converse intelligently with English gentlemen on ordinary subjects.

This is the simple cause of Mohan Lal's elevation of character: and can it be doubted that, under the Divine blessing, the same means which have produced such a decided effect in raising an individual in the scale of civil-isation and honour, will, if properly applied, lead to the same result in re-gard to the entire population of this great country?[63]

Mohan Lal thus stood, in the eyes of these British 'modernizers', as the pioneer that all Indians should follow up 'the scale of civilisation and honour' towards Europeans. But even sympathetic British critics, who felt his work 'most creditable', qualified that praise by adding: when 'considered as the work of an Asiatic in a foreign tongue'.[64]

For the Indian, Central, and West Asian rulers with whom Mohan Lal dealt as well, his expertise in English and access to British know-ledge made him distinctive, but also dangerous. They tried to in-duce Mohan Lal to influence British policy on their behalf.[65] They

---

[61] Lal, *Travel*, p. 296; Hinnells, *Zoroastrians*, p. 103.

[62] Lal, *Travel*, pp. 62, 288.

[63] Trevelyan, 'Memoir of Mohan Lal', in Lal, *Travel*, p. xxvii.

[64] Havelock, *Narrative*, vol. 1, p. 150. C.f., Sir William Jones' comments on Emin, in Chapter 2.

[65] Lal, *Travel*, pp. 129, 264.

honoured him with the Persian 'Order of the Lion and Sun' and the Afghan 'Order of the Durrani Empire', but his life was often threatened. Mohan Lal openly tested and disgraced an Afghan rival who falsely claimed to know English.[66]

Mohan Lal's experiential education among these Muslim peoples clearly affected his self-conceptualization profoundly. Initially, he identified himself with his natal traditions. He retained a Kashmiri Brahmin cook, arranging to eat separately from both the British and Muslim members of their party, and declining to share food or drink with their local hosts, despite the dangers of disclosure of his Brahmin identity that this entailed.[67] Early in his journal, he recorded his critical responses against the Muslim practices and Islamic beliefs which he watched. Over time, however, his journal evinces his movement towards the culture and values of his step-mother and his Muslim hosts. At first as part of his disguise, but later in more intimate ways, Mohan Lal assumed the alias and identity 'Agha Hasan Jan'. With this shift came his distancing from Hinduism.

His close socializing with Muslims and Christians put him ritually outside the Brahminic fold. In 1834, members of the Kashmir Pandit community in Delhi formally excommunicated him.[68] He protested that, to that point, he 'always observed the outward form of the Hindoo religion' and never dined with Muslims or Christians.[69] This excommunication, 'hurt the feelings of my old parents and mortif[ied] their hearts'. He could not, however, get this excommunication reversed, even by appealing to the British law-court in Delhi.

At this point in his journal, Mohan Lal started to ridicule Hindu practices and beliefs: 'Hindus of both sexes, after bathing themselves, worship[ed] the pictures of their deities, which were painted on walls, some of them being represented with four heads, and others with monkeys' heads, which they presented with offerings of flowers and fruits . . . Here is a display of utter ignorance and prostitution of all sense—rational creatures turned fools, and deceived into a belief in stones, water, and fire, all of which I am sure can do them no good.'[70]

[66] Ibid., p. 128.
[67] Ibid., pp. 91, 108, 197–8.
[68] Ibid., p. 225.
[69] Lal cited in Hari Gupta, *Life*, pp. 63, 66.
[70] Lal, *Travel*, pp. 226–7.

He also found distasteful the deportment of only partly Anglicized Hindus who, for example, continued to 'rub mustard-oil over their bodies, which makes them disagreeable to those whom they approach to converse with.'

His books, written primarily for a British audience, never explicitly specified his religious identity. When quizzed by the missionary Reverend Joseph Wolff (1795–1862, himself a convert from Judaism to Christianity), Mohan Lal pleased him by saying 'that my religion consisted in the worship of one sole Supreme Being.'[71] When questioned by the Iranian emperor, 'whether I was a Sunni or Shia', Mohan Lal pleased this Shi'ite ruler by replying 'I am a friend of Panjtan, or five persons [of the family of the Prophet Muhammad]', a suggestively Shi'ite answer.[72] Indeed, in his journal, Mohan Lal began to associate himself with the martyrs of Shi'ism: 'I suffered much from thirst, and remembered the hardships of Ali's family, which were caused by the scarcity of water in the dasht [desert] of Karbala.'[73] He also repeatedly participated in Shi'ite congregational prayer and visited the shrines of Shi'ite Imams.

At some point, Mohan Lal indeed seems to have adopted Shi'ism, at least in part as a matter of conviction. He began to dine with Muslims and Christians. When his Brahmin cook died in 1837, for example, he employed a Shi'ite 'Persian cook, Mohammed Taher'.[74] Yet, many Muslims he met identified him as a Hindu. He thus crossed the boundaries of all these cultures.

During the first Afghan War (1839–42), Mohan Lal served as a main interpreter and supply agent for the invading British army, with Rs 1,000 being his monthly salary. In Kabul's insurrection of 1841, Mohan Lal was one of the first on the British side captured, yet he continued to negotiate on their behalf, even while he received little support from British authorities. Of all his relatives and friends, only classmate Shahamat Ali (then stationed at Indore) pledged the Rs 10,000 ransom demanded by his Afghan captors. However Mohan Lal eventually escaped to the protection of the Shi'ite party in Kabul.

From there he continued to represent and advance British interests.

[71] Ibid., pp. 40–1. See Wolff, *Researches*.
[72] Lal, *Travel*, pp. 135–6.
[73] Ibid., pp. 70, 99, 135–6, 147.
[74] Ibid., p. 236.

As authorized by his desperate British employers, he promised large amounts of money to buy support, including promising bounty for the assassination of Afghan leaders. He borrowed heavily on his own credit for these sums. Indeed he proved successful in negotiating the ransom of British prisoners. Despite Mohan Lal's financial and moral pledges on behalf of the British government to various Afghan leaders, however, most were subsequently abandoned by that government.

While clearly one of the few heroes in this British disaster, Mohan Lal also generated British resentment and became a scapegoat for their failures. British critics of the assassinations he organized on the instructions of his British employers reviled him as 'endowed with a genius for traitor-making, the lustre of which remained undimmed to the very end of the war.'[75] The death of Burnes and other British officers who had authorized his loans left him and other creditors with no proof of their large financial claims due from the government.

After Mohan Lal finally escaped Afghanistan and returned to India in 1843, he received little recognition or reward for what he had done. He requested appointment as Persian Secretary in the prestigious Lucknow or Hyderabad Residencies; instead he was sent to the political agency at Lahore, at a much reduced monthly salary of Rs 350.[76] This was work as a mere assistant, instead of an independent agent. Even more humiliating, the British officials under whom he served distrusted him, due to his complex financial and moral relations in Afghanistan with the British, and their sense that he had risen above his station.

Frustrated, Mohan Lal obtained eighteen months' leave of absence, nominally in order to visit Bombay but actually to go to Britain. Along the way, he consulted his friend Shahamat Ali and collected letters of introduction from many British officials who knew his work or that of his father or grandfather. Indians with experience in Britain also gave letters of introduction to their British friends, explaining Mohan

[75] Kaye, *History of the War*, vol. 1, p. 459. Various newspapers debated Mohan Lal's achievements. *Englishman* 20/10/1842, 7/12/1842; *Bombay Times* 5/11/1842 717a–c, 21/12/1842 819–22, 28/12/1842 836a.

[76] FPC 15/3/1843, no. 107, 27/1/1844, no. 211, 6/5/1848, nos 127–8, 3/6/1848, nos 93–4, NAI; Broadfoot Papers ADD 40128, vol. 2, ff. 81–4, BL.

Lal's three goals: 'to see the *beautiful England*, the wonders of which he has heard so much about', 'to deliver some valuable papers belonging to his late patron [Alexander Burnes] to his father personally', and 'to have his particular services in Cabool substantially acknowledged by the Court of directors.'[77]

Mohan Lal sailed from Bombay with one Afghan Muslim servant, reaching Britain via Egypt in September 1844. On his arrival, he recorded his warm welcome, how he socialized and dined with his British 'friends in England, [who were] desirous to shew me every attention whose continued civilities and interest in my behalf made me feel as comfortable as if I were among my own kindred, and in my native land.'[78] Many of the directors dined with him; the chairman even called upon him in his hotel. He was impressed with steam-powered industrialization and railways, and the electric telegraph.

Mohan Lal admired British culture, but recognized its limitations. For example, in his comments on the London theatre, he critiqued the morality of actresses and, by extension, the British élite who consorted with them:

> the gaudy attire of the actors and actresses . . . will at once bring into the mind of an Asiatic the fabulous tales of the gardens of the fairies. I could not say much in commendation of the beauty or modesty of the females who appear on the stage. However, they attract the attention and respect of the spectators; and some of them have made conquests, and have become wives of noblemen, and associate with ladies of the highest birth.[79]

He also remarked at length how money determined a woman's marriage prospects, leaving many unmarried. He showed great pity for the grinding poverty he saw.

Late in 1844, Mohan Lal made a much publicized presentation of the late Alexander Burnes' papers to Burnes' father in Scotland. The *Times*, echoing the *Edinburgh Witness* and the *Montrose Review*, recounted the honoured reception of this 'celebrated Oriental stranger, the companion and protégé of the late lamented Sir Alexander

---

[77] Cursetjee letter 19/12/1844, Elphinstone Papers, F.88/126, BL.
[78] Lal, *Travel*, p. 300.
[79] Ibid., p. 305.

Burnes . . . He has a remarkably pleasant and highly intellectual cast of countenance, and is dressed in a magnificent Hindoo costume . . . His countenance beams with intelligence; and his intercourse with Europeans has enabled him to adapt himself, with perfect tact, to all their habits and modes of thinking, so that he can sustain with care and propriety, his part in any general conversation.'[80] Mohan Lal display- ed British social graces but also highlighted his attractive distinctive- ness by wearing Indian clothes and his Afghan and Persian orders (Image 23). Mohan Lal later returned to Scotland, at the invitation of 'my kind masonic brother, Mr Laurie, secretary to the Grand Lodge of Scotland.'[81] He also made celebrated tours of England, Ireland, and the continent.[82]

In Britain, Mohan Lal gained powerful supporters. He had audi- ences with Queen Victoria and Prince Albert—although as a private individual in light of his ongoing financial claims against the Govern- ment of India—and they invited him to a Royal Ball. He boasted of being made an honourary member of 'the Oriental, Carlton, Travel- lers', Junior, United Service, Star, and Victoria Yacht Clubs'.[83] He repeatedly visited Elphinstone, complaining that his work in Kabul was 'successful, but not rewarded'.[84] He attended the burial of Dwarka- nath Tagore in 1846, which suggests a nascent Indian community in London. While Mohan Lal did not record his romantic affairs, his family later claimed to receive repeated letters from Mohan Lal's 'Eng- lish wife' and her children allegedly by him.[85]

In response to his petition of January 1845, the Company granted him an extraordinary annual pension of Rs 6,000 plus a special dona- tion of Rs 15,000. Yet these were not as much as Mohan Lal felt he

---

[80] *Times* 25/10/1844 5a; 7/11/1844 5b.

[81] Lal, *Travel*, p. 308.

[82] Lal Letter 28/7/1846, Elphinstone Papers, F.88/129; Lal to Mayor of Liverpool 16/12/1844, MSS EUR A.84, BL. Calotypes of Mohan Lal by David Octavius Hill and Robert Adamson are in the Scottish National Portrait Gal- lery. Stevenson, *David*, pp. 78, 294 and *Facing*, pp. 91, 94, 98.

[83] Lal, *Travel*, p. 317.

[84] Mohan Lal joined other Indian visitors in praising Elphinstone. Lal Letters 27/9/1844, 7–13/10/1844, 6/11/1844, Elphinstone Papers F.88/126, BL; Lal, *Travel*, p. 306.

[85] Hari Gupta, *Life*, p. 293n2.

Image 23: Portrait of Mohan Lal Kashmiri,
etching by T. Peiken, 1846.

deserved, in light of what British officials had received for lesser service in Afghanistan. He and his supporters, including Members of Parliament, felt that the grant of a tax-free estate would be more appropriate to his achievements.[86] The directors then raised his pension to

[86] Lal Letters 18/1/1845, 9/6/1845, Willock Letter 3/2/1845, Elphinstone Papers F.88/127–8; Political and Military References, January 1845,

Rs 10,000, retroactively from the date of his leaving Afghanistan, in addition to his salary.[87] The British popular press regarded the pension as a 'munificent reward' that would inspire other 'native servants in the East'.[88] The directors and Board of Control, however, refused to deal with his huge financial claims from his loans in Afghanistan, instructing him to settle those with authorities in India.[89]

While in Britain, Mohan Lal participated in the heated public debate about the disastrous Afghan war, and about British policies in India generally. His position, defending Burnes and also himself, was highly enmeshed in partisan politics. While Mohan Lal disdained writing letters to the editor to answer his critics, he instead published huge books publicizing his career and claims. He expanded and republished his first book, *Travel* (London: W. H. Allen, 1846) adding an account of his triumphant trip to Britain. He also wrote and published a two-volume (900-page) *Life of Amir Dost Mohammed Khan of Kabul* (London: Longman, Brown, Green, and Longmans, 1846) filled with documentary evidence that justified his own and Burnes' actions in Afghanistan. Mohan Lal dedicated his *Life* to Queen Victoria and Prince Albert, presented a copy to Sir Robert Peel, and used it to lobby other British notables.[90] These works cost him £300 to publish and were also apparently intended to capitalize on the current public fascination with Afghanistan.

Many Britons purchased and admired his books. Some British book reviewers (particularly those hostile to Burnes and Mohan Lal's political allies), however, criticized him for his 'absurd . . . mimicry of John Bull phraseology, and the thoroughly Asiatic modes of thinking and feeling which have survived all his Feringhee training.'[91] They

---

nos 1437–9, May 1845, no. 3106, June 1845, nos 158, 3506, July 1845, nos 550, 917, December 1845, no. 4540, BL.

[87] Court Minutes 16/4/1845 to 30/7/1844; Military Papers 29–31/7/1845 L/MIL/2/220, BL.

[88] *Times* 23/5/1845 5c.

[89] Political and Military References April 1846, no. 2314, May 1846, no. 3007, June 1846, no. 3097, BL.

[90] Peel Papers ADD 40597, vol. 417, f. 45; Lal Letter 23/1/1845, Elphinstone Papers, F.88/127; Auckland letter 21/8/1846, Broughton Papers, MSS EUR F.213/17, BL.

[91] *Quarterly Review* 78, 156 (September 1846), pp. 463–510.

found it incongruous that an 'Oriental' would write a book in order to sell it and make money 'as a publisher's hack'.[92] Yet even these critics regarded the insights he inadvertently provided into 'the Oriental' mind as valuable.

In his publications, Mohan Lal also censured official British actions, for example their betrayal of the amirs of Sindh. As instructed by his British supervisors, he himself had assured these rulers that, if they cooperated, they would be kept on the throne. When the British deposed them, Mohan Lal felt personally dishonoured.[93] Mohan Lal also expressed sympathy with the case of the deposed ex-maharaja of Satara, but supported the directors' critiques of paid Indian diplomats like Rungo Bapojee—who was also in London at the time.[94]

Mohan Lal argued that Anglicization was the key to India's future: 'India will never regain the zenith of its former glory, nor even prosper, until the whole population becomes acquainted with the language of the government, and then, entertaining the pacific sentiments of loyalty and homage to her present honourable British masters, claim and enjoy her rights like the other subjects of Britain.'[95] He found, however, that this expected equality was denied by Britons.

Despite his substantial pension, Mohan Lal believed it was inadequate to his accomplishments. Even as he was leaving Britain late in 1846, he continued to solicit a British knighthood, to go with his Persian and Afghan orders.[96] The directors, however, saw this as presumptuous in an Indian and refused to support his request.

After his return to India, Mohan Lal never again received employment from the Government of India, despite his many applications.[97] His friends from Britain continued their interest in him.[98] Many British officials in India, however, felt him corrupted by his honoured reception in London, which they felt had raised his aspirations above

---

[92] *Blackwood's Edinburgh Magazine* 60, 373 (November 1846), pp. 539–54.

[93] Lal, *Life*, vol. 1, p. 399; vol. 2, pp. 81–3.

[94] Ibid., vol. 2, p. 369.

[95] Lal, *Travel*, p. 319.

[96] Court Minutes 16/12/1845 to 14/10/1846; Political and Military References July 1846, no. 168, August 1846, no. 515, September 1846, no. 1186, October 1846, no. 1842, BL.

[97] FPC 6/5/1848, nos 127–8, NAI.

[98] Political and Military References August 1850, no. 2154, BL.

his place as a colonized Indian, and also his complex financial claims on the government. British officials charged Hodges (his friend, half-sister's husband, and father-in-law) with corruption—concerning some of the Afghan loans and for extortion based on Mohan Lal's famous influence with the British—and dismissed him from his post.[99] Mohan Lal's direct supervisor stopped his salary of Rs 320 monthly until London expressly ordered it to be restored. He also never received the Rs 79,496 which he claimed he had personally paid for supplies for the British army in Afghanistan.[100] In 1853, his multiple appeals finally led to the creation of a commission to investigate his claims. The conclusions of the individual commissioners varied but they settled on Rs 12,000, which was the mean average of their recommendations. The governor-general, however, vetoed any repayment whatever.

For the last thirty years of his life, Mohan Lal remained frustratingly marginal to all the cultures around him. His various business undertakings failed, he fell into debt despite his Rs 10,000 pension, and he had to hide from prosecution by his creditors. A British official mourned the waste of his potential: 'a man who had been so well received in England and other parts of Europe by the very first people, Kings and Queens not excepted, should not be ignored by the British Society of this country as I found Mohan Lal was, and thus be driven back on his heathen and ignorant associates to the inevitable deterioration of the enlightened ideas he had acquired in his European tour'.[101] Mohan Lal reportedly sent two of his daughters to England to be Anglicized, but they died of smallpox on their way back to India.[102] He often used the name Agha Hasan Jan, and patronized Shi'i religious institutions. Ironically, during the 1857 fighting, he had to flee as a man associated with the British, and his neighbour and in-law, Hodges, was assassinated. Mohan Lal died in Delhi in 1877. Not all Anglicized Indians felt as betrayed by British promises and then humiliations as Mohan Lal, although all paid some price.

Mir Shahamat Ali, Mohan Lal's classmate, also served the British, first teaching at Delhi English College and then, from 1832 rising

[99] FSC 25/10/1845, nos 78–81, NAI.
[100] Hari Gupta, *Life*, pp. 296–301, 308.
[101] FPC 10/2/1854, nos 272–4, NAI.
[102] Hari Gupta, *Life*, pp. 309–12.

rapidly as the protégé of Sir Claude Wade.[103] At the encouragement of Mohan Lal, he too published his personal journal as a book explaining his accomplishments, embedded in a narrative and analysis of British political intercourse in Afghanistan: *The Sikhs and Afghans in Connexion with India and Persia Immediately before and after the Death of Ranjeet Singh from the Journal of an Expedition to Kabul, through the Panjab and the Khaibar Pass by Shahmat Ali, Persian Secretary with the Mission of Lieut. Col. Sir C.M. Wade, C.B. to Peshawar in 1839, and now Mir Munshi to the Political Resident in Malwa* (London: J. Murray, 1847).[104] He intended this to be his entrée to Britain.[105]

Indeed, he visited Britain the next year, publishing on his arrival *Notes and Opinions of a Native on the Present State of India and the Feelings of Its Peoples* (Ryde, Isle of Wight: George Butler, 1848). He wrote this book to warn the British public about the widening resentment among 'natives of India, who have hitherto been patient spectators of the scene, [but] are now becoming alive to their own interests and welfare, and are beginning to grow loud in their complaints of the condition to which they have been reduced; a continuance of which state they instinctively consider oppressive, and degrading to them as a nation.'[106] Among these alienating policies were 'distinctions of colour and creed . . . which . . . have marked . . . the policy of the British towards its Indian subjects, [and] which has proved to be not only ruinous to them and their country, but to have destroyed the good name of the English in the estimation of the Asiatic nations in general.'[107] Like Rungo Bapojee at this same time, he expressed to the British public the growing and widespread Indian hostility to British colonial discrimination based on 'colour'.

He particularly protested how alienated his own class of Anglicized officials had been made by their own communities: 'such of the natives as receive an English education, and imitate the customs and manners of the English, are looked upon with disgust, and apparently with sufficient reason, because many of these young men, being very little

---

[103] FPC 18/1/1841, nos 99–100, 3/5/1841, nos 55–9, 28/6/1841, no. 108, 27/3/1857, no. 40, NAI.

[104] Lal, *Life*, vol. 2, p. 250n.

[105] Shahamat Ali, *Sikhs and Afghans* (1986), p. xiii. *Times* 30/12/1846 7c.

[106] Shahamat Ali, *Notes*, p. 6.

[107] Ibid., p. v.

acquainted with their own habits, religious and national feelings, begin to assail their own countrymen summarily, like their European masters.'[108] Such men were underemployed by the Government of India, and subordinated to less qualified British officials.[109] Using the example of Mohan Lal, he showed how even the inadequate honours he had received only 'prejudiced the minds of the European part of the service generally against him, as if being a native, he was unworthy of this distinction. The consequence is, that, instead of being employed in some suitable situation, where by his services he might have given further testimonies of his gratitude and usefulness, he is allowed to lead an idle and inactive life in retirement.'[110] In a prescient warning, he argued that British policies of interference in religion and lack of respect for Indians in British employ would provoke the Indian Army into a mutiny—as would happen nine years later. Like other Indian writers, he contrasted the 'arrogance' of Britons in India with how 'natives of India generally meet with every civility and politeness in England, as if the English at home and the English in India belonged to two different races of people.'[111]

While in Britain, Shahamat Ali sought to imitate Mohan Lal by demonstrating his literary skills and hinting that the directors honour his accomplishments. He published *Picturesque Sketches in India; with Notices of the Adjacent Countries of Sindh, Afghanistan, Multan, and the West of India* (London: J. Madden, 1848—also titled *History of Bahawalpur*). This was his translation of a Persian manuscript which described the dynastic history of that state, with his additional few pages of remarks on Britain and its institutions. The directors, however, did not provide the financial help he requested.[112] Nor did he receive the honours or monetary recognition from the directors that he felt he deserved.[113]

[108] Ibid., p. 75.

[109] He uses the example of another Anglicized Indian official who went to Britain: Peer Ibrahim Khan, see Chapter 10. Shahamat Ali, *Notes*, p. 93n.

[110] Shahamat Ali, *Notes*, pp. 93–4.

[111] Ibid., p. 76n.

[112] Court Minutes 2–9/8/1848, 22/11/1848, 29/12/1848; Political and Military References March 1849, no. 2392, April 1849, no. 2579; Shahamat Ali Letter 30/11/1848 and reply 2/12/1848, Elphinstone Papers F.88/137, BL.

[113] Court Minutes 7/3/1849, 4/4/1849.

Less controversial than Mohan Lal, Shahamat Ali's later career in India prospered as far as 'a native is allowed' (as he put it).[114] After his return in 1850, he received appointments as Deputy Bhil Agent and then Joint Superintendent of the princely state of Sellana, as a member of the Regency Board. In March 1857, he was appointed Native Agent in Malwa. He rose to be Superintendent of Rutlam state and received the honour Commander of the Star of India. Thus, he specialized as an intermediary, supervising Indian rulers for the Government of India. Other men of their class, inspired by Mohan Lal's handsome pension and undiscouraged by his later treatment in India, also ventured to Britain, with very mixed results.[115]

Bengali Businessmen, Students, and Christians

As the capital of British rule in India, Calcutta emerged as one of the most intense sites of interactions between Indians and Britons. By the 1840s, Bengali businessmen, Christian converts, and students with already extensive connections to the British began to make the voyage to Britain in larger numbers. Each sought further advancement there and brought back deeper knowledge of Britain. Given the growing number of such travellers, we will highlight only one case of each type to illustrate the variety of their receptions and agency.

One of Calcutta's leading merchants and civil leaders, Dwarkanath Tagore (1794–1846), decided to tour Britain and also improve his commercial and political influence there. He sailed with much publicity in January 1842 on his own steamship, the *India*, accompanied by his British personal physician, a nephew, and five attendants.[116] Like his close friend Rammohun Roy, Tagore arrived in Britain with

[114] FPC 22/5/1851, nos 103–9, 27/3/1857, nos 40–4, 1/1/1857, nos 483–6, 4/3/1859, nos 337–8, 25/3/1859, nos 192–4, 30/12/1859, nos 702–7, supp., NAI.

[115] Men citing Mohan Lal's example included Peer Ibrahim Khan who went in 1851–2 and Ghulam Mahomed who went in 1857.

[116] See *Bombay Times* 2/10/1841, 635b–c, 19/1/1842 46a–b, 17/12/1842 814–15; *Friend of India* 6/1/1841; *India News* 10/10/1842; Kling, *Partner*, especially pp. 168–75; Kripalani, *Dwarkanath Tagore*; Mittra, *Memoir*; *Times* 1/8/1842 5c. Other Calcutta businessmen also turned to London. Soloman Zalmon, a Jewish merchant of Calcutta, failed in London to recoup his fortunes.

an already established reputation as a social reformer, as well as an entrepreneur. After his arrival, he received a distinguished welcome from Queen Victoria and many of Britain's prominent politicians and businessmen.[117] He dined, drank, and socialized with them, responding graciously to their plaudits with effusive words of gratitude for all that Britons had done for India. Britons conquered India, he proclaimed, not for selfish motives but 'from mere love of doing good', including saving it from 'the tyranny and villainy of the Mahometans . . .'.[118] Since he had no political mission, he did not face the same humiliations in London as Rammohun Roy or other Indian diplomats (but his pro-British declarations later ostracized him back in Calcutta).

He educated himself about Britain at large. On arrival via France, he was surprised by how impressed he was: 'After seeing everything on the Continent, I did not expect that I should be so much taken by this little island; but really London is the *wonderful city*; the bustling of the city, the carriages, the shops, and the people quite bewildered me . . . If a man has wealth, this is the country to enjoy it in.'[119] In a reverse of orientalism, he regarded Englishwomen as embodying his own exotic Persian fantasies: 'The beauty of the ladies in England puts me in mind of the fairy tales. What I read in my younger days in the Persian tales, I begin to see in London.'[120] Talking to élites and enjoying London's tourist sites, he inspected British factories and mines, finding steam-powered printing presses particularly noteworthy. He made a walking tour of the countryside.[121]

His supporters angled for a knighthood for him, but instead the directors promised him a 'gold medal' as 'a testimonial of their esteem

---

Revenue, Judicial, and Legislative Committee References L/PJ/1/51, no. 385, BL.

[117] Tagore Letter 21/9/1842, Peel Papers ADD 40515, vol. 335; Babbage Correspondence ADD 37192, vol. 11, f. 214, BL.

[118] Dwarkanath Tagore's Toast at Lord Mayor's dinner, quoted in *Friend of India* 22/9/1842, p. 690.

[119] Tagore to his son, Debendranath, quoted in Mittra, *Memoir*, pp. 88–9. See also Dwarkanath's personal diary quoted and paraphrased by Kling, *Partner* and Mittra, *Memoir*.

[120] Tagore Letter 29/6/1842 in *Friend of India* 15/9/1842, p. 581.

[121] Rendel Letter 19/8/1842, MSS EUR A.146, BL.

and of the approbation with which they regard the public benefits conferred by him upon British India.'[122] He returned via France, reaching Calcutta (December 1842) on the same ship as George Thompson (see Chapter 7).

Back in Calcutta, Tagore's leadership flagged. His interdining with Britons, as well as his rumoured sexual affairs with British and Indian women, alienated him from the more conservative members of his family and community. His pro-British statements in London distanced him from the more progressive political leaders of Calcutta. Further, the Union Bank, which he controlled, was financially unstable, and he sold out just prior to its collapse.

Based on his first trip, Tagore became more firmly convinced that knowledge of Britain and education there would bring advantages for the next generation of Indians. Despite his financial difficulties, in 1845 he returned to Britain, taking young men for study and training there: his youngest son, Nagendranath, his nephew, Nabin Chandra Mukherji, and four Bengali medical students (discussed below).

After his return to Europe, he resumed his munificent hospitality and élite socializing. He also honoured his late friend Rammohun Roy, shifting his grave to Arno's Vale Cemetery near Bristol and erecting a monument. That proved prophetic, since Dwarkanath himself died in 1846 and was buried (without any religious ceremony) in Kensal Green, London.[123] His son and nephew returned to Calcutta, while the medical students continued their education.

Significantly, the earliest students to regularly enrol in a formal course of study in Britain went to master British medical science. European-style medicine proved attractive to some Indians as offering new cures. Further, the government medical service was more open to Indians because Britons ranked it lower in prestige than some others, like the civil service.

The Calcutta Medical College (established 1835) taught a British scientific curriculum. In 1845, four advanced students agreed to accompany their British Professor of Anatomy, Henry Hurry Goodeve (1807–84), to Britain for advanced training and qualification

---

[122] Court Minutes 19/10/1842, 2/11/1842, 5/7/1843.
[123] Carpenter, *Last Days*, pp. 130–1.

at University College, London.[124] In Britain, these Indian medical students competed successfully against British classmates and also practised on British bodies, including women's bodies. Given growing British attitudes towards the moral and even physical inferiority of Indians, their British hosts were astonished at the fact that these Indians could surpass Britons in a rigorous and technical subject like medicine.

The most senior student, Dwarkanath Bose, was enabled to make the journey through a public subscription from the leaders of Calcutta society. Bholanath Das Bose and Gopal Chandra Seal, who had each won a gold medal in the annual Calcutta Medical College awards, received funding from Dwarkanath Tagore. The expenses and tuition of the youngest, Soojee Comar Chuckerbutty, were paid by the directors. They enrolled in April 1845 and settled at 7 Upper Woburn Place, under Goodeve's direct supervision.[125]

In May, they attended the Holborn Public Baths where Dwarkanath Bose expressed his competitiveness by challenging the British youth for prizes in a swimming contest. Clearly, the British public did not regard the sharing of water sports with these men as threatening.[126] Although he did not win in this physical competition with young Britons, he and his fellows would stand out in more scholarly contests.

College and Company authorities monitored both their academic progress, which was measured against their British fellow students, and their social life with the Britons around them, which was reportedly minimal.[127] They stood apart from the Britons around them. Goodeve recognized they competed on 'national' lines against Britons, writing of 'their anxiety to distinguish themselves and to rival their English fellow students'. He also praised the students' 'gentle and obedient' conduct, and also how they 'have easily conformed themselves to European manners . . . Their whole time is given to study,

---

[124] Brown, 'Indian Students'; Lahiri, *Indians*, p. 3.

[125] Court Minutes 30/4/1845, 11/6/1845, 9–16/7/1845, 6/8/1845; Revenue, Judicial, and Legislative Committee References L/PJ/1/39, no. 170; L/PJ/1/40, nos 247, 260a, BL.

[126] *Times* 2/5/1845 7d.

[127] Court Minutes 8–22/7/1846.

they appear very regardless of amusements in any shape when it inter-feres with the great object of their coming to England.'[128] While he lamented the 'sedentary life' that their devotion to their studies entailed, he also sought to isolate them from 'general society, or being frequently present at places of public amusement, lest they be injured by the interest and attention they might thus create.' Goodeve and the British authorities projected an image onto these students which conformed to developing British ethnic typecasting of Bengalis gen-erally: intelligent but effeminately weak, physically and morally. They mostly spent their holidays with Goodeve touring Britain's country-side and industry. On one journey, they paid homage at Rammohun Roy's grave.[129]

While these four men lived together, their experiences in Britain varied. The eldest, Dwarkanath Bose, proved least obedient to Goodeve and college discipline, and received the least recognition from them. Goodeve wrote that he 'obtained only a certificate in Midwifery;—this certainly is not encouraging on his part and I regret to say I am not surprised at his want of success, for though possessing considerable ability he has not the industry of the rest and he is wholly deficient in zeal for the cause in which they are all embarked.' Goodeve went on to report that Bose's 'moral character . . . is certainly inferior to his friends, and though not naturally vicious, is easily led into temptation by others.' Since he showed least promise, and so that he should not 'deteriorate rather than improve by remaining comparatively idle in London', Goodeve arranged his return to Calcutta in December 1846 (with Dwarkanath Tagore's son, Nagendranath).[130] He subsequently received an appointment as Assistant Demonstrator of Anatomy in the Calcutta Medical College at a monthly salary of Rs 200, and also began private practice.[131]

The remaining three made such 'remarkable' achievements that the

[128] Revenue, Judicial, and Legislative Committee References L/PJ/1/42, no. 27, BL.

[129] Court Minutes 27/8/1845.

[130] Revenue, Judicial, and Legislative Committee References L/PJ/1/45, no. 13, BL.

[131] Carpenter, *Last Days*, p. 253.

directors approved continuing their education longer.[132] Gopal Seal
and Bholanath Bose both earned first division Bachelor of Medicine
degrees.[133] Seal lagged behind the other students in English yet he
earned certificates in Surgery, and Medicine. Bholanath won gold
medals in Botany and in Comparative Anatomy, silver medals in Chemistry and Materia Medica. He earned certificates in Surgery, the
Practice of Medicine, and Midwifery. The University College Senate
agreed to waive the requirement of an additional year of practice in his
case before receiving the M.D. degree, which he did. Both thus became
members of the Royal College of Surgeons of England. They left with
Goodeve for Calcutta in January 1848.[134] Seal tragically drowned
soon after his return to India while Bose held medical service appointments.[135]

The youngest, Chuckerbutty, adapted himself most to British society. He also took a first degree in the Bachelor of Medicine examination, with certificates in Anatomy, Physiology, Materia Medica,
and Chemistry. He won the gold medal in Comparative Anatomy
(judged best for the last ten years) plus the silver medal in Zoology. He
specialized in Surgery, as dresser and then clinical clerk. On successive
six week annual holidays, a leading faculty member, Dr Grant, took
Chuckerbutty on tour with him to Paris and then to central Europe,
meeting specialists there.[136]

Chuckerbutty also decided to convert to Christianity. Although
Goodeve said he had not pushed his students in this direction, he was
pleased. Chuckerbutty also added 'Goodeve' to his name. Thus, of the
four, he most adopted British culture.

After the others returned to India with Goodeve, Chuckerbutty
stayed on, since he was too young yet to receive the M.D. degree and
wanted to pursue further specialized training. The directors continued
to support him, including his request for a month in Scotland 'for the

[132] Court Minutes 14–28/10/1846, 6/1/1847.

[133] Revenue, Judicial, and Legislative Committee References L/PJ/1/47,
nos 166, 326, 345, 349, BL.

[134] Court Minutes 14/7/1847, 15/10/1847, 17–24/11/1847, 15–21/12/
1847.

[135] Carpenter, *Last Days*, p. 253.

[136] Revenue, Judicial, and Legislative Committee References L/PJ/1/43,
no. 156, BL.

benefit of his health and mental improvement'.[137] When he reached the legal age, he passed his examination and became a member of the Royal College of Surgeons.[138] In November 1848, he requested a further two year extension of training in London. The directors, agreeing his accomplishments had been 'praiseworthy', allowed him to study Pathological Anatomy for another fifteen months at his annual stipend of £160 plus fees.[139] The directors did not, however, grant his request for 54 pounds 19 shillings 6 pence for the purchase of a 'Microscope, and the Medical Books . . . with a view to the prosecution of Scientific enquiries'.[140]

In the autumn of 1849 he submitted his testimonials and certificates, and the directors recommended to the Bengal government his appointment to a suitable post in the Calcutta Medical College with a salary 'commensurate with his high attainments'. In this way, he could 'have an opportunity of communicating to his countrymen the scientific knowledge and practical acquirements attained by him in this country.'[141] After his return to Calcutta, he was appointed assistant surgeon in the Bengal government service. Chuckerbutty regarded his achievements as a proof of the success of 'one of the most arduous experiments ever yet undertaken by our countrymen.'[142] In 1854 he returned to England to be examined and qualified by the Board of Examiners.[143] He topped the list in the Indian Medical

[137] Court Minutes 19/7/1848.

[138] Revenue, Judicial, and Legislative Committee References L/PJ/1/49, no. 183, BL.

[139] Court Minutes 7–14/6/1848, 1–29/11/1848, 13/12/1848, 10/1/1849, 11/4/1849; Revenue, Judicial, and Legislative Committee References L/PJ/1/49, no. 183, BL.

[140] Court Minutes 17/10/1849, 18–28/12/1849, 30/1/1850, 27/2/1850; Revenue, Judicial and Legislative Committee References L/PJ/1/52, no. 379, BL.

[141] Court Minutes 4–18/7/1849, 29/8/1849, 26/9/1849, 10/10/1849; Revenue, Judicial, and Legislative Committee References L/PJ/1/51, nos 9, 118, 204, 273, 278–9, 348, BL.

[142] Chuckerbutty letter 26/2/1850, Miscellaneous Letters Received E/1/190, f. 110, BL.

[143] Court Minutes 29/12/1854, 31/1/1855; Revenue, Judicial, and Legislative Committee References L/PJ/1/68, no. 3; Political and Military References Memoranda April 1855, no. 4387(a), BL.

Service examination of January 1855, earning a covenanted appointment in that service.[144] He published in the *British Medical Journal* and rose to be the first Indian Professor of Medicine and Materia Medica at Calcutta Medical College in 1867.[145]

The superior performance of these students demonstrated to the British public, as well as the medical profession, that Indians were capable of 'acquiring the sciences and professional knowledge of the Western World, and that in such contests they are equal to their European fellow Subjects.' They also reassured Indians that British ideologies of superiority were unfounded. Many other Indian medical students would follow over the course of the nineteenth century.[146]

Despite the strong evangelical Christian orientation of many Britons, including colonial officials, relatively few Indians converted. Nor did those who did convert necessarily find the acceptance and support from Britons that they expected. Further, the number of Indian Christians and converts who came to Britain in the early nineteenth century was relatively limited.[147] This statement needs to be qualified in that many of the Indian settlers and also visiting seamen and servants seem to have converted, in name if not for theological reasons, as part of their interactions with British society. Men like William Munnew and Dean Mahomet converted as part of living in Britain, but their reason for coming to Britain does not seem to have been based primarily on their Christian identity.

For a few, however, their identity as Christians in India was apparently the main factor that drew them to Britain. In 1847, a Christian convert from Calcutta, A.C. Mazoomdar, living in Bedminster (near

[144] Brown, 'Indian Students'; Carpenter, *Last Days*, p. 253.

[145] Chuckerbutty, 'Present State'.

[146] Court Minutes 10/2/1858.

[147] As British authority extended directly and indirectly across India, many groups sought influence in London, including the Syrian Christian community of Malabar. In 1841 and 1855–6, Mar Athanasius, Syrian Bishop of Malabar, came seeking the support of British authorities in London. Mar Athanasius letter, 20/5/1841, Elphinstone Papers F.88/119, Moh Ibraheem letter 14/8/1844, Elphinstone Papers F.88/126, BL; Court Minutes 7/11/1855, 25/4/1856.

Bristol), wrote plaintively to the directors for assistance.[148] He explained that he had gone to a Christian school in Bengal founded by the Reverend Dr Alexander Scottam. Despite the opposition of his wealthy family, he 'was led to renounce the heathen superstition of my fathers and embrace the Gospel of Christ.' Disinherited, he moved to Britain in order to be among supportive Christians. Instead, he found a 'strong apathy towards a stranger and a foreigner', which frustrated all his applications for employment. He used his wife's small capital in a business speculation that failed. Thus, he appealed to the directors for 'pecuniary assistance to alleviate our present misery'. He appealed in vain. Other converts to Christianity sometimes received more attention.[149] Nevertheless, as Gauri Viswanathan, Antoinette Burton and other scholars have shown for the later nineteenth century, Indians who converted to Christianity often had quite different expectations about their roles than did British Christians.[150]

Military Men

While the Company's armies employed vast numbers of Indian men, relatively few Indian soldiers successfully made the voyage to Britain. In 1857 alone, there were some 228,000 Indian soldiers serving the

[148] Court Minutes 18/8/1847; Finance and Home Committee Minutes 25/8/1847; Mazoomdar letter 16/8/1847, Finance and Home Committee Papers, L/F/2/111, BL.

[149] In 1843, a Parsi convert to Christianity, Dhunjeebhoy Nowrojee, went to Edinburgh, where he studied at the Free Church College, received ordination in 1846 and then returned to India to preach. Calotypes and a portrait of Dhunjeebhoy Nowrojee as a minister active in the creation of the Free Church of Scotland by David Octavius Hill and Robert Adamson are in the J. Paul Getty Museum and Scottish National Portrait Gallery. J. Paul Getty, *In Focus*, p. 146, and Stevenson, *David*, pp. 96, 155. He was followed by Wuzeer Beg, 'the son of a Mahomedan messman in Poona', who received ordination as a Presbyterian minister in Edinburgh, and then spent his career preaching in Australia. Ishuree Dass, who came from a north Indian agricultural jati, was an orphan, raised and converted by British Christians. After his return to India in 1848, he wrote a small book about his time in Britain and America. Brown, 'Indian Students'; Dass, *Brief Account*.

[150] Viswanathan, *Outside* and Burton, *At the Heart*.

Company (versus 43,000 Europeans). They enlisted for a range of reasons. For many, the army represented access to advancement and honour, in a career traditional for their family; for others, financial reasons may have been more compelling.[151] In exchange for expected rewards, however, Indian soldiers necessarily accepted the hierarchies of obedience inherent in all armies, with the addition of the racial hierarchy imposed by European colonial armies in Asia. Codes of military regulations carefully specified procedures for discipline, trial for indiscipline, and modes of appeal. When these regulations were violated by their officers and all recourses available in India had failed, however, a few intrepid soldiers travelled to Britain for redress. While they obtained new hearings, and participated variously in the British public sphere, their hopes for justice were rarely sustained.

Although their number remained small, Indian soldiers had been going to Britain since the mid eighteenth century, seeking advancement or justice.[152] Travelling to Britain was expensive and functioning there was difficult without a knowledge of English (or the money to hire intermediaries) as even Indian diplomats discovered. Nevertheless, over a dozen Indian soldiers overcame these obstacles and reached Britain. Their specific motivations varied. For example, in 1810, Drill Havildar Shaick Bassoon appealed to the directors against his court-martial conviction for 'sorcery', which he felt sure they would overturn as irrational.[153] In 1825–6, cavalryman Alyar Khan protested in London his dismissal by an influential British officer whom he had (apparently justly) accused of cowardice.[154] Both men received hearings from the directors (hearings which had been denied for years in India),

---

[151] See Fisher, *First Indian Author*, pp. 17–27.

[152] In 1748, fourteen *topasis* (soldiers with mixed Indian and European, particularly Portuguese, descent or comportment) arrived in London from Bombay. Court Minutes 3/6/1748, see also 4–6/3/1761. In addition, some sepoys came on duty, like the six whom King George III reviewed in 1796. *Times* 16/7/1796 2c.

[153] Board Collections F/4/294, no. 6770a, BL; Court Minutes 30/5/1810.

[154] Nevertheless, the officer, Lieutenant William Mactier (1793–1855) eventually rose to be Brevet Colonel and Companion of the Order of the Bath. Court Minutes 4–18/5/1825, 21/3/1826; Correspondence Committee Minutes 11–25/5/1825, 23–30/8/1826, 6/9/1826, 29/12/1826; Letters from Court to Bengal, Military Department 8/6/1825 L/MIL/3/2076, BL.

orders to the Indian Army for extensive reinvestigations of their claims, and free passage home. While neither man was reinstated, in 1831 Alyar Khan received a Rs 10 monthly pension. Nonetheless, the directors also repeatedly warned their officials in India to prevent the 'impropriety' of other 'worthless individuals similarly situated to resort to England for the purpose of presenting petitions.'[155] These patterns were similar to those encountered by most Indian representatives and diplomats: official denials of their right to appeal in London, but nonetheless hearings by the directors, free passage home, and—rarely—some limited benefits.

While pursuing their appeals in London, such Indian soldiers also participated in British public culture. In a particularly rich example, we can contrast their perspective with that of Britons around them. In March 1834, a much impoverished three-man delegation of Indian non-commissioned officers reached London, headed by Khwaja Bukhsh, a dismissed cavalry petty officer.[156] They argued that they were among 25 officers and 79 men of the 4th Local Horse Regiment who had been unjustly dismissed four years earlier without a trial. They had been fired because they complained about embezzlement of their pay by the Hindu clerks attached to their regiment, in collusion with their British officers. These dismissed cavalrymen had fruitlessly spent years in India seeking a hearing of their case. Their immediate commander, Captain Charles Montauban Carmichael Smyth, maintained that the sums taken from their pay were not embezzlement but legitimate deductions for a fund to purchase new horses and maintain the current ones. He blamed the trouble on clan- and tribal-based rivalries by known trouble-makers who had to be dismissed immediately to prevent a mutiny. Yet, the Persian petition this delegation presented to the directors contained all the dismissed men's names, which indicated that not all were even Muslim, discrediting this 'tribe' argument.

The three-man delegation had travelled over seventeen months via

---

[155] Letters from Court to Bengal, Military Department 8/6/1825, 23/8/1826, 13/9/1826, 29/10/1828, 2/3/1831 L/MIL/3/2076–8; Secretary's Memorandum 6/11/1834, Military Collections L/MIL/5/409, no. 278, BL; Correspondence Committee Minutes 13/6/1810.

[156] He had been *Jemadar* and *Naib Resaldar*. Court Minute 16–23/4/1834, 17–25/6/1834, 11–16/7/1834, 13–27/8/1834.

Egypt to appeal directly to the directors against this mass dismissal without trial. On reaching Egypt, the British consul had arranged for them to sail to Britain in a Maltese ship, but they had to borrow the £12 passage fare. On reaching London, they went to Captain Grindlay who guided them in their negotiations with the directors. The directors refused to pay their expenses to Britain, but allocated £32 for them at Gole's depot (at a rate of 2 shillings 6 pence per man per day, ensuring accommodation superior to that of mere lascars) and promised to pay their return passage if they would go back 'immediately'. They refused to leave and called as witness on their behalf upon Captain Gavin Ralston Crawfurd, the assistant agent of the governor-general in Saugor and Narbada territories, who had just reached Britain.[157] He testified that they had been unjustly dismissed without court-martial.

Faced with such contradictory evidence from British officers, the directors wrote to Bengal instructing a full investigation into the apparently inappropriate salary deductions that had sparked the conflict. They also promised the men that their cases would be investigated and that the Indian government would maintain them until it was settled. They also allocated £200 to get the three back to Bombay.[158]

Over their year in London, these three cavalrymen also negotiated their representations before the British public. While waiting for justice at East India House in April 1835, they captured the attention of Sir David Wilkie. This famous artist had been commissioned by the widow of Sir David Baird (1757–1829) to commemorate her late husband's triumph over Tipu Sultan in 1799.[159] For authenticity, Wilkie had obtained Tipu Sultan's own pelisse and trousers and also abundant weapons from that war which had been taken to Britain as booty. Yet Wilkie wanted Indian life-models, particularly since he had never been in India and could find no picture of Tipu Sultan's face to copy.[160] He therefore went to India House and hired these three cavalrymen to pose for him, 'both in face and dress perfect for what I

[157] Court Minutes 27/8/1834.

[158] Court Minutes 26/8/1835.

[159] 'Sir David Baird Discovering the Body of Sultaun Tippoo Saib ...' in National Gallery of Scotland. See Miles and Brown, *Sir David Wilkie*, pp. 251–7.

[160] Cunningham, *Life*, vol. 3, pp. 96–9, 110–11, 223–5, 530. See also Tobin, *Picturing*.

want'.[161] Wilkie had no interest in who these men really were, calling them Hindus, or why these men had come, only dimly aware they ventured 'to complain of some grievance'.

Using an interpreter, Wilkie posed Khwaja Bukhsh as Tipu 'reclining with his head supported by one of his lieutenants, and his hand held by the other, with his finger on his pulse to know if he were alive or dead. The group was magnificent, and I was all ecstasy to realize such a vision of character and colour.' (Image 24). When the men realized that Wilkie was portraying them as the infamous Tipu Sultan, they immediately objected, breaking from their poses, protesting (as Wilkie recorded): "'Me no Tippoo!" . . . "No Tippoo I!" "No Tippoo I!" and . . . no persuasion I could use could induce them to resume them'. Wilkie clearly failed to understand the reasons why these men would object, attributing it to 'superstition'. Wilkie was further surprised when Khwaja Bukhsh agreed to model if 'allowed to stand like a soldier' of the Company's army, a status which indeed he had come to Britain to recover. Wilkie judged him 'evidently pleased with his new position; for I had put a sword in his hand, and placed him in the attitude of an assailant' over Tipu Sultan's body. Yet, after two days, Khwaja Bukhsh and his companions abruptly ceased attending Wilkie's studio. What Wilkie did not know was that they had finally and reluctantly left London for India in June 1835.[162]

In their place, Wilkie hired 'some native Lascars, who have been sitting to me daily . . . I am getting the chief of the Indian heads painted in.'[163] Wilkie proudly exhibited this large canvas at the Royal Academy in 1839.[164] Indeed various other Indians, including seamen and servants, also agreed to work as models for British artists, although they found the atmosphere chilling, especially since they were costumed in thin Indian dress and the studios were often unheated. Thus, for Wilkie and some other British artists of the mid nineteenth century, Indians were virtually interchangeable props, useful mainly to illustrate British military triumphs.

[161] Cunningham, *Life*, vol. 3, pp. 96–9, 110–11.
[162] Court Minutes 29/10/1834, 2/1/1835, 27/5/1835, 25/9/1835; Political and Military Committee Minutes 14/7/1835, 23/9/1835; Military Collections L/MIL/5/409, no. 278, BL.
[163] Cunningham, *Life*, vol. 3, pp. 223–5.
[164] Heleniak, *William Mulready*, pp. 102–4.

Other Indian soldiers continued to have faith that they would receive justice if only they could reach London.[165] The most persistent was Manohar, who made four futile trips over a decade, protesting his unjust dismissal for alleged desertion.[166] Most soldiers received no more than free passage back to India with orders that the local Company authorities should investigate their cases. This was more than they had without this venture, but it was by no means all they anticipated.

Improving Oneself in Britain

Especially from the 1830s, increasing numbers of Indians spent their careers in service with the British, as officials, colleagues, students, or soldiers. They tended to be more Anglicized than in earlier generations, producing multiple alienations. Their own communities often saw them as having marginalized themselves. Their British supervisors usually regarded them as having left their place as 'real Indians' by their vary act of moving closer to the British. Nor did many Britons in mid-nineteenth-century Britain consider them as fully British. Further, on their return to India, Britons and Indians often viewed their experiences in Britain as mixed.

In Britain, some Indian men studied British technology or medicine, observed and commented on British culture and society, or sought to improve their condition or obtain justice. As we saw for diplomats and envoys, men about town, and tourists, once there they still had some agency in shaping British perceptions—publishing, socializing, petitioning—but they also faced deepening British colonial attitudes against them. By the 1850s, the various groups of Indians in Britain had begun to form a range of communities there.

[165] See the cases of Mahommud Hameed in 1838, Adge Mahomed (former soldier turned dervish) in 1846, Madras sepoy Syud Komal in 1853, and Maulvi Ghulam Mahomed in 1857. Court Minutes 8/8/1838, 30/12/1846, 22/12/1857, 23/3/1858, 6/4/1858; Political and Military Committee Minutes 7/12/1853; PDHC, L/PS/3/108, f. 74; Revenue, Judicial, and Legislative Committee References L/PJ/1/44, no. 248, L/PJ/1/45, no. 12; Political and Military References 18/7/1838, no. 1323, BL; FPC 17/3/1854, nos 147–9, 12/11/1858, nos 280–3, NAI.

[166] Court Minutes 6/5/1846; Political and Military Committee Minutes 12–19/11/1851; Military Papers 1–9/5/1846, L/MIL/2/244; Political and Military References August 1847, no. 3428, BL.

CHAPTER 10

Indian Communities in Britain during the Decades to 1857

Developing Indian Social Circles and Neighbourhoods

By the mid nineteenth century, various classes of Indians in Britain expanded in number and increasingly related with each other. Indian seamen established a substantial community in east London, where some Indian servants also found companionship. The dozens of Indian diplomats, emissaries, and noblemen and women who travelled or settled in Britain formed social circles among themselves, while their numerous retainers also came together. Several Indians worked as professional intermediaries, both teaching Britons about India and guiding Indian employers through British culture and politics. Overall, as the cross-connections among many Indians developed, they individually and collectively faced changing attitudes and conditions in Britain, shaped largely by spreading colonialism.

Britain's worldwide domination of international trade and manufacturing depended to a significant measure on Indian maritime labourers. Their numbers rose with political, economic, and technical changes, even as official controls over them weakened. Consequently, they formed lively and supportive enclaves in Britain's docklands, which conversely appeared to many Britons as alien territory.

Indian servants became more numerous, cheaper, and less valued in Britain due to declines in international ship-passage fares, Britain's increasing wealth, and India's relative impoverishment. Yet Indian servants could also more readily find fellowship with other working-class Indians. Nonetheless, the events of 1857 cast doubt in British minds about the trustworthiness of all Indians, including those in their households.

By 1857, over thirty Indian political missions had reached London
to advance the interests of rulers or deposed dynasties. These formed
a counterflow against the larger forces of British colonial expansion.
Given the scale of British political aggression in India, British officials
were relatively successful in suppressing such Indian deputations. By
1857 the British had annexed hundreds of Indian states covering
1,577,000 square kilometres and containing 165,000,000 people.
Dozens of deposed Indian dynasties still retained their status as hereditary (albeit pensioned) royalty. A few managed to get to Britain where
they found pleasure and even increased their pensions and status. The
other 800,000 square kilometres of India remained under approximately 550 nominally sovereign Indian 'princes' who kept their thrones
but were subject to British indirect rule.[1] A few of these rulers sent
Indian embassies to lobby in London.

For virtually all Indians in Britain during these decades, their reception and roles differed from earlier times. Although British opinions about Indians were never uniform by class or gender, overall they
changed with spreading colonialism. For the twenty years prior to
1854, Parliament largely relieved the East India Company of its paternalistic supervision and support of Indians in Britain. Thus, there was
now no longer a system in place to manage them there. Even between
1854, when Parliament restored the Company's responsibility, and
1858, when the Company finally lost its authority over India, the
directors only marginally regulated working-class Indians in Britain.
Further, while many British women were often receptive to Indians in
Britain, their menfolk were frequently less so. Many British working-
men, especially seamen, feared competition from Indians. For many
British middle-class men, Indians, even royalty, had only vestiges of
their earlier exotic attraction. Yet various British aristocrats continued
a patronizing recognition of their Indian peers.

The bloody fighting of 1857 especially alienated Britons and Indians from each other. In India, the deaths of hundreds of Britons, including women and children, often carried out by Indian soldiers or
servants who had worked under them, aroused British national horror

---

[1] Studies of relations between Indian rulers and the British include Ashton,
British Policy; Copland, *British Raj* and *Princes of India*; Fisher, *Indirect Rule*;
Jeffrey, *People, Princes*; McLeod, *Sovereignty*; and Ramusack, *Princes*.

and demands for retribution. British indiscriminate execution of thousands of Indians, often without evidence or trial, and the looting of Indian property, estranged many Indians against Britons generally. Following 1857, Parliament formally took over the administration of India from the Company; the British Raj turned from policies of annexation, which intended to model Indians after Britons, to ones that relied on India's remaining princes as its 'natural leaders', presupposing that Indians were inherently different from Britons.[2]

In Britain now, Indians of all classes found far less sympathy, and often felt compelled to proclaim their loyalty to the British, whatever their private feelings. Many Britons suddenly regarded Indian men as physical threats, especially to White women, reinforcing widespread British ideas about Indians as biologically and immutably different and inferior by race.

London's Oriental Quarter

Especially after 1834, a largely working-class Indian community, centred on lascars, evolved in London's East End. Various British policies and developments, mostly outside the control of Indians, shaped its growth. For many Britons, this area came to hold exotic and dangerous connotations as London's 'Oriental Quarter'. For many Indians, however, it provided shelter, food, companionship, and opportunities to earn by serving the needs of other Indians.

Earlier, lascars in Britain had primarily dealt with the Company. However, the 1834 Act of Parliament which suspended for twenty years the Company's charter to trade in Asia, simultaneously removed most of its legal responsibility for Indians in Britain.[3] Consequently, the directors ended their contracts with Gole's depot and other suppliers of medical care and clothing for lascars. While most Britons still

[2] See Metcalf, *Aftermath* and *Ideologies*.

[3] Each presidency struggled, until Government of India Act I of 1859, to gain control over the recruitment of Indian maritime labour. E.g., *Asiatic Journal and Monthly Register* (December 1838), Asiatic Intelligence, p. 294b; General Department Proceedings 28/3/1838, nos 35–6; Marine Department Proceedings 17/4/1839, nos 1–4, 22/5/1839, no. 15, 14/8/1839, no. 17, 20/11/1839, nos 32–4, WBSA; Home Miscellaneous Proceedings 25/2/1859, nos 10–12; 27/7/1859, nos 20–49, NAI.

believed that the Company had moral accountability for all Indian indigents in Britain, the directors did not live up to these expectations. In 1842, for example, Parliament lamented the 'large number of lascars wandering about London' and hoped that the government and directors would somehow remedy 'the sufferings of these poor people'.[4] When conditions worsened, in 1844 Parliament ordered the British Navy to assume responsibility for returning every Asian (and also every African) seaman who might be found in distress, charging the shipowner who brought him.[5] This was not an effective arrangement, since the admiralty had no real system for tracking or providing for these men: instead, it mainly responded to individual 'problem' cases.

Further, after 1834 many more British merchants began to trade with India, bringing larger numbers of Indian seamen to Britain. Under existing laws (see Chapter 5), arriving ship-captains still had to report all Asian seamen aboard and were legally liable for their maintenance and return but, in practice, they often made no provision for them. Additionally, in 1844, the Government of India ended its system of taking bonds from departing captains for their Asian seamen, reducing their financial commitment to caring for them in Britain (the system of bonds for Indian servants had also become less rigorous). Thus, many Indian seamen who became indigent in Britain, either due to disability or lack of employment opportunities, had to survive on the streets or were taken into workhouses or charity homes, or found places in the Oriental Quarter.

In 1849, after heated debate, shipowners who wanted cheap Indian labour overcame British seamen who feared that competition, persuading Parliament to repeal the Navigation Acts' limitation on Indian maritime employment returning to India.[6] Thereafter, the expense

---

[4] Commons Debate 3/3/1842, *Hansard,* series 3, vol. 60, p. 1377. For treatment of lascars see, e.g., *Times* 20/11/1843 5b.

[5] Act 7 and 8 Victoria, *c.* 112. Symons, *Law,* p. 153; *Hansard,* series 3, vol. 76, *passim; Times* 10/6/1852 7d.

[6] Hence, the earlier distinction between lascars and Indian sailors diminished, making the former a generic term for the latter. Lords Debate 8/4/1853, *Hansard,* series 3, vol. 125, pp. 791–802; Palmer, *Politics;* Shipping Committee Minutes 1/6/1821. The opposition of British seamen to Indians would continue. See: Balachandran, 'Circulation'; Dixon, 'Lascars'; Tabili, 'Construction'.

of employing lascars dropped by about half, since they could work the passage home. Further, the concurrent emergence of steam power on international voyages created the need for unskilled and poorly-paid workers to shovel coal into ships' furnaces. Many ships hired Indians for this torrid and dangerous task. Thus, as their cost and status declined, the number of Indian maritime workers reaching Britain rose significantly to 3000–3,600 annually by the 1850s.[7] Even those with employment going home, however, needed places to stay while in Britain and usually found it in the Oriental Quarter.

Since Parliament recognized that many Indian seamen were being neglected by the admiralty, it belatedly sought to assign responsibility elsewhere. In 1854, Parliament ordered shipowners to take care of their Asian seamen: if in the first six months after an Indian seaman's arrival he 'becomes chargeable upon the Poor Rate, or . . . be convicted as an idle or disorderly Person, or (commits) any other Act of Vagrancy', the owner who brought him could be fined up to £30.[8] Again, this legislation had limited efficacy (especially since shipowners were exonerated after six months). Later in 1854, Parliament reinstated the Company's legal responsibility for all destitute Indians in Britain.[9] Nonetheless, the directors established no extensive or comprehensive system of management and control (although they did subsidize an evangelical charity home, see below). A few years later, in 1858, the British crown terminated the Company's administrative functions in India, reopening the issue of responsibility over Indians in Britain.

As the consequence of all these changes over the decades following 1834, Indian seamen, individually or in groups, dealt more directly with British society. Some stayed in Shadwell, where ships from India still occasionally landed, but they faced increasing hostility as that neighbourhood urbanized. A glimpse into their lives, and the attitudes they faced, comes through a controversy in 1838 over a lascar burial there.[10] Mr Estes, an employee of the Company, had leased

---

[7] See Thorner, *Investment*. Estimate by Colonel Hughes of the Strangers' Home for Asiatics, cited in Visram, *Ayahs*, p. 52.

[8] Act 17 and 18 Victoria, *c.*120.

[9] Act 18 and 19 Victoria, *c.* 91. *Hansard*, series 3, vol. 138–9, *passim*; Court Minutes 14–28/11/1855.

[10] *Times* 5/10/1838 3f, 8/10/1838 3a.

ground behind a former Dissenter's chapel off Cannon Street Road. He allowed Catholics, Dissenters, and lascars to bury their dead there, for a fee of 7 shillings. One lascar burial was observed by 'several thousands' of British gawkers and described in detail by the *Times* as a curiosity, suggesting both the rarity of such burials and the continuing British fascination, if not respect, for the 'exotic' in their midst. The Anglican Minister of nearby St. George's in the East protested such practices, castigating lascars (as well as Dissenters and 'the lower orders of the poor Irish Papists') who 'swarm in the neighbourhood', and who collectively had 'a rooted aversion to the settled order of things both in church and state'. This Victorian antipathy to Asians (and others outside the established order) was growing. The 1850s saw many stories in the British press about lascars as arsonists of British ships.[11]

Indians also moved extensively throughout Britain. During the early 1840s, Indians in Bourn (Cambridgeshire), Bradford (West Yorkshire), Coventry (West Midlands), Greenock (near Glasgow), Kingston-upon-Hull (East Yorkshire), Ilkeston (Derbyshire), Leicester (Leicestershire), and Nottingham (Nottinghamshire), as well as London were all visited by one British evangelist.[12] Conversely, many Indians travelled among British towns and villages. Jhulee Khan of Calcutta arrived in 1841 as a lascar. He remained in Britain as a professional musician, playing his fiddle in taverns across the countryside. After about sixteen years of this itinerant life, he became a protégé of a British lady in Tottenham. He converted to Christianity, took the name John Carr, married, and began to evangelize by preaching and playing and singing hymns in streets and churches. In 1866, he returned to India, along with his British wife and five children, his passage subsidized with £100 from his Christian supporters.[13]

Lascars and other Indian working-class people found a variety of occupations in Britain. As we saw, some worked as artists' models, particularly when a British triumph in India was to be illustrated, or an exotic person to be depicted.[14] In 1853 when the Dublin Great

[11] E.g., *Annual Register* (1851) Chronicle 4/3/1851, pp. 20–1; *Times* 8/10/1853 10b, 18/10/1853 10b, 20/10/1853 9f.

[12] Peggs, *Lascars' Cry*, pp. 3–4.

[13] Salter, *Asiatic*, p. 170.

[14] 'Etched Thoughts by the Etching Club', *Blackwood's Edinburgh Magazine* 56, 346 (August 1844), pp. 153–60; Mayhew, *London*, vol. 3, pp. 185–9.

Industrial Exhibition wanted to portray Indian folk-life, it recruited lascars from London to work the *charkha* (hand-spinning wheel).[15] Indians came to predominate among crossing-sweepers (Image 25). Since horse-drawn transportation littered the streets with dung, respectable men and women (particularly in long skirts) tipped men with brooms to clear their path across the street. Possession of some crossings became recognized and even protected (presumably for a consideration) by the police. After British veterans of the Napoleonic Wars died off in the 1830s–1840s, Indians (and Africans) largely took possession of this niche.[16]

Other street professions identified with Indians were selling Christian religious tracts and 'lucifer' matches. By peddling these, they skirted vagrancy laws against direct begging. Indeed, many Asians who settled in London became Christians there, at least nominally. Additionally, Indian street-singers and musicians strolled through London's more fashionable and wealthy West End.[17] Indians were, of course, only a small proportion of the many indigents on London's streets.[18]

In a widely publicized case in 1852, a blind lascar, Mahomet Abraham of Calcutta, was arrested for begging.[19] Mahomet had reached London in 1844 but, blinded during the voyage, was abandoned by his ship-captain. For eight years he had lived in London by begging, accompanied by his brown dog. What precipitated his arrest by officers of the Mendicity Society was the 23-year-old Englishwoman, Elizabeth Allen, found in his company. Elizabeth, the daughter of a gentleman and his wife, had earlier eloped with a married Englishman, been abandoned, and discovered by her parents in a workhouse infected with 'loathsome disorders'. After again escaping confinement by her parents, she worked in a milliner's but, when that failed, lived by singing ballads in London's streets. As Mahomet described their meeting:

> I went out one night to buy some victuals for my dog. It was late, and I called out to the people I heard passing by, 'Where can I get any dog's

[15] Revenue, Judicial, and Legislative Committee References 3–17/8/1853, BL.

[16] Mayhew, *London*, vol. 1, pp. 241–2, 308; vol. 4, p. 440.

[17] Ibid., vol. 3, pp. 184–9.

[18] Ibid., p. 406.

[19] *Times* 7/6/1852 7b–c, 23/6/1852 8a.

Image 25: An Indian Crossing Sweeper, Berkeley Street,
by Carl Hartmann, *c*.1847.

meat?' At last, Eliza heard me, and she came and took me to a catsmeat shop, where I got what I wanted, and I asked her to come home and take a cup of tea with me, and I would try and make her comfortable. So she agreed to come home with me, and we had our tea, and then she said, as it was a quarter to 11 o'clock, she was shut out, and she did not know where to go.[20]

They lived together for 9–10 months in a single room at 7 Little Halifax Street, claiming to have been wedded in nearby Whitechapel Church. She posted him outside the Sir Paul Pindar Tavern, Bishopsgate, with a begging petition pinned to his breast.[21] He reportedly took home a substantial 7–15 shillings daily. Their 'perverted' relationship, however, drew the shocked notice of the Mendicity Society. The *Times* called him 'jet black . . . a particularly revolting object'. Most troubling for London's lord mayor was why Eliza, who was of gentle birth and had inherited a small house in Devonshire, would accept living in sin with Mahomet; he chastised her for 'the disgrace with which you cover yourself and your family'. She responded by clasping Mahomet's hand and affirming that she had 'both respect and affection for him'.

The British authorities determined to separate them. Mahomet resisted returning to India and pleaded that begging in London was his only livelihood. Unable to deport him, the lord mayor sent him to the poorhouse. To redeem Eliza, the authorities and her parents arranged her emigration, conveying marriage proposals from British 'tradesmen and others about to proceed to Australia and California . . . [who promised] to treat her with the greatest kindness in [those] distant countries . . .'.[22] Thus, these British authorities in the 1850s regarded her marriage with an unknown British emigrant as far more appropriate, because of their class and ethnicity, than life with the Indian beggar she knew well. Also problematic for British authorities were the growing numbers of street-children who were, from their physical features, visibly the children of Asian men and British women.[23]

---

[20] *Times* 10/6/1852 7d.

[21] Sir Paul Pindar was a seventeenth-century merchant, sometime ambassador to Turkey, so the setting (and tavern's signboard) was apt for Mahomet. The front of this house is now in the Victoria and Albert Museum.

[22] *Times* 21/6/1852 7e.

[23] Mayhew, *London*, vol. 3, pp. 384–6; Salter, *Asiatic*, pp. 69–70.

The largest Indian community developed in Poplar and Limehouse, in London's East End near the East India Docks. There, a few entrepreneurial Indians joined Britons in running rooming houses which specialized in serving, and thereby profiting from, Indian visitors. Given the exclusively male population of arriving seamen, and the common cultural expectation that women were necessary to provide particular services, a distinctive pattern developed. The Indian male rooming-house operator often had a British woman partner. The patriarchic nature of both British and Indian society meant the woman took her identity from him. One British ethnographer, Joseph Salter of the London City Mission, noted critically:

> in the Oriental quarter; there are several houses here devoted to Asiatics, presided over by Chinese, Malays, and Indians, according to the country of the Asiatic seeking companionship . . . Each of the proprietors is assisted by an English mistress, some of whom have lived so long in this element, that they use the Oriental vernacular, and have even been known to act as interpreters at the Police-courts when the oft-repeated quarrels of Asiatics have brought them into trouble. We have indications here of their position in the names which the women bear . . . such as Mrs Mohammed, Mrs Peeroo, Mrs Janoo, oriental names derived from the proprietors of the houses above referred to; or Chinese Emma, Calcutta Louisa, and Lascar Sally, names which in themselves may justly be considered to suggest the mode of life adopted.[24]

While the British commentator disapproved, his evidence accords with gender patterns we have seen throughout this book.

One of these proprietors, Abdool Rahman of Surat, came to England as a lascar in the 1840s. He first established himself as a crossing-sweeper at St. Paul's Churchyard and learned much about British society. When the Nepali ambassador Jung Bahadur visited London in 1850 (see Chapter 7), Abdul Rahman joined his suite as a translator, supplementing (and independent of) British escort officers.[25] He then used the money he received to establish himself as operator of two lodging-houses designed for lascars in Blue Gate Fields, Limehouse. Allegedly, he also provided opium. After some twenty years there,

[24] Salter, *Asiatic*, pp. 26–7.

[25] *Indian News* 16–17/6/1850 cited in Whelpton, *Jang Bahadur*, pp. 232–3.

Abdul Rahman finally sold his houses and shipped back to India as a serang.[26]

Many male members of the British establishment viewed the Oriental Quarter as creating new 'problems', especially what they saw as promiscuous mixing of Asian and British cultures and people there. Salter described with dismay the shift of an English public house, the Royal Sovereign (12 Blue Gate Fields), into a haven for lascars and British lower-class women:

> The skittles have long vanished, and the rough walls and roof have long ceased to echo with boisterous European voices—for Asiatics have taken possession of it, and twenty beds are spread out for the repose of the Lascars who seek shelter [in the skittle-ground]. The jagree dust, crazy hookas, and dirty lotas give evidence of the free use made of it. But, hark! what is that uproarious shout of discordant Asiatic and European voices mingled?— the sound of excited men and women together . . . only a jollification and a spree these Lascars have with the ladies of the neighbourhood . . .[27]

This house was still owed by a British man, but a Goan Indian, Francis Kaudery, operated it.

The City Mission Magazine (August 1857) echoed these protestations about promiscuous intercourse between Asian men and British women:

> Men of all colours, and half a score of nations, are accompanied by a host of women. Many are drunk, and all are riotous; the women have sailors' hats on their heads, and sailors' belts round their waists; they are quarrelling and pulling each other about; some have been robbed, and the police are amongst them; the language uttered is such as Satan only could suggest, and the whole scene calls up in the mind of the spectator an idea of the orgies of hell.[28]

For many reformers, this disorder by the 'nomadic races' (their constructed category which included British street-people, peddlers, seamen, and travellers, as well as Asians in Britain) posed a danger to the 'settled races' (meaning established British society).[29] Yet, despite the

[26] Salter, *Asiatic*, pp. 30–1, 275–8.
[27] Ibid., pp. 31–2, 69.
[28] Ibid., p. 34.
[29] Mayhew, *London*, vol. 1, pp. 1–2.

reformers' optimistic hopes of 'cleaning up' this area, it remained a centre for lascars and other Asiatic seamen.

In 1842 the Church Missionary Society surveyed and reported the 'State of the Lascars in London'. Evangelicals proposed a charity house, and gathered £15,000 (including Indian donations totaling £5,000).[30] In 1856, 'The Strangers' Home for Asiatics, Africans, and South Sea Islanders' opened in Commercial-road, Limehouse, under the leadership of its Secretary and Manager, Lieutenant-Colonel R. Marsh Hughes, late of the Company's army.[31] This linking of various ethnicities of the working classes collectively as 'Strangers' reflected current British attitudes. Since Parliament had reimposed legal responsibility for lascars on the Company, its directors contributed hundreds of pounds of the Company's money annually to this Home.[32] This home assumed many of the paternalistic functions of Gole's former depot, including identifying, maintaining, and managing lascars (and other indigent Indians), working with their serangs in prosecuting police and legal charges against defaulting shipowners, and arranging for lascar employment or passage home. Even as the Oriental Quarter developed, the servants of the increasingly numerous Indian diplomatic and political missions interacted with it.

Surat's Successive Missions
(1844, 1854–1857)

Many Indian delegations—containing some two hundred royalty, diplomats, emissaries, and their staff and servants—travelled to Britain during the dozen years prior to 1857. But they functioned in a rapidly changing environment. Their exotic appeal diminished, since many Britons assumed superiority over 'orientals', even royalty. The more experienced directors and Board of Control deployed time-tested policies to repulse these missions. Nonetheless, some particularly astute and informed Indians developed expertise in manoeuvring

[30] FPC 1/5/1857, NAI; Hughes Letter 24/1/1879, PDHC, L/PJ/2/59; *Illustrated London News* 56 (1870), pp. 253–4; Salter, *Asiatic*, pp. 6–7.

[31] Court Minutes 14–28/11/1855, 16/4/1856, 22–30/12/1857, 12–26/1/1858, 3–10/2/1858, 3–10/3/1858; Political and Military Committee Memoranda 22/12/1857, BL; Salter, *Asiatic*, pp. 66ff; *Times* 20/11/1855 9e.

[32] Court Minutes, 1856–8, *passim*. The Home continued until 1927.

within the British public sphere; they advanced their causes with great sophistication, using Parliament and London law-courts, allying with or hiring influential Britons. In contrast, other Indian delegations still arrived with little chance of success, due to their ineffective preparation or their specific goals or timing. The events of 1857 significantly altered their political and cultural positions in Britain. To examine the changing dimensions of these missions, we begin with one of the more successful among them, comparing its earlier and later experiences.

Meer Jafur Ali Khan Bahadur (d.1863) turned a tenuous claim to aristocracy into a secure, titled, handsomely pensioned status for himself and his daughters, through a dozen years of effort, two trips to Britain, and the employment of many Indian experts in dealing with the British. In 1844, Meer Jafur, a son-in-law of the pensioned nawab of Surat, ventured to Britain to obtain for his wife her inheritance—with little success. He returned leading a more experienced delegation in 1853, claiming the title and estate as nawab in his own right—with much greater success after four years of political and legal manoeuvring. We saw (in Chapter 5) that two earlier claimants to the nawab of Surat's estate had gone to Britain (1806 and 1809–10), being royally received there but later degraded in India. Meer Jafur clearly learned much during his trips, as the results show.

When the Bombay government had annexed Surat in 1800, the treaty gave the deposed nawab a pension of Rs 150,000 annually. This treaty was renewed in 1818 with his successor. The British also verbally promised that the pension would be perpetual.

In 1833, Meer Jafur, son of a courtier to the Gaikwad of Baroda, married the nawab's eldest daughter, Bukhtyaroonnisa Begum, with the explicit expectation that she would inherit, since the nawab had no sons. Her mother was a slave whom the nawab had emancipated and legally married. When the nawab died in 1842, the Bombay government investigated fully and decided that the title should terminate, but that Bukhtyaroonnisa should receive half the pension, the rest divided among other family members. Meer Jafur argued that the estate of the nawab, as royalty, should be inherited entire under primogeniture by Bukhtyaroonnisa, with himself succeeding to the title. The Bombay governor dismissed his claims as 'absurd'.[33] Overriding the governor,

---

[33] Bombay Political Consultation 7/9/1842, no. 139, f. 446, MSA.

however, the governor-general ordered the entire estate confiscated and the pension terminated, with only a modest provision for the nawab's family. Meer Jafur protested: 'a despotic stroke of the pen of . . . [the] governor-general in India, deprived [him] of his rights, and so compelled him to proceed to England to seek for justice.'[34] Thus, in 1844, Meer Jafur headed to London with an entourage including a Briton he employed, Mr T.J.A. Scott, Scott's wife and child, and seven Indians including an expert on the British, Lutfullah.[35]

Like a growing number of other Indian scholar-officials, Lutfullah (1802–74) had long served as an intermediary in India between Britons and Indians. During his early career, he taught Persian, reportedly to over one hundred Britons.[36] Subsequently, he taught English and British culture to various Indian royalty, including Meer Jafur.[37] Lutfullah later wrote his account of this mission in English.[38]

In London, like other Indian dignitaries, Meer Jafur met a mixed response. The British public welcomed him as 'his Asiatic Highness'. Even the lord chancellor received him with full honours at the courts of Chancery, where the assembled crowd of barristers, solicitors, and spectators pronounced him 'a very good-looking fellow'.[39] (There Meer Jafur briefly attended the lunacy trial of another Indian notable, Dyce Sombre, see Chapter 8.) The *Times* opined: 'certainly he is a princely-looking personage, and his features are of a very fine cast'. Meer Jafur supported this image by appearing in public 'splendidly dressed in crimson and richly embroidered oriental costume, with three attendants in eastern dresses . . . .'[40]

While these attendants made an exotic display, they complained

[34] Lutfullah, *Autobiography*, pp. 367ff.

[35] Lutfullah regarded Scott (secretary to the Bombay Chamber of Commerce) as arrogant, demanding, and useless. Lutfullah, *Autobiography*, pp. 248–60, 367ff.

[36] Lutfullah, *Autobiography*, p. 147.

[37] Ibid., pp. 200–1, 230.

[38] This was edited by Colonel W.H. Sykes and Captain Edward Eastwick and published by them in London, just as the 1857 conflict was beginning. Lutfullah, *Autobiography*, Introduction; Court Minutes 12/8/1857.

[39] *Times* 12/7/1844 7b.

[40] *Times* 29/8/1844 6d.

privately that their Indian clothing also attracted the gawking and constraining curiosity of the British whenever they went out.[41] In contrast, Lutfullah donned Turkish-style clothes which he purchased at Cairo, thus retaining his Islamic identity but also appearing less exotic before the British public. The mission also consulted the Ottoman ambassador to London about how to deal with the British.[42]

This mission worked to mobilize influence from prominent Britons. Meer Jafur delivered a letter from his father to an old acquaintance, Mountstuart Elphinstone, requesting his 'impartial kindness in my son's behalf'.[43] Meer Jafur socialized with the British royal family and other aristocrats.[44] While declining to eat with non-Muslims, he entertained many Europeans who ate in his presence.[45] Indeed, Lutfullah (like many other Indians) contrasted welcoming British society with the condescending or contemptuous attitudes of Britons in India: 'The fact is, that the more you proceed on towards England, the more you find the English people endowed with politeness and civility . . .'.[46]

The members of the delegation savoured London's attractions. They were impressed by Britain's engineering feats, especially with iron construction, other architectural innovations, gas-lighting, and the Diorama.[47] Lutfullah particularly admired British advances in surgery: 'the summit of the science of anatomy in both theory and practice.'[48] They went to London's Italian opera, but were shocked by its immodest display of female bodies there. Indeed, Luftullah noted and decried the generally excessive license given to British women by their men: 'the freedom granted to womankind in this country is great, and the mischief arising from this unreasonable toleration is most deplorable'.[49]

[41] Lutfullah, *Autobiography*, pp. 403–4.
[42] Ibid., pp. 432–3.
[43] Elphinstone proved evasive. Elphinstone Correspondence F.88/125–6, 168, *passim*, BL.
[44] Lutfullah, *Autobiography*, p. 416.
[45] Salter, *Asiatic*, p. 45.
[46] Lutfullah, *Autobiography*, pp. 387, 398, 413, 421.
[47] Ibid., pp. 407ff, 422.
[48] Ibid., p. 423, see also p. 415.
[49] Ibid., p. 43.

The directors, many of whom met socially with Meer Jafur, proved less sympathetic when he officially submitted his wife's claims.[50] After much debate, they first voted that this appeal was 'inadmissible' in London and must be handled by local authorities in India. Nevertheless, they directed the governor of Bombay to 'bestow' an appropriate and 'adequate' stipend gratuitously on Bukhtyaroonnisa.[51] The next month, following Meer Jafur's further appeals and lobbying, and more heated debate, they amended their orders. By a majority of one, they supported the governor-general's termination of the title and confiscation of the late nawab's personal property, but reopened the governor-general's decision on the £15,000 pension, which 'may be considered to bear the interpretation of an hereditary grant'. To determine whether it was indeed inheritable property, Bukhtyaroonnisa should file suit in the 'Zillah Court of Surat or in the Court of Sudder Dewany Adowlut or in H.M. Supreme Court of Bombay', as was the right of any Indian under 'the compact contracted with the People of India'.[52]

Meer Jafur expressed 'severe disappointment' with this result and requested further reconsideration, submitting even more documentary evidence. He then personally received what he regarded as informal 'assurances' from the Company's chairman that virtually all his claims would be recognized, if only he would return to India.[53] Finally, grudgingly accepting this, he requested a loan of £1,000 from the directors for the passage home; parting reluctantly from the sensual pleasures of London, he left in October 1844.[54] This first trip revealed to him how he could enjoy a royal reception among the British public and establishment. It also clearly gained him strong, albeit not decisive, support among the directors and showed him how to deal with authorities there more effectively.[55]

[50] Political and Military Committee References May 1844, no. 846 and 17/7/1844, no. 1848; see also August 1844, no. 2230, L/MIL/1/59, BL.

[51] Court Minutes 21/5/1844, 17/7/1844; Lutfullah, *Autobiography*, p. 411.

[52] Court Minutes 7/8/1844.

[53] Anonymous, *Case of Meer Jafur Alee*, pp. 8–9; Lutfullah, *Autobiography*, p. 432.

[54] Court Minutes 7/8/1844, 4/9/1844; Military and Political Committee Minutes 4/9/1844; Lutfullah, *Autobiography*, p. 432.

[55] Lutfullah, *Autobiography*, p. 434.

Just two months after his return to India, however, Bukhtyaroonnisa died. Rather than crushing his claims, this occasioned him to demand for himself the late nawab's entire personal estate, Rs 150,000 annual pension, and title. The Bombay government refused all these, offering him only Rs 12,000 annually for life, with the same amount to his two daughters.

Over subsequent years, his appeals in Bombay to the law courts and government there dragged on, with no progress. As his father wrote in 1846, 'the debts are amounting to lacs of Rupees, he lives in Bombay in the state of anxious expectation.'[56] Then, in 1848, due to his continued applications, the directors ordered the family pension more than doubled to Rs 52,000. The Bombay Legislative Assembly, however, passed a special act, placing the matter of the late nawab's estate outside judicial review. Meer Jafur objected, citing his legal right to sue (reiterated in the directors' 1844 resolution) and asserting that this act proved the Bombay government had squandered the late nawab's property in its custody and was covering up. In 1851, one of Meer Jafur's British supporters brought his case up before a Company stockholders meeting. A commission of inquiry by the Bombay government in 1852 awarded Meer Jafur half the late nawab's personal property, but he considered this inadequate.

In 1853, nearly a decade after his first trip, Meer Jafur returned to London to renew his claims. This time, he brought a far more knowledgeable entourage and put his own experience in Britain to work. His achievements as a result of this second visit were striking, although less than he demanded.

The first part of his suite of twelve attendants went in advance, with Meer Jafur himself arriving after they had prepared his reception into official and public arenas. The *Times*, granting him the title he claimed, announced the arrival of this advance party: 'The nawab's servants were dressed in the picturesque costume of their country . . . They cooked for themselves on board . . . the only thing they would eat which had been touched by Christians was bread. They killed the fowls they ate, and cut the throats of the sheep, which furnished flesh for their own table.'[57] This account stressed their 'picturesque' difference

[56] Elphinstone Correspondence F.88/129, BL.
[57] *Times* 8/12/1853 8c.

from Britons but not the respectful deference that earlier delegations (including his own a decade before) had received.

His entourage included several men able to manoeuvre knowledgably in the British legal and political systems. In Meer Jafur's previous delegation, only Lutfullah had been fluent in English (Lutfullah did not make this second trip, instead remaining in Surat).[58] In his place, Meer Jafar brought several men who, the *Times* patronizingly noted, 'spoke English fluently and grammatically'.[59] One was an elderly 'English Secretary', an Indian man who thereafter stayed on in Britain for years and wrote defending Islam against Christianity.[60] Also included as 'Interpreter' was Mohammed Ali, 'a young man, a Persian by birth, but educated in India; he was conversant with three Eastern languages, besides having acquired English at a [Christian] school in Kurrachee.' Further, he had married Meer Jafur's niece. Mohammed Ali reportedly had earlier gone to the recently begun Crimean War to fight alongside the British and Ottomans against the Russians there, a cause popular among some Muslims.[61] He and Meer Jafar would later associate with the suite of the Queen Mother of Awadh (see below). In addition, Meer Jafar brought Rahim (his *hajam*, or barber), Mishameeram (his elderly *durban*, or doorkeeper), Shaik Mohammed (his cook), Noor Mohammed (a manservant), and Dost Mohammed Shah (his hereditary valet and personal attendant). Of this party, only Mishameeram performed *namaz* (prayer) regularly but most observed Islamic dietary restrictions. In addition, Ali Ackbar, a man very experienced in working with and around the British, but also hostile to them, joined this delegation as 'Persian Secretary'.

Five years earlier, Mirza Ali Ackbar Khan Bahadur (b.1817) had achieved the peak of his profession as munshi under British officials. His father had served in the Company's Bushire Residency and Bombay Native Education Society, among other positions, for twenty-three years until his death in 1831. Ali Ackbar was himself educated

[58] Lutfullah, *Autobiography*, pp. iii–iv.

[59] *Times* 8/12/1853 8c.

[60] Salter does not name him, *Asiatic*, pp. 44–8.

[61] Hafiz Ludroo Islam Khan, a Carnatic Stipendiary, also volunteered from London to fight in Crimea. Azimullah (see Chapter 7) visited the site of battle, but perhaps not in support of the British.

by that society but, at age fourteen when his father died, he started working for Britons. From 1838, he rose as expert in Persianate protocols in Sindh, where various rulers sparred against the British, and against each other. Over the years, his British employers had honoured him with the title Khan Bahadur, a set of elegant pistols, and many glowing testimonials.[62] His monthly salary had risen to Rs 520. His appointment as chief munshi, confidential secretary, and Persian translator to Sir Charles Napier made him one of the most influential Indians in Sindh.[63]

Yet, his career was also controversial (as was that of Napier). When charged with accepting bribes in 1842, Ali Ackbar had satisfied his British supervisor that his enemies were trying 'frame' him. Yet, in 1845, when he had sued an Indian merchant for a Rs 100,000 debt in a Bombay court, that merchant reported him to that government as corrupt.[64] The Bombay government began a long investigation which found his income disproportionate to his assets, allegedly including a palatial house in Karachi, private gardens, and a string of race-horses. Both he and Napier rejected these charges as malicious and inaccurate. Ali Ackbar denied his house was very valuable or that he had any race-horses, and that his property was legitimately acquired. Specifically, he explained the Rs 100,000 as one-third inherited, one-third borrowed, and one-third earned by private trading. Unconvinced, the Bombay government suspended him without pay in 1848 on suspicion, and then added more accusations including that he had stolen British secret documents and sold them to one of the many competing Sindh rulers, Ameer Ali Morad.[65] Although Ali Ackbar largely won his case in the Bombay Supreme Court and the investigation could find no firm proof of his guilt, the Bombay government dismissed him anyway in 1849 without a pension. He fought this in Bombay and then, when unsuccessful there, went to Britain to continue his cause, officially as

[62] FSC 25/1/1843, nos 79–81, 7/10/1843, nos 113–14, 25/5/1844, nos 44–6, 27/4/1844, nos 103–6, NAI.
[63] See Lambrick, *Sir Charles Napier*; Eastwick, *Glance*.
[64] Court Minutes 28/3/1855; Broughton Correspondence ADD 36,478, vol. 23, ff. 233–47, BL; FSC 30/5/1844, nos 70–4, 26/6/1847, nos 37–49, 25/9/1847, nos 75–80, 18/8/1849, nos 50–3; FPC 21/7/1849, nos 1–16, NAI.
[65] PDHC, L/PS/3/108, ff. 190–7.

Persian Secretary in the suite of the Meer Jafur but allegedly also secretly in the pay of Ameer Ali Morad.[66]

In London, Ali Ackbar submitted to the directors his own case for reinstatement or pension. They adopted their usual position that all such matters must be handled only in India. He nevertheless continued for years to appeal and lobby to defend his honour and obtain his pension.[67] The Napier faction in London backed him during bitter partisan disputes that raged in Parliament, the Company, and the public throughout this period. Ali Ackbar and his British supporters got Parliament on three separate occasions to demand all the papers relevant to his dismissal.[68] Using these hitherto confidential British documents, Ali Ackbar published a rebuttal: *Reply to Attacks upon his Character Made by H. M. Frere, Esq., of the Bombay Civil Service, Without Proof or Inquiry* (London: I.R. Taylor, 1858). After the Company lost its authority over India, Ali Ackbar petitioned the India Office which replaced it.[69]

While in London, Ali Ackbar supported himself by working as advisor and translator to at least four Indian royalty, diplomats, and emissaries, as he explained, 'writing pamphlets and taking opinions'.[70] In addition to the missions of Meer Jafur, Ali Morad, and Awadh (discussed below), he also assisted the deposed ruler of Coorg, Veer Rajunder Wadiar (r. 1820–34, d. 1859), who had retired in London.[71] Among other services, Ali Ackbar witnessed the late Coorg ruler's will, which bequeathed him £100 and his horses and three carriages. British

[66] Court Minutes 28/3/1855, 2/5/1855; Political and Military Committee Minutes 2/5/1855.

[67] E.g., Court Minutes 14/4/1858, 28/5/1858, 30/6/1858.

[68] PP, Returns (Commons), 1857–8, vol. 43, paper 159, pp. 207ff; 1860, vol. 52, paper 352, pp. 439ff; 1861, vol. 46, paper 242, pp. 89ff; Court Minutes 23/3/1858, 14/4/1858.

[69] E.g., Ali Ackbar Petition to Secretary of State for India and Reply 14/10/1858, PDHC, L/PS/3/108.

[70] PP, Returns (Commons) 1857–8, vol. 12, paper 115, pp. 369ff.

[71] PP, Returns (Commons) 1863, vol. 45, paper 480, pp. 475ff; FPC 13/6/1856, nos 355–6, NAI; Ali Ackbar Letters 13/4/1858, 28/5/1858, 1–9/6/1858 and replies 27/4/1858, 30/6/1858, PDHC, L/PS/3/108; Salter, *Asiatic*, p. 255; *Times* 8/5/1852 5d, 17/6/1858 11b.

critics remarked snidely how Ali Ackbar prospered in London through such work on behalf of other Indians.

Meer Jafur and his party established themselves in London. He met with other Indian noblemen and representatives there, including Gholam Mohamed, the sole surviving son of Tipu Sultan, and Awadh emissary Museehood-Deen (both discussed below). The various members of his suite socialized with people of their own classes, including Indian settlers. For example, his servants frequently hosted Sheikh Hameed, who resided in London's Dudley Refuge for the Destitute.[72] Sheikh Hammed introduced to them Joseph Salter of the London City Mission. Salter then studied Hindustani with Meer Jafur's valet, Dost Mohammed Shah, two evenings every week, so Salter could evangelize among the many Indians in London. They used as their guides both Duncan Forbes' *Hindustani Manual* (London: W.H. Allen, 1853) and the published Christian Testament in Hindustani translation. In exchange, Salter taught Dost Mohammed Shah both English and Christianity. In the evenings, other Indian and Persian servants would congregate in the kitchen of Meer Jafur's rented house in Paddington (near Chapel Street), for food, cards, tea, smoking, and music: 'the dhol or native drum would be brought forward, a series of native songs sung.'[73]

In addition to enjoying London's pleasures, Meer Jafur had two goals. First he wanted the full pension and title that he believed was guaranteed in the 1800 treaty. Second, he insisted the directors intervene in the ongoing legal case about the late nawab's personal property by overturning the Bombay government's humiliating decree that it be liquidated by public auction prior to distribution among the heirs. He claimed this property entire, by virtue of his late wife's rights.[74] Meer Jafur, aware on this trip of the cost of living in Britain, also requested that his current pension be paid in London. The directors initially rejected all these requests, refusing to even deal with him or his

[72] According to Salter, Sheikh Hammed later married (without benefit of clergy) a British servant, but allegedly fell into drink, poverty, and crime as part of London's underworld. Salter, *Asiatic*, pp. 42ff.

[73] Salter, *Asiatic*, p. 47.

[74] Court Minutes 4/1/1854; Political and Military Committee Minutes 11/1/1854.

claims and referring him to the Bombay courts.[75] In 1853, British lawyers (acting for another Indian nobleman in London, Hyder Jung
Bahadur, a Carnatic stipendiary) challenged the directors routine rejection of direct Indian appeals and their customary redirection to
local authorities, asking whether it was justified by act of Parliament
or a regulation of the Company. The directors could only unconvincingly reply that this rule, 'though not prescribed by Act of Parliament,
is one to which the Court inviolably adhere.'[76]

This rebuff, however, did not dissuade Meer Jafur. He employed
a British law firm, Gregory Faulkner and Company, to advance his
claims.[77] They obtained written legal opinions in his favour from Her
Majesty's Solicitor-General, and other prominent legal authorities.[78]
In the face of the directors' continued refusal to hear his case, he appealed to Her Majesty's Privy Council. The council decided that they
did not have jurisdiction, but in light of the 'anomalous and extraordinary proceeding' of the Bombay government against him, recommended Meer Jafur's case favourably to the Board of Control.[79] The
board, however, rejected his appeal.

Much intense negotiation followed. At one point, Meer Jafur reached
a compromise with the directors in which he and his daughters would
receive £7,500 annually, retroactively from 1842 (the date of the late
nawab's death). The faction hostile to him in the court of directors,
however, amended this agreement back to the current £5,200 annual
pension and refused him the nawab's personal property.[80] To generate
public support, Meer Jafur had a pamphlet published and distributed
that argued his case in persuasive detail: *Case of Meer Jafur Alee, Khan
Bahadoor, of Surat* (London: John Robert Taylor, 1855).

Meer Jafur, like Ali Ackbar and other astute Indians, had learned
that he could use Parliament to gain his ends if he could muster (or

[75] Court Minutes 11–18/1/1854.

[76] Court Minutes 8–23/3/1853, 22/2/1854, 3/1/1855; Political and Military Committee Minutes 22/2/1854.

[77] Court Minutes 18/1/1854.

[78] Court Minutes 15/5/1854, 5/4/1854; Political and Military Committee
Minutes 5/4/1854, 12/9/1855.

[79] Anonymous, *Case of Meer Jafur Alee*, p. 15; PDHC, L/PS/3/108, ff. 204–
9. See also PP, Returns (Commons) 1854, vol. 49, paper 483, pp. 1ff.

[80] Court Minutes 13/6/1856, 12/9/1855.

buy) sufficient political clout. He had leading Members of Parliament Sir Erskine Perry and Sir Fitzroy Kelly introduce a petition and a private bill on his behalf in 1856, legislating the full £15,000 pension in perpetuity and the entire estate of the late nawab.[81] Parliament appointed a select committee to investigate and report, which unanimously supported him; several other inquiries by the Commons and Lords followed.[82] The directors fought Meer Jafur's Parliamentary bill and publicity campaign.[83] His example, however, apparently inspired Mehdee Alee Khan Bahadur, husband of the daughter of the late nawab of Rampur, to venture to London (1856–7) on a similar mission, although with less success.[84]

Meer Jafur's bill passed the Commons strongly, up to the third and final reading. On the eve of this decisive vote in June 1856, Meer Jafur and the directors finally reached what the chairman called a 'timely compromise'. Meer Jafur would have the bill withdrawn and, in exchange, would receive the full pension of £15,000 annually (retroactive from 1842 but only for the lives of Meer Jafar and his daughters), while the inheritance of the nawab's personal estate (then worth about £10,000) would be decided by the Privy Council.[85] The majority of the directors, however, rejected their chairman's proposal and voted to continue to fight in Parliament.[86] Meer Jafur's bill then passed the Commons 213 to 27, displaying widespread support among almost all

[81] Commons Debate 19/2/1856, 1–8/4/1856, *Hansard*, series 3, vol. 140, pp. 277, 639, 979–80; Court Minutes 5–28/3/1856.

[82] PP, Returns (Commons) 1856, vol. 10, papers 265, 265(I), 265(II), pp. 441ff; vol. 45, paper 63, 305, pp. 159ff; 1857(I), vol. 11, paper 82, pp. 107 ff; (Lords) 1856, vol. 27, papers 199, 199(I), 199(II), pp. 441ff.

[83] Court Minutes 16–30/4/1856; Political and Military Committee Memoranda March 1856, nos 425–7, April 1856, no. 804, June 1856, no. 2089, BL.

[84] Mehdee Alee claimed Rampur for his wife, Shumsa Tajdar Begum. He also submitted a petition to Parliament. PDHC, 25/11/1857, L/PS/3/108. Meer Jafur also advised the Awadh ruler about which British lawyers to hire, and the Awadh mission generally. *Times* 29/5/1858 11a–b.

[85] Further, the pension of the late nawab's two widows would rise from £1,440 to £2,000 each, the late nawab's servants would continue to receive their established pensions. Court Minutes 23/6/1856.

[86] Political and Military Committee Memoranda July 1856, no. 2712, October 1856, nos 216, 4155, December 1856, no. 783, January 1857, no. 1599, April 1857, nos 2839, 2941, July 1857, no. 652, August 1857, no. 1069, BL.

parties, since the treaty clearly stated the family's property rights and the bill astutely separated this legal issue from more contentious political ones.[87] But the directors continued to fight in the House of Lords, where they ultimately triumphed the next month.[88] Meer Jafur then appealed again to the Privy Council and petitioned the queen.[89]

Meanwhile, furious parleys continued behind the scenes. The directors finally decided that the political cost of further fighting was not worth the expense of these pensions, which would anyway end with the inevitable death of the principal parties. They offered him and his daughters £10,000 annually, plus a cash payment of £20,000 as the arrears on that pension, with a year's delay ordered on the sale of the late nawab's property in India so that there would be time for the Privy Council to decide whether to accept the case.[90] While less than he wanted and his Parliamentary conflict continued, it was much more than he currently received, so Meer Jafur accepted this compromise, as he lamented, 'worn out . . . in the unequal and protracted struggle to obtain justice at the hands of the British government.'[91] Further, news of the bloody fighting of 1857 in India began reaching London, making the environment more hostile to Indians there.

In August 1857 Meer Jafur returned home. Yet, he continued to assert, as a matter of honour, his legal right to the entire personal estate of his late father-in-law. In 1858, after multiple appeals, he won some vindication when the Privy Council disallowed the Bombay government's 1848 act (which had put the matter of the nawab's estate outside judicial review).[92] In the government's custody, however, the

[87] Commons Debate 24/6/1856, *Hansard*, series 3, vol. 142, pp. 1898–1905.

[88] Court Minutes 25/6/1856, 2–9/7/1856. Lords Debate 7/7/1856, *Hansard*, series 3, vol. 143, pp. 383–97. *Times* 8/7/1856 5d–f.

[89] Court Minutes 16–18/7/1856.

[90] Court Minutes 22/10/1856 to 26/8/1857.

[91] Commons Debate 6–16/3/1857, *Hansard*, series 3, vol. 144, pp. 1943, 2375–81; PP, Returns (Commons) 1857(II), vol. 29, papers 31, 71, pp. 215ff; 1857–8, vol. 43, paper 167, pp. 277ff; *Times* 26/5/1857 11b; Court Minutes 8/4/1857; PDHC 7/7/1857, L/PS/3/108. Before going, he reportedly advised other Indian royalty, including the Awadh heir. *Morning Advertiser* cited in *Bombay Times* 9/2/1857 238c–d.

[92] PDHC 31/7/1858, L/PS/3/108.

estate had shrunk to only £4,000, a fraction of its earlier value.[93] Meer Jafur finally purchased the remnants of it from the other heirs. Clearly, if he had not gone to England and harnessed political and legal forces there, he would never have accomplished so much, but he remained bitter about the treatment he received.

Meer Jafur achieved more in Britain than most other missions, in part because his was a legal case about property (although fought politically) rather than an administrative or policy matter. He travelled twice to Britain, but was not unique in any of his tactics there. For six years (1851–7), the Indian agents of the maharaja of Jodhpur struggled vainly to reverse a British decision which took Ahmednagar away from their master's family.[94] Ali Morad of Sindh, looking to overturn his conviction of forgery and demotion from amir to landowner, himself went to Britain (1856–7), where he added to the extensive controversy about Sindh but gained little for himself despite much political manoeuvring.[95] These and other Indian royalty and envoys purchased the services of members of Parliament, published books and pamphlets in London, and sued through British courts, in addition to lobbying the directors and Board of Control.[96] Simultaneously, other pensioned princes availed themselves of London's delights.

[93] PP, Returns (Commons) 1857(II), vol. 29, papers 31, 71, pp. 215ff; 1857-58, vol. 43, paper 167, pp. 277ff; Commons Debate 6–16/3/1857, *Hansard*, series 3, vol. 144, pp. 1943, 2375–81; PDHC, L/PS/3/108, ff. 204–13, 236–9.

[94] Court Minutes 12–19/8/1857, 16/9/1857; PDHC, L/PS/3/108, ff. 53–5; PP, Returns (Commons) 1859(I), vol. 18, paper 125, pp. 73ff.

[95] Court Minutes 24/11/1852, 20/5/1857 to 2/9/1857; Political and Military Committee Memoranda September 1856, no. 3488, November 1856, no. 713, December 1856, no. 965, August 1857, nos 1062, 2708, October 1857, nos 3871, 3881; Tract 553 on Sind, BL; Ali Morad, *Petition of His Highness Ameer Ali Morad Khan Talpoor* and *Case of Meer Ali Morad Khan*; Lords Debate 29/3/1852, Commons Debates 23–4/6/1852, 18/3/1853, *Hansard*, series 3, vol. 120, pp. 238–64; vol. 122, pp. 1241–57, 1273–7; vol. 125, pp. 434–6; PP, Returns (Commons) and (Lords) 1852–64, various.

[96] In order to get the case before Parliament, Ali Morad's solicitor, David Coffey, allegedly arranged £10,000 payment to Isaac Butt, Q.C., M.P. Butt was later charged with Breach of Parliamentary Privilege for this. Commons Debate 19/2/1858, *Hansard*, series 3, vol. 148, pp. 1730–2, 1855–67; PP (Commons), 1857–8, vol. 12, paper 115, pp. 369ff; Court Minutes 3/6/1857, 18/3/1858.

Counterflows to Colonialism

Pensioned Son of Tipu Sultan and
His Servant Settler

London became a resort for growing numbers of Indian royalty. They had their own financial and political interests to advance and also sought pleasure, particularly contrasted with life in confinement in India. We saw (in Chapter 8) how Jamh ood-Deen, a son of Tipu Sultan, moved to London and flourished there until his death in 1842. Following him were other pensioned princes, including the deposed maharajas of Coorg, Veer Rajunder Wadiar, and the Punjab, Duleep Singh (1838–93, r. 1843–9), and two descendants of the nawab of the Carnatic, Hafiz Lodroo Islam Khan and Hyder Jung.[97] Also emulating Jamh ood-Deen was his sole surviving brother, Gholam Mahomed (1795–1872). Each had to convince the British to grant them 'leave' from their confinement in India and travel to Britain; some claimed that only the British climate would recover their health, others that they or a family member wished to become Christian or get an English education.[98] Once in London, they enjoyed themselves, lobbied for more money, and often successfully resisted British efforts to compel them to leave.[99]

It took Gholam Mahomed several years to gain permission to leave India, since British officials feared further embarrassments for them

[97] Bell, *Annexation of the Punjaub*; Login, *Lady Login's Recollections* and *Sir John Login*; Singh, *Correspondence*; Victoria, *Letters*, vol. 3, pp. 49, 59–61, 69, 278–9, 315, 320; Court Minutes 7/6/1854 to 3/3/1858; EUR MSS F. 78/48, BL; Maharajah Duleep Singh to Editor, *Times* 13/11/1877 8a.

[98] E.g., Veer Rajunder Wadiar, the deposed maharaja of Coorg. Wadeer, *Memorial*; Court Minutes 21/12/1852 to 16/12/1857; Political and Military Committee Minutes 12–26/1/1853, 18/5/1853, 6/7/1853, 24/8/1853; Political and Military Committee Memoranda March 1856, no. 729 to March 1857, no. 2614; FPC 1/9/1849, nos 109–13; PDHC, L/PS/3/108, ff. 113, 241ff; Wilson Correspondence EUR MSS E.301/13, BL; Lords Debate 21/7/1856, *Hansard*, series 3, vol. 143, pp. 1065–7; PP, Returns (Commons), 1857(I) vol. 8, paper 39, pp. 301ff; 1863, vol. 45, paper 480, pp. 475ff; Salter, *Asiatic*, p. 255; *Times* 17/6/1858 11b. He was buried in an 'unconsecrated catacomb' at Kensal Green, London.

[99] E.g., Hafiz Ludroo Islam Khan. Court Minutes 18/8/1852, 26/1/1853, 9/2/1853; Political and Military Committee Minutes 25/8/1852, 29/9/1852, 26/1/1853, 5/4/1854, 16/5/1855; Braid, *Statement*.

from this family in London. His late brother, Jamh ood-Deen, and his son-in-law, the Nepali ambassador Jung Bahadur, had advised him how to negotiate with the British. He finally persuaded the government of India to let him visit, arriving in 1854, aged 59. He was accompanied by his son, Feroz Shah, and a large suite, including a servant Joaleeka (discussed below). He hired a British officer in the Company's army, Captain Johnson, to be his escort and guide.[100] The party stayed in the fashionable Oriental Hotel (Vere Street, off Oxford Street). He socialized with British aristocrats and also many other Indian notables there, including Meer Jafur of Surat.[101]

While he sought pleasure, he also desired to increase his pension and those of his family members, making these hereditary for future generations.[102] To build his case, he and his British lawyers requested from the directors all the documents in the Company's archives about their family; the directors declined to provide these.[103] In addition, Gholam Mahomed asked the directors to help him sort out and recover Jamh ood-Deen's pilfered property in Calcutta and in Europe.[104]

While in London, 'His Highness' Gholam Mahomed, like his late brother, received royal treatment from many British élites.[105] The former British commander-in-chief in India, Lord Combermere, hosted him graciously and received his portrait in return.[106] In particular, he gained the ear and personal sympathy of Queen Victoria. He sat at her

[100] Political and Military Committee Minutes 20/5/1854.

[101] His Highness Prince Gholam Mahomed Affidavit 7/7/1854, L/L Box 64 (441), vol. 2, ff. 306–8, BL.

[102] Court Minutes 29/12/1854, 24/1/1855, 14/2/1855, 28/3/1855, 4/4/1855; Political and Military References June 1854, no. 337, December 1854, no. 2359, January 1855, no. 2964, March 1855, no. 3876, BL; FPC 2/1/1852, no. 3, NAI; PP (Commons) 1861, vol. 46, paper 44, pp. 95–225.

[103] Court Minutes 10–30/5/1854; Letter from Court, Political Department 4/1/1854, no. 1, NAI.

[104] Court Minutes 13/6/1855; Military and Political Committee Minutes 28/3/1855.

[105] In contrast, some British newspapers had become dismissive of visiting Indian royalty, calling Gholam Mahomed's 'physiognomy . . . very peculiar— almost Jewish in appearance' and comparing his magnificent dress to that of high Catholic ecclesiastics. *Globe* cited in *Times* 6/4/1854 10e.

[106] Stapleton Cotton, *Memoirs*, vol. 2, pp. 327–8, 388–9.

table (although probably avoiding haram food there) and attended her royal balls. Victoria was particularly supportive of Indian royalty generally. In 1854, she expressed to the Company's authorities her special interest in Gholam Mahomed and advocated creating a hereditary landed Indian aristocracy:

> she *feels* strongly [about] . . . old Prince Gholam Mohammed, and his son Prince Feroz Shah. The Queen understands (though she is not sure of the fact) that the old man is here in order to try to obtain his pension continued to his son. This is very natural, and it strikes the Queen to be an arrangement difficult to be justified, in a moral point of view, to give these poor people—who after *all* were once so mighty—*no* security beyond their lives. Whilst we remain permanently in possession of their vast Empire, they receive a pension, which is not *even* continued to their descendants. Would it not be much the best to allow them, instead of a pension, to hold, perhaps under government, a property, which would enable them and their descendants to live respectably, maintaining a certain rank and position? . . . Nothing is more painful for *any* one than the thought that their children and grandchildren have no future, and may become absolute beggars. How much more *dreadful* must this be to proud people, who, like Prince Gholam, are the sons and grandsons of great Princes like Hyder Ali and Tippoo Sahib! Besides it strikes the Queen that the more kindly we treat Indian Princes, whom *we* have *conquered*, and the more consideration we show for their birth and former grandeur, the more we shall attach Indian Princes and governments to us, and the more ready will they be to come under our rule.[107]

Victoria clearly expected the governor-general to act upon her request and establish Gholam Mahomed as a titled and propertied aristocrat, as was worthy of his noble birth. Her attitudes found support among many Indian pensioned nobility, and also in the post-1858 British Raj.[108] Victoria especially favoured Indian royalty who converted to Christianity, including standing as godmother to Gauriamma, daughter of the ex-maharaja of Coorg, and vainly attempting to engage her

---

[107] Victoria to Dalhousie 2/10/1854 in Victoria, *Letters*, vol. 3, pp. 49, 59–61.

[108] Carnatic Stipendiary Hyder Jung also sought this. Jung, *Petition*; PDHC, L/PS/3/108, ff. 356–7, 383; Political and Military Committee Minutes 16/3/1853; FPC 25/8/1854, nos 45–6, NAI.

to ex-maharaja Duleep Singh of the Punjab, another convert to the Church of England and settler in Britain.

The sympathetic attitude of influential British royalty and nobility induced the directors in 1855 to enhance Gholam Mahomed's annual pension by 25 per cent to £6,000, and to grant him an additional £3,000 to enable him to return to India in 'a manner suitable to his rank'.[109] Gholam Mahomed thought he could have gotten even more except that the Board of Control, which was very divided on the budgetary implications of such pensions, restrained the directors' munificence.[110]

Unlike his brother, Gholam Mahomed returned to India after only a year in England. Yet, in India, he found less support and respect. Once the 1857 fighting was over, he returned to London with his son and grandson, again asking for increased pensions and benefits. He received in 1859 the honour Knight Commander of the Star of India, guaranteed hereditary pensions for his family, and the enhanced title Shahzada ('Son of a King') for the next generation.[111] The Government of India objected in vain to these pension enhancements, arguing they would encourage other princes to go to Britain in imitation. Thus, several Indian royalty who came to Britain achieved some success financially and socially, which they would evidently not have achieved in India.

Indian servants also were effected by going to London. Indeed, one Bengali servant in Gholam Mahomed's suite, Joaleeka (181?–6?), remained in Britain as a settler. Over the years, Joaleeka had travelled across India a servant for a series of British soldiers. He thus learned not only several regional languages but also basic English, although from lower-class Britons soldiers since his accent was 'cockney'.[112]

[109] Court Minutes 20–7/6/1855, 4/7/1855, 1/8/1855, 6–14/4/1858; Military and Political Committee Minutes 11/7/1855; Political and Military References June 1855, no. 543, July 1855, no. 1155, August 1855, no. 1443, BL.

[110] Stapleton Cotton, *Memoirs*, vol. 2, pp. 327–8.

[111] Tupper, *Index*, vol. 3, pp. 222–3, para 790; FPC 26/11/1858, nos 169–74, 30/12/1859, nos 386–7, NAI; PP (Commons) 1861, vol. 46, paper 44, p. 95.

[112] Joaleeka's oral autobiography recorded in 'Hindoo Beggars' written by Andrew Halliday in Mayhew, *London*, vol. 4, pp. 423–5.

When Gholam Mohamed assembled an entourage for London, he recruited Joaleeka, not as his own interpreter but as 'interpreter to his servants'.

While the delegation stayed at the Oriental Hotel, Joaleeka fraternized with British women of his class, although he was in his forties: 'I formed a connection with a white woman. She was a servant in the hotel. I broke my caste and from that moment I knew that it would not do for me to go back to India. The girl fell in the family-way . . .' The hotel manager discovered her condition while Gholam Mahomed was away visiting Paris, and his brother's grave there, with most of the other servants. The manager fired her and Joaleeka apparently abandoned her as well.

While Joaleeka feared the anger of his employer, he felt protected by living in Britain: 'I also knew that by the English laws in England I was a free man and that my master could not take me back against my will.' Thus, when Gholam Mahomed promised to forgive him and bring him back to Calcutta, Joaleeka pretended to accept this: 'I salaamed and thanked him, and said I was his slave for ever; but at the same time I knew that he would break his word and that when he had me in his power, he would put me to death. He was a very severe man about caste.' The day Gholam Mahomed left London, Joaleeka hid:

I changed my clothes at the house of a girl I knew—not the same one as I had known at the hotel, but another. This one lived at Seven Dials. I stopped indoors for many days till this girl, who could read newspapers, told me that my master had sailed away. I felt very glad, for though I knew my master could not force me to go back with him yet I was afraid for all that, for he knew the King and the Queen, and had been invited by the lord mayor to the City.

Once safe, he used her and a series of other British women to fit into local society:

The girl in whose house I hid showed me how to beg. She persuaded me to turn Christian, because she thought that it would do me good—so I turned Christian. I do not know what it means, but I am a Christian, and have been for many years. I married that girl for some time. I have been married several times. I do not mean to say that I have ever been to church as rich folks do; but I have been married without that . . . I am living now in Charles Street, Drury Lane. I have been married to my present wife six years. We have three children and one dead. My eldest is now in the hospital with a bad arm . . . My present wife is Irish, and fought two women about it. They were taken to Bow street by a policeman but the judge would not hear them. My wife is a very good wife to me, but she got drunk too often. If it were not for that, I should like her better. I ran away from her once, but she came after me with all the children.

In his eyes at least, he was a man British women found worth fighting over.

As an Indian settler, Joaleeka had access to sources of income not as easily available to British men of his class. After his master left, he worked for two years as a crossing-sweeper. He also earned some occasional cash by interpreting between Indians and British authorities. He estimated his income at up to 12 shillings weekly.

British attitudes toward Joaleeka, however, changed in 1857: 'After the mutiny . . . I did very badly. No one would look at a poor Indian then—much less give to him . . . All that knew me used to chaff me about it, and call me Johnny Sepoy.' His Indian identity turned from a competitive advantage into a liability, despite his protestations of loyalty to the British and his denigration of other Indians. His three acknowledged children, Catholic like their mother, presumably knew little of India except through his stories. Many such servants as Joaleeka thus assimilated into British society. While Indian delegations continued to arrive, they often met with relatively unpromising receptions.

The Awadh Queen Mother and Suite

In India during the decade leading up to 1857, British annexations and depositions of rulers increased in pace, particularly using, as Rungo Bapojee warned, the 'Doctrine of Lapse'. These often prompted futile and expensive missions.[113] When the British annexed the large state of Awadh in 1856, its dethroned ruler, Wajid Ali Shah (r. 1847–56,

[113] For example, Maulvi Gholam Khan and Syed Ibrahim represented the widowed maharanis of Nagpur in 1854–6, vainly lobbying to reverse this annexation. Court Minutes 12–25/4/1855, 10–24/10/1855; Military and Political Committee Minutes 25/4/1855; Political and Military References, August 1854 to June 1856; Kaye, *History of the Sepoy War*, vol. 1, pp. 85–96.

d. 1887), refused the proffered £150,000 annual pension (although this meant severe financial hardship for his many dependents, both those who went with him into exile in Calcutta and those who stayed behind in Lucknow). Instead, he determined to go to London personally to petition Queen Victoria, Parliament, and the directors, protesting this immoral act. When the British discouraged him from travelling to London, he reported illness and instead dispatched a delegation of 113 people headed by his mother, Jenabi Auliah Taj Ara Begum (d. 1858), one of his brothers, General Mirza Sikunder Hushmat Bahadoor (1822–58), and his son and proclaimed heir, Mirza Mohummud Hamid Allie Mirza Wallee Ahud Bahadoor (1826/28-1874). Despite its pomp, the mission failed to impress most Britons favourably. Then, the 1857 conflict further turned most British attitudes against it. Like the earlier three missions from the Awadh royal family we have considered, this cost much and gained little politically, although every member of the delegation experienced Britain in powerful ways.

Wajid Ali Shah, in addition to family members and British courtiers, also recruited for his mission Indians very experienced in working with the British: Moulvee Mohummud Musseehood-Deen Khan Bahadur (b.1804) and Mirza Ali Ackbar (discussed above). Musseehood-Deen's family had long served the Awadh rulers but for the last three generations had worked for the British as intermediaries and judges. Musseehood-Deen himself had been twelve years employed by the British, receiving the title Khan Bahadur and rising to the high office of Mir Munshi in the Persian department, the peak in his profession.[114] After someone leaked a confidential British document to the Awadh ruler, the British accused and fired Musseehood-Deen in 1844, with none of the charges against him ever proven, or even made explicit. After this dismissal, he found work with the Awadh ruler, despite British insistence that he be dismissed.[115] The British annexation of Awadh deprived his family of their landholdings there. Thus, he had extensive experience with the British but also antipathy toward them.

[114] FPC 31/10/1838, nos 119–21, 10/4/1839, nos 189–90, 24/4/1839, nos 147–8, 6/12/1841, no. 81, NAI.
[115] FPC 11/12/1847, no. 194, 7/10/1848, nos 224–6, 28/3/1856, no. 165, NAI.

The Awadh delegation reached Southampton via Alexandria in August 1856 with a grand display and much initial fascination by the British public and also other Indians already in London.[116] By this point, British public opinion had well-established expectations about 'oriental' royalty and how they should be regarded. In this environment, the British press reflected competing efforts by supporters and opponents of this mission to put their own 'spin' on its particular significance.

Even before the envoys arrived, Wajid Ali Shah's hired British agent—Major Robert Wilberforce Bird, the former assistant resident to Awadh—apparently supplied the *Times* with details and perhaps prose as well. In the tone of a British royal court calendar, the *Times* listed by name the mission's nine leading dignitaries.[117] This article assured the British public that they would receive 'every accommodation' and noted that its ladies observed seclusion and therefore the embassy would hire entire hotels. A subsequent *Times* article announced: 'The disembarcation of these illustrious individuals has excited the greatest curiosity, and a vast number of people congregated in the docks to witness it. The *suite* and attendants are most gorgeously attired in the Oriental costume. The Queen-mother was brought on shore in a sedan-chair, closely veiled, and the same seclusion was observed in reference to the landing of her daughters.'[118] This article also indicated their vast and easy wealth by recounting that jewels worth £50,000 had fallen overboard in the Red Sea. A few days later, the *Times* publicized some of the many British personages who paid their respects to the delegation: 'the Earl and Countess of Hardwicke, Lady St John, the Ladies Yorke, Sir George Pollock, Sir George Wombwell, Admiral Ayscough, Viscount Royston, the Mayor of Southampton . . . .'.[119] It reminded readers that only respectable British women could meet the Awadh Queen Mother.

Sentiment soon shifted against the delegation, however, despite the lobbying of its hired publicists. The *Times* marked the Awadh nobles

[116] Salter, *Asiatic*, p. 52.
[117] *Times* 19/8/1856 6f. See also Syed Abdoollah Letter to Editor, *Times* 12/11/1855 9d.
[118] *Times* 22/8/1856 12e.
[119] *Times* 27/8/1856 7f.

for their exotic display, but their attendants appeared as dirty opium-smoking loafers who alienated the space in Britain that they occupied:

> Although the appearance of the Princesses and principal attendants is most superb by reason of the elaborate and costly dresses with which they are attired, the mass of the inferior servants present an unusually filthy and unsightly group. Ranging on the basement floors of the hotel are large numbers continually to be seen lounging in the most careless manner, or squatting before a charcoal fire either cooking some article of food or indulging in the fumes derived from a dirty opium pipe. The entire floor of this portion of the hotel is strewed with the clothing of the inhabitants, and in appearance much resembles the back premises of an extensive rag merchant, the whole being rendered more unpleasant by the quantity of dirt which each article of dress apparently contains.

We can contrast these mid-nineteenth-century images with those of earlier periods, when even Indian servants were exotic rarities.

At the same time, the *Times* described common Britons as mesmerized by this insubstantial oriental luxury and veiled sexuality:

> at present the interest excited is one of mere vulgar curiosity on the part of the multitude, who desire only to see the dresses and appointments of the servants and followers, and greedily drink in the absurd tales of the fabulous wealth and jewels belonging to the Royal party, which have been industriously circulated. Besides the usual rabble of boys consequent on such occasions, numbers of respectably dressed persons, with now and then a carriage filled with occupants, are to be seen intently gazing at the exterior of the Royal York Hotel, where the illustrious party is located, and great pains are frequently taken to secure a sight of the ladies of the Royal party, who sometimes take a sly peep from the upper apartments upon the congregated numbers assembled in the streets below.

Thus, some British newspapers recorded the British masses and Indian visitors observing each other.

The *Globe* depicted vulgar British delight in the Awadh delegation as a 'raree-show'.[120] This newspaper also ridiculed the obsession with seclusion by the Awadh women and their servants. It compared the members of the mission to the monster Caliban, and called them 'charlatan'; the mission's goal was 'ill-advised and preposterous'. It debunked Bird's rhetorical efforts to sway the British mob. The *Times*,

[120] Article in *Globe* reprinted in *Times* 28/8/1856 12f.

which had initially published more favourable representations of the delegation, reprinted this scathing article. The *Times* thus shifted against the mission within ten days of their arrival, portraying it as a nuisance to the British rather than a source of pride, profit, or even entertainment: 'The strangely dressed natives stroll and lounge about the street without apparently the slightest notice being taken of them . . . Altogether the natives appear a very good-tempered race, and amuse themselves principally by troubling shopkeepers to explain the quality and use of the articles exposed for sale, but in few instances making purchases at the prices which they are called upon to tender for the transfer of the goods.'[121] In addition to their reluctance to spend money, the *Times* attributed unpleasant odours to them. Indeed, the hotel that they rented would allegedly be unfit for respectable people (i.e., Europeans) for some time: 'Mr White, the proprietor, received 100£ for the use of his premises during the 10 days they have been occupied; and we do not doubt that it will be at least as many more days before the establishment will be again rendered fit to be used as the residence of a European.'[122]

By the time of their departure by train from Southampton for London, the delegation retained only its curiosity factor. The *Times* stressed the childish disorganization and impracticality of these 'natives' and 'Orientalists'. Again the press highlighted as comical and ineffectual the efforts of the eunuchs and other servants to protect the modesty of their queen, 'this curious specimen of Eastern royalty', as she moved from covered carriage to the train. Yet, the eunuchs were defeated by plucky Britons who climbed onto the roof of the railroad carriage to peer over the inadequate screening.

The two Britons attached to the mission, Bird (long-time Awadh agent in London) and Captain J. R. Brandon (who travelled with it), squabbled over their respective roles. Ultimately, they arranged that the former would take care of the mission's political business while the latter would manage its accommodation and social intercourse. In London, Brandon rented the Duke of Brunswick's Harley House on New Road for a year at £550 rent, although it was not very secluded. Nor was it large enough for the entire entourage; they also hired nearby

[121] *Times* 30/8/1856 10c.
[122] *Times* 1/9/1856 12a, 8/5/1852 5d; Salter *Asiatic*, p. 54.

houses for the rest. Newspapers pictured their moving in as a great bustle of effeminate activity and expense: 'The [British] mob . . . gaze and laugh at the barbaric crowd in feminine garb, who, with their semi-virile chiefs, throng the ante-rooms of the New-road harem, or cluster on the tops of the neighbouring cabs . . . The wrongs of the Oudean [Awadh] dynasty have produced a less intense effect than the number, the costume, and the dirt of the Oudean domestics.'[123] This delegation thus had thus become not a great honour to Britain but a comic Oriental farce.

The mission's many nobility, scribes, and servants interacted with the growing number of other Indians in London, according to their respective classes. These included various people in the nawab of Surat's and other delegations, and also Britons with Indian connections.[124] Indian settlers, including scholar-official Syed Abdoollah (discussed below), met with and advised this mission.[125] Awadh servants went to east London's Oriental Quarter to find fellowship and pleasure. For example, during the fast of Ramzan, which the Awadh and Surat delegations officially respected, unobservant attendants went there to eat and drink.[126] In exchange, Indian servants often visited their peers at Harley House.[127]

As the Awadh emissaries mobilized their campaigns to win over the directors, Parliament, Queen Victoria, and the British public, they met a particularly hostile response. The Awadh Queen Mother wrote officially announcing her arrival and submitting the Awadh ex-ruler's appeal to reverse the annexation; the directors and Board of Control rejected these.[128] They hired a firm of British lawyers, Gregory, Skirrow and Company, to formally request all the relevant papers in the Company's files, all unavailable in India. At first, the directors refused to

[123] *Times* 2/9/1856 10b, 17/11/1856 8b–c.

[124] Stapleton Cotton, *Memoirs*, vol. 2, pp. 331–3.

[125] FPC 11/3/1859, nos 862–7, NAI; *Times* 12/9/1857 9d–e, 24/4/1858 11d. He also translated documents between Persian and English for the mission. Lucas, *Dacoitee*, pp. 153–60.

[126] Salter, *Asiatic*, pp. 203–4.

[127] E.g., Ameen Adeen in Salter, *Asiatic*, p. 69; *Times* 21/5/1858 12f.

[128] Political and Military Committee Memoranda September 1856, no. 3521, BL.

provide them. The delegation, however, induced Parliament to demand them, which made these accessible for the Awadh mission to refute.[129] Not until early 1857, six months after their arrival, were they received at the Company's headquarters, and then only as a courtesy not as ambassadors.[130] Bird published a pamphlet outlining the wrongs perpetrated against them: *Spoliation of Oudh* (London: W.S. Johnson, 1857), expanded by Samuel Lucas into *Dacoitee in Excelsis* (London: Nassau Steam Press, 1857). Members of the delegation wrote letters to prominent British authorities and many newspapers.[131] They also arranged for the delegation's leading men to be portrayed as dignitaries in London newspapers (Image 26).

By this time, however, the British press usually regarded the mission as a contest between British purity and Oriental debauchery, calling the delegates: 'parasites . . . lapped and nurtured in an atmosphere of venality, and hardened in the routine of those vile arts by which Eastern courtiers rise and fall . . .'.[132] Yet, in fact, British and Indian swindlers bilked gullible Britons across Britain, using the scam that they represented the Awadh delegation.[133]

The outbreak of the 1857 fighting destroyed most remaining public or official sympathy for their cause. Nevertheless, Musseehood-Deen published a book: *Oude: Its Princes and Its Government Vindicated*

[129] Musseehood-Deen Letters 22/12/1856, 5/2/1857, 11-30/3/1857, 7/4/1857, 3/6/1857 and replies 3/1/1857, 19/2/1857, 7/5/1857, PDHC, L/PS/3/108; Court Minutes 24/12/1856, 7/1/1857, 11/2/1857, 8/4/1857, 22/7/1857; PP, Returns (Commons) 1856, vol. 45, Command Paper 2086, pp. 341ff.

[130] *Times* 17/1/1857 12d.

[131] Musseehood-Deen Letter 23/1/1857 and Reply 5/2/1857, PDHC, L/PS/3/108; Court Minutes 28/1/1857; Petition from Queen Mother of Oude 26/5/1857, Miscellaneous Letters Received E/1/194, BL; Bird and Mohd. Musseh Ooddeen Letter to Editor, *Times* 2/2/1857 5d; *Illustrated London News* 18/7/1857 71b–c and Supplement 1/8/1857. See the extensive correspondence between the directors and Musseehood-Deen, the Awadh principals, and their lawyers, in Political and Military Committee Memoranda, December 1856 to April 1857, BL.

[132] *Times* 17/11/1856 8b–c.

[133] Article reprinted from *Manchester Guardian* in *Times* 12/9/1856 6e; article reprinted from *Birmingham Journal* in *Times* 20/9/1856 10d–e; *Times* 13/9/1856 9e, 12/9/1857 9d–e, 21/5/1858 12f.

Image 26: Leading Men of the Oude Delegation (from left to right: Moonshee Mahommed Rufe, Secretary; General Secundar Hushinah, brother of the King; Mirza Mohummud Hamid Allie Mirza Wallee Ahud Bahadoor, Heir; Jallesood Dowlah Syed Allee Khan Bahadoor, Aide-de-Camp to the King; Maulvi Museeh al-Daula, Agent to the King), 1857.

(London: J. Davy and Sons, 1857). British authorities in Britain and India seized all the copies they could.[134] Nevertheless, the mission persisted. Rebuffed by the directors, they submitted a petition to the House of Lords.[135] In it they expressed their '. . . sincere regret [at] the tidings which have reached the British kingdom of disaffection prevailing among native troops in India.' They assured the British that they themselves were 'a Royal race, ever faithful and true to their friendship with the British nation'. Nevertheless, the Lords rejected their petition on a technicality, since it omitted the required term 'Humble' in places where protocol repeatedly demanded it. Even the petition's sponsor, Lord Campbell, excused himself for having submitted it, which he said he did out of duty alone.

In November 1857, the delegation unrealistically offered to reconquer and rule India for Victoria: 'We propose that the Prince Mirza Md. Hamid Allie Bahadur Heir Apparent to the King of Oude now resident in England should immediately proceed to India supported by a British Force and in the name of the King of Oude should assume the government of the Country and call upon the People to rally round the Standard of the Sovereign against the revolted Sepoys.'[136] They cited the precedent of Dost Muhammad, ruler of Afghanistan, whom the British had once imprisoned in Calcutta but who was supporting them in 1857. This proposal met no encouragement from the British. Indeed, they continued to hold the Awadh ex-ruler in confinement in Calcutta throughout the 1857 conflict.[137]

Meanwhile, the delegation's funds dwindled. The Awadh ex-ruler sent them £4,783 in October 1857, but as they wrote: 'The expenses in London [were] so much greater than what Her Majesty and the Princes could possibly have expected.'[138] Yet appeals to the directors

[134] See Introduction by Ahmad, *British Aggression.*

[135] *Times* 8/8/1857 6b; Court Minutes 17–29/4/1857, 13/5/1857, 24/6/1857, 1–22/7/1857, 2/9/1857; Lords Debate 6/8/1858, *Hansard,* series 3, vol. 147, pp. 1119–22.

[136] Musseehood-Deen Letter 28/10/1857, PDHC, L/PS/3/108; Court Minutes 25/11/1857, 2/12/1857; Political and Military Committee Memoranda November 1857, no. 4876, BL.

[137] Court Minutes 16–21/10/1857.

[138] Court to Musseehood-Deen 22/10/1857, 28/12/1857 and Reply 23/11/1857, PDHC, L/PS/3/108.

about their financial exigencies received a cold shoulder.[139] They, gave up Harley House as inauspicious (after two women servants had died there) and rented four attached houses on Warwick Road (one leased by Jafur Alee of Surat), plus a country home in Richmond for the Queen Mother.[140] Finally, they received another £7,156 from Wajid Ali Shah in January 1858.[141]

The Awadh king, however, further confused the issue by sending Colonel Richard Ousely (who had just been suspended from the Bengal Army) to take over as 'chief agent for the conduct of His Majesty's affairs in this country' at a lavish salary. The Awadh mission recognized his status but refused to give him any money.[142] After six months unpaid, unrecognized by the directors, and becoming unwell, Ousely withdrew from further involvement with this cause.

Indicative of the internal conflicts within the delegation, Musseehood-Deen wrote to the directors requesting that they ignore any communications that came directly from the Queen Mother, since she had come under the influence of people opposed to him.[143] Some of the Awadh mission, finding no support in London, decided to go to Paris and from there to Mecca and back to Calcutta.[144] Although the British government rejected their request for passports, the French government issued them.[145]

In Paris, the Queen Mother died (24 January 1858), as supporters in Parliament said, 'of a broken heart'.[146] Next month, her son died in

[139] Court Minutes 2/12/1857.

[140] FSC 29/1/1858, no. 609, NAI; *Times* 18/11/1857 6d.

[141] *Times* 21/4/1858 10b; Musseehood-Deen Letter 9/1/1858 and Reply 22/1/1858, PDHC, L/PS/3/108, ff. 89–91; Court Minutes 12–26/1/1858, 10/3/1858.

[142] Desborough Letter 22/12/1857 and Reply 8/1/1858, PDHC, L/PS/3/108, ff. 117ff; Court Minutes 23–30/12/1857.

[143] Musseehood-Deen Letter 22/9/1857, PDHC, L/PS/3/108; Political and Military Committee Memoranda September 1857, no. 3379, BL.

[144] Sikunder Hushmut to Court 9/12/1857, PDHC, L/PS/3/108, f. 88; Commons Debate 16/2/1858, *Hansard*, series 3, vol. 147, pp. 1477–1543.

[145] Musseehood-Deen Letter 9/9/1857 and Reply 14/10/1857, PDHC, L/PS/3/108; Court Minutes 16–30/9/1857, 14/10/1857, 16/12/1857; Political and Military Committee Memoranda September 1857, nos 3639, 3665, October 1857, no. 3873, December 1857, no. 5300, BL.

[146] Commons Debate 16/2/1858, *Hansard*, series 3, vol. 147, p. 513.

Paddington, London (25 February 1858). Then the young Awadh heir tried to take leadership of the mission away from Musseehood-Deen, who had control over whatever funds remained. The heir (who was below the age of majority in British law) therefore, acting in the name of his father, used the mission's British lawyers to sue Musseehood-Deen, who countersued using his own lawyer, Mr T.J. Angell. Musseehood-Deen had one of the prince's supporters jailed for forgery, which charge the courts dismissed. Musseehood-Deen was eventually compelled by British courts to turn over the remaining £4,000 of the mission's funds.[147] Various servants of the Awadh mission then sued to get their unpaid wages.[148] Several stayed on or went home separately, often in dire financial straits.[149]

Musseehood-Deen blamed the youth of the heir and the 'unworthy and self-interested intriguers [in margin] Mehdi Koolie and Allie Ackbar'.[150] The former was a Persian who claimed to be the great grandson of Nadir Shah. The latter, Ali Ackbar, (discussed above) had advised three other delegations.[151] In response, the heir asserted that Musseehood-Deen 'was ready to betray us'. This internecine conflict divided many other Indians in London.[152] After a further vain petition to Parliament, the heir then went via Marsailles and Alexandria back to India in 1861, taking the remaining valuables.[153] Although the

[147] He retained his £948 annual salary, however. Skirrow Letter 28/4/1858, 1/6/1858 and replies 31/5/1858, 9/6/1858, Court to Hamid Ali 2/10/1858 and Reply 19/8/1858, Angell to Musseehood-Deen 6/8/1858, Skirrow to Hamid Ali 24/8/1858, PDHC, L/PS/3/108 ff. 121ff, 260, 266–9; *Times* 21/4/1858 10b, 23/4/1858 11c, 27/4/1858 11d, 10/5/1858 11c, 29/5/1858 11a–b.

[148] *Times* 10/5/1858 11b–c; FSC 29/1/1858, no. 609, NAI.

[149] E.g, Musseehood-Deen fired his long-time personal servant, Kadir Bukhsh, who had also married a British woman. With the help of Syed Abdoolah, Kadir Bukhsh took work in a Turkish Bath in Finsbury, and later sued Musseehood-Deen. *Times* 19/12/1861 10f, 20/12/1861 8a–b. See also Jaleesood Dowlah to Court 7/1/1859, PDHC, L/PS/3/108, f. 259.

[150] Musseehood-Deen letter 1/7/1858, PDHC, L/PS/3/108, f. 123.

[151] Court to Foreign Secretary 2/7/1858, PDHC, L/PS/3/108, ff. 124–5.

[152] Meer Jafur of Surat allegedly advised the Awadh heir, in exchange for a share of any gains. *Morning Advertiser* republished in *Bombay Times* 9/2/1857 238c–d.

[153] Musseehood-Deen Letter 26/8/1858, PDHC, L/PS/3/108, f. 125; Hameed Ali Petitions to Parliament presented to Lords by Lord Mounteagle

Awadh ruler replaced Musseehood-Deen in 1859, he remained in Britain, marrying an Englishwoman, Miss Bilk.[154] During the 1857 fighting, his two houses in Agra had been looted, then confiscated by the British government. His request for employment or a pension from the British was rejected.[155] He finally retired to India in November 1863, leaving his young but estranged British wife behind with no means of support.[156] Other Indian intermediaries, however, did better in Britain.

Indian Intermediaries in London

From the eighteenth century, a growing number of Indian scholar-officials went to Britain to advance their careers. By the mid nineteenth century, their status had clearly been reduced by Anglicization and Orientalism but their expertise in Indian culture and languages and their ability to intermediate between the British administration and the Indian people still enabled them to make places for themselves under the British. In June 1851, two men of slightly different standing arrived together, Peer Ibrahim Khan and Syed Abdoollah.[157] The former had a more prominent trip to Britain but soon returned to India, the latter remained as a settler, finding a number of entrepreneurial ways to live there as a professional.

When the holy Sufi family of Peer Ibrahim Khan (*c.* 1825–56) lost their lands to the Sikhs, he had taken service under the British, rising

---

29/6/1858, 29/7/1858. For a critical epitaph on this mission see Kaye, *History of the Sepoy War*, vol. 1, pp. 402–4.

[154] Musseehood-Deen, *Oudh*, pp. 170–2; *Times* 17/12/1861 8d–9a, 6/8/ 1862 11a–b. The Awadh ex-king later sent eunuchs Ahsanuddaula and Mean Mahboob to England as his representatives. FPC 18/11/1859, NAI; *Calcutta Englishman* 2/11/1859 cited in *Times* 20/11/1865 6a.

[155] Political Dispatch from Secretary of State 24/7/1860, no. 58, BL; Musseehood-Deen to Secretary of State October 1859, PDHC, L/PS/3/108, ff. 364–6.

[156] *Times* 16/1/1860 10f–11a, 2/10/1861 9f, 17/11/1865 11f, 20/11/1865 6a.

[157] They shared 77 Connaught Terrace, Edgeware Road. Court Minutes 4/6/1851.

to the high office of 'Native Agent at the Court of the nawab of Bha-
walpore', with the title Bahadur.[158] Despite his noble birth, evident
abilities, and expertise, however, younger and less qualified Britons
superseded him.[159] Nonetheless, when he requested permission to go
to Britain, the governor-general granted him two years leave at full
salary, although his supervisor recommended that he be guided by a
Briton: 'As it is very desirable that such an intelligent Gentleman
should make the most of his visit . . . [He should be] placed under
charge of some [British] officer proceeding to England, who by his
advice and assistance, will be able to render the journey instructive and
agreeable.'[160] Yet no suitable Briton agreed to accompany him, so he
travelled with Syed Abdoollah.

Peer Ibrahim soon entered into the highest social circles in London,
sponsored by his patrons, Sir Claude Wade and Sir Henry Lawrence.
Just before he arrived, his élite origins and service to the British were
rehearsed by the *Times*.[161] Queen Victoria soon received him and
invited him to a Royal Ball where he met many of the British aristocracy.[162]

Even as he developed his social connections, he worked to advance
himself, as Mohan Lal and Shahmat Ali had done earlier (see Chapter 9). In Peer Ibrahim's autobiographical letter to the directors,
he recounted his distinguished family history and sought restoration
of their landed estate, a British title to go with his Indian one, and
increased salary.[163] The directors appreciated his breeding and accomplishments but were reluctant to grant him anything substantial: they
considered whether offering him a sword of honour would be sufficient.[164] Finally, they followed the advice of British officials in the
Punjab and granted a Persian title: Mubariz al-Daula ('Hero of the

[158] Letter from Court, Political 31/7/1850, no. 22, NAI.
[159] Shahamat Ali, *Notes*, p. 93n.
[160] Financial Papers 21/11/1851, L/F/2/147, BL.
[161] *Times* 21/4/1851 7f.
[162] Wade Letters 18/5/1851, 30/5/1851 and replies 18/5/1851, 7/6/1851,
Broughton Papers MSS EUR F.213/19; Peer Ibraheem Khan to Court 20/1/
1852, Miscellaneous Letters Received E/1/191, f. 6, BL.
[163] Court Minutes 8/10/1851; FPC 7/5/1852, nos 44–6, NAI.
[164] Hobhouse Letter 28/7/1851, Broughton Papers MSS EUR F.213/15,
BL; FPC 7/5/1852, nos 44–6, NAI.

State'). In order to get him out of London, the directors loaned him £600 (a full year's salary in advance) and granted him free passage back to Bombay, first class for himself, as well as appropriate lesser accommodation for his two Muslim servants. Unlike his friend, Syed Abdoollah, he resumed his career in India, leaving England 20 January 1852.[165]

Syed Abdoollah (b.1825) was not as high born or high ranked as Peer Ibrahim. He had been born at Pushkar, Rajasthan, and followed his father and other relatives into service to the British. By 1851, he held the modest office of 'Persian, Oordoo, Hindee, and English Translator to the Board of Administration for the Affairs of the Punjab.' Nor did he receive the same support from the British as Peer Ibrahim; when he took two years leave he only received half pay. Nonetheless, he was an accomplished composer of Urdu and Persian poetry and prose.[166]

Five months after reaching Britain and exploring 'the English language, laws, and customs', Syed Abdoollah applied to the Company for appointment as 'Moonshee or Teacher of the Persian, Oordoo, and Hindee Languages' at Haileybury or Addiscombe. He enclosed glowing testimonials in support of his application, proposing:

> at least a trial as a Teacher to judge my capacity for a permanent Office in England; a Country to which I have become attached by my recent observation of its many noble Institutions and the kindness I have received from numerous persons of rank and worth. I am prepared to undergo an examination in the most difficult Persian and Oordoo works and I flatter myself that if I receive the appointment I seek the effect of my humble zeal and application will be apparent at the next ensuing College Examination in the improved pronunciation of such students as may be committed to my care.[167]

The directors declined his offer; as we have seen the college had long refused to appoint Indians.

Meantime, however, Syed Abdoollah incurred 'heavy expenses of living in this Metropolis'. To generate income, he taught independently 'giving lessons in the Oriental Languages to gentlemen preparing

[165] He died in office in 1856, succeeded by his brother. Court Minutes 24/12/1850, 19/11/1851, 3–24/12/1851; FPC 17/10/1856, nos 367–8, 17/4/1857, nos 590–1, 8/4/1859, nos 100–6, NAI.
[166] Syed Abdoollah Letter, 27/8/1856, Elphinstone Papers F.88/175, BL.
[167] Syed Abdoollah Letter, Financial Papers 26/11/1851, L/F/2/147, BL.

to enter [Company] service.' He also taught for two years at Hanwell College and also at Grove, Blackheath, as a 'Teacher of Hindustanee'.[168] While he did not explain this to the directors, part of his expenses stemmed from his marriage to a Scottish woman, Margaret Wilson Henderson, the daughter of Captain John Henderson. They wedded first in a civil ceremony and then, when her family and friends objected, again in the Parish Church of St James, Paddington (13 December 1852).[169] In order to legally marry in the parish church, Syed Abdoollah swore under oath there was no impediment to this marriage (i.e. he had become Anglican).

In 1853, Syed Abdoollah renewed and reframed his argument for his appointment to Haileybury: 'The importance of the acquisition of the languages of the East has been dwelt upon by successive [Company] chairmen in their excellent and instructive addresses to the students of the Colleges and it has occurred to me that perhaps the assistance of a Native of the Country who has made philology his peculiar study would not be unacceptable to the students.'[170] The directors again declined his offer.[171]

After the directors' second rejection, Syed Abdoollah decided to return to India with his wife: 'As the love of one's country is great, and I have no permanent situation here'.[172] He applied to the directors for 'an appointment [in India] as Deputy Collector, Assistant Magistrate, or whatever other office your Hon'ble Court may think me fit to hold.' As they were accustomed, the directors redirected him to the Government of India.[173] They did, however, provide free first class passage back to Jabalpur (where his father, Meer Syed Mohummud, was a

[168] Syed Abdoollah also become close to Reverend Mr Miller's family, Sydenham Street, Perry Hill. Testimonials of Emerson, Hanwell College, 5/5/1853, and Keiser, 4/5/1853, Revenue, Judicial, and Legislative Committee References L/PJ/1/64, no. 235a, BL.

[169] They settled at 11 Bedford Street, Bedford Square. Bishop of London, Marriage Allegations 13/12/1852 Guildhall.

[170] Syed Abdoollah Letter 28/6/1853, L/PJ/1/64, no. 235a, BL.

[171] Hafiz Ludroo Islam Khan offered as well. Political and Military Committee Minutes 25/8/1852, 29/9/1852, 26/1/1853, 5/4/1854, 16/5/1855; Court Minutes 18/8/1852, 26/1/1853, 9/2/1853, 14–20/3/1855, 16/5/1855.

[172] Court Minutes 28/6/1853.

[173] Court Minutes 29/6/1853, 13/7/1853.

Native Magistrate) for him—but it declined to pay for his wife's passage or give him the £50 he repeatedly requested to cover her costs.[174] He left England via the Cape of Good Hope, early in 1854.[175] His return to India was brief. He visited his father and presumably asked approval for all that he had done, including his marriage. He again reached England in August 1855.[176]

Syed Abdoollah resumed his career in London as a teacher and entrepreneur, based on his expertise in 'oriental' culture. He presented to the directors for their Museum his translation of an Urdu poem by Wajid Ali Shah, called 'Ocean of Love'.[177] He also proposed to Mountstuart Elphinstone translating into Urdu Elphinstone's *History of India*; Elphinstone, however, declined paying him for this project and generally scorned Indian linguists.[178] Other Indian translators living in London were more successful; for example, Hafiz Ludroo Islam Khan (a descendant of the nawab of the Carnatic) translated into Urdu and published in 1853 an abridgement of Oliver Goldsmith's 1764 *An History of England in a Series of Letters from a Nobleman to His Son*, which the directors graciously allowed him to dedicate to their chairman.[179]

Syed Abdoollah continued to seek work as a professor of Indian languages. In March 1858, he submitted to the directors a pamphlet

[174] Political and Military Committee Minutes 14/12/1853, 8/2/1854; Court Minutes 20/11/1853, 14/12/1853.

[175] It is not evident if his wife accompanied him on this visit or not. Court Minutes 8–22/2/1854; Political and Military Committee Minutes 8/2/1854.

[176] He lived with his family at Park Cottage, Park Place, Paddington and later at 8 Grove-terrace, St John's Wood. Court Minutes 1/8/1855; *Times* 21/11/1857 9c.

[177] Syed Abdoollah Letter 5/9/1855, Miscellaneous Letters Received, E/1/192, f. 296, BL.

[178] Syed Abdoollah Letter 27/8/1856 and Reply 28/8/1856, Elphinstone Papers F.88/175, BL. Mountstuart Elphinstone lamented in 1838 that the Indian scholar he found in London differed so much in approach as to be useless: Elphinstone wanted a summary translation of the Persian text but the teacher insisted on explaining the full meaning of every word before going on to the next. Journal of Elphinstone 22/1/1838, 19/4/1838 F.88/14, ff. 185, 188–9, BL.

[179] Court Minutes 2–30/11/1853, 21–30/12/1853.

arguing for the establishment of an 'Oriental College' in London (under his own direction).[180] Indeed, as the Company colleges terminated, other educational institutions, both private commercial and public, expanded their teaching of Indian languages to Britons going to India.

One of the largest employers of Indian faculty from the mid nineteenth century was University College, London. This institution appointed (on a part or full-time basis) eight Indian faculty, offering a wide range of languages. Syed Abdoollah applied for and received the position of Professor of Hindustani there (1859–66).[181] A fellow faculty member for much of that period was a Parsi scholar and merchant from Bombay, Dadabhai Naoroji, who was Professor of Gujarati (1856–66). Naoroji later entered politics, becoming the second Indian elected to Parliament and a leader of the Indian National Congress. Also on the faculty were R. Cowasjee, Lecturer in Gujarati (1866–9), Ganendra Mohan Tagore, Professor of Bengali and Indian Law (1860–5), Khitter Mohun Dutt, M.D., Lecturer in Bengali (1865–6) and Hindustani (1867–9), G. Hyder, Lecturer in Bengali (1866–71) and Hindustani (1869–71), D.K. Shahabudin, Professor of Hindustani, Gujarati, and Marathi (1871–4), and Chee Yui Tang Lecturer in Chinese (1861–4). The salaries of these Indian faculty was relatively low, however, so Syed Abdoollah continued to teach privately.[182]

Syed Abdoollah also retained an ongoing interest in the condition of other Indians in Britain. In 1856, he orated to the dignitaries gathered for the opening of the Strangers' Home (see above).[183] He mixed socially with the large delegation from Awadh, and even tried to gain from Wajid Ali Shah a salary for his work as consultant to it, in vain.[184] In 1869, he proposed to the British government restoring the system of deposits from employers who brought Indian servants to Britain,

[180] Court Minutes 31/3/1858.

[181] Bellot, *University College*, Chart 2.

[182] Syed Ameer Ali, *Memoirs and Writings*, p. 24; Haldar, *English Diary*, pp. 23, 32; Salter, *Asiatic*, pp. 118–19; Visram, *Ayahs*, p. 63.

[183] Salter, *Asiatic*, pp. 66–7. See also Abdoolah's Letters to the *Times* 28/6/1859 9f, 25/10/1859 6e, 17/1/1860 9a, 15/11/1860 7f, 15/8/1862 4c, 28/2/1865 12f.

[184] FPC 11/3/1859, nos 862–7, NAI; *Times* 24/4/1858 11d, 20/11/1865 6a.

thus protecting them from destitution there.[185] The diverse Indian presence in Britain from the mid nineteenth century onward, however, lies beyond the scope of this book.

Indians in British Society

Over the decades to 1857, on the eve of 'high colonialism', significantly more Indians of various classes and backgrounds entered Britain, yet their receptions by Britons and their own attitudes towards Britain and other Indians there altered. The Anglocentric world system that extended colonialism also enabled and enticed more Indians to travel to Britain. Increasingly, Britons regarded Indians collectively as inferior colonized peoples, although individual Indians in Britain established a range of roles, depending on their class, gender, ethnicity, and particular deportment and circumstances.

More numerous than ever before, Indian travellers and settlers formed their own communities and social circles in Britain. Annually, several thousand Indian seamen arrived, working the ships that imported Indian raw materials and exported British finished goods. Many Indian servants found work in prosperous Britain not as available in relatively impoverished India. Yet, following 1834, the East India Company's system of supervision and management of these arriving working-class Indians ended without effective replacement. Thus, they—and the British women and entrepreneurs who served their needs and lived off their wages—created an Oriental Quarter in east London which centred on them and other Asians, largely outside of British control. This transient community, and its cultural, racial, and sexual mixing, generated growing élite British disapproval.

As knowledge spread among Indian rulers and former rulers about the sometimes conflicted political relationships among authorities in London and those in India, ever more Indian political delegations arrived and deployed a variety of strategies. Particularly charismatic and insightful envoys learned how to function there. They consulted with each other and sympathetic Britons, hired British lawyers and

---

[185] He calculated the numbers of such poor Indians on Britain's streets at 900. Syed Abdoollah Letter 17/1/1869 and Replies 27/1/1869, 16/2/1869, L/PJ/2/49, BL.

agents, and employed experienced Indian experts in dealing with the British. The increasing involvement of Parliament in the affairs of India, at the cost of the authority of the directors, meant that new political arenas opened up for Indian missions. They petitioned, lobbied, and bribed rival politicians, particularly those in opposition who were seeking ways to discredit the government. They publicized their cases through articles, pamphlets, and books, and made sartorial and dietary choices that shaped their self-presentations. Some representatives and royalty achieved much, particularly those who claimed legal rights using British law courts or Parliament, or obtained the support of the British aristocracy. Others faced antipathy among the British public; no longer attractive oriental rarities, they often seemed either picturesque or corrupting aliens. While many enjoyed the manifold pleasures of the British capital, living as men about town, they faced British constraints on them back in India.

Other classes of Indians in Britain also met with each other, and mixed with Britons as well. Anglicized officials went there to advance themselves. For those who sought to enter British society, marriages or liaisons with British women, often combined with conversion to Christianity, formed a prime means of assimilation. Their incomes often depended both on their entrepreneurial expertise in British culture and their distinctive ability to convey Indian cultures and languages to Britons.

The events of 1857, which ended both the East India Company's administration of India and also the period considered in this book, clearly altered the situation of Indians in Britain. Working-class Indians appeared to even more Britons as threatening aliens in their midst. Many Indians of all classes were forced to protest their loyalty to the British and their hostility to Indians fighting against them in India; some, including those from Awadh and Jodhpur, promised to devote all their resources to crushing the insurrection against the British.[186] Yet, the Board of Control and directors increasingly pressured delegations to leave, for example instructing Ali Morad of Sindh to go

[186] Court Minutes 26/8/1857, 6–14/10/1857; Ali Morad to Court 20/8/ 1857, Coffey to Court 17/2/1858, Ali Ackbar to Secretary of State 20/12/1858 and Reply 10/2/1859, Syed Uckber Ally (of Jodhpur) to Court 11/8/1857, PDHC, L/PS/3/108; *Times* 18/11/1857 6d, 23/12/1857 9f.

'manifest your zeal and fidelity in the service of the British government' there.[187] On their return to India, however, a few Indian envoys were arrested on suspicion of 'treason'.[188]

For many Indians living in London, the degrading effects of colonialism and their distinctive perspective on India as a whole, reshaped their understandings of the British and themselves. Mixing with Indians from many regions often overcame traditional cultural and political distinctions among them. Their common treatment by the British as 'other' made some conscious of their shared condition. Several explicitly expressed their hostility to the British as they were departing, others returned to India and fought the British.[189] Many leaders of India's later nationalist movements likewise had their political consciousness formed by their living and learning in Britain.

---

[187] Ali Morad to Court 6/7/1857 and Reply 19/8/1857 PDHC, L/PS/3/108.

[188] PP, Returns (Commons) 1859(I), vol. 18, paper 125, pp.73ff.

[189] Ali Ackbar to Court 9/9/1857, PDHC, L/PS/3/108.

Conclusions and Beyond 1857

Early Indians in Britain

Between 1600 and 1857, tens of thousands of Indians from all classes formed counterflows into Britain, interacting in diverse ways with Britons and other Indians there. Such Indian passages pre-dated colonialism but expanded in number and variety as it developed. The experiences of these travellers and settlers differed, based on their class, gender, religion, and individual circumstances. Despite efforts by many British officials to prevent their journey and control them after arriving, Indians manoeuvred and negotiated among often conflicting British authorities in colony and metropole. Indians not only represented themselves in Britain, they also explored its diversity and disseminated that knowledge in India, often contesting British colonial agendas. Nonetheless, despite their immediate and (more subtle) long-term effects on British and Indian societies, their lives and writings over time became 'homeless texts', hitherto largely absent from both British and Indian national histories but vital to our deeper understanding of both.[1]

Indians produced knowledge in Britain about India and in India about Britain against which British authorities in both places had to contend. Most British colonial authorities in India tried to project an image of Britain as monolithic and hegemonic. These projections often jarred with Britain's internal political, ethnic, class, and gender inequities and conflicts that Indians saw for themselves there, described for British audiences, and also sent or carried back to India. Many Indians wrote autobiographies, histories, journals, letters, newspaper advertisements, petitions, and travel-narratives in English that they

[1] See Targhi-Tavokoli, *Refashioning Iran*.

intended to influence audiences in Britain directly—either a wide, anonymous readership or a focused one, depending on the genre. The writings of other Indians reached those audiences only through the mediation of Britons who interpreted, edited, or otherwise appropriated their voices. Those Indians who wrote in Persian, Urdu, Arabic, or Nepali targeted readers in India; their writings, however, often remained in manuscript, with limited readership for years, or even until today. A few Anglicized Indians wrote in English, not for British audiences primarily, but rather for other Indians like themselves. In addition, Indians gave oral accounts of India and of Britain (although these are most difficult to recover today). Thus, the variety of knowledge produced by these Indians had uneven distribution and effects, particularly in the face of British representations about both Britain and India.

Indians in Britain were also subjects of British national, local, personal, and colonial accounts. Sometimes official records included them simply because they were present in Britain. For instance, the British national censuses from 1841 onwards indiscriminately sought comprehensive identification of everyone living in every house in Britain—including all Indians. Also intermingled with Britons, testimony by Indians appeared in British legal and Parliamentary records, their position-wanted notices in newspapers, their baptisms, marriages, children's births and deaths in local parish registers, and their payments in borough tax rolls. Further, British autobiographies, diaries, letters, visual art, and fiction depicted Indians, real or imagined. Colonial records, mostly generated by the East India Company, concentrated on them because they were distinctly Indian and produced the largest volume of information on them.

Each kind of evidence provides distinctive perspectives, although not all Indians appeared equally. Often for working-class Indians we must piece together scattered fragments. The lives of Indian women of all classes were generally—by their gendered roles and customary dependence on their husbands or employers—more obscured than men's. But even the lives and words of higher class male travellers or settlers must be recovered from various primary sources since they have been largely ignored in conventional secondary histories of Britain and India.

Colonialism formed the overall context for interactions between Indians and Britons. Between 1600 and 1857, the identity 'Indian' and what that meant changed significantly in contested ways. Initially, people from what became India reached England relatively rarely, encountering there little concrete knowledge about their homelands. They thus had more scope to shape their receptions and roles. Conversely, in the pre-colonial period (and even well into the colonial period), many people from India arrived with little realistic understanding about what life in England would actually entail. The re-lations between Europeans and these early travellers and settlers gradually informed all parties, although asymmetrically because Europeans exerted ever further power over Asians.

The spread of colonialism also brought official British efforts to dichotomize people as Indian or British, colonized or colonizer. People who crossed boundaries, including most of the subjects of this book, presented particular problems of classification to British officials. Many came from transnational communities, or were of part-Indian ancestry, or had changed class status or religion in Britain, or had settled there. One of this book's central concerns has been to show how contingent were identities, how and why they were constructed somewhat differently in India and Britain, and the ways diverse people from India dealt with and shaped them through history.

In the century prior to 1857, British-commanded armies conquered India, Britain established itself as the dominant core of its economic world system, Britain's colonial officials and Orientalists sought to control knowledge about India, and Anglicizers devalued Indian learning. Britain's self-image, both internally and projected into its colonies, also shifted with its rising power. All these factors altered the condition and identities of Indians in Britain and India. In many British minds, India went from the seat of a potent empire, a land of fabled wealth and wisdom, to a relatively impoverished and appropriately subjected colony exporting cheap labour and raw materials. The collective image and status of Indians in British correlated with these changes, and their counterflow efforts to sway British opinion were largely overmatched by British colonial forces.

Over time, various Indian communities, classes, and individual men and women responded diversely to opportunities to travel to

Britain, and functioned differently once there. Many of the earliest travellers and settlers came from already diasporic or transregional communities, like Armenians, Parsis, and Indo-Portuguese. Muslims, whose cultural worlds already linked India and Europe, more readily made the voyage than did high-born Hindus who were apprehensive of the degradation it entailed. Indians who were or became Protestant Christians generally received from Britons more acceptance than those who adhered to Islam, Zoroastrianism, Hinduism, or even Catholicism.

The largest number of Indians reaching Britain were working class. Tens of thousands were seamen, men who expected to make long voyages to unknown places. Their labour made British worldwide commerce possible, yet they proved resistant to British efforts to control their recruitment, service, and lives in Britain. Thousands of Indian men and women servants also accepted employment sailing to or living there. They entered British domestic spaces and negotiated their identities, i.e. how much they should Anglicize their names, dress, diet, and religion. For those who became indigent, the East India Company was their reluctant and paternalistic patron of last resort.

Hundreds of Indian élites made the passage to Britain to pursue their own agendas. Many represented themselves in the public sphere through writing and publishing books and pamphlets, teaching, making speeches, lobbying, and testifying in law courts. Some influenced Parliament as expert witnesses, petitioners, observers, bribe-givers, or (in one case) Member. Dozens of middle class Indian scholar-officials, experts in Persianate literary and administrative cultures, went to instruct Britons in these. Many established themselves as professionals whose mastery over Indian languages and cultures distinguished them from their British rivals and enabled them to support their British wives and families. Indian rulers (or former or would-be rulers) deployed or led over thirty Indian diplomatic and political missions that sought to shift the site of their disputes with British colonial authorities to London. There they could with more agency enter political debates and assert their legal rights, usually in direct conflict with the Company and often in alliance with opposition political factions in Parliament. Indian merchants and officials, soldiers, and other employees of the Company also sought to advance their interests there—

protesting British policies, seeking honours or justice, exploring Britain's pleasures, or mastering its technology or science.

An Indian's class could rise while in Britain, if she or he was willing to adapt and had sufficient resources. Sartorial and religious choices as well as particular circumstances shaped their reception in society. Indian clothing might add an oriental allure while 'cross-dressing' as British helped one mingle with Britons of one's class. Being or becoming even nominally Protestant Christian made a significant difference. With the support of a British patriarch, Indian women and their children sometimes won acceptance and legitimacy in Britain that colonial society in India denied them. Indian slaves customarily achieved emancipation by Anglicizing themselves, including converting to the Church of England. Servants occasionally earned places in the middle-class. Scholars and officials passed as princes. Pensioned noblemen socialized with British peers. A few diplomats, emissaries, and royalty managed, through skilfull direct appeals to authorities in London, to reverse or modify the adverse decrees of British officials in India. Many Indian men hired British servants, sex workers, or lawyers, purchased politicians, or took wives. Yet, all these gains required struggle and entailed costs, while their putative status occasionally met mixed and contested responses there.

Gender crosscut other identities. Indian women servants and the Indian wives or daughters of Britons usually experienced Britain quite differently from Indian males, even males of their own class and religion. Reflecting both British and Indian social norms, Indian women participated less in the public sphere. Conversely, Indian men generally subordinated the British women they employed, lived with, or married. Sexual relations between Indian men and British women attracted little official or popular notice. What little there was tended to cast Indian men as the victims of predatory British women, especially women of the lower classes or of the morally bankrupt aristocracy. Further, Indian male assessments of British culture and society often used their relative valuations of the treatment and status of British and Indian women in ways reciprocal to British gendered denigrations of India.

Over time, Indian visitors and settlers created spaces for themselves in Britain. The houses and rooms rented by individual or groups of

Indians provided places where they could dine, dress, worship, and socialize largely on their own terms. There they hosted Britons and also, increasingly, members of their own class and religious community from across India. Many thereby discovered commonalities with people from regions of India unfamiliar to them. From the nineteenth century, Indian working-class people and entrepreneurs developed the Oriental Quarter in east London's docklands, where Asian and British cultures and peoples intermingled, although under the critical eyes of British officials, social reformers, and evangelicals. Indeed, spreading British attitudes that increasingly lumped Indians in Britain generally together tended to foster their collective consciousness as colonized subjects. Several Indians, after experiencing frustrations in Britain firsthand, fought violently in 1857 to expel colonialism. Further, some Indians of every class decided to remain in Britain as individual settlers, usually marrying and leaving descendants who are part of British society today. These early Indian travellers and settlers, arriving during the pre-colonial and early-colonial periods, thus held complex positions in Indian and British history. Those who came later continued some of these same patterns, but also faced some new and quite different conditions during the high colonial and the post-colonial eras.

Indians during High-colonialism and Post-colonialism

From the late nineteenth century, a series of related factors shifted the weight of British public opinion against Indians collectively. The bloody 1857 conflict (among other anti-colonial struggles like the Jamaica insurrection of 1865), followed by their violent suppressions by British forces, made alleged biologically defined racial difference the basis for identity on all sides. Insurgents killed Europeans solely on the grounds of their physical appearance; Britons killed Indian males on the basis of their appearance and sex. Subsequently, many Britons interpreted Darwinian theories of evolution as giving a scientific validity to their evolving concepts of distinct races as inherited, immutable, and hierarchically ranked.[2] Indeed, many Britons came to regard colonialism as advantageous to all parties and the result of their own

[2] Metcalf, *Ideologies.*

moral superiority over other peoples of the world. The concept of essential racial 'difference' also seemed to many Britons to legitimize their suppression or rejection of bourgeois nationalist democratic movements by Asians, even when these movements were led by Anglicized but non-White lawyers like Mahatma Gandhi and Jawaharlal Nehru, who had been trained and qualified in England itself. Further, Britons largely succeeded in conflating ideas of 'progress' and 'modernity' with westernization.

During this high-colonial period, Indians of all classes travelled and settled in Britain in ever greater numbers, building on the experiences of their predecessors but contending with these changing conditions. Their lives and experiences have drawn the insightful attention of a growing number of scholars.[3] We can only suggest some of the salient contrasts and continuities with the hitherto less studied first 250 years of Indians in Britain that enrich our understanding of these later developments.

Under the British Raj (1858-1947), India's princes no longer faced systematic official opposition to their presence in Britain. The earlier diplomatic delegations we studied battled against the Company to reach and manoeuvre in Britain, usually protesting adverse colonial policies including annexation of their states. In contrast, the British Raj ceased annexations, leaving a third of India indirectly controlled through approximately 550 'princes'. Further, the Raj encouraged these princes to personally submit themselves to their 'feudal suzerain', the British monarch. During the decades of negotiations leading up to Indian and Pakistani independence, the British tried to use the princes as a 'third force' against Hindu and Muslim nationalists, for example by inviting a delegation of them to the Round Table Conferences in London (1930-32). Thus, these later political roles of Indian royalty in Britain strongly contrast with the patterns we have seen earlier.

Yet, certain patterns persisted. We have seen that over the early nineteenth century, popular British respect for visiting Indian royalty was largely giving way to condescending perceptions of them as primarily providing oriental pageantry and spectacle to the British imperial capital.[4] Nonetheless, some princes revelled in Europe's sensual

---

[3] For example, Innes, *History*; Lahiri, *Indians*; and Visram, *Asians*.
[4] See Burton, 'Making'; Cannadine, *Ornamentalism*.

pleasures, empowered by their wealth, aristocratic status, and residual oriental exotic attractiveness. Princes continued to produce scandals and confrontations embarrassing to the British government; many resisted British controls overtly or covertly. Thus, the later lives in Britain of royalty like Duleep Singh and Ranjitsinhji (both as a putative prince and then as the Jam Saheb of Nawanagar) should be understood in the larger historical context, which reveals both significant contrasts and continuities with their predecessors.[5]

Indian middle-class men and women increasingly went to Britain for education, advancement, pleasure, or justice. They generally brought with them far deeper preconceptions and knowledge about Britain than had their predecessors. The British Raj deliberately sought to instil among educated Indians respect and appreciation for an idealized Britain. As Gauri Viswanathan demonstrates, the official curriculum in India stressed English literature as a way to indoctrinate Indian students.[6] Missionaries also proselytized a highly selective model of Christianity. Further, the accumulated travel accounts by prior Indian visitors purveyed different information and knowledge that also shaped the expectations of those who came after.[7] Thus, as Partha Chatterjee explains, a late-nineteenth-century visitor knew what he would find: He 'would have no doubt that what he was experiencing, and what he would need to convey to his countrymen back home, was a moral and civilisational essence, expressed in such virtues of the modern English people as the spirit of independence, self-respect and discipline, their love for art, literature and sport, and above all, their cultivation of knowledge.'[8]

Nonetheless, compared with earlier travellers, later Indian visitors also usually better understood the structure and functioning of British culture, economics, law courts, politics, and society. They also had many more compatriots with whom to associate and share accumulated experiences. Consequently, many Indians discovered in Britain and articulated discrepancies between British pretensions to liberal

[5] See Satadru Sen, *Migrant Races*.

[6] Viswanathan, *Masks*.

[7] See Raychaudhuri, *Europe*; Mukhopadhyay, 'Writing'; and Simonti Sen, 'Travels' (Ph.D., 1995).

[8] Partha Chatterjee, 'Five Hundred Years'.

humanism and British practices of British colonialism and racism. We saw several early Indians return frustrated with the injustices they encountered in Britain. Many later Indian students became political leaders—including B.R. Ambedkar, S.C. Bose, Mohandas Gandhi, Aurobindo Ghose, M.A. Jinnah, Dadabhai Naoroji, Jawaharlal Nehru, and V.D. Savarkar. As has been extensively studied, all these men found their experiences in high colonial Britain helped them formulate their own political and cultural nationalisms. Additionally, Indian male and female social leaders—including Behramji Malabari, Saraswati Ramabhai, and Cornelia Sorabji—also engaged critically with British society, opposing British efforts to control their lives and impressions.[9] Nor did all Indians respond the same way. Some, including Sir Mancherjee Merwanjee Bhownaggree, M.P., remained staunch Tories.[10] Thus, the later lives of Indians in Britain and the later images of Britain that prevailed in India built on patterns established earlier, but were altered by high colonialism.

During this period, working-class Indian men and women expanded their communities in Britain, struggling to make places in its shifting economy and society. Indian seamen sailed British ships, but the dominance of steam power often reduced them to unskilled labour. Further, many faced exclusion by British fellow seamen as more rigid racial patterns spread through British society.[11]

Nonetheless, as we saw for east London's Oriental Quarter, Indian neighbourhoods and enclaves in Britain's port cities grew in cooperation and conflict with the surrounding communities. Further, during the first and second world wars, hundreds of thousands of Indian troops fought in the trenches of Europe. Like their predecessors, many of these Indian men found companionship and support with British women of their social class. As we saw, from the mid nineteenth century, the British male establishment disapprovingly noted as subversive, but failed to prevent, their extensive relations.[12]

[9] Burton, *At the Heart*; Viswanathan, *Outside*.

[10] See McLeod, 'Indian Tory'.

[11] Balachandran, 'Conflicts'; Benjamin, 'British and Indian Sailors'; Broeze, 'Underdevelopment'; Dunlop, 'Lascars'; Hood, *Blight*; Myers, 'Black Poor'; Prescott, 'Lascar Seamen'; Visram, *Asians*.

[12] Levine, 'Race'; Omissi, *Indian Voices*.

The substantial post-colonial movement to Britain by Indians from South Asia, Africa, and the Caribbean drew new and intensified attention from both supporters and opponents. Following the independence of India and Pakistan, many people from the former colonies regarded Britain as a place to prosper. Britain also appeared a refuge for Indians who had worked as intermediaries in Britain's other Asian and African colonies, but were then rejected by local nationalist movements. Especially from the 1960s, as Asians became Britons in ever larger numbers, their presence in British society became more highly politicized by organizations like the British National Party.

During the last four decades, scholars and commentators have begun more fully to consider the roles of Indians in Britain, and representations by and about them, especially concentrating on the post-1857 period. Writing in the post-colonial era, they have sometimes, however, projected today's issues and concepts back through time. Further, debates about race and ethnicity that convulsed late-twentieth-century Britain tended to dichotomize Black and White, colonized and colonizer, alien Asian other and native English self, victim and oppressor.

Yet, post-modern understandings of the contingency and fluidity of all cultural categories and social roles complicate such dichotomous characterizations. Indeed, recent fiction by Indian travellers and settlers and their descendants—including Dhondy, Kureishi, and Rushdie—portrays Britain as filled with a variety of people with shifting, unstable, and multiple identities. These authors and fictional characters engage in complex social interactions, living among a range of people with diverse ethnic, class, and gender characteristics.[13] Our historical evidence suggests that such a contingency of categories prevailed during the pre-colonial and early-colonial periods as well. Thus, while Britain from the late nineteenth to the late twentieth centuries exhibited starker racial and other cultural distinctions, these mainly developed with the transition to high colonialism, becoming more fluid again in the post-colonial world. Today's 'multi-cultural Britain' thus reflects centuries of change, beginning with the first 250 years of counterflows discussed in this book.

[13] Dhondy, *Bombay*; Kureishi, *Buddha* and *London Kills Me*; Rushdie, *Satanic*.

Bibliography

PUBLISHED BOOKS AND ARTICLES CITED

Abbott, James, *Narrative of a Journey from Heraut to Khiva, Moscow, and St Petersburgh*, 2 vols (London: William H. Allen, 1843).

'Abdulhaq, *Marhum Dilli Kalij* (Dehli: Anjuman Taraqqi-yi Urdu, Hind, 1945).

Abu Talib Khan, Mirza, *Masir Talibi fi Bilad Afranji*, reprint, ed. Hosein Khadive-Jam (Tehran: Hosein Khadive-Jam, 1983); ed. Mirza Husain Ali and Mir Qudrat Ali (Calcutta: Fort William College, 1812).

Abu-Lughod, Ibrahim, *Arab Rediscovery of Europe: A Study in Cultural Encounters* (Princeton: Princeton University Press, 1963).

Abu-Lughod, Janet, *Before European Hegemony: The World System A.D. 1250–1350* (New York: Oxford University Press, 1989).

Adam, William, *Slavery in India* (Finsbury: J. Haddon, 1840).

Aitchison, C.U., *Collection of Treaties, Engagements, and Sanads*, 3rd ed. (Calcutta: Superintendent of Government Printing, 1892).

Alam, Muzaffar and Seema Alavi, eds, *A European Experience of the Mughal Orient: The I'jaz-i Arsalani (Persian Letters 1773–1779) of Antoine-Louis Henri Polier* (New Delhi: Oxford University Press, 2001).

Ali, M. Athar, *Apparatus of Empire: Awards of Ranks, Offices, and Titles to the Mughal Nobility, 1574–1658* (Delhi: Oxford University Press, 1985).

Ali, Mir Shahamat, *Notes and Opinions of a Native on the Present State of India and the Feelings of Its People* (Ryde, Isle of Wight: George Butler, 1848).

———, *Picturesque Sketches in India; with Notices of the Adjacent Countries of Sindh, Afghanistan, Multan, and the West of India* [also titled *History of Bahawalpur*] (London: J. Madden, 1848).

———, *Sikhs and Afghans, in Connexion with India and Persia, Immediately Before and After the Death of Ranjeet Singh* (London: J. Murray, 1847).

Ali, Mrs Meer Hassan, *Observations on the Mussulmauns of India*, 2 vols (London: Parbury, Allen, 1832).

Ali, Syed Ameer, *Memoirs and Writings* (Lahore: People's Publishing House, 1968).

Ali Morad, Ameer, *Case of Meer Ali Morad Khan, Lately the Sovereign of the State of Khyrpoor, in Upper Scinde* (London: John Robert Taylor, 1855).

———, *Petition of His Highness Ameer Ali Morad Khan Talpoor of Khyrpoor, of Upper Scinde, in India as Presented in Parliament 29 June 1856* (London: Waterlow and Sons, 1856).

Allen, William, *Life of William Allen, with a Selection from His Correspondence*, 2 vols (London: Charles Gilpin, 1846).

Al-Najjar, Mustaffa A., Abdul Amir M. Amin, and Abdul Waheed Khan, eds, *Bussorah Diaries*, 2 vols (Basrah: University of Basrah, 1980).

Andrews, C.F., *Zaka Ullah of Delhi* (Cambridge: W. Heffer, 1929).

Anonymous, *Biographical Sketch and Portrait of George Thompson* (Calcutta: J. A. Gibbons, 1843).

———, *Historical Description of the Tower of London* (London: Francis Power, 1792).

———, *Life and Adventures of James Lovewell* (Calcutta: India Gazette Press, 1829).

———, 'Nana Sahib', *Chambers Journal of Popular Literature*, series 3, 9, 222 (3/4/1858): 223–4.

———, *Raja of Sattara* (London: Tyler and Reed, 1848).

———, *Short Address to Young Men of the Several Orthodox Denominations of Christians* (London: W. Harris, 1814).

———, *Short Statement Relative to the Presents Transmitted to England in 1834 by the King of Oude* (London: R. Clay, 1837).

———, *Treaties, Etc. between the Nawabs of the Carnatic and the Hon. East India Company, and also a Letter from His Late Majesty King George III to Nawaub Walajau* (London: James Madden, 1856).

Ackbar, Mirza Ali, *Reply to Attacks upon his Character Made by H. M. Frere, Esq., of the Bombay Civil Service, Without Proof or Inquiry* (London: I.R. Taylor, 1858).

Archer, Mildred, *India and British Portraiture 1770–1825* (London: Sotheby, Parke, Bernet, 1979).

Arnold, David, 'European Orphans and Vagrants in India in the Nineteenth Century', *Journal of Imperial and Commonwealth History* 7 (1979): 104–27.

Ashley-Brown, W., *On the Bombay Coast and Deccan* (London: Society for Promoting Christian Knowledge, 1937).

Ashton, S.R., *British Policy Towards the Indian States* (London: School of Oriental and African Studies, 1982).

Aslanyan, M.M., 'Hovsep Emine ev Angliats'i Arevelaget Uilyam Jonse [Joseph Emin and the English Orientalist William Jones]', *Patma-Banasirakan Handes. Istoriko-Filologicheskii Zhurnal* 4 (1987): 73–81.

As-Saffar, Muhammad, *Disorienting Encounters: Travels of a Moroccan Scholar in France in 1845–1846*, ed. Susan Gilson Miller (Berkeley: University of California Press, 1991).

Bacon, Thomas, *First Impressions and Studies from Nature in Hindostan*, 2 vols (London: W.H. Allen, 1837).

Balachandran, G., 'Circulation through Seafaring: Indian Seamen, 1890–1945', in Claude Markovits, Jacques Pouchepadass, and Sanjay Subrahmanyam, eds, *Society and Circulation: Mobile People and Itinerant Cultures in South Asia, 1750–1950* (New Delhi: Permanent Black, 2003), pp. 89–130.

———, 'Conflicts in International Maritime Labour Markets: British and Indian Seamen, Employers and the State, 1890–1939', *Indian Economic and Social History Review*, 39, 1 (2002): 71–100.

———, 'Searching for the Sardar: The State, Pre-capitalist Institutions, and Human Agency in the Maritime Labour Market, Calcutta, 1880–1935', in Burton Stein and Sanjay Subrahmanyam, eds, *Institutions and Economic Change in South Asia* (Delhi: Oxford University Press, 1996): 206–36.

Baladouni, Vahe and Margaret Makepeace, *Armenian Merchants, Transactions of the American Philosophical Society* 88, 5 (1998).

Baldwin, Marjorie, *Story of the Forest* 2nd ed. (Colgate: St Savior's Church, 1985).

Ballantyne, Tony, *Orientalism and Race: Aryanism in the British Empire* (Houndmills: Palgrave, 2002).

Banaji, D. R., *Slavery in British India* (Bombay: D.B. Taraporvala, 1933).

Banerjee, Brajendra Nath, *Rajah Rammohun Roy's Mission to England* (Calcutta: N.M. Raychowdhury, 1926).

Bapojee, Rungo, *Annexation of Sattara* (London: G. Norman, 1849).

———, *Letter to the Right Hon. J. C. Herries* (London: G. Norman, 1852).

———, *Letter to the Right Honourable Sir John Cam Hobhouse* (London: the Author, 1848).

———, *Rajah of Sattara* (London: G. Norman, 1852).

———, *Statement . . . at a Great Meeting in the Hanover Square Rooms [of the Literary Association], Wednesday, December 2, 1846* (London: the Author, 1846).

Barber, Jill, *Celebrating the Black Presence*, vol. 2, *Hidden Lives* (Westminster: City of Westminster Archives Centre, 2000).

Barendse, R. J., *Arabian Seas, 1640–1700* (Leiden: Leiden University, 1998).

Barker, Anthony J., *African Link: British Attitudes to the Negro* (London: Frank Cass, 1978).

Barnett, Richard, *North India between Empires: Awadh, the Mughals, and the British, 1720–1801* (Berkeley: University of California Press, 1980).

Barron, Arthur and Alfred Austin, *Report of Cases of Controverted Elections* (London: S. Sweet, 1844).

Basham, A. L., 'Notes on Seafaring in Ancient India', in A.L. Basham, ed., *Studies in Indian History and Culture* (Calcutta: Sambodhi Publications, 1964): 162–6.

Basu, Baman Das, *Story of Satara*, ed. Ramananda Chatterjee (Calcutta: Modern Review Office, 1922).

Batten, Charles, *Pleasurable Instruction: Form and Convention in Eighteen-century Travel Literature* (Berkeley: University of California Press, 1978).

Bayly, C.A., *Empire and Information: Intelligence Gathering and Social Communication in India, 1780–1870* (Cambridge: Cambridge University Press, 1996).

———, *Imperial Meridian: The British Empire and the World, 1780–1830* (New York: Longman, 1989).

———, *Origins of Nationality: Patriotism and Ethical Government in the Making of Modern India* (Delhi: Oxford University Press, 1998).

———, *Raj: India and the British, 1600–1947* (London: National Portrait Gallery, 1990).

Beaconsfield and District Historical Society, *Beaconsfield Parish Register* (Beaconsfield: Beaconsfield and District Historical Society, 1937).

Bell, Evans, *Annexation of the Punjaub and the Maharajah Duleep Singh* (Ludhiana: Lyall Book Depot, 1969).

Bellot, H. Hale, *University College London, 1826–1926* (London: University of London Press, 1929).

Benjamin, N., 'British and Indian Sailors', in P.M. Joshi and M.A. Nayeem, eds, *Studies in the Foreign Relations of India* (Hyderabad: Andhra Pradesh State Archives, 1975): 485–96.

Bennett, Edward, *Tower Menagerie* (London: Robert Jennings, 1829).

Bevan, Vaughan, *Development of British Immigration Law* (London: Croom Helm, 1986).

Bhabha, Homi, *Location of Culture* (New York: Routledge, 1994).

Bird, Robert Wilberforce, *Spoliation of Oudh* (London: W.S. Johnson, 1857).

Birdwood, George and William Foster, *Register of Letters &c. of the Governour and Company of Merchants of London Trading into the East Indies, 1600–16* (London: Bernard Quaritch, 1893).

Bland, Humphrey, *Treatise of Military Discipline* (London: S. Buckley, 1727).

de Boigne, Charlotte, *Memoirs*, ed. Sylvia de Morsier-Kotthaus (London: Museum Press, 1956).

Bolt, Christine, *Victorian Attitudes to Race* (London: Routledge and Kegan Paul 1971).

Bolts, William, *Considerations on Indian Affairs* (London: J. Almon, 1772, 1775).

Boot, H.M., 'Real Incomes of the British Middle Class, 1760–1850', *Economic History Review*, 52, 4 (1999): 638–68.

Bowen, H.V., *Revenue and Reform: The Indian Problem in British Politics, 1757–1773* (Cambridge: Cambridge University Press, 1991).

Boye, Jerome, ed., *L'Extraordinaire Aventure de Benoit de Boigne aux Indes* (Paris: Echanges Culturels et Actions de Development, 1996).

Boyle, M., *Court Guide* (London: Saunders and Otley, 1800–).

Braid, William David, *Statement of the East India Company's Conduct towards the Carnatic Stipendiaries* (London: T. Scott, 1853).

Braidwood, Stephen J., *Black Poor and White Philanthropists: London's Blacks and the Foundation of the Sierra Leone Settlement, 1786–1791* (Liverpool: Liverpool University Press, 1994).

Brigg, William, *Register Book of the Parish of St Nicholas Acons, London* (Leeds: Walker and Laycock, 1890).

British and Foreign Anti-Slavery Society, *Slavery and the Slave Trade in British India* (London: T. Ward, 1841).

Broeze, Frank, 'Underdevelopment and Dependence', *Modern Asian Studies* 18, 3 (1984): 429–57.

Broughton, Lord (John Cam Hobhouse), *Recollections of a Long Life*, 6 vols, ed. Lady Dorchester (London: John Murray, 1909–11).

Brown, F.H., 'Indian Students in Britain', *Edinburgh Review*, 217, 443 (January 1913): 138–56.

Buckler, F.W., *Legitimacy and Symbols: The South Asian Writings of F.W. Buckler*, ed. M.N. Pearson (Ann Arbor: University of Michigan, 1985).

Burke, Edmund, *Correspondence*, 10 vols, ed. Thomas W. Copeland (Cambridge: Cambridge University Press, 1958–78).

Burleigh, Charles, *Reception of George Thompson in Great Britain* (Boston: Isaac Knapp, 1836).

Burnes, Alexander, *Travels into Bokhara*, 3 vols (London: John Murray, 1839).

Burton, Antoinette, *At the Heart of the Empire: Indians and the Colonial Encounter in Late-Victorian Britain* (Berkeley: University of California Press, 1998).

———, 'House/Daughter/Nation: Interiority, Architecture, and Historical Imagination in Janaki Majumdar's "Family History" ', *Journal of Asian Studies*, 56, 4 (November 1997): 921–46.

————, 'Making a Spectacle of Empire: Indian Travellers in Fin-de-Siecle London', *History Workshop*, 42 (Fall 1996): 126–46.

Cannadine, David, *Ornamentalism: How the British Saw Their Empire* (New York: Oxford University Press, 2001).

Carlyle, Thomas, *Love Letters of Thomas Carlyle and Jane Welsh*, 2 vols, ed. Alexander Carlyle (London, John Lane, 1909).

————, *Reminiscences*, ed. James Anthony Froude (New York: Harper and Brothers, 1881).

Carlyle, Thomas and Jane, *Collected Letters*, 26 vols, ed. Charles Richard Sanders *et al.* (Durham: Duke University Press, 1970–93).

Carpenter, Mary, *Last Days in England of the Rajah Rammohun Roy* (London: Trubner, 1866).

Chancellor, Valerie, *Political Life of Joseph Hume* (London: the Author, 1986).

Chanda, Ramaprasad and Jatindra Kumar Majumdar, eds, *Selections from Official Letters and Documents Relating to the Life of Raja Rammohun Roy* (Calcutta: Calcutta Oriental Book Agency, 1938).

Chatterjee, Indrani, *Gender, Slavery, and Law in Colonial India* (New Delhi: Oxford University Press, 1999).

Chatterjee, Kumkum, *Merchants, Politics, and Society in Early Modern India: Bihar, 1733–1820* (Leiden: E.J. Brill, 1996).

Chatterjee, Partha, 'Five Hundred Years of Fear and Love', *Economic and Political Weekly*, 33, 22 (30 May–5 June 1998): 1330–6.

Chattopadhyay, Amal Kumar, *Slavery in India* (Calcutta: Nagarjun Press, 1960).

Chaudhuri, K.N., *English East India Company: The Study of an Early Joint-stock Company, 1600–1640* (London: Frank Cass, 1965).

————, *Trade and Civilisation in the Indian Ocean: An Economic History from the Rise of Islam to 1750* (Cambridge: Cambridge University Press, 1985).

Choksey, R.D., *Raja Pratapsinh of Sattara* (Poona: Bharata Itihasa Samshodhaka Mandala, 1970).

Chopra, H.L., *Life of Pandit Mohan Lal* (Delhi: the Author, 1979).

Chuckerbutty, S. Goodeve, 'Present State of the Medical Profession in Bengal', *British Medical Journal* (23, 30 July 1864): 86–8, 109–12.

Clutton, Sir George, 'Cheetah and the Stag', *Burlington Magazine*, 112 (1970): 539–40.

Cobbett, William, *Parliamentary History of England*, 36 vols (London: Hansard, 1806–20).

Cohn, Bernard S., *Colonialism and Its Forms of Knowledge: The British in India* (Princeton: Princeton University Press, 1996).

Cole, Juan, 'Invisible Occidentalism', *Iranian Studies,* 25, 3–4 (1992): 3–16.

Collet, Sophia Dobson, *Life and Letters of Raja Rammohun Roy* (London: Harold Collet, 1900).

Colley, Linda, *Britons: Forging the Nation, 1707–1837* (New Haven: Yale University Press, 1992).

Compton, Herbert, *Particular Account of the European Military Adventurers in India, from 1784 to 1803* (London: T. Fisher Unwin, 1893).

Conner, Patrick, *George Chinnery, 1774–1852: Artist of India and the China Coast* (Woodbridge, Suffolk: Antique Collector's Club, 1993).

Copland, Ian, *British Raj and the Indian Princes: Paramountcy in Western India, 1857–1930* (Bombay: Orient Longman, 1982).

———, *Princes of India in the Endgame of Empire, 1917–1947* (Cambridge: Cambridge University Press, 1997).

Cotton, Sir Evan, 'Begum in Sussex', *Bengal Past and Present,* 46 (1933): 91–94.

———, *Journals of Archibald Swinton* (Calcutta: Government of India Press, 1926).

Cotton, Stapleton (Viscount Combermere), *Memoirs and Correspondence,* 2 vols, ed. Mary Woolley Gibbings Cotton (London: Hurst and Blackett, 1866).

Cowley, Robert, *Hogarth's Marriage a-la-mode* (Ithaca: Cornell University Press, 1983).

Cunningham, Allan, *Life of Sir David Wilkie: With His Journals, Tours, and Critical Remarks on Works of Art; and a Selection from His Correspondence,* 3 vols (London: John Murray, 1843).

Cursetjee, Ardaseer, *Diary of an Overland Journey from Bombay to England and of a Year's Residence in Great Britain* (London: Henington and Galabin, 1840).

Dabydeen, David, *Hogarth's Blacks: Images of Blacks in Eighteenth Century English Art* (Mundelstrup, Denmark: Dangaroo Press, 1985).

Dale, Steven F., *Indian Merchants and Eurasian Trade, 1600–1750* (Cambridge: Cambridge University Press, 1994).

Dalrymple, William, *White Mughals: Love and Betrayal in Eighteenth-century India* (London: HarperCollins, 2002).

Danvers, Frederick Charles, *Letters Received by the East India Company,* 6 vols (London: Sampson, Low, Marston, 1896–1902).

Darukhanawala, H.D., *Parsi Lustre on Indian Soil* (Bombay: G. Claridge, 1939).

Das, Harihar, 'Early Indian Visitors to England', *Calcutta Review* 3rd series, 13 (1924): 83–114.

Das, Sisir Kumar, *Sahibs and Munshis: An Account of the College of Fort William* (Calcutta: Orion, 1978).

Das Gupta, Ashin and M.N. Pearson, eds, *India and the Indian Ocean, 1500–1800* (Calcutta: Oxford University Press, 1987).

Dasgupta, B.N., *Rajah Rammohun Roy: The Last Phase* (New Delhi: Uppal, 1982).

Dass, Ishuree, *Brief Account of a Voyage to England and America by Ishuree Dass of Futtehgurh* (Allahabad: Presbyterian Mission Press, 1851).

Daunton, Martin and Rick Halpern, eds, *Empire and Others: British Encounters with Indigenous Peoples, 1600–1850* (London: University College, London Press, 1999).

Davis, Rose Mary, *Good Lord Lyttelton: A Study in Eighteenth Century Politics and Culture* (Bethlehem, P.A.: Times Publishing Company, 1939).

de Tassy, Garcin, 'Karim Khan', *Revue de l'Orient et de l'Algérie et de colonies: bulletin et actes de la Société orientale* (Paris: Société orientale, 1865) 4. sér., t. l (1865): 105–41, 641–63.

————, *Rudimens de la langue hindoustani, à l'usage des élèves de l'École royale et spéciale des langues orientales vivantes* (Paris: Imprimerie royale, 1829).

Dhondy, Farrukh, *Bombay Duck* (London: Jonathan Cape, 1990).

Digby, Simon, 'Eighteenth Century Narrative' in Christopher Shackle, ed., *Urdu and Muslim South Asia: Studies in Honour of Ralph Russell* (London: School of Oriental and African Studies, 1989): 49–65.

Dirks, Nicholas B., *Castes of Mind: Colonialism and the Making of Modern India* (Princeton: Princeton University Press, and Delhi: Permanent Black 2001).

Dixon, Conrad, 'Lascars: The Forgotten Seamen', in Rosemary Ommer and Gerald Panting, eds, *Working Men Who Got Wet: Proceedings of the Fourth Conference of the Atlantic Canada Shipping Project, July 24–July 26, 1980* (Newfoundland: Memorial University, 1980): 265–81.

Duff, James Grant, *History of the Mahrattas*, 3 vols (London: Longmans, Rees, Orme, Brown, and Green, 1826).

Dunlop, Anne, 'Lascars and Labourers', *Scottish Labour History* 25 (1990): 40–57.

Dyce Sombre, David Ochterlony, *Dyce Sombre against Troup, Solaroli (Intervening) and Prinsep and the Hon. East India Company . . . In the Perogative Court of Canterbury* (London: Henry Hansard, n.d.).

————, *Humble Petition of David Ochterlony Dyce Sombre Addressed to the Lords Temporal, Spiritual and Commoners Assembled in Parliament* (Paris: the Author, 1850).

————, *In Lunacy: In the Matter of David Ochterlony Dyce Sombre, a Person Found to Be of Unsound Mind* (London: Hansard, 1851).

————, *Mr Dyce Sombre's Refutation of the Charge of Lunacy brought against Him in the Court of Chancery* (Paris: the Author, 1849).

East India College, *Directions for the Guidance of the Students of the East-India College* (Hertford: East India College, 1814).

————, *East India Company Debates at the India House: August 22nd, 23rd, and September 24th, 1845* (London: E. Wilson, 1845).

————, *Proceedings of a Special General Court of Proprietors . . . 12 and 13 February 1840* (London: John Wilson, 1840).

————, *Sattara papers*, 4 vols (London: J.L. Cox, 1841–3).

Eastwick, E.B., *Glance at Sind . . . Dry Leaves from Young Egypt* (London: J. Madden, 1849, 1851).

Eastwick, Robert, *Master Mariner: Being the Life and Adventures of Captain Robert William Eastwick*, ed. Herbert Compton (London: T. Fisher Unwin, 1891).

Elers, George, *Memoirs of George Elers: Captain in the 12th Regiment of Foot (1777–1842) . . .*, ed. Augustus Monson and George Leveson-Gower (London: W. Heinemann, 1903).

Emin, Joseph, *Hovsep Emini Keankn u Arkatsnere [Life and Adventures of Joseph Emin]* trans. H. Khashmanean (Peyrut: Tparan Mshak, 1958).

————, *Life and Adventures of Joseph Emin, An Armenian, Written in English by Himself* (London: the Author, 1792); 2nd edn, ed. A. Apcar (Calcutta: Asiatic Society of Bengal, 1918).

Equiano, Olaudah, *Interesting Narrative of the Life of Olaudah Equiano, or Gustavus Vassa, the African. Written by Himself* (Leeds: James Nichols, 1814).

Feilding, Cecilia, *Royalist Father and Roundhead Son: Being the Memoirs of the First and Second Earls of Denbigh, 1600–1675* (London: Methuen, 1915).

Ferrier, R.W., 'Armenians and the East India Company', *Economic History Review*, 26, 1 (1973): 38–62.

Fisher, Michael H., *The First Indian Author in English: Dean Mahomed (1759–1851) in India, Ireland, and England* (Delhi: Oxford University Press, 1996).

————, *Indirect Rule in India: Residents and the Residency System, 1764–1858*, 2nd ed. (Delhi: Oxford University Press, 1998).

————, 'Persian Professor in Britain: Mirza Muhammed Ibrahim at the East India Company's College, 1826–44', *Comparative Studies in South Asia, Africa and the Middle East*, 21, 1&2 (October 2001).

———, *The Politics of the British Annexation of India, 1757–1857* (New Delhi: Oxford University Press, 1997).

———, 'Representing "His" Women: Mirza Abu Talib Khan's 1801 "Vindication of the Liberties of Asiatic Women" ', *Indian Economic and Social History Review*, 37, 2 (2000): 215–37.

Foote, Samuel, *Nabob* (London: the Author, 1772).

Forbes, Duncan, *Hindustani Manual: Intended to Facilitate the Essential Attainments of Conversing with Fluency, and Composing with Accuracy, in the Most Useful of All Languages Spoken in Our Eastern Empire* (London: W.H. Allen, 1853).

Forbes, Thomas Roger, *Chronicle from Aldgate: Life and Death in Shakespeare's London* (New Haven: Yale University Press, 1971).

Forbes-Mitchell, William, *Reminiscences of the Great Mutiny, 1857–59: Including the Relief, Siege, and Capture of Lucknow, and the Campaigns in Rohilcund and Oude* (London: Macmillan, 1894).

Forrest, George W., ed., *Selections from the Letters . . . in the Bombay Secretariat* (Maratha Series), vol. 1, part 2 (Bombay: Government Central Press, 1885).

Foster, William, *English Factories in India*, 13 vols (Oxford: Clarendon Press, 1906–27).

Foster, William, 'India Board', *Transactions of the Royal Historical Society*, series 3, 11 (1917): 79–80.

Fox, Caroline, *Memories of Old Friends: Being Extracts from the Journals and Letters of Caroline Fox, of Penjerrick, Cornwall, from 1835 to 1871*, ed. Horace N. Pym. 2nd ed. (Philadelphia; Lippincott, 1882).

Frank, Katherine, *Lucie Duff Gordon* (London: Hamish Hamilton, 1994).

Fryer, Peter, *Staying Power: The History of Black People in Britain* (London: Pluto, 1984).

Frykenberg, R.E., ed., *Delhi through the Ages: Essays in Urban History, Culture, and Society* (Delhi: Oxford University Press, 1986).

Furber, Holden, *Rival Empires of Trade in the Orient, 1600–1800* (Minneapolis: University of Minnesota, 1976).

Gash, Norman, *Lord Liverpool: The Life and Political Career of Robert Banks Jenkinson, Second Earl of Liverpool, 1770–1828* (Cambridge: Harvard University Press, 1984).

George III, King, *Correspondence of King George the Third, from 1760 to December 1783, Printed from the Original Papers in the Royal Archives at Windsor Castle*, 6 vols, ed. Sir John Fortescue (London: Macmillan, 1927–8).

Gerzina, Gretchen, *Black London: Life Before Emancipation* (New Brunswick: Rutgers University Press, 1995).

Ghosh, Durba, 'Changing Names and Converted Subjects', *Gender and History* (forthcoming).

Gilchrist, John, *Dictionary, English and Hindoostanee*, 2 vols (Calcutta: Stuart and Cooper, 1787–90).

Gilroy, Paul, *'There Ain't No Black in the Union Jack': The Cultural Politics of Race and Nation* (London: Hutchinson, 1987).

Gopal, Surendra, 'Armenian Traders in India in the 17th Century', in Amalendu Guha, ed., *Central Asia: Movement of Peoples and Ideas from Times Prehistoric to Modern* (New Delhi: Vikas, 1970): 200–13.

Gordon, Andrew, *Our India Mission: A Thirty Years' History of the Indian Mission of the United Presbyterian Church of North America* (Philadelphia: the Author, 1886).

Gordon, Stuart, *Marathas, 1600–1818* (Cambridge: Cambridge University Press, 1993).

Government of India, *Gazetteer of the Bombay Presidency* (Bombay: Government Central Press, 1877).

Grant, Colesworthy, *Sketches of Oriental Heads* (Calcutta: Thacker, 1850?).

Great Britain, Public Record Office, *Calendar of State Papers, Colonial Series*, 27 vols, ed. W. Noel Sainsbury *et al.* (London: Public Record Office, 1860–1926).

Gundara, Jagdish S. and Ian Duffield, eds, *Essays on the History of Blacks in Britain: From Roman Times to the Mid-Twentieth Century* (Aldershot: Avebury, 1992).

Gupta, Hari Ram, *Life and Work of Mohan Lal Kashmiri* (Lahore: Minerva, 1943).

Gupta, Narayani, ed., *Delhi between Two Empires, 1803–1931: Society, Government and Urban Growth* (Delhi: Oxford University Press, 1981).

Guptara, Prabhu, *Black British Literature: An Annotated Bibliography* (Sidney: Dangaroo Press, 1986).

H. J., *King of Oude, His Brother, and Attendants* (London: Ackermann, c. 1838).

Haldar, Rakhal Das, *English Diary of an Indian Student, 1861–62* (Dacca: Asutosh Library, 1903).

Hallward, N.L., *William Bolts: A Dutch Adventurer under John Company* (Cambridge: Cambridge University Press, 1920).

Hansard, T.C., ed., *Parliamentary Debates* (London: Hansard, 1812–).

Bibliography

Harrison, Mark, *Climates and Constitutions: Health, Race, Environment and British Imperialism in India, 1600–1850* (Delhi: Oxford University Press, 1999).

Hasan, Mushirul, 'Resistance and Acquiescence in North India: Muslim Responses to the West', in Mushirul Hasan and Narayani Gupta, eds, *India's Colonial Encounter: Essays in Memory of Eric Stokes* (Delhi: Manohar, 1993): 39–63.

Havelock, Henry, *Narrative of the War in Afghanistan in 1838–39*, 2 vols (London: Henry Colburn, 1840).

Hawes, Christopher J., *Poor Relations: The Making of a Eurasian Community in British India 1773–1833* (London: Curzon, 1996).

Hawkins, William, *Hawkins' Voyages during the Reigns of Henry VIII, Queen Elizabeth, and James I*, ed. Clements R. Markham (New York: B. Franklin, 1970).

Hayward, Arthur L., *Lives of the Most Remarkable Criminals* (London: George Routledge, 1927 reprint).

Heber, Reginald, *Narrative of a Journey through the Upper Provinces of India, from Calcutta to Bombay, 1824–1825*, 2nd edn (London: John Murray, 1827).

Hedges, William, *Diary of William Hedges, Esq. (Afterwards Sir William Hedges) During His Agency in Bengal as well as on His Voyage Out and Return Overland 1681–1687)*, 2 vols, ed. Henry Yule (London: Hakluyt Society, 1888).

Heiton, John, *Castes of Edinburgh* (Edinburgh: John Menzies, 1860).

Heleniak, Kathryn Moore, *William Mulready* (New Haven: Yale University Press, 1980).

Henriques, Fernando, *Children of Conflict: A Study of Interracial Sex and Marriage* (New York: Dutton, 1975).

Hewlett, Maurice, 'Armenian Knight's Entertainments', *London Mercury* 6 (1922): 69–76.

Hickey, William, *Memoirs of William Hickey*, 4 vols, ed. Alfred Spencer, 3rd edn (London: Hurst and Blackett, 1919–25).

Hinnells, John R., *Zoroastrians in Britain: The Ratnabai Katrak Lectures, University of Oxford 1985* (Oxford: Clarendon Press, 1996).

Hodson, V.P.C., *List of the Officers of the Bengal Army 1758–1834*, 4 vols (London: Constable and Phillimore, 1927–47).

Hogarth, William, *Complete Works*, 2 vols (London: London Printing, n.d.).

Holder, Heidi J., 'Melodrama, Realism and Empire on the British Stage', in J. S. Bratton *et al.* eds. *Acts of Supremacy: The British Empire and the Stage, 1790–1930* (Manchester: Manchester University Press, 1991): 29–32.

Holzman, James Mayer, *Nabobs in England: A Study of the Returned Anglo-Indian, 1760–1785* (New York: the Author, 1926).

Hood, W.H., *Blight of Insubordination: The Lascar Question, and Rights and Wrongs of the British Shipmaster, including the Merchantile Marine Committee Report* (London: Spottiswoode, 1903).

Huch, Ronald K. and Paul R. Ziegler, *Joseph Hume, Memoirs of the American Philosophical Society*, 163 (Philadelphia: American Philosophical Society, 1985).

Hume, Joseph, *Rajah of Sattara* (London: G. Woodfall and Son, 1845).

Hunter, William, *Essay on the Diseases Incident to Indian Seamen, or Lascars* (Calcutta: Company's Press, 1804).

Hyam, Ronald, *Empire and Sexuality: The British Experience* (Manchester: Manchester University Press, 1990).

Imperial Record Department, *Calendar of Persian Correspondence*, 7 vols (Calcutta: Superintendent of Government Printing, 1911) [*CPC*].

Impey, Elijah B., *Memoirs of Sir Elijah Impey* (London: Simpkin, Marshall, 1846).

Inden, Ronald B., *Imagining India* (Bloomington: Indiana University Press, 2001).

Innes, C.L., *A History of Black and Asian Writing in Britain, 1700–2000* (Cambridge: Cambridge University Press, 2002).

Ioannisian, A.R., *Iosif Emin* (Erevan: Izd-Vo Armenianskoi SSR, 1989).

I'tisam al-Daula, *Shigurf Namah-i Velaet*, ed. James Edward Alexander and Munshi Shumsher Khan (London: Parbury, Allen, 1827).

———, *Wonders of Vilayet: Being the Memoir, Originally in Persian, of a Visit to France and Britain*, trans. Kaiser Haq (Leeds: Peepal Tree Press, 2001).

J. Paul Getty Museum, *In Focus: Hill and Adamson* (Los Angles: J. Paul Getty Museum, 1999).

Jacquemont, Victor, *Letters from India: Describing a Journey in the British Dominions of India*, 2 vols (Karachi: Oxford University Press, 1979).

Jafur Ali, Meer, *Case of Meer Jafur Alee, Khan Bahadoor, of Surat* (London: John Robert Taylor, 1855).

Jeffrey, Robin, ed., *People, Princes and Paramount State: Society and Politics in the Indian Princely States* (Delhi: Oxford University Press, 1978).

Jones, Sir William, *Memoirs of the Life, Writings, and Correspondence of Sir William Jones*, ed. John Shore Teignmouth (London: John Hatchard, 1804).

Jones Brydges, Sir Harford, *Case of the Rajah of Sattara* (London: John Wilson, 1843).

Jung, Hydur, *Petition of Hydur Jung Bahadoor to the Honorable Commons of Great Britain* (London: the Author, 1853).

Kabir, Humayun, *Mirza Abu Talib Khan* (Patna: Patna University, 1961).

Kamps, Ivo and Jyotsna G. Singh, *Travel Knowledge: European 'Discoveries' in the Early Modern Period* (New York: Palgrave, 2001).

Kapur, Narinder, *Irish Raj: Illustrated Stories about Irish in India and Indians in Ireland* (Antrim: Greystone, 1997).

Kaye, J.W., *History of the War in Afghanistan*, 3 vols (London: Richard Bentley, 1857).

———, *History of the Sepoy War in India, 1857–1858*, 3 vols, 9th edn (London: Longmans, Green, 1896).

Keene, Henry George, *Hindustan under Free Lances, 1770–1820* (London: Brown, Langham, 1907).

———, *Servant of 'John Company': Being the Recollections of an Indian Official* (London: W. Thacker, 1897).

Kelly, Hugh, *Romance of an Hour: A Comedy of Two Acts* (London: the Author, 1774).

Kesavan, B.S., *History of Printing and Publishing in India* (New Delhi: National Book Trust, 1985).

Khan, Ali Ackbar, *Reply to Attacks upon his Character Made by H.M. Frere, Esq., of the Bombay Civil Service, Without Proof or Inquiry* (London: I.R. Taylor, 1858).

Khan, Gulfishan, *Indian Muslim Perceptions of the West during the Eighteenth Century* (Karachi: Oxford University Press, 1998).

Khan, Karim, *Siyahatnama*, ed. 'Ibadat Barelvi (Lahore: Majlis-i Isha'at-i Makhtutat, Idarah-yi Adab o Tanqid, 1982 reprint).

Khan, Yusuf, *Ajaibat-i Farang*, ed. Joseph Johannes (Lucknow: Joseph Johannes, 1873); (Lucknow: Mission Printing Press and Nevil Kishore, 1898); (Lahore: Makkah Books, 1983).

Khan, Yusuf, *Tarikh-i Yusufi, Travels in Europe by Yoosoof Khan Kummulposh* [title page English, rest of book Urdu] ed. Pandit Dharm Narayan (Delhi: al-Alum Madrasa, 1847).

Kling, Blair B., *Partner in Empire: Dwarkanath Tagore and the Age of Enterprise in Eastern India* (Calcutta: Firma KLM, 1976).

Kopf, David, *British Orientalism and the Bengal Renaissance* (Berkeley: University of California Press, 1969).

Kripalani, Krishna, *Dwarkanath Tagore: A Forgotten Pioneer: A Life* (New Delhi: National Book Trust, 1980).

Kuiters, Willem G.J., 'Law and Empire', *Journal of Imperial and Commonwealth History*, 28, 2 (May 2000): 1–22.

Kulkarni, Sumitra, *Sattara Raj* (New Delhi: Mittal Publications, 1995).

Kureishi, Hanif, *The Buddha of Suburbia* (New York: Viking, 1990).

——, *London Kills Me* (London: Faber and Faber, 1991).

Lahiri, Shompa, *Indians in Britain: Anglo-Indian Encounters, Race and Identity, 1880-1930* (London: Frank Cass, 2000).

Lal, Munshi Mohan, 'Account of Kala Bagh on the Right Bank of the Indus' and 'Brief Account of the Origin of the Daud Putras . . .' *Journal of the Asiatic Society*, series 3, 7 (January 1838): 25–33.

——, 'Brief Account of Masu'd, Known by the Name of Farid Shakarganj or Shakarbar' and 'Description of Uch-Shari'f', *Journal of the Asiatic Society*, series 3, 5 (October 1836): 635–8, 796–8.

——, 'Letter to Editor', 'Brief Description of Herat', 'Further Information Regarding the Siah Posh Trive, or Reputed Descendants of the Macedonians', *Journal of the Asiatic Society* 3rd series 3, 3 (February 1834): 9–18, 76–9.

Lal, Mohan, *Life of Amir Dost Mohammed Khan of Kabul*, 2 vols (London: Longman, Brown, Green, and Longmans, 1846); (Karachi: Oxford University Press, 1978).

——, *Travel in the Punjab, Afganistan and Turkistan to Balk, Bokhara and Herat and a Visit to Great Britain and Germany* (Calcutta: the Author, 1834); (London: W.H. Allen, 1846); (Calcutta: K.P. Bagchi, 1977).

Lambert, Sheila, ed., *House of Commons, Sessional Papers of the Eighteenth Century*, 147 vols (Wilmington: Scholarly Resources, 1975).

Lambrick, H.T., *Sir Charles Napier and Sind* (Oxford: Clarendon Press, 1952).

Land, Isaac, 'Customs of the Sea: Flogging, Empire, and the 'True British Seaman' 1770 to 1870', *Interventions*, 3, 2 (July 2001), pp. 169–85.

Lang, John, *Wanderings in India* (London: Routledge, Warne, and Routledge, 1861).

Lawson, Philip, *East India Company* (New York: Longman, 1993).

Lawson, Philip and Jim Phillips, ' "Our Execrable Banditti": Perceptions of Nabobs in Mid-Eighteenth Century Britain', *Albion* 16, 3 (Fall 1984): 225–41.

Lelyveld, David, *Aligarh's First Generation* (Princeton: Princeton University Press, 1978).

Leslie, Charles Robert and Tom Taylor, *Life and Times of Sir Joshua Reynolds*, 2 vols (London: John Murray, 1865).

Levine, Philippa, 'Race, Sex, and Colonial Soldiery in World War I', *Journal of Women's History*, 9, 4 (Winter 1998): 104–30.

Lewis, Bernard Oxford, *Muslim Discovery of Europe* (London: Weidenfeld and Nicolson, 1982).

Lindborg, Ruth H., ' "Asiatic" and the Boundaries of Victorian Englishness', *Victorian Studies* 37, 3 (Spring 1994): 381–404.

Llewellyn-Jones, Rosie, *Engaging Scoundrels* (Delhi: Oxford University Press, 2000).

———, 'Indian Travellers in Nineteenth Century England', *Indo-British Review*, 18, 1 (1990): 137–41.

———, *A Very Ingenious Man: Claude Martin in Early Colonial India* (Delhi: Oxford University Press, 1992).

Lock, F.P., *Edmund Burke*, vol. 1 (Oxford: Clarendon Press, 1998).

Login, Lena Campbell, *Lady Login's Recollections*, ed. E. Dalhousie Login (London: Murray, 1917).

———, *Sir John Login and Duleep Singh* (London: W.H. Allen, 1890).

London Oriental Institution, *Annual Reports* (London: London Oriental Institution, 1819–).

Long, Edward, *History of Jamaica*, 3 vols (London: T. Lowndes, 1774).

Lorimer, Douglas A., *Colour, Class and the Victorians* (Leicester: Leicester University Press, 1978).

Louis, William Roger, ed., *Oxford History of the British Empire*, 5 vols (Oxford: Oxford University Press, 1998–9).

Lowe, Lisa, *Critical Terrains: French and British Orientalisms* (Ithaca: Cornell University Press, 1991).

Lucas, Samuel [Robert W. Bird], *Dacoitee in Excelsis; or the Spoilation of Oude by the East India Company* (London: Nassau Steam Press, 1857).

Lutfullah, *Autobiography of Lutfullah: A Mohamedan Gentleman . . .*, ed. Edward B. Eastwick and S.A.I. Tirmizi (London: Smith, Elder, 1857); (New Delhi: International Writer's Emporium, 1985, 1987 reprint).

Lutfullah, Syed, *Azimullah Khan Yusufzai: The Man Behind the War of Independence, 1857* (Karachi: Mohamedali Educational Society, 1970).

Mackenzie, John M., 'Empire and Metropolitan Cultures', in Andrew Porter, ed., *Nineteenth Century, Oxford History of the British Empire*, vol. 3 (Oxford: Oxford University Press, 1999): 270–93.

Magnus, Philip, *Edmund Burke: A Life* (London: John Murray, 1939).

Mahomet, Dean, *Travels of Dean Mahomet* (Cork: the Author, 1794).

Majumdar, Jatindra Kumar, *Raja Rammohun Roy and the Last Moghuls* (Calcutta: Art Press, 1939).

Malabari, B.M., *Indian Eye on English Life, or, Rambles of a Pilgrim Reformer* (Bombay: Apollo Printing Works, 1891).

Marshall, P.J., *East Indian Fortunes: The British in Bengal in the Eighteenth Century* (Oxford: Clarendon Press, 1976).

———, 'Edmund Burke and India', in Rudrangshu Mukherjee and Lakshmi Subramanian, eds, *Politics and Trade in the Indian Ocean: Essays in Honour of Ashin Das Gupta* (Delhi: Oxford University Press, 1998): 250–69.

———, 'English in Asia to 1700', in Nicholas Canny, ed., *Origins of Empire, Oxford History of the British Empire*, vol. 1 (Oxford: Oxford University Press, 1998): 264–85.

———, 'Indian Officials under the East India Company in Eighteenth-Century Bengal', *Bengal Past and Present* 84 (1965): 95–120.

Martin, Gregory, *Flemish School, circa 1600–circa 1900* (London: National Gallery, 1970).

Marx, Karl, 'East India Question', *New York Daily Tribune* (25/7/1853).

Matar, Nabil, *Islam in Britain, 1558–1685* (Cambridge: Cambridge University Press, 1998).

———, *Turks, Moors, and Englishmen in the Age of Discovery* (New York: Columbia University Press, 1999).

Matthews, C. M., *Haileybury Since Roman Times* (London: Butler and Tanner, 1959).

Mayhew, Henry, *London Labour and the London Poor*, 4 vols (London: Griffin, Bohn, and Company, 1861–2).

McLeod, John, *Sovereignty, Power, Control: Politics in the State of Western India, 1916–1947* (Leiden: Brill, 1999).

Metcalf, Thomas, *Aftermath of Revolt, circa 1600–circa 1900* (Princeton: Princeton University Press, 1964).

———, *Ideologies of the Raj* (Cambridge: Cambridge University Press, 1995).

Miles, H.A.D. and David Blayney Brown, *Sir David Wilkie of Scotland, 1785–1841* (Raleigh: North Carolina Museum of Art, 1987).

Minault, Gail, 'Qiran al-Sa'adain', in Jamal Malik, ed., *Perspectives of Mutual Encounters in South Asian History* (Leiden: Brill, 2000): 260–77.

Misra, Anand Swarup, *Nana Saheb Peshwa and the Fight for Freedom* (Lucknow: U.P. Government, 1961).

Mittra, Kissory Chand, *Memoir of Dwarkanath Tagore* (Calcutta: Thacker, 1870).

Mittra, Peary Chand, *Life of Colesworthy Grant* (Calcutta: Bose, 1881).

Montagu, Elizabeth, *Elizabeth Montagu, the Queen of the Bluestockings*, 2 vols, ed. Emily J. Climenson (London: John Murray, 1906).

Mukhopadhyay, Bhaskar, 'Writing Home, Writing Travel', *Comparative Studies in Society and History* 44, 2 (April 2002): 293–317.

Musseehood-Deen Khan Bahadur, Moulvee Mohummud, *Oude: Its Princes and Its Government Vindicated* (London: John Davy and Sons, 1857); reprinted as *British Aggression in Awadh*, ed. Safi Ahmed (Meerut: Meenakshi Prakashan, 1969).

Myers, Norma, 'Black Poor of London', *Immigrants and Minorities* 13, 2–3 (1994): 7–21.

————, *Reconstructing the Black Past: Blacks in Britain, c. 1780–1830* (London: Frank Cass, 1996).

Naoroji, Dadabhai, *Poverty and Un-British Rule in India* (London: S. Sonnenschein, 1901).

National Archives of India, *Fort William-India House Correspondence*, 17 vols (Delhi: National Archives of India, 1949–81).

Neill, Edward D., *Memoir of Rev. Patrick Copland* (New York: Charles Scribner, 1871).

Ng, Kwee Choo, *Chinese in London* (Oxford University Press, 1968).

Nicholson, W.N., *Statement of the Case of the Deposed Raja of Sattara* (London: G. Norman, 1845).

Norris, Charles, *Case of the Raja of Sattara* (London: Fisher, 1843).

Nowrojee, Jehangeer and Hirjeebhoy Merwanjee, *Journal of a Residence of Two Years and a Half in Great Britain* (London: William H. Allen, 1841).

Omissi, David, ed., *Indian Voices of the Great War: Soldiers' Letters, 1914–18* (New York: St Martin's Press, 1999).

Palmer, Sarah, *Politics, Shipping and the Repeal of the Navigation Laws* (Manchester: Manchester University Press, 1990).

Panayi, Panikos, *Immigration, Ethnicity and Racism in Britain: 1815–1945* (Manchester: Manchester University Press, 1994).

Parasnis, D.B., 'Original Correspondence between the English and the Marathas', *Indian Historical Record Commission, Proceedings*, 5 (1923): 91–9.

Parker, David, 'Chinese People in Britain', in Gregor Benton and Frank N. Pieke, eds, *Chinese in Europe* (New York: St Martin's, 1998): 67–95.

Peacock, Daniel J., *Lee Boo of Belau: A Prince in London* (Honolulu University of Hawaii Press, 1987).

Peggs, Reverend James, *Lascars' Cry to Britain* (London: the Author, 1844).

————, *Slavery in India*, 3rd edn (London: G. Wightman, 1840).

Pennant, Thomas, *Synopsis of Quadrupeds* (Chester: J. Monk, 1771).

Penny, Nicholas, *Reynolds* (London: Royal Academy, 1986).

Penny, Frank, *Church in Madras* (London: Smith, Elder, 1904).

Philips, C.H., *East India Company, 1784–1834* (Manchester: Manchester University Press, 1940).

Pissulencar, P. Panduranga, 'Some Unknown Dealings between Raghoba and the Portuguese', *Indian Historical Records Commission, Proceedings*, 11 (1928): 124–30.

Pointon, Marcia, *Mulready* (London: Victoria and Albert Museum, 1986).

Polier, Antoine Louis Henri, *Shah Alam II and His Court* (Calcutta: Asiatic Society, 1989).

Pratt, Mary Louise, *Imperial Eyes: Travel Writing and Transculturation* (London: Routledge, 1992).

Prescott, R.G.W., 'Lascar Seamen on the Clyde', in *Scotland and the Sea*, ed. T.C. Smout (Edinburgh: John Donald, 1992): 199–212.

Qadir, A.F.M. Abdul, 'Early Muslim Visitors to Europe from India', *Proceedings of the 6th All-India Oriental Conference* (1930): 83–96.

Rabi ibn Muhammad Ibrahim, Muhammad, *Ship of Sulaiman*, tr. John O'Kane (New York: Columbia University Press, 1972).

Ram, Malik, *Qadim Dilli Kalij* (Delhi: the Author, 1975).

Ramdin, Ron, *Making of the Black Working Class in Britain* (Aldershot: Gower, 1987).

———, *Reimagining Britain: 500 Years of Black and Asian History* (London: Pluto, 1999).

Ramusack, Barbara, *Princes of India in the Twilight of Empire: Dissolution of a Patron-client System, 1914–1939* (Columbus: Ohio State University Press, 1978).

Rawlinson, H.G., *British Beginnings in Western India, 1579–1657; An Account of the Early Days of the British Factory of Surat* (Oxford: Clarendon Press, 1920).

Raychaudhuri, Tapan, *Europe Reconsidered: Perceptions of the West in Nineteenth Century Bengal* (Delhi: Oxford University Press, 1988).

Reeves, Frank, *British Racial Discourse: A Study of British Political Discourse about Race and Race-related Matter* (New York: Cambridge University Press, 1983).

Rich, Paul B., *Race and Empire in British Politics*, 2nd edn (Cambridge: Cambridge University Press, 1990).

Rizvi, Saiyid Athar Abbas, *Socio-Intellectual History of the Isna 'Ashari Shi'is in India*, 2 vols (Delhi: Munshiram Manoharlal, 1986).

Roberts, Frederick Lord, *Forty One Years in India*, 2 vols (London: Richard Bentley, 1897).

———, *Letters Written during the Indian Mutiny* (London: Macmillan, 1924).

Robertson, Bruce Carlisle, *Raja Rammohan Ray: Father of Modern India* (Delhi: Oxford University Press, 1999).

Robinson, Mary, *Memoirs*, 2nd ed. (London: Cobden-Sanderson, 1930).

——, *Poetical Works*, 3 vols (London: R. Phillips, 1806).

Roy, Rammohun, *English Works*, ed. Jogendra Ghose (New Delhi: Cosmo, 1906).

——, *Exposition of the Practical Operation of the Judicial and Revenue Systems of India* (London: Smith Elder, 1832).

——, *Precepts of Jesus* (New York: B. Bates, 1825).

——, *Treaty with the King of Delhi* (London: John Nichols, 1831).

Roy, S.N., 'Rajaram, the Adopted Son of Rammohun Roy', *Modern Review* (Calcutta) 60, 4 (October 1936): 446.

Royal Academy, *Catalogue of the Royal Academy Exhibitions* (London: Royal Academy, 1819).

Rushdie, Salman, *Satanic Verses* (New York: Viking, 1989).

Russell, Constance, *Rose Goddess and Other Sketches of Mystery and Romance* (London: Longmans, Green, 1910).

Russell, William Howard, *My Diary in India, in the Year 1858–9* (London: Routledge, Warne and Routledge, 1860).

Sadrul Ola, Qazi Mohamed, *History of the Family of Mirza Sheikh I'tesammudin* (Calcutta: the Author, 1944).

Said, Edward W., *Culture and Imperialism* (New York: Knopf, 1993).

——, *Orientalism* (New York: Vintage, 1978).

Salter, Joseph, *Asiatic in England: Sketches of Sixteen Years' Work among Orientals* (London: Seely, Jackson, and Halliday, 1873).

Sanders, Charles Richard, *Strachey Family, 1588–1932* (Durham: Duke University Press, 1953).

Sankhdher, B.M., 'Mirza Abu Talib Khan', *Islamic Culture*, 44 (1970): 245–8.

Sarkar, Tanika, 'A Book of Her Own, A Life of Her Own: Autobiography of a Nineteenth-Century Woman', *History Workshop Journal* 36 (Autumn 1993): 35–65.

Scobie, Edward, *Black Britannia: A History of Blacks in Britain* (Chicago: Johnson Publishing Company, 1972).

Scott, A.F., *Every One a Witness* (London: White Lion, 1974).

Scott, Jonathan, *Observations on the Oriental Department* (Hertford: the Author, 1806).

Scott, Sir Walter, *Surgeon's Daughter* (Edinburgh: R. Cadell, 1830).

Seddon, Felix John Vaughan, *Address delivered in King's College, London . . . on the languages and literature of Asia.* (London: the Author, 1835).

Sen, Satadru, *Migrant Races: Empire, Idendity and K.S. Ranjitsinghji* (Manchester: Manchester University Press, 2004).

Sen, Sudipta, *Distant Sovereignty: National Imperialism and the Origins of British India* (New York: Routledge, 2002).

———, *Empire of Free Trade: The East India Company and Making of the Colonial Marketplace* (Philadelphia: University of Pennsylvania Press, 1998).

Sen, Surendra Nath, *Eighteen Fifty-Seven* (New Delhi: Government of India, 1957).

Sender, Henny, *The Kashmiri Pandits: A Study of Cultural Choice in North India* (Delhi: Oxford University Press, 1988).

Seth, Mesrovb J., *History of Armenians in India* (London: Luzac, 1897).

Shakespear, Captain Sir Richmond, 'Personal Narrative of a Journey from Heraut to Ourenbourg, on the Caspian, in 1840', *Blackwood's Edinburgh Magazine* 51, 320 (June 1842): 692–720.

Shakespear, John, *Grammar of the Hindustani Language* (London: Cox and Baylis, 1813).

Sharga, B.N. and Rajni Sharga, 'Zutshis of Bazaar Sitaram, Delhi', *Vitasta*, 33 (1999–2000), n.p.

Sharma, Mahendra Narain, *Life and Times of Begam Samru of Sardhana* (Sahibabad: Vibhu Prakashan, 1985).

Shepherd, W.J., *Personal Narrative of the Outbreak and Massacre at Cawnpore during the Sepoy Revolt of 1857* (New Delhi: Academic Books, 1980 reprint of 1879).

Sherer, J.W., 'Bishop in Partibus', *Gentleman's Magazine*, 280 (January–June 1896): 459–69.

Shreve, Nicholas, *Dark Legacy* (Arundel: Bookwright, 1996).

———, *Indian Heir: David Ochterlony Dyce Sombre* (Arundel: Bookwright, 2001).

Shyllon, Folarin, *Black People in Britain, 1555–1833* (London: Institute of Race Relations, 1977).

Simha, Pratapa [Rungo Bapojee], *Letter to the Right Hon. Sir Henry Hardinge* (London: Alex, Munro, 1845).

Simond, Louis, *Journal of a Tour and Residence*, 2 vols (New York: the Author, 1815).

Sindh, Vakeels of, *Translation of a Paper given to Lord Ashley by the Vakeels of the Ameers of Sinde, 15 August 1845* (London: the Authors, 1845).

Singh, Maharajah Duleep, *Correspondence*, ed. Ganda Singh (Patiala: Punjabi University, 1977).

Sinha, Mrinalini, *Colonial Masculinity: The 'Manly Englishman' and the 'Effeminate Bengali' in the Late Nineteenth Century* (Manchester: Manchester University Press, 1995).

Sleeman, William Henry, *Rambles and Recollections of an Indian Official,* 2 vols (London: J. Hatchard, 1844).

Spear, Percival, *Nabobs: A Study of the Social Life of the English in Eighteenth-Century India* (London: Oxford University Press, 1963).

———, *Twilight of the Mughuls: Studies in Late Mughul Delhi* (Cambridge: Cambridge University Press, 1951).

Standing Committee on the Hindu Sea-Voyage Question, *Hindu Sea-Voyage Movement in Bengal* (Calcutta: S.N. Banerjee, 1894).

Steensgaard, Niels, *Carracks, Caravans and Companies: The Structural Crisis in the European-Asian Trade in the Early 17th Century* (Lund: Studentlitteratur, 1973).

Stevenson, Sara, *David Octavius Hill and Robert Adamson: Catalogue of Their Calotypes taken between 1843 and 1887 in the Collection of the Sccoottish National Portrait Gallery* (Edinburgh: National Galleries of Scotland, 1981).

———, *Facing the Light: The Photography of Hill & Adamson* (Edinburgh: Scottish National Portrait Gallery, 2002).

Steward, James Christen, *New Child* (Berkeley: University of California, 1995).

Stewart, Charles, *Original Persian Letters, and Other Documents, with Facsimiles* (London: The Author, 1825).

Stoler, Ann Laura, *Race and the Education of Desire: Foucault's History of Sexuality and the Colonial Order of Things* (Durham: Duke University Press, 1995).

Strachey, Edward, 'Romantic Marriage of Major J.A. Kirkpatrick', *Blackwood's Magazine* 154 (July–December 1893): 18–29.

Strachey, G[eorge], 'Carlyle and the "Rose-Goddess" ', *Nineteenth Century* 185 (September 1892): 470–86.

Stullybrass, Peter, 'Marx and Heterogeneity', *Representations* 31 (Summer 1990): 69–95.

Subrahmanyam, Sanjay, *The Portuguese Empire in Asia, 1500–1700: A Political and Economic History* (London: Longman, 1993).

Sutherland, Lucy, *East India Company in Eighteenth-Century Politics* (Oxford: Clarendon Press, 1962).

Symons, Edward William, *Law Relating to Merchant Seamen,* 3rd edn (London: Longman, Brown, Green, and Longmans, 1844).

Tabili, Laura, 'Construction of Racial Difference in Twentieth-Century Britain: The Special Restriction (Coloured Alien Seamen) Order, 1925', *Journal of British Studies* 33,1 (January 1994): 54–98.

————, 'We Ask for British Justice': Workers and Racial Difference in Late Imperial Britain (Ithaca: Cornell University Press, 1994).

Tagore, Dwarkanath, 'Letters', Friend of India (September 1842): 548, 564–5, 581, 690.

Taifoor, Syed A.S.M., 'Sheikh I'tesamuddin of Nadia', Bengal Past and Present, 49 (1935): 117–29.

Tate Gallery, George Stubbs (London: Tate Gallery, 1984).

Targhi-Tavokoli, Mohamad, 'Imagining Western Women: Occidentalism and Euro-eroticism', Radical America 24, 3 (1993): 73–87.

————, Refashioning Iran (New York: Palgrave, 2001).

Taylor, Basil, 'George Stubbs's Painting of a Cheetah with Two Indians', in Philip Wilson and Annamaria MacDonald, eds, Art at Auction 1969–70 (New York: Viking, 1970).

Taylor, P.J.O., A Companion to the Indian Mutiny of 1857 (Delhi: Oxford University Press, 1996).

Thackeray, William Makepeace, Newcomes (London: Harper and Brothers, 1899).

Thompson, George, Address . . . to the Electors of the Tower Hamlets (London: the Author, 1847).

————, 'Fragment verbatim et literatum from my journal in Upper India (4 July 1843), Liberty Bell (1846): 1–6.

————, Raja of Sattara (London: W. Tyler, 1841).

————, Speeches, ed. Raj Jogeshur Mitter (Calcutta: S.K. Lahiri, 1895).

Thompson, Henry Frederick, Intrigues of a Nabob (London: the Author, 1780).

Thomson, Mowbray, Story of Cawnpore (London: R. Bentley, 1859).

Thorner, Daniel, Investment in Empire: British Railway and Steam Shipping Enterprise in India, 1825–1849 (Philadelphia: University of Pennsylvania Press, 1950).

Tobin, Beth Fowkes, Picturing Imperial Power: Colonial Subjects in Eighteenth-century British Painting (Durham: Duke University Press, 1999).

Toon, Mrs M[abel] Chan, Love Letters of an English Peeress to an Indian Prince (London: Digby, Long, 1911).

Trautmann, Thomas, Aryans and British India (Berkeley: University of California Press, 1997).

Trevelyan, George Otto, Cawnpore (London: Macmillan, 1894).

Tupper, C.L., Index to Indian Political Practice, 4 vols (Calcutta: Superintendent of Government Printing, 1895).

United Kingdom. Parliament. Sessionals, 1660–1858.

Vadgama, Kusoom, *India in Britain: The Indian Contribution to the British Way of Life* (London: Robert Royce, 1984).

Verelst, Harry, *View of the Rise, Progress, and Present State of the English Government in Bengal* (London: J. Nourse, 1772).

Vibart, Colonel H.M., *Addiscombe: Its Heroes and Men of Note . . .* (Westminster: Archibald Constable, 1894).

Victoria, Queen, *Letters: A Selection from Her Majesty's Correspondence*, 3 vols, eds Arthur Christopher Benson and Viscount Esher (London: John Murray, 1907).

Vindex [Rungo Bapojee], *Dethroned Rajah of Sattarah, Extract from the Supplement to the Bombay Gazette, January 27, 1843* (London: Munro and Congreve, 1843).

Visram, Rozina, *Asians in Britain: 400 Years of History* (London: Pluto, 2002).

———, *Ayahs, Lascars and Princes: Indians in Britain, 1700–1947* (London: Pluto, 1984).

Viswanathan, Gauri, *Masks of Conquest: Literary Study and British Rule in India* (New York: Columbia University Press, 1989).

———, *Outside the Fold: Conversion, Modernity, and Belief* (Princeton: Princeton University Press, 1998).

Wadeer, Veer Rajundur, *Memorial of Veer Rajundur Wadeer to the Court of Directors* (London: the Author, n.d.).

Wadia, Ardeshir Ruttonji, *Bombay Dockyard and the Wadia Master Builders*, 2nd edn (Bombay: R.A. Wadia, 1957).

Wadia, Ruttonjee Ardeshir, *Forgotten Friend of India* (Baroda: J.B.H. Wadia, 1946).

———, *Scions of Lowjee Wadia* (Bombay: Krishnamurthi, 1964).

Walker, Richard, *Regency Portraits*, 2 vols (London: National Portrait Gallery, 1985).

Waller, Derek, *Pandits: British Exploration of Tibet and Central Asia* (Lexington: University Press of Kentucky, 1990).

Ward, Andrew, *Our Bones are Scattered: The Cawnpore Massacres and the Indian Mutiny of 1857* (New York: Henry Holt, 1996).

Washbrook, D.A., 'Orients and Occidents', in Robin W. Winks, ed., *Historiography, Oxford History of the British Empire*, vol. 5 (Oxford: Oxford University Press, 1999): 596–611.

Wecter, Dixon, *Edmund Burke and His Kinsmen* (Boulder: University of Colorado, 1939).

Wheeler, Roxann, *Complexion of Race: Categories of Difference in Eighteenth-century British Culture* (Philadelphia: University of Pennsylvania, 2000).

Whelpton, John, *Jang Bahadur in Europe: The First Nepalese Mission to the West* (Kathmandu: Sahayogi Press, 1983).

White, Captain W., *Mirzas Kaiwan Jah, or the Dethroned King of Oude in Chains!!!* (London: William Strange, 1838).

White, David L., *Competition and Collaboration: Parsi Merchants and the English East India Company in 18th-Century India* (New Delhi: Munshiram Manoharlal, 1995).

Williams, L.F. Rushbrook, *Black Hills: Kutch in History and Legends: A Study in Indian Local Loyalties* (London: Weidenfeld and Nicolson, 1958).

Williamson, Thomas, *East India Vade-Mecum* (London: Black, Parry, and Kingsbury, 1810).

Wilson, Kathleen, *Island Race: Englishness, Empire, and Gender* (New York: Routledge, 2003).

Wink, Andre, *Al-Hind: The Making of the Indo-Islamic World*, 2 vols (Leiden: Brill, 1990–7).

Wolff, Joseph, *Researches and Missionary Labours among the Jews, Mohammedans and Other Sects*, 2nd edn (London: the Author, 1835).

Young, Desmond, *Fountain of the Elephants* (New York: Harper and Brothers, 1959).

Zastoupil, Lynn, 'Defining Christians, Making Britons', *Victorian Studies* 44, 2 (January 2002): 215–43.

Zastoupil, Lynn and Martin Moir, eds, *Great Indian Education Debate: Documents Relating to the Orientalist-Anglicist Controversy, 1781–1843* (Richmond: Curzon, 1999).

PERIODICALS CITED

The Age
Annual Register
Asiatic Journal and Monthly Register
Blackwood's Edinburgh Magazine
Bombay Times
British Indian Advocate
Calcutta Gazette
Calcutta Monthly Journal
Chambers Journal of Popular Literature
Daily Advertiser
Daily News
Edinburgh Review
European Magazine, and London Review

Friend of India
Gentleman's Magazine
Howitt's Journal of Literature and Popular Progress
Journal of the Asiatic Society
Illustrated London News
Indian Gazette
Liberty Bell
London Gazette
Morning Chronicle
Morning Herald and Daily Advertiser
Morning Post and Daily Advertiser
New York Daily Tribune
Public Advertiser
Quarterly Review
Statesman
Times

RECORDS CITED, NATIONAL ARCHIVES OF INDIA [NAI]

Bengal Military Consultations.
Bengal Public Consultations.
Bengal Secret and Military Consultations.
Foreign Political Consultations. [FPC]
Foreign Secret Consultations. [FSC]
General Return of the Troops.
Home Public Consultations.
Home Miscellaneous, volumes.
Home Miscellaneous Proceedings.
India Political Consultations.
Letters to and from Court of Directors.
Political Dispatch from Secretary of State.
Proceedings of Military Department.

RECORDS AND MANUSCRIPTS CITED, BRITISH LIBRARY, INCLUDING ORIENTAL AND INDIA OFFICE COLLECTION

Akbar, Moonshee Ali, 'Case of 1849', Broughton Correspondence, ADD 36478.
Ali, Meer Hasun, tr. 'Gospel of St Matthew translated into Hindoostanee' ISL 3063.
Archdeaconry of Calcutta, Quarterly Ecclesiastical Returns, N/1/36.
Babbage Correspondence, ADD 37192.

Bentham Papers, ADD 33546.
Board (of Control) Collections, Minutes, and Letter Books, F/ series.
Broadfoot Papers, ADD 40128.
Broughton Correspondence, ADD 36478.
Broughton Papers, MSS EUR F.213/ series.
College Committee, J/ series.
Correspondence Committee, Reports, Memoranda, and Minutes, D/ series.
Court of Directors Minutes, B/ series [Court Minutes].
Dyce Sombre Papers and Diary, L/L/Boxes 63–5.
Elphinstone Papers, MSS EUR F.88 series.
Finance and Home Committee Minutes and Reports, L/F/ series.
Financial Papers, L/F series.
Forbes, Forbes and Company, Balance Sheet, MSS EUR C.549.
General Register of Pensions, L/AG/21 series.
Hamilton and Greville Papers, ADD 42073.
Hastings, Warren, General Correspondence, ADD 29134, 29171.
Hickey, William, Autobiography, MSS EUR G.118.
Home Miscellaneous Series, HMS series. [HMS]
Home Department, Military Papers, L/MIL/2 series.
Itisam al-Din, 'Shigrif Namah-i Wilayat', MSS OR 200.
Khan, Karim, 'Siyahatnama', MSS OR 2163.
Khan, Mirza Abu Talib, 'Masir Talibi fi Bilad Afranji', Persian ADD 8145–7.
Kirkpatrick, J. A., Letterbook, MSS EUR F.228/55.
Lal, Mohan to Mayor of Liverpool 16/12/1844, MSS EUR A.84.
Landsdowne Papers, ADD 40856.
Letter Book from Managers, E/3 series.
Letters to and from Bengal/India, E/4 series.
Madden, Sir Frederick, Correspondence, EG 2838.
Marine Department, L/MAR/B/ series.
Marine Department, Papers Relating to the Care of Lascars, 1793–1818, L/MAR/C/902, vols 1–2. [Lascar Papers]
Memorandum on Haileybury, Oriental Department, MSS EUR F.303/445.
Military Papers, L/MIL/ series.
Miscellaneous Letters Received and Sent, E/ series.
Organization of the Home Establishment, L/AG/30/12.
Peel Papers, ADD 40515, 40597.
Personnel Papers, O/ series.
Political and Military Committee Minutes and References, L/MIL series.
Political Department, Home Correspondence, L/PS/ series. [PDHC]

Register of Deposits, General Treasury, L/MAR/C/ series.

Roy, Rajah Rammohun, Letters, ADD 29747, 59655, 70844.

Roy, Rajah Rammohun, Papers, MSS EUR B.399.

Roy, Rajahram, letter, 17 September 1844, MSS EUR C.161.

Rendel, James, letter 19 August 1842, MSS EUR A.146.

Revenue, Judicial, and Legislative Committee Minutes and References, L/PJ/ series.

Seminary Committee Reports, L/MIL/1/10 series.

Shipping Committee Minutes, L/MAR series.

Storm, John, letter, 12 August 1844, MSS EUR C.174.

Sutton Court Collection, MSS EUR F.128 series.

Wilson, H. H., Correspondence, MSS EUR E.301/13.

Wood, Sir Charles, Collection, MSS EUR F.78/47.

OTHER MANUSCRIPTS AND RECORDS CITED

Bengal, General Proceedings, West Bengal State Archive, Kolkata, India. [WBSA].

Bengal, Marine Department Proceedings, WBSA.

Bombay, Political, Public, and Secret Diaries, Maharashtra State Archive, Mumbai, India. [MSA].

Bombay, Public and Political Outward or Order Books, MSA.

Church of Jesus Christ of Latter-Day Saints, International Genealogical Index [IGI].

Clarey, Helen Winifred, 'Lady Forester', University of Keele, M.A., 1986.

Divekar, Bhaskar R., 'Raghunathrao Peshwa', St Xavier's College, Bombay, M.A., 1933.

Dyce Sombre Papers, D.1788/398/2 series, Stafford County Record Office, Stafford, England.

Eaton, Natasha. 'British Art in India *c.* 1772–1795', University of Warwick, Ph.D., 2001.

Gaikwad, S.D., 'Life of Peshwa Raghunathrao', Bombay University, Ph.D., 1970.

Ghosh, Durba, 'Colonial Companions: Bibis, Begums and Concubines of the British in India, 1760–1830', University of California, Berkeley, Ph.D., 2000.

Great Britain, Censuses, 1841–1901, in Family Records Centre, London.

Jervis, Mary Anne, 'Notes on the Jervis Pedigree by Lady Forester', copied by William Bowers, 34/17/68, William Salt Library, Stafford, England.

Land, Isaac Edward, 'Domesticating the Maritime', University of Michigan, Ph.D., 1999.

McLeod, John, 'Indian Tory: A Biography of Sir Mancherjee Merwanjee Bhownaggree', forthcoming.

Mir Muhammad Husain Isfahani, 'Risalah-i Ahwal-i Mulk-i Farang', Maulana Azad Library, Arabic No. 33; Persian No. 18/1, Aligarh, India.

Montagu Manuscripts MO 714, 937, 938, 1328, 1511, 1575, 4367, Huntington Library, San Marino, U.S.A.

National Register of Deaths, Family Records Centre, London.

Old Bailey Proceedings, Guildhall Library, London. [OBP]

Parish and other Ecclesiastical Registers in:

> Greater London Record Office, London. [GLRO]
> Guildhall Library, London.
> Hertford Local Library and Archives, Hertford, England.
> Westminster Archives Centre [WAC], London.

Schofield, G.E., 'Foundation and Establishment of the East India College, Hertford, 1805–17', University of London Institute of Education, M.A., 1985.

Sen, Simonti, 'Travels in Europe: 'Self' and 'Other' in the turn-of-the-century Bengali Travel Narratives, 1870–1910', Calcutta University, 1995.

SP/34/22, Public Record Office [PRO], Kew, England.

Travers, Robert, 'Contested Notions of Sovereignty in Bengal', Cambridge University, Ph.D., 1998.

Westminster Ratebooks and Poll Books, WAC.

OTHER SOURCES CITED

Dalrymple, William, personal communication, 20/6/2001.

http://familytreemaker.genealogy.com/users/p/a/l/Jeanne-Shirley-Palowkar/index.html

http://ikashmir.org/Vitasta/2000/5.4.html

Wilson, David, personal communication, 19/6/2002.

www.oldbaileyonline.org

www.starcourse.org/emd/emdwho.htm

www.vandemataram.com/biographies/patriots/akhan.htm

Index

COUNTERFLOWS TO COLONIALISM

Indian Travellers and Settlers
in Britain 1600–1857